Employment Tribunal Procedure

A users' guide to tribunals and appeals

Second edition

Jeremy McMullen, MA, MSc, is a Circuit Judge. He was formerly a part-time chairman of employment tribunals, chair of the ILO Joint Panel, and of the Industrial Law Society and the Employment Law Bar Association.
Jennifer Eady, BA, is a member of the English and Northern Irish Bars practising at Old Square Chambers, London, she is also a part-time chairman of employment tribunals, a member of the 'A' panel of junior Treasury counsel, standing junior counsel to the NUM and NUJ and formerly chair of the Industrial Law Society. She is co-author of *Discrimination (Quantum and Remedies)* (Sweet & Maxwell, 2nd edn, 2001).
Rebecca Tuck, BA, is a barrister at Old Square Chambers in London specialising in employment and discrimination law.

Employment Tribunal Procedure

A users' guide to tribunals and appeals

SECOND EDITION

Jeremy McMullen, Jennifer Eady
and Rebecca Tuck

 Legal Action Group
2002

This edition published in Great Britain 2002
by LAG Education and Service Trust Ltd
242 Pentonville Road
London
N1 9UN

First edition published 1996 and reprinted 1998 by Jeremy McMullen QC
and Jennifer Eady

British Library Cataloguing in Publication Data
A CIP catalogue record for this book is available from the British Library

ISBN 1 903307 07 4

Typeset by RefineCatch Ltd, Bungay, Suffolk
Printed in Great Britain by Bell & Bain, Glasgow

Foreword to the First Edition

By LORD ARCHER OF SANDWELL QC
Chairman, Council on Tribunals

Industrial tribunals are the offspring of two historical processes. First was the stormy relationship between organised working people and the law. Where the common law had been left to develop according to the predelictions of judges, employees in general, and trade unions in particular, found no greater understanding of their needs and aspirations among the judiciary than among their own employers. It is scarcely surprising, then, that employees felt greater confidence in a forum labelled 'tribunal' than they would have felt in a court.

Secondly, the rule of law had traditionally been declared to reside in the historic courts which dealt with disputes between individuals or between the individual and the executive. It was not until the Franks Report, in 1957, that specialist tribunals were accepted not as an exception to the rule of law, but as a constitutional part of it.

These two processes, then, converged in the mid-1960s, when newly-recognised rights to security in employment were enshrined in a succession of statutes. Since then successive governments have sought to reconcile the trade union movement to a system of adjudication without the unhappy associations of the courts, and in the last 30 years the jurisdiction of industrial tribunals has expanded to meet new forms of dispute and new needs. Unusually among tribunals, they deal largely, although by no means exclusively, with disputes not between citizen and government, but between citizen and citizen.

One consequence is that the jurisdiction is exercised in a relatively informal atmosphere, with a lawyer in the chair, and two colleagues whose contribution is not legal expertise, but some knowledge of the context in which industrial disputes arise. Yet the law administered in industrial tribunals is far from simple, and if it is to meet the varied situations found in a complicated world, it is likely to defy attempts at simplification. Even more confusing are the jurisdictional and procedural rules which are necessary to ensure that proceedings are heard in an orderly way, that everyone concerned understands the issues in the case, and that no-one is taken by surprise.

At the heart of such dispute resolution must be access to justice. Those who litigate in industrial tribunals are likely to need a guide through this labyrinth. *Employment Tribunal Procedure* will ensure that applicants throughout the country do not enter the process blind to the perils ahead. Those unfamiliar with this forum will benefit from its lucid guidance. The appendices are of particular value and the chronological approach of the text will help clarify and demystify tribunal procedure.

Few employees, and only a moderate proportion of smaller employers, are in a position to pay the fees of solicitors and counsel. If neither party has had access to advice, the tribunal is confronted with the dismaying task of extracting the essential issue from the evidence, while if one party enjoys competent representation and the other is denied it, we know from the research of Professor Hazel Genn and others that no tribunal, however competent and conscientious, can ensure a level playing field. If an issue is raised, or evidence is produced, at the hearing without previous warning, the tribunal is confronted with the options of excluding the new material, or of adjourning the hearing, with additional costs and delay to the parties, and the wasting of such time could have been allocated to other cases.

Everyone, then, has an interest in ensuring that litigants understand the jurisdiction which they are invoking, and take the proper procedural steps at the proper time. As yet, legal aid is not available for proceedings before industrial tribunals. Sometimes, competent help is obtainable from a trade union, a CAB, a law centre or the Free Representation Unit, but for many reasons, it is not always to hand at the necessary place and time. In this situation, there is an urgent need for a book setting out clearly in non-technical language the provisions which form the jurisdiction and procedure of industrial tribunals. This is such a book. It presents all the provisions clearly and accurately, and in a form which takes the reader quickly to the relevant information. While it comes to the aid of the puzzled litigant, it will also prove a blessing to trade union officials, personnel officers and others who help to prepare and present cases. For lawyers, too, it should provide a *vade mecum* which will spare much time-consuming research.

I venture to hope that it may inspire similar procedural guides to other systems of tribunals.

Preface

This book is written mainly to help advisers of people facing a tribunal hearing. We also hope it will be accessible to people bringing their own claims without the help of lawyers or specialist advisers. We have tried to show how working people can enforce their rights through the tribunal procedure; we take this commitment as being consistent with the legislation, which is about employment *rights* and anti-discrimination. What we say will be equally useful to employers and their advisers responding to claims.

It may seem odd that, as lawyers, we advocate using the tribunal procedures in the way we describe *only as a last resort*. Legal steps are no substitute for handling workplace problems at the workplace in accordance with agreed procedures. All parties will be better off if a dispute can be settled by negotiation without resort to a tribunal, or even to arbitration. New rights on union recognition should assist this.

There have been many changes in legislation since the first edition, on working time, part-timers, race discrimination, workplace representation, giving a huge extension of rights to working people, new procedure rules for tribunals and appeals to deal with them, and arbitration for unfair dismissal. Also the Human Rights Act 1998 has radically affected employment rights and the adjudication of them. New approaches to discrimination and other evils have been shaped by tribunals and courts in the UK and Europe.

We are grateful to many legal, trade union and tribunal colleagues and clients who have given us ideas for this book and in particular Tony Pullen, Isabel Manley, Vereena Jones, Emma Smith, Alice Leonard and Colette Chesters for detailed comments on the text. What appears is not their fault. We also thank Adam Brett for his assistance on Northern Ireland law, and our clerks for their support. We thank the Employment Tribunal Service, and the staff at London North West Region for use of the standard letters.

Throughout this book we have used 'chairman' to describe those who preside over employment tribunals. This is in accordance with the language of the legislation. References to tribunals are to employment tribunals in Great Britain and to the industrial tribunal in Northern Ireland, and to the Employment Appeal Tribunal. References in statutes to *industrial* tribunals were replaced by statute in 1998.

We state the law as we see it on 1 October 2001.

Note on the law in Scotland and Northern Ireland
The procedure in tribunals in Scotland and Northern Ireland is similar to that in England and Wales, although each has its own set of rules. The substantive law of contracts of employment differs slightly in Scotland, and the terminology is quite different.

References in this book are to the regulations and rules for England and Wales, and wherever there is a Scottish or Northern Irish variation, we say so.

J McM
J E
R T
Old Square Chambers, London.
1 September 2001

Contents

Table of cases

Table of statutes

Table of statutory instruments

Table of European legislation

Abbreviations

2001 Regs	Employment Tribunals (Constitution and Rules of Procedure) Regulations 2001 SI No 1171
2001 Rules	Employment Tribunals Rules of Procedure (contained in SI 2001 No 1171, Sch 1)
ACAS	Advisory, Conciliation and Arbitration Service
CAB	citizens advice bureau
COET	Central Office of Employment Tribunals
CPR	Civil Procedure Rules
CRE	Commission for Racial Equality
DRC	Disability Rights Commission
ECJ	European Court of Justice
EDT	effective date of termination
EOC	Equal Opportunities Commission
EqPA 1970	Equal Pay Act 1970
ERA 1996	Employment Rights Act 1996
ERelA 1999	Employment Relations Act 1999
ETA 1996	Employment Tribunals Act 1996
ETS	Employment Tribunal Service
GMF	genuine material factor
IE	independent expert
JES	job evaluation study
NIRC	National Industrial Relations Court
NMWA 1998	National Minimum Wage Act 1998
PD 1996	*Practice Direction (EAT: Procedure)* [1996] ICR 422; [1996] IRLR 430
PTW Regs 2000	Part-time Workers (Prevention of Less Favourable Treatment) Regulations 2000 SI No 1551
ROET	regional office of employment tribunal
RRA 1976	Race Relations Act 1976
SDA 1975	Sex Discrimination Act 1975

TICE Regs 1999	Transnational Information and Consultation of Employees Regulations 1999 SI No 3323
TULRCA 1992	Trade Unions and Labour Relations (Consolidation) Act 1992
TUPE	Transfer of Undertakings (Protection of Employment) Regulations 1981 SI No 1794
WT Regs 1998	Working Time Regulations 1998 SI No 1833

Constitution

General

1.1   Employment tribunals were first established by the Industrial Training Act 1964. Since then, the role of tribunals has changed dramatically and they now have jurisdiction to hear many types of claim (see chapter 2), but the vast majority of cases involve unfair dismissal or redundancy pay.

1.2   In performing a judicial function, tribunals are creatures of statute. Unlike the courts, they have no inherent jurisdiction: if a tribunal is to exercise a particular power, it is necessary to find out which statute creates the power. There is no general power, except that a tribunal is required to give effect to European Union law and the ECHR rights incorporated by the Human Rights Act 1998.[1]

1.3   The aim of employment tribunals has always been to provide 'an easily accessible, speedy, informal and inexpensive procedure for the settlement of . . . disputes . . . and to remove the . . . multiplicity of actions'.[2] To some extent these goals have been achieved: tribunals are not bound by the rules of evidence or procedure which govern most courts. Instead they can moderate their own procedure as they see fit.[3] Equally, there is no monopoly on rights of audience before tribunals, so anyone can represent a party or can choose to represent themselves, and no one wears wigs or gowns. The tribunal, representatives and witnesses remain seated for the hearing and modes of address are relatively informal: Sir or Madam are acceptable and usual, without being too obsequious; Mr or Ms may be used for representatives, parties and witnesses.

1.4   On the other hand, for most litigants in person and many lay representatives, tribunals will seem highly formal and legalistic. Evidence is usually given on oath or affirmation, witnesses are cross-examined, legal language is used and legal submissions are made. At times the issues before the tribunal will be complex and involve quite complicated legal analysis. Frequently parties will employ legal professionals who are trained in and used to the greater formality of the courts. All this increases the formality and costs of the proceedings, and sometimes causes delays.

1.5   In the vast majority of cases the issues are quite simple ones of

1   *Secretary of State for Scotland v Wright* [1991] IRLR 187, EAT, applying *Pickstone v Freemans plc* [1987] ICR 867; [1987] IRLR 218, CA. See para 1.11 below.
2   Royal Commission on Trade Unions and Employers' Associations under Lord Donovan 1968, Cmnd 3623, para 578.
3   Employment Tribunals Rules of Procedure 2001 ('2001 Rules') rr11(1) and 15(1).

fact and there is no reason why the tribunal should not be able to adjudicate on these cases without the 'assistance' of detailed rules of evidence and procedure and lawyers. In doing so, the tribunal will have regard to the overriding objective of the Employment Tribunal Rules of Procedure 2001 (2001 Rules), which is to enable it to deal with cases justly. That means, so far as practicable, (a) ensuring that the parties are on an equal footing; (b) saving expense; (c) dealing with the case in ways which are proportionate to the complexity of the issues; and (d) ensuring that the case is dealt with expeditiously and fairly.[4] This objective is similar, although not identical to that applied in the High Court and county court under the Civil Procedure Rules (CPR). Unlike the 2001 Rules the CPR refer to dealing with a case in a way proportionate not just to the complexity of the issues but also to the amount of money involved, the importance of the case and the financial position of each party. The CPR also require the court to allot to a case 'an appropriate share of the court's resources . . . taking into account the need to allot resources to other cases'.[5] The omission of these provisions may provide a useful indication as to how it is intended that tribunals should approach their task in applying the overriding objective to the conduct of cases before them.

Position of employment tribunals in the legal system

1.6   Employment tribunals are the first stage in the legal process for enforcing most statutory employment rights. The decisions of one tribunal are not binding on any other tribunal or court, although they may be persuasive.

1.7   The next stage is the Employment Appeal Tribunal (EAT), to which an appeal lies from decisions of employment tribunals. There is a division of the EAT in England and Wales (sitting in London) and in Scotland (sitting in Edinburgh). It has the status of a court of record, which means its decisions are binding on employment tribunals, and on county courts in England and Wales and sheriff courts in Scotland, and create legal precedents which should be followed.[6]

---

4   Employment Tribunals (Constitution and Procedure) Regulations 2001 SI No 1171 ('2001 Regs') reg 10.
5   CPR 1.1(2)(e).
6   Employment Tribunals Act (ETA) 1996 s20(3).

1.8   The EAT in England and Wales has the status of the High Court and hearings are presided over by a High Court judge or a circuit judge appointed under Supreme Court Act 1981 s9, or a recorder appointed part-time under the Employment Tribunals Act 1996 (ETA 1996). The judge sits with two (or, exceptionally, four) lay members drawn from separate panels nominated by the different sides of employment relations, appointed by the Lord Chancellor in conjunction with the secretary of state. In Scotland, EAT cases are heard by a judge of the Court of Session sitting with two lay members appointed by the same system.

1.9   Appeals from the EAT in England and Wales lie to the Court of Appeal (Civil Division) and in Scotland they go to the Court of Session (Inner House). Appeals must be on points of law (not fact) and can only be made with the permission (consent) of the EAT or, if it refuses, the Court of Appeal or Court of Session. From there they go to the House of Lords. Permission to do so is required in England and Wales and Northern Ireland but not in Scotland.[7]

1.10   Appeals from tribunals sitting in Northern Ireland, where there is no EAT, are heard by the Northern Ireland Court of Appeal, by way of case stated.[8] Appeal from this court lies to the House of Lords.

1.11   Since 2 October 2000, when the Human Rights Act 1998 came into force, the tribunal must take into account any judgment or decision of the European Court of Human Rights when considering any matter in respect of which a human rights issue has arisen. Neither ETs nor the EAT may make a declaration that a piece of legislation is incompatible with the European Convention on Human Rights, that power being limited to the House of Lords, Court of Appeal and High Court.

Contempt

1.12   Although tribunals are not courts of record, for the purposes of the Contempt of Court Act 1981,[9] which provides the power for the Divisional Court to punish contempt of other courts, they are inferior courts and any person acting in contempt of them can be punished by imprisonment: see *Peach Grey & Co (a firm) v Sommers*.[10] In this

---

7 Court of Session Act 1988 s40.
8 Industrial Training (Northern Ireland) Order 1984 art 31 and Rules of Supreme Court (Northern Ireland) 1980 Order 61.
9 See CPR Procedural Guide D1–031; County Court Rules Order 29 and Rules of the Supreme Court Order 52.
10 [1995] 2 All ER 513; [1995] ICR 549; [1995] IRLR 363, DC.

case, the applicant to the tribunal proceedings had indirectly tried to persuade a witness to withdraw his evidence. The court held that it did have the power to commit the applicant to prison for that contempt of the proceedings of the tribunal as an inferior court.[11]

Location and administration

1.13   The Employment Tribunal Service (ETS) has its head office at 7th Floor, 19–29 Woburn Place, London, WC1H 0LU. The Public Register of Applications and Decisions for England and Wales is situated at the ETS Field Support Unit, 1st Floor, 100 Southgate Street, Bury St Edmunds, IP33 2AQ; its role is administrative. There are also 22 regional offices of ETs (ROETs). The postal address of the applicant's workplace determines to which of the 22 offices the application is made and by which it is administered (see list of tribunals in appendix D) within one of the regions.

1.14   The head of all employment tribunals in England and Wales is the President of Employment Tribunals, who must have held a 'general qualification' for at least seven years.[12] This will mean a barrister or solicitor with rights of audience in part of the Supreme Court and the county courts, appointed by the Lord Chancellor. He or she may hold office until the age of 72[13] (age 70 for appointments in and after 1995). Recently the presidents have been circuit judges. The chief administrative officer of the ETS is the Secretary of Tribunals. The secretary is the named officer to whom all originating applications must be first presented at the address of the appropriate tribunal offices. At each tribunal office there is a regional secretary, who may exercise any of the functions of the Secretary of Tribunals.

1.15   There are 22 regional chairmen, one at each ROET, who take charge of the administration of cases by the tribunals in their regions and also hear cases.

1.16   In Scotland there is a separate ETS, based at Eagle Building, 215 Bothwell Street, Glasgow G2 7TS and three offices of tribunals (see list of addresses in appendix D). All applications in Scotland should be sent to the ETS. Presiding over the Scottish tribunals is a president appointed by the Lord President of the Court of Session.[14]

---

11 More recently confirmed in *Ex p Kane* (2000) *Daily Telegraph* 7 November.
12 2001 Regs reg 3(1) and Courts and Legal Services Act 1990 s71.
13 Ibid reg 3(3).
14 Employment Tribunals (Constitution and Rules of Procedure) (Scotland) Regulations 2001 SI No 1170 reg 3(1).

1.17   The equivalent to the ETS in Northern Ireland is the Office of the Employment Tribunals and the Fair Employment Tribunal, Long Bridge House, 20–24 Waring Street, Belfast BT1 2EB.

Composition of tribunals

Chairman

1.18   A legally qualified chairman presides over the hearing and advises his/her lay colleagues on the tribunal of the relevant law and its application. The chairman must be a barrister (in Scotland, an advocate) or solicitor holding a 'general qualification'[15] of at least seven years' standing in part of the Supreme Court and the county courts. He or she is appointed by the Lord Chancellor or, in Scotland, by the Lord President. Part-time chairmen are also appointed who undertake to serve up to 30 days each year; in practice, they sit on about one third of all tribunals.

1.19   It is the chairman's role to set out the tribunal's decision in any case and give the reasons for that decision. Chairmen do not, however, carry any more weight on the tribunal than their colleagues: they can be outvoted by the lay members of the tribunal and will then give the majority decision of the lay members and their own minority decision. The majority decision is binding.

Chairman sitting without lay members

1.20   Tribunal chairmen can, however, make certain decisions alone, without lay members, either considering the relevant application on the papers or sitting alone with the parties present. The chairman's power to make decisions without lay members present is strictly limited and, subject to the following exceptions, does not extend to making final decisions on substantive questions of fact or law, or to reviewing a decision of the tribunal.[16] The power to sit alone is achieved by one of two routes.

1) By 2001 Rules r15(8), 'any act' required to be done by a tribunal may be done by a chairman alone except:
   – hearing an originating application under r10;

---

15   Within the meaning of Courts and Legal Services Act 1990 s71; see 2001 Regs reg 5(1)(a).
16   2001 Rules r15(8).

- acts incidental to the hearing of an originating application by a full tribunal as implied by rr11 and 12;
- the review of a tribunal decision under r13(1); and
- the ordering of a rehearing under r13(7).

In practice this means that all interim stages (including jurisdiction decisions under r6 about entitlement to bring proceedings) and pre-hearing reviews are conducted by a chairman sitting alone (r7). The powers also include:

- dismissal of proceedings on withdrawal by the applicant (r15(2)(a));
- a decision in accordance with the written agreement of the parties (r15(2)(b));
- striking out of proceedings (r15(2)(c) and(d));
- postponement or adjournment (r15(7)) and extension of time (r17));
- giving directions (r4);
- joining parties and proceedings and creating representative actions (rr19 and 20).

2) In addition to these general powers, financial constraints have gradually slimmed down the number of cases which must or may be heard by a full tribunal. By ETA 1996 s4(2)–(4)[17] the following proceedings 'shall' be heard by a chairman alone, subject only to the caveat in s4(5) (see below):

- (a)applications for interim relief in trade union membership, health and safety and other cases (Employment Rights Act 1996 (ERA 1996) ss128, 131 and 132 and Trade Unions and Labour Relations (Consolidation) Act 1992 (TULRCA 1992) ss161, 165 and 166);
- complaints concerning unauthorised deductions of union subscriptions (TULRCA 1992 s68A);
- claims for remuneration under protective award (TULRCA 1992 s 192);
- complaints concerning failure to consult under TUPE s11(5);
- complaints under Pension Schemes Act 1993 s126;
- applications under the insolvency provisions (ERA 1996 s182);
- applications for a redundancy payment from the secretary of state in the event of an employer's insolvency, or refusal/failure to make the payment (ERA 1996 s170)

17   As amended by Employment Rights (Dispute Resolution) Act 1998 s3.

- complaints relating to unlawful deductions from wages (ERA 1996 s23);
- applications for written statement of particulars of employment, itemised pay statement, guarantee payments, or relating to claims for remuneration on suspension on medical grounds (ERA 1996 ss11, 34 and 64);
- claims for breach of the contract of employment (ETA 1996 s3);
- complaints concerning failure to keep records, appeals against enforcement notices and against penalty notices under the National Minimum Wage Act 1998 (ss11, 19 and 22);
- proceedings where the complainant has given written notice withdrawing his/her claim;
- proceedings where the parties have given written consent to the case being heard by a chairman alone (even if they subsequently withdraw it);
- proceedings where the respondent no longer contests the case.

These cases are subject to the caveat in ETA 1996 s4(5) that they *may* be heard by a full tribunal following a decision by a chairman sitting alone, who must have regard to:

- the likelihood of a dispute arising on the facts which makes it desirable for the hearing to be in front of a full tribunal;
- whether there is a likelihood of an issue of law arising which would make it desirable for the case to be heard by a chairman alone;
- any views expressed by the parties; and
- whether there are other proceedings concurrently being heard which must be heard by a full tribunal.

1.21   Tribunals had regarded the statute as requiring chairmen to sit alone in those cases set out in ETA 1996 s4(2)–(4), unless under s4(5) a chairman exercises his discretion to make an exception, and sit with lay members. However, there are now conflicting decisions of the EAT about whether the discretion under s4(5) must always be considered before a chairman may proceed to sit alone; in *Sogbetun v Hackney LBC*,[18] Morison J held that chairmen were under a mandatory duty to exercise their discretion under s4(5), and always to explain why they had elected to sit alone. A different division of the EAT in *Post Office v Howell*[19] disagreed with *Sogbetun*, holding that

18 [1998] IRLR 676; [1998] ICR 1264.
19 [2000] IRLR 224.

even if there is such a mandatory duty, a chairman's failure to exercise it will neither go to jurisdiction, nor render any decision a nullity. A further division of the EAT had now held, in *Arriva Kent Thameside Ltd v Clarke*,[19a] that whether a failure to consider the s4(5) discretion renders the decision a nullity, or is merely an irregularity makes no real difference. The effect is the same; it is an error for a chairman to fail to explain the decision to sit alone.

1.22   None of these decisions lays down any requirement to consult the parties although Morrison P in *Sogbetun* stated that this is preferable. (Note also the requirement under s4(5)(c) is only that regard is taken of '*any* views expressed by the parties'.)[20] However, it is clear that if the parties are consulted, their representations must be considered. This might usefully be done at a directions hearing (see para 12.45). The notice of hearing will indicate that the case will be heard by a chairman alone and if a party wants a hearing by a full tribunal, representations should be made at the time the notice is received.

1.23   Although a preliminary point on jurisdiction under 2001 Rules r6 can be heard by a chairman sitting alone, considering a preliminary point of law is held to be the hearing of an originating application, or an integral part of it, and so is regulated by ETA 1996 s4, which indicates whether either a chairman sitting alone or a full tribunal is appropriate.

1.24   The EAT in *Mobbs v Nuclear Electric Plc*,[21] held that where it was necessary to hear evidence and reach a decision of fact in a preliminary hearing, it was not permissible for a chairman to sit alone. However, this decision was swiftly overturned by another division of the EAT in *Tsangocos v Amalgamated Chemicals Limited*.[22] In this case it was confirmed that a chairman sitting alone does have jurisdiction, without qualification, to determine jurisdictional points and to hear all other matters in connection with an originating application.

1.25   The *Tsangocos* decision was approved in *United Airlines v Bannigan and others*,[23] although it was emphasised in that case that a chairman should consider carefully the wisdom of sitting alone where there are disputes of fact, as the experience of lay members in such circumstances may be especially valuable. These sentiments were repeated

---

19a EAT/0341/00, 20 August 2001, available from the EAT website www.employmentappeals.gov.uk.
20 Emphasis added.
21 [1996] ICR 536.
22 [1997] IRLR 4; ICR 154.
23 EAT 192/97, 15 September 1997.

in *Sutcliffe v Big C's Marine*,[24] ('the quality of justice must not be allowed to deteriorate because of resource implications'), and in *Co-operative Wholesale Society Ltd v McGurran*.[24a]

1.26   The EAT stated, in *Wellcome Foundation v Darby*,[25] that it is not every preliminary issue that will be suitable for a preliminary hearing, but rather that some cases will require a full hearing of evidence and argument. Consideration should be given to whether the issue is one which is properly to be taken in advance of a full hearing.

Lay members

1.27   The chairman of a tribunal usually sits with two lay members, drawn from two panels of people representing employers and employees. Lay members are appointed to serve on tribunals by the secretary of state after consultation with representative bodies such as the Confederation of British Industry and the Trades Union Congress. They are entitled (and encouraged) to utilise their industrial knowledge and experience in assessing tribunal cases and are seen as forming (together with the chairman) the 'industrial jury'.

1.28   If any member (including the chairman) of a tribunal has a personal or financial interest in a particular case, he or she should declare that interest to the parties and should not sit on that case unless all parties consent. All those coming before tribunals should be able to have complete confidence in the independence and integrity of those hearing the case. Any direct interest in the case will automatically exclude a person from sitting.[26] The Human Rights Act 1998, by incorporating article 6(1) of the European Convention on Human Rights, provides that civil rights should be determined by an 'independent and impartial tribunal'. Given what might appear to be close links between the tribunal members and the appointing secretary of state, it has been questioned whether a sufficient degree of independence is achieved in cases involving that government department; see *Smith v Secretary of State for Trade and Industry*.[27]

---

24   [1998] IRLR 428.
24a EAT/395/00, 26 April 2001.
25   [1996] IRLR 538.
26   *R v Gough* [1993] AC 646, HL (and, in the employment law context, *Greenaway Harrison Ltd v Wiles* [1994] IRLR 380, EAT); *Re Pinochet Ugarte (No 2)* [1999] 2 WLR 272, HL; *Locabail v Bayfield Properties* [2000] IRLR 96, CA; *Re Medicaments and Related Classes of Goods (No 2)* [2001] ICR 564, CA.
27   [2000] ICR 69; [2000] IRLR 6.

More recently, however, the EAT has confirmed that sufficient guar-
antees of independence are provided by the terms on which tribunal
members hold their office, *Scanfuture UK Ltd and Link v Secretary of
State for Trade and Industry.*[28] The occasions when the question of bias
might arise are considered in more detail in chapter 18, which also
sets out guidance for parties who need to raise the question during
the course of the hearing.

1.29   In these circumstances, or if one of the lay members is absent for
any other reason, and the parties both consent, the chairman may sit
with just one lay member. While lay members are expected to give
fair consideration to all cases whichever panel they are drawn from,
the whole purpose of the composition of a tribunal is to try and
ensure that both perspectives are present. Clearly this is not achieved
if the chairman sits with just one lay member. In such circumstances,
a party always has the right to insist that a tribunal is fully
constituted.

National security cases

1.30   The 2001 Regs introduced a requirement that a further panel be
maintained, listing chairmen and lay members who are suitable
people to act in cases involving national security.[29]

Equal pay and sex and race discrimination claims

1.31   There is no requirement that members of a particular gender or
ethnic background sit on tribunals considering these cases, nor that
any member hearing such a case has any specialised knowledge. In
these classes of case, however, selection of the tribunal will generally
be made by the ROET so as to have a representative membership or
at least one member with specialised knowledge or training. This is a
particular concern in cases involving allegations of race discrimination following the government's undertaking at the time of passing
the Race Relations Act 1976 to take steps to appoint people to the
panels of lay members with specialised knowledge or experience of
race relations matters. It remains, however, a goal, not a legal
requirement.[30]

---

28 [2001] IRLR 416, EAT.
29 The Employment Tribunals (Constitution and Rules of Procedure) Regulations
    2001 reg 6.
30 *Habib v Elkington & Co Ltd* [1981] ICR 435; [1981] IRLR 344, EAT.

Tribunal clerks

1.32   A tribunal clerk is appointed for each hearing. The clerk will introduce him or herself to the representatives or parties and take details of witnesses (their full name, position, which oath or affirmation they will take) and observers, and collect any additional documents and the legal authorities which will be referred to during the course of the hearing. If the applicant has been claiming jobseeker's allowance or income support, the clerk will also take details of the benefit office concerned. Any subsequent award of compensation will be notified to that office should the recoupment provisions apply to an award of compensation.[31]

1.33   The clerk to the tribunal also sits in at the beginning of most cases to administer the oath or affirmation but tends not to stay throughout. Limited assistance can be sought from tribunal clerks before and during the course of a hearing but their primary function is to assist the tribunal.

Tribunal consultative groups

1.34   Most ROETs now have consultative groups which meet about three times a year and liaise with representatives of regular users of tribunals in the relevant area. An adviser with a general query on the practices or procedures in a particular ROET may find it helpful to ask the appropriate representative on the consultative group (eg, the law centre or CAB representative) to ask them to raise the issue. If there appears to be no such representative, advisers should contact the secretary to the relevant ROET with any query.

---

31 Employment Protection (Recoupment of Jobseeker's Allowance and Income Support) Regulations 1996 SI No 2349; ETA 1996 s16.

CHAPTER 2
Types of claim

13

Jurisdiction: general

2.1   Tribunals are created by statute and have no powers other than those given them by parliament. If a case falls outside a tribunal's jurisdiction, it is not permitted to consider the matter. Even if the parties do not raise the point, the tribunal must always be satisfied that it has the power to hear a particular case before it goes on to do so: '[it] cannot merely by silence confer upon [itself] a jurisdiction which [it does] not have'.[1] Furthermore, even if the point is not taken before the tribunal, lack of jurisdiction can always be raised on review or appeal.

2.2   Not all jurisdictional questions are dealt with in this book, as many give rise to questions of substantive law rather than procedure. Reference should be made to other texts (and the relevant Acts) to ensure that a particular applicant has the right to bring a complaint before a tribunal. Where the jurisdictional issue is of a procedural nature it is referred to in this chapter or in chapter 5 on time limits.

2.3   After para 2.7 below there is a list of rights in which legislation provides that employment tribunals have jurisdiction in England and Wales; there is not room in this book for a complete list for Scotland and Northern Ireland, but the headings are roughly the same. In Northern Ireland the Fair Employment Tribunal also has a parallel jurisdiction under the Fair Employment (NI) Acts 1976 and 1989 in cases of religious and political discrimination which does not exist for tribunals in Great Britain.

Territorial jurisdiction

2.4   Tribunals in England and Wales are permitted to hear claims only where:

- any respondent resides or carries on a business in England or Wales; or
- if the claim could have been determined by a county court, the cause of action would have arisen wholly or in part in England or Wales; or

---

1   *British Midland Airways v Lewis* [1978] ICR 782, EAT.

– the proceedings are to determine a question which has been referred to the tribunal by a court in England or Wales.[2]

2.5 A company with a registered office in England or Wales is within these territorial limits.[3] A check on the registered address of a company[4] can be made by a search of its records at Companies House.

2.6 Even if a company has no registered office in England or Wales but the cause of action arises within the jurisdiction, for example, the employee is dismissed in England or Wales, a tribunal will have jurisdiction to hear that claim.

2.7 Similar provisions apply to tribunals in Northern Ireland and in Scotland except that there is no reference to county courts and in Scotland jurisdiction also arises if the contract of employment is executed or performed in Scotland.

---

2   Employment Tribunals (Constitution and Procedure) Regulations 2001 SI No 1171 reg 11(5).
3   *Odeco (UK) Inc v Peacham* [1979] ICR 823, EAT.
4   As required to be notified by Companies Act 1985 s691.

EMPLOYMENT TRIBUNAL JURISDICTION AND TIME LIMITS

	Statutory right	Time limit
Equal Pay Act 1970		
s2	Breach of equality clause.	6 *whole* months from termination of employment (s2(4)).
s7A	Complaint by member of armed forces regarding breach of term equivalent to equality clause.	9 whole months from the end of the service out of which the complaint arose (s7A(8)).
Health and Safety at Work Act 1974		
s24	Appeal against improvement or prohibition notice.	As specified in the notice (s24(2)).
s80	Safety Representatives and Safety Committee Regs 1977 SI No 500 reg 11(1): time off with pay for safety representative.	3 *whole* months from failure to pay (reg 11(2)).
Sex Discrimination Act 1975		
s63	Discrimination on the ground of sex or against a married person.	3 months (s76(1)).**
s68	Appeal against non-discrimination notice.	6 *whole* weeks from service of notice (s68(1)).
s72(2) and s72(4)	Application by EOC relating to discriminatory advertisement, etc.	6 months or 5 years (s76(3)).**
s73	Preliminary action by EOC relating to persistent discrimination, advertisements, etc.	6 months (s76(4)).**
s77	Complaint that contract, rule, collective agreement is void.	None (SDA 1986 s64A).

Race Relations Act 1976

s54	Discrimination on the ground of race.	3 months (s68(1)).
s59	Appeal against non-discrimination notice.	6 *whole* weeks from service of notice (s59(1)).
s63(3)(a)	Application by CRE relating to discriminatory advertisements, etc.	6 months or 5 years (s68(4)).
s64	Preliminary action by CRE relating to persistent discrimination, advertisements, etc.	6 months (s68(5)).

Transfer of Undertakings (Protection of Employment) Regulations 1981, *as amended 1987 and 1995*

reg 11(1)	Failure to inform or consult appropriate representatives of employees of transfer of undertaking.	3 months (reg 11(8)(a)).
reg 11(5)	Failure to pay compensation.	3 months of order (reg 11(8)(a)).

Industrial Training Act 1982

s12	Appeal by employer against assessment of industrial training levy.	As specified by the relevant levy order.

Sex Discrimination Act 1986

s6(4A)	Invalidity of discriminatory collective agreements and other rules.	6 months (SDA 1975 ss63, 76(1), (5)).**

Trade Union and Labour Relations (Consolidation) Act 1992 *as amended 1993, 1996, 1998 and 1999*

s66(1)	Union member not to be unjustifiably disciplined.	3 months (s66(2))* (and extended where internal appeal).
s67(1) and (2)	Compensation for unjustifiable discipline.	4 weeks to 6 months from declaration (s67(3)).
s68(A)	Unauthorised or excessive union subscription deducted from wages.	3 months (s68(1)).*
s70C	Refusal to conduct collective bargaining concerning training.	3 months (s70C(2)).*

EMPLOYMENT TRIBUNAL JURISDICTION AND TIME LIMITS

	Statutory right	Time limit
s87(1)	Wrongful deduction of political fund contribution or employer's refusal to make deduction.	3 months s87(2).*
s116(4)	Trade union's secret ballot on employers' premises (repealed from 1 April 1996).	3 months (s116(5)).*
s137(2)	Refusal of employment on ground related to union membership or non-membership.	3 months (s139(1)).*
s138(2)	Refusal of service by employment agency on ground related to union membership.	3 months (s139(1)).*
s146(5)	Action short of dismissal relating to union membership and activities.	3 months (s147).*
ss152 and 161(1)	Interim relief in dismissal cases relating to union membership or non-membership.	7 days following termination (s161(2)).
s168(4)	Time off for union duties.	3 *whole* months (s171).*
s169(5)	Time off with pay for union duties.	3 *whole* months (s171).*
s170(4)	Union member's time off for union activities.	3 *whole* months (s171).*
s174(5)	Exclusion or expulsion from union.	6 months (s175).*
s176(2)	Compensation for unlawful exclusion/expulsion.	4 weeks to 6 months from declaration (s176(3)).
s189(1)	Failure to consult or inform employee representative/union/employee on redundancies.	Before the date of the last dismissal and 3 months thereafter (s189(5)).*
s192(1)	Remuneration under protective award.	3 months (s192(2)).*
s238	Unfair dismissal during certain official industrial action (including maternity or health and safety grounds s238(2A)).	6 months (s239(2)).*

Sch A1 para 156(5)	Detriment short of dismissal in cases concerning trade union recognition/bargaining arrangements.	3 months (Sch A1 para 157(1)).*

Pension Schemes Act 1993

s11(5)(e)	With Occupational Pension Schemes (Contracting-out) Regulations 1984 SI No 380 (amended by SI 1985 No 1323 and SI 1986 No 1716): contracting out.	None.
s113(1)	With Occupational Pension Schemes (Disclosure of Information) Regulations 1986 SI No 1046 reg 10: questions whether union is recognised.	None.
s126(1)	Failure to pay contributions to scheme by the secretary of state.	3 months from communication of decision (s126(2)).*

Pensions Act 1995

s62	With Occupational Pension Schemes (Equal Treatment) Regulations 1995 SI No 3183, equal treatment rules in pension schemes for people of different sex and family or marital status.	6 *whole* months from termination of employment (Equal Pay Act 1970 s2(4) as amended by Pensions Act 1995 s63(4)).

Disability Discrimination Act 1995

s8	Discrimination/detriment on grounds of disability.	3 months (Sch 3 para 3).**

Employment Rights Act 1996

s11(1)–(2)	Reference of question relating to written statement of particulars of employment (s1) and itemised pay statement (s8).	While employed and 3 months beginning with termination of employment (s11(4)).*

EMPLOYMENT TRIBUNAL JURISDICTION AND TIME LIMITS

Statutory right		Time limit
s23	Unlawful deduction from wages.	3 months from deduction or last in series (s23(2)).*
s34	Guarantee payment.	3 months (s34(2)).*
s48(1)	Detriment in health and safety/shop workers/ betting workers/Sunday trading cases/ performing functions of employee representative.	3 months (s48(3)).*
s48[1A]	Detriment for making a protected disclosure.	3 months (s48(3)).*
s48[12A]	Detriment in working time cases.	3 months (s48(3)).*
s51(1)	Time off for public duties.	3 months (s50(2)).*
s54(1)	Time off to look for work or make arrangements for training.	3 months (s54(2)).*
s57(1)	Time off for ante-natal care.	3 months (s57(2)).*
s57(B)(1)	Time off for dependants.	3 months (s57B(2)).*
s60(1)	Time off for pension scheme trustees.	3 months (from date failure occurred) (s60(2)).*
s63(1)	Time off for employee representatives.	3 months (s63(2)).*
s63C	Time off for training.	3 months (s63C(2)).*
s64	Remuneration on suspension on medical grounds.	3 months (s70(2)).*
s67	Alternative work on maternity/medical grounds.	3 months (s70(2)).*
s80	Complaints concerning parental leave under Maternity and Parental Leave etc Regulations 1999 SI No 3312.	3 months (s80(2)).*
s92(1)	Written statement of reasons for dismissal.	3 months from EDT (ss93 and 111).
s94	Unfair dismissal.	3 months from EDT (s111).*

s128	Interim relief in dismissal cases relating to certain health and safety issues.	7 days after EDT (s128(2)).
s163	Reference of question relating to failure by employer to make redundancy payment.	6 months (s164).
s170	Reference of question relating to payment equivalent to redundancy rebates in respect of civil servants, etc.	None.
s182	Payment by secretary of state on insolvency of employer.	3 months (s188(2)).*
Employment Tribunal Act 1996 and Employment Tribunal (Extension of Jurisdiction Order) 1994		
s3 and reg 7	Contract claims.	3 months. *
Employment Tribunal Act 1996 and Employment Appeal Tribunal Rules 1993 as amended by 2001 Regs and Rules of the Supreme Court Order 94 r8(3)		
s21 and EAT Rules r3(2)	Appeal to EAT (or High Court).	42 days from promulgation of employment tribunal decision.
Working Time Regulations 1998		
reg 30	Failure to permit exercise of rights or failure to pay annual leave.	3 months (reg 30(2)).* (6 months in armed forces cases).
Human Rights Act 1998		
s7	Infringement of human rights (to a court; unless rules are made under s7(11)).	1 year (s7(5)).**
National Minimum Wage Act 1998		
s11(1)	Refusal to produce records.	3 months from end of 14-day period within which records ought to have been produced (s11(2)).*

EMPLOYMENT TRIBUNAL JURISDICTION AND TIME LIMITS

Statutory right	Time limit
s19(5) Appeal against enforcement notice.	4 weeks from date of service.
s22(2) Appeal against penalty notice.	4 weeks from date of service.
Employment Relations Act 1999	
s11(1) Refusal of right to be accompanied to disciplinary/grievance hearing.	3 months (s11(2)).*
Tax Credits Act 1999	
Sch 3 para 2 Detriment concerning tax credit rights.	3 months (ERA 1996 s48).*
Disability Rights Commission Act 1999	
Sch 3 para 10(2) Appeal against non-discrimination notice.	6 weeks (para 10(1)).
Transnational Information and Consultation of Employees Regulations 1999	
reg 27 Refusal of right to time off or to give information.	3 months (reg 27(2)).*
reg 32 Complaints relating to detriment in respect of rights connected with European Works Councils.	3 months (ERA 1996 s48).
Part Time Workers (Prevention of Less Favourable Treatment) Regulations 2000	
reg 8 Less favourable treatment/detriment.	3 months (reg 8(2))* (6 months for the armed forces).

ACAS arbitration scheme

Introduction

3.1   The Advisory, Conciliation and Arbitration Service (ACAS) arbitration scheme came into force on 21 May 2001.[1] The scheme provides a voluntary alternative to the employment tribunal (ET) for the resolution of unfair dismissal disputes in the form of arbitration. It is only if both parties agree to arbitrate that this means of determining a dispute can be used. It applies to disputes involving an employer who resides or carries on business in England or Wales.[2] A code of practice supplements the scheme. Additional jurisdictions may be given to arbitrators by the secretary of state in due course.[3]

Terms of reference

3.2   The terms of reference given to the arbitrator are as follows:

In deciding whether the dismissal was fair or unfair, the Arbitrator shall:
(i)   have regard to the general principles of fairness and good conduct in employment relations (including, for example, principles referred to in any relevant ACAS 'Disciplinary and Grievance Procedures' Code of Practice or 'Discipline at Work' Handbook), instead of applying legal tests or rules (eg, court decisions or legislation).
(ii)   apply EU Law.
The Arbitrator shall not decide the case by substituting what he or she would have done for the actions taken by the Employer.
    If the Arbitrator finds the dismissal unfair, he or she shall determine the appropriate remedy under the terms of this scheme.

---

1   The Scheme is made under Trade Unions and Labour Relations (Consolidation) Act 1992 (TULRCA 1992) s212A, which implements Employment Rights (Dispute Resolution) Act 1998 s7. See ACAS Arbitration Scheme (England and Wales) Order 2001 SI No 1185 at Appendix D.
2   An arbitration scheme for Scotland is due to come into force at the end of 2001, and a scheme for Northern Ireland is being drafted under the Employment Rights (Dispute Resolution) (Northern Ireland) Order 1998 SI No 1265.
3   TULRCA 1992 s212A(1).

Scope of the scheme

3.3 The scheme applies only to complaints of unfair dismissal which allege contravention of Employment Rights Act 1996 (ERA 1996) Part X. Any associated claim which an employee may have, such as a discrimination claim, or breach of contract claim, must either be withdrawn or else referred to the ET, as the arbitrator is limited to dealing solely with the unfair dismissal issue.

3.4 Before submitting a dispute to arbitration the parties must agree to waive jurisdictional issues, and a specific pro forma set out in appendix A to the scheme must be completed. The scheme is not designed for disputes raising jurisdictional issues such as whether the applicant is an employee, whether the necessary continuous service had been completed, or whether a claim was submitted within the appropriate time limit. There is assumed to be no jurisdictional barrier to the claim. Furthermore, in agreeing to an arbitration parties will be treated as having agreed that a dismissal has taken place.

3.5 The arbitrator is under a duty to act fairly and impartially, giving each party an opportunity to put their case, and to deal with the other's case; and also to avoid delay and expense so as to provide a fair means of access for the resolution of disputes.

3.6 The parties must comply 'without delay' (which is not defined) with any determination or direction of the arbitrator, and all procedures under this scheme are strictly confidential.

Access to the scheme

3.7 Any agreement to submit a dispute to arbitration must:
- be in writing;
- concern an existing dispute;
- not alter or vary any provision of the scheme;
- have been reached either:
  - where a conciliation officer has taken action under Employment Tribunals Act 1996 s18; or
  - through a compromise agreement where the conditions regulating such agreements under ERA 1996 are satisfied;
- be accompanied by a completed waiver form for each party.

3.8 In circumstances where a dispute other than unfair dismissal is settled, and the unfair dismissal complaint is referred to arbitration, separate settlements must be reached.

3.9   Within six weeks of signing an arbitration agreement ACAS must be notified, and the following documents must be sent to the ACAS Arbitration Section:

- arbitration agreement;
- IT1;
- IT3;
- waiver form.

If ACAS is not notified within the six-week period, it will only accept the referral if it is shown that it was not reasonably practicable to have submitted the referral within time. It is assumed that the interpretation given by tribunals when considering whether it was reasonably practicable to lodge unfair dismissal complaints on time will be applied, since it arises from analogous legislation.[4]

Withdrawal and settlement

3.10   An employee can withdraw his or her complaint at any stage of the arbitration process, provided the withdrawal is in writing. However, an employer cannot unilaterally withdraw once it has entered into the arbitration agreement.

3.11   Parties are free to reach an agreement settling the dispute at any stage and, on receipt of a joint written request, the ACAS Arbitration Section will terminate the proceedings. If the parties want the form of words of settlement to be recorded, this can be done, but the arbitrator may only record the parties' wording and may not approve, interpret or ratify any settlement.

Appointment of arbitrator

3.12   The arbitrator will be selected from an ACAS arbitration panel. This is made up of people who have practical knowledge and experience of discipline and dismissal issues in the workplace, recruited via an open recruitment exercise. Appointments are for an initial period of two years, but may be renewed at the discretion of

4   See para 5.24.

ACAS. Payment is on the basis of time spent in connection with arbitral proceedings.

3.13   The parties have no choice of arbitrator. Following their selection, the arbitrator must state in writing any circumstances known to them which would give rise to any justifiable doubts about their impartiality, or confirm in writing that there are no such circumstances. If a party objects to an arbitrator, they must apply to the ACAS Arbitration Section setting out their grounds of objection. The only grounds of objection permissible are those set out in Arbitration Act 1996 s24(1)(a) and (c), ie, justifiable doubts about impartiality or physical or mental incapability of conducting the proceedings, or justifiable doubts about such ability. If ACAS refuses the application, a party may apply to the High Court, or to the Central London County Court.

3.14   If an arbitrator needs to be replaced, whether because of death or because he or she ceases to hold office for any reason, a further arbitrator will be appointed. The replacement will have complete discretion about whether, and if so to what extent, the previous proceedings should stand.

The hearing

3.15   A hearing must be held in every case, and will be arranged by the arbitrator as soon as is reasonably practicable. In any event, the arbitrator must decide the date and venue within two months of the initial notification being sent to ACAS. Any venue can be used, though it should not be 'partisan', such as the workplace, unless both parties agree. ACAS will meet the reasonable expense of hiring a venue if necessary. There is no provision for any expenses to be paid to those involved in arbitrations, other than in circumstances in which assistance is required from interpreters, signers and others. Once the hearing date has been fixed, any requests for it to be moved must be made in writing within 14 days of notification.

3.16   At least 14 days before the hearing each party must send to the ACAS Arbitration Section a statement of case together with supporting documentation and a list of the names and title/role of all those people who will attend the hearing, as witnesses or otherwise. The likely nature of 'supporting documentation' is explained in the scheme and, just as in ETs, is likely to include contracts of employment, time sheets and attendance records, performance appraisals, warning and dismissal letters, company handbooks, wage slips, P60s, though this is not an exhaustive list

3.17   Parties must also be prepared to deal with the issue of remedy, including the practicability or otherwise of reinstatement or re-engagement, details of jobseeker's allowance or income support received, along with details of all attempts to find work or otherwise mitigate losses arising from dismissal. Details of any other awards made by a tribunal or court in connection with the subject matter of this dispute must be disclosed.

3.18   The arbitrator has no power to compel the disclosure of documents, or the attendance of witnesses, but may draw adverse inferences from a party's failure to co-operate. If a party fails to attend a hearing, it may take place in their absence or be adjourned. Their written submissions will be considered. If a matter is adjourned, but an employee fails to demonstrate sufficient cause for his or her non-attendance, the complaint may be dismissed.

3.19   During a hearing, no party or witness shall be cross-examined by a party or representative or examined on oath or affirmation. This means that the role of the arbitrator is to take the initiative so as to ascertain the facts. Strict rules of evidence will not apply.

European Union and human rights

3.20   While parties may be represented by legal advisers, they will not be able to cross-examine witnesses, and strict rules of law will not apply. However, the exception is where questions arise concerning EU law or the Human Rights Act 1998 (HRA 1998). Here the arbitrator has the power, on application of either party or on their own initiative, to appoint a legal adviser who will assist to the extent that the law is relevant to the resolution of the dispute. The parties may make submissions about the content of any advice offered by the legal adviser, following which the arbitrator will take all the information into account before determining the dispute.

Awards

3.21   The awards which can be made by the arbitrator are the same as those which can be made by a tribunal in unfair dismissal claims. As in the tribunal, reinstatement and re-engagement are to be considered before a monetary award. Monetary awards are calculated and can be enforced in the same way as tribunal awards via the county court. The main difference is that the arbitrations are confidential.

3.22   It is not likely that the recoupment of benefit regime[5] applies to arbitration awards since they are not *tribunal* awards, and there is no parallel requirement on the arbitrator to make inquiries and record the data relating to benefit. The scheme itself does not mention this issue.

Challenges and appeals

3.23   There are very limited opportunities for parties to appeal against, or otherwise challenge the result of an arbitration. There is no general right to appeal on either a point of law or fact; with the exception that points of EU law, or matters under the HRA 1998 may be appealed. If there are no points under either EU law or the HRA 1998, the only challenge which can be made is under Arbitration Act 1996 ss67–69, namely on grounds of substantive jurisdiction, serious irregularity or a question of law. If any party continues to take part in proceedings without making an objection about substantive jurisdiction, proceedings being conducted improperly or any failure to comply with the arbitration agreement or scheme, or any other irregularity, they will lose their right to object at a later time.

---

5   Employment Protection (Recoupment of Jobseeker's Allowance and Income Support) Regulations 1996 SI No 2349.

CHAPTER 4

Stages before the originating application

The correct respondent

4.1   After checking to make sure that the tribunal has jurisdiction to hear the case, the applicant needs to consider who is the correct respondent to name on the originating application. This will generally be the employer but it may also be a fellow employee or other individual, in claims under the Sex Discrimination Acts (SDA) 1975 and 1986, Race Relations Act 1976 (RRA 1976), or the Disability Discrimination Act 1995 (DDA 1995), or possibly a trade union.

4.2   Sometimes it will not be clear who the relevant employer is, for example, in cases arising out of transfer of a business or where there is a complicated arrangement of associated companies. Difficulties in naming the correct respondent may sometimes be resolved by a reply given to a letter before action.[1] If in doubt, the applicant should name all possible respondents and explain the reasons for doing so in the details of the complaint.

4.3   Where a purely technical error has been made in the naming of a respondent and no prejudice has been caused, the tribunal may take a pragmatic approach, allowing an amendment late on in the proceedings.[2]

4.4   A tribunal is given a broad discretion to join a party to proceedings as a respondent 'at any time',[3] and can do so even after the time limit for presenting a claim against a new respondent has expired.[4] It can also be done after a decision on the merits of the case has been given: in *Linbourne v Constable*[5] the Employment Appeal Tribunal held that an amendment should be allowed to substitute a respondent even after a decision had been given. The guidelines to be taken into consideration by the tribunal in such cases were set out by the National Industrial Relations Court in *Cocking v Sandhurst (Stationers) Ltd*:[6]

– Did the unamended application comply with the rules relating to the presentation of originating applications (see para 5.45) and was it presented within the relevant time limit? If not, there is

---

1   See para 4.12.
2   *Chapman v Goonvean and Rostowrack China Clay Co Ltd* [1973] ICR 50; [1972] IRLR 124, NIRC.
3   Employment Tribunals Rules of Procedure 2001 ('2001 Rules') r19(1).
4   *Drinkwater Sabey Ltd v Burnett* [1995] ICR 328; [1995] IRLR 238, EAT, following *Gillick v BP Chemicals Ltd* [1993] IRLR 437, EAT. See also chapter 12.
5   [1993] ICR 698.
6   [1974] ICR 650.

no power to amend and a new originating application must be presented within the relevant time limit.
- If it did comply with the rules on presentation, the tribunal has discretion to allow an amendment that would add or substitute a new party. It should do so only if satisfied that the mistake sought to be corrected was a genuine mistake and was not misleading or such as to cause reasonable doubt about the identity of the person intending to claim or, as the case may be, to be claimed against.
- In deciding whether or not to exercise its discretion, the tribunal should have regard to all the circumstances of the case, including any injustice or hardship which may be caused to any of the parties or potential parties if the amendment were allowed or refused. If allowing the amendment might cause unnecessary additional cost to one party, the tribunal might properly conclude that this was an appropriate case for the amending party to be ordered to pay the additional costs caused by the late amendment (see para 20.5 on costs).

4.5   When an amendment is allowed after a decision has been given, as in the *Linbourne* case (above), the tribunal will give the new respondent an opportunity to be heard on the merits of the case unless there would be no prejudice by not doing so.

4.6   Generally, see chapter 8 on amendments.

Unincorporated associations

4.7   One word of warning: proceedings must be commenced against some legal 'person' or body, whether that 'person' is an individual, a collection of individuals or a company. If the employer is an unincorporated association, the claim cannot be made against the association in the abstract, as it is not a legal body. The correct respondent in these cases is the individual or individuals with effective day to day control of the association, often the chairman or members of the management or executive committee.[7] Applicants can bring a claim against 'representative' respondents in such circumstances, as in *Affleck v Newcastle Mind*.[8]

7   *Bradley Egg Farm v Clifford* [1943] 2 All ER 378.
8   [1999] IRLR 405, EAT.

Insolvent employers

4.8   As with court proceedings, tribunal proceedings may be commenced or continued against a company in administration only with the leave of the High Court or the administrator.[9] The administrator is an interested party and may be joined to the proceedings. However, failure to obtain the leave of the court does not make the originating application a nullity. The proper course is for the tribunal to stay (*sist*, in Scotland) the proceedings while the leave of the court is obtained.[10] It is highly likely that a similar approach would be taken where the company is in compulsory liquidation under Insolvency Act 1986 s130(2).

4.9   If the administrator adopts the contracts of employment of a company's employees, he or she will be liable to be sued personally, so leave of the court is not required. The Insolvency Act 1986 ss19 and 44 were amended by the Insolvency Act 1994 with effect from 15 March 1994 to limit the responsibilities of administrators, which in *Powdrill v Watson*[11] had been held to be unlimited once the administrator adopts or is deemed to adopt a contract of employment.

4.10   If one of the parties is bankrupt, the trustee in bankruptcy will have a clear interest in the outcome of the proceedings and would be entitled to apply to be joined as a party. In these cases a directions hearing (para 12.45) may assist in clarifying the position of the insolvent party and the interests of others who may wish to be joined in the proceedings.

4.11   The secretary of state is likely to be interested in most claims against insolvent employers, since there is likely to be a payment out of the National Insurance Fund under Employment Rights Act 1996 s182. The tribunal will notify the department of these claims and the secretary of state may be joined as a party.

---

9   Insolvency Act 1986 s11(3), applied in *Carr v British International Helicopters Ltd* (*in administration*) [1994] ICR 18, EAT.

10   *Carr*, above.

11   [1995] 2 AC 394; [1995] ICR 1100; [1995] IRLR 269, HL, confirming [1994] ICR 395, CA (the *Paramount Airways* case).

Letter before action

4.12   While applicants are under no obligation to notify their employers (or other potential respondents) of a claim before presenting it to a tribunal, a letter before action can serve to resolve some of the issues between the prospective parties before tribunal proceedings are commenced and may even render such proceedings unnecessary if the employer makes the payment or takes the action sought by the employee. If there is no risk of time limits being missed, it is generally worth writing a letter notifying the prospective respondent of the complaint which may be made.

4.13   This is particularly helpful where the employee is unsure about the precise identity of the employer. If, subsequently, an application has to be made to change the name of the respondent after tribunal proceedings have been commenced (para 4.1), the fact that the first named respondent took no steps to correct the mistake on receipt of the letter before action, or that the correct respondent had already been put on notice by such a letter, will assist the employee in making the application and/or in applying for any costs incurred by the failure to clarify the position at an earlier stage.

4.14   The letter before action should set out the broad nature of the complaint and indicate that the writer will commence proceedings in the tribunal unless steps are taken to remedy the situation within a specified period of time. Obviously, a prospective applicant should have in mind at this stage what he or she hopes to get out of the proceedings and the limitations on tribunals' remedies. The letter should be 'open': it should express the full claim and not deal with proposals for settling the claim as a form of compromise. Such proposals, if made, should be contained in separate correspondence, specifically marked 'without prejudice'.

4.15   It is not necessary to go into much detail at this stage and it would be unwise to do so without full instructions and advice. Be warned: respondents will often seek to cross-examine on the basis of any inconsistencies, however slight, between correspondence before action and the case as stated in the course of the proceedings. On the other hand, if the applicant is confident that a full account can be given at this stage, the fact it has been given even before proceedings are commenced can make the case easier to sustain subsequently in the tribunal. This is especially true in constructive dismissal and discrimination cases, where the applicant's contemporary perception of events is very important.

4.16   Furthermore, if there is no reasonable defence to the complaint and the case is one where there is a real chance of the applicant obtaining an order for costs against the respondent (para 13.1), the fact that the nature of the complaint and the relief sought has been detailed before the commencement of tribunal proceedings will be a relevant factor in any application for costs against a respondent who failed to take that opportunity to resolve the matter.

Questionnaires

4.17   In race, sex and disability discrimination cases, information can be requested from an employer or other respondent by use of a questionnaire *before* any claim is presented to a tribunal.[12] There are also proposals to extend this procedure to equal pay claims, although these are often brought alongside a claim under the SDA 1975 in any event (and, arguably, as the EqPA 1970 is incorporated as a Schedule to the SDA 1975, the questionnaire procedure under the SDA 1975 can already be used in any event).

4.18   The questionnaire enables a prospective applicant to find out background information which may assist the claim, for example, the relative numbers of men and women or the racial background of employees in each grade within the workplace; and to question the prospective respondent on the reasons for the action which has led to the grievance. It may also lead to the provision of relevant statistical evidence, even if the employer has to create documentation in order to provide such information. As a respondent cannot be ordered to create documents which are not already in existence, this is an unusual and potentially very useful procedure. A failure to answer the questionnaire or an inadequate or incomplete answer may lead the tribunal to draw an inference of unlawful discrimination. Answers given to a questionnaire can also form the basis of cross-examination. All in all, the questionnaire procedure is often a very useful tool for an applicant in a discrimination complaint.

4.19   Copies of the prescribed forms for the questionnaire and reply are set out in appendix A. Chapter 9 deals with the procedure.

---

12   SDA 1975 s74(1); RRA 1976 s65(1); DDA 1995 s56.

Financing a case and costs implications

4.20   Legal help is not available for representation at tribunals in England
and Wales. Legal aid is now available in limited cases in Scotland,
having been introduced in order to satisfy the Human Rights Act
1998 requirement that parties have a fair trial. There are however, no
moves to extend legal help to assist parties bringing claims in
England and Wales.[13] A prospective applicant may, however, be eligible to receive legal assistance (which may include representation)
from the following sources:

– a trade union or professional association;
– in sex discrimination or equal pay cases, the Equal Opportunities
  Commission (EOC);
– in race discrimination cases, the Commission for Racial
  Equality (CRE);
– in disability discrimination cases, the Disability Rights Commission (DRC);
– law centres or citizens advice bureaux;
– other free advisory bodies, such as the Bar Pro Bono Scheme,[14]
  and various other local and community-based projects;[15]
– solicitors who have a franchise under the 'legal help' scheme
  (for advice and all steps other than actual representation);
– under an insurance scheme – increasingly a feature of many
  household insurance policies;
– ACAS (basic, non-partisan advice only).

4.21   Respondents may also be eligible for assistance from the above
sources, although corporate respondents are less likely to be in need
of financial assistance in obtaining legal advice or representation.
Respondents who are members of particular trade associations may
be entitled to free advice and representation under the terms of their
membership.

4.22   Both lay and professional advisers may also refer appropriate
cases to the EOC, CRE or DRC, or act as a referral agency to the Free

---

13 For information on legal aid in Scotland, contact the Scottish Legal Aid Board
    (see address in appendix E) or on their website: www.slab.org.uk. For Northern
    Ireland contact the Northern Ireland Legal Aid Department (see address in
    appendix E).
14 See addresses in appendix E.
15 See the website of the Community Legal Service: www.justask.org.uk.

Representation Unit, which may be able to provide preliminary advice and representation at the hearing. Addresses for the above organisations are set out in appendix E.

4.23   Although anyone can appear at a tribunal, it stands to reason that the more and the better informed the advice and assistance that a party receives before or during the hearing, the better prepared he or she is likely to be.

4.24   The successful party in a tribunal case is, however, unlikely to be able to reclaim from the other side any legal costs incurred during the proceedings. The general rule in tribunals is that costs will not be awarded unless a party has acted vexatiously, abusively, disruptively or otherwise unreasonably or the bringing or conduct of the proceedings is misconceived.[16] If one party believes that there may be a good argument for obtaining costs against the other, it is worth bringing this to the other side's attention in writing before making the application. If the other side continues to act in the same vexatious or unreasonable (etc) manner, the letter will assist any application to the tribunal for costs. On the other hand, letters threatening applications for costs in tribunals are often made where there is really no ground for such an application. The recipient of such a letter should consider its contents seriously and take further advice if necessary, but should not be deterred from bringing or defending a claim by a groundless threat.

4.25   The subject of costs orders is dealt with in more detail in chapter 20.

16   2001 Rules r14(1).

Checklist: Pre-action considerations

- Is the applicant eligible for 'legal help' or any other financial aid in respect of the claim?
- Do questions of sex, race, or disability discrimination or of equal pay arise where advice and assistance might be obtained from the EOC, CRE or DRC?
- Is the complaint one which a tribunal can properly hear or should it be brought in the county court or some other court or tribunal?
- Does the applicant meet the jurisdictional conditions in relation to pursuing a particular claim in a tribunal?
- Is the correct respondent named?
- Are any of the parties insolvent?
- Has a letter before action been sent to give the respondent the opportunity of meeting the claim without the necessity of tribunal proceedings?
- In cases under SDA 1975, RRA 1976, and DDA 1995, has the appropriate questionnaire been served?

CHAPTER 5

Time limits

continued

General principles

5.1   The table at para 2.7 sets out the time limits applicable to the initiation of all of the statutory claims which may be made before a tribunal. Different considerations apply to time limits for presenting a notice of appearance, which are less strict, and for complying with interlocutory orders. There are three general principles:

1) There are time limits for most statutory claims.
2) Most statutory claims are subject to an escape clause allowing the claim to be presented within a further time limit by the exercise of the tribunal's discretion.
3) All time limits operate according to rigid rules based on a determination of the precise relevant date. These time limits are matters of jurisdiction, and not of discretion or procedure.

Time limits in general

5.2   Almost all statutory rights are subject to a time limit, but the following require particular attention:

Failure by employer to make redundancy payment

5.3   Reference under Employment Rights Act 1996 (ERA 1996) s163 of a question relating to a failure by an employer to make a redundancy payment. The reference is to the secretary of state, who may make a payment out of the National Insurance Fund. There is no time limit on this reference by a former employee.

Redundancy payments to public office holders

5.4   Reference of a question relating to payment of the equivalent of a redundancy payment to civil servants and other public office holders, under ERA 1996 s171. These are subject to the normal contractual limitation period of six years.[1] This is because the claim arises not under statute but under contract and the mechanism for resolving this particular contractual issue is referral of the question to a tribunal.

---

1   Limitation Act 1980 s5.

Discriminatory terms

5.5   A complaint under Sex Discrimination Act 1975 (SDA 1975) s77(1) and SDA 1986 s6(4A) that a term in a contract, or a rule, or a collective agreement is void on the grounds that it is discriminatory. No time limit is prescribed.

UK claims affected by EU law

5.6   Claims based directly on the Treaty of Rome, for example, article 141 (equal pay), are not subject to any specific time limit under the Treaty. The European Court of Justice (ECJ) has held that such matters are for the member states' own jurisdictions to apply as matters of procedure.[2] This was followed in relation to time limits for enforcing claims under a directive which was intended to be directly effective (ie, not the Treaty itself) in *Emmott v Minister for Social Welfare*,[3] a case from the Irish Republic where the ECJ held:

> In the absence of Community rules on the subject, it is for the domestic legal system of each member state to determine the procedural conditions governing actions at law intended to ensure the protection of the rights which individuals derive from the direct effect of Community law, provided that such conditions are not less favourable than those relating to similar actions of a domestic nature nor framed so as to render virtually impossible the exercise of rights conferred by community law.[4]

5.7   In *Livingstone v Hepworth Refractories plc*[5] it was held that analogous time limits to those in domestic procedures should be applied to claims under article 141. In that case a time limit of three months was appropriate for a sex discrimination claim under article 141 as that is the time provided by the SDA 1975.

5.8   In *Biggs v Somerset CC*[6] the Court of Appeal held that rights under the Treaty are not justiciable as free-standing claims in tribunals. Tribunals have jurisdiction only when given it by statute. Although they must apply EU law in the application and enforcement of domestic law, and even disapply domestic law inconsistent with it, they cannot hear cases founded solely on directly effective European

---

2   *Rewe-Zentralfinanz eG and Rewe-Zentral AG v Landwirtschaftskammer für das Saarland* (No 33/76) [1976] ECR 1989; [1977] CMLR 533, ECJ.
3   [1993] ICR 8; [1991] IRLR 387, ECJ.
4   See para 16 of the judgment.
5   [1992] ICR 287; [1992] IRLR 63, EAT.
6   [1996] IRLR 203, CA.

provisions. The claim was made by a woman part-time teacher dismissed in 1976 who thought she must have a claim for unfair dismissal once she read of the judgment of the House of Lords in *R v Secretary of State for Employment ex p EOC*.[7] She argued that the exclusion of part-timers from the right to claim unfair dismissal was discriminatory (as had been held in that case) and that she should be entitled to bring a claim within three months of the Lords' judgment.

5.9   The Court of Appeal held that this was a matter of domestic law and procedure, as unfair dismissal was not within the Treaty, nor had the Equal Treatment Directive[8] 1976 then become operative. There was no free-standing right of unfair dismissal in EU law which could be taken before a tribunal. Furthermore, it was possible for the applicant to have lodged a claim of unfair dismissal in 1976 and fought the battle then.

5.10   In the light of the acceptance at many judicial levels of an individual's right to commence proceedings in the tribunal this judgment is surprising. In view of this difficulty, as a safe rule three months should be considered the appropriate limitation from the date of the relevant act by the employer. Where unfair dismissal is claimed, this might start to run from the date of dismissal or from the date of a significant court decision.

5.11   It is also submitted that the Court of Appeal was wrong to dismiss the right of individuals to bring claims in the tribunal based on EU law. Since the domestic procedures must not make it more difficult for individuals to enforce European rights than similar rights in domestic law, it cannot be right for an individual to have to use the courts rather than the more accessible tribunals for such enforcement.

5.12   If there is a right to bring a claim under directly effective EU provisions, the same principles apply to claims brought under relevant directives, for example, the Equal Treatment Directive, as to claims directly under the Treaty of Rome, with the exception that time runs only from the date when a directive is properly and fully transposed into UK law.[9]

5.13   For claims based on the Treaty the date appears to run from 'the date upon which it could reasonably be said to be clear to any person affected . . . that such a claim could properly be made'.[10] One

7 [1994] ICR 317; [1994] IRLR 176.
8 EEC/76/107.
9 See *Emmott*, note 3 above.
10 See *Rankin v British Coal Corporation* [1995] ICR 774; [1993] IRLR 69.

interpretation is to make time run for equality of redundancy pay (and arguably pensions) from the date of the judgment of the ECJ in *Barber v Guardian Royal Exchange Assurance Group*.[11] This seems to treat judgments of the ECJ in a different way from judgments of the High Court in the UK, where the principle is maintained that judgments of, for example, the House of Lords do not change the law, but simply make clear what the law always was.

5.14   It is always necessary to apply domestic legislation with its own time limit and other procedural restrictions to cases where there is no directly effective EU right. According to the Court of Appeal, the existence of a statutory bar is not a good reason for contending that it was not reasonably practicable to present a claim, or that it is just and equitable to extend time.[12]

5.15   The principle of equivalence as set out in *Emmott* (above) was restated again by the ECJ and the House of Lords in the joined cases of *Preston and others v Wolverhampton Healthcare Trust*.[13] In this case part-time employees brought claims under Equal Pay Act 1970 (EqPA 1970) s2(4) and the Occupational Pension Schemes (Equal Access to Membership) Regulations 1976,[14] complaining of having been denied access to occupational pension schemes. The ECJ held that the time limit in EqPA 1970 s2(4), requiring claims to be brought within six months of the termination of the applicant's contract of employment, was not contrary to European law. The Lords held that comparable claims in contract and for direct breach of article 141, were not more favourable taken as a whole. But it held that the EqPA 1970 s2(4) time limit for bringing a claim is unlawful in so far as it requires an employee who is engaged on a series of fixed-term contracts to initiate tribunal proceedings within six months of the termination of each of those contracts.

5.16   Claims under the Human Rights Act 1998 (HRA 1998) must be made within one year of the act complained of, unless the complaint is raised by a victim in proceedings instigated by a public body.[15]

11   [1990] ICR 616; [1990] IRLR 240.
12   See *Biggs*, note 3 above (unfair dismissal claim refused to part-time worker 18 years late); *R v Secretary of State for Employment ex p EOC* [1994] ICR 317; [1994] IRLR 176, HL (the part-time workers' case).
13   [2001] IRLR 237; [2001] ICR 216, HL.
14   SI No 142.
15   HRA 1998 ss7 and 22.

Time limits and escape clauses

5.17 Most of the time limits are softened by words such as those relating to unfair dismissal complaints,[16] which introduce a secondary time limit:[17]

> an employment tribunal shall not consider a complaint . . . unless it is presented to the tribunal –
> (a) before the end of the period of three months beginning with the effective date of termination, or
> (b) within such further period as the tribunal considers reasonable in a case where it is satisfied that it was not reasonably practicable for a complaint to be presented before the end of the period of three months.

5.18 A different formulation applies in relation, for example, to complaints of sex, race, disability, and part-timer discrimination:

> A court or tribunal may nevertheless consider any such complaint . . . which is out of time if, in all the circumstances of the case, it considers that it is just and equitable to do so.[18]

These latter claims have only one limitation period. Claims which are subject to an escape clause carry with them their own limitation periods, each of which is capable of shutting out an applicant.

5.19 Provisions which do not give the tribunal any flexibility are:

- claims under EqPA 1970 s2(4);
- a claim for time off with pay for a safety representative (Health and Safety at Work Act 1974 s80 and Safety Representatives and Safety Committees Regulations 1977[19] reg 11(2));
- appeals against non-discrimination notices under SDA 1975 s68 and Race Relations Act 1976 (RRA 1976) s59;
- an application for interim relief (Trade Unions and Labour Relations (Consolidation) Act 1992 (TULRCA 1992) s161(2) and ERA 1996 s128);
- complaints by union members for a declaration following findings of unjustifiable discipline (TULRCA 1992 s66(3)) and expulsion/exclusion (TULRCA 1992 s176(3));
- applications for compensation following findings of unjustifiable

---

16   ERA 1996 s94.
17   Ibid s111(2).
18   SDA 1975 s76(5), RRA 1976 s68(6), DDA 1995 Sch 3 para 3, Part-time Workers (Prevention of Less Favourable Treatment) Regulations (PTW Regs) 2000 SI No 1551 reg 8(3).
19   SI No 500.

discipline or unlawful expulsion/exclusion from a trade union (TULRCA 1992 ss67 and 174).

Jurisdiction

5.20   Almost all of the statutory rights which are subject to a time limit are affected by a jurisdictional bar. Tribunals have no jurisdiction to hear a case brought outside the time limit.[20] This means that the parties cannot waive a time limit, for example, by agreeing to have the case heard even though a complaint was not made within time. (Although parties can agree to submit an unfair dismissal claim to ACAS Arbitration even if such complaint is out of time in the tribunal, see chapter 3.) It also means that the tribunal itself can and should take the point if it is aware of it.[21] Furthermore, a new point relating to jurisdiction may be taken on appeal to the Employment Appeal Tribunal (EAT) even though not raised at the tribunal.[22] The vast majority of statutory rights are qualified by words such as 'an employment tribunal shall not consider a complaint . . . unless it is presented . . .' within the appropriate period.[23]

5.21   A similar bar in different words appears in EqPA 1970 s2(4) and ERA 1996 s11(4) (claims for written particulars). Although the National Industrial Relations Court (NIRC) in *Grimes v Sutton LBC*[24] felt the latter provision was not jurisdictional, the better view, it is submitted, is now found in *Rogers*[25] and *Secretary of State for Employment v Atkins Auto Laundries Ltd*,[26] which related to the comparable provision on redundancy pay now in ERA 1996 s164(3).

5.22   Time limits, therefore, are rigid and jurisdictional.

20   *Biggs v Somerset CC* [1996] IRLR 203; [1996] ICR 364, CA.
21   *Rogers v Bodfari (Transport) Ltd* [1973] ICR 325; [1973] IRLR 172, NIRC and *Dedman v British Building and Engineering Appliances Ltd* [1974] ICR 53; [1973] IRLR 379, CA.
22   *House v Emerson Electric Industrial Controls* [1980] ICR 795, EAT. *JF Knight (Roadworks) Ltd v Platfoot* [2001] ICR Part 3 p xvi.
23   ERA 1996 s104(2) (on unfair dismissal).
24   [1973] ICR 240.
25   See note 21 above.
26   [1972] ICR 76, NIRC.

When does time start running?

5.23   All the statutory rights depend on the identification of a relevant event from which time begins to run. Once that date is clear, the rules relating to the counting of time can be applied.

Unfair dismissal

5.24   Time runs from the effective date of termination (EDT) as defined in ERA 1996 s97(1). A specific exception is provided by ERA s104(3) so that an applicant can present a claim after notice has been given but before the EDT. The same goes for an applicant claiming constructive dismissal under ERA 1996 s95(1)(c) who, instead of terminating summarily (as he or she would be entitled to do), gives notice and between the giving of notice and the EDT lodges a complaint.[27]

5.25   Since the termination of a fixed term contract on its due date is not a termination by notice, a complaint presented before the due date does not fall within the exception in ERA 1996 s97(4).[28] If you know the contract is not going to be renewed, you must wait until after it has expired before presenting a claim.

Redundancy pay

5.26   A claim for redundancy pay must be made within six months of the 'relevant date'. This is defined by ERA 1996 s145 and is a slightly expanded version of that applying to unfair dismissal under ERA 1996 s97(1). A claim is in time if within the six months counting the EDT:[29]

- a redundancy payment has been agreed and paid;
- the employee has made a claim in writing to the employer for redundancy pay;
- a question has been referred to a tribunal by originating application; or
- an unfair dismissal complaint has been presented in time, ie, within three months.

This means that the applicant need not present a claim to the tribunal

---

27   *Presley v Llanelli BC* [1979] ICR 419; [1979] IRLR 381, EAT.
28   *Throsby v Imperial College of Science and Technology* [1978] ICR 357; [1977] IRLR 337, EAT.
29   ERA 1996 s164.

but can stop time running by writing to the employer and claiming redundancy pay.

5.27   Extension of time can be granted by the tribunal if during a *further* limitation period of six months the employee does the second, third or fourth things above *and* the tribunal considers it just and equitable in all the circumstances to allow the complaint to go ahead, having regard to the reason for the failure to take any of the above steps in the original six-month limitation period.

Equal pay

5.28   Claims under EqPA 1970 s2 for breach of an equality clause should be brought during the existence of the contract, or within six months of the employee leaving.[30] It should be noted that in *Preston v Wolverhampton*[31] the ECJ held that a where a person is engaged on a series of fixed term contracts, he or she is *not* required to initiate proceedings within six months of the termination of each of those contracts.

Written particulars

5.29   Claims under ERA 1996 s11(4) seeking written particulars of contractual terms, or an itemised pay statement, must be brought during the existence of the contract or within three months of the employee leaving.

Interim relief

5.30   Claims for interim relief (ERA 1996 s128) in cases of dismissal on the grounds of trade union activity or membership (TULRCA 1992 ss152 and 161), or health and safety complaints (ERA 1996 s100) or taking action as an elected employee representative (ERA ss101A(d) and 103) or making a protected disclosure under the whistle blowing jurisdiction of the Public Interest Disclosure Act 1998 (ERA 1996 s103A) must be brought at any time up to seven days after the EDT. A claim can be brought *before* the EDT, and the period of seven days runs from the day *after* the EDT, so a dismissal with or without notice taking effect on a Tuesday would require presentation of a claim by the end of the following Tuesday.

5.31   None of these claims attracts an escape clause giving the tribunal discretion to extend the deadline.

30 EqPA 1970 s2(4).
31 See note 13 above.

Discrimination

5.32 Special time limits apply to bringing discrimination claims. These are generally where the act complained of extends over a period of time. Time runs from the date of the act complained of. But 'any act extending over a period shall be treated as done at the end of that period'.[32] Discrimination against someone on the grounds of raising health and safety issues, 'whistle blowing', working time issues or raising the issue of parental leave is actionable within three months of the act complained of, or '. . . where that act . . . is part of a series of acts . . . the last of them'.[33] A similar provision applies in respect of action short of dismissal on trade union grounds.[34]

5.33 When a contractual term is unlawful by way of discrimination, it is treated as extending throughout the duration of the contract.[35] Where discrimination arises in respect of other matters than terms of the contract, it continues throughout the duration of the regime in which the discrimination is carried on. In *Barclays Bank plc v Kapur*[36] Asian workers, formerly employed by the bank in East Africa, who joined the bank's pension scheme in England in 1970 were denied recognition of their previous service in Africa, arguably on discriminatory grounds. This was held not to be a one-off act of discrimination but a continuing regime providing unfavourable pension rights as long as the employees remained in employment (although, having succeeded in the preliminary procedure, the employees lost at the hearing of the substantive claim).[37] Similarly, a failure to take proper remedial action following an act of discrimination has a continuing effect until that remedial action is taken.[38] The critical distinction is between a single act such as a decision on grading, and a general regime which has a continuing discriminatory effect.[39]

5.34 This distinction between single, and continuing acts was

---

32 SDA 1975 s76(6)(b), RRA 1976 s68(7)(b), DDA 1995 Sch 3 para 3(2)(b), PTW Regs 2000 reg 8(2).

33 ERA 1996 s46(3)(a).

34 TULRCA 1992 s147(1)(a).

35 SDA 1975 s76(6)(b) and RRA 1976 s68(7)(a).

36 [1991] ICR 208; [1991] IRLR 136, HL.

37 [1995] IRLR 87, CA.

38 *Littlewoods Organisation plc v Traynor* [1993] IRLR 154, EAT.

39 *Sougrin v Haringey HA* [1991] ICR 791; [1991] IRLR 447, EAT; *Owusu v London Fire and Civil Defence Authority* [1995] IRLR 574, EAT. See also *Lindsay v Ironsides, Ray and Vials* [1994] ICR 384; [1994] IRLR 318, EAT: preliminary issue should be tried as to whether a single discriminatory act is out of time.

considered in *Owusu v London Fire and Civil Defence Authority*[40] where the EAT held that a failure to promote or shortlist was a complaint of a one-off act, but a repeated failure to upgrade the applicant, or to allow him to act at a higher grade when the opportunity arose was considered to amount to a discriminatory practice, ie, a continuing act. In *Cast v Croydon College*[41] a series of refusals concerning a benefit were held by the Court of Appeal to amount to a continuing act if there was further consideration of each request, rather than merely a reference back to the earlier decision.

5.35   Where the act complained of is the refusal by employers to accept a grievance, time begins to run from the date on which the decision was communicated to the complainant, not the date on which the decision was made.[42] Where the employee invokes an internal appeal which is unsuccessful, the operative date depends on whether, as a matter of contract, the employment continues pending appeal.[43]

5.36   For deliberate omissions which are claimed to be discriminatory, time runs from the date on which a 'decision' is taken 'at a time and in circumstances when [the employer] was in a position to implement that decision'. So *Swithland Motors plc v Clarke*[44] when a car dealership seeking to take over the assets of a dealership which went into receivership interviewed but refused to appoint male car salesmen, allegedly on discriminatory grounds, it made the 'decision' not at the time of the interview but at the time of the takeover when it was in a position to implement the decision. But where the discrimination takes the form of *dismissal*, the time limit runs from the date of the expiry of the notice (if given) and not the date of the decision to dismiss or the giving of the notice.[45]

5.37   Even if acts outside the three-month period do not constitute part of a series of discriminatory acts or a continuing regime, they may nevertheless be adduced as evidence of discrimination occurring within the time limit.[46] Similarly, acts which prove discrimination occurring *after* the presentation of a valid claim may also be adduced.[47]

---

40 [1995] IRLR 574, EAT.
41 [1998] IRLR 318; [1998] ICR 500, CA.
42 *Aniagwu v Hackney LBC* [1999] IRLR 303, EAT.
43 *Adekeye v Post Office (No 2)* [1997] IRLR 105; [1997] ICR 110, CA.
44 [1994] ICR 231; [1994] IRLR 275, EAT.
45 *Lupeti v Wrens Old House Ltd* [1984] ICR 348, EAT.
46 *Eke v Customs and Excise Commissioners* [1981] IRLR 344, EAT.
47 *Chattopadhyay v Headmaster of Holloway School* [1982] ICR 132; [1981] IRLR 487, EAT.

Wages protection and Sunday trading cases

5.38   Claims relating to unlawful deductions from wages in respect of a series of deductions must be made within three months of the *last* deduction.[48]

5.39   Claims of detrimental treatment for refusing to do Sunday shop work following a series of acts must be brought within three months of the *last* of them.[49]

The rules on counting time

5.40   Having identified the date of the relevant event which triggers a claim, complaint, application or appeal to a tribunal, by reference to the appropriate statute, it is possible to determine the time limit for presentation of the originating application. The rules for calculating time were comprehensively summarised in *Pruden v Cunard Eller-man Ltd.*[50] Following citation of relevant authorities and reference to the Interpretation Act 1978, Wood J said:

> Where time is specified to run from a particular date, the word 'date' means the whole of the period of 24 hours from midnight to midnight, and the law takes no account of a fraction of a day unless special reasons require it . . . Where a complaint is required to be presented within a specific period – 'from', 'after' or 'of' – a particular date, that date is to be excluded from the calculation . . . However, where a complaint is required to be presented within a specified period beginning with 'a particular date' that date is to be *included* in the calculation . . . Those principles are well established.[51]

5.41   An expanded analysis appears in Civil Procedure Rules Part 2.8 and the accompanying notes, and the 2001 Regs add guidance on counting time in reg 2(7)–(10). In the table at para 2.7 the expression 'whole' weeks or months refers to time periods which begin from, after or on a particular date. For example, a dismissal for trade union activities occurring on a Tuesday triggers a limitation period of seven whole days so that an originating application must be presented on or

---

48   ERA 1996 s23(2) and (3).
49   Ibid s48(3).
50   [1993] IRLR 317, EAT. See also *RJB Mining (UK) Ltd v NUM* [1995] IRLR 556, CA.
51   At para 6.

before the following Tuesday. A claim for equal pay by a woman who left her job on 15 June must be presented on or before 15 December.

5.42   However, most claims under employment protection legislation must be brought 'before the end of the period of three months beginning with [the relevant event]', for example, unfair dismissal, a claim for which must be brought within the period of three months beginning with the effective date of termination. In such a case a claim for a dismissal arising on 15 June must be presented on or before 14 September. The date of the relevant event, in this case dismissal, is day 1 of the limitation period.

5.43   The EAT in *Pruden*[52] resolved the problem which arises when the trigger event is the last day of a month, because months consist of different numbers of days, ie, 28, 29, 30 or 31. Only four months have the same number of days as the corresponding month three months later (May, June, July, October). For all other months, the approach in *Pruden* will produce the correct answer. In that case, an originating application presented on 30 November in respect of a dismissal on 31 August was within time. If there is no corresponding date in the month in which limitation occurs, take the next earlier date. So a dismissal on 30 November must generate an originating application by 28 February in the succeeding year (or 29 February in a leap year).

5.44   The only slight surprise in applying these rules is that a dismissal on the last day of the month of February (ie, 28) must generate an originating application on 27 May, which is, of course, four days before the end of the month. However, a dismissal on the next day, 1 March, must generate an originating application by 31 May, four days later.

Commencement of proceedings

5.45   Time ceases to run when proceedings are properly commenced. By 2001 Rules r1(1), proceedings 'shall be instituted by the applicant presenting to the Secretary an originating application . . .' (although some proceedings are commenced by an *appellant* with a notice of appeal, for example, those under the Health and Safety at Work Act 1974). Presentation is a unilateral act. It does not require any response by the tribunal office.[53] As long as the originating applica-

---

52   See note 50 above.
53   *Hetton Victory Club Ltd v Swainstone* [1983] ICR 341; [1983] IRLR 164, CA.

tion is physically delivered to the relevant office before midnight at the end of the last day in the limitation period, the application is validly presented. So if a letter box is available at the office, posting through it will be effective presentation. If there is no provision for postal delivery through a letter box at the relevant office, service can be effected on the next available date when the office is open.[54]

5.46   Presentation must be made to 'the Secretary'. This means the Secretary of the Tribunals in England and Wales at Bury St Edmunds and in Scotland at Glasgow. The regulations provide for regional offices with regional secretaries who are established 'under the Office of the Tribunals for an area specified by the President' of the Tribunals.[55] Presentation at a regional office is valid and there seems to be no reason why this definition should not extend also to sub-offices within a region, for example, Watford, part of London North West Region.

5.47   Presentation may be effected by fax. In such a case the IT1 expressly discourages following this up with a hard copy, but it would be prudent to do so with a covering letter as soon as practicable. There is of course always a risk that there may be a fax transmission problem, or some simple practical problem such as lack of paper, which means that the fax is not 'presented' at the tribunal. Arguably, a claim is validly presented if it is transmitted and stored electronically at the tribunal awaiting paper and printout. When e-mail presentation is available, that too will suffice.

5.48   If it is impossible to 'present' the originating application within the time scale, for example because there is no letter box at the tribunal office available for use when the office is closed, as on a weekend, or possibly where a fax machine malfunctions, *either* the deadline is extended until the next working day *or* it would be possible to argue that it was not 'reasonably practicable' to present the claim on time and to make use of the secondary limitation period (see below).

Extending the deadline

5.49   Extensions of time can be granted in the two categories of case cited in para 5.17. For those situations where power is given to the tribunal to extend the deadline on the grounds that 'it was not reasonably

54 *Ford v Stakis Hotels and Inns Ltd* [1987] ICR 943; [1988] IRLR 46, EAT.
55 2001 Regs reg 2(1).

practicable' to present the claim on time, a *further* limitation period applies which is itself subject to legal constraint. So, for unfair dismissal, the tribunal must make a finding in relation to the limitation period that it was not reasonably practicable to present the claim on time, and then go on to consider whether the claim was presented 'within such further period as the tribunal considers reasonable . . .'.[56]

Failure to meet the deadline: 'not reasonably practicable'

5.50   The limitation period may be extended by reason of an 'escape clause'. The following general principles were laid down in *Walls Meat Co Ltd v Khan:*[57]

> The performance of an act . . . is not reasonably practicable if there is some impediment which reasonably prevents, or interferes with, or inhibits, such performance. The impediment may be physical, for instance the illness of the complainant or a postal strike; or the impediment may be mental, namely, the state of mind of the complainant in the form of ignorance of, or mistaken belief with regard to, essential matters. Such states of mind can, however, only be regarded as impediments making it not reasonably practicable to present a complaint within the period of three months, if the ignorance on the one hand or the mistaken belief on the other, is itself reasonable. Either state of mind will, further, not be reasonable if it arises from the fault of the complainant in not making such enquiries as he should reasonably in all the circumstances have made, or from the fault of his solicitors or other professional advisers . . .

Each of these triggers for the operation of the escape clause is considered below.

Onus of proof

5.51   Since the issue relates to jurisdiction, it is for the applicant to prove the facts necessary for establishing jurisdiction and for establishing that it was not reasonably practicable to comply with the deadline.[58]

Physical inability

5.52   Physical illness and mental depression may well make it not reasonably practicable for the applicant to make a claim in time. But if the

56   ERA 1996 s111(2).
57   [1979] ICR 52 at 60 per Brandon LJ; [1978] IRLR 499, CA.
58   *Porter v Bandridge Ltd* [1978] ICR 943; [1978] IRLR 271, followed in *Walls Meat v Khan*, note 57 above: '. . . the burden of proof being on the employee . . .'.

applicant is in touch with an adviser, it seems the applicant will be assumed to have passed the responsibility for ensuring the necessary steps are taken to the adviser and may not rely on his or her own incapacity.

5.53   The Court of Appeal in *Schultz v Esso Petroleum Ltd*[59] held that the question of reasonable practicability must be considered against the background of the surrounding circumstances and the aim to be achieved. Mr Schultz was dismissed due to long-term absence, caused by depression. He initially attempted to instigate an appeal procedure, and for the first seven weeks of the limitation period he was capable of giving instructions to his solicitor. Thereafter however he was too ill to do so. The Court of Appeal disagreed with the tribunal and the EAT which had both held that it was reasonably practicable to have presented the application in time; it was held not to have been fair to give the same weight to a period of disabling illness regardless of which part of the limitation period it falls within.

Postal delays

5.54   If the originating application is correctly addressed but is either lost or delayed in the post, it may not be reasonably practicable to have presented it on time. Evidence must be produced by the applicant or his or her adviser to show that the originating application was posted and was correctly addressed. Evidence can be brought to show that a letter posted first class one day will be delivered to the same town the next. But in *St Basil's Centre v McCrossan*[60] it was suggested that the time scale set out in the practice direction applying in the High Court for the service of documents[61] should apply. This says that in the normal course of post documents are deemed to have been served (a) in the case of first class mail, on the second working day after posting and (b) in the case of second class mail, on the fourth working day after posting.

5.55   This is a slightly odd approach to the meaning of 'practicable' and is more akin to 'feasible', the meaning attached to it by the Court of Appeal in *Palmer v Southend-on-Sea BC*.[62] It is likely that the time scale specified in the practice direction will be held to be 'reasonable' as an

---

59 [1999] 3 All ER 338; [1999] IRLR 488.
60 [1992] ICR 140; [1991] IRLR 455, EAT.
61 [1985] 1 All ER 889.
62 [1984] ICR 372; [1984] IRLR 119, CA; followed in *London Underground v Noel* [2000] ICR 109, CA.

expectation by the applicant and his or her advisers. A shorter period may also be reasonable in the circumstances. What is unlikely to be reasonable, however, is a delay between the preparation of the originating application and its being taken to the post. A postal delay may excuse the presentation of the application within time, but will not excuse a failure to take the prepared originating application to the post, since it cannot be said that it was 'not reasonably practicable' to present the claim within time. The lesson is: do not delay.

5.56   Objective circumstances which might provide justification for the escape clause may be affected by the applicant's actions during that time so as to defeat the escape clause. In *Capital Foods Retail Ltd v Corrigan*[63] the EAT held that part and parcel of the reasonableness of the applicant complying with the deadline is a duty to follow up the presentation of a complaint which has been unacknowledged. Rule 2(1) of the 2001 Rules requires the tribunal office to notify the parties (including the applicant) of the case number and address for further communications 'upon receiving an originating application'. Failure to do anything about an unacknowledged originating application may jeopardise the escape clause in the limitation period. In other words, if you post an originating application which ought to arrive with one month to spare, hear nothing for two weeks and yet do nothing further until after the deadline, you cannot complain that it was not 'reasonably practicable' to present the claim on time, since with due diligence the failure to acknowledge could have been investigated and a new claim presented within time.

Ignorance of rights and facts

5.57   This comes within the category of 'mental impediment – namely the state of mind of the complainant' as Brandon LJ put it:[64]

> if . . . an employee was reasonably ignorant of either (a) his right to make a complaint for unfair dismissal at all, or (b) how to make it, or (c) that it was necessary for him to make it within a period of three months from the date of dismissal, an industrial tribunal could and should be satisfied that it was not reasonably practicable for his complaint to be presented within the period concerned.

5.58   In *Walls Meat* itself, the applicant was under the impression that his claim for unfair dismissal was being handled by the tribunal

---

63 [1993] IRLR 430.
64 *Walls Meat v Khan*, note 57 above, at 61.

adjudicating his claim for unemployment benefit. His mistake was held to be reasonable. The escape clause will be more readily available to someone who was totally ignorant of all these factors, than to someone who knew of the right to claim unfair dismissal but was unclear about how and when to exercise it. In the latter case, the applicant would be on notice and would find it more difficult to make out the justification for a late claim.

5.59 In assessing the reasonableness of the applicant's belief, the tribunal will find such a claim more difficult to accept if it comes from a highly articulate applicant. In *Avon CC v Haywood-Hicks*[65] it was held that an intelligent and well-educated applicant ought to have investigated his rights within the time limit. Clearly, since compensation for unfair dismissal has been in existence since 1971, it will be increasingly difficult to claim ignorance of the right to claim and of the need to seek advice.

5.60 To ignorance of rights can be added an extra category: ignorance of a material fact. In *Machine Tool Industry Research Association v Simpson*[66] an employee accepted her redundancy but after the deadline for claiming unfair dismissal had expired discovered some facts which led her to believe she had not been dismissed for redundancy and claimed unfair dismissal. Her claim was allowed to proceed. Purchas LJ said (at 564):

> 'reasonably practicable' imports three stages, the proof of which rests on the employee. The first proposition . . . is that it was reasonable for the employee not to be aware of the factual basis on which she could bring an application to the tribunal during the currency of the three months limitation period . . . [I]f that is established, it cannot be reasonably practicable to expect an applicant to bring a case based on facts of which she is ignorant. Secondly, the applicant must establish that the knowledge which she gains has, in the circumstances, been reasonably gained by her and that that knowledge is either crucial, fundamental or important . . . to her change of belief . . . [T]hat concept . . . is an objective qualification of reasonableness, in the circumstances, to a subjective test of the applicant's state of mind. The third ground . . . is that the acquisition of this knowledge had to be crucial to the decision to bring a claim in any event.

5.61 So the discovery of facts which for the first time enable the applicant to put forward a claim justifies escape from the limitation period. Illustrations of this approach are found in:

65 [1978] ICR 646; [IRLR] 118, EAT.
66 [1988] ICR 558; [1988] IRLR 212, CA.

- *James W Cook & Co (Wivenhoe) v Tipper,*[67] where employees made redundant were entitled to bring their claims for unfair dismissal when, after the deadline, they realised that all chances of getting their jobs back disappeared on the closure of the yard they were working in. It was not reasonably practicable to bring proceedings during the relevant period.
- *Churchill v Yeates & Son Ltd,*[68] where it was held that it was not reasonably practicable for an employee to bring a complaint 'until he is aware of a fundamental fact which renders his dismissal unfair'. There was doubt about the correctness of the employer's reason for dismissal as being, inter alia, redundancy.

5.62   In all cases of timing, the essential ingredient is the employee's reasonable and genuine belief. It is not necessary for the applicant to establish the truth of the new fact, only the reasonableness of a belief in it.[69]

Advisers: wrong advice or delay

5.63   The general rule is that you cannot use the escape clause where your advisers have been at fault.[69a] As Lord Denning MR said:

> If a man engages skilled advisers to act for him – and they mistake the time limit and present [the claim] too late – he is out. His remedy is against them.[70]

5.64   Within this category are solicitors, citizens advice bureaux, trade union full-time and lay officers including shop stewards, and representatives of trade, employers' and professional associations.[71] In *Riley v Tesco Stores*[72] the applicant received incorrect advice from a citizens advice bureau but was not excused.

5.65   But a different test is applied to employees of tribunals and job centres. In *Jean Sorelle Ltd v Rybak*[73] it was held that a tribunal could decide that information given by an employee of the tribunal office

---

67   [1990] ICR 716; [1990] IRLR 386, CA.
68   [1983] ICR 380; [1983] IRLR 187, EAT, approved in *Marley*, note 69 below.
69   *Marley (UK) Ltd v Anderson* [1996] IRLR 163, CA.
69a Contrast the position under the CPR where the Court of Appeal, in *Steeds v Peverel Management Services Ltd* [2001] ENCA Civ 419, held that the sins of the lawyer should not be visited upon the client in this context.
70   *Dedman v British Building and Engineering Appliances Ltd* [1974] ICR 53; [1973] IRLR 379, CA.
71   See *Hammond v Haigh Castle & Co Ltd* [1973] ICR 148; [1973] IRLR 91, NIRC.
72   [1980] ICR 323; [1980] IRLR 103, CA.
73   [1991] ICR 127; [1991] IRLR 153, EAT.

did not fall within the category of skilled advice, so that if it were incorrect and relied on by the applicant so that he or she missed the deadline, he or she would be saved by the escape clause. The distinction between advisers retained by the applicant and staff of official bodies was also drawn in *London International College Ltd v Sen*.[74] Here the applicant received advice from a solicitor and also contacted the tribunal office. It was held that the fact that the applicant had consulted a solicitor did not automatically make it reasonably practicable for the applicant to present an originating application in time. The proper approach is to ask what was the substantial cause of the late application, and since in *Sen* this was the information given by the tribunal office, the escape clause was operated in favour of the applicant.

5.66 Of course, failure by a skilled adviser to ensure that the claim posted on time has been received in time remains inexcusable, and unreasonable conduct during the intervening time might exclude the operation of the escape clause.[75]

Delay caused by internal appeals

5.67 It is often thought by applicants, particularly those in jobs where there is sophisticated appeal and disciplinary machinery, that time does not begin to run against them until the exhaustion of the relevant appeal procedures. This is wrong.

5.68 Where there is an appeal against a decision to dismiss, the date from which time will run depends on whether, during the period between the decision to dismiss and the outcome of the appeal, the employee stands dismissed with the possibility of reinstatement, or whether he or she is suspended with the possibility of the proposed dismissal not being confirmed.[76]

5.69 However, in most cases, the decision of management to dismiss causes an effective date of termination for the purposes of the commencement of a relevant limitation period, and is not affected by any internal appeal machinery. To err on the side of caution, the earlier date should be taken as the one from which time will begin to run. Naturally, in such cases, if the applicant is successful at the internal appeal, reinstatement occurs and there has been no dismissal.[77] If the

---

74 [1993] IRLR 3339, CA.
75 See *Capital Foods (Retail) Ltd v Corrigan* [1991] IRLR 430, EAT.
76 *Drage v Governors of Greenford High School* [2000] IRLR 314, CA.
77 See *J Sainsbury Ltd v Savage* [1981] ICR 1; [1980] IRLR 109, CA.

effective date of termination starts the limitation period running, however, an internal appeal can have no effect on it; nor is it a sufficient ground for finding that presentation of a complaint of unfair dismissal was not reasonably practicable.[78]

5.70   This approach was approved in *Palmer v Southend-on-Sea BC.*[79] There, two local government workers were convicted of stealing petrol and dismissed, but the council's appeal committee indicated that should their conviction be overturned, the dismissals might be reconsidered. The Court of Appeal did overturn their convictions but the council refused to reinstate them. The tribunal's decision that it had been reasonably practicable to present claims to the tribunal within three months was upheld.

5.71   The moral is that if there is an internal appeal procedure, a claim for unfair dismissal should still be lodged in any event. The tribunal hearing can always be postponed on the ground that an internal procedure is operating and will imminently decide the matter. Most employers would accept the lodging of an originating application in such circumstances as simply a protective measure and not in any way an attempt to threaten them or short-circuit existing procedures.

5.72   The only clear case in which it is likely that the escape clause will be operated in favour of the applicant is when the employer itself encourages the applicant to forego making a claim in time. In *Owen v Crown House Engineering Ltd,*[80] negotiations took place with the applicants' union following redundancy notices. The employers invited the union official to 'hold his hand' in submitting claims to the tribunal so that the employers' board could consider the matter in more detail. The NIRC upheld the 'vital importance of attempting to settle all differences by amicable negotiation' and that had claims been made 'it would almost certainly have killed any hope of a fruitful outcome to the negotiations'.[81] So, action by employers causative of the applicant missing the deadline can give rise to the operation of the escape clause. For safety's sake, however, it is still advisable to present the originating application within the time scale.

Criminal or other proceedings

5.73   It can sometimes be reasonable to misunderstand the nature of proceedings where a similar issue is being judged by social security and

78   *Bodha v Hampshire AHA* [1982] ICR 200.
79   [1984] ICR 372; [1984] IRLR 119, CA.
80   [1973] ICR 511; [1973] IRLR 233, NIRC.
81   Per Sir Hugh Griffiths at 516.

employment tribunals.[82] A safe rule is to make a claim in time. The existence of criminal proceedings will certainly affect many tribunal claims for unfair dismissal based on dishonesty, and the appropriate course is to apply for a stay of the tribunal hearing. In such a case it is more likely than not that the applicant will have or has access to legal advice. This should include advice on, at the very least, time limits for presenting an unfair dismissal claim. In these circumstances, it is unlikely that the escape clause would be operated in favour of the applicant if no claim were lodged at the employment tribunal.

Failure to meet the deadline: time limits on the escape clause

5.74   When the tribunal is satisfied that it was not reasonably practicable to present the originating application during the limitation period (for example, three months), it must then go on to decide whether it was presented 'within such further period as the tribunal considers reasonable . . .'.[83] A broader discretion is thus given to the tribunal than in respect of the original limitation period. The length of time permitted is strictly a matter of fact for the tribunal to determine. In *Marley (UK) Ltd v Anderson*,[84] the EAT held that, although the Court of Appeal in *James W Cook*[85] did express views about the time scales in that particular case (four to six weeks 'were simply too long'), there was an error of law when the tribunal felt itself *bound* by that approach. Similarly, the tribunal must not simply consider the length of the delay, but also the circumstances in which the delay occurred and the reasons for it extending beyond the limitation period.

Failure to meet the deadline: 'just and equitable'

Sex, race, disability and part-timer discrimination cases

5.75   Questions of reasonable practicability do not arise in relation to claims of sex, race, disability and part-timer discrimination, since the limitation period of three months may be set aside if 'in all the circumstances of the case [a tribunal] considers that it is just and

---

82   See *Riley v Tesco*, note 72 above.
83   ERA 1996 s111(2).
84   [1994] IRLR 152.
85   See note 42 above.

equitable to do so'.[86] Because of the wide discretion given to tribunals, it is unlikely that a decision can successfully be appealed. The 'circumstances of the case' appear to be those related to the reason for the delay, and tribunals are not required to investigate them in full.

5.76   That different statutory considerations apply is apparent from *Trust House Forte (UK) Ltd v Halstead*,[87] where late claims were made in respect of unfair dismissal and racial discrimination. The tribunal gave the applicant the benefit of the escape clause in respect of both claims. On appeal, the EAT refused to uphold the unfair dismissal claim, but did not interfere with the exercise of discretion in relation to the discrimination claim.

5.77   Given the breadth of the discretion, it would be appropriate to call evidence relating to the degree of prejudice should the tribunal exercise its discretion, for example, whether the length of the delay and the circumstances attending it make it more difficult for the employer to defend the case, and whether the employer has in any way contributed to the delay or acquiesced in it. In general, though, the approach is that the tribunal can take account of anything it considers relevant.[88]

5.78   It is worth recalling that time does not begin to run until the *end* of a period during which a continuing act of discrimination has occurred, or the last of a series of acts of discrimination, and may not have begun to run in respect of a continuing policy which is held to be discriminatory. A claim can be made at any time during its currency.

Redundancy pay

5.79   A *further* limitation period applies in respect of redundancy payments (see para 5.26).

---

86   SDA 1975 s76(5); RRA 1976 s68(6); DDA 1995 Sch 3 para 3; PTW Regs 2000 reg 8(3).
87   EAT 213/86, unreported.
88   *Hutchinson v Westwood Television Ltd* [1977] ICR 279; [1977] IRLR 69, EAT.

CHAPTER 6

The originating application

continued

Introduction

6.1   The originating application is the title given to the document which starts tribunal proceedings: the means by which an applicant actually makes his or her claim and the first formal step in the tribunal complaint procedure. In this respect it is the tribunal equivalent of a particulars of claim in the High Court or county court, but it is not a formal 'pleading' (see below) and should not be treated as such.

6.2   Two or more originating applications may be presented in a single document by applicants who claim relief in respect of or arising out of the same set of facts.[1] This is particularly useful where multi-applicant claims arise, for example, in a large-scale redundancy case where a number of dismissed employees claim to have been unfairly dismissed in like circumstances or in an equal pay case involving a challenge to pay arrangements applicable to many female employees.

6.3   The time limits within which proceedings must be brought in the tribunal are dealt with in chapter 5 and any potential applicant should pay particular attention to these.

Minimum requirements and Form IT1

6.4   Generally the originating application takes the form of the Central Office of Employment Tribunals' (COET's) Form IT1[2] (see appendix A). This can be obtained from any local office of the Employment Service, including job centres, and from most advice centres. An explanatory booklet (ITL 1) can also be obtained from the same sources. In Scotland, the IT1 is known as the 'IT1 (Scot)' and in Northern Ireland, as the 'IT1 (NI)', where the explanatory booklet is referred to as the 'IT1 (L) (NI)'. In Northern Ireland, forms and booklets may be obtained from any local training and employment agency.

6.5   Using Form IT1 is by far the easiest way of submitting a claim to the tribunal: by completing it properly, an applicant can be sure that he or she has provided all the information necessary to commence a claim. Tribunal proceedings may, however, be commenced by other means: by using a home-made form or even by a letter sent to the

---

1   See Employment Tribunals Rules of Procedure (2001 Rules) (contained in SI 2001 No 1171, Sch 1) r1(2).

2   The reference is to the former title 'Industrial Tribunal', the form reference does not appear to have been updated to 'ET'.

Tribunal Office.[3] Any claim made, whether by IT1 or by any other document, must be in writing and should contain the following details:

− the applicant's name and address and, if different, an address within the UK to which notices and other documents relating to the claim can be sent;
− the names and addresses of the person or people against whom relief is sought; and
− the grounds, with particulars, on which relief is sought (r1(1)).

Although an originating application to a tribunal should meet all these requirements, a fairly flexible approach has been taken to claims presented which fail to comply with these conditions.

6.6   In *Burns International Security Services (UK) Ltd v Butt*,[4] where the applicant had failed to give any particulars of the grounds of his unfair dismissal complaint, the Employment Appeal Tribunal (EAT) stated that this was not fatal, the only mandatory requirement being that the application must be made in writing and the other requirements being of a directory rather than a mandatory nature. In particular, the EAT pointed out that the tribunal could order further particulars of a complaint to be provided if necessary (see r4(3)), so that failing to give full particulars in the originating application was a rectifiable omission. This reasoning is strengthened by the fact that (since 1993), a tribunal can make such an order of its own motion; and is consistent with the emphasis on good case management under the 2001 Rules.

6.7   Similarly, in *Gosport Working Men's and Trade Union Club Ltd v Taylor*,[5] the fact that the applicant had merely given his name and telephone number but not his address was held not to be fatal, as he had provided sufficient details to enable him to be identified.

6.8   As the bare minimum, it seems that if the originating application is in writing and contains sufficient details to identify the person making the claim and the person or people against whom the claim is made, it will be allowed, although the applicant may be required to provide further particulars of the claim.

---

3   *Smith v Automobile Pty Ltd* [1973] ICR 306, NIRC.
4   [1983] ICR 547; [1983] IRLR 438.
5   [1978] 13 ITR 321, EAT.

The originating application distinguished from court documents

6.9   This flexible approach to the originating application is consistent with the distinction between it and the more formal documents required in the civil courts – in particular, there is no equivalent in the tribunal rules to the Civil Procedure Rules (CPR) requirements relating to the contents of the claim form and defence (CPR Part 16) and the truth in them. Generally speaking, an applicant in tribunal proceedings should not be held rigidly to the particulars given in the originating application at any later hearing in the case, although obvious inconsistencies may be the subject of adverse inference. If a respondent has failed to ask for further particulars of the complaint, then the applicant cannot be criticised too greatly for failing to provide them. If the factual basis for making a complaint of, for example, unfair dismissal is included in a claim expressly stated to be of race or sex discrimination, then the applicant should be allowed to make that complaint as well. Failure to provide full details from the start should not be fatal.

6.10   The correct approach for the tribunal in cases where the originating application provides little (if any) detail of the complaint (or one of the complaints) that the applicant seeks to make at the substantive hearing will often be to allow an amendment to be made, and to consider any representations the respondent wishes to make in respect of the need for an adjournment in the light of the amendment and/or in respect of the additional costs incurred due to the amendment (see chapter 8).

6.11   Furthermore, while the rules require an applicant to set out the grounds of complaint in respect of which relief is sought, there is no requirement to specify the relief itself. If the facts particularised in the originating application lead the tribunal to conclude that the applicant's dismissal was by reason of redundancy but was unfair in all the circumstances, then it will not be fatal to a finding of unfair dismissal that the applicant has indicated that he or she is claiming only a redundancy payment on the face of the originating application. In *Chapman v Goonvean and Rostowrack China Clay Co Ltd*[6] Sir John Donaldson P said:

> [if there were] the slightest doubt whether an applicant's claim is or

should be for a redundancy payment or for compensation for unfair dismissal, or for both . . . the applicant should be encouraged to put forward or maintain both such claims until all the facts are known.

This view was affirmed by the Court of Appeal.[7]

Presentation of the originating application

6.12   This subject is dealt with in full in chapter 5. In England and Wales the originating application should be 'presented' to the tribunal office in the postal district where the applicant is or was employed[8] (see appendix A – where to send your application). In Scotland, all originating applications should be presented to the Central Office in Glasgow.

6.13   It can be delivered by hand, sent by post or faxed, but the time limits for presentation must be complied with. Originating applications which are sent to tribunal offices are accepted as having been duly 'presented'.[9]

6.14   Those acting for applicants should take all steps to make sure that the originating application has been received by the tribunal in time. If it is sent by post, it appears that the onus is on representatives to telephone the COET to make sure that it has been received.[10]

6.15   Applications sent by fax are 'presented' when they arrive at the tribunal, not when sent, so where a solicitor was unaware of the change of telephone code such that the IT1 was not sent, the EAT held that it was reasonably practicable to have found out the correct code earlier, and to have presented it on time.[11]

Action on receipt of the originating application

6.16   As soon as an originating application is received at a tribunal office, it is date-stamped. As a matter of evidence, this will generally be taken to be the date on which the application was 'presented'. The relevant date is, however, not the date of 'receipt' but the date of actual 'presentation' and if there is evidence that the application was presented,

---

7   [1973] ICR 310.
8   2001 Rules r1(1).
9   Ibid r23(2) and *Bengey v North Devon DC* [1977] ICR 15, EAT.
10   See *Capital Foods (Retail) Ltd v Corrigan* [1993] IRLR 430, EAT (para 5.56 above).
11   *Hartley v HFC Bank* EAT/1468/99, 17 March, 2001, unreported.

for example, by the applicant putting it through the letter box of the tribunal office in person the day before, then this will be the crucial date in respect of any time limit.[12]

Initial vetting procedure

6.17   If an originating application is received which the secretary to the tribunal believes seeks relief which is outside the jurisdiction of the tribunal, then notice will be sent to the applicant to that effect, indicating the reasons for that view and stating that the originating application will not be registered unless written indication of an intention to proceed with the claim is received from the applicant (2001 Rules r1(2)).

6.18   As the secretary to the tribunal performs an administrative, not a judicial function, this step should not be seen as a form of striking out and is in fact rarely used. It would be appropriate in obvious cases of mistaken forum. Indeed, even if the applicant has manifestly made such a mistake, if he or she states that he or she wishes to proceed, despite the notice sent by the secretary, then the application will be duly registered and will proceed as normal (2001 Rules r1(3)), although it may subsequently be the subject of a pre-hearing review or an application for costs.

The register

6.19   Within 28 days of receiving the originating application, or as soon as reasonably practicable thereafter, particulars of the application will be entered in the register (2001 Rules r2(2)). The register is a public record of all tribunal applications, appeals and decisions which is open to inspection (2001 Regs reg 9)[13] and which is often used by members of the press to obtain prior information on the nature of particular tribunal cases. Due to the public nature of the register, where an application appears to involve allegations of the commission of a sexual offence, any particulars which might allow the identification of the person making the allegation, or affected by it, must be omitted (2001 Rules rr2(2) and 13(6)).

---

12 *Post Office v Moore* [1981] ICR 623, EAT.
13 Employment Tribunals (Constitution and Rules of Procedure) Regulations 2001 (2001 Regs) SI No 1171.

Informing others of the originating application

6.20   Many applicants will send a copy of their originating application to the respondent or respondents at the same time as presenting it to the tribunal office. While this is good practice, it is not obligatory.

6.21   As well as entering particulars of the originating application in the register, the secretary to the tribunal will send a copy of it to the respondent with a notice stating the means and time for entering an appearance, the consequences of failing to do so and the right to receive a copy of the decision (2001 Rules r2(1)(a) and (c)) (see appendix A). When an application is entered in the register, it is allocated to a regional office and given a case number. These details are sent to all parties to the proceedings (2001 Rules r2(1)(b)).

The contents of the originating application

6.22   While the essential requirements for a valid originating application may be minimal, it is always preferable to give the details specified in the 2001 Rules so far as this is possible, including sufficient particulars to enable the nature of the complaint being made to be clearly identified. If at all possible:

– use a Form IT1;
– type in the entries on the IT1 and complete all parts after reading the notes accompanying it.

Box 1: Type of complaint

6.23   Specify the type of complaint made, such as, 'Unfair dismissal' or 'Entitlement to a redundancy payment'.

6.24   If more than one complaint is being made, list each complaint separately, for example, '(1) Unfair dismissal; and/or (2) Entitlement to a redundancy payment'.

6.25   If different complaints are being made in respect of different respondents, say so, for example, (in a transfer of undertakings case) 'In respect of the First Respondent: (1) Unfair dismissal; and/or (2) Entitlement to a redundancy payment. In respect of the Second Respondent: (1) Unfair dismissal; and/or (2) Declaration of terms and conditions'.

Box 2: The applicant's details

6.26 Although not all the items set out in the IT1 are required under the 2001 Rules, as much information should be included as possible; the applicant's date of birth, for example, will often be relevant in determining the calculation of any basic award or redundancy payment due.

6.27 If the applicant is not represented, the address given here will be that to which all subsequent notices and other correspondence relating to the proceedings will be sent. It is for the applicant to ensure that the correct information is supplied. Any changes to the contact address should be notified to the tribunal and all other relevant parties (2001 Rules r23(5)).

6.28 Where the same facts are relied on, more than one applicant can make an application on the same IT1.[14] Although this is convenient in large-scale, multi-applicant claims, in many cases it will still be preferable for separate applications to be completed and individual details given. Even in the larger-scale claims, schedules should be provided giving relevant individual particulars for each applicant separately.

Box 3: Details of the applicant's representative

6.29 If the applicant is represented, then the address given here will be the one to which the tribunal will send all notices and other documents relating to the proceedings. Any adviser who is 'on the record' on the IT1 must be prepared to keep his or her client properly informed as to the conduct of the proceedings and as to the times and dates of any hearings. Any changes to the named representative or to the contact address should be notified to the tribunal and all other relevant parties (2001 Rules r23(5)).

Box 4: Dates of employment

6.30 The details given here may give rise to questions relating to the tribunal's jurisdiction to hear the complaint in question and may be used in any calculation of basic award or redundancy payment and should therefore be completed as accurately as possible. The start date should be the date the applicant's continuous employment

---

14 *Gosport Working Men's and Trade Union Club Ltd v Taylor* (1978) 13 ITR 321, EAT and see 2001 Rules r1(2).

commenced (whether it was with a previous employer or under a different contract of employment) and the date of termination will be the date on which notice expired or (if no notice was given or if the applicant was paid in lieu) the actual date on which the applicant left the employment. Regard should be had to the relevant statutory provisions applicable to a particular complaint where the start or leaving date of employment might be in issue. If the start or end date is likely to be in contention, then an applicant might find it useful to give further particulars of such matters in the details of complaint (see below).

Box 5: Details of the respondent

6.31   Sufficient details should be given to enable the tribunal to identify and communicate with the appropriate respondent. More than one respondent can be named, for example, in a transfer of undertakings case against transferor and transferee, or where the allegation is one of discrimination and the complaint is made, for example, both against the individual discriminator and vicariously against the employer.

6.32   If an applicant is unsure of the correct identity of the respondent (ie, where the employer is one of a group of companies or in a transfer of undertakings case), then all possible respondents should be identified and the reasons for doing so set out in the particulars of the complaint; a complaint against a particular respondent can always be withdrawn at a later date. Mistakes over the identity of the correct respondent should not be fatal, as an application to amend the identity of the respondent can be made at a later date (see chapter 8).

Box 6: Connection with the respondent

6.33   Generally this will be the applicant's job title, although if the relationship is other than that of employer/employee (for example, where the applicant is complaining of discrimination in his or her application for a job or where the respondent is a colleague who is alleged to have committed acts of discrimination against the applicant) then the connection which has led the applicant to make the application to the tribunal should be explained.

Box 7: Normal basic hours

6.34   Although not required by the 2001 Rules, this information will indicate whether there might be a problem relating to the calculation of any payments claimed and might be of particular relevance in certain cases, for example, under the Working Time Regulations 1998.[15]

6.35   Generally speaking the 'normal working hours' will be the contractual minimum hours the applicant was required to work, and this may include overtime where there is a contractual obligation to work it.[16]

Box 8: Details of earnings

6.36   This information may be used in establishing, for example, any basic award or redundancy payment or compensatory award and should be given as accurately as possible, although an applicant will not be held to a mistaken weekly rate if he or she later seeks to amend these details. The 'basic wage/salary' is the gross amount the applicant was due; the 'average take home' is the net amount (ie, after deduction of tax and national insurance). It is up to the applicant whether to give weekly, monthly or yearly figures, but it helps if the information is given for a consistent period throughout. If the applicant's wage varied from week to week, the average amount for the last 12 calendar weeks of the employment should be taken. Under 'bonuses/benefits', all additional 'perks' should be listed, including any pension benefit, etc. While these will not be included as part of a 'week's pay' for the purposes of a basic award or redundancy payment, they are part of the applicant's loss in terms of any compensatory award or equal pay order.

Box 9: Date of action complained of other than dismissal

6.37   This will generally apply in relation to discrimination cases (race, sex, disability and trade union), victimisation and breach of statutory rights cases, wage protection complaints, equal pay cases and applications for a declaration of terms and conditions. This information may also give rise to an issue relating to the tribunal's jurisdiction to hear the complaint (ie, as to whether the claim has been presented in time) and should be completed carefully.

15   SI No 1833.
16   *Gascol Conversions v Mercer* [1974] ICR 420; [1974] IRLR 155, CA.

6.38   If it is difficult to specify one date, for example, where the complaint relates to a continuing course of conduct in a discrimination case (see para 5.32), then this can be clarified in the more detailed particulars of complaint. In such cases, it might be advisable merely to state in the box provided 'from [date] and continuing' and then expand on the point in the details of complaint.

Box 10: Remedy sought in unfair dismissal cases

6.39   This is not a requirement of the 2001 Rules and can be left blank without rendering the application a nullity. It does, however, give a clear indication to the respondent of the relief sought by the applicant and, consequently, of its potential liability. This is all the more important given the large sums tribunals can (and do) now award and the need for respondents to ensure that the costs expended in defending a claim are proportionate to its ultimate value. Where insufficient particulars are given, tribunals are increasingly sympathetic to the need for applicants to provide a schedule of loss (and see chapter 9).

6.40   Whether reinstatement or re-engagement has been indicated as a remedy sought, it is of relevance when considering whether the employer was entitled to engage a permanent replacement. However, whatever the applicant states under this head will not be binding and the tribunal should address the question again if and when it considers remedies at the full hearing of the complaint.

Box 11: Details of complaint

6.41   This is the applicant's opportunity to set out the nature of his or her case. It will generally be the first document the tribunal members hearing the case actually read in relation to the complaint: care should therefore be taken to present the details to the applicant's best advantage (which may mean setting out the details on a separate sheet attached to the IT1 rather than trying to work within the confined space given on the form). While there may be some advantage in keeping certain matters open, for example, in an unfair dismissal case, in not admitting the reason given for dismissal straight away but putting the respondent to proof, the purpose of the originating application is to set out the case the respondent has to meet and to make it clear what is and what is not in issue. It is often useful to give detailed particulars especially where the burden of proof is on the applicant, for instance in *constructive* unfair dismissal cases.

6.42   In cases where the applicant is relying on a number of different incidents (for example, where there has been on-going harassment or in a 'last straw' constructive dismissal case),[17] it is advisable to set out details of all incidents which are relied on; in this way the applicant cannot be accused of raising them for the first time at the hearing of the claim.

6.43   It is not necessary to set out the relevant law in the originating application, although reference to the relevant sections can assist in making the nature of the claim clear to those reading the document (for example, in specifying that the claim is one of indirect sex discrimination under Sex Discrimination Act 1975 s1(1)(b), of unlawful racial discrimination on the grounds of victimisation under Race Relations Act 1976 s2, etc). Furthermore, the relevant law should be borne in mind when completing the originating application to ensure that important points are not left out, such as the size and administrative resources of the respondent in an unfair dismissal case.

6.44   It is not helpful to include background detail if this is not relevant to the type of claim being made: if the issue in an unfair dismissal by reason of redundancy case is the fairness of the selection procedure, details of the applicant's views on the need for redundancies and the business decisions which led to the redundancy situation in the first place are unlikely to assist the tribunal.

6.45   On the other hand, where information is relevant and may later form the subject of a request for further particulars or for written answers, it will help to expedite the applicant's claim to provide the details from the start: where relevant, name names, give dates, set out the gist of conversations relied on and so on.

6.46   Examples of details of complaints which might by used in originating applications are set out in appendix B.

17 *Lewis v Motorworld* [1986] ICR 157; [1985] IRLR 465, CA.

CHAPTER 7

Notice of appearance

Introduction

7.1   The notice of appearance is the respondent's 'defence' to any application to the tribunal and provides the opportunity for the respondent to set out its case and to state where there are specific points of dispute or agreement. The notice of appearance is not a 'pleading' and should not be treated in the same way as might a defence in High Court or county court proceedings – there is, for instance, no equivalent in the tribunal rules to Civil Procedure Rules Part 16 which specifies the requirements of a claim form and defence. On the other hand, the notice of appearance, together with the originating application, will generally be one of the first documents read by the tribunal and will form the starting point for any consideration of the respondent's case. It is, therefore, good practice to ensure that the notice of appearance accurately sets out the case the respondent wishes to present.

Minimum requirements and Form IT3

7.2   Generally the notice of appearance takes the form of the Central Office of Employment Tribunals' Form IT3 (see example in appendix A). A copy will be sent to the respondent(s) of an application to the tribunal with a copy of the originating application.

7.3   Two or more notices of appearance may be presented in a single document where:
   – they relate to originating applications in which the relief claimed is in respect of or arises out of the same set of facts; and
   – in respect of those originating applications, the respondent either does not intend to resist the claims or intends to resist the claims made but on the same grounds in each case (see 2001 Rules r3(2)[1]).

7.4   As with the originating application, use of Form IT3 is the recommended although not the only means of entering a notice of appearance. Generally speaking, completing the IT3 will be the most convenient means open to a respondent to state its case. It will give a clear indication of precisely what information the tribunal requires to be able to consider how best to progress the claim further.

---

1   Employment Tribunals Rules of Procedure (2001 Rules) (contained in SI 2001 No 1171, Sch 1).

7.5   A respondent may choose to enter a notice of appearance by other means providing it meets the basic requirements provided for in 2001 Rules r3, ie, it must be in writing and should contain the following details:

- the respondent's full name and address and, if different, an address within the UK to which notices and other documents relating to the claim can be sent;
- whether or not the respondent intends to resist the application; and
- if the respondent does intend to resist the application, sufficient particulars to show on what grounds the application is resisted.

7.6   As with the originating application, apart from the necessity of submitting a written notice of appearance, the other requirements are of a directory rather than mandatory nature. This has been held to be the case in relation to the requirement to set out particulars of the grounds on which the application will be resisted, see *Seldun Transport Services Ltd v Baker.*[2]

7.7   While the rules may not set out absolute standards for the notice of appearance, reasonably full particulars are to be encouraged; although the Employment Appeal Tribunal (EAT) in *Seldun* recognised that a lack of detail could be corrected by ordering further particulars to be provided of the grounds of resistance, it did not thereby seek to encourage this course of action.

7.8   Like the originating application, the notice of appearance in tribunal proceedings is not to be considered as a formal 'pleading' in the same way as a defence in a High Court or county court action. While some corporate respondents may be able to utilise the services of lawyers in drafting the notice of appearance, it is recognised that many respondents are not in this position and that the notice of appearance may well have been completed by someone entirely unfamiliar with court or tribunal proceedings.

7.9   If the respondent really believes that it is unable to answer the case set out by the applicant in the originating application because insufficient details have been presented, the proper course is to write to the applicant asking for further particulars of the originating application and also to write to the tribunal enclosing details of the request made and formally applying for an extension of time to enter the notice of appearance. If the request is not satisfactorily answered on a voluntary basis, an application can be made for the applicant to be

2   [1978] ICR 1035, EAT.

ordered to respond under 2001 Rules r4(1)(a) (see 2001 Rules r3(2)(b) and para 9.15 onwards).

7.10   This is not a course of action which should be lightly embarked on by a respondent: a tribunal may well take a different view as to the sufficiency of detail required in the originating application (particularly on a fairly straightforward unfair dismissal claim) before the respondent is able to enter a notice of appearance. The safer course of action in most cases will be for the respondent to enter a notice of appearance on Form IT3 and state under part 8 of the form that insufficient details of the applicant's case have been given to enable the respondent to give details of the grounds of resistance, but that further particulars have been sought and fuller details of the respondent's case will be given once these further particulars are received. This type of 'holding IT3' may often be preferable to seeking to extend time for presentation of the notice of appearance altogether, and protects the respondent from any of the adverse consequences which can flow from not having entered a notice of appearance (see para 7.16).

Time limits

7.11   The notice of appearance should be submitted within 21 days[3] after a copy of the originating application has been received from the regional office,[4] except where the claim made is against a foreign state, where the time limit is two months by virtue of the provisions of State Immunity Act 1978 s12(2). Unlike originating applications, this time limit is not rigidly adhered to and there is usually great flexibility allowed to respondents in entering a notice of appearance. An extension of time should, however, be sought under 2001 Rules r17(1). Whether an extension of time is granted is a matter for the discretion of the tribunal, and any prejudice suffered by the applicant by an unnecessary delay might result in a costs award against the respondent concerned.

7.12   There is no time limit for an application to extend time under 2001 Rules r17(1). A tribunal therefore has the power to consider an application for an extension of time in which to enter a notice of appearance at any stage, even after the registration of the tribunal's substantive decision in the case *St Mungo Community Trust v Colleano*,[5]

3   See paras 5.40–5.44.
4   2001 Rules r3(1).
5   [1980] ICR 254, EAT.

although in *St Mungo* the EAT observed: 'There must inevitably be a very heavy burden on a respondent who applies for an extension of time, after notice of the proceedings and after judgment, to justify the application'. In *Kwik Save Stores Ltd v Swain*[6] Mummery J stated that in exercising its discretion to extend time the tribunal must take account of all relevant factors and reach a conclusion which is 'objectively justified on the grounds of reason and justice'. In particular the reason given for the delay is important, as is the likely prejudice to each party and the merits of the respondent's defence.

7.13 The decision to grant an extension of time under 2001 Rules r17(1) can be made without any consultation with the applicant or other parties to the proceedings. On the other hand, any order made without notice to the other side has been said to be provisional in nature and open to further consideration, because it is always open to the absent party to challenge it.[7]

7.14 The question of the time limit in relation to a notice of appearance is a procedural not a jurisdictional matter. In practice, tribunals are encouraged to be flexible in extending time for respondents, as the consequences of not doing so would mean that a respondent would be debarred from defending the claim. Where a respondent fails to enter a notice of appearance within the 21-day time limit, a further copy of the originating application will again be sent, this time by recorded delivery, with a reminder of the consequences of not entering a notice of appearance and a notice giving a further seven days' extension of time. Even where the application for an extension of time is made late on in the proceedings, a tribunal may well still allow the late notice of appearance to be presented, provided serious prejudice is not then suffered by the applicant (ie, prejudice other than merely having to prove a case which is disputed). A refusal by the tribunal to exercise its jurisdiction may be challenged by way of appeal.[8]

Action on receipt of a notice of appearance

7.15 As the case will have been assigned to a tribunal office after the receipt and registration of the originating application, the respondent

---

6   [1997] ICR 49, EAT.
7   *Reddington and others v S Straker & Sons Ltd and others* [1994] ICR 172, EAT.
8   *Practice Direction (EAT: Procedure)* [1996] ICR 422; [1996] IRLR 430, para 16 – see appendix C.

will be asked to return the notice of appearance to the secretary to that particular office. Once a notice of appearance has been received, the secretary sends a copy of it to all the other parties to the proceedings (2001 Rules r3(1)). Best practice would suggest that a respondent copy the notice of appearance to all other parties at the same time as sending it to the tribunal but there is no obligation to do so.

The consequences of not entering a notice of appearance

7.16   Where a respondent fails to enter a notice of appearance it will be debarred from taking any further part in the proceedings save in the following limited respects:

- to apply for an extension of time for entering a notice of appearance under r17(1) (2001 Rules r3(3)(a));
- to apply for further particulars of the originating application under r4(1) (2001 Rules r3(3)(b));
- to apply for a review of the tribunal's decision under r13(4) on the ground that the respondent never received notice of the proceedings (2001 Rules r3(3)(c));
- to be called as a witness by another person (2001 Rules r3(3)(d)); and
- to be sent a copy of the tribunal's decision (2001 Rules r3(3)(e)).

7.17   Except for the actions specified in these exceptions, the respondent concerned is no longer considered to be a 'party' to the proceedings (2001 Rules r3(3)).

7.18   If a respondent who has not entered a notice of appearance attends the substantive hearing, its attendance is to be treated as an application for an extension of time in which to submit a notice of appearance – an application which will then be considered in accordance with the principles set out in *Kwik Save v Swain*.[9]

Contents of the notice of appearance

7.19   Although the essential requirements for a valid notice of appearance may be minimal, it is always preferable to give the details specified in the rules so far as this is possible, including sufficient particulars to enable the nature of the grounds on which the claim is resisted to be clearly identified. If at all possible:

9   See note 6 above. See also *Tull v Severin* [1998] ICR 1037, EAT.

- use a Form IT3;
- type in the entries on the IT3 and complete all parts after reading the contents of the originating application.

Box 1: The respondent's details

7.20   While not all the items requested in Form IT3 are required under the rules, as much information should be given as possible. If the respondent is not represented, the address given here will be that to which all subsequent notices and other correspondence relating to the proceedings will be sent. It is for the respondent to ensure that the correct information is supplied. Any changes to the contact address should be notified to the tribunal and all other relevant parties (2001 Rules r23(5)).

Box 2: Details of the respondent's representative

7.21   If the respondent is represented, the address given here will be the one to which the tribunal will send all notices and other documents relating to the proceedings. Any adviser who is 'on the record' on the IT3 must be prepared to keep the client properly informed of the conduct of the proceedings and of the times and dates of any hearings. Any changes to the named representative or to the contact address should be notified to the tribunal and all other relevant parties (2001 Rules r23(5)).

Box 3: Whether the application is resisted

7.22   Even if the respondent does not wish to contest all or part of the claim, it is advisable still to complete a notice of appearance, as there are a number of adverse consequences which arise for a respondent who has failed to enter a notice of appearance. In circumstances where liability is not contested but the remedy is, the appropriate course is to tick the second box under this part of the form, but make it clear that there remains a dispute as to remedy; the case will then be listed for a hearing before the tribunal on the question of remedy only.

Box 4: Whether dismissal is admitted and, if so, the reason for that dismissal

7.23   In certain cases (most obviously claims of unfair dismissal), the applicant's case will depend on the tribunal first establishing that there was in fact a dismissal. If this is admitted by the respondent, as indicated by ticking the relevant box under this part of the form, the tribunal will move straight away to consider the fairness or otherwise of that dismissal. If dismissal is not admitted (for example, in a constructive dismissal claim or in a case where the meaning of the words taken by the applicant to terminate the employment is in dispute), this should be made clear on the face of the IT3. The tribunal can then go on either to consider the question of dismissal as a preliminary point or, more likely, to identify this as an issue to be determined as part of the substantive hearing into the whole claim. The latter course may be the most appropriate in a constructive unfair dismissal case where the issues relating to the question of whether there was a dismissal are likely also to determine the question of the fairness of the dismissal if so found. Identifying this as an issue between the parties is, however, also likely to dictate which side goes first in the tribunal hearing: the applicant will bear the burden of proving dismissal if this is not accepted and will generally present his or her case first in such circumstances.

7.24   Where dismissal is admitted, the respondent is invited to state the reason for that dismissal. Employment Rights Act 1996 (ERA 1996) s98(1) and (2) sets out the reasons for dismissal which will be found to be prima facie fair and the respondent should consider that section before completing this part of the IT3 in an unfair dismissal case. In a case involving a dismissal arguably in connection with the transfer of an undertaking, particular regard should be had to the Transfer of Undertakings (Protection of Employment) Regulations 1981[10] before completing the IT3.

7.25   A respondent should try to state clearly the reason (or principal reason) for any dismissal in this part of the IT3. The important point is to ensure that the facts and matters set out at box 7 (details of grounds of resistance) accurately reflect the respondent's case on the reason for the decision to dismiss. A respondent should not be penalised for using the wrong 'label' if it is clear throughout which matters are actually relied on as having given rise to the dismissal in any

10   SI No 1794.

particular case, although it may still be necessary to apply to amend the reason given in the IT3 if the wrong label has been used initially. In *Blue Star Ship Management Ltd v Williams*[11] it was held that an amendment to allege a different reason for a dismissal would generally not be allowed at a late stage in the proceedings unless 'it can genuinely be said that the amendment is no more than for the purpose of giving an appropriate label to a fully established set of facts'.

7.26   Where the facts and matters relied on for the dismissal are clearly put forward by the respondent, the tribunal may even find that the dismissal was fair, although for a different reason under ERA 1996 s98 than the label given by the respondent, provided the grounds relied on are those set out by the respondent. A tribunal will not be entitled to find a dismissal fair on a ground not 'pleaded' or argued for by the respondent where the difference in grounds goes to the facts or substance of the dismissal or where there might have been some difference in the way in which the applicant conducted the case in the light of the reason relied on. If, however, the different grounds are in fact just different labels and there was no basis for thinking that the applicant has been prejudiced in the presentation of his or her case, it will be open to a tribunal to find the dismissal fair for a different reason to that stated by the respondent.[12] In *Hannan*, the tribunal held that the dismissal was not by reason of redundancy (as had been argued by the respondent), but was by reason of some other substantial reason which was fair in all the circumstances of the case. As the grounds relied on by the tribunal for this conclusion were the same as those initially relied on by the respondent in seeking to claim that the dismissal was by reason of redundancy and as there was no reason to think that the applicant's case would have been differently conducted had 'some other substantial reason' been the label used by the respondent on the IT3, the EAT refused to allow the employee's appeal against the tribunal's decision.

7.27   Alternative reasons should be given when appropriate, such as '(1) redundancy or (2) business reorganisation amounting to some other substantial reason of a kind such as to justify the dismissal of an employee holding the position which the applicant held'. Furthermore, where the respondent's primary case is that there was no dismissal, it is still advisable to put forward a reason for the termination of the applicant's employment by way of alternative (although,

---

11 [1978] ICR 770; [1979] IRLR 16, EAT.
12 *Hannan v TNT-IPEC (UK) Ltd* [1986] IRLR 165, EAT.

realistically, it may be hard to demonstrate that any dismissal found to have taken place was 'fair' in such circumstances).

Box 5: The dates of the applicant's employment

7.28   The dates given here may give rise to questions relating to the tribunal's jurisdiction to hear the complaint in question and may be used in any calculation of a basic award or redundancy payment and should therefore be completed as accurately as possible. The start date should be the date on which the applicant's period of continuous employment commenced (whether it was with a previous employer or under a different contract of employment) and the date of termination will be the date on which notice expired or (if no notice was given or if the applicant was 'paid in lieu') the actual date on which the applicant left the employment. Attention should be paid to the relevant statutory provisions applicable to a particular complaint when the start or end date of employment might be in issue. Where this might be a matter of contention between the parties, fuller particulars can be provided in the details of the grounds of resistance (see para 7.32).

Box 6: Details of the applicant's earnings

7.29   This information may be used in establishing any basic award or redundancy payment or compensatory award. If the respondent disagrees with the information supplied by the applicant, this should be made clear by ticking the appropriate box and supplying the information the respondent believes to be correct. Often the respondent may be in a better position to supply details relating to net earnings, pension contributions, etc, and it is helpful to all concerned if the information is provided at this early stage. If it remains in dispute, at least all parties then know of the issue between them and can endeavour to find material (for example, actuarial evidence, etc) to support their particular position. The information should be given as accurately as possible, although a respondent will not be held to a mistaken weekly rate if it later seeks to amend these details.

7.30   The 'basic wage/salary' is the gross amount the applicant was due, the 'average take home' is the net amount (ie, after deduction of tax and national insurance). It is up to the respondent whether weekly, monthly or yearly figures are given but it helps if the information is given for a consistent period throughout and in such a way as would provide a ready comparison with the details supplied by the applicant.

7.31   If the applicant's wage varied from week to week, the average amount for the last 12 calendar weeks of the employment should be taken. Under 'bonuses/benefits', all additional 'perks' should be listed, including any pension benefit, etc. While these will not be included as part of a 'week's pay' for the purposes of a basic award or redundancy payment, they are part of the applicant's loss in terms of any compensatory award.

Box 7: Details of the grounds of resistance

7.32   This is the respondent's first opportunity to set out the nature of the defence and will generally be the first document relating to the respondent's case read by the members of the tribunal. Care should therefore be taken to present the details to the respondent's best advantage, which may mean setting out the details on a separate sheet attached to the IT3 rather than trying to work within the confined space given on the form.

7.33   The purpose of the notice of appearance is to set out the respondent's case in answer to the allegations made by the applicant in the originating application and to make it clear what is and what is not in issue.

7.34   Where the respondent bears the burden of proof, it is particularly important to make sure that the case set out in the notice of appearance accurately reflects the way in which the respondent in fact wishes to present the case.

7.35   Sufficient details should be given to show how the respondent views the facts and matters which led to the decision to dismiss or take the other action complained of, for example, if there was a history of warnings and/or a number of disciplinary meetings, details should be provided so that the applicant knows in advance the events on which the respondent intends to rely.

7.36   Even where dismissal is not admitted, if it is subsequently found that the applicant was in fact dismissed, the tribunal will go on to consider whether that dismissal was fair. In such cases the respondent should consider 'pleading' in the alternative grounds on which it might be considered that any dismissal found was in fact fair. In particular, if a respondent intends to continue to contest liability once it is found that there was a dismissal, a reason should be put forward for that dismissal as an alternative to the respondent's primary case as soon as possible. Although a respondent can subsequently apply to amend and put forward a reason for the dismissal, leave will not be given if this would require further evidence to be adduced and considered or an adjournment of the hearing.[13]

7.37   It is not necessary to set out the relevant law in the notice of appearance, although reference to the relevant sections can assist in making the nature of the defence clear to those reading the document (for example, by specifying that a claim of indirect sex discrimination is contested on the basis of a defence of justification under Sex Discrimination Act 1975 s1(1)(b)(ii)). Furthermore, the relevant law should be borne in mind when completing the notice of appearance to ensure that important points are not left out, such as the size and administrative resources of the respondent in an unfair dismissal case.

7.38   It is not helpful to include background detail if this is not relevant to the type of claim being made, for example, if the issue in an unfair dismissal by reason of redundancy case is the fairness of the selection procedure, details of the applicant's capability will only be relevant if this formed part of the selection criteria.

7.39   On the other hand, where information is relevant and may later form the subject of a request for further particulars or for written answers, it will help to provide the details from the start and will avoid the possibility that the respondent will be accused of having raised matters for the first time at the substantive hearing of the case. Where relevant, name names, give dates, set out the gist of conversations relied on and so on.

Incorrect identification of the respondent

7.40   If the body named as respondent by the applicant is in fact wrong (or, at least, it intends to argue that this is the case), this should be detailed as a preliminary matter in the body of the notice of appearance. If identification of the correct respondent requires resolution of some preliminary legal or factual point (for example, when there might have been a transfer of an undertaking), the tribunal is likely to consider this at a preliminary hearing under 2001 Rules r6 (see chapter 14). The tribunal has a broad discretion to join other parties as respondents and/or to allow an amendment to the identification of the respondent in the originating application (see para 4.1).

---

13   *Ready Case Ltd v Jackson* [1981] IRLR 312, EAT.

Jurisdictional points

7.41   If a jurisdictional point is apparent to a respondent on receipt of the originating application (for example, the application was presented out of time or the applicant fails to meet the qualifying requirements for the type of claim submitted), the best course is to raise this as a preliminary point in the notice of appearance, before going on to set out the details of the grounds on which the claim is resisted. If appropriate, the respondent should also apply for the jurisdictional point to be determined at a preliminary hearing under 2001 Rules r6.

7.42   As a jurisdictional point cannot be waived by a party or by the tribunal, it would in fact be open to the respondent to raise the matter not in the notice of appearance but at some subsequent stage in the proceedings, even as late as an appeal. If the respondent is aware of the point at the stage of completing the notice of appearance, however, there is no good reason why it should not be raised in that document, particularly if leaving it to some later stage (for example, just before the hearing) might take the applicant by surprise and lead to an adjournment or postponement of the case. Where a respondent was intending to raise a jurisdictional issue in a case at the time of completing the notice of appearance and yet failed to raise it until shortly before the hearing, thereby necessitating an adjournment or postponement, it might well be open to the tribunal to conclude that such conduct was unreasonable and should result in the respondent being ordered to pay the wasted costs incurred by the applicant.

7.43   If liability is in dispute, a respondent should not seek to rely exclusively on a jurisdictional question but should look ahead to consider what might happen if the tribunal in fact finds that it does have jurisdiction to hear the complaint. The substantive defence to the claim should be put forward 'without prejudice' to the respondent's contention that the tribunal has no jurisdiction to hear the complaint.

7.44   Examples of details of grounds of resistance which might be used in notices of appearance are set out in appendix B.

The applicant's notice of appearance

7.45   Where an applicant makes a complaint of breach of contract, the respondent may well include a (counter)claim in addition to the 'defence' entered by way of the notice of appearance. As the counterclaim will be a positive claim by the respondent, it obviously would help to clarify the issues between the parties if the applicant were to make his or her position clear in relation to the contentions of the counterclaim at an early stage in the proceedings. In order to enable the applicant to do this, Form IT3(c) will be sent to the applicant for completion with the notice of appearance when this raises a counterclaim.

CHAPTER 8

Amendment

Introduction

8.1   Within its general power to regulate its own procedure under 2001 Rules r15(1),[1] a tribunal may at any stage of the proceedings consider an application to amend the originating application or notice of appearance. While there are no formal 'pleadings' in tribunals, the principal grounds on which a claim is to be brought or defended should be clear on the face of the originating application or notice of appearance. In so far as the initial document presented fails to set out the claim or defence relied on properly, the party concerned should seek to amend it as soon as possible. Any application to amend should make clear the precise terms and intended effect of the amendment sought, preferably setting out the nature of the amendment clearly in writing.[2]

8.2   The guidelines which will be considered by the tribunal when faced by an application to amend are set out below. Generally a tribunal will permit an amendment to be made providing the other side is not thereby prejudiced. A late amendment, even shortly before the commencement of the substantive hearing, may well be allowed: any prejudice suffered by the other side may be remedied by granting an adjournment of the hearing with an order for costs against the person applying to amend so late in the day.

Amendment of the originating application

8.3   The guidelines which tribunals should follow when considering any application to amend an originating application, whether to add or substitute respondents or to change the basis of the claim made, were set out by the National Industrial Relations Court (NIRC) in *Cocking v Sandhurst (Stationers) Ltd:*[3]

   – Did the unamended originating application comply with the rules relating to the presentation of originating applications (see chapter 6) and was it presented within the relevant time limit (see chapter 5)?

   – If not, then there is no power to amend and a new originating application must be presented within the relevant time limit if this is still possible.

1   Employment Tribunals Rules of Procedure (contained in SI 2001 No 1171, Sch 1).
2   *Harvey v Port of Tilbury London Ltd* [2000] ICR 1030; [2000] IRLR 693, EAT.
3   [1974] ICR 650.

- If it was, the tribunal has a discretion to allow an amendment which would add or substitute a new party but should only do so if satisfied that the mistake sought to be corrected was a genuine mistake and was not misleading or such as to cause reasonable doubt over the identity of the person intending to claim or to be claimed against.
- In deciding whether or not to exercise its discretion, the tribunal should have regard to all the circumstances of the case, including any injustice or hardship which may be caused to any of the parties if the amendment were allowed or refused. If allowing the amendment might cause unnecessary additional cost to one party, the tribunal might properly conclude that this was an appropriate case for the amending party to be ordered to pay the additional costs of, or occasioned by, the amendment (see chapter 20).

8.4   The NIRC's decision in *Cocking* has since been approved by the Court of Appeal in *British Newspaper Printing Corporation (North) Ltd v Kelly*.[4] Although, to the extent that *Kelly* suggests that no rules relating to time limits apply to amendments of claims before the employment tribunal, the Employment Appeal Tribunal (EAT) in *Harvey*[5] disagreed.

8.5   A detailed review of the practice and procedure relating to applications to amend was undertaken by the EAT in the case of *Selkent Bus Co Ltd v Moore*[6] and the *Cocking* guidance should be read in conjunction with this. It was stated in *Selkent* that the general guiding principle is that the tribunal's discretion should be exercised in a way that is consistent with the requirements of 'relevance, reason, justice and fairness inherent in all judicial discretions'.

8.6   If a party seeks to add or substitute a new cause of action, but one which is linked to or arises out of the same facts as the original claim, judicial discretion will usually permit the amendment. For example, in *Capek v Lincolnshire CC*[7] a claim for breach of contract to recover arrears of pay was held to have been made prematurely and therefore the tribunal did not have jurisdiction to hear the claim, but in reaching this conclusion the Court of Appeal ordered that the matter be remitted to the tribunal to consider whether there had been an unlawful deduction of wages which the tribunal had jurisdiction to

---

4   [1989] IRLR 222.
5   See note 2 above.
6   [1996] ICR 836.
7   [2000] IRLR 590.

hear under Employment Rights Act 1996 (ERA 1996) Part II. In substance the two claims were the same.

8.7   If the amendment sought relates to an entirely new claim unconnected with the original claim as pleaded and is otherwise out of time, it will not be permitted. In *Housing Corporation v Bryant*[8] the failure of an applicant to make any reference in her unfair dismissal claim to alleged victimisation defeated her subsequent application to amend to include a claim under the Sex Discrimination Act 1975.[9]

8.8   If a purely technical error is made in the naming of a respondent, *and* no prejudice has been caused, the tribunal may take a pragmatic approach, allowing an amendment late on in the proceedings, even after the issue of a consent order.[10] A tribunal is given a broad discretion to join a person to proceedings as a respondent and can do so at any time, even when the time limit for bringing a claim has expired by the time of the application to amend. The person whom it is sought to join should be given the opportunity to be heard on the application.[11] A new respondent may even be joined after a decision on the merits of the case has been given; although in that case, the new respondent must be afforded the opportunity to be heard, either by a rehearing after the presentation of an IT3 or by review.[12]

Amendment of the notice of appearance

8.9   Similar principles apply to any application to amend the notice of appearance. The later a respondent seeks to amend the basis of the defence relied on, the less likely it is that the tribunal will allow the amendment to be made. In particular, the tribunal will be reluctant to allow a respondent to amend in order to claim a new reason for a dismissal,[13] or to put forward a reason for a constructive dismissal where previously none was claimed,[14] unless the *substance* of the case was already contained within the original notice of appearance, ie, the

---

8 [1999] ICR 123, CA.
9 See also *Harvey v Port of Tilbury (London) Ltd* [1999] ICR 1030; [1999] IRLR 693, EAT.
10 *Milestone School of English Ltd v Leakey* [1982] IRLR 3, EAT.
11 *Gillick v BP Chemicals Ltd* [1993] IRLR 437.
12 *Linbourne v Constable* [1993] ICR 698, EAT.
13 *Kapur v Shields* [1976] ICR 26, QBD.
14 *Ready Case Ltd v Jackson* [1981] IRLR 312, EAT.

amendment is no more than for the purpose of giving an appropriate label to a fully described set of facts.[15]

Amendment and striking out

8.10   By 2001 Rules r15(2)(c) a tribunal may (of its own motion or on application) order any part of an originating application or notice of appearance to be amended or struck out on the grounds that it is scandalous, misconceived or vexatious. See also paras 12.34 and 20.8.

---

15   *Blue Star Ship Management Ltd v Williams* [1978] ICR 770; [1979] IRLR 16, EAT.

CHAPTER 9

Defining the issues: questionnaires, further particulars, written answers

Introduction

9.1   Anyone contemplating or conducting tribunal proceedings needs to be able to make the best assessment possible of the prospects of success at all stages in the process. In chapter 4 the basic steps which can be taken to assess the strengths and costs of a case before commencing tribunal proceedings were described. This chapter builds on these steps, describing the special 'pre-action' procedure available in discrimination cases in the form of the questionnaire and detailing this and other interlocutory steps which can be used before a full hearing to learn as much as possible about the way in which the other side intends to conduct the case.

9.2   An order made by an tribunal in respect of any of these procedures will be interlocutory in nature and, therefore, not open to review (see chapter 22). Where, however, an interlocutory order is initially made after considering representations from only one party, the order is essentially provisional and may be reconsidered by the tribunal upon application by an absent party.[1]

Questionnaires

Scope

9.3   A person considering bringing a complaint under the Sex Discrimination Act 1975 (SDA),[2] the Disability Discrimination Act 1995 (DDA 1995) and/or the Race Relations Act 1976 (RRA 1976) should use the questionnaire procedure (see paras 4.17–4.19) to decide whether to institute proceedings and, if so, to formulate and present the complaint in the most effective manner. SDA 1975 s74(1), DDA 1995 s56(2) and RRA 1976 s65(1) provide that the secretary of state may by order prescribe the forms by which a potential complainant might question the respondent and by which the respondent might then reply. The relevant forms are to be found in the schedules to the Sex Discrimination (Questions and Replies) Order 1975,[3] the Race

---

1   *Reddington v Straker & Sons Ltd* [1994] ICR 172, EAT.
2   Many equal pay claims are linked to SDA 1975 claims and, arguably, the SDA 1975 questionnaire procedure can be applied to claims under the EqPA 1970 which is incorporated as a schedule to the SDA 1975. The government has, however, proposed introducing a EqPA 1970 questionnaire, see clause 42 of the Employment Bill 2001.
3   SI No 2048, as amended.

Relations (Questions and Replies) Order 1977,[4] and the Disability Discrimination (Questions and Replies) Order 1996.[5]

9.4   The forms provided consist of a questionnaire which the applicant or potential applicant may use to direct questions at the respondent about the reasons for doing any relevant act (ie, some act which might amount to unlawful discrimination under the SDA 1975 and/or RRA 1976) or on any other matter which is or may be relevant, and a form of reply for the respondent to use by way of answer.

Use of the questionnaire procedure

9.5   Any applicant or potential applicant complaining of sex, race or disability discrimination should be aware of the questionnaire procedure and the uses to which it can be put.

9.6   First, the questionnaire provides a means for a potential applicant to question the respondent before bringing a claim. It allows the complainant to obtain detailed information that might assist the presentation of the complaint and to find out more about the case the respondent is likely to present by way of a defence. In some cases (particularly those involving complaints of indirect discrimination), the answers provided to a well-formulated questionnaire might be the best means by which a complainant can assess the prospects of succeeding in a claim.

9.7   Furthermore, provided it has been served within the relevant time limits (see below), the questionnaire and any answers given by way of reply can be used as evidence in any tribunal proceedings. The replies given are admissible as evidence, whether or not the prescribed form has been used by the respondent.[6] If the respondent fails to answer or replies in an equivocal or evasive fashion, this might in itself be used as evidence of discrimination (see para 9.10).

9.8   In many discrimination cases, particularly those involving allegations of indirect discrimination, statistical information about the respondent's workforce may provide the best evidence available from which to draw an inference of discrimination. Where no existing document contains the statistical information sought, discovery will be useless and an order for further particulars is unlikely to be

4   SI No 842.
5   SI No 2793.
6   SDA 1975 s74(2)(a); RRA 1976 s65(2)(a); DDA 1995 s56(3)(a).

considered appropriate in these circumstances.[7] Furthermore, some tribunals have indicated that they will not order that information be provided by way of written answers (see para 9.33) where a questionnaire would be the appropriate means for requesting the details concerned.

9.9   The basic form of questionnaire set out in the Questions and Replies Orders provides a useful starting point for any complainant. Part 4 allows for other questions to be included in the form and these will obviously depend on the particular circumstances of the case which is to be brought. As a general rule, details of the sex or racial breakdown of the relevant part of the workforce will provide useful background to the claim, as will any information on the maintenance and operation of any equal opportunities policy by the employer. Specialist assistance in the drafting of questionnaires may be obtained from the Commission for Racial Equality, the Disability Rights Commission or the Equal Opportunities Commission, either from members of their staff or by way of reference to local advisers with relevant experience.

Responding to the questionnaire

9.10   The recipient of a questionnaire is not obliged to serve a reply nor can he or she be ordered to do so. If, however, the tribunal finds that a respondent has deliberately and without reasonable excuse omitted to reply to a properly presented questionnaire within a reasonable period of time, or that the replies given are evasive or equivocal, it may draw any inference from that fact that it considers just and equitable to draw, including an inference that the respondent committed an unlawful act (ie, an act of unlawful sex, race or disability discrimination).[8] Any respondent on the receiving end of a questionnaire would be well-advised to answer clearly and promptly.

Time limits on questionnaires

9.11   Article 5 of the SDA and RRA Questions and Replies Orders, and article 3 of the DDA Questions and Replies Order each provide for time limits within which the questionnaire must be served if it is to be utilised as evidence before a tribunal. These limits are as follows:

---

7   *Carrington v Helix Lighting Ltd* [1990] ICR 125; [1990] IRLR 6, EAT.
8   SDA 1975 s74(2)(b); RRA 1976 s65(2)(b); DDA 1995 s56(3)(b).

- If the questionnaire is served *before* the presentation of an originating application: three months beginning with the date of the act complained of.
- If the questionnaire is served *after* the presentation of an originating application: 21 days beginning with the day on which the application was presented.

9.12   A questionnaire served outside these time limits must be served with the leave of the tribunal if it is to be admissible as evidence. Where leave is given by a tribunal to serve a questionnaire, the time limit within which it must then be served will be specified by the tribunal itself. If an applicant wishes to serve a questionnaire out of time, the best course is to send a copy to the respondent, giving notice of the intention to apply to the tribunal for leave to serve out of time. At the same time an application to the tribunal should be made, including with the application a copy of the proposed questionnaire together with all relevant correspondence. The tribunal which considers whether or not to grant leave will consider matters such as the length of any delay and the reasons for it and the possible prejudice to the respondent, as well as the relevance or oppressiveness of the questions included within the questionnaire itself.[9]

9.13   If on receipt of the reply to the original questionnaire it is apparent that further questions need to be asked, there is nothing to stop an applicant from applying to the tribunal for leave to serve further questionnaires, although they will be unable to ask for further particulars of the original questionnaire itself (see para 9.31 below). Indeed, the service of further questionnaires is a practice which the Employment Appeal Tribunal has endorsed in appropriate circumstances as a 'sensible and necessary part of the procedure'.[10]

9.14   The service of further questionnaires must, however, be distinguished from the service of a request for further particulars of matters raised in the reply. Just as the tribunal cannot order that a respondent reply to a questionnaire, it has no power to order that further particulars of a reply be provided.

9 *Williams v Greater London Citizens Advice Bureaux Service* [1989] ICR 545, EAT.
10 *Carrington v Helix*, note 7 above.

Further particulars

9.15   A party to tribunal proceedings may ask the other party to provide
further particulars of the originating application or notice of appearance. Although there are no formal 'pleadings' in tribunal proceedings, the process is similar in many respects to requests for further
information in High Court or county court cases under Civil Procedure Rules (CPR) Part 18 (although there is no requirement for a
signed statement of truth in any such document before the tribunal).

9.16   The purpose of a request for further particulars is to ensure that a
party is properly informed of the other side's case, so he or she can be
prepared to meet it at hearing. If an employer's notice of appearance
contains the allegation that the applicant was unable to perform his
or her duties satisfactorily, the applicant would be entitled to further
particulars as to which duties are referred to and the manner in
which it is alleged that their performance was unsatisfactory.[11] Or if
an applicant claims he or she was treated in a way which was inconsistent with the treatment of other employees and with the general
practice within that employment, the employer would be entitled
to request further particulars of the general practice alleged, and
citation of instances involving other employees.[12]

9.17   As a general rule, a party should not be required to supply further
particulars in respect of an issue on which the other side bears the
burden of proof.[13] Where a party puts forward a positive case, however, further particulars may be ordered of the allegations made even
though they do not bear the burden of proof. For instance, in a case
where dismissal is admitted (where the employer will bear the burden of proving the reason for that dismissal), it has been held that an
applicant who speculates on the real reason for the dismissal may be
required to provide further particulars of any positive assertion
made.[14]

9.18   The necessity of requesting further particulars arises when the
other side has failed fully to particularise its case. If the replies given
to a request are still not sufficiently particularised, a further request
can be made: a request for further particulars of the further particulars. But requests should not develop into an attempt to carry out
the trial of the issues on paper. Tribunals will not order further

11 *White v University of Manchester* [1976] ICR 419; [1976] IRLR 218, EAT.
12 *International Computers Ltd v Whitley* [1978] IRLR 318, EAT.
13 *James v Radnor CC* (1890) 6 TLR 240, QBD.
14 *Colonial Mutual Life Assurance Society Ltd v Clinch* [1981] ICR 752, EAT.

particulars requested solely for the purpose of ascertaining who are the witnesses the other party is likely to call to give evidence.[15]

9.19   Tribunals have historically been reluctant to order that further particulars be provided which go solely to compensation when the issues on liability have not yet been determined,[16] even though this might be useful for an employer seeking to make a realistic offer of settlement. Tribunals are, however, increasingly willing to direct that proper particulars be provided of loss at an early stage, which may include directing that a full schedule of loss be prepared and that discovery of documents relevant to loss and mitigation is given. While this practice is by no means automatic, it might be expected where:

–   the claim is one of unlawful discrimination or is otherwise one where damages are at large or might be significant;
–   the tribunal intends to consider the question of remedy concurrently with that of liability or has provisionally listed the issue of remedy to be considered immediately after the liability hearing;
–   it is helpful to allow all concerned to direct a proportionate amount of resources to the case. In particular, this might allow a respondent to take a 'commercial view' as to the value of resisting the claim.

9.20   Where an originating application is insufficiently particularised for a respondent to understand the nature of the case made by the applicant, even to the extent of being able to present a properly formulated notice of appearance, an order can be made for further particulars to be supplied even before a notice of appearance is served (2001 Rules rr3(3)(b) and 4(1)). This is one of the few steps which can be taken by a respondent which has not entered a notice of appearance (see para 7.16)

9.21   When responding to a request for further particulars, a party is not obliged to supply information which has not been sought, although it may be advisable to expand the answer if it is not otherwise possible to answer the request properly. At the same time, parties should be wary of requests which require 'all facts and matters relied on in support of the allegation that . . .'. An incomplete answer to such a request may result in an objection to the subsequent introduction of further matters relied on in support of the allegation concerned but not specified in the reply. This is an attempt to use the

---

15 *P&O European Ferries (Dover) Ltd v Byrne* [1989] ICR 779; [1989] IRLR 254, CA.
16 *Colonial Mutual Life Assurance Society Ltd v Clinch*, note 14 above.

further particulars as a means of defining the limits of the opponent's case. If, after responding to a request for further particulars, new information comes to light which adds to the case a party wishes to put forward, or if it has left out certain matters by mistake, it is better to raise these points either by amendment or by voluntary additional further particulars, rather than to wait until the hearing of the case.

9.22   In making a request for further particulars, or in responding to such a request, the basic principles to be applied should be borne in mind, as summarised by Wood J in *Byrne v Financial Times Ltd*:[17]

> General principles affecting the ordering of further and better particulars include that the parties should not be taken by surprise at the last minute; that particulars should only be ordered when necessary in order to do justice in the case or to prevent adjournment; that the order should not be oppressive; that particulars are for the purpose of identifying the issues, not for the production of the evidence; and that complicated pleadings battles should not be encouraged.

The power to order further particulars

9.23   A request for further particulars should first be made directly to the other party without seeking an order from the tribunal. It is always better to try to obtain further details from the other side on a voluntary basis and this is certainly the practice encouraged by tribunals.

9.24   Rule 4(1) and (3) of the 2001 Rules sets out the tribunal's power to order that a party provide further particulars of the grounds on which that party relies, and of any facts and contentions relevant to those grounds. Such an order can be made on the application of a party or by the tribunal of its own motion.

9.25   Whether made directly to the other party or by way of application to the tribunal, a request for further particulars should be in writing and should ideally set out the passage in respect of which the particulars are sought before stating the nature of the request made.

9.26   As with all interlocutory orders, a tribunal's decision whether or not to order further particulars will be largely a matter for its discretion and will be very difficult to overturn on appeal. This is also true of the tribunal's power to vary or set aside orders for further particulars and of any decision whether or not to strike out or debar for failure to comply with an order.

17 [1991] IRLR 417 at 419, EAT.

Application to vary or set aside an order

9.27 If an order requiring a person to supply further particulars is made by the tribunal in his or her absence, that person may apply to the tribunal to vary or set aside the order under 2001 Rules r4(7). Such an application should be made by notice to the secretary before the date by which the tribunal has ordered that the particulars be supplied. Notice of the application to vary or set aside will then be sent to all other parties.

Failure to comply with an order

9.28 If a party does not comply with an order made under 2001 Rules r4(1), the tribunal may, before or at the hearing:

- make a costs order under 2001 Rules r14(1)(a); *or*
- strike out the whole or part of the originating application or notice of appearance and, where appropriate, debar a respondent from further defending the application (see 2001 Rules r4(8)).

9.29 It would seem that 2001 Rules r4(8) envisages that an order to strike out in these circumstances will not be accompanied by an order relating to costs (note the use of the word *or*). There seems, however, to be no reason why the two orders should be mutually exclusive and nothing to prevent the tribunal from exercising its general jurisdiction to award costs under 2001 Rules r14 in any event. After all, if a party has conducted the proceedings in such an unreasonable way as to be struck out in these circumstances, why should the remaining party not be reimbursed for the costs it has thereby incurred?

9.30 A tribunal cannot exercise its power under 2001 Rules r4(8) without having sent notice to the party in default giving it an opportunity to show cause why the tribunal should not do so. The notice cannot be sent out before expiry of the time limit ordered for the further particulars to be provided.[18]

Further particulars of questionnaires

9.31 A tribunal will not order a respondent to provide further particulars of a reply to a questionnaire. The proper course of action if a complainant wishes to ask further questions of the respondent in such cases, is to seek leave to serve a further questionnaire (see para 9.13).

---

18 *Beacard Property Management and Construction Co Ltd v Day* [1984] ICR 837, EAT.

Equal pay cases

9.32   In an equal pay case, where the respondent seeks to rely on the genuine material factor defence provided by Equal Pay Act 1970 s1(3), an applicant can request precise details of the percentage pay differentials which are said to be explained by the material factor relied on; see the case of *Enderby v Frenchay Health Authority and Secretary of State for Health*.[19] The arguments previously relied on by respondents to resist any such request for further particulars of this defence[20] would now be contrary to the decision of the European Court of Justice in *Enderby*.

Written answers

9.33   A further means of seeking information about another party's case is to ask that answers be given in writing to specific questions in respect of that case (2001 Rules r4(3)). Written answers are likely to be viewed in the same way as orders for further information (formerly 'interrogatories') in the High Court or county court and the same guidelines are likely to be applied. Indeed the earlier wording of the 1993 Employment Tribunal Rules relating to written answers (also r4(3)) used language similar to that of the CPR, ie, that such an order may be made if the tribunal 'considers (a) that the answer of the party to that question may help to clarify any issue likely to arise for determination in the proceedings, and (b) that it would be likely to assist the progress of the proceedings for that answer to be available to the tribunal before the hearing'.

9.34   Like information given in court proceedings, written answers are unlikely to be ordered where other procedural processes would be more appropriate, for example, where the answer could be sought by way of a request for further particulars or where it would be resolved on discovery. Some tribunals have indicated that they will not be prepared to order written answers to questions in sex, race or disability discrimination cases where the information could be sought by using the questionnaire procedure (see paras 9.5–9.9), although where the time limit has already passed for the issue of the questionnaire, such an application might be viewed more sympathetically.[21] As

19   [1994] ICR 112; [1993] IRLR 591, CA and ECJ.
20   *Byrne and others v Financial Times Ltd* [1991] IRLR 417, EAT.

with further particulars, tribunals will be reluctant to order that written answers be provided where the questions asked amount to an attempt to try the issues in the case on paper rather than at a hearing.

9.35 Written answers will be considered by the tribunal not as part of the 'pleading' process but as representations made by the party concerned as part of its case.

The power to order written answers

9.36 The other party should first be asked to provide written answers on a voluntary basis. If this is refused, 2001 Rules r4(1) and (3) provides that the party may be ordered to do so by the tribunal, either on the application of a party or of its own motion. If an application is made by a party, the tribunal may require it to send notice of the application to all other parties. When a tribunal makes an order, it will state the time within which the answers must be supplied and a copy of the order will be sent to all other parties by the secretary.

Application to vary or set aside an order to provide written answers

9.37 If an order requiring a party to supply written answers is made by the tribunal in his or her absence, 2001 Rules r4(7) provides that the person may apply to the tribunal to vary or set aside the order. Such an application should be made to the secretary before the expiry of the date by which the tribunal has ordered that the particulars be supplied. Notice of the application to vary or set aside will then be sent to all other parties.

Failure to comply with an order

9.38 If a party does not comply with an order under 2001 Rules r4(1), the tribunal may, before or at the hearing:
- make a costs order under 2001 Rules r14(1)(a); *or*
- strike out the whole or part of the originating application or notice of appearance and, where appropriate, debar a respondent from further defending the application (see 2001 Rules r4(8) and para 9.29).

---

21 A questionnaire remains the best option for applicants if possible given the formal way in which inferences can be drawn from a failure to answer or from an unsatisfactory or inadequate answer.

9.39   A tribunal cannot strike out or debar, however, without having sent notice to the party in default giving him or her an opportunity to show cause why the tribunal should not do so (2001 Rules r4(7)); such notice must not be sent out before expiry of the time limit ordered for the written answers to be provided (by analogy with requests for further particulars).[22]

22   *Beacard Property Management and Construction Co Ltd v Day*, note 18 above.

CHAPTER 10

Disclosure

continued

Introduction

10.1   The documentation relevant to a particular case will generally provide the best evidence to the issues in that case. It avoids the need to rely on selective recollection of events, and can provide a useful indication of the real view taken by a particular individual at the time an event occurred rather than that which he or she might adopt when giving evidence after proceedings have commenced. Finding out about the existence of those documents and gaining sight of them is effected by *disclosure* and *inspection* (*recovery* in Scotland). It may well be the most crucial step taken by the parties. The documents available in a case will often be the best weapon available and the earlier inspection of the documents takes place, the earlier a party can use the weapon to its advantage, whether by way of requests for further disclosure, or further particulars, or for use in assessing the merits of the case generally and in settlement negotiations.

General principles

10.2   Unlike in High Court or county court proceedings (see Civil Procedure Rules (CPR) Part 31), there is no general duty to make disclosure in tribunal proceedings. Unless a party requests disclosure, the other side is not obliged to disclose any documents at all. Late production of documents, on the morning of the hearing, may, however, give good grounds for seeking an adjournment with an order for costs to be made against the party with previously undisclosed documents. Where the late disclosure involves just one or two short documents, the tribunal may expect the hearing to go ahead after a short adjournment on the morning to enable the other party to read the new papers. The principle is that no party should be prejudiced by late disclosure of documents.

10.3   Such difficulties can be overcome to a large extent by seeking disclosure before the hearing. As there is no general duty to disclose all documents, this can often be a very imprecise procedural instrument. As an employee will not know all the documents in the employer's possession, *specific* requests may miss the most important document in the case. The crown jewels may be a board minute or confidential memo referring to the employee as a dangerous militant who will have to be removed (in a union reasons case), or stating he or she they does not 'fit in' (in a discrimination case). General requests for disclosure of an employee's personnel file, or for all documents on which the other side intends to rely, may not produce the goods: damning policy documents, for instance, may not be specific to that employee. While tribunals dislike general orders for disclosure, a request for all documents relevant to the issues in the case may be the best way to ensure at the hearing that all the cards are on the table. Assistance might also be derived from the wording of the CPR, which provide that 'standard disclosure' will include the following:

– the documents on which a party relies; and
– the documents which:
  • adversely affect that party's case;
  • adversely affect another party's case; or
  • support another party's case.

See CPR 31.6, and para 10.7, below.

10.4   Moreover, when giving disclosure, a party should not be selective as to the documents to be disclosed within a particular class and should not allow a misleading impression to be gained by partial disclosure. The principles were set out by Waite J in *Birds Eye Walls Ltd v Harrison:*[1]

> Once . . . a party has disclosed certain documents . . . it becomes his duty not to withhold . . . any further documents in his possession or power . . . if there is any risk that the effect . . . might be to convey to his opponent or to the tribunal a false or misleading impression as to the true nature, purport or effect of any disclosed document.
>   . . . [T]wo principles [are] to be borne in mind if injustice is not to be suffered . . . the duty of every party not to withhold from disclosure any document whose suppression would render a disclosed document misleading is a high duty which the tribunals should interpret broadly and strictly . . . Tribunals should . . . ensure that if any party can be . . . at risk of having his claim or defence unfairly restricted by the denial of an opportunity to become aware of a document . . . material to the just prosecution of his case, he does not suffer any avoidable disadvantage as a result.

10.5   Part of a document may be disclosed if it is made clear that the document is not complete, and the whole of the document *must* be offered to the tribunal or the other side if it is requested.[2]

10.6   *Disclosure* means providing a list of documents; *inspection*, which

1   [1985] ICR 278; [1985] IRLR 47, EAT.
2   *C J O'Shea Construction Ltd v Bassi* [1998] ICR 1130, EAT.

may include the taking of copies of documents, is what is required to see them. In practice, parties generally agree to conduct disclosure by mutual exchange of copies of relevant documentation. Rarely, a charge is made for copying and, if it is reasonable, it should be paid. Reliance on the more technical form of disclosure by list arises where the great majority of documents are with one party, usually the employer, the request is generalised, and providing extensive copies might be unduly burdensome. In these circumstances, or where the party in question is just being bloody-minded, disclosure may well be by list, the other party being expected to request inspection of specific items (usually at the other side's premises or at the offices of their solicitors) or to undertake the copying.

The power to order disclosure

10.7   The power to order disclosure is provided by 2001 Rules r4(5)(b).[3] A tribunal may, on the application of a party or of its own motion, order one party to grant to another such disclosure or inspection of documents (including the taking of copies) as might be granted by a county court. The procedure of the county court is set out in CPR Part 31 (Disclosure and Inspection). The essence of the CPR is that orders for disclosure are now limited to 'standard disclosure' unless the court directs otherwise (CPR 31.5), such that a party is only required to disclose those documents on which he relies, documents which adversely affect his own or another party's case, or which support another party's case, and documents which he is required to disclose by a relevant practice direction (CPR 31.6 and 31.8). A party must make a reasonable search for documents (CPR 31.7), but as in all aspects of the operation of the CPR, the principle of proportionality must be considered, and a party will not be compelled to do that which would be disproportionate in the circumstances of a particular case.

10.8   As under the old rules, orders will not be granted if the request for disclosure amounts to a 'fishing expedition' (see further para 10.20).

10.9   Tribunals encourage parties to avoid the need for formal applications for disclosure and inspection and, instead, to agree to the mutual exchange of documents and the creation of an 'agreed bundle' for use in any tribunal hearing. An agreed bundle does not mean that all

3   Employment Tribunals Rules of Procedure (contained in SI 2001 No 1171, Sch 1).

parties agree on the relevance of the documents it contains or as to the truth of their contents. All it means is that there is no live dispute about the existence and authorship of the documents involved, so the writer need not be called as a witness simply to prove that he or she created the document. Of course, the writer should be called if there is dispute about the reasons for what is written. So a director who signed a disciplinary procedure agreement need not be called but the manager who wrote the dismissal letter under the procedure should be.

10.10   Although the tribunal's power in relation to disclosure and inspection is quite limited, the notice of hearing, Form IT4 (see appendix A), expressly suggests that mutual disclosure by list should take place voluntarily and that sufficient copies should be provided for other parties, before the hearing, and for the tribunal members and the witness table at the hearing.

10.11   A decision relating to disclosure may be made by a tribunal chairman sitting alone (2001 Rules r15(8)) and may arise from the tribunal acting of its own motion (2001 Rules r4(5)).

10.12   Before determining an application for disclosure, a tribunal may require the party making the application to give notice of it to all other parties, giving particulars of the application and the address to which and the time within which any objection should be made (both of which will be specified by the tribunal) (2001 Rules r15(5)).

10.13   If the tribunal determines an application for disclosure on the papers, or in the absence of any party, the absent party against whom any order is made may apply to the tribunal to vary or set aside the requirement (2001 Rules r4(7)). Any order for disclosure is an interlocutory order and not a decision. There is no power for the tribunal to review it (see chapter 22) but it can be appealed.[4] The decision in any instance is, however, largely a matter for its discretion and it will be difficult for any party to appeal against that decision.

Failure to comply

10.14   If a party fails to comply with an order for disclosure, the tribunal may, at or before the hearing, make an order for costs under 2001 Rules r14(1)(a), or strike out the whole or part of the originating application or notice of appearance, and debar a respondent from defending the

4   *Science Research Council v Nasse* [1980] AC 1028; [1979] ICR 921; [1979] IRLR 465, HL.

proceedings altogether (2001 Rules r4(8)). The tribunal cannot, however, strike out or debar unless prior notice has been sent to the party concerned giving an opportunity to show cause why the tribunal should not do so (2001 Rules r4(8)).

10.15 In considering whether to strike out or debar, the tribunal will take into account similar considerations to those applied in the High Court or county courts.[5] The main test is whether there is a real or substantial risk that, as a result of the default, a fair trial will no longer be possible.[6]

10.16 Failure to comply with an order for disclosure, without reasonable excuse, may also render the party concerned liable on summary conviction to a fine not exceeding level 3 on the standard scale.[7]

No duty to create documents

10.17 Disclosure applies only to existing documentation; there is no obligation under this procedure for a party to create a document. Where statistics are sought which will have to be created for that case, the questionnaire in discrimination cases, or the written answer procedure under 2001 Rules r4(3), might provide the only means of obtaining such information (see paras 9.3 and 9.33).

Disclosure and inspection: general principles

Documents

10.18 A 'document' is widely defined for the purposes of disclosure. It is not limited to writing or print on paper but includes anything on which information or evidence is recorded, for example, tape recordings,[8] photographs, videotapes, microfilms,[9] computer disks, e-mails and so on.

10.19 In High Court and county court proceedings, the documents used at court hearings should be the originals whenever possible. This rule does not apply to tribunal proceedings, although the original should be available for inspection if any question is raised (or is likely to be raised) as to its authenticity, or its alteration.

---

5   *National Grid Co Ltd v Virdee* [1992] IRLR 555, EAT.
6   *Landauer Ltd v Comins & Co* (1991) *Times* 7 August, CA.
7   Employment Tribunals Act 1996 (ETA 1996) s7(4); r4(6).
8   *Grant v Southwestern and County Properties Ltd* [1974] 2 All ER 465, ChD.
9   Bankers' Books Evidence Act 1879.

Relevance

10.20   A document of which disclosure is sought must first be shown to be material and relevant to the issues in the proceedings. A document is 'relevant' when:

> it is reasonable to suppose [it] contains information which *may*, not which *must*, either directly or indirectly enable the party [applying for disclosure] either to advance his own case or to damage the case of his adversary [including] a document which may fairly lead him to a train of enquiry which may have either of these two consequences . . .[10]

10.21   A document is not 'relevant' if it is intended to be used merely to attack a witness's credibility;[11] nor if it is being sought to find out the names of the other side's witnesses.[12]

10.22   Relevance is not the only criterion. If the tribunal is satisfied that the documents are material and relevant to the case, it may still exercise its discretion to decide not to order disclosure. Relevant to the tribunal's exercise of discretion are the following questions:

- Will refusing disclosure hinder a fair hearing?
- Will refusing disclosure cause delay and thereby increase costs?
- Is the request proportionate? Regard may be had to the number of documents involved, the nature and complexity of the proceedings, the ease and expense of retrieval and the significance of the document.
- Would an order for disclosure in the terms sought be oppressive?
- Are there any other relevant considerations, such as confidentiality, which need to be balanced against the question of relevance?

10.23   It is for the party applying for disclosure to show that the document is relevant to an issue or issues already clearly defined in the proceedings, ie, it is not a fishing expedition and disclosure is necessary at that stage in the proceedings.[13]

Privilege

10.24   *Privilege* protects a document from disclosure or inspection in the interests of the administration of justice. For public policy reasons, a

---

10   *Compagnie Financière du Pacifique v Peruvian Guano Co* [1882] 11 QBD 55, CA.
11   *George Ballantine & Son Ltd v F E R Dixon & Son Ltd* [1974] 2 All ER 503, ChD.
12   *Knapp v Harvey* [1911] 2 KB 725, CA.
13   *Rolls Royce Motor Cars Ltd v Mair and others* EAT/794/92, unreported.

party will not be obliged to hand over certain classes of documents. Privilege may arise in a number of instances which are considered below.

Confidentiality

10.25 General guidelines as to confidentiality of documents and disclosure in tribunal cases were set out by Lord Wilberforce in *Science Research Council v Nasse; Vyas v Leyland Cars*[14] and can be summarised as:

- If a tribunal is satisfied that disclosure of a document is necessary in order fairly to dispose of the proceedings, it must order disclosure of the document, even though the document is confidential. There is no principle in law by which documents are protected from disclosure by reason of confidentiality by itself.[15]
- There is no presumption against disclosure of confidential documents.
- Where there is an objection to disclosure of documents on the grounds of confidentiality, the tribunal should inspect the documents to decide whether disclosure is necessary for the fair disposal of the case or for saving expense.
- In exercising its discretion as to whether to order disclosure, the tribunal should have regard to the fact that documents are confidential and should consider whether the necessary information can be obtained by other means, not involving a breach of confidence.
- Confidentiality is a relevant factor in deciding whether to order disclosure: relevance is not the only factor and general orders for disclosure are not always appropriate in tribunal proceedings.

10.26 A party will not be able to claim privilege against disclosure solely on the ground that the document, or its contents, was supplied in confidence by a third party.[16]

10.27 It is for the tribunal in its discretion, rather than as a matter of strict entitlement by a party, to decide questions of confidentiality and disclosure. It can decide them at some interlocutory stage or as they arise during the hearing.[17] Often the most appropriate course is to

---

14 [1980] AC 1028; [1979] ICR 921; [1979] IRLR 465, HL.
15 *Alfred Crompton Amusement Machines Ltd v Customs and Excise Commissioners (No 2)* [1974] AC 405; [1973] 2 All ER 1169, HL. Although considerations of the right to privacy might now arise under ECHR article 8, incorporated under the HRA 1998, see para 10.45 below.
16 Ibid.
17 *BRB v Natarajan* [1979] ICR 326; [1979] IRLR 45, EAT.

consider all arguments relating to disclosure and the confidentiality of documents at a separate directions hearing. This has been particularly encouraged by the Employment Appeal Tribunal (EAT) for complex cases.[18]

10.28   If the tribunal, at whatever stage, considers it appropriate that there should be an examination of the documents, it should consider how the facts in the documents can be disclosed without divulging the confidential parts. As a general rule, names and addresses of those against whom comparison is being made (for example, in a case alleging discrimination at interview for a job) should not be disclosed, although qualifications may well be, as might other factors necessary for the tribunal to make a proper assessment of the value of the evidence.

Public interest immunity

10.29   All claims of privilege rely on general principles of public policy. Public interest immunity goes further and asserts protection from disclosure on the ground that disclosure would be injurious to the public interest.[19] When public interest immunity is claimed, the tribunal will have to balance that claim against the importance of the documents to the proceedings, the extent of injustice caused by their non-disclosure and the public interest in fair administration of justice.[20] There is no 'right' to resist disclosure on such a ground but the party seeking to do so should be able to show some public duty which outweighs the public policy considerations in favour of disclosure.

10.30   The circumstances in which public interest immunity might arise have been identified as falling within two types: immunity extending to a whole class of documents and immunity simply in relation to the contents of a particular document. The distinction has been described by Lord Wilberforce as follows:

> . . . with a 'class' claim it is immaterial whether the disclosure of the particular contents of particular documents would be injurious to the public interest – the point being that it is the maintenance of the immunity of the 'class' from disclosure in litigation that is important;

18   See *Brooks v British Telecommunications plc* [1991] ICR 286; 1991 IRLR 4, EAT (affirmed [1992] ICR 414; [1992] IRLR 66, CA) and *Halford v Sharples* [1992] ICR 146, EAT (affirmed [1992] ICR 583, CA).

19   See CPR 31.19.

20   *D v NSPCC* [1977] 1 All ER 589, HL.

whereas in a contents claim, the protection is claimed for particular 'contents' in a particular document. A claim remains a 'class' even though something may be known about the contents; it remains a 'class' even if parts of the documents are revealed and parts disclosed.[21]

10.31   Where immunity is claimed on a 'class' basis, an order for inspection should be made with extreme care and should not be exercised before giving the party claiming the immunity the opportunity to appeal.[22]

10.32   If a claim of 'class' immunity is accepted and documents are excluded on that basis, no use whatever can be made of the documents and no reliance placed on anything contained in them by any of the parties to the proceedings.

10.33   Police complaints files containing documents prepared under the Police and Criminal Evidence Act 1984, and files compiled under the police disciplinary regulations, are discoverable as a 'class'. But immunity or other kinds of privilege may be claimed in respect of the contents of *particular* documents within those categories.[23]

10.34   'Class' immunity has also been held not to apply to files held by the Association of Chief Police Officers consisting of confidential reports kept on each individual chief officer[24] (subject to the exclusion of particular documents relating to positive vetting and the private lives of individual officers). Nor does it apply to statements made in the course of police grievance proceedings.[25]

National security

10.35   Where the disclosure of any information would, in the opinion of a minister, be contrary to the interests of national security, any disclosure of that information will be prohibited.[26] Even without this statutory prohibition, which could be applied in most proceedings before a tribunal,[27] whenever public interest immunity is claimed, courts and tribunals will generally not look behind that certificate to

21   *Burmah Oil Co Ltd v Bank of England* [1980] AC 1090 at 1111, HL.
22   *Halford v Sharples* [1992] ICR 146 at 155–158, EAT and [1992] ICR 583 at 609–610, CA.
23   *R v Chief Constable of West Midlands Police ex p Wiley* [1995] 1 AC 274, overruling *Neilson v Laugharne* [1981] QB 736, CA.
24   *Halford v Sharples* [1992] ICR 146, EAT.
25   *Metropolitan Police Commissioner v Locker* [1993] ICR 440; [1993] IRLR 319, EAT.
26   Employment Rights Act 1996 (ERA 1996) s195.
27   ERA 1996 s193(2).

assess the likely danger themselves. In *Balfour v Foreign and Com-monwealth Office*[28] the Court of Appeal held that while a tribunal should be vigilant to ensure that a claim of public interest immunity was raised only in appropriate circumstances, and was particularised, once a certificate of a minister demonstrated that the disclosure of documentary evidence posed an actual or potential risk to national security, the tribunal should not exercise its right to inspect that evidence.[29]

Diplomatic privilege

10.36   Embassy documents are protected by absolute privilege.[30]

Legal privilege

10.37   Legal privilege falls under two heads:

- *Legal advice privilege*: communications between client and legal adviser which are confidential and made for the purpose of obtaining or providing legal advice. These include documents which come into being in contemplation of litigation, but are not limited to that classification. The basis of the privilege is the principle that any person should be entitled to seek and obtain legal advice at any time without fear that it might later be disclosed to another; the privilege is therefore owned by the client, not the lawyer, and continues indefinitely.

- *Legal proceedings privilege*: communications between client, legal adviser and third parties which are made for the purpose of existing or contemplated legal proceedings. This privilege is more limited in nature and has a restricted life. It can no longer be relied on once the litigation concerned has come to an end.

10.38   'Legal adviser' is defined as a qualified lawyer: a barrister, advocate, solicitor or salaried legal executive, whether in independent practice or employed 'in-house'.[31] It does not extend to other professional advisers such as personnel consultants and, presumably, trade union officials and other advice workers even though the advice is

28 [1994] ICR 277.
29 Also see *Conway v Rimmer* [1968] AC 910, HL.
30 *Fayed v Al-Tajir* [1987] 2 All ER 396, CA.
31 See *Halsbury's Laws of England*, 4th ed, Vol 13, paras 71 onwards.

clearly in the nature of legal advice.[32] The difficulty with this restriction in tribunal proceedings is that because of the open nature of the forum and the lack of legal aid, applicants (in particular) are often likely to have received advice from those who are not legal professionals. If that advice-giver is merely acting as the means of communication between the applicant and a professionally qualified legal adviser, the communication will still be privileged, but if the advice comes direct from a non-qualified source, no privilege will attach.

Without prejudice communications

10.39   It is a rule of evidence that without prejudice communications between the parties should not be disclosed to a court.[33] This rule applies to tribunals, as confirmed in the case of *Independent Research Services Ltd v Catterall*.[34] In *Catterall* the public policy behind the rule was described: parties should be free to try and settle their differences without fear that anything they say in the course of negotiations will be used in evidence as a sign of weakness or lack of confidence in their case. On the assumption that negotiations are 'genuine' and not a pretext to hide a threat, without prejudice correspondence – for example, describing an offer made by an employer to settle an applicant's case – will be excluded as inadmissible and cannot be ordered to be disclosed.

10.40   Usually such correspondence is headed 'without prejudice' but the presence or absence of these words is not conclusive. Material can be excluded if it forms part of a series of negotiations, some of which are properly headed 'without prejudice' and some are not.[35] In *Catterall* the EAT held that an exception could be made to the rule excluding the without prejudice material only if excluding it would allow a dishonest case to be advanced.

10.41   On the other hand, just because a letter is headed 'without prejudice' does not mean to say it will be privileged; it will be the contents of the letter which matter. If these are written with a view to settlement, the communication will be privileged; if not, then the fact that it is so labelled will do nothing to create a privilege where none exists.[36]

---

32   *New Victoria Hospital v Ryan* [1993] ICR 201; [1993] IRLR 202, EAT.
33   *Cutts v Head* [1984] Ch 290, CA.
34   *Independent Research Services Ltd v Catterall* [1993] ICR 1, EAT.
35   *South Shropshire DC v Amos* [1986] 1 WLR 1271, CA.
36   *Chocoladefabriken Lindt & Sprungli AG v Nestle Co Ltd* [1978] RPC 287, ChD.

Communications with ACAS conciliation officers

10.42   In tribunal proceedings, this 'without prejudice privilege' extends to communications between a party and an Advisory, Conciliation and Arbitration Service (ACAS) conciliation officer unless the privilege is expressly waived by the party communicating with the conciliation officer.[37]

Medical reports

10.43   Medical reports will often be confidential documents. It is even possible that an applicant might be the subject of the report in question, but has never seen it before the tribunal proceedings and may be surprised and even distressed by its contents. Such considerations, however, should not outweigh the need to order disclosure and inspection to the applicant in an appropriate case.[38] Safeguards may, however, be employed, such as covering up irrelevant parts of the report or limiting disclosure to legal advisers.[39] Even where disclosure could be detrimental to a party's mental health, this consideration may be outweighed by the need to ensure that he or she is not prejudiced in presenting his or her case.[40]

10.44   Disclosure of medical reports obtained by an employer will rarely be refused in a case where the reason given for the applicant's dismissal is incapability due to ill-health.[41]

10.45   Arguments that a person's right to privacy and family life under article 8 of the European Convention on Human Rights means that he or she should not therefore be obliged to undergo a medical examination or disclose his or her medical records even where he or she is claiming damages for personal injuries,[42] have received short shrift from the tribunal. This was seen in *De Keyser v Wilson*[43] where Lindsay P stated that a request for a medical report could not give rise to any actionable breach of article 8. Just as courts in personal injury cases may stay proceedings indefinitely in the event of a party refusing to

---

37   ETA 1996 s18(7) and *M & W Grazebrook Ltd v Wallens* [1973] ICR 256; [1973] IRLR 139, NIRC (see chapter 16).
38   *McIvor v Southern Health and Social Services Board* [1978] 1 WLR 757; [1978] 2 All ER 625, HL.
39   *DHSS v Sloan* [1981] ICR 313, EAT.
40   *DHSS v Sloan (No 2)* EAT 342/81, unreported.
41   *Ford Motor Co Ltd v Nawaz* [1987] ICR 434; [1987] IRLR 163, EAT.
42   See *Sherrif v Klyne Tugs* [1999] IRLR 418, CA.
43   [2001] IRLR 324, EAT.

give permission to disclosure of his or her medical records, employment tribunals too have this option open to them. However, *De Keyser* stopped short of considering whether there would be a breach of article 8 if there was a request for confidential medical records, limiting itself to the issue of requiring a person to attend a medical examination, in circumstances where the medic carrying out the examination would be bound by conventional medical confidence.

Medical Reports Act 1988

10.46 This Act gives an employee a statutory right to access to medical reports prepared for employment purposes by a medical practitioner with responsibility for the clinical care of the employee, ie, the employee's own general practitioner or hospital doctor or consultant or the company's doctor where the employee has been under his or her care and so the report is not the result of a one-off examination.

10.47 The Act also protects the employee in the normal course of his or her employment as it places restrictions on the obtaining of medical information by the employer from the employee's own adviser.

Waiver of privilege

10.48 The privilege which attaches to certain documents can be lost if the party who could claim it chooses to 'waive' that protection. Where this occurs, the document becomes as any other and can no longer be claimed to be 'privileged' from disclosure or production.

10.49 In most cases, the privilege will be the property of the client and not the lawyer or other adviser; consequently, only the client can waive the privilege which attaches to a particular document. A lawyer or adviser can, however, waive privilege on his or her client's behalf. In the case of 'without prejudice' communications, the privilege belongs to both parties to the document and it can only be waived by them jointly; it is not capable of unilateral waiver.[44]

10.50 Diplomatic privilege can only be waived by the state to whom it belongs or by the ambassador on behalf of that state.[45]

10.51 In High Court and county court proceedings, a formal list is used for disclosure, which must accord with CPR 31.10. Documents which are privileged must be identified as such. While there is no standard form of list in tribunal proceedings, caution must still be taken not to

44 *Walker v Wilsher* (1889) 23 QBD 335, CA.
45 *R v Madan* [1961] 2 QB 1, CA.

list as available for inspection those documents in respect of which privilege may be claimed (see para 10.53).

10.52   Privilege may be lost by reference to the document concerned during the course of a hearing. This may occur by the party owning the privilege giving evidence with reference to that document or by the party's representative mentioning it in the course of speeches or in questioning a witness. If it is not intended for privilege to be waived, then the party wishing to claim it should be careful not to rely on the document during the course of the proceedings.

Mistaken disclosure

10.53   When a privileged document is mistakenly included in a list of documents on disclosure, the privilege is not necessarily to be taken as having been 'waived': in such circumstances the party wishing to claim privilege should seek as soon as practicable to rectify the mistake by amending the list of documents. If, however, the other party is allowed to inspect the document concerned or is even supplied with a copy, it may be far more difficult subsequently to seek to assert privilege in respect of it. In such circumstances, the party wishing to claim privilege should seek to rectify the situation as soon as possible by notifying the other side of the mistake which has occurred and identifying the document as one in respect of which privilege is claimed. Whether or not privilege will still attach to the document will depend on the circumstances of the disclosure and the conduct of the parties. If the party to whom the document has been disclosed consciously took advantage of the opponent's mistake to obtain a copy, the tribunal may be persuaded to rectify that mistake so that the privilege may be reclaimed.[46]

Partly privileged documents

10.54   A party claiming privilege in respect of a document will not be permitted to rely on parts of that document on a self-selected basis.[47] Just as with other documents, a party is under a duty not to give partial disclosure:

> Where a party is deploying in court material which would otherwise be privileged, the opposite party and the court must have an opportunity of satisfying themselves that what the party has chosen to

---

46   *Derby & Co Ltd v Weldon (No 8)* [1991] 1 WLR 73, CA.
47   See *O'Shea v Bassi*, note 2 above.

release from privilege represents the whole of the material relevant to the issue in question. To allow an individual item to be plucked out of context would be to risk an injustice through its real weight or meaning being misunderstood.[48]

10.55   Where a document deals with more than just one subject-matter and privilege is claimed in respect of one distinct part, then it will be possible to disclose the other part or parts of the document without having been taken to have waived privilege in respect of the whole.[49] If the privileged part of the document is not so self-contained, however, part disclosure may be taken to be a waiver of the whole.

10.56   If there is any doubt, no part of the document should be disclosed but the guidance of the tribunal should be sought at an interlocutory stage. If the tribunal then orders that part of the document can be edited out, there can be no doubt but that the party claiming the privilege has not thereby waived its right to protection from disclosure of the concealed part.

Documents from third parties

10.57   Rule 4(5)(b) of the 2001 Rules only provides the tribunal with the power to order disclosure as between parties. If disclosure is desired from another person who is not a party to the proceedings, and who is not prepared to produce the document(s) in question voluntarily, then the tribunal is given the power by 2001 Rules r4(5)(a), either on the application of a party or of its own motion, to order the attendance of any person at an appointed time and place and to require that person 'to produce any document'.[50]

10.58   Such an order may be required in a number of cases, for example, cases involving a transfer of an undertaking where the previous employer (the transferor) or the receiver is reluctant to release certain documents on a voluntary basis.

10.59   Furthermore, as the tribunal's power is not limited merely to requiring a non-party to attend before a hearing of the tribunal, the order made can require the person concerned to produce the document before any substantive hearing in the case. This may be the best means of securing sight of the document before a full hearing, giving

---

48   *Nea Karteria Maritime Co Ltd v Atlantic and Great Lakes Steamship Corp* [1981] Com LR 139, QBD per Mustill J.
49   *Great Atlantic Insurance Co v Home Insurance Co* [1981] 1 WLR 529, CA.
50   See also CPR 31.17.

all parties prior knowledge of its contents and thus time to prepare their respective cases properly in the light of this, without the need to adjourn a full hearing.

10.60   In considering whether to order production of documents by someone who is not a party to the proceedings, the tribunal will apply the same tests of relevance and necessity as already outlined above. Furthermore, the person subject to such an order will also be able to rely on privilege from production in the circumstances already set out in this chapter. It should also be borne in mind that non-parties can only be ordered to attend and produce documents if they are present within Great Britain.

10.61   Any person who fails, without reasonable excuse, to comply with an order to attend and produce documents is liable on summary conviction to a fine not exceeding level 3 on the standard scale.[51]

Oppressive requests

10.62   In considering whether or not to order disclosure and inspection of documents, tribunals will also bear in mind the extent of the demand being made on the party who will have to produce the documents in question. This is particularly so given the overriding objective which requires the examination of proportionality (see 2001 Regs reg 10(2)(c)[52]). Usually the respondent will hold most of the relevant documentation and where the evidence sought by the applicant relates (as it may in a discrimination or equal pay case) to a large number of people or a period of many years, the respondent may well have grounds for claiming that an order for full disclosure would be oppressive. In such a case, the order made may be limited to selective disclosure, as in *Perera v Civil Service Commission*,[53] where the application for disclosure would have involved the disclosure of documents relating to some 1,600 people.

10.63   Much will depend on the particular circumstances of the case and tribunals will be prepared to order quite wide-scale disclosure where necessary to determine the issues which arise in a particular case. In *Selvarajan v Inner London Education Authority*[54] the EAT held, in a race

---

51   ETA 1996 s7(4); r4(6).
52   Employment Tribunals (Constitution and Rules of Procedure) Regulations 2001 SI No 1171.
53   [1980] ICR 699; [1980] IRLR 233, EAT.
54   [1980] IRLR 313, EAT.

discrimination case, that documents which had come into existence over a period of some 15 years before the Race Relations Act 1976 would be the subject of an order for disclosure as they could be logically probative of subsequent discrimination.

10.64 Where an application is given for selective disclosure in such cases, it is always open to the tribunal to reconsider the matter subsequently and make a fuller order if appropriate. The proper course of action for the tribunal is first to isolate the issues to which disclosure is relevant and then make orders for disclosure which address those issues if necessary. If it subsequently turns out that the issues are broader than it first appeared, or if further disclosure is required to meet those issues, then this can be reconsidered by the tribunal later in the proceedings, as in *Rolls Royce Motor Cars Ltd v Mair and others*,[55] a case involving some 150 claims of unfair dismissal in a large-scale redundancy exercise over various divisions of the employing company.

10.65 It has also been held that there is no general principle whereby applicants are entitled to gain disclosure of appraisal scores in a redundancy selection exercise.[56]

Equal pay and discrimination cases

10.66 In cases claiming equal pay, documentary evidence of previous wage-bargaining or of the background to a collective agreement may well be relevant and necessary to a determination of the issues between the parties, even though it requires consideration of matters which now appear to be ancient history. Disclosure may be sought to assist the applicant in identifying an appropriate comparator, although there should be some evidence that a prima facie case is made out so the application can be shown to be more than a mere fishing expedition.[57]

10.67 Where an applicant claims discrimination, very often that claim will depend on documentary evidence relating to the treatment of other employees, including statistical and monitoring information. Guidance was given on the approach which should be taken in

---

55 EAT 794/92, unreported.
56 See *Eaton Ltd v King* [1995] IRLR 75, EAT, and *British Aerospace plc v Green and others* [1995] IRLR 433, CA; however, a more generous view was taken in *FDR Ltd v Holloway* [1995] IRLR 400, EAT.
57 See *Clwyd CC v Leverton* [1985] IRLR 197, EAT.

respect of disclosure in such proceedings in *West Midlands Passenger Transport Executive v Singh.*[58] In that case, the Court of Appeal held that, in determining whether information sought in a discrimination case was relevant, the special features of discrimination proceedings should be borne in mind, ie:

– The document(s) in question need not conclusively prove that the employer has discriminated; for the purposes of the disclosure application it need only be established that the document(s) *may tend to prove* that such discrimination has taken place.

– Direct discrimination means that the complainant has not been assessed according to individual merit but has been treated less favourably as a member of a particular group. Statistical information may establish a discernible pattern in the treatment of that particular group (for example, under-representation in certain jobs, lack of promotion) which may in turn give rise to an inference of discrimination against members of the group.

– If a practice is being operated against a group, then, in the absence of a satisfactory explanation, it will be reasonable to infer that the complainant, as a member of that group, has been treated less favourably on the grounds of race or sex.

– Evidence of discrimination against a group in relation to promotion may be more persuasive evidence of discrimination in the particular case than previous treatment of the applicant, which may be indicative of personal factors peculiar to the applicant.

– As suitability of candidates can rarely be measured solely by objective means but will generally involve subjective judgments, evidence relating to the success or failure of members of a particular group may indicate that the real reason for failure is a conscious or unconscious discriminatory attitude which involves stereotyped assumptions about members of that group.

– As employers are permitted to adduce evidence demonstrating that in practice they operate a policy of non-discrimination, the employee must be entitled to seek evidence to the contrary.

10.68   *West Midlands Passenger Transport Executive v Singh* involved allegations of race discrimination, but the principles set out by the Court of Appeal apply to complaints of discrimination generally.[59]

10.69   As disclosure in discrimination cases may include applications and

---

58 [1988] ICR 614; [1988] IRLR 186, CA.
59 These guidelines will be less relevant in cases of sex discrimination as the burden of proof is reversed.

assessments in relation to other candidates or employees, questions of confidentiality might well arise. Often these can be resolved by covering up references which name or otherwise identify the particular individual, but this should not be at the expense of obtaining the necessary information from the document, ie, relating to the sex or race and to the qualifications and experience of the person concerned.

Checklist: Disclosure

- Before making an application to the tribunal, ask the other side for voluntary disclosure of documents: if there are likely to be equal quantities of documents on both sides, propose mutual exchange of copy documents; if the other side holds the bulk of the documentation, be prepared to pay the reasonable photocopying charges for the documents to be provided in full or seek inspection so that copies of the actual documents (or parts) required can be sought specifically.
- If you are aware of the existence (or likely existence) of certain documents, be specific in your request. If you are unsure as to the documentation in the other side's possession, ask more generally for disclosure of documents relevant to the issues in the case. In any event, it is often useful to add a 'catch-all' request for all relevant documents: however certain you are as to the existence of particular documents, you are unlikely to have full knowledge of all documentation in the other side's possession.
- If necessary, make the appropriate application to the tribunal for disclosure of the documents sought, making the basis for the request clear and indicating that you have already sought voluntary disclosure but without success.
- If you are not satisfied with the disclosure given, keep the tribunal informed, making clear your reasons for dissatisfaction.
- If an order for disclosure has been made against you in your absence with which you are unhappy, apply to the tribunal as soon as possible (and certainly within the time period specified) for that order to be varied. If you feel it would assist, ask at the same time for an oral hearing on the question.
- When considering the documents you have to disclose, bear in mind the protection offered by the principles relating to confidentiality and privilege. Be careful not to waive privilege unless that is what you really want.

- If you realise that you have included a privileged document in a list sent to the other side without indicating that privilege is claimed, immediately amend that list to make the claim clear.
- If a privileged document has actually been sent to the other side by mistake, immediately seek the return of that document, making it clear that privilege is claimed in respect of the document concerned.
- If questions of confidentiality or privilege arise in relation to *part* of a document, consider whether it is possible to reach agreement with the other side on a means of presenting that document without disclosure of the confidential or privileged part. If you do reach agreement, make it clear that disclosure is being given on the basis of that agreement and that you do not waive privilege in respect of the document as a whole. If agreement cannot be reached and if in doubt as to the severability of that part of the document which you regard as privileged, do not disclose the document in part but refer the dispute to the tribunal.
- If a person who is not a party to the tribunal proceedings has relevant documents and is unwilling to give these up voluntarily, apply for an order for that person to attend and produce them.
- If at all possible, seek to 'agree' a bundle of documents for use before the tribunal. If agreement cannot be reached in relation to particular documents, put the rest into an agreed bundle and deal with the issues relating to the disputed documents at an interlocutory hearing or as a preliminary issue or at some other appropriate time at the substantive hearing.

CHAPTER 11

Interim relief

Introduction

11.1   Tribunals have additional powers to intervene at an interlocutory stage in dismissal cases arising under seven different statutory provisions: those involving trade union activities, campaigning for or against union recognition, employee representation on transfers, redundancies and working time, health and safety at work, pension fund trustees, whistle blowing. The first is set out in Trade Unions and Labour Relations (Consolidation) Act 1992 (TULRCA 1992) s152 and the others are known as the 'specified reasons' under Employment Rights Act 1996 (ERA 1996) s129(1). In this chapter they are referred to as 'trade union and other specified' reasons for interim relief. The powers are to grant temporary remedies pending the hearing of the case, notably to provide for continuation of the contract of employment. This is felt to be an important safeguard to the rights of union activists and certain others and operates as a kind of injunction preserving the situation as it was before the dismissal, or at least allowing the employee to be treated as suspended rather than as dismissed.

Dismissal for trade union and other specified reasons

11.2   The right to claim interim relief is confined to cases of dismissal where the principal reason is alleged to be the applicant's involvement in the representation of employees or in health and safety at work. Such dismissals are automatically unfair. The right to interim relief arises only if the principal reason for dismissal was that the applicant:[1]

- was or proposed to become a member of an independent trade union;
- took part or proposed to take part at an appropriate time in its activities;
- was *not* a member of any union or a particular union, or refused to join or proposed to refuse to join or remain in a union;

---

1   See TULRCA ss152 and 161 (union involvement); Sch A1 para 161(2) (union recognition); ERA 1996 s128 together with s100(1)(a) and (b) (health and safety); s101A(d) (working time); s102(1) (pension fund trustees); s103 (employee representative or candidate); s103A (protected disclosure).

- acted or proposed to act in various ways with a view to obtaining or preventing recognition of a trade union; or
- performed or proposed to perform the functions of a health and safety representative or a member of a safety committee; or
- carried out or proposed to carry out activities in connection with preventing or reducing risks to health and safety at work, having been designated by the employer to do so; or
- performed or proposed to perform functions as a workforce representative, or candidate, under Working Time Regulations 1998[2] Sch 1; or
- performed or proposed to perform functions as an occupational pension scheme trustee; or
- performed or proposed to perform functions as an employee representative for the purposes of consultation under Transfer of Undertakings (Protection of Employment) Regulations (TUPE) 1981[3] or TULRCA 1992 s188 (mass redundancies); or
- made a protected disclosure under the whistle blowing provisions of ERA 1996 s47B.

11.3   There are other forms of automatically unfair dismissal which are not eligible for interim relief, such as that the applicant was *selected for redundancy* for one of the above trade union reasons (TULRCA 1992 s153), or was dismissed for refusing to work in dangerous conditions (ERA 1996 s92(1)(c)–(e)), or was a protected shop or betting shop worker (ERA 1996 s93), or had asserted a statutory right (ERA 1996 s104).

Procedural steps

11.4   References to the statutory procedure described here are to dismissals for union involvement but the nature of the procedure applies equally to the other specified cases under ERA 1996 ss128–129.

11.5   The application for interim relief is separate from the originating application claiming unfair dismissal but may be made on the same IT1 form, or on a different form at the same or a different time. It must be presented not later than seven days after the dismissal.[4] An

2   SI No 1833.
3   SI No 1794.
4   TULRCA 1992 s161; see para 5.41 above.

applicant claiming infringement of union rights, rather than non-union or other specified rights, must also present a certificate signed by an official of his or her union authorised to give such a certificate, and the union must be independent. The official should say that:

– the applicant was or proposed to become a member of the union at the date of dismissal; and
– there appear to be reasonable grounds for supposing that the reason for the dismissal was the one alleged, ie, union involvement.[5]

11.6   The certificate must deal with the reasonableness of the belief and not simply assert the opinion of the union official, although it is axiomatic that the official would consider his or her beliefs to be founded on reasonable grounds.[6]

The hearing

11.7   Interim relief is one of the cases which will usually be heard by a chairman alone (see para 1.20). The tribunal is required to secure a hearing and make a determination as soon as practicable. This has three effects. First, the employer is to be given copies of the application (and union certificate) and at least seven days' notice of the hearing. Provision is made in union cases for additional parties to be joined on three days' notice (TULRCA 1992 s162). Second, the tribunal is not to exercise its ordinary powers to postpone the hearing unless 'it is satisfied that special circumstances justify' it. Third, the tribunal is required to announce its findings at the hearing (TULRCA 1992 s163, ERA 1996 s129(2)). The intention is that a decision should be made as quickly as practicable.

11.8   The central issue at the hearing is whether it appears likely that the tribunal hearing the full case will find that the applicant was unfairly dismissed for the alleged reason, ie, union involvement or other specified reason. This is really a balance of probabilities rather than a higher test, but it has more than a reasonable prospect of success.[7] If some other reason emerges which will also lead to a finding of unfair dismissal, the tribunal is not entitled to make an interim relief order.

11.9   Frequently, no witnesses are called but a submission is made by the applicant's representative and documents and a chronology are

5   TULRCA 1992 s162.
6   *Bradley v Edward Ryde & Sons* [1979] ICR 488, EAT.
7   *Taplin v C Shippam Ltd* [1978] ICR 1068; [1978] IRLR 450, EAT.

referred to. Since the evidence is likely to be controversial and subject to lengthy cross-examination, it is often counter-productive to call witnesses, since the main facets of the applicant's case will have been exposed. In the face of predicted long cross-examination, it is sometimes felt more useful to go straight to an expedited full tribunal hearing. Nevertheless there are no rules as to the type of evidence adduced and in many cases brief evidence from the applicant or the union official is appropriate.

Remedies

11.10   It is assumed that the applicant wants reinstatement, so the tribunal must ask the respondent if it is willing to reinstate or re-engage on no less favourable terms and conditions of employment. If the respondent is willing to re-engage on different terms and conditions of employment in another job, the tribunal will decide whether any refusal by the applicant is reasonable. If the respondent refuses both, or the applicant reasonably refuses re-engagement, the tribunal must make an order for continuation of the contract of employment.[8]

11.11   This is an order that for the purposes of the benefits of the contract of employment, seniority and pensions, and for continuity of employment under statute, the contract continues from the date of termination until determination or settlement of the case, including the hearing of any appeal.[9] The tribunal specifies the amounts and dates of payment of wages.

11.12   Between the hearing and final determination or settlement either party can apply (to any tribunal, not just the one which decided it) for a revocation or variation of the order on the ground of a relevant change in circumstances.[10] These are not defined and appear to be widely drafted. The same urgent time scale is to be observed. There is no reason why the same tribunal should not deal with variations but it may be unfair for it to deal with interim relief and the full hearing, because it will already have expressed a view.[11]

11.13   The applicant may complain to a tribunal that the employer has

---

8   TULRCA 1992 s163(6).
9   *Zucker v Astrid Jewels* [1978] ICR 1088; [1978] IRLR 385, EAT.
10   TULRCA 1992 s165 and *British Coal Corporation v McGinty* [1988] IRLR 7, EAT.
11   *British Coal*, note 10 above.

not complied with the terms of an order for reinstatement or re-engagement and the tribunal may then order the continuation of the contract of employment *and* order compensation to be paid.[12]

12   TULRCA 1992 s166.

CHAPTER 12

Interim stages

Introduction

12.1   A case involves many steps before it is heard. The regulations still refer to 'interlocutory matters' (2001 Regs reg 2(2)[1]). The Civil Procedure Rules (CPR) generally refer to them as 'interim proceedings'. Here we use the modern term.

Joining and dismissing respondents in the proceedings

12.2   A tribunal can order that:

– a person against whom a remedy is claimed may be joined (added), or in Scotland 'sisted', as a party to proceedings (2001 Rules r19(1)) – from this formulation it is clear that the party is to be a respondent; or

– a respondent be dismissed from being a party to proceedings (2001 Rules r19(2)); or

– one party represent a number of parties who have the same interests (2001 Rules r19(3)).

These orders may be made either by the tribunal on its own initiative or on an application by a party usually to a chairman alone (para 1.20).

12.3   The tribunal's powers are limited to the people against whom relief is sought. So a tribunal cannot join a person if the relief sought cannot be ordered against that individual or organisation. In *Sandhu v Department of Education and Science*,[2] an order joining the Department as respondent to a race discrimination claim was refused on the basis that it was not the applicant's employer, nor was there any evidence to show that the Department had aided the employer in any discriminatory act.

12.4   When it is apparent to a tribunal that an individual or a body should be joined (sisted) in the proceedings, but the applicant has failed to include that person in the originating application, this power enables the tribunal to resolve the problem of its own accord. It is a power which might conveniently be exercised in a case involving the

---

1   Employment Tribunals (Constitution and Rules of Procedure) Regulations 2001 SI No 1171.

2   [1978] IRLR 208, EAT.

transfer of an undertaking, where the applicant might not be sure who the correct legal respondent is.

12.5 The tribunal may require any party making an application under 2001 Rules r19 to serve notice of that application on other parties (2001 Rules r15(5)), although there is no requirement that notice be served on the person whom it is sought to join. If an order for joinder is made under 2001 Rules r19(1) without first hearing the person to be joined, the order will be treated as having been provisionally made without the other side being there and it will be open to the additional party to apply to be disjoined. The application is treated as an application for 'consequential directions' under 2001 Rules r19(1).[3]

12.6 If the actions or advice of third parties are relevant to the issues in a claim, for example, an Advisory, Conciliation and Arbitration Service officer's involvement in a conciliated settlement, or an adviser's negligence in a claim made out of time, the tribunal cannot order that they be joined as parties unless relief can be ordered against them in the tribunal proceedings – this is the basis of the rule. But the tribunal may be able to order that they attend as witnesses (see para 10.57).[4]

Industrial pressure from third parties

12.7 More specifically, the question of joinder of parties is raised by Trade Unions and Labour Relations (Consolidation) Act 1992 (TULRCA 1992) ss150 and 160, which provide that where a dismissal (TULRCA 1992 s160) or action short of dismissal (TULRCA 1992 s150 – for claims brought under TULRCA 1992 s146) takes place due to trade union or shop-floor pressure, an employer *or* the dismissed employee may request that the tribunal join the trade union or other people exerting the pressure as additional respondent(s) to the proceedings.

12.8 If this request is made before the hearing begins, the tribunal *must* allow it; if it is made later, the tribunal may refuse it. If it is made after the tribunal has already given its determination as to the appropriate remedy, it must refuse it (ss150(2) and 160(2)). If the request is made before the hearing, the tribunal has no choice but to order that the joinder take place: the person making the application for joinder does not even have to show an arguable case. Once joined,

---

3   *Reddington v S Straker & Sons Ltd* [1994] ICR 172, EAT.
4   *Marshall v Alexander Sloan & Co Ltd* [1981] IRLR 264, EAT and *Riley v Tesco Stores Ltd* [1980] ICR 323; [1980] IRLR 103, CA.

however, the trade union (or other individual concerned) has the right to seek an adjournment, to ask for a pre-hearing review, or to make any other appropriate application under the 2001 Rules,[5] as if it had been a party from the outset.

Race and sex discrimination cases

12.9   Other instances where it may be appropriate to join an individual to tribunal proceedings include race, sex, disability and part-time worker discrimination cases when an individual employee might be held to be personally responsible for discriminatory acts for which his or her employer is also liable.

National Insurance Fund

12.10   Claims can be made against the secretary of state for payments from the National Insurance Fund for redundancy or on an employer's insolvency. The secretary of state has rights under the 2001 Rules even when not joined as a party: to receive notices of applications, to make interim applications, to make representations on a pre-hearing review, to appear as if a party and to be heard at any full or interlocutory hearing.[6]

12.11   In addition, the tribunal may join the secretary of state as a party under the general provisions of 2001 Rules r19.

Combined proceedings

12.12   On the application of a party or on its own initiative, a tribunal (which may consist of a chairman sitting alone) may order that applications be considered together (2001 Rules r20(1)) where:

– some common question of law or fact arises in two or more applications; or
– the applications arise out of the same set of facts; or
– there is some other reason which makes it desirable that those cases are heard together.

12.13   This power might be exercised where there are several unfair

---

5   Employment Tribunals Rules of Procedure (contained in SI 2001 No 1171, Sch 1).
6   2001 Rules r8(6).

dismissal claims arising out of a large-scale redundancy exercise, where there are common issues of law and fact; or where an applicant has made separate applications, for example, for unfair dismissal and racial discrimination, arising out of substantially the same set of facts.

12.14   An order that cases be considered together is not the same as a decision that there will be a test case (see para 12.19): the tribunal is still hearing separate applications. Any decision should deal separately with points of difference in the cases, even if that means that separate decisions are given.[7] For instance, in a redundancy resulting in a number of unfair dismissal claims, while there may be common questions relating to the selection criteria and collective consultation, individual application of the selection criteria and consultation might vary considerably.

12.15   Before making an order that cases be combined under 2001 Rules r20, the tribunal must *either* give all parties concerned the opportunity at a hearing to show cause why this order should not be made, *or* send notice to parties giving them the opportunity to show such cause (2001 Rules r20(2)). On the application of a party or of its own initiative, the tribunal also has the power, under 2001 Rules r20(3), to vary or set aside an order made for the combining of cases under 2001 Rules r20(1). The tribunal must give each party the opportunity to make oral or written representations (2001 Rules r20(3)).

12.16   In many cases where there are multiple applications involving similar issues of fact or law, an order combining cases is in everyone's interest. It saves having to adduce evidence or to make legal submissions more than once. It can lead to a substantial saving in costs and time, particularly when many witnesses are involved.

12.17   Parties may, however, have genuine concerns about combining applications, particularly if this may prejudice one person's case. In *Dietmann and Wahlstrom v Brent LBC*,[8] a case arising out of the public inquiry into the death of the child Jasmine Beckford, two social workers, each claiming that she had been unfairly dismissed, argued against their cases being combined. Each said that her answers to the allegations against her might be used to cross-examine the other. Their appeals were rejected. The Court of Appeal held that justice

---

7   See *Paine & Moore v Grundy (Teddington) Ltd* [1981] IRLR 267, EAT.
8   [1987] IRLR 146, CA.

could not be said to be done if there were two separate hearings at which each applicant was exonerated by the tribunal and the blame laid at the feet of the other. The court also emphasised the discretionary nature of the tribunal's decision in ordering that cases be combined. Once the tribunal has made its decision, it will, therefore, be difficult to appeal against that exercise of its discretion.

12.18   When cases have been combined, the tribunal can make further directions as to how it will go about hearing the different applications (2001 Rules r20(1)). In some cases, all the applicants' evidence will be heard together; in others the tribunal will hear each case in total, giving its reasons in one case before moving on to the next. This latter procedure may be of assistance where cases involve identical issues of law; the finding in the first case might well be decisive for the parties in other cases (and see para 12.19). Ultimately the tribunal hearing the cases which have been combined has the right to control its procedure as it sees fit, although a directions hearing is useful to canvass such questions with the parties in advance of the hearing.

Test cases

12.19   Tribunals do not have the same powers as the courts to order that representative applications be heard as 'test' cases which would bind all others bringing claims on the same grounds.[9] The only way of proceeding with a test case in the tribunal is to use the provision for combining proceedings under 2001 Rules r20. For example, a number of cases can be combined and a few 'test' applications heard which are representative of all the other cases. Findings of the tribunal will be decisive in all other cases. This is particularly useful where there are numerous applicants with equal pay applications.[10]

12.20   There is no power to allow representative actions to be brought and subsequently relied on by individuals who did not themselves bring claims within the specified time limit. This means that all potential applicants must still present their claims as individuals within the time limit. They cannot rely on claims brought by others.

12.21   While test cases can be mutually advantageous for the parties in expediting matters and saving costs, it is often difficult to select lead cases which are truly representative of all classes of applications. In

9   CPR Part 19.
10   See *Ashmore v British Coal Corporation* [1990] ICR 485; [1990] IRLR 283, CA.

many multi-applicant cases arising out of the same facts or involving the same issues of law, it is not possible to carry out this exercise because the applications each raise individual issues which will need separate consideration; hence the need for individual hearings in the Ministry of Defence pregnancy discrimination claims in the early 1990s. Before ordering that cases be combined and test cases selected for initial consideration, the tribunal should be satisfied that exactly similar issues arise so as to justify the same result in each case.

12.22   In selecting test cases, assistance may be derived from the Supreme Court Procedure Committee's *Guide for Use in Group Actions:*[11]

> It is important that a sufficient number of lead cases should be chosen to obtain decisions on all the points required for the disposal of as many of the cases as possible. Equally, to achieve the greatest saving in interlocutory costs, the selection of the lead cases should be made as soon as possible. On the other hand, some issues may not become apparent until fairly late in the preparations for trial. A measure of flexibility will usually be appropriate in Group litigation . . .

12.23   A decision in a test case binds all the other cases in the combined proceedings in so far as the issues are similar. Where a party to an application which has been combined seeks to pursue a tribunal case despite the test case decision, the tribunal may exercise its powers under 2001 Rules r15(2)(e) to strike out the originating application or notice of appearance in that case.[12]

Witness orders

12.24   By 2001 Rules r4(5) a tribunal (which may be a chairman sitting alone (2001 Rules r15(8))) may on application by any party or of its own initiative order any person within Great Britain, including a party, to attend as a witness. It will specify the time and place at which the individual concerned is to attend.

12.25   If an order is made against a person in his or her absence, whether a party or not, he or she may apply to the tribunal to vary or set aside the order by sending notice to the secretary before the time when he or she is required to attend as a witness (2001 Rules r4(7)).

---

11   May 1991, ch 3D.
12   *Ashmore v British Coal Corporation* [1990] ICR 485; [1990] IRLR 283, CA.

The secretary will serve notice of the application to set aside or vary on all other parties to the proceedings.

12.26   The power given to tribunals to order a witness to attend is analogous to the power of the High Court or county courts under CPR Part 34 to summon a person to attend before it. A person who is subject to a tribunal witness order and who fails to comply with its terms, is liable on summary conviction to a fine (Employment Tribunals Act 1996 s7(4)).

12.27   The tribunal's power to order a witness to attend is discretionary in nature and it is therefore difficult to appeal against it. Since it is interim, there is no power to review the order. It is, therefore, all the more important for anyone applying for a witness order to make sure that all the facts relied on are clearly set out. Similarly, an application to set aside or vary the order should be made as soon as possible, clearly setting out the grounds relied on. If necessary, an oral hearing should be requested.

12.28   The relevant considerations to be borne in mind by tribunals before deciding whether or not to make a witness order were set out by Sir John Donaldson in *Dada v Metal Box Co Ltd*:[13]

> The first is that the witness prima facie can give evidence which is relevant to the issues in dispute . . . We do not suggest that the tribunal should ask the applicant to give a full proof of his evidence but the applicant should indicate the subject-matter of his evidence and show the extent to which it is relevant. The second . . . is that it is necessary to issue a witness order . . . [W]itnesses should always be invited to attend by the applicant before he applies for witness orders. If they agree to attend and the applicant is quite satisfied that they will attend, then it is unnecessary to issue witness orders . . . A witness may not reply to the request for an undertaking that he will attend. In those circumstances, it may be necessary to issue such an order. He may refuse, in which case . . . a witness order is clearly needed. Again, he may equivocate . . . In such circumstances it will . . . be a matter for the judgment of the tribunal . . . Finally, although not exclusively . . . there is the . . . the witness who says, 'Certainly I will come and give evidence, but it would be very much easier for me to come if I had a witness order requiring me to come'. That situation can arise if an employer is unwilling to release a witness. Again that would be a reason for granting a witness order.

12.29   In *Noorani v Merseyside TEC Ltd*[14] the Court of Appeal emphasised

13   [1974] ICR 559; [1974] IRLR 251, NIRC.
14   [1999] IRLR 184.

that the tribunal has a broad discretion, and that it must inquire as to whether the evidence a witness could give is sufficiently relevant to justify the order. There is, however, no requirement that any evidence which might be relevant must be admitted. In practice, tribunals are prepared to grant witness orders subject to any subsequent application to vary or set aside.

12.30   In most cases, a witness order should not be necessary: those witnesses who will give evidence in your favour are unlikely to refuse to attend, although they may prefer to do so under a witness order for the reasons outlined in the *Dada* case. A potential witness who is reluctant to attend on your behalf is unlikely to co-operate before the hearing in the drafting of a witness statement. As a general rule, if you are unsure what a person may say when called to give evidence, it is unwise to call him or her. Applying for a witness order to require the attendance of someone who may be hostile to the client's case would be giving a hostage to fortune. It is far better to leave it to the other side to call a witness, so that there is the opportunity to cross-examine (see chapter 18).

12.31   In limited circumstances, if the witness displays no desire to tell the truth and is resistant to the party calling him or her, it is possible to ask the tribunal for permission to treat the witness as 'hostile'. If granted, the party calling the witness may cross-examine but cannot present evidence to show that the witness should not be believed. Such applications are rarely granted.

12.32   In some cases, a party may have little choice but to apply for a witness order to require the attendance of a person whose evidence may or may not be favourable. For instance, in a transfer of undertakings case, the respondent-transferee may apply for a witness order requiring the receiver who carried out the dismissals of the applicant employees to attend, although that receiver may not be prepared to provide a witness statement in advance.

12.33   When calling witnesses subject to a witness order, you should bear in mind that the order may need to be amended to state a different date and time if the hearing goes part-heard before that witness's evidence is completed. When the witness has finished giving evidence, it is necessary to ask the tribunal if he or she may be 'released', so that he or she will not be in breach of the order by leaving the tribunal after having given evidence but before the expiry of the time period specified in the order.

Striking out

Scandalous, misconceived or vexatious applications or notices of appearance; scandalous, unreasonable or vexatious conduct

12.34   At any stage of the proceedings, a tribunal may order any originating application or notice of appearance, or anything contained within those documents, to be struck out or amended on the basis that it is 'scandalous, misconceived or vexatious', or the conduct of a party is 'scandalous, unreasonable or vexatious' (2001 Rules r15(2)(c) and (d)). Before exercising its power to strike out, the tribunal must either give the party against whom such an order is proposed the opportunity to show cause orally why it should not be made or send notice to that party giving him or her an opportunity to show such cause orally or in writing (2001 Rules r15(3)).

12.35   When considering whether the originating application or notice of appearance or a party's conduct offends this rule, the tribunal will adopt much the same approach towards those expressions as it would towards an application for costs (see para 20.8). 'Vexatious' includes matters which constitute an abuse of process; a term which may be widely construed and is not limited to dishonest claims or defences, or to conduct which is in bad faith. In *Ashmore v British Coal Corporation*[15] Stuart-Smith LJ expressed the following view:

> A litigant has a right to have his claim litigated, provided it is not . . . vexatious or an abuse of the process. What may constitute such conduct must depend on all the circumstances of the case; the categories are not closed and considerations of public policy and the interests of justice may be very material.

12.36   In *Ashmore*, the originating application was struck out as an abuse of process; the applicant was one of 1,500 women canteen workers who brought equal pay claims against British Coal. The claims had been combined and 14 sample cases selected for consideration. While these were expressly stated not to be 'test' cases, all the other claims had been stayed. When the sample cases were determined against the applicants, Ms Ashmore applied to have the stay on her case lifted. British Coal's application to have her claim struck out on the ground that it was vexatious was upheld by the tribunal. It was held to be an abuse of the process to seek to relitigate an issue which

15   [1990] ICR 485; [1990] IRLR 283, CA.

had already been fully litigated in the sample cases which were representative of all the other claims. There were no material differences between the sample cases and hers, and her union (the Union of Democratic Mineworkers) had been present when the lead cases had been selected, yet had made no representations against this procedure.

12.37   In an application to strike out a claim on grounds similar to those in *Ashmore*, a prima facie burden lies with the party making the application. There is an entitlement to relitigate the same issues between different parties unless it can be shown that there are special reasons (such as those applying in *Ashmore*) which would render it an abuse of process.[16]

12.38   Tribunals rarely exercise the power to strike out proceedings, even where there seems to be little left for the applicant to gain by pursuing a complaint. In *Telephone Information Services Ltd v Wilkinson*,[17] an employer had made an offer to pay to an employee bringing a claim of unfair dismissal the maximum statutory compensation which could be awarded for this kind of claim. The employee was not prepared, however, to withdraw the originating application and the Employment Appeal Tribunal (EAT) upheld the tribunal's refusal to strike it out. The employee was entitled to pursue a claim in the expectation that a finding of unfair dismissal might be made regardless of any extra monetary compensation.

12.39   If an applicant withdraws a claim, the tribunal dismisses it, and the applicant then seeks to institute the same complaint within the time limit for commencing proceedings, the tribunal will strike out the second claim if it is wholly misconceived.[18] In these circumstances, however, the appropriate course of action is for the applicant to apply for a review of the tribunal's decision to dismiss the first application on withdrawal by the applicant. When the remedy of review is still open to the applicant, the EAT has held that it *would* be appropriate to strike out the second application, as in *Acrow* (*Engineers*) *Ltd v Hathaway*,[19] a case from which the applicant withdrew on the grounds of ill-health.

12.40   The originating application or notice of appearance may be struck out if the manner in which proceedings are conducted, whether by the party or his or her representative, is 'scandalous, unreasonable or

16 *Department of Education and Science v Taylor and others* [1992] IRLR 308, QBD.
17 [1991] IRLR 148, EAT.
18 *Mulvaney v London Transport Executive* [1981] ICR 351, EAT.
19 [1981] ICR 510, EAT.

vexatious'. When a respondent's representative assaulted the applicant's representative in the tribunal waiting room, the notice of appearance was struck out.[20] Similarly, in *Bennett v Southwark LBC*,[21] the tribunal struck out an applicant's complaints. Her representative, having been refused an adjournment said 'If I were an Oxford educated white barrister with a plummy voice I would not be put in this position'. Since there were no grounds for finding that the tribunal had been biased, this was said to amount to scandalous conduct; and as the comments were made after numerous adjournment requests, the conduct was also vexatious.

The vexatious litigant

12.41   When an individual is persistently and unreasonably vexatious in making applications to the tribunal or in instituting appeals to the EAT, the EAT has the power (on application by the Attorney General or Lord Advocate), by way of a restriction of proceedings order, to prevent proceedings by that person being instituted or continued, either in the tribunal or EAT, unless permission is given to do so.[22]

Want of prosecution

12.42   The tribunal has the power, on the application of a respondent or of its own initiative, to strike out an originating application for want of prosecution, ie, failing to press on with the claim at a reasonable speed (2001 Rules r15(2)(e)). In exercising its discretion the tribunal will apply the same guidelines as apply under the CPR 3.4 and the Practice Direction thereto.[23] These are laid down by the House of Lords in *Birkett v James*[24] which distinguished between two types of case:

– where there has been 'intentional and contumelious' default by the applicant, ie, where the applicant has failed to comply with an order of the tribunal and it has been made clear that the originating application would be struck out unless the applicant complied with the order within the time allowed;

– where there has been (i) inordinate and inexcusable delay on the part of the applicant or his or her lawyers *and* (ii) that delay will give

20 *Harmony Healthcare Plc v Drewery* (2000) *Independent* 20 November, EAT.
21 EAT 1273/97 and 878/99, 11 January 2001, unreported.
22 ETA 1996 s33 (see para 24.34).
23 *Evans v Metropolitan Police Authority* [1993] ICR 151; [1992] IRLR 570, CA.
24 [1978] AC 297 and see Arbitration Act 1950 s13A(2).

rise to a substantial risk that it is not possible to have a fair trial of the issues in the action or is such as is likely to cause or to have caused serious prejudice to the respondent.

12.43   In the first type of case, the normal rules for striking out or debarring will be followed where a party acts in default of an order for further particulars, disclosure or written answers (2001 Rules r4(8) and see paras 9.28, 10.14 and 9.38 respectively).

12.44   Before the tribunal strikes out an originating application for want of prosecution, the applicant must be given the opportunity to show cause orally why this order should not be made, or notice must be sent giving an opportunity to show cause orally or in writing (2001 Rules r15(3)).

Directions hearings

12.45   A tribunal may at any time, either on the application of a party or of its own initiative, give directions on any matter arising in connection with the proceedings before it 'as appear . . . appropriate' (2001 Rules r4(1)). An application for directions *may* be made by written notice to the secretary, setting out the title of the case and the grounds of the application (2001 Rules r4(2)(a)) but it need not be. It may also be made at the hearing (2001 Rules r4(2)(b)). Directions are frequently given following a case management hearing, or a preliminary determination under 2001 Rules r6 or a pre-hearing review under 2001 Rules r7.

12.46   Directions can either be given at a hearing, usually an interlocutory hearing, or merely on written application without any hearing having taken place. Any directions given without notice to the other party will remain provisional until all parties have had the opportunity to make representations to the tribunal.[25]

12.47   Hearings for directions in the tribunal are analogous to pre-trial reviews or case management conferences in the civil courts, for example, under CPR Parts 27, 28 and 29 for small claims, fast and multi-track cases. They are often useful in ensuring that the case proceeds to a final hearing in an orderly and coherent manner and their use has been encouraged by the EAT in a number of cases.[26] As there are no automatic directions in tribunals, hearings can be

---

25 *Reddington v S Straker & Sons Ltd* [1994] ICR 172, EAT.
26 See *Brooks v British Telecommunications plc* [1991] ICR 286; [1991] IRLR 4, EAT; *Goodwin v Patent Office* [1999] ICR 302; [1999] IRLR 4, EAT; *Martins v Marks and Spencer plc* [1998] IRLR 326, CA.

helpful in ensuring that matters such as disclosure and inspection take place in good time to allow the parties to prepare for the substantive hearing. Directions can be given not just as to the form of the hearing of the case (for example, the order in which the issues will be considered or the way in which combined applications will be heard), but also as to the time table for all further interim stages. In *Kuttapan v Croydon LBC*[27] the EAT held that the power to give directions includes a power to set aside or revoke a striking-out order: in that case the order was a mandatory one as the applicant had failed to comply with an order to pay a deposit.

12.48   In *Halford v Sharples*[28] the EAT emphasised the desirability of directions hearings in many tribunal cases and sought to make a number of suggestions for the conduct of these interlocutory hearings. Many of these suggestions were taken up in the 1994 *Practice Direction No 1*[29] (see appendix C). Of those not implicitly submerged by the overriding objective (2001 Regs reg 10) and the case management powers (2001 Rules r4), these may survive:

– where there is a preliminary determination under 2001 Rules r6 or where there has been a pre-hearing review, a directions hearing may follow on immediately;
– the hearing will not involve lay members but ideally the hearing will be conducted by the chairman who will have conduct of the case at the substantive hearing (except where this chairman has been involved in a pre-hearing review); and
– the date for the full hearing should be fixed.

12.49   Mummery LJ in the course of his judgment in *Martins v Marks and Spencer plc*[30] suggested that in race discrimination cases it would be good practice to hold a meeting for 'preliminary directions' so that the issues are identified before the hearing of a case commences. The need for clear directions in disability discrimination cases was emphasised by the EAT in *Goodwin v Patent Office*.[31] In these cases the EAT stated that it 'will generally be unsatisfactory for the disability issue to remain unclear and unspecific until the hearing itself', and if expert evidence is to be called, parties should be given advance notice,

27 [1999] IRLR 349.
28 [1992] ICR 146.
29 *Guidance on Judicial Procedure for the Employment Tribunals in England and Wales*, COET, November 1994.
30 [1999] IRLR 326, CA.
31 [1999] IRLR 4, EAT.

and the medical report disclosed. Appellate courts will be very slow to interfere with directions given (or not given), as the Court of Appeal in *X v Z Ltd*[32] emphasised that 'tribunals themselves are the best judges of case management decisions which crop up every day as they perform their function ... of trying to do justice with the maximum flexibility and the minimum of formality'.

12.50   To make the best use of a directions hearing in the tribunal, the parties should be represented by those who have so far had conduct of the case and/or will be presenting the case. If agreement can be reached with the other side as to the directions to be made and the interlocutory time table to be observed, this should be put to the chairman, preferably in the form of a schedule. If no agreement can be reached, the parties should at least try to identify the issues on which directions are required in advance of this hearing. The parties should bring their full files to the directions hearing, and those attending should be prepared to fix a date for the substantive hearing and so should attend with a clear, and preferably agreed, time estimate and with the dates when representatives, parties and witnesses are able to attend.

Checklist: Interim stages

- Are there one or more applications involving common questions of law or fact, or is there other good reason why cases should or should not be considered together?
- If cases have been combined, what would be the best way for them to be heard?
- Can any of these issues be resolved by agreement with other interested parties?
- Would a directions hearing be useful, either to resolve these issues or to consider generally any further issues which might arise, such as length of hearing, number of witnesses, time table for each day of the hearing, preparation of documents, a list of issues to be decided, chronology, list of main characters.

Pre-hearing review

Introduction

13.1   The pre-hearing review under 2001 Rules r7(4)[1] is a procedure for institutionalising the threat of costs against an applicant or, very rarely, a respondent. Its purpose is to weed out whole cases, or single contentions in any given case, which 'have no reasonable prospect of success'. The tribunal may order the party to pay a deposit which may be used to defray a later award of costs.

Procedure

13.2   The procedure can be initiated by either party or by giving notice to the secretary, or by the tribunal on its own initiative. The tribunal can refuse the application without a hearing (2001 Rules r7(2)). This is a 'determination', but not one under 2001 Regs reg 2(2) and so not appealable. There appears to be no requirement under the rules to give reasons, but failure to do so, coupled with the lack of an appeal, may be a breach of article 6(1) of the European Convention on Human Rights.

13.3   If it goes ahead, the tribunal must provide an opportunity for the parties to be heard and to make written and oral representations. The hearing, which is not the hearing of the originating application, may take place before a chairman sitting alone by virtue of 2001 Rules r15(8).

13.4   The material available to the tribunal is strictly limited and the tribunal's consideration is confined by 2001 Rules r7(1) to:

- the contents of the originating application and notice of appearance;
- any representations in writing; and
- any oral argument.

13.5   Since there is no live evidence, the only way in which evidence can be considered is by way of written representation. There is no reason why the written representation should not include either extracts from or the totality of witness statements to be used at the hearing. Legal argument can of course be addressed both in writing and orally.

13.6   If the tribunal considers that there is *no reasonable prospect of success* in any given contention, it must record its reasons in *summary* form. There is no right to demand or obligation to provide extended

1   Employment Tribunals Rules of Procedure (contained in SI 2001 No 1171, Sch 1).

reasons (2001 Rules r7(6)). That document is then sent to the parties with an explanatory note.

Order to pay a deposit

13.7   Once the tribunal has made such a determination, it may make a deposit order as a condition of a party being allowed to continue to take part in the proceedings in relation to the contention or to the case as a whole. The order is still discretionary (2001 Rules r7(4)), but it would be difficult for a tribunal to justify a finding of no reasonable prospect without an order against a party who has the means to comply with it. The order itself is that the party must pay a deposit of up to £500 as a condition of being permitted to continue to take part in the proceedings 'relating to that matter'. Before making the order, the tribunal must take reasonable steps to ensure that the party against whom the order is made can comply with the order, and it must take account of information received in determining the amount (2001 Rules r7(5)). See appendix A for the form sent out by the Tribunal requesting information as to means.

13.8   Once the order has been served, the party has 21 days in which to pay the deposit. There are conflicting decisions of the Employment Appeal Tribunal (EAT) as to when this 21-day period commences: in *Immigration Advisory Service v Oommen*[2] it was held that the commencement date is the date when the document recording the making of the order is deemed to have been effected in the ordinary course of post, not the day on which it is posted by the tribunal. This was followed in *Kuttapan v Croydon LBC*.[3] But Morison P expressly disagreed with this in *Hammersmith and Fulham LBC v Ladejobi*[4] and *Mock v Inland Revenue Commissioners*.[5] The better view, since it is at least more precise in locating a 'date sent' rather than a 'date received', is to follow *Ladejobi* and *Mock* until such time as the Court of Appeal makes a definitive ruling.

13.9   A further period of up to 14 days' grace is allowed if representations are made within the initial 21 days. If the order is not complied with, the tribunal has no discretion and must strike out either the originating application or the notice of appearance or the relevant

2   [1997] ICR 683, EAT.
3   [1999] IRLR 349, EAT.
4   [1999] ICR 673, EAT.
5   [1999] IRLR 785, EAT.

part of either to which the order relates. So, when an order has been made, it is a condition for continuing with the case, or with that part of the case covered by the order, that the deposit is paid.

13.10   The deposit is refundable in full as a general rule. It is refundable on withdrawal of the originating application, since proceedings would then be at an end. The rules do not provide this but the deposit ought to be refundable as soon as the party agrees to take out the offending part of the originating application or the notice of appearance; or if at the pre-hearing review the tribunal makes the determination, it could, in its discretion, decline to order the deposit to be made if the document is amended.

13.11   The deposit is also refundable at the end of the proceedings *unless* (2001 Rules r7(7)):

– the tribunal hearing the originating application finds against the party on the specific matter for which he or she was ordered to pay the deposit; *and*

– the tribunal has made an award of costs, either arising out of the matter for which the deposit was ordered or for any other reason.

Costs at the main hearing after a deposit order

13.12   In a case where a deposit has been ordered, even if no award of costs is made at the substantive hearing, the tribunal must still go on to consider whether to award costs against the party 'on the ground that he conducted the proceedings relating to the matter unreasonably in persisting in having the matter determined by a tribunal' (2001 Rules r14(7)). It must consider the reasons set out by the first tribunal when it ordered a deposit, and the second tribunal must have come to the opinion that the first tribunal's reasons were 'substantially the same' as its own reasons.

13.13   The issue of costs is in the discretion of the second tribunal and it does not follow automatically that because a deposit order has been made, and an adverse finding has been reached for substantially the same reasons at the full hearing, that costs must be awarded (2001 Rules r12(7)). If they are, the deposit is set off against and used to discharge any award of costs made by the tribunal, whether for the matters covered by the deposit or otherwise (2001 Rules r12(8)).

13.14   At the substantive hearing, no member of the tribunal who sat on the pre-hearing review may take part (2001 Rules r7(9)), even if no order was made. There is no reason why the second tribunal should not know and have read the reasons of the first tribunal if it made an order, but in practice the decision recording the making of the order or refusing to make one is kept in a sealed envelope on the file and not read until the end of the substantive hearing.

Preliminary hearings

Introduction

14.1   It is sometimes useful, but often counter-productive, for a preliminary hearing to take place on an issue before full consideration of all the issues in a case. If a case can be disposed of by taking one short preliminary point, it is obviously sensible to do so. But often the issues raised in a preliminary point overlap into matters more appropriate for a substantive hearing. Sometimes preliminary points of law are taken to the highest level before the facts have been determined, only to frustrate or exhaust one of the parties. Preliminary points were taken to the House of Lords in, for example, *Barclays Bank plc v Kapur*,[1] where it was held that failure by the bank to give pension credit for previous service in East Africa was a continuing act and the claim was not time-barred. On trial of the merits of the claim, however, the Employment Appeal Tribunal (EAT) and Court of Appeal overturned the tribunal's finding that the action was based on race discrimination,[2] thus rendering pointless the findings in the preliminary hearings.

14.2   It is important to distinguish three forms of proceeding: preliminary hearings on jurisdiction, the hearing of a preliminary point of law, and reference of a preliminary point to the European Court of Justice (ECJ).

Preliminary hearings on jurisdiction

14.3   A tribunal can at any time 'before the hearing of an originating application', either on application by a party or of its own motion, 'hear and determine any issue relating to the entitlement' of a party to bring or contest proceedings (2001 Rules r6(1)). Notice must be given to all the parties in writing and an opportunity given to advance oral argument before the tribunal. A tribunal may decide to hear a preliminary issue of its own initiative, but it should not do so without giving parties an opportunity to be heard.[3] Rule 6(2) of the 2001 Rules makes specific reference to the right of parties to make representations in writing, and to advance oral argument, but makes no reference to the hearing of evidence. However, the EAT has confirmed that

1   [1991] ICR 208; [1991] IRLR 136, HL.
2   [1995] IRLR 87, CA.
3   *Sutcliffe v Big C's Marine* [1998] IRLR 428, EAT.

to 'hear' an issue must include the right to hear evidence.[4] Since a preliminary hearing does not constitute the hearing of the originating application itself, it is likely that 2001 Rules r15(8) empowers a chairman sitting alone to determine the preliminary issue, and *Practice Direction No 1* carries this into effect (see appendix C).

14.4   The scope of this rule is pre-eminently designed for issues of jurisdiction, for example, to determine whether an applicant has sufficient qualifying service to bring a claim for unfair dismissal, or whether a claim is brought within the relevant limitation period. At first sight, a dispute about whether a respondent is properly joined in a transfer of undertakings case might be one about the entitlement of a party to contest proceedings. But here it would be necessary for the tribunal to make findings of fact clearly overlapping with the task of the tribunal hearing the substantive originating application. It is for this reason that the EAT and the Court of Appeal have been keen to restrict the use of preliminary hearings in employment law, reflecting the warnings against these procedures given in *Allen v Gulf Oil Refining Ltd*.[5] In *Secretary of State for Education v Birchall*[6] Mummery J said:

> there are . . . dangers in isolating an issue from the main dispute and ordering it to be determined as a preliminary point on the basis of assumed facts. It is often quicker and cheaper to find all the facts first and then to resolve the issues.

That statement arose in a case where allegations of race discrimination, normal retirement age and fixed term contracts were all raised.

14.5   Cases dealing with jurisdiction are different from those where 'the complaint itself fails in some essential or fundamental element'.[7] In Equal Pay Act 1970 cases, the defence under EqPA 1970 s1(3) that the difference in pay between men and women is due to a genuine material factor other than sex is frequently taken as a preliminary point; and this may usefully avoid expenditure and further delays on requisitioning an independent expert.[8]

14.6   In constructive dismissal cases, where the entitlement of an employee to bring a claim depends on him or her proving a dismissal (and therefore that the tribunal has jurisdiction), it is frequently

---

4   *Tsangacos v Amalgamated Chemicals Ltd* [1997] ICR 154; [1997] IRLR 4, EAT.
5   [1981] AC 1001, HL. See *Munir v Jang Publications Ltd* [1989] ICR 1; [1989] IRLR 224, CA; *Post Office Counters Ltd v Malik* [1991] ICR 355.
6   [1994] IRLR 630, EAT.
7   *Post Office Counters v Malik*, note 5 above, per Wood J.
8   *British Coal Corporation v Smith* [1994] ICR 810; [1994] IRLR 342, CA (see para 21.28).

counter-productive to hear evidence relating to a dismissal without consideration of all of the surrounding facts. This would make it inappropriate to hold a preliminary hearing either on jurisdiction or on a preliminary point of law.

Preliminary point of law

14.7   An entirely separate concept is a hearing to determine an issue of law which might either finally conclude the case or finally conclude one aspect of the case. There is no dispute on the power of the tribunal to hear the case, but it is contended that a material aspect of the claim will fail and, if so, it should be decided on its own. It *is* the hearing of the originating application but it proceeds in stages, starting with evidence and submissions on a preliminary point which, once decided, will affect the further stages in the case.[9]

14.8   This may be achieved by raising a preliminary point on assumed facts, as for example in *Pickstone v Freemans plc*[10] on the construction of the EqPA 1970. In such a case the parties should seek to agree facts in writing by exchange with each other,[11] or alternatively call sufficient evidence to enable findings to be made, and then make submissions as to the law. The Court of Appeal has warned that parties should not seek to foreshorten the hearing by deciding the point on *assumed* facts; it is usually necessary to find or agree facts before it can be determined whether there is a legal argument at all. In *Smith v Gardner Merchant*[12] a tribunal determined, without hearing evidence, that a claim of discrimination on the grounds of sexual orientation did not fall within the Sex Discrimination Act 1975, and it had no jurisdiction. Ward LJ described the case as an:

> . . . example of an attempt to shorten proceedings which results in their being prolonged and ultimately inconclusive in nine cases out of ten.

14.9   The tribunal had asked itself whether sexual orientation was within the SDA 1975, rather than asking whether the applicant, a male homosexual, had been discriminated against on the ground of his sex, a question which could not be answered on the assumed facts.

9 *Post Office Counters v Malik*, note 5 above.
10 [1988] ICR 697; [1988] IRLR 357, HL.
11 See *Waters v Metropolitan Police Commissioner* [1995] IRLR 531, EAT.
12 [1998] IRLR 510; [1999] ICR 134, CA.

The Court of Appeal remitted the matter to the tribunal to decide the facts and answer the proper question.[13]

14.10 If substantial disputed evidence has to be brought, tribunals are more inclined to allow a full hearing to determine all issues. There is much to be said for allowing a tribunal to make findings on the substantive point in addition to the preliminary point, so that, if the case is pursued to appeal, the relative strength of the parties' cases on the substantive merits is known to them, and indeed to the higher court. This is why constructive dismissal claims are unsuitable for preliminary rulings, whereas a preliminary point such as the existence of a contractual term for the purposes of deductions under the wages protection legislation can readily be determined.

Reference to the European Court of Justice

14.11 By article 234 of the Treaty of Rome, a preliminary ruling can be sought from the ECJ on the interpretation of the Treaty and subordinate EU legislation, and the validity and interpretation of acts of the institutions of the European Union. This will include directives and the effect of directives. Power to refer is given to any national court or tribunal, but in all cases the ruling must be sought on a preliminary point and the ruling must be 'necessary' for the tribunal to reach its decision. The ruling, in other words, must be sought before the decision of the tribunal is reached. Generally speaking it will be more convenient to leave it to the EAT or the Court of Appeal to make a reference but some landmark cases such as *Johnston v RUC*[14] have been referred directly by tribunals.

14.12 The reference will not be sent to the ECJ until the time for appealing the order has expired 2001 Rules r22. By analogy with the High Court, the reference should include the questions to be decided together with a summary of the facts, an outline of the parties' cases and the relevant provisions of national law.[15]

---

13 The legal answer, that under the SDA 1975 and the Equal Treatment Directive EC/76/207 discrimination on the ground of sex does not include sexual orientation, was provided in *Secretary of State for Defence v MacDonald* [2001] IRLR 431 by the Court of Session; the Court of Appeal in *Pearce v Governing Body of Mayfield Secondary School* [2001] IRLR 669 left open the question of whether the answer might be different when the SDA 1975 is read with the Human Rights Act 1998.

14 [1987] ICR 83; [1986] IRLR 263, ECJ.

15 Rules of the Supreme Court Order 114, as set out in Civil Procedure Rules Sch 1.

Adjournment and postponement

Introduction

15.1   The tribunal has power to regulate its own procedure (2001 Rules r15(1)[1]) and to extend time (2001 Rules r17) and it has a general power in the interests of justice to adjourn or postpone. There is also a specific power under 2001 Rules r14(4) to order costs to be paid when a party has sought a postponement or an adjournment.

15.2   There is a further specific power to adjourn or postpone where by statute conciliation procedures are available, in order to give an opportunity for the case to be settled by conciliation or withdrawal (2001 Rules r15(7)).

15.3   Apart from such specific cases, the tribunal has a wide discretion to postpone or adjourn proceedings, as was made clear in *Jacobs v Norsalta Ltd*,[2] a case where tribunal proceedings were stayed pending High Court proceedings involving complicated questions of compensation:

> . . . the tribunal has a complete discretion, so long as it exercises it judicially, to postpone or adjourn any case provided there is good, reasonable ground for so doing.

15.4   An application for a postponement or adjournment should generally be made in writing and may lead to an oral hearing. The tribunal should not adjourn or postpone without giving all parties an opportunity to make representations.[3] A postponement or adjournment should not be granted dependent on payment of costs which have been ordered against a party.[4]

The party making the application

15.5   It is relevant to bear in mind who is making the application, since there are sometimes tactical advantages associated with delay. For example, postponement of a hearing on compensation following a finding on liability against an employer would have the beneficial effect (from the employer's point of view) of delaying the running of interest from an award of compensation. Generally, tribunals will be

---

1   Employment Tribunals Rules of Procedure (contained in SI 2001 No 1171, Sch 1).
2   [1977] ICR 189, EAT per Phillips J.
3   *Bowater plc v Charlwood* [1991] ICR 798; [1991] IRLR 340, CA.
4   *Cooper v Weatherwise (Roofing and Walling) Limited* [1993] ICR 81, EAT.

astute to look carefully at the reasons given in support of the application and to balance these against the possible prejudice to other parties.

Factors relevant to a decision

15.6   The following factors are relevant to the decision whether or not to grant an application to postpone or adjourn.

Ill-health or unavailability of parties and witnesses

15.7   In order to avoid uncertainty, an application based on the ill-health of a party or a witness should be accompanied by a doctor's certificate. Unavailability of a witness, for example by being on holiday abroad or working abroad, could also provide grounds for postponing or adjourning. On the other hand, proceedings could commence to some extent without a relevant witness and then adjourn part-heard in order to accommodate the witness's availability.

15.8   A last-minute change of representation might also justify an application. Plainly the interests of justice, as well as the provisions of article 6 of the European Convention on Human Rights, require a party to be represented properly. A sudden change of representation might frustrate this if the new representative was unprepared. On the other hand, the tribunal will need to balance this against the article 6 requirement to provide a fair hearing to all parties, a requirement that might not be assisted by delay. Obviously the reason for any such change of representation at a late stage will be relevant. *Practice Direction No 1*[5] (see appendix C) makes no allowance for difficulties caused to advocates by a case being adjourned unfinished (part-heard) to another date when they are booked for another case. This common practical problem could be overcome with sympathetic and realistic exercise of discretion in relisting cases.

Proceedings in other cases

15.9   Sometimes a case raises a legal issue which is waiting to be determined in another case by a higher UK court, or the European Court

---

5   *Guidance on Judicial Procedure for the Employment Tribunals in England and Wales*, COET, November 1994.

of Justice (ECJ), and this might affect the outcome of a given case. Although it could make sense and save costs to postpone a hearing which might become abortive as a result of the outcome of different proceedings in a different court, the parties and the tribunal have no control over those other proceedings. The tribunal will wish to consider whether the other case will really determine all relevant issues and whether it might be preferable to proceed to make findings of fact in the case before it in any event. It should not be assumed that the existence of a 'test case' raising similar issues will necessarily result in a general stay of proceedings: each case should be considered individually.

15.10   For example, in *Financial Times v Byrne (No 2)*[6] it was argued that the hearing of a preliminary point on equal pay should be stayed pending the determination by the ECJ of *Enderby v Frenchay Health Authority*.[7] The application was rejected partly because the *Enderby* case would not determine all of the relevant issues in the *Financial Times* case; but also because the applicants in that case had no control over the *Enderby* proceedings, which might have been settled without a hearing, have been further delayed or determined without reference to the issue relevant in the *Financial Times* case.

15.11   An example however, of when tribunals were ordered, by the President of the Employment Tribunals,[8] to stay applications pending the outcome of another case, was seen when *Ex p Seymour-Smith*[9] was due to be heard in the ECJ. A possible outcome of the case was that those with one year's service could have been given the right to make a claim for unfair dismissal. Therefore, tribunals adjourned all applications in unfair dismissal cases where applicants had more than one year of service, but less than two (at that time the necessary qualifying service to bring an unfair dismissal claim) unless the case could be determined without reference to the question of qualifying service. In the event, the ECJ did not find the rule that an applicant needed two years' service to be discriminatory at the dates in question.

---

6   [1992] IRLR 163, EAT (leave to appeal refused by CA).
7   [1994] ICR 112; [1993] IRLR 591.
8   [1998] IRLR 351, EAT.
9   *R v Secretary of State for Employment ex p Seymour-Smith* [1999] 2 AC 554; [1999] All ER (EC) 97; [1999] 3 WLR 460; [1999] ICR 447; [1999] IRLR 253, ECJ, applied [2000] 1 All ER 857; [2000] ICR 244; [2000] IRLR 263, HL.

High Court proceedings

15.12   A tribunal is more likely to stay proceedings if there is a very similar issue to be determined in the High Court (or the county court) and it is likely to bring about a final conclusion of all or the major issues in the tribunal proceedings. An applicant who claims unfair dismissal and wants to reserve the right to issue proceedings for wrongful dismissal in the High Court, should present an unfair dismissal claim by way of originating application in the usual way, but seeking at the same time, a stay of tribunal proceedings.[10] An applicant would generally be well advised to do this if the wrongful dismissal claim is worth more than the limit on contract claims in the tribunal or if he or she is seeking remedies other than damages.[11]

15.13   Where there is such a potential overlap between the facts to be determined in the tribunal and those raised in High Court proceedings, it is generally desirable for the same issues to be determined by the High Court rather than by a tribunal[12] – otherwise 'the Judge would be put in a strait jacket'.[13]

15.14   Considerations which might point to waiting until after the High Court case has been decided generally relate to the more stringent procedural requirements of that forum, ie:

   – the desirability for strict rules of evidence to be applied;[14]
   – the use of more formal 'pleadings';[15]
   – the total amount of damages may be higher than a tribunal can award;
   – complexity of the issues;[16]
   – the availability of more stringent rules on discovery, the power to award costs, better remedies, and the prospect of delay.[17]

If these are not important considerations, there is no reason to postpone the tribunal.

---

10   *Warnock v Scarborough Football Club* [1989] ICR 489, EAT.
11   See Employment Tribunals (Extension of Jurisdiction) Orders 1994 SI No 1623 (England and Wales) and SI No 1624 (Scotland).
12   *Green v Hampshire CC* [1979] ICR 861, ChD.
13   *Automatic Switching Ltd v Brunet* [1986] ICR 542, EAT per Sir R Kilner Brown.
14   *Bowater plc v Charlwood* [1991] ICR 798; [1991] IRLR 340, EAT.
15   Ibid.
16   *Jacobs v Norsalta*, note 2 above.
17   Ibid.

Foreign proceedings

15.15   A postponement was granted pending the imminent issue of High Court proceedings in England coupled with the existence of other actions abroad in *JMCC Holdings Ltd v Conroy*.[18] Again, similarity of issues together with convenience of location are matters to be considered.

Criminal proceedings

15.16   In cases involving allegations of dishonesty, such as unfair dismissal for misconduct, and a concurrent prosecution in the Crown Court, it is desirable for tribunal proceedings to be stayed so as to allow complete flexibility for the applicant and their advisers in the criminal trial. Yet in *Bastick v James Lane (Turf Accountants) Ltd*[19] the EAT declined to interfere with a chairman's decision to refuse a postponement sought by an applicant charged with theft in circumstances leading to a claim for unfair dismissal. The chairman decided that the issues were not sufficiently similar. Of course, the issues *are* different: whether there was sufficient material before the employer to justify a dismissal, compared with whether the employee committed theft beyond reasonable doubt. There are however very strong policy reasons for allowing criminal proceedings to go first. Given the very different tasks of the tribunal and the Crown Court, however, an applicant should not build up false hopes that an acquittal in the criminal proceedings will mean a finding of unfair dismissal in the tribunal.

15.17   In Scotland, the practice is generally to adjourn the hearing of the tribunal application until the resolution of the criminal proceedings.

Appeal

15.18   There is no obligation on a tribunal to adjourn pending an appeal, for example, on a preliminary point or a ruling on procedure against a party. Similarly, there is no obligation on a tribunal to stay a hearing on remedies pending an appeal by an employer on liability. It may be in the parties' interest to agree to stay further proceedings for the saving of costs, but in the absence of agreement, there is no reason

18   [1990] ICR 179, EAT.
19   [1979] ICR 778.

why an applicant's case should be held up. A solution might be to agree subject to appeal that time for computing interest on any award is deemed to run from the date a compensation hearing would have taken place. This would not, however, safeguard against the potential prejudice caused by delay should issues of fact have to be determined.

Internal procedures

15.19   The tribunal rules contain no requirement for a party to try and exhaust internal procedures before commencing tribunal proceedings. Nevertheless, the possibility of a settlement through conciliation is always a ground for exercising discretion in favour of a stay. The hearing of an internal appeal might be just such a ground, since it is possible that a favourable result for the applicant would avoid the need to continue tribunal proceedings. The Employment Rights (Dispute Resolution) Act 1998 provides that where there is a procedure for appealing and a party does not make use of it, that party may be penalised in damages.[20] This points to a legislative policy of wanting parties to exhaust internal routes before resorting to litigation, but, as set out in chapter 5, waiting for the result of internal appeals will generally not be a good excuse for failing to file proceedings in time – proceedings should be issued and an adjournment sought.

Costs on adjournment and postponement

15.20   Once the interests of justice have identified a reason for granting a stay, any resulting disadvantage to the other party can be compensated in costs. There is no requirement that the pejorative terms of 2001 Rules r14(1), 'vexatiously, abusively, disruptively or otherwise unreasonably', etc, should be complied with. Rather, 2001 Rules r14(4) is entirely neutral and allows the tribunal to exercise its discretion to award costs on the application of a party for a postponement or an adjournment without the need to attribute unreasonableness to a party. Costs can be awarded in favour of or against the party applying.

---

20   See ERA 1996 s127A, inserted by s13 of the Employment Rights (Dispute Resolution) Act 1998.

CHAPTER 16

Settlement and conciliation

General considerations

16.1   In tribunal proceedings, as in any litigation, there are often a number of advantages in settling the case before (or during) the full hearing. Settling a case means entering into an agreement with the other side, with both parties being bound by the terms of that agreement without having to have the issues in the case determined by the tribunal.

16.2   Concluding an action by this means is often advantageous for both parties because:

   – agreeing to settle an action avoids the risk of losing as well as the unpleasantness of a hearing;
   – the recoupment provisions[1] do not apply to settlements;
   – both parties avoid the costs of fighting the case to the end (apart from legal costs, there will generally be costs in preparing for and attending the tribunal, whether in terms of taking time off work or loss of management time);
   – while the remedies open to the tribunal are limited by statute, the parties may agree to include in the agreement matters which are outside the tribunal's jurisdiction, such as an agreed form of reference or a confidentiality clause.

16.3   The advantages of resolving tribunal proceedings have long been recognised by parliament and a statutory conciliation procedure is available through the offices of the Advisory, Conciliation and Arbitration Service (ACAS).

16.4   Settlements in tribunal proceedings are not, however, without risk. Anyone entering into an agreement to settle a case should only do so if they understand and agree to the terms on which the case is to be compromised. The terms of the settlement form a binding contract between the parties which can be enforced in the ordinary courts. Those terms may include an agreement by the employee to waive certain legal rights arising out of the employment relationship. Care should be taken not to surrender legal rights unintentionally. If it is not intended to compromise any future claims relating, for example, to accidents at work or to pension rights, then the agreement should make this clear. If a settlement includes terms relating to pension rights, then particular care should be taken to ensure that the agreement comes within the terms of the pension scheme.

---

1   Employment Protection (Recoupment of Jobseeker's Allowance and Income Support) Regulations 1996 SI No 2349.

16.5   Generally speaking, any attempt to contract out of an employee's statutory employment rights will be invalid.[2] Apart from the specific statutory exceptions to this rule (for example, on the failure to renew a fixed-term contract where the requirements of Employment Rights Act 1996 (ERA 1996) s197 are met), an employee can only contract out of his or her right to bring tribunal proceedings in relation to statutory employment rights by:

- entering into a settlement through ACAS;
- entering into a compromise agreement after having been advised by a suitably qualified (and insured) relevant adviser; or
- entering into an agreement during the course of a hearing before a tribunal which forms the basis of a tribunal's decision by consent.

16.6   These protections do not apply to contract claims arising out of the employment relationship which can be brought in the tribunal. Such claims are founded on common law principles and are treated as they would be in any court: an agreement between the parties can effectively contract out of the right to pursue the complaint in question provided it meets the normal requirements for legally binding contracts at common law, ie:

- there has been a valid offer and acceptance;
- consideration (such as compensation) has been provided for the agreement;
- there is an intention to create legal relations between the parties; and
- a party's consent to the agreement is not rendered void by reason of duress, undue influence, misrepresentation or mistake.

Compromising statutory rights

16.7   Employment rights given by statute can be taken away only by statute and the protections provided apply until all questions of liability and remedy have been determined by the tribunal. Therefore, even where the question of liability has been determined and the issue of remedy has been adjourned to another day, an agreement between the parties will be void unless it conforms with one of the methods of compromising a claim provided by statute.[3]

---

2   See ERA 1996 s203, SDA 1975 s77, RRA 1976 s72, DDA 1995 s9.
3   *Courage Take Home Trade Ltd v Keys* [1986] ICR 874; [1986] IRLR 427, EAT.

16.9   There are, however, ways in which an employer can circumvent these protective measures, even in relation to the employee's statutory rights. Those acting for employees should not be surprised by the use of such tactical devices (particularly as part of a termination package) which give employers some guarantee against future claims without having to face the obstacles presented by the statutory means of settlement.

16.9   If an agreement is concluded with the employee which does not purport to exclude the employee's right to go to a tribunal but does provide (for example) for the payment of a sum of money by way of an agreed settlement of all claims (including statutory claims) for compensation, the employee's subsequent application to a tribunal may enable the employer to argue that the original agreement has been breached by the employee. This would not stop the employee continuing with the claim to the tribunal but may render it inadvisable to do so: he or she may lose the entitlement to receive the money promised under the original agreement. To give the employer greater certainty, this form of agreement may expressly provide that payment of the money is conditional on no legal proceedings (including tribunal proceedings) being commenced in relation to the (for example) dismissal, or for the money (or at least part of it) to be paid only after the relevant time limits for making a claim have expired. This does not breach the statutory provisions against contracting out, as it does not purport to stop the employee going to the tribunal but merely states that they will have to seek compensation via the tribunal and not under the terms of the agreement, if they choose to do so.

16.10   In any event, if an employee did still proceed with a claim in the tribunal after accepting such a payment it is likely that this sum would be deducted from any compensatory award if he or she succeeded in a complaint. The question for the tribunal would be whether it was just and equitable to deduct the sum paid. Clearly if, for example, an employer has sought to put undue pressure on the employee to contract out of his or her rights, it would be difficult to see how that employer could contend that it would not be just and equitable to make any further award. Furthermore, even if the employer agreed to pay a sum equal to the statutory maximum, there is no guarantee that a further sum will not be awarded. The compensatory award is calculated by assessing the employee's loss from the date of the dismissal, less sums received from the employer and by way of mitigation. It is only after this calculation that the statutory ceiling is applied. If the employee's overall loss is very high, the ex gratia (voluntary) payment by the employer may do little to offset the compensatory award.

16.11   Sums paid by the employer voluntarily may also be taken to reduce any liability in respect of a redundancy payment or basic award, but only if it can be established that the payment made was clearly meant to represent settlement of this liability.[5] This will depend on the particular circumstances of each case. If a payment is intended to cover any liability for redundancy entitlement or for a basic award in an unfair dismissal claim, this should be made clear. An employer who makes a payment without expressly stating what that money is intended to cover risks having to make a further payment to cover a basic award in any subsequent tribunal proceedings.[6]

16.12   Alternatively, where an employer has already conceded liability (for example, by admitting that the dismissal was unfair) and has made an open offer to pay the maximum sum the tribunal could award to an employee who succeeds in his or her claim, pursuing an application to the tribunal may result in an award of costs being made against the employee concerned. Without a concession as to liability, however, a tribunal should not award costs against an employee simply because an open offer has been made of the maximum award possible.[7]

16.13   Thus, while such offers do not purport to restrict the employee's right to bring tribunal proceedings, pursuing a claim is rendered pointless and puts the employee at risk of costs.

Advisory, Conciliation and Arbitration Service

16.14   ACAS was established under the Employment Protection Act 1975, expressly to promote the improvement of industrial relations.[8] The secretary of state appoints the members of ACAS after consulting both employers' and workers' organisations (TULRCA 1992 s248). ACAS is organised into regional offices, a list of the addresses of which is set out in appendix E.

5   *Chelsea Football Club and Athletic Co Ltd v Heath* [1981] ICR 323; [1981] IRLR 73, EAT.
6   *Boorman v Allmakes Ltd* [1995] IRLR 553, CA.
7   *Telephone Information Services v Wilkinson* [1991] IRLR 148, EAT.
8   See now TULRCA 1992 s209.

16.15   The primary function of ACAS is to conciliate in trade disputes and the majority of its work falls outside the terms of this book. ACAS does, however, have express duties in individual employment disputes and plays an important role in conciliation in tribunal cases. Since 21 May 2001 ACAS also administers the arbitration scheme.[9]

The role of ACAS in tribunal claims

16.16   Conciliation officers may (and must if asked to do so by a party to a complaint) attempt to conciliate any complaints which could form the basis of a claim to a tribunal. They will only get involved in such cases *before* the presentation of a claim, however, if expressly asked to do so by one of the prospective parties (Employment Tribunals Act 1996 s18). ACAS cannot be used as a 'rubber-stamp' for agreements entered into between employers and employees.

16.17   The July 1990 *ACAS Practice Direction* sets out three conditions which must be met before ACAS will agree to be involved in any conciliation process:

- the employee must have been dismissed, or received notice of dismissal (or ACAS has to be satisfied that the employee believes him or herself to have been constructively dismissed);
- the employee's employment rights must have been infringed; and
- the parties must not have agreed all the terms of the settlement, ie, there must remain some role for the services of ACAS.

16.18   Once a claim has been presented to the relevant regional office of employment tribunals, a conciliation officer is appointed by ACAS for all claims of:[10]

- unfair dismissal;
- unlawful sexual discrimination or breach of an equality clause under the Equal Pay Act 1970;
- unlawful racial discrimination;
- unlawful deduction of wages;
- infringement of rights listed under TULRCA 1992 s290;
- unlawful discrimination under the Disability Discrimination Act 1995;
- infringement of the National Minimum Wage Act 1998;

9   See chapter 3.
10   As set out in ETA 1996 s18(1).

- breach of the Working Time Regulations (WT Regs) 1998;[11]
- breach of the Transnational Information and Consultation of Employees Regulations (TICE Regs) 1999;[12]
- breach of the Part-time Workers (Prevention of Less Favourable Treatment) Regulations (PTW Regs) 2000.[13]

16.19   Where a claim is presented to a tribunal and any of the above provisions applies, the secretary of the tribunals will send copies of all documents and notices relating to that claim to the conciliation officer concerned (2001 Rules r23(8)[14]).

16.20   The conciliation officer appointed to a claim presented to the tribunal under these provisions is under a duty to endeavour to promote a settlement between the parties before its determination by the tribunal, either:

- on a request to do so by the parties; or
- where, in the absence of such a request, the conciliation officer considers there are reasonable prospects of settling the claim.

16.21   In most cases, the conciliation officer will contact the parties as a matter of course. If no such contact has been made, a party can find out which conciliation officer has been appointed to the case by contacting the relevant ACAS office (see appendix E).

16.22   In unfair dismissal cases, and cases of sex, race or disability discrimination, where the complainant has ceased to be employed by the employer, the conciliation officer has a specific duty to promote the reinstatement or re-engagement of a dismissed employee (ETA 1996 s18(4)). This obligation will only arise, however, if appropriate in the circumstances of any particular case; the officer is not under an absolute duty to promote reinstatement or re-engagement if it would clearly be futile to do so.[15]

16.23   The conciliation officer's duty does not end when a case goes to hearing but continues until the determination of all questions of liability and remedy. Clearly the services of a conciliation officer may be of great assistance where liability has been determined but the question of compensation has been left open for a further hearing, even if attempts at conciliation were previously to no avail.

---

11   SI No 1833.
12   SI No 3323.
13   SI No 1551.
14   Employment Tribunals Rules of Procedure (contained in SI 2001 No 1171, Sch 1).
15   *Moore v Duport Furniture Products Ltd* [1982] ICR 84; [1982] IRLR 31, HL.

16.24   If the services of the conciliation officer are utilised, it is worth bearing in mind the following:

- the conciliation officer is independent and does not have the same relationship with a party as, for example, a lawyer or adviser;
- the conciliation officer is not an arbiter of tribunal cases and is not there to judge the merits of the case or to try to review the evidence;
- the conciliation officer will also be talking to the other side and will pass on information given, although he or she could not be called to give evidence about a matter raised during negotiations if that was properly the subject of privilege and the communicator had not given permission;
- any settlement reached with the help of a conciliation officer is still an agreement between the parties: the conciliation officer is not there to impose terms on the parties or even to recommend a particular settlement.

The effect of an agreement through ACAS

16.25   Before the presentation of a claim or at any point after the commencement of a claim of unfair dismissal, an agreement through the conciliation officer to forego the right to pursue a claim to the tribunal will be upheld in so far as it relates to the rights set out under ETA 1996 s18(1)(d). This will not, however, preclude the applicant from bringing a claim under (for example) the Sex Discrimination Act 1975 (SDA 1975) or the Race Relations Act 1976 (RRA 1976) or the Disability Discrimination Act 1995 (DDA 1995) or under European law *unless* the agreement *specifically* prohibits all such possible claims. An agreement 'in full and final settlement of all claims' will not suffice.[16] In other words, to ensure that the agreement does dispose of all possible employment claims, it should expressly be stated to be in settlement of all claims, whether under ERA 1996, TULRCA 1992, SDA 1975, RRA 1976, DDA 1995, WT Regs 1998, National Minimum Wage Act 1998 (NMWA 1998) or EU law.

16.26   The words of a general exclusion can debar subsequent claims, provided that such claims were intended by the parties to have been excluded. Unidentified claims, ie, those of which an applicant is ignorant, may be covered by a general exclusion but '. . . a long and . . . salutary line of authority shows that, in the absence of clear

16 *Livingstone v Hepworth Refractories plc* [1992] ICR 287; [1992] IRLR 63, EAT.

language, the court will be very slow to infer that a party intended to surrender rights and claims of which he was unaware and could not have been aware', per Lord Bingham in *Bank of Credit and Commerce International SA (in compulsory liquidation) v Ali*.[17] The *BCCI* case also served as a reminder that the scope of general words of a release will depend on the context furnished by the surrounding circumstances in which the release was given (see per Lord Nicholl) – in that case the applicant was not precluded from pursuing a claim for stigma damages notwithstanding the 'general release' contained within his settlement agreement with BCCI.

16.27   The powers of conciliation officers in assisting in the settlement of tribunal claims have generally been liberally construed and the courts have demonstrated a reluctance to interfere with the actions of conciliation officers providing they have been carried out in good faith.[18]

16.28   Conciliation officers usually record agreements on Form COT3 (see appendix B), although this form does not have to be used for the parties to be bound by the agreement. Indeed, terms agreed in this way may still be binding on the parties even though they have not been reduced to writing at all.[19] Provided the conciliation officer has 'taken action' under ETA 1996 s18, the contract will be binding unless it is expressed to be part of the agreement that it should be recorded in a particular document.

16.29   Once a settlement has been achieved through a conciliation officer, it will be extremely difficult to challenge it later. It would probably require evidence that the conciliation officer acted in bad faith or adopted unfair methods in seeking to achieve a settlement before the agreement could be set aside.[20]

16.30   Any agreement entered into through the conciliation officer on behalf of a party by their adviser or representative will be binding on that party provided the adviser or representative concerned has been held out as having authority to act on that party's behalf and no notice has been given to the contrary: the adviser or representative has ostensible authority to act as the party's agent for these purposes. If, in fact, that authority has not been given, the party concerned will have an action in the normal courts against the adviser or representative but will still be bound by the agreement apparently entered into on his or her behalf. This principle applies to all types of adviser or

17 [2001] UKHL 8; [2001] IRLR 292, HL.
18 *Hennessy v Craigmyle & Co Ltd and ACAS* [1986] ICR 461; [1986] IRLR 300, CA.
19 *Gilbert v Kembridge Fibres Ltd* [1984] ICR 188; [1984] IRLR 52, EAT.
20 *Slack v Greenham (Plant Hire) Ltd* [1983] ICR 617; [1983] IRLR 271, EAT.

representative, not just to qualified lawyers: in *Freeman v Sovereign Chicken Ltd*[21] the adviser was a citizens advice bureau (CAB) worker who signed a COT3 in full and final settlement of the applicant's claims. The applicant later sought to lodge a further IT1, arising from the same facts, but was prevented by law ('estopped', see para 18.57 below) from asserting this because of the compromise agreement in place. His argument that the CAB worker had not had his authority to compromise his claim was not successful, as the CAB worker had ostensible authority to sign, and it mattered not that she did not have actual authority. Anyone acting for a party should make sure that they have express authority to enter into a particular agreement, checking that the client has seen the terms of the agreement and approved the wording of the settlement before it is finalised.

Compromise agreements and contracts

16.31   Another means by which parties (or potential parties) to tribunal claims can effectively agree to 'contract out' of their statutory employment rights is by entering into a compromise agreement or contract under ERA 1996 s203(3) and (4), SDA 1975 s77, RRA 1976 s72, TULRCA 1992 s288(2A), DDA 1995 s9(2), WT Regs 1998 reg 35, NMWA 1998 s49, TICE Regs 1999 regs 40 and 41, and PTW Regs 2000 reg 9. The term 'compromise agreement' is used in relation to all claims under ERA 1996, WT Regs 1998, NMWA 1998, TICE Regs 1999. For those under SDA 1975, RRA 1976, TULRCA 1992 and DDA 1995 the appropriate term is 'compromise contract': there is no substantive difference between the two. A compromise agreement is narrowly defined and must comply with the strict requirements laid down if it is to be effective. The importance of satisfying the strict requirements was seen in *Riverside Health Authority v Chetty and others*[22] where the tribunal and Employment Appeal Tribunal (EAT) refused to strike out a claim which did not meet these requirements.

16.32   As one of the requirements is that the employee has received advice from a 'relevant independent adviser' before entering into the agreement, some applicants (who do not have access to such an adviser) will inevitably fall back on to the services of ACAS.

16.33   The compromise agreement procedure was really intended to

21   [1991] ICR 853; [1991] IRLR 408, EAT.
22   EAT 1168/95, unreported.

assist those parties who knew precisely where they stood and wanted to enter into a binding agreement without subsequent claims in the tribunal. In such cases ACAS had taken the view that it should not be used merely as a rubber stamp where agreement had already been reached and issued a practice direction in July 1990 to this effect.

16.34 To provide for cases which did not fall within the ACAS conditions, the compromise agreement exception to the prohibition on contracting out was provided by Trade Union Reform and Employment Rights Act 1993 s39, which amended the previous statutory position.

16.35 Compromise agreements or contracts may relate to potential claims under ERA 1996, SDA 1975, RRA 1976, TULRCA 1992, DDA 1995, WT Regs 1998, or NMWA 1998, and may be made in order to prevent any proceedings being instituted or may relate to cases where proceedings have already been instituted. However, a compromise cannot seek to exclude potential complaints which have not yet arisen on the off chance that they might be raised – so the formula 'in full and final settlement of all claims that the applicant has or may have against the respondent, howsoever arising', should not be used.

16.36 A breach of contract claim brought under the Employment Tribunal (Extension of Jurisdiction) Order 1994[23] can be settled without the use of a compromise agreement.[24] Such agreements are enforceable in the employment tribunal.[25]

Requirements of an effective compromise agreement

16.37 The conditions relating to such agreements are as follows:

- the agreement must be in writing;
- the agreement must relate to the specific complaint;
- the employee must have received independent legal advice from an independent legal adviser (defined below) on the terms and effect of the proposed agreement and in particular its effect on his or her ability to pursue his or her rights before a tribunal;
- there must be in force, when the adviser gives the advice, a contract of insurance or an indemnity provided by the members of a professional body, covering the risk of a claim by the employee in respect of loss arising in consequence of taking the advice;
- the agreement must identify the adviser; and

---

23 SI No 1623, see appendix C.
24 See *Carter v Reiner Moritz Associates Ltd* [1997] ICR 881.
25 *Rock-It Cargo Limited v Green* [1997] IRLR 581.

– the agreement must state that the conditions regulating compromise agreements under the relevant Act are satisfied.[26]

16.38   Advice previously had to be given by a 'qualified lawyer'; however, the Employment Rights (Dispute Resolution) Act 1998 widened the range of people entitled to give advice, essentially to include trade unions and advice centres. Section 9 of the above Act (now incorporated into ERA 1996 s203(3A)) defines a 'relevant independent adviser' as:

– a qualified lawyer (solicitor or barrister, or a person who is an 'authorised advocate' or 'authorised litigator' within the meaning of the Courts and Legal Services Act 1990);
– a trade union officer, employee or member, who is certified by the union as competent to give such advice, or who is authorised to do so on behalf of the union;
– a worker at an advice centre who is certified by the centre as competent to give such advice, or who is authorised to do so on behalf of the union;
– a person of a description specified in an order made by the secretary of state (to date no such orders have been made).

16.39   An adviser will not be 'independent', in relation to legal advice given to the employee (set out in ERA 1996 s203(3B)), if he or she is:

– a lawyer who is acting in the matter for the employer or a person connected with the employer;
– a trade union or advice centre which is the employer, or is connected with the employer;
– in the case of an advice centre, if the employee has to make payment for the advice received;
– in the case of a trade union or advice centre adviser, if he or she is not certified or authorised to act on behalf of that organisation.

16.40   The requirement that the lawyer must be covered by a 'policy of insurance' has been replaced by a requirement that the adviser be covered by a 'contract of insurance, or an indemnity provided for members of a profession or professional body'. This makes it clear that the cover that can be provided by the Solicitors' Indemnity Fund is sufficient to sign off on compromise agreements.

16.41   The requirement that the agreement or contract must relate to a

26 *Lunt v Merseyside TEC Ltd* [1999] ICR 17, EAT – the agreement should specifically set out that the conditions regulating agreements under that statute for each statute relied on.

specific complaint means that this form of settlement cannot rule out all possible future claims and cannot exclude potential claims on the off chance that these might be raised at some point in the future. There is, therefore, no way of avoiding the difficulties which arose in *Livingstone v Hepworth Refractories plc*[27] (see para 16.25). Where the employee has raised a number of grievances in an originating application or in a letter before action, however, there seems no reason why one compromise agreement cannot deal with all those specific complaints raised which the parties have now agreed to settle, although each such complaint should be dealt with separately within the agreement and it should be clear that terms have been agreed by way of settlement under each head.

16.42   If a compromise agreement or contract is entered into which meets these requirements, then the claims specified in it will have been effectively compromised and it can be relied on as overriding statutory rights.

Decisions by consent

16.43   Many agreements between parties take place at the door of the tribunal (either just before or during a tribunal hearing). While this means that costs will already have been expended and tribunal time wasted, it is an inevitable aspect of litigation: very often parties will not have assessed the relative strengths of their cases until late in the day or just before the hearing, when they know (for example) which witnesses the other side intends to call. There is also something about the prospect of walking into a court or tribunal which seems to focus minds and encourage parties to be more favourably disposed to the idea of a settlement of the case.

16.44   One way of disposing of the tribunal proceedings at that stage is for the applicant simply to withdraw the complaint. The tribunal may then make an order dismissing the claim on the applicant's withdrawal under 2001 Rules r15(2)(a). If the respondent subsequently reneges on the agreement, the applicant will not, however, be able to reinstate the tribunal claim but will have to seek a remedy for breach of contract (breach of the agreement) in the county court. Even where the relevant time limit in respect of the claim in question has not expired, a subsequent claim brought by the employee in these

27 [1992] ICR 287; [1992] IRLR 63, EAT.

circumstances may be struck out as frivolous or vexatious.[28] In such circumstances, it may be possible to apply to the tribunal to review its decision, on the ground that the interests of justice require a review (2001 Rules r13(1)(e)), or to commence fresh proceedings where the circumstances of the case could justify this approach[29] and where a review has been refused. The better course, however, would be for the tribunal to order that the case be stayed until a specified date (by when, for example, the applicant will be sure that the respondent will have paid the sums agreed) when it will be dismissed as withdrawn by the applicant, with both parties having liberty to apply for the matter to be reinstated at any time before that date. If an applicant is concerned about the respondent complying with an agreement to pay a particular sum, then it would be sensible to specify a time period during which any cheque should have been received and have cleared in the applicant's bank account. Tribunals are usually amenable to making an order in these terms and it provides a particularly useful safeguard where there is a risk that the respondent might become insolvent before the terms of the agreement are met – in such circumstances the applicant may need to reinstate proceedings before the tribunal in order to recover monies from the secretary of state. The fact that such an order specifies that the application will be dismissed as withdrawn on a particular date gives administrative certainty to all concerned. See also para 16.47.

16.45   Alternatively, where parties to a tribunal case have come to an agreement, the tribunal has the power to make a decision in the terms of that agreement (2001 Rules r15(2)(b)). A tribunal 'decision' includes a declaration, an order, a recommendation or award or a determination but not any 'other' interlocutory order or decision (2001 Regs reg 2(2)[30]).

16.46   A decision 'by consent' can be expressed directly in the terms agreed between the parties, ie, that the respondent is ordered to pay the applicant a certain sum of money. This order will be recorded as a decision of the tribunal and will be enforceable in the county court. A decision in this form, however, has a number of disadvantages: it can only include matters within the tribunal's jurisdiction – if a tribunal would not usually have the power to make an order in the terms sought, then the fact that the parties have agreed to it will not change

---

28 *Acrow (Engineers) Ltd v Hathaway* [1981] ICR 510.
29 *Mulvaney v London Transport Executive* [1981] ICR 351, EAT.
30 Employment Tribunals (Constitution and Rules of Procedure) Regulations 2001 SI No 1171.

the situation. Furthermore, if the agreement is for the payment of money from the respondent to the applicant and this is recorded as a decision of the tribunal, the recoupment provisions[31] apply, ie, money received by an employee in jobseeker's allowance or income support may be recouped from the sum agreed to be paid in the tribunal proceedings.

16.47   To avoid these problems, as indicated above, parties can instead ask the tribunal to make a decision merely to stay or adjourn the proceedings on terms scheduled to the tribunal's order. This decision can use the form of order used in civil courts generally called the '*Tomlin* order': ie, that all further proceedings in the case be stayed on the terms scheduled to the order save for the purpose of carrying such terms into effect, with liberty to apply for that purpose. The form of words approved in civil courts generally is set out in CPR 40.6, and the related practice directions. As the terms of the agreement are not actually part of the tribunal's decision but are merely scheduled to it, they can include matters which are outside the tribunal's jurisdiction (such as the terms of a reference, a confidentiality clause, etc) and payments of money will not attract the attention of the recoupment provisions.

16.48   If the proceedings are stayed or adjourned with liberty to apply, where an employer defaults on the agreement the employee can chose to reinstate the proceedings by applying to lift the stay or to seek an order from the tribunal or the county court in the terms of the agreement (although the tribunal would only be able to make such an order in so far as the terms were within its powers). If there is no provision for liberty to apply, the employee would be restricted to reinstating the proceedings, by lifting the stay, or pursuing a claim for breach of the agreement in the county court.

16.49   The right to reinstate proceedings in the tribunal can be extremely important for employees. Not only does it reinstate the threat of the hearing against the employer, with the costs and publicity implications that that entails; it also means that where the employer has been found to be insolvent, the employee can still pursue a claim for a basic award or redundancy payment which can then be recovered from the secretary of state under the provisions relating to the protection of employees on an employer's insolvency.

16.50   Where a party is represented in tribunal proceedings and the representative (whether a lawyer, adviser or lay representative) agrees to a decision being made 'by consent', it will be assumed that the party

31 See note 1 above.

concerned has *in fact* consented, even if the representative acted without taking proper instructions. The party's remedy, if any, lies against the representative.[32] Those acting for parties in the settlement of a case by these means should adopt the same cautious approach as when entering into an agreement through a conciliation officer or by any other means: it is the representative's duty to make sure that the individual is properly advised on the terms and effect of the agreement and that he or she does in fact consent to that compromise of the claim.

Checklist: Settlement and conciliation

For employees:

- If an offer of settlement has been made, how does it compare to the value of the claim as it is likely to be assessed by a tribunal?
- Are there advantages to you in compromising the claim rather than going ahead with the hearing, ie, the provision of a reference (without subsequent retraction or amendment), avoidance of the recoupment provisions, saving of costs?
- Could acceptance of the offer mean that rights other than those pursued in the tribunal proceedings might be lost (for example, a personal injury claim, pension rights, etc)?
- If considering entering into a compromise agreement, do so only on taking *independent* advice.
- Make sure the mechanism by which you settle the claim meets your requirements – make sure you understand and are happy with the terms of any agreement and utilise any safeguards necessary, ie, for exempting certain claims from a general release or for staying proceedings in the tribunal to enable the terms of the agreement to be carried out.
- Before accepting any offer: if in doubt, get advice.

For employers:

- Is the employee willing and able (ie, independently advised by a qualified, insured independent adviser) to enter into a binding compromise agreement or contract? If so, can an agreement be reached which would avoid the risk of subsequent proceedings?

---

32 *Times Newspapers Ltd v Fitt* [1981] ICR 637, EAT.

- If the employee is unwilling or unable to enter into any agreement but there is a risk of subsequent tribunal proceedings, consider making an offer which includes a concession of liability, without prejudice save as to costs.
- If any payment is to be made to the employee, consider whether it should be made in open correspondence or 'without prejudice'.
- If a payment is made to the employee, make it clear what that payment is intended to cover: if it includes an amount in respect of a possible basic award, this should be expressly stated.
- If tribunal proceedings are contemplated or have been commenced, consider utilising the services of ACAS and entering into an agreement through a conciliation officer, recorded on Form COT3.

For advisers:

- Is your client in a sufficiently well-informed position to assess the pros and cons of settlement properly?
- If advising the employee, do you meet the definition of a relevant independent adviser for the purposes of entering into a compromise contract or agreement?
- Has an ACAS conciliation officer been involved in seeking to reach a compromise of the claim?
- If an agreement has been reached, does your client understand the full implications of the terms of the agreement?
- Keep a record of any agreement reached, signed by your client and those acting for the other party.
- Pay attention to time limits (for payment of money, etc) set out in the agreement and consider restoring the claim in the tribunal if these are not met.
- If the recoupment provisions apply to your client, is the settlement recorded in such a way as to avoid recoupment?

CHAPTER 17

Preparing for the hearing

Notice of the hearing

17.1   Notice must be given at least 14 days before the hearing unless the parties agree with the tribunal office to a shorter period (2001 Rules r5(2)[1]). The notice of hearing includes guidance to the parties on witnesses and documents (see para 17.10). The notes accompanying the notice of hearing include advice on attendance, making representations in writing, disposal of the case against a respondent who has not entered a notice of appearance, the possibility of the case not getting on, witness statements (see para 17.10), and a note to employers to be prepared to deal with the issue of reinstatement and expenses.

Listing

17.2   The tribunal office will make arrangements for the listing of the case according to the practice operated in that particular region. The length of time the case is likely to take to present and for the tribunal to reach a decision needs to be carefully evaluated and reasons given. It is better to be conservative, and give ample time; no one complains if the hearing ends before the scheduled day and it is preferable to adjourning the case part-heard, with all parties coming back weeks or even months later.

17.3   It is necessary to check the availability of all witnesses and any representative, and then send the tribunal the estimate of length and dates to avoid.

Preliminary points of law

17.4   An application to seek a preliminary hearing should already have been made by now but if not, it should be made forthwith (see chapter 14).

Chairman sitting without lay members?

17.5   If either party wants the case to be heard either by a chairman sitting alone, or by a full tribunal, and there is a discretion given to the

1   Employment Tribunals Rules of Procedure (contained in SI 2001 No 1171, Sch 1).

tribunal to decide this (see para 1.20 for when this arises), the preference should be made known to the tribunal, with reasons.

Hearing in public

17.6   The hearing of an originating application must be in public unless a government minister directs otherwise (or the tribunal so decides on grounds of national security (2001 Rules r8(2) and (3)). If there are allegations of a sexual offence or sexual misconduct, and in disability discrimination cases, orders protecting the identity of those involved can be sought at this stage under 2001 Rules r16. This is discussed at para 18.20.

Written representations

17.7   Written representations can be made to the tribunal. They should be sent seven days before the hearing with copies to other parties within seven days of the hearing (2001 Rules r10(5)).

Skeleton arguments

17.8   In practice the tribunal will welcome the presentation of written arguments in skeleton form, as is the requirement under the Civil Procedure Rules (CPR).[2] A short summary of the issues in opening, or a skeleton argument and draft findings of fact presented in closing, are usually accepted gratefully. They save time and release the tribunal from making detailed notes on oral submissions. There is no need to send them in advance to the tribunal or the other side unless there is an agreement or direction to do so.

Agreed facts

17.9   Some cases are heard without any live evidence being called because there is no dispute on the facts. Transfer of undertakings cases and wages protection claims might usefully centre on issues of law alone.

---

2   See Practice Guide 1 of the CPR, paras 59–63.

So it might be worthwhile to draft a statement and send it to the other side to see if agreement is possible.

Witness statements

17.10   Each party should decide which witnesses it is likely to call and take a detailed statement from them.

17.11   Evidence from non-expert witnesses is generally called for in the form of written statements, for which power is given by the case management provisions of 2001 Regs reg 10 and 2001 Rules r4(3) (see para 18.75). The notes to accompany the notice of hearing in England and Wales include the following (see appendix C):

> The length of the hearing and the consequent expense may be reduced if you prepare written statements for yourself and your witnesses. Such statements may help you and your witnesses to include all the matters that you consider important. You may then apply at the hearing for the evidence you wish your witness to give to be read by him or her from the statement. It will be for the tribunal to decide whether the witness can do so after hearing what you and the other party have to say about it. If the written statement is read, the witness may be questioned by the other party, and the tribunal.

17.12   The statement should therefore be in a form which can be disclosed in full to the other side and to the tribunal. There is no general requirement to exchange or send it in advance, although this may be ordered by the tribunal under 2001 Regs reg 10 and 2001 Rules r4. Witness statements are rarely used in Northern Ireland. They were never used in Scotland before the power was given to order this to be done by rule 4 of the 2001 Rules applicable in Scotland.

17.13   A party should also consider whether an expert is needed, for example, on job evaluation in an equal pay case, or on the issue of whether an applicant is 'disabled' in claims under the Disability Discrimination Act 1995. Evidence given by an expert in the form of an opinion in the civil courts must be provided in advance of the trial, and there is now a presumption that oral evidence will not be given by that expert, unless the court gives permission.[3] CPR 35.7 encourages the use of a jointly instructed expert in all but the most complex of cases. The EAT in *DeKeyser Ltd v Wilson*[3a] have stated that

---

3   CPR 35.5. See also the Practice Direction to Part 35.
3a   [2001] IRLR 324, EAT.

the instruction of a joint expert is the 'preferred course', going on to set out guidelines to be followed when drawing up joint instructions. There is no specific requirement for a report to be provided in advance at a tribunal but if an expert witness is produced without prior notice or an indication of the nature of his or her evidence, an application for adjournment is likely to be granted and costs could be awarded against the party producing the expert evidence. It is obviously unsatisfactory for one party to be unprepared for the evidence of an expert. Without advance access to its own expert, the other side is unable properly to evaluate, cross-examine and challenge any opinion given.

Documents

17.14   Parties are encouraged to agree what documents are going to be put to the tribunal, and this may be ordered by the tribunal (2001 Rules r4(3)). In unfair dismissal cases the employer will usually open the case and the preparation of the index and paginated bundles should be up to its representative in the first place. Both sides should have a clear idea of the relevant material and the best way to present it. Usually this will be in chronological order, but there may be separate issues, or separate originating applications which justify discrete bundles or sections.

17.15   If an application for the costs to be paid by the losing side is to be made, perhaps on the ground of being put to unnecessary preparation, a separate bundle should be prepared for this purpose to use at the end of the hearing (see para 20.31).

Authorities to be referred to

17.16   It is necessary to consider what law is relevant to the case. A list of cases to be referred to should be handed in to the clerk at the tribunal on the hearing day, and exchanged with the other side before that. It is helpful to the tribunal and to your own submissions if a bundle of photocopies is provided for each tribunal member so that they and the representatives can highlight the relevant passages.

17.17   Tribunals and the Employment Appeal Tribunal are not required to follow the practice which applies in all civil courts[4] of requiring

4   [2000] 1 WLR 1001.

advocates to cite only one authority for each proposition and to cite the proposition for which the case stands. But as a matter of common sense, representatives should adopt this practice. Nor do they follow the practice of the Court of Appeal[5] in requiring cases to be cited in the *Industrial Cases Reports* (ICR) if there is a choice of law report; *Industrial Relations Law Reports* (IRLR) and other reports may be used. Tribunals are flexible. The IRLR are provided free to all chairmen and are more readily available to lay and professional representatives, with good CD-ROM and index facilities. To maintain uniformity, it is sensible to use either IRLR or ICR consistently.

17.18   The tribunal chairman (but not the lay members) will have access to the legislation, so if it is necessary to refer to several statutes and European directives, it will help the case to have these photocopied for all three members too.

Warning witnesses to attend

17.19   A representative on the record is responsible for ensuring that the client is warned of the hearing date and that notice of the hearing is given to witnesses. A witness should be sent the final version of his or her statement and asked to sign it. There is nothing wrong in all witnesses seeing each others' statements, and indeed it saves time if a witness can comment in his or her own statement on evidence in other statements, especially if both people were at the same meeting or saw the same events. This is not encouraged in Scotland, where witnesses do not know other witnesses' testimony, and are not permitted to sit in the tribunal hearing before they give their own evidence.

5   [1995] 1 WLR 1096.

CHAPTER 18

The hearing

continued

Introduction

18.1   This chapter sets out the principal features of a tribunal hearing, and refers to the law relating to procedure, and advice on the best practice in conducting a hearing. The right of every person to have a fair hearing by an independent and impartial tribunal is now *guaranteed* through the Human Rights Act 1998 (HRA 1998), which incorporates the European Convention on Human Rights ('the Convention') into UK law. (See particularly ECHR article 6).

Administration

Arrangements at the tribunal

18.2   All tribunal hearing centres have a reception check-in to enable parties and witnesses to register. It is important for all who are likely to be called as witnesses to register either personally or through their representative. This is because the list of witnesses is then seen by the tribunal who can quickly decide whether their knowledge of any witness might cause them to be excused from hearing the case. Representatives will also find it useful to see the list of the other side's witnesses, especially where no statements have been given in advance.

18.3   In most hearing centres there are separate rooms for parties and witnesses for each side of the case, ie, applicants and respondents. This appears to be the only civil forum where separation is deemed necessary – the civil courts do not have separated waiting areas. In some centres conference rooms are available free of charge on a first come, first served basis.

18.4   In some hearing centres rooms are made available for members of the tribunal adjacent to the hearing rooms. This enables the members to enter and withdraw while the parties are in the room. In other centres, no facilities are available and so the tribunal is already seated on the bench when the parties are ushered in by the tribunal clerk. Whenever possible, it is useful for clients and witnesses to see the tribunal room's layout before the hearing starts in order to feel comfortable.

18.5   While waiting for the case to come on, applicants are frequently asked if they are claiming jobseeker's allowance or income support and if so, to give the name of the office where they are registered and their national insurance number. This is in case an award of compensation is made and recoupment of benefits provisions apply. At the same time the tribunal clerk will take a note of the full name and job title or position of each witness and establish whether the witness is to swear an oath and if so, on which holy text, or whether the witness will affirm.

Listing

18.6　Parties are warned in the advance notes sent to them that the case may not start on time. This is because the policy of the tribunals is to overbook so that on any given day there will be a number of 'floaters' which will be slotted in as and when any of the cases are settled or disposed of. These floaters are not attached to any particular tribunal and will go to the first one which becomes available. If there is no reasonable prospect of the floater being reached, parties will be advised by the tribunal clerk. Another date will be fixed. Sometimes this decision is not reached until midday.

18.7　　From time to time, a major mistake occurs in listing, for example, a party is not sent a notice of hearing, or a chairman fails to appear. In such circumstances it is possible to make a claim against the Department of Trade and Industry, which administers tribunals, although there is no guarantee that such claims will be met.

Documents

18.8　Copies of documents which will be referred to should be handed in to the tribunal clerk. This enables the tribunal to have a more detailed look at the documents in the few minutes available before the hearing. In practice, tribunals do not see any documents in advance of the day of the hearing. On the day, a small bundle is prepared of the tribunal documents, ie, originating application, notice of appearance, relevant correspondence with the tribunal, orders made and directions given, but this is all that will be available to the tribunal unless the parties themselves provide a more detailed bundle. It is advantageous to hand in bundles of documents at once so that the tribunal can start reading and get a picture of the case.

18.9　　Witness statements are in a different category and are dealt with at para 17.10.

Authorities to be referred to

18.10 A list of cases to be referred to or a bundle of photocopies of the law reports should be handed in to the clerk and exchanged with the other side. It is helpful to the tribunal and to your own submissions if a bundle of photocopies is provided for each tribunal member. Otherwise only the chairman will be provided with a copy by the tribunal clerk, making it invidious for the lay members.

Procedure

18.11 By 2001 Rules r11,[1] tribunals are enjoined to avoid formality and are not bound by rules of evidence in the same way as courts are. They must make inquiries of advocates and witnesses so as to clarify the issues and handle the proceedings justly, and are of course required to carry out the overriding objective (2001 Regs reg 10)[2]. Subject to the rules of procedure which govern particular aspects of the tribunal's powers, 'a tribunal may regulate its own procedure' (2001 Rules r15(1)).

18.12 Despite the encouragement of informality, tribunals are usually conducted very formally. The requirement that tribunals should make inquiries entitles the tribunal to be more inquisitorial and directive than the courts: indeed a tribunal has the power to call a witness itself (2001 Rules r4(5)(a)). Almost all the rules of procedure may be activated by the tribunal of its own motion, whether or not any party makes an application. This combination of informality and inquiry provides the legal justification for a tribunal to take an interventionist line if it wants to.

Chairman and members

18.13 The cases where a chairman can sit without lay members are set out at para 1.20.

---

1 Employment Tribunals Rules of Procedure (contained in SI 2001 No 1171, Sch 1).
2 Employment Tribunals (Constitution and Rules of Procedure) Regulations 2001 (2001 Regs) SI No 1171.

Challenge to composition of tribunal

18.14   Given the local composition of tribunals, it is inevitable from time to time that members will know parties or witnesses in a case they are about to hear. Any direct interest in the case would automatically exclude a member from sitting.[3] That constitutes bias in the technical sense of having a pecuniary or proprietary interest in the outcome of proceedings. But objection can be made to the composition of the tribunal on far less tangible grounds, since it is important to avoid any possibility of a challenge during or after a tribunal hearing. Particularly following the incorporation of the Convention into UK law, emphasis is placed not only on bias being avoided, but also any appearance of bias.

18.15   The members should be selected at random from the panels of people drawn from both sides of employment relations. In cases of race discrimination, effect is given to an assurance given during debates on the Race Relations Act 1976 that there should be at least one member with special knowledge or experience of race relations in the employment field. A separate list of people so qualified is kept by the tribunals. The absence in a race discrimination case of such a person will not invalidate the proceedings, but administrative arrangements are generally made to ensure such a person sits.[4] A similar assurance was not given in debates on the Sex Discrimination Act 1975, but in practice administrative arrangements are usually made to ensure that members of both sexes sit on cases of sex discrimination and equal pay. No particular arrangements are made in disability cases. There are panels of chairmen and lay members who may sit in cases involving issues of national security.[4a]

18.16   The most appropriate time to make an objection about the composition of the tribunal is before the hearing starts, while it remains a potential problem and before it becomes an actual problem. In *Halford v Sharples*[5] a member had 'specialist' knowledge of personnel practices in police forces and was specifically chosen to sit on a claim

---

3   *R v Gough* [1993] AC 646, HL; see also *R v Bow Street Stipendiary Magistrate ex p Pinochet Ugarte (No 2)* [2000] 1 AC 119; [1999] 1 All ER 557, HL; *Locabail (UK) Ltd v Bayfield Properties Ltd* [2000] QB 451; [2000] IRLR 96, CA; *Director General of Fair Trading v Proprietary Association of Great Britain* [2001] 1 WLR 700, CA; *Re Medicaments and Related Classes of Goods (No 2)* [2001] ICR 564, CA.

4   *Habib v Elkington & Co Ltd* [1981] ICR 435; [1981] IRLR 344, EAT.

4a   2001 Regs reg 6.

5   [1992] ICR 146, EAT.

of sex discrimination brought by a senior officer. The Employment Appeal Tribunal (EAT) decided the tribunal should be selected at random and not by reference to any specialist experience. The proper test is:

> Could the reasonable and disinterested observer present at the hearing . . . reasonably take the view . . . that the continued presence of the member was undesirable in that a party could reasonably feel that injustice might occur during the hearing?[6]

And in *University College of Swansea v Cornelius*[7] a tribunal decision was overturned because one of the members was the mother-in-law of a person who had sat on an internal appeal.

18.17   If a list of potential witnesses has been handed in at the outset, the tribunal can consider whether any person on the list is known to any member. The proper approach is for the chairman to draw this to the attention of the parties and invite comments. Generally speaking, any objection which is not 'irresponsible, frivolous or wholly without content'[8] will be acted on. If no objection is made once the possible conflict is pointed out, the case can go on; if objection is made, the tribunal should consider whether the member should stand down.

Absence of a member

18.18   If a conflict arises before or during the course of the hearing and a member stands down, or becomes indisposed, the hearing cannot continue without him or her without consent of all parties (2001 Regs reg 9(3)). If consent is given, a decision can be made by a member and a chairman together and if they disagree the chairman has a casting vote (2001 Rules r12(1)). It is therefore imperative to weigh carefully the advantages of making an objection, since it may abort the proceedings. It is useful to know which panel (in shorthand known as TUC or CBI) the member comes from. One of the longest cases ever before a tribunal was heard by a chairman and one member following the death of the other – the claims of unfair dismissal on the grounds of trade union activity raised by dockworker shop stewards lasted for 197 days, the member dying after seven days.[9]

18.19   Consent need not be obtained from a person who is debarred from participating.

---

6   Ibid per Wood J.
7   [1988] ICR 735.
8   *Halford v Sharples*, note 5 above, at 171.
9   *Port of London Authority v Payne* [1994] ICR 555; [1994] IRLR 9, CA.

Hearing in public

18.20   The hearing of an originating application must be in public (2001 Rules r10(2)). But it can be in private if a minister so directs on the grounds of national security (2001 Rules r8(2) and Employment Tribunals Act 1996 (ETA 1996) s10). If a direction is made by a minister, it cannot be challenged in the tribunal; the only way of making a challenge is by way of judicial review.[10] The tribunal has discretion to hear certain evidence in private (2001 Rules r10(3)), but this applies only in respect of specific evidence and not speeches and other evidence or aspects of the case. In addition to the interests of national security, the grounds are that public disclosure of evidence would:

- involve breach of a statutory provision;
- involve disclosure of information given to the witness in confidence;
- cause substantial injury to any undertaking, excluding matters relating to the effect on collective bargaining.

A decision as to whether a hearing should be held in private must be made by the full tribunal[11] and there is no right for the application itself to be heard in private.

18.21   It was previously thought that there was no need for interlocutory applications to be heard in public, and a practice developed whereby they were heard by a chairman alone in chambers.[12] This was because a 'hearing', defined in 2001 Regs reg 2(1), must be in public but a 'decision' does not include the making of 'any other interlocutory order or any other decision on an interlocutory matter than striking out an originating application or notice of appearance' (2001 Regs reg 2(2)). However in *Storer v British Gas plc*[13] the Court of Appeal set aside the decision of a chairman relating to jurisdiction, which had been reached following a hearing which took place in his chambers due to the fact that there were no tribunal rooms available. As access to the chairman's chambers was only via a door secured by a push button coded lock, beyond a door marked private, there was an infringement of 2001 Rules r8(2) requiring a hearing to be in public. The *Jones* case was not considered by the Court of Appeal in *Storer*,

---

10   *Fry v Foreign and Commonwealth Office* [1997] ICR 512, EAT.
11   *Milne v Waldren* [1980] ICR 138, EAT.
12   *Jones v Enham Industries* [1983] ICR 580, EAT.
13   [2000] IRLR 495, CA.

although the view of Henry LJ was that the employment tribunal rules do not provide for any 'chambers-type procedure' as in civil courts.

18.22   In England and Wales, and Northern Ireland, witnesses are generally permitted to sit in the tribunal room before giving evidence. In Scotland those who may be called to give evidence remain outside the tribunal until they are called.

Allegations of sexual offences and sexual misconduct, and disability cases

18.23   Provisions introduced by Trade Union Reform and Employment Rights Act 1993 s40 (now ETA 1996 s11) allow tribunals to restrict reporting of cases involving sexual misconduct. Sexual misconduct means:

> . . . the commission of a sexual offence, sexual harassment or other adverse conduct (of whatever nature) related to sex, and conduct is related to sex whether the relationship with sex lies in the character of the conduct or in its having reference to the sex or sexual orientation of the person at whom the conduct is directed.[14]

18.24   In such a case (and in cases under the Disability Discrimination Act 1995 involving evidence of a personal nature, under 2001 Rules r16(2)) the tribunal, having given the opportunity to the parties to advance oral arguments, can decide to make a restricted reporting order (2001 Rules r16(3)). The order specifies the person who may not be identified in reports of the case; the order should be no wider than is necessary to prevent identification of the 'persons affected', and the tribunal must take an 'individual by individual' approach, and not simply apply a blanket ban.[15] The ban remains in force until the decision of the tribunal is promulgated unless it is revoked earlier. The EAT made it clear in *Chief Constable of the West Yorkshire Police v A*[16] that if there is a liability hearing followed by a remedies hearing, the promulgation of the decision refers to the date on which the whole proceedings are at an end, after the decision as to remedy.

18.25   A restrictive reporting order cannot be granted to prevent the identification of a body corporate.[17]

18.26   The rules require a notice to be affixed to the door of the tribunal

---

14   ETA 1996 s11(6).
15   *Associated Newspapers Ltd v London (North) Industrial Tribunal* [1998] IRLR 569, QBD.
16   [2000] IRLR 465 at 468.
17   *Leicester University v A* [1999] IRLR 352, EAT.

and to the list of cases on the notice board at the tribunal office (2001 Rules r16(5)). The effect of such a notice is to provide a warning to all journalists in the hearing centre. Breach of a restricted reporting order exposes people who publish the identity of a person to a fine (ETA 1996 s11(2)). For newspapers and other media, liability rests on the proprietor and the editor, and in respect of broadcast programmes, the company providing the service and anybody fulfilling functions corresponding to an editor. A person publishing the identity in any other form is also liable. Ignorance and lack of suspicion of the existence of an order is a defence (ETA 1996 s11(3)).

18.27   In addition to a restricted reporting order, tribunals must take certain steps where a case involves allegations of the commission of a sexual *offence*. This is defined as offences specified in the Sexual Offences (Amendment) Acts 1976 and 1992 and the Criminal Procedure (Scotland) Act 1995 s274(2) (ETA 1996 s11(6)). The tribunal office must omit from the register, or delete from it, any document recording the proceedings available to the public, and any material which might 'lead members of the public to identify any person affected by or making such an allegation' (2001 Rules r16(6)). The (possibly unintended) effect of this is to restrain publication of identifying material until the decision is promulgated and then to permit publication of names which must, on the other hand, be omitted from or deleted from the official record.

Representation at the tribunal

18.28   There is no restriction on the kind of person who may represent a party at the proceedings and so representation by counsel, solicitor, trade union official, employer's association, voluntary worker, friend or anyone at all is permitted. This is an unqualified right (ETA 1996 s6), so in *Bache v Essex CC*[18] where the tribunal dismissed a representative and directed an applicant to represent herself, the tribunal was held by the Court of Appeal to have acted outside its powers. On the facts of that case however, there would have been no difference in the outcome had this infringement not occurred, so the decision stood.

18.29   Any party may give evidence, call witnesses, question witnesses and address the tribunal (2001 Rules r11(2)). In addition, the secretary

18   [2000] IRLR 251, CA.

of state can be treated as a party in proceedings which may involve payment out of the National Insurance Fund (2001 Rules r10(7)).

18.30   A respondent who fails to comply with an order for further particulars, discovery or written answers to questions may have its notice of appearance struck out and 'where appropriate' be debarred from defending altogether (2001 Rules r4(8)). A respondent who has not entered an appearance at all cannot take part in the proceedings except to the extent that it is necessary for the purposes of an application for further particulars, an extension of time and an application for review (2001 Rules r3(3)). (See para 7.16.)

18.31   If a party which has been given notice of the hearing fails to attend or be represented, the tribunal has a wide range of powers. For an applicant, the case may be dismissed, the application may be disposed of or the hearing may be adjourned. But if the application is to be dismissed or disposed of, the tribunal must consider the originating application, notice of appearance, any written representations and any answers provided in accordance with the question and answer procedure under 2001 Rules r4(3) (2001 Rules r11(3)). In practice, some tribunal offices make inquiries to ensure that the applicant has had proper notice of the hearing by making phone calls, for example, to his or her home and employer (although this is not a requirement and no assumption should be made that a tribunal will do this). A tribunal is likely to allow some leeway to an applicant, and may take another case while waiting for the applicant to arrive. It will be reluctant to determine or dismiss the case in the absence of any explanation from the applicant, but it certainly has the power to do so and frequently regards it as inappropriate to make inquiries. In such a situation an award of costs might be appropriate under 2001 Rules r14 (see chapter 20). If there is an explanation, the decision can be set aside on an application for a review under 2001 Rules r13(1)).

Written representations

18.32   Written representations can be made to the tribunal. They should be sent seven days before the hearing with copies to other parties, but the tribunal has power to consider them even if they have been submitted within seven days of the hearing (2001 Rules rr10(5) and 15(2)(c)). In practice the tribunal will welcome the presentation of written arguments in skeleton form. A short summary of the issues in opening, or a skeleton argument and draft findings of fact presented in closing, are usually accepted gratefully. They save time and release the tribunal from making detailed notes on oral submissions.

18.33 The real purpose of the rule allowing for written submissions is not clear: they do not replace oral evidence, especially as the tribunal has power to call witnesses and ask questions (2001 Rules r4(5)). In pre-hearing reviews, however, written representations are crucial (see chapter 13).

Adjournment or postponement

18.34 The circumstances in which an adjournment or postponement is ordered are dealt with in chapter 15. The tribunal has a very wide discretion and in addition has a discretion specifically in relation to costs caused by a postponement or adjournment (2001 Rules r14(4) and (5)).

The issue to be determined

18.35 In most cases the issue to be determined will be clear: unfair dismissal, unlawful deduction, sex discrimination, etc. But in unfair dismissal cases, for example, tribunals often preferred to take evidence and make a decision on liability before dealing with remedies. This practice (which did not apply in Scotland) is now firmly discouraged, since the parties are warned in the listing letter to allow for all the time needed for the tribunal to reach a decision on all issues including remedy. It is important at the outset that the tribunal should announce, having considered representations, what issue it is about to determine. If, rarely, liability and remedy are to be determined at a split hearing, it should also be made clear by the tribunal whether or not evidence is to be heard relating to liability for contributory fault or other conduct under Employment Rights Act 1996 (ERA 1996) ss122(2) and 123(6).[19]

18.36 It would be contrary to the rules of natural justice for a tribunal which had announced it was to deal with only one issue to make findings on more than one without giving the parties an opportunity to make representations and call further evidence. If an announcement has not been made at the outset, it must be assumed that evidence should be called relating to mitigation, remedies, reinstatement, a *Polkey*[19a] reduction and so on.

---

19 See *Iggesund Converters Ltd v Lewis* [1984] ICR 544; [1984] IRLR 431, EAT.
19a *Polkey v EA Dayton Services Ltd* [1987] IRLR 503, HL.

18.37   If remedies are to be dealt with after a finding, or evidence, on liability, it is important to ensure that a date is fixed for the resumed hearing on remedies, should the tribunal make a finding in favour of the applicant. It is also convenient for all issues of liability, ie, liability and contributory conduct, to be dealt with at a single hearing, since the evidence will be more or less the same, and it will enable the parties to make headway on negotiating a settlement following a successful result for the applicant once it is known whether, and if so to what extent, the applicant contributed to the dismissal.

18.38   Separate hearings are usually convenient for testing the material factor defence in equal pay claims.

18.39   In constructive dismissal cases, it is usually unhelpful to separate the issue of breach of contract from unfair dismissal (see para 14.6). Again, the evidence is likely to be coterminous so that the applicant will be producing evidence to show that the employer behaved so badly that there was a breach of contract, and the employer will produce material either denying the facts said to constitute a breach of contract or seeking to show it behaved fairly.

18.40   In these circumstances, not much is to be gained by splitting the legal issues from the factual issues under ERA 1996 ss95(1) and 98(4). Most tribunals hearing an application to separate these considerations will hear all the evidence and make determinations on dismissal, ie, repudiation under ERA 1996 s95, reason for dismissal under ERA 1996 s98(1) and reasonableness of the dismissal under ERA 1996 s98(4). If the tribunal finds there was no dismissal, it is useful (for any future appeal) to invite the tribunal before the end of the hearing to make decisions on the alternative hypothesis that if there *was* a dismissal, it was fair or alternatively unfair.

Late amendment, new allegations, late disclosure

18.41   Disputes about documents should be resolved at the outset of the hearing; as should any last minute amendments to the originating application, notice of appearance and answers given to written requests. Concessions should also be made at this stage. Of course, amendments and concessions can be made during the course of proceedings. They are usually made orally, and if necessary can be reduced into writing at the end of the day.

Who goes first?

18.42   The running order should normally depend on where the onus of proof lies. As a rule of thumb, first in, last out operates so that the party who has to prove any particular issue goes first and finishes last, ie, gives evidence first and makes the last speech. Once the onus of proof falls on a party, that party has not only the duty but the right to go first.[20] In unfair dismissal cases the onus of proof lies initially on the employer: to show the reason for dismissal and that it falls within the categories of fair dismissal in ERA 1996 s98(1) and (2). The practical effect is that the employer goes first.

18.43   If the dismissal is not admitted, the onus of proof is on the employee. This assertion will be made either in the notice of appearance or at the outset of the hearing. If the employer disputes that there has been a constructive dismissal and claims the employee resigned or retired, the onus of proof is on the employee.

18.44   The onus is on the employer where there is a challenge to the jurisdiction of the tribunal, for example, because the applicant is said not to have the one year's continuous service entitling him or her to bring a claim of unfair dismissal, or in a DDA 1995 case where there are less than 15 employees. This practice has been approved by the EAT in *Post Office Counters Ltd v Heavey*.[21] But since the tribunal is free to adopt its own procedure, subject to the rules it can decide to ask the employee to go first.[22]

18.45   Certain practical factors affect the way in which tribunals make this decision. If the applicant is unrepresented and is making allegations of unfair dismissal in a general way, it is often useful for the applicant to go first, not least because the concept of 'putting your case' is difficult to grasp (it means ensuring that every part of the case is put first to an employer's witness). If the employer is represented by a solicitor or counsel, the tribunal often invites the lawyer to outline briefly the facts and legal issues before inviting the applicant to give evidence.

18.46   Although in almost all unfair dismissal cases where the dismissal is admitted the employer's evidence is taken first, there is logically no reason why this should be the case when a dismissal for a particular reason is accepted by the applicant. For example, the applicant claims

---

20   *Gill v Harold Andrews Sheepbridge Ltd* [1974] ICR 294; [1974] IRLR 109, NIRC.
21   [1990] ICR 1; [1989] IRLR 513.
22   *Hawker Siddeley Power Engineering Ltd v Rump* [1979] IRLR 425, EAT.

she was dismissed, the reason given is dishonesty and the applicant accepts that that was the reason but argues that the facts do not disclose dishonesty or do not give grounds for a dismissal in the circumstances. Here the employer has discharged the onus of proving the reason and a potentially fair reason and therefore, there being no onus of proof under ERA 1996 s98(4), it is more logical to allow the applicant to make her allegations first and then to hear the evidence relating to the employer's explanation.

18.47   In both discrimination and dismissal cases there can be a very real advantage to the applicant in going first which should be seized if at all possible. In lengthy dismissal cases where the respondent opens, the first the tribunal hears from the applicant is after several days of evidence given by managers painting a very negative picture of his or her behaviour. In sex discrimination cases, the applicant naturally wishes to establish at the outset the wrong done to him or her. If the tribunal allows an opening speech to be made (see para 18.51), this is the ideal opportunity for a statement to be made. And of course the press is more likely to be in attendance at the start of a hearing than halfway through.

18.48   In claims for redundancy payments there is a presumption that a dismissal is on account of redundancy (ERA 1996 s163(2)). So an employer who claims the reason for dismissal was not redundancy would go first, the onus being on the employer to prove this.

18.49   In claims combining unfair dismissal and discrimination,[22a] we suggest that as between the duty of the employer to show a reason for a dismissal and the right of an applicant to open a discrimination case, priority should be given to the applicant's right so that he or she would open all aspects of the discrimination and dismissal cases.

18.50   In equal pay cases where a material factor defence is raised under Equal Pay Act 1970 s1(3), the onus is on the employer. But the applicant is still required to show an employment relationship and establish the basic facts against which (it is contended by the employer) a material factor defence exists to a claim for equal pay. Again, on a purely practical basis, the applicant should be allowed to open his or her case and call evidence. Although the focus of attention will quickly shift to the employer's material factor defence, at least the applicant will have established elementary components in his or her claim and the tribunal will have heard from him or her. At least one

22a For instance, race or disability discrimination, where there is a difference of sex and less favourable treatment then the burden of proof is on the respondent to show this was not unlawful discrimination.

major equal pay case went to the Court of Appeal, back to the tribunal, then was referred to an independent expert, and it was more than five years before any claimant gave evidence.[23]

The opening speech

18.51   There is a right to make an opening speech only in appeals against training levies, prohibition, improvement and non-discrimination notices.[24] Otherwise there is no formal right. Rule 11(2) of the 2001 Rules entitles a party 'to address the tribunal' but this does not require the address to be made at the start of the case. Furthermore, 2001 Rules r11(2) is subject to 2001 Rules r11(1), which gives the tribunal a wide discretion as to the handling of the proceedings. In Scotland, opening speeches are never made, except for appeals (above). In England and Wales, and Northern Ireland, a brief opening is sometimes permitted. If there are several applicants, each should be given the same right to open, as should multiple respondents if they open. If a respondent employer opens a case, the applicant employee coming second does not in practice make an opening speech.

18.52   The purpose of an opening speech is to make a brief impression on the tribunal and to give a summary of the principal issues of law and of where disputes of fact will lie, together with a statement of what the person opening the case hopes to achieve. An outline of the evidence to be called and the names of witnesses is often given but is not necessary. As a matter of practicality, it is important to direct the tribunal to the relevant statutes (not quite so necessary in respect of ERA 1996 s98) and the names and at least the headnotes of relevant authorities which should be borne in mind by the tribunal during the hearing.

18.53   It is not necessary to explore the bundles of documents. These will have to be examined by the relevant witnesses in any event – for example a letter written by the manager dismissing the applicant will be examined by the writer and the recipient when they give their evidence. A brief introduction to the issues of law and fact to be decided will generally be welcomed by the tribunal, but its patience will be tried if the documents are read at the outset. The law should be described neutrally but there is nothing wrong in making tendentious statements on your case at this stage.

---

23   *Bromley v H & J Quick Ltd* [1988] ICR 623; [1988] IRLR 249, CA.
24   2001 Regs Schs 4–6 (SI No 1171).

Conduct of the hearing

18.54   Within the scope of the tribunal's duty under 2001 Rules r11(1) to avoid formality and conduct the proceedings 'in such manner as it considers most appropriate for the clarification of the issues . . . and the just handling of the proceedings', the tribunal has a very wide discretion. The duty clearly envisages a 'hands-on' approach if a tribunal cares to take it. The following issues may well arise in a hearing.

Natural justice: a fair hearing

18.55   The conduct of the hearing is subject to the rules of procedure (but not the civil law of evidence) and the rules of natural justice. They are now crystallised in the jurisprudence under article 6 of the Convention, incorporated by the HRA 1998. These are that each side should be given the opportunity to present its case through evidence and argument and to cross-examine each other's witnesses. A decision should not be made on any issue about which a party has not been given the opportunity to present evidence and address arguments.[25] As Lord Bridge said in *Lloyd v McMahon*:[26]

> . . . the so-called rules of natural justice are not engraved on tablets of stone . . . [W]hat the requirements of fairness demand when any body, domestic, administrative or judicial, has to make a decision which will affect the rights of individuals depends on the character of the decision-making body, the kind of decision it has to make and the statutory or other framework in which it operates . . .

And in *Wiseman v Borneman*[27] Lord Reid said:

> Natural justice requires that the procedure before any tribunal which is acting judicially should be fair in all the circumstances, and I would be sorry to see this fundamental general principle degenerate into a series of hard and fast rules.

The right to a hearing under ECHR art 6 does not include a right to legal representation where no criminal charge is involved.[27a]

---

25   *Laurie v Holloway* [1994] ICR 32, EAT.
26   [1987] AC 625 at 702.
27   [1971] AC 297 at 308.
27a See, for example, *R v Securities and Futures Authority Ltd and another ex p Fleurose* [2001] IRLR 764.

Formality

18.56 In *Aberdeen Steak Houses v Ibrahim*[28] the EAT laid down its own summary of what was required of tribunals under the rules of natural justice:

> Over the years a number of cases have given guidance on the appropriate procedure and on rules of evidence . . .
> a) Decisions bearing upon the party who should present his case first: *Gill v Harold Andrews Sheepbridge Ltd* [1974] ICR 294 and *Oxford v DHSS* [1977] ICR 884.
> b) It is for the party and not the tribunal to decide the order in which he calls his witnesses: *Barnes v BPC (Business Forms) Ltd* [1975] ICR 390.
> c) It is the duty of the parties to ensure that all relevant evidence is put before the tribunal and that it is not for the tribunal themselves to do this: *Craig v British Railways (Scottish Region)* (1973) 8 ITR 636; *Derby City Council v Marshall* [1979] ICR 731; *Mensah v East Hertfordshire NHS Trust* [1998] IRLR 531, CA.
> d) A tribunal should not allow a party to be taken by surprise by an allegation of dishonesty made at the last minute, but should adjourn and give directions: *Hotson v Wisbech Conservative Club* [1984] ICR 859.
> e) Where a party specifically states that he will not be calling evidence, he will normally be bound by his statement: *Stokes v Hampstead Wine Co Ltd* [1979] IRLR 298.
> f) Tribunals cannot refuse to admit evidence which is admissible and probative of one or more issues: *Rosedale Mouldings Ltd v Sibley* [1980] ICR 816.

Nevertheless in the same case the tribunal eschewed informality in accordance with 2001 Rules r11 and said:

> It is possible for informality to go too far and it is important for parties appearing before any judicial body and for their legal advisers in preparing for trial to know the rules normally to be applied during the hearing. It is important there should be consistency . . . Total informality and absence of generally recognised rules of procedure and evidence can be counter-productive.

The application of these judgments would ensure that tribunals do behave quite formally.

---

28 [1988] ICR 550 at 557 per Wood J; [1988] IRLR 420.

Admissibility of evidence

Estoppel

18.57   Estoppel is a rule of evidence which prevents cases, or issues in cases, being litigated twice. It operates as a defence and can be raised in tribunal proceedings.[29] An issue decided by a tribunal between the same parties will prevent either of the parties reopening the issue in, for example, subsequent tribunal proceedings or parallel county court or High Court proceedings.[30]

18.58   The rule can prevent the reopening of a single issue or a whole cause of action. But the original decision must have been within the competence of the original tribunal and have been essential for the decision in that case. Otherwise the decision will be obiter dicta, not binding on subsequent tribunals and courts.

18.59   The EAT held in the case of *AKO v Rothschild Asset Management Limited and another*[31] that where a claim was dismissed by the employment tribunal on withdrawal by the applicant at a stage before the respondent had even entered a notice of appearance, such that there was merely an administrative step by a chairman, rather than a considered decision of a tribunal, that applicant was not estopped from raising the same points in subsequent proceedings. The EAT therefore distinguished this situation from *Barber v Staffordshire CC*[32] where an applicant who had lodged a claim in the employment tribunal, which was dismissed on withdrawal on the day of the hearing, was estopped from launching further proceedings on the same factual basis, in circumstances where the case had been going on for six months, a notice of appearance was entered, directions given, and a panel of three members were presented with a compromise agreement wherein the applicant withdrew her claim and the respondent undertook not to make any applications (the clear inference being costs application).

Hearsay

18.60   A statement made by a person who is not a witness in proceedings, adduced for the purpose of establishing the truth of what that person

---

29 *Henderson v Henderson* [1843] Hare 100; *Munir v Jang Publications Ltd* [1989] ICR 1; [1989] IRLR 224, CA.

30 *Green v Hampshire CC* [1979] ICR 861 and *O'Laoire v Jackel International Ltd* [1990] ICR 197; [1991] IRLR 70, CA.

31 EAT/103/00, 20 April 2001, available on EAT website at www.employmentappeals.gov.uk.

32 [1996] IRLR 209, CA.

said, is hearsay and would be admissible in a court to the extent permitted by the Civil Evidence Act 1995. Tribunals may and frequently do take hearsay evidence. It is quite proper, albeit tactically injudicious, to object to it being heard at the time, and to lay down a marker so that in a closing speech the tribunal can be asked to pay less attention to that evidence because it was not subject to cross-examination. But it must be borne in mind that since the 1995 Act, hearsay is generally let in, and objecting to it is generally pointless. Once in, it can be criticised as being of light weight, but that is different.

18.61   Quite often the issue before a tribunal is not the truth, but what was known to an employer at the time a decision to dismiss was made. So in *Coral Squash Clubs Ltd v Matthews*[33] it was held that it was quite proper and indeed necessary for hearsay evidence to be adduced before the tribunal about information given to the employer. It did not matter whether the information was correct or not; the central question was what material was available before the employer decided to dismiss. Clearly, if the information is unsatisfactory and requires further investigation, it will often be unreasonable for the employer to dismiss on that basis.

18.62   The short point about hearsay evidence is that anyone who has relevant evidence must be brought to the tribunal as a witness. The more important their evidence, the more necessary it is for them to be there. If they are going to give evidence, hearsay evidence from another witness is unnecessary. If they are not going to give evidence, hearsay evidence is of limited weight. Objection at the moment of its being given is often counter-productive, but the point should be made when addressing the tribunal in a closing speech.

Material before and after the relevant event

18.63   As a general rule, events after the relevant date are immaterial, for example, after the date of dismissal in an unfair dismissal case.[34] In such a case the central question is the information available to the employer at the time of the dismissal.

18.64   In cases of discrimination, particularly where the applicant still works for the employer, events before and after the event giving rise to the claim may be introduced in evidence 'if logically probative of a relevant fact'. In *Chattopadhyay v Headmaster of Holloway School*,[35] for

---

33   [1979] ICR 607; [1979] IRLR 390, EAT.
34   *Devis Ltd v Atkins* [1977] ICR 662; [1977] IRLR 314, HL.
35   [1982] ICR 132; [1981] IRLR 487, EAT.

the purpose of proving racial discrimination, evidence was admissible of hostility to the applicant both before the relevant event and after it.

18.65   If what is alleged is a series of discriminatory acts, then of course all evidence within the relevant time period will be admissible.

Without prejudice communications

18.66   These should not be introduced in the proceedings in evidence-in-chief or cross-examination (see para 10.39). If you want to protect your position on an offer to settle, mark the offer 'without prejudice except as to costs'. It can then be opened up once the decision has been made and the only argument is over costs, or costs after a good offer has been made and rejected, either to offer or to accept a certain sum.

Credibility and collateral matters

18.67   As Wood J said in *Aberdeen Steak Houses Ltd v Ibrahim*:[36]

> When in cross-examination questions go to credit only, the party cross-examining should be bound by the answers of the witness.

18.68   This means strictly that it is not possible to call evidence to contradict evidence given by a witness going to the witness's credibility. It is part of a rule which prevents the admission of collateral evidence as to character or disposition indicating (largely to create an aura of prejudice) that the witness is inclined on previous occasions to have done wrong and therefore is likely to have done so on the occasion in question.

18.69   In *Snowball v Gardner Merchant Ltd*[37] an applicant complaining of persistent sex discrimination was cross-examined as to her propensity to talk to fellow employees freely about sexual matters. She denied this and it was anticipated that evidence would be called by the employers to show that she was lying. The EAT upheld the admissibility of this evidence. The applicant argued that her attitude was in any event irrelevant to the question of whether she had been sexually harassed, but the EAT held that such evidence was relevant to any injury or detriment she may have claimed. It was therefore admitted even though indirectly it went to her credit (as was its purpose).

18.70   The general rule, more likely to be enforced in the light of the rule relating to the non-disclosure of the identity of those affected by allegations of sexual misconduct (para 18.23), is that evidence given in

---

36 [1988] ICR 550.
37 [1987] ICR 719; [1987] IRLR 397, EAT.

cross-examination relating to credit is binding on those doing the cross-examining, and no new evidence may be brought to contradict it. Furthermore, evidence of an alleged propensity to sexual permissiveness is not relevant, and is therefore collateral, to the central issue of liability for sexual harassment. It is also unlikely to stand up to the right to privacy in article 8 of the Convention.

18.71   It follows that, contrary to cases in criminal courts, evidence as to character is seldom going to be admissible.[38]

Sworn evidence

18.72   Tribunals are given power to administer oaths by 2001 Rules r11(4). In practice, an oath or affirmation is invariably taken from witnesses. Similarly, in cases where interpreters are used, they are required to take an oath or affirmation that they will interpret truthfully and faithfully what the witness says. The usual practice in the absence of a clerk is for the chairman to administer the oath or affirmation. A supply of holy books is available in all tribunals, and staff have been instructed to pay particular attention to the respectful preservation and handling of them.

18.73   Interpreters can also be used to assist disabled parties and witnesses, and the tribunal may award fees expenses to enable them to attend. An application should be made at an early stage to the tribunal.

Notes of evidence

18.74   There is no statutory requirement for the chairman or other members to take notes. However, it has been held that a clear note should be taken of the relevant evidence by the chairman which should be made available if directed by the EAT in an appeal alleging, for example, perversity.[39] The Tribunals and Inquiries Act 1992 s10, which regulates tribunals, requires the relevant tribunal to give reasons; this is specifically required by 2001 Rules r12(3); and is a requirement of a judicial body such as a tribunal under article 6 of the Convention. If the reasons cannot be traced to the notes of evidence, or the agreed documents, the tribunal decision is perverse.

---

38 Although, in criminal courts, it is now the case that cross-examination as to a complainant's sexual history is not permitted without leave of the court, such leave only being granted when belief as to consent is in issue: Youth Justice and Criminal Evidence Act 1999 s41.

39 *Houston v Lightwater Farms Ltd* [1990] ICR 502; [1990] IRLR 469, EAT.

Witness statements

18.75 Evidence from non-expert witnesses is increasingly called for in the form of written statements (see 2001 Rules r4(1) and para 17.13, note 3). This almost corresponds to the production of witness statements by exchange in the civil court.[40] The practice in the tribunals is to encourage parties to exchange witness statements, and this may be the subject of an order.

18.76 The witness statement itself is not evidence until it is adduced by the relevant witness. Practice varies from region to region but it is usual for a witness to read his or her own statement. He or she may be asked supplementary questions by the representative of the party for whom he or she is giving evidence, but permission is required to do this. It is most likely when this party's case is presented second, since the witness may need to deal with any conflicts which have emerged in the case thus far.

18.77 Witness statements are a very powerful tool. Given proper attention, a witness's evidence can be honed to perfection by skilled advisers. Since they are not always exchanged in advance, it is difficult to cross-examine immediately on every line in the statement. Examination-in-chief in the traditional way, without handing in a statement, gives more time to absorb the material and prepare cross-examination in addition to that prepared in advance. Mutual exchange is now common practice where parties are represented at a tribunal. Sometimes the procedure is shortened even further – if there are no other people present in the tribunal apart from the parties and their witnesses, the tribunal itself may retire to read the witness statements. Even if the public is present, statements can be taken 'as read' if a copy is left on the clerk's table for the public to read.

18.78 Live evidence given by a person who has not presented a written statement cannot be excluded on that ground alone, and it will be a breach of the rules of natural justice and article 6 of the Convention to refuse to hear it.

18.79 Witnesses who provide a written statement for lawyers and other representatives should carefully read the statement, making alterations and corrections as appropriate, and sign it if correct. One advantage of written statements is that the parties can see where the conflict lies if, before the hearing, there has been an exchange of statements.

40 See CPR 32.4.

The sequence of evidence

Evidence-in-chief

18.80   On the assumption that the employer is opening the case, evidence-in-chief from the primary witness will be called first. If a witness statement exists, it should be read. Questions may be asked in non-leading form. The best answers are monosyllabic or at most one-liners. It is important that the witness gives evidence in relation to all matters about which he or she has any information. In particular, he or she should be asked about all documents in the bundle for which he or she is responsible, ie, those he or she has written, or, for example, if the personnel manager, documents relevant to the personnel function – procedure agreements, disciplinary codes and so on. Witnesses should also be asked about letters which they have received so that they can say what they did when they received them and what their reaction was to them. All relevant matters must be spoken to.[41]

18.81   Leading questions must not be asked without the tribunal's permission.

Cross-examination

18.82   The (usually elusive) goal of cross-examination is extraction of an admission on one of the main issues in favour of the party cross-examining. Such admissions are quite rare and admissions as to motives may be of limited value. Even an admission that the employer did not behave fairly or reasonably is not conclusive of the issue; the tribunal will still have to make up its own mind irrespective of admissions made by a witness for one of the parties. That in a sense is a question of opinion. Admissions as to facts will however be important.

18.83   The more prosaic purpose of cross-examination is to ensure that all points of the applicant's case have been put to the respondent. The applicant cannot raise evidence about matters which they have not given the respondent witnesses an opportunity to comment on. If such questions are raised, it is likely to invoke an application to recall one of the respondent's witnesses which will have the attendant disadvantage of reinforcing that witness's testimony by leaving in the mind of the tribunal the enduring image of the witness.

18.84   Cross-examination consists of asking leading questions and is not

---

41   *Aberdeen Steak Houses v Ibrahim* [1988] ICR 550; [1988] IRLR 420, EAT.

restricted to material which has been adduced in-chief. Questioning can be on any matter relevant to the issues to be decided, but a party does not have 'an absolute right to cross-examine come what may'; the issue being asked about must be 'of assistance' to the tribunal.[42] Any document about which the witness has some relevant input can also be put in cross-examination.

Questions by the tribunal

18.85 The most appropriate time for this to occur is immediately following cross-examination, but practices vary. For example, some tribunals ask questions throughout the hearing, some remain silent until after re-examination. The advantage in having the tribunal ask questions immediately following cross-examination is that it cuts down on the number of opportunities given to the representatives to ask further questions and therefore saves time. If questions are asked at this stage, the tribunal ought, in accordance with the rules of natural justice, to allow an opportunity to cross-examine on any new matter arising out of questions by the tribunal.

Re-examination

18.86 This ought to be strictly confined to matters which have been raised in cross-examination and in questions by the tribunal. If a document has been raised in cross-examination, the whole of the document can be the subject of re-examination. As before, questions must be in non-leading form. If you have forgotten to put a point, it is better to own up, seek leave from the tribunal, and offer the other side an opportunity to cross-examine on it.

Power of tribunal to call witnesses of its own initiative

18.87 Rule 4(3) of the 2001 Rules states that the tribunal may, on application of either party or of its own motion, require the attendance of any person, including a party as a witness. In *Clapson v British Airways*[43] the EAT held that, in a case where the applicant decided not to give evidence, the tribunal was entitled to issue a witness order compelling him to do so. Furthermore, under 2001 Rules r11(1) the tribunal could then decide that both sides be permitted to cross-examine that witness. The EAT stated that the procedure in an employment

---

42 *Zurich Insurance Co v Gulson* [1998] IRLR 118, EAT.
43 [2001] IRLR 184.

tribunal was part inquisitorial and part adversarial; it is a procedure peculiar to itself and not equivalent to the Civil Procedure Rules followed in county courts (where a judge cannot order that a person gives evidence).

Rulings during the course of the hearing

18.88   Depending on the degree of intervention by the chairman, tribunals make rulings from time to time or throughout a hearing. Parties are encouraged to move on in their questioning and to give more attention to certain points, and they 'need not be troubled by' a particular point. A chairman might openly reflect on what appear to the tribunal to be the essentials of the case. Most of this is done as directions without being the subject of a formal ruling. However, three situations may call for a ruling in the course of the hearing.

Admissibility of evidence

18.89   If there is a dispute on the admissibility of evidence, with arguments addressed by both sides, the chairman should be asked to give a ruling. The ruling may be accompanied by reasons at the time or by an undertaking that the reasons will form part of the reasons for the substantive decision.

Half-time submission of no case to answer

18.90   After the presentation of the whole of one side's evidence and the closing of its case, it is sometimes possible to make a submission that there is no case to answer. The EAT has approved this practice for both simple unfair dismissal cases and for constructive dismissals.[44] The device is particularly appropriate where there is a burden of proof and the party with the burden has a very weak case, or where an essential component for liability is missing. Such submissions are, however, rare.

18.91   The party making the submission is not required by the tribunal to make an 'election' as is the rule in criminal cases. In other words, the party does not have to choose between a submission and calling no evidence. If the submission fails, evidence can still be called. The only danger to representatives is that the submission should not include a statement that no evidence will be called. This happened in

---

44   *George A Palmer Ltd v Beeby* [1978] ICR 196; *Walker v Josiah Wedgwood & Sons Ltd* [1978] ICR 744; [1978] IRLR 105.

Stokes v Hampstead Wine Co Ltd[45] and so when the submission was rejected, the tribunal refused to allow the party to call any evidence. There is thus no formal risk to the case except the inherent danger that in making the submission you draw attention to a weakness or missing component in the other side's case, which may be put right on cross-examination of your own witnesses.

18.92   It is dangerous to call no evidence if the submission has been rejected. The tribunal will have made clear that it needs further persuasion and probably more evidence before it makes a decision in the respondent's favour on the merits.

18.93   Because of the tripartite character of the tribunal, it is less likely than a court or a chairman sitting alone to accept such a submission. Tribunals generally prefer to have both sides give their evidence. This is particularly so when the party going first is unrepresented and the party going second is represented.

18.94   In *Coral Squash Clubs Ltd v Matthews*[46] Slynn J said:

> . . . this Appeal tribunal has never said that the industrial tribunal cannot stop a hearing at the end of the case of the party whose evidence and submissions come first. It clearly is a power which must be exercised with caution; but if the tribunal is satisfied that the party upon whom the onus lies and who goes first has clearly failed either in law or in fact to establish what he set out to establish, then . . . the tribunal is entitled to decide the case at that stage.

18.95   A middle road which often emerges is encouragement by the tribunal to the parties to 'consider their positions' and try and settle. This practice, if done subtly and without expressing a firm view, is encouraged by the EAT as a means of shortening cases. For example, having heard the employer's witnesses about the circumstances of a dismissal and the absence of a proper procedure to deal with it, there may be little the applicant needs to add for a finding of unfair dismissal to be made, at least on procedural grounds. If the tribunal takes the provisional view that the employer's case is hopeless when it is closed, there is no reason to give the employer the chance to improve its case by exposing the applicant to cross-examination.

Unfairness during the hearing

18.96   The conduct of the hearing by the chairman or the interventions by members can be the subject of a complaint of bias, apparent bias or

---

45   [1979] IRLR 298, EAT.
46   [1979] ICR 607; [1979] IRLR 390, EAT.

unfairness. Indeed a complaint may now be made under article 6 of the Convention. Bias in its strict sense, and prior knowledge of members either of the subject matter of the case or of the witnesses, are grounds for complaint at the start (see para 18.14). The proper objective test to apply to the conduct of a hearing is whether a reasonable person with some knowledge of the facts would have a legitimate ground for thinking the tribunal may not be impartial.[47]

18.97   Complaints of bias should be raised by way of appeal – parties are not expected to raise such matters during the course of the hearing.[48] In *Simper* an application was made criticising the chairman's biased comments at the end of the applicant's cross-examination and before an adjourned hearing. In fact the case was remitted to a fresh tribunal, but it was stressed that the proper course is to wait until the case is concluded:

> Save in extraordinary circumstances, it cannot be right for a litigant, unhappy with what he believes to be the indications from the tribunal as to how the case is progressing, to apply, in the middle of the case, for a re-hearing before another tribunal.

This is because it is undesirable for the tribunal to have to adjudicate on its own bias.[49]

18.98   Although the test in complaints of bias is an objective one, Lord Goff has said:

> ... having ascertained the relevant circumstances, the Court should ask itself whether, having regard to those circumstances, there was a real danger of bias on the part of the relevant member of the tribunal in question, in the sense that he might unfairly regard, or have unfairly regarded, with favour, or disfavour, the case of a party to the issue under consideration by him.[50]

In applying this test, the Court of Appeal in *Locabail*[51] stated that:

> It will very often be appropriate to enquire whether the judge knew of the matter relied on as appearing to undermine his impartiality,

---

47   *Director General of Fair Trading v Proprietary Association of Great Britain* [2001] 1 WLR 700, CA and see *Greenaway Harrison Ltd v Wiles* [1994] IRLR 380, EAT.
48   *Peter Simper & Co Ltd v Cooke* [1986] IRLR 19, EAT, per Peter Gibson J.
49   *Simper* was affirmed by the EAT in *Bennett v Southwark LBC* EAT 1273/97 and 878/99, 11 January 2001, unreported. In this case the EAT held that a tribunal had been wrong to discontinue proceedings without giving the parties an opportunity to comment, in circumstances where a black representative had made allegations that he would have been treated differently if white.
50   *R v Gough* [1993] AC 646 at 670, HL; see also note 3 above.
51   *Locabail (UK) Ltd v Bayfield Properties Ltd* [2000] IRLR 96, CA.

because it if is shown that he did not know of it the danger of it having influenced his judgment is eliminated and the appearance of possible bias is dispelled.

18.99 Tribunal members frequently raise matters themselves if they consider that a party could take objection. A common sense approach was taken in the case of *Williams v HM Inspector of Taxes*, one of the cases heard with *Locabail*,[52] where the Court of Appeal held that the suggestion of there being apparent bias on the part of a tribunal chairman who had once worked for the Inland Revenue in a junior capacity 35 years before, was fanciful.

18.100 If the conduct of the tribunal does become unacceptable, it is worth bearing in mind the *EAT Practice Direction* of April 1996[53] which provides (at para 9) that full particulars of any complaint must be given in the notice of appeal, and affidavits must be sworn by the complainant or relevant witnesses and advisers. These will all be sent to the chairman for appropriate comments.

18.101 This means that a party will need to be ready to justify fully any allegation made. In practice, complaints are rare and successful complaints even rarer.

18.102 On the other hand, complaints about the conduct of the hearing which do not fall into the categories of bias or apparent bias should be raised forthwith. So, a complaint that a member is not paying attention or has fallen asleep should be raised at once.[54]

Recall of witnesses

18.103 If new material emerges during the evidence of the party giving evidence second, it is right to allow the recall of evidence by witnesses whose case was presented first. But it would not be right to allow a represented party to make an allegation in cross-examination which could have been dealt with in evidence-in-chief by his or her own witness, in order to have a second bite at the cherry. For example, in an unfair dismissal case with the employer giving evidence first, allegations relating to contributory fault must be made during that evidence and should not be put for the first time in cross-examination of the applicant.

18.104 Given the requirement to attempt informality, most tribunals

---

52 [2000] IRLR 96.
53 See appendix C.
54 *Red Bank Manufacturing Co Ltd v Meadows* [1992] ICR 204; [1992] IRLR 209, EAT.

would allow an application to recall the witness either because of the mistake by an advocate or an unrepresented party in not addressing the issue properly first time around, or because the interests of justice require it. It should be borne in mind that as a matter of weight, little would be attached to the recall of a witness to deal with a matter which could have been dealt with by evidence-in-chief; it rather gives the impression of second thoughts or a last-ditch attempt to win the case.

Closing speeches

18.105   According to the rule of 'last in, first out', which is usually followed in English and Welsh tribunals, the party giving evidence second goes first with closing speeches. In Scotland, closing speeches generally follow the order in which the evidence in the case was led. This will be the party's first opportunity to address the tribunal and is the manifestation of the right to do so contained in 2001 Rules r11(2). In a well-conducted case, any authorities either party relies on will have been notified to each other and to the tribunal at the outset, and may have been described briefly by the representative opening the case. A representative is obliged to produce and deal with all authorities relevant to the case, whether helpful or unhelpful to their own argument, and in particular you must not wait for the other side to cite an authority first and hope to be given the opportunity to reply to it.

18.106   The closing speech summarises the main points of the evidence. Where there is a conflict, the tribunal should be invited to make findings of fact in accordance with the evidence as that party or their representative sees it. Submissions are made on the law. On some points the tribunal may interrupt and give a right to reply once it has heard the way the other side puts it. It will do this where, during the course of the hearing, the argument may have become much more difficult for the other side to oppose.

18.107   A closing speech for the party which has the burden of proof comes last. Since this party may at least briefly have opened on the central issues of law, it is not so necessary to deal in detail with all the authorities. It is quite proper to ask the other side when reading passages from an authority to read out passages in addition to those already read so as to draw the tribunal's attention to parts of the case on which it is intended to rely, and avoid repetition when making the closing speech. Otherwise it is best to keep quiet.

18.108   At this stage it is permissible for the tribunal to indicate its likely finding on any particular point. It does so by 'not calling on' the representative to deal with any particular point. In other words, it is convinced of the facts and the legal arguments relating to a particular point in that side's favour, and having given the other side an opportunity to deal with it, it is unnecessary to ask for the point to be elaborated further. If a representative is stopped in his or her tracks in this way, it will be a breach of the rules of natural justice for the tribunal to find against his or her client on that point.

18.109   The other side is not usually entitled to say anything after the party going first has made a closing speech. Occasionally, where new points of law or new cases are referred to in the closing speech, the other side has a right to reply but it does require a careful application and a sympathetic tribunal. If the other side has been informed of the cases on which it is intended to rely, the fact that they are raised for the first time in the closing speech does not entitle the other side to come back in reply and have the last word. It should have dealt with them in its own closing speech.

CHAPTER 19

The decision

19.1 Introduction

Introduction

19.1   The decision of the tribunal must have formal characteristics. It includes a declaration, an order, a recommendation, an award, and sometimes a determination as to who is entitled to bring or contest proceedings, but does not include interlocutory orders or decisions on interlocutory matters (2001 Regs reg 2(2);[1] see para 22.28). It also includes a direction under the Health and Safety at Work Act 1974 where an appeal has been lodged (2001 Regs reg 2(4)) and a direction following appeals under the Sex Discrimination Act 1975 and the Race Relations Act 1976 (2001 Regs reg 2(5)).

19.2   The decision is entered on the register, which is open for public inspection (2001 Regs reg 12). Any parts of the decision or of the reasons which identify people involved in an allegation of a sexual offence must be omitted from the register (2001 Rules rr12(7) and 15(6)), as must the reasons in a case where there has been a national security direction or the tribunal has for other reasons sat in private (2001 Rules r12(6)).

19.3   The decision must be signed by the chairman or, if he or she is unable to do so because of incapacity, it must be signed by the other members. The decision of the tribunal can be by a majority but if only two people constitute the tribunal, the chairman has a casting vote (2001 Rules r12(1) and (11)).

19.4   The tribunal must give reasons for its decision, which can either be in summary or extended form (2001 Rules r12(3)). The decision and the reasons need not be given at the same time. The requirement is for tribunals to give reasons in summary form (2001 Rules r12(4)) except where the rules require them to be in extended form. This is in relation to proceedings:

- of sex, race or disability discrimination or equal pay;
- in which a request has been made orally at the hearing;
- in which a request is made in writing at any time before summary reasons have been sent or within 21 days of the date on which they were sent; or
- where the tribunal considers 'that reasons given in summary form would not sufficiently explain the grounds for its decision'.

According to 2001 Rules r12(2) the decision can be given orally at the

---

1   Employment Tribunals (Constitution and Rules of Procedure) Regulations 2001 SI No 1171.

end of a hearing or reserved (ie, kept secret until promulgated in writing) or a decision can be given with reasons to follow.

19.5 What is important is for the chairman to explain precisely the form in which the reasons are or are to be given. In simple cases, the chairman explains in general terms the reasons for the decision and says that the definitive form will appear as summary reasons in due course. If extended reasons are given orally, they should be recorded on tape at the time, as no other reasons in writing can be adduced without a caveat.[2] The caveat is that the official reasons will be those promulgated in writing in due course.

19.6 *Practice Direction No 1* of November 1994 (see appendix C) encourages reasons to be given orally and recorded on tape, in extended and summary form at the same time. The summary form is transcribed and becomes the reasons sent to parties. If parties request extended form reasons, the earlier part of the tape is transcribed and promulgated.

19.7 If a party has lost, or looks likely to lose, it is worth asking at the hearing for reasons to be given in extended form. An appeal to the Employment Appeal Tribunal (EAT) may only be made if accompanied by reasons in extended form. On the other hand, there is no reason why a successful party should make life easier for the other side by seeking full reasons in writing.

19.8 A mistake in the chairman's reasons relating to a fact such as a date or the name of a person should be pointed out and (tactfully) invite a correction. Leaving errors on the record is undesirable and encourages false hopes of an appeal.

19.9 If both parties agree in writing on the terms of a decision, the tribunal can make a decision in those terms (2001 Rules r15(2)(b)). This power is not affected by provisions relating to compromise agreements (see chapter 16), since under this provision the case is disposed of by the tribunal rather than by the parties. Decisions by consent are dealt with at para 16.43.

19.10 In an equal value case, the report of an independent expert must be attached to the reasons (2001 Rules r12(4A) inserted by Sch 3 para 4).

19.11 The content and depth of the reasons vary from tribunal to tribunal. In summary form, they rarely extend beyond two pages. The adequacy of the reasons can be considered on appeal to the EAT, since extended reasons must be attached to the appeal. The reasons should:

... contain an outline of the story which has given rise to the

2 *Trollope & Colls v Sharpe* EAT/812/92, unreported.

complaint and a summary of the tribunal's basic factual conclusions and a statement of the reasons which have led them to reach the conclusion which they do on those basic facts. The parties are entitled to be told why they have won or lost. There should be sufficient account of the facts and of the reasoning to enable the EAT . . . to see whether any question of law arises; and it is highly desirable that the decision of an industrial tribunal should give guidance both to employers and trade unions as to practices which should or should not be adopted.[3]

19.12   When making findings of fact where evidence is disputed, tribunals are not required to give detailed pros and cons for accepting or rejecting any witness's evidence. It is the conclusion (rather than the detailed reasoning) which must be ascertainable.[4] On disputed issues, the reasons should specify the conclusion drawn by the tribunal, (although if a decision cannot be made between two conflicting sets of evidence, the tribunal may find that the party which bears the burden of proof has failed to discharge it). Where inferences are relied on, the primary facts giving rise to the inference should be set out.[5] Sir John Donaldson in *Martin v MBS Fastenings (Glynwed) Distribution Ltd*[6] said: 'So far as the findings of fact are concerned, it is helpful to the parties to give some explanation for them but it is not obligatory.' More recently Peter Gibson LJ giving judgment in *High Table Ltd v Horst*[7] stated that 'whilst the tribunal must consider all that is relevant it need only deal with the points which were seen to be in controversy relating to those issues, and then only with the principal important controversial points'.

19.13   Codes of practice must be taken into account if they are relevant, although as they lack statutory force they will not by themselves be determinative of the case. In cases under the Disability Discrimination Act 1995 the tribunal should, according to the EAT in *Goodwin v Patent Office*[8] always make explicit reference to any relevant provision of the guidance or code which has been taken into account in arriving at their decision.

19.14   If multiple complaints are heard together, the tribunal must deal with each complaint, as to both liability and remedy, separately, so for

---

3   *Meek v City of Birmingham DC* [1987] IRLR 250, CA at 251 per Bingham LJ.
4   *Levy v Marrable & Co Ltd* [1984] ICR 583, EAT.
5   *British Gas plc v Sharma* [1991] ICR 19; [1991] IRLR 101, EAT.
6   [1983] ICR 511; [1983] IRLR 198.
7   [1997] IRLR 513 at 518, CA.
8   [1999] IRLR 4.

example a complaint of both unfair dismissal and discrimination must be considered separately.[9]

19.15   Once a decision has been made and registered, it can be changed to correct clerical mistakes and accidental slips and omissions only (2001 Rules r12(8)).[10] Otherwise a review under 2001 Rules r13 is required. Before registration, the tribunal has limited powers. If it has announced no oral decision, it clearly has power to recall the parties to hear additional evidence and additional arguments. After it has announced an oral decision with or without reasons, its powers are much more limited. In *Hanks v Ace High Productions Ltd*[11] it was held that the power did not extend to hearing further arguments 'when already a clear decision has been reached'; and yet in that very case the tribunal, which *did* allow further argument, had its decision upheld. There is a conflict of authorities on the power to recall a case after a decision and/or reasons have been given.

19.16   On the one hand, it is arguable that a decision is not a decision until it is signed by the chairman (2001 Rules r12(2)) but this rule expressly includes oral decisions, and tribunals have been overruled for giving a decision and reasons orally and changing them in writing.[12] This was because the decision was changed, rather than because it was doubted that there is power in a tribunal to do so. Obviously the EAT and the Court of Appeal are more likely to intervene when a decision has been changed, and that is the only case they are likely to be dealing with. The better view is that the tribunal is not discharged from its duty as soon as it announces its oral decision but remains seized of the case until promulgation of the decision and reasons. However, if it wishes to reconsider its decision, it must give the parties an opportunity to be heard.

9   *British Sugar v Kirker* [1998] IRLR 624, EAT.
10   This is akin to the 'slip rule' in civil proceedings: CPR 40.12.
11   [1978] ICR 1155; [1979] IRLR 32, EAT.
12   *Arthur Guinness Son & Co (Great Britain) Ltd v Green* [1989] ICR 241; [1989] IRLR 288, EAT; *Lamont v Fry's Metals Ltd* [1985] ICR 566; [1985] IRLR 470, CA.

CHAPTER 20

Costs

Introduction

20.1   The costs of bringing a case to a tribunal should have been considered at an early stage (see para 4.24).

20.2   Unlike in cases in the High Court and most cases in the county court, a party cannot usually expect to be awarded costs if he or she wins, but nor will he or she generally have to pay the other side's costs if he or she loses. This fact can encourage parties to seek to keep costs down and to take a 'commercial view' in tribunal proceedings. It is also in keeping with the aims of ensuring that tribunals are not expensive to use and remain the forum of the parties and not their lawyers.

20.3   The reality is, however, that many parties will use lawyers or other advisers to assist them in their tribunal case and will incur costs in doing so. At all times it should be borne in mind that those costs will probably not be recoverable. Advisers should be careful to consider whether there is some way of meeting the costs of legal or other professional representation, for example, by use of the 'legal help' scheme (advice only, not representation, though assistance is now available from the Legal Aid Board in Scotland in limited cases[1]), by recourse to a trade union or other professional body or trade association, by using the assistance of bodies such as the Commission for Racial Equality, the Equal Opportunities Commission or the Disability Rights Commission, or by applying for assistance under the increasingly common provisions for legal costs in many home and vehicle insurance policies. Morison J in *R v Securities and Futures Authority Ltd and another ex p Fleurose*[1a] commented, obiter, that a right to a fair trial under ECHR art 6 may include a right to the assistance of a lawyer if that is indispensable for effective access to court, for example, because of the complexity of the case. This raises the question of how such 'assistance' would be funded – it is unlikely to be via legal aid.

20.4   A threat to apply for costs can be a powerful weapon in tribunal proceedings, and with the changes introduced by the 2001 Rules[2] so that tribunals may award up to £10,000 without ordering a detailed assessment of costs, the consequence must be that parties pay closer attention, at an ever earlier stage, to the prospects of success and the danger of having an award of costs made against them.

1   See appendix E for address of Scottish Legal Aid Board.
1a   [2001] IRLR 764
2   Employment Tribunals Rules of Procedure (contained in SI 2001 No 1171, Sch 1).

When costs can be awarded

20.5   There are four circumstances in which specific provision is made for costs orders. They are:

- unreasonable (etc) conduct;
- failure to accede or reply to request for reinstatement;
- conduct leading to adjournment or postponement of a hearing (see para 15.20);
- following determination of a pre-hearing review (see para 13.12).

Unreasonable, etc, conduct

20.6   Tribunals have no power to order costs or witness allowances except in limited circumstances. In general the duty on the tribunal to consider awarding costs will only arise where:[2a]

> ... in the opinion of the tribunal, a party has in bringing the proceedings, or a party or a party's representative has, in conducting the proceedings acted vexatiously, abusively, disruptively or otherwise unreasonably, or the bringing or conducting the proceedings by a party has been misconceived ...

20.7   In the previous 1993 Rules[3], costs could only be awarded if a party behaved 'frivolously, vexatiously, abusively, disruptively or otherwise unreasonably', and there was no duty on the tribunal to consider making an award. The 2001 Rules remove the 'frivolous' test, and significantly, add the duty, and power, to consider awarding costs where a claim is 'misconceived'.

'Vexatiously'

20.8   This term was considered in *Marler Ltd v Robertson*,[4] where it was held that:

> ... [i]f an employee brings a hopeless case not with any expectation of recovering compensation but out of spite to harass his employers or for some other improper motive, he acts vexatiously, and likewise abuses the procedure.[5]

2a   2001 Rules r14(1).
3   Industrial Tribunal Rules of Procedure 1993 (contained in Industrial Tribunals (Constitution and Rules of Procedure) Regulations 1993 SI No 2687 Sch 1).
4   [1974] ICR 72, NIRC.
5   In the context of a decision to strike out a notice of appearance because of vexatious conduct on the part of a representative, see *Bennett v Southwark LBC* EAT 1273/97 and 878/99, 11 January 2001, unreported – see para 12.40.

'Abusively, disruptively'

20.9   These terms were added by the 1993 Rules and are maintained in the 2001 Rules, to be applied where a party has been abusive during the course of a tribunal hearing or has sought to disrupt it. The 2001 Rules make it abundantly clear that the behaviour of a representative will be considered as well as that of a party.

'Otherwise unreasonably'

20.10   This expression is wider than the expressions that precede it in the 2001 Rules. This separate categorisation suggests that 'otherwise unreasonably' is not to be read as merely another way of saying 'frivolously' or 'vexatiously' but refers to conduct of a different kind. Tribunal decisions suggest, however, that this kind of distinction is not a precise science, with many orders based on 'unreasonable conduct' which could also be considered as 'frivolous' or 'vexatious' within the *Marler* guidelines. In *Stein v Associated Dairies Ltd*,[6] costs were awarded because of the applicant's unreasonable behaviour in pursuing a claim where he ought to have known that he had no prospect of succeeding, knowing that another employee dismissed for the same offence on the same day had failed in his unfair dismissal claim.

'Misconceived'

20.11   This is defined in the 2001 Regs as 'including having no reasonable prospects of success' (reg 2(2)), the definition therefore not being exhaustive. It is clear that the addition of this test gives the tribunal a great deal of discretion when considering awarding costs. It is likely to cover scenarios that would previously have been termed frivolous, but also to go beyond that. Guidance on the meaning of the term frivolous was given in *Marler* where it was indicated that conduct would be frivolous if:

> the employee knows that there is no substance in his claim and that it is bound to fail, or if the claim is on the face of it so manifestly misconceived that it can have no prospect of success . . .

Of course, what applies to the employee must equally be true of the employer (or other respondent) where the conduct of the 'defence' to a claim was misconceived.

20.12   It had also been held that 'frivolously' might cover those cases where a party ought to have known it had no prospect of success, as

---

6   [1982] IRLR 447, EAT.

in *Cartiers Superfoods Ltd v Laws.*[7] This view met with some approval in the *Marler* case, with the caveat that it cannot be said that a party 'ought' to have known that which it has taken the tribunal some time to find out, through fully testing the evidence available.[8] The Employment Appeal Tribunal (EAT) in Scotland in *Lothian Health Board v Johnstone*[9] also sounded a cautionary note in considering the *Cartiers* case, warning that it does not lay down any general proposition and must be considered in the light of its particular facts.

20.13   The precise scope of this added provision is potentially very broad, but it will be a matter for individual chairmen to apply as they see fit. Certainly more applications for costs are likely to be made.

Costs against respondents

20.14   Costs may be awarded against respondents if they behave in a manner outlined above. In *Cartiers*, however, it was stated that 'great care' should be exercised by tribunals before making an award against a respondent as 'obviously, a respondent must be entitled to defend proceedings brought against him'.

20.15   However, the right to defend proceedings does not mean that the defence can be conducted unreasonably, and a respondent guilty of such conduct is just as liable to face an order for costs as an applicant in similar circumstances.

20.16   An award of costs cannot, however, be made against a respondent in respect of the conduct leading to the dismissal or other act complained of. It is the behaviour of the respondent *as* respondent that is relevant, ie, how the employer reacts to the applicant's claim rather than its conduct before any complaint has been made.[10]

Reinstatement and re-engagement

20.17   Under 2001 Rules r14(5), the tribunal *must* make an order of costs or for the payment of allowances where, in an unfair dismissal complaint:

- the applicant has expressed a wish to be reinstated or re-engaged and has communicated that wish to the respondent at least seven days before the hearing of the complaint; but

7 [1978] IRLR 315, EAT.
8 [1974] ICR 72, NIRC, per Sir Hugh Griffiths at 77.
9 [1981] IRLR 321.
10 *Davidson v John Calder (Publishers) Ltd and Calder Educational Trust Ltd* [1985] ICR 143; [1985] IRLR 97, EAT.

– the proceedings have to be postponed or adjourned due to the respondent's failure, without special reason, to adduce reasonable evidence as to the availability of the job from which the applicant was dismissed.

20.18   The power does not depend on the respondent having behaved in the ways provided for by 2001 Rules r14(1). The tribunal *must* make an order in the circumstances set out in 2001 Rules r14(5), *unless* 'special reasons' are made out to excuse the respondent's failure to adduce the evidence required.

Relevant considerations for a costs order under 2001 Rules r14(1)

20.19   The tribunal will consider whether the conduct complained of falls under one or more of the heads set out in 2001 Rules r14(1) and then what (if any) costs have been occurred as a result of that conduct. A party may have conducted proceedings quite disgracefully, but if this has not led to any additional costs being incurred, a tribunal is most unlikely to make any order for costs to be paid. While 2001 Rules r14(1)(a) and (b) are not expressly limited to costs *caused by* the specified conduct, the award of costs is compensatory, not punitive, in its nature.[11] Costs will not be awarded unless it can be shown that they were incurred as a result of the behaviour complained of.

20.20   The tribunal will generally take into account the ability to pay of the party against whom it is minded to make a costs order. In *Wiggin Alloys Ltd v Jenkins*[12] a tribunal refused to award costs against an applicant who was in prison and was unlikely to be able to meet an order for costs in the foreseeable future. On the other hand, the fact that a party is wholly without funds does not always mean that no order will be made. It remains a matter for the tribunal's discretion in each case, and it may make an award but order that it should not be enforced without further application.[13] The EAT in *Omar v Worldwide News Inc*[14] held that the means of an individual should always be considered before an order of costs is made against him or her. It further held that it was only in exceptional circumstances that the means

11   Ibid.
12   [1981] IRLR 275.
13   *Nial v Baxters (Butchers) Ltd* (1985) *Times* 9 February, EAT.
14   [1998] IRLR 291, EAT.

of a trade union which had been backing an action brought by one of its members should be taken into account, specifically where the union has brought a claim on behalf of a member which it knows to be without merit, or where the union has pursued a particular test case.[15] Both these propositions were disagreed with by another division of the EAT in *Beynon v Scaddon*.[16] Lindsay P pointed out that the rule as to costs (rule12 of the 1993 Rules, now 2001 Rules r14):

> . . . neither requires nor provides any machinery for an inquiry into a party's means. If, in every case, as a precondition of any order as to costs, there had to be an inquiry into the prospective payor's means, one might reasonably expect the employment tribunal to have been empowered to so enquire. It is not as if the draftsman of the Rules had no such empowerment in mind; on a little earlier in the Rules, rule 7(5) [concerning orders for deposits] makes the taking of reasonable steps to ascertain ability to pay a precondition of an order. Whilst it will no doubt, usually be desirable to look into means, when that is possible, before an order for costs is made, it cannot be said that a failure to do so necessarily makes the order an improper exercise of discretion.[17]

20.21   There is now disagreement in the authorities concerning not only the extent to which a tribunal may consider the ability of the party to pay costs, but also of the body representing the party, especially trade unions. While agreeing that costs ought not to have been awarded against the union in *Omar*, where the applicant had fabricated his evidence, Lindsay J in the *Beynon* case held that it was wrong to formulate types of circumstances in which a discretion might be exercised, and concluded that the discretion must be unfettered. In subsequent cases[18] the *Beynon* case has been followed, and, being the latest pronouncement of the EAT on the subject, should prevail.

20.22   Rule 14(1) of the 2001 Rules states that costs may only be awarded against a 'party', which the EAT in *Beynon* interpreted as including, at least in relation to an evaluation of conduct in the bringing and conduct of proceedings, the conduct of the representatives, on the ground that it would be absurd if a party's representative could conduct proceedings abusively or disruptively or could require costly adjournments, and yet be immune to costs.

15   See also *Carr v Allen-Bradley Electronics Ltd* [1980] ICR 603; [1980] IRLR 263, EAT.
16   [1999] IRLR 700.
17   Ibid para 19.
18   See *Queen Mary & Westfield College and Royal Hospital NHS Trust v Kovacs* EAT/ 1157/99, 16 March 2001, unreported.

In-house lawyers and other representatives

20.23   The legal costs incurred in tribunal litigation by in-house lawyers are as much recoverable as are the costs incurred by employing independent solicitors.[19]

Volunteer representatives

20.24   More difficult to recover, however, are costs in respect of representation by volunteers or by other representatives or advisers who appear at no direct cost to the party they represent: union or citizens advice bureau advisers, law centre or Free Representation Unit representatives, and lawyers whose costs are met by an insurance policy. The difficulty in such cases is establishing that any costs have been incurred by the party using these services. On the other hand, there seems to be no reason in principle why the basic cost incurred by the representing body should not be recoverable in the same way as the costs of in-house lawyers. Ultimately the party using the services of that representative is likely to have to pay something towards the cost (whether directly by means of some claw-back provision or indirectly through trade union subscription or insurance policy premiums) and the difficulty in quantifying this sum should not prevent an order for costs being made in appropriate circumstances.

Wasted costs

20.25   Costs may only be ordered in favour of a party or against a party: there is no scope for a costs order against lawyers who have wasted costs by their conduct of the proceedings as there is in the courts, since the Courts and Legal Services Act 1990 s4 (CPR 48.7) does not apply to tribunals. (Note however, the remarks of Lindsay P in the *Beynon* case, at para 20.20 above.)[20]

Contingency fees

20.26   Costs will not be ordered if the obligation of the party to pay an adviser or representative arises only if the tribunal should make an finding on liability or an order for costs in his or her favour. This would be an unlawful contingency arrangement. The tribunal cannot

---

19   *Wiggin Alloys*, note 12 above.
20   Clause 22 of the Employment Bill 2001 proposes an amendment to ETA 1996 s13 to allow for future Regulations to explicitly provide a mechanism for costs to be awarded against a party's representative.

order a respondent to pay an applicant in respect of sums that a party is not liable to pay to his or her adviser.[21]

Equal value claims

20.27 Similar rules apply to equal value claims; although in such cases costs may include those incurred in connection with any investigations carried out by the independent expert in preparing the report.[22]

When the application should be made

20.28 The 2001 Rules do not provide any specific time within which an application for costs should be made. In *Johnson t/a Richard Andrew Ladies Hairstylists v Baxter*[23] the EAT stated that an application for costs should be made within a reasonable time. If the tribunal does not reserve its decision, the application should be made forthwith.

20.29 Even where the decision is reserved, then it should be made in advance of the decision (at the end of the substantive hearing) if at all possible so as to avoid an additional hearing on costs alone. In practice, this decision may be difficult to assess, and sensitive to make, since the result of the case and the reasons are not known at that stage. Yet the application should still be made on the footing that the tribunal will make a favourable finding and the tribunal will be invited to deal with it in its reserved decision.

20.30 As the power to make a costs order is discretionary, any delay in the making of the application will be a relevant consideration for the tribunal, particularly when it might have caused prejudice to the party against whom the order is sought. In *Lothian Health Board v Johnstone*[24] the Scottish EAT indicated that any application for costs should be made as soon as possible – in that case only two members of the original tribunal were able to hear the application for costs made some seven months after the original decision.

---

21 *British Waterways Board v Norman* (1994) 26 HLR 233, DC.
22 2001 Regs Sch 3 r5, which modifies Sch 1 r14.
23 [1984] ICR 675; [1985] IRLR 96.
24 [1981] IRLR 321.

How to make the application

20.31 Many applications for costs in tribunals fail because of inadequate preparation. If, in advance of the hearing, it seems likely that such an application will need to be made, it is important to ensure that all relevant documentation, including correspondence and evidence in relation to the costs claimed, is put together in an easily readable form – a separate costs bundle if necessary. Now that sums of up to £10,000 can be awarded by the tribunal, good preparation is more important than ever before.

20.32 The costs bundle will include correspondence relied on, such as pre-hearing warnings as to the vexatious or misconceived nature of the complaint or grounds of resistance and early attempts to put the other side on notice as to an application for costs. The bundle may also include letters written 'without prejudice save as to costs' (see para 10.39) or which might show the unreasonable conduct of the party against whom the order is sought. (It should be noted that the absence of any warning that a costs application will be made, will not serve as a bar to costs being awarded, though it is clearly good practice to give the warning in a letter should an application be likely).

20.33 Ideally, a separate schedule will also be made available to the tribunal, setting out the costs incurred at the different stages of the proceedings (see below). Where the costs in question are significant, then a schedule of costs should be served on the other side in advance of the application. Where a party is faced with such an application and is taken by surprise by late service of a schedule of costs, they would have good grounds for objecting to a summary assessment of the award to be made by the tribunal without further time to consider the amounts claimed and prepare any representations necessary. Although there is no separate provision in the 2001 Rules for the prior service of schedules of costs and no formula for summary assessment has been laid down, best practice would suggest that something akin to the procedure of the Civil Procedure Rules is adopted where possible, ie, the schedule should be served on the other side not less than 24 hours before the relevant hearing and the kind of information listed in CPR *Practice Direction 44* should be provided.

Amounts to be awarded

20.34   The tribunal may order the party against whom the award is made to pay:

- the costs of another party to that party; and/or
- the allowances payable by the secretary of state to any party or witness for attendance at the tribunal, which includes a party's expenses (2001 Rules r14(1)) and an independent expert (2001 Regs Sch 3 r5).

In other words, the tribunal has power both to compensate another party in respect of costs incurred and to protect the public purse.

20.35   An order for costs can be made in one of three ways under 2001 Rules r14(3), ie, that one party must pay to the other:

- a specified sum not exceeding £10,000;
- a sum which has been agreed between the parties; or
- the whole or a specified part of the costs to be assessed.

20.36   If the costs involved are less than £10,000 the tribunal will itself be able to carry out the assessment of how much should be paid. If a party wants the tribunal to make this order, it should be prepared to submit details when making the application. It should set out in the form of a schedule the costs incurred at each stage, including both solicitor and counsel costs if appropriate. If there has been no time to prepare a schedule, a party should still be in a position to advance some figures and evidence relating to costs so that the tribunal can carry out the assessment. It is always good practice for the case file to be available at the hearing with an up-dated print-out of the bill of costs included. If counsel has been instructed, the tribunal may wish to see the brief fee marked on the back sheet to the instructions or to be told what fee has been agreed. Anyone who wants an order for costs must be in a position to give the tribunal the material it needs (and see CPR *Practice Direction 44*).

20.37   If the costs are greater than £10,000, and no agreement can be reached, the tribunal will merely order an award for the whole or some proportion of the costs incurred (ie, those relating to a particular application or part of the claim) but will not specify any amount. The bill of costs claimed will then be subject to 'detailed assessment', which the tribunal will order to be on the appropriate county court scale depending on the nature of the claim (2001 Rules r14(6)).

20.38   Detailed assessment of costs (previously called 'taxation') is the process by which the bill of costs claimed by a party is considered by a district judge (or deputy district judge) of the county court.[25] The court orders to be paid only costs that have been reasonably incurred and that are proportionate. In other words, if the party in whose favour the award is made has run up legal costs which were unnecessary, or has paid over the odds, it will not be entitled to recover these from the other party. It is only entitled to such costs as it can establish were reasonably incurred. The only exception to this will be where the tribunal orders that the costs should be assessed on an 'indemnity basis', in which case it will be for the party against whom the order has been made to establish that those costs were unreasonably incurred. The EAT in *Beynon* made it clear that ordering costs on an indemnity basis is not penal, rather it is compensatory.

20.39   The additional burden of submitting a bill of costs to assessment can encourage a party in whose favour an award has been made to try to agree a sum with the other side. However, since the amount of costs which may now be awarded by the tribunal has increased from £500 in the 1993 Rules to £10,000, the number of cases which are sent for assessment is likely to decrease and the task of assessing costs summarily will fall on tribunals, who must consider whether costs incurred are proportionate.

Allowances

20.40   The allowances paid by the secretary of state to parties and witnesses attending the tribunal (regardless of the outcome) cover loss of wages, travel costs and other expenses. They will rarely fully compensate a person for any loss of wages, and fixed scales are set out under each head (ETA 1996 s5(3)). They do not extend to the costs of professional representatives.

20.41   In the circumstances set out by 2001 Rules r14, it is open to the tribunal to order that these are repaid to the secretary of state by a party against whom an order for costs has been made. In practice, tribunals rarely make such an order.

25   Costs are dealt with in CPR Parts 43–48.

Equal pay claims

Introduction

21.1   The procedures for claiming equal pay differ from other tribunal actions and merit a chapter of their own. Section references in this chapter are to the Equal Pay Act 1970 (EqPA 1970) unless otherwise indicated.

21.2   Equal pay claims may be brought (by women or men[1]) on three grounds under the EqPA 1970 and the Treaty of Rome:

- the applicant claims to be employed on 'like work' with a comparator of the opposite sex (EqPA 1970 s1(2)(a));
- the applicant claims to be employed on work 'rated as equivalent' to that of the chosen comparator under a job evaluation study (JES) (EqPA 1970 s1(2)(b));
- the applicant claims to be employed on work which is different but of equal value to that of the comparator (EqPA 1970 s1(2)(c)).

European law

21.3   An applicant may claim equal pay for the same work, or for work done on a job classified as equal, or for work which is of equal value, but nevertheless find that the EqPA 1970 gives no effective remedy. Article 141 of the Treaty of Rome ('the treaty') and Directive 75/117/EEC (the Equal Pay Directive), which has been held to facilitate article 141 (see *Jenkins* below), can be relied on in the tribunal.[2]

21.4   Article 141 can be relied on directly only if it is clear and can be operated to give equal pay without recourse to national implementing measures necessary to define discrimination.[3] In *Pickstone v Freemans plc*[4] the Court of Appeal held that article 141 could be relied on directly in an equal value case where the discrimination is obvious on a direct comparison of the two types of work.[5] Because most equal value claims are not so obvious, and require some form of expert or at least

---

1   Although, for convenience, references in this text assume the claim to have been brought by a woman against a male comparator.

2   *Secretary of State for Scotland and Greater Glasgow Health Board v Wright and Hannah* [1991] IRLR 187, EAT.

3   *Worringham v Lloyds Bank* [1981] ICR 558, ECJ at 589; [1981] IRLR 178.

4   [1987] ICR 867; [1987] IRLR 218, CA (affirmed on different grounds [1988] ICR 697; [1988] IRLR 357, HL).

5   [1987] ICR 867 per Purchas LJ at 895 and Nicholls LJ at 880.

experienced evaluator, it must still be doubted if article 141 may be directly enforced in many claims.[6]

21.5   No enforcement procedure is specified in the treaty or the directive, so the UK's own procedures governing tribunals are operated.[7]

Procedures under the Equal Pay Act 1970

21.6   The procedure is designed to lead to a declaration that the woman's contract contains an equality clause, so that *any* term of her contract which is or becomes less favourable than his is a breach of contract.

21.7   The basis of a *like work* claim is that a woman is doing work which is the same as, or is of a broadly similar nature to, that of a man. A claim that the woman is doing work that has been *rated as equivalent* will be based on a job evaluation study (JES) that has been conducted by the employer and which gives equal rating to the jobs of the woman and her comparator. The procedure involved in bringing cases based on like work and on a JES is generally the same as that for other types of tribunal claims described in this book.

21.8   In *equal value* cases, different (and more complex) rules apply, varying the procedure in a number of respects. These are known as the Equal Value Complementary Rules of Procedure.[8]

A comparable male worker

21.9   The applicant in each type of case has to show that a man is doing this work:

- in the same establishment for the same employer; *or*
- at a different establishment in Great Britain for the same employer where common terms and conditions of employment are observed.[9]

21.10   For practical purposes the applicant must cite a male comparator at an early stage, although the choice of comparator is hers alone.[10]

6   See the view of Lord Oliver in [1988] ICR 697 at 723, strictly obiter and the only speech containing a reference to this problem.

7   *Pickstone v Freemans plc*, note 4 above, and *Livingstone v Hepworth Refractories plc* [1992] ICR 287; [1992] IRLR 63, EAT.

8   Employment Tribunals (Constitution and Rules of Procedure) Regulations 2001 (2001 Regs) SI No 1171 Sch 3.

9   EqPA 1970 s1(6) and *British Coal Corporation v Smith* [1994] ICR 810; [1994] IRLR 342, CA.

10   *Ainsworth v Glass Tubes and Components Ltd* [1977] ICR 347; [1977] IRLR 74, EAT.

So it has been held that she need not prove the comparator is representative of a particular group of employees.[11] Difficulties may arise if a wholly anomalous comparator is chosen, since the respondent is likely to justify a material factor other than the difference of sex as the reason for the different pay under EqPA 1970 s1(3). This defence was argued unsuccessfully in *McPherson v Rathgael Centre for Children and Young People*,[12] where it was held that even a 'gross but understandable error' (comparator was paid higher by mistake and the employer refused to reduce his pay when the mistake discovered) did not justify unequal pay.

21.11   The combined effect of the EqPA 1970 and article 141 allows claims to be made with a comparator who is not working simultaneously with the applicant, for example, when she is appointed to replace him but on a lower salary.[13] It is also strongly arguable that if there is *no* male comparator in sight but it can be shown that a male would have been paid at a higher rate for the same work, the EqPA 1970 will not apply but a claim can be based on article 141.[14]

21.12   Restricting inter-establishment claims to Great Britain and not the whole of the UK is probably open to a successful challenge that the treaty and the Equal Pay Directive are not properly implemented in the UK because of the subdivision of the member state. Comparison is prevented as between establishments in Northern Ireland and Great Britain, even though Northern Ireland has its own equivalent legislation.

Burden of proof

21.13   This is initially on the applicant,[15] although each element of the defence of a genuine material factor under EqPA 1970 s1(3) is for the employer to prove.[16] The employer must also prove the existence of a JES under EqPA 1970 s2A(2). Furthermore, it seems that the employer is under a duty to show that any pay structure or policy is not discriminatory when it is not transparent (that is, so as to enable a

11 *Thomas v National Coal Board* [1987] ICR 757; [1987] IRLR 451, EAT.
12 [1991] IRLR 206, NI CA.
13 *Macarthys Ltd v Smith (No 2)* [1980] ICR 672; [1980] IRLR 209, CA.
14 *Hammersmith and Queen Charlotte's Special Health Authority v Cato* [1988] ICR 132; [1987] IRLR 483, EAT.
15 Although the Burden of Proof Directive covers equal pay, the Sex Discrimination (Indirect Discrimination and Burden of Proof) Regulations 2001 (SI No 2660) do not amend the EqPA 1970 as the government took the view that it already falls to the employer to prove that there has been no sex discrimination if pay differs.
16 *Financial Times v Byrne* [1992] IRLR 163, EAT.

woman to see how her pay and others' is made up),[17] or has the effect of placing women on average below men (ie, is indirectly discriminatory on the ground of sex).[18]

Procedure

21.14 Claims for equal pay for *like work* under EqPA 1970 s1(2)(a) and article 141 of the treaty are made to a tribunal in accordance with the 2001 Rules.[19] The treaty and the Equal Pay Directive, which facilitates implementation of the treaty (see *Jenkins v Kingsgate Ltd*[20]) are directly enforceable in the tribunal in respect of like work.[21] In this case the tribunal will apply its normal rules of procedure including those relating to time limits.[22]

Claims based on a job evaluation study

21.15 A JES is relevant under the EqPA 1970 in two different situations (as noted by Dillon LJ in *Bromley v H & J Quick Ltd*):[23]

– it can form the basis of a claim for equality based on EqPA 1970 s1(2)(b);
– it can defeat a claim for equal value without reference to an independent expert.

The applicant's claim for equal pay

21.16 In these circumstances, if the applicant and the comparator are not doing like work, the applicant can say under EqPA 1970 s1(5) that:

a) there has been a JES;
b) it was made using an evaluation of the demand of the job on the jobholder under headings such as effort, skill and decision (ie, decision-making);
c) it compared her job and the comparator's;
d) it rated the work as equivalent, or would have if the system had

---

17 *Handels-og Kontorfunktionaerernes Forbund i Danmark v Dansk Arbejdsgiverforening (acting for Danfoss)* [1991] ICR 74; [1989] IRLR 532, ECJ.
18 *Enderby v Frenchay Health Authority* [1994] ICR 112; [1993] IRLR 591, ECJ.
19 Employment Tribunals Rules of Procedure (contained in SI 2001 No 1171, Sch 1).
20 [1981] ICR 592 at 614; [1981] IRLR 228, ECJ.
21 *Pickstone v Freemans plc*, note 4 above.
22 *Livingstone v Hepworth Refractories plc*, note 4 above, and see para 5.7.
23 [1988] ICR 623 at 627; [1988] IRLR 249, CA.

not given different values for men and women under the same
headings; and

e)   she has not been given equal pay.

21.17   By definition the work of each will be different. A JES which
meets the test in (b) is properly described as 'analytical', since it
compares the components of different jobs by analysing the special
features demanded in each job, by reference to several factors
common to all the jobs evaluated.

21.18   A JES will not meet the test in (d) if gender bias has entered into
the scheme, or its application. The Court of Appeal has approved the
use of the booklet *Job Evaluation Schemes Free of Sex-Bias* (EOC, 1993)
on the need to avoid such bias.[24]

The respondent's defence based on a job evaluation study

21.19   An applicant has the right to have her claim considered under the
equal value provisions unless her claim is clearly hopeless (EqPA
1970 s2A(1)). As a specific illustration, EqPA 1970 s2A(2) declares
conclusively ('there shall be taken') that a claim is unreasonable if a
non-sexist, truly analytical JES has already concluded that her job is of
less value than that of her comparator.

21.20   When there is a JES, the procedural steps in dealing with a claim
for equal pay for work of equal value, which is not based on EqPA
1970 s1(2)(b) but on EqPA 1970 s1(2)(c), are:

– the applicant claims equality;
– the respondent claims there has been a JES;
– the respondent is able to establish that the JES was made using an
   evaluation of the demand of the job on the jobholder under headings such as effort, skill and decision (ie, decision-making); and
– there are no reasonable grounds for saying the JES was based on a
   system which discriminated (either directly or indirectly) on the
   grounds of sex (EqPA 1970 s2A(2)(b) and (3));
– the JES compared her job and the comparator's;
– the JES did not rate the work as equivalent.

21.21   This might even be a JES carried out *after* the commencement of
the tribunal proceedings.[25] But there is no reason why an equal value
claim should be held up to await the carrying out of a JES by an
employer after proceedings have been commenced.[26] Any JES relied

---

24 Ibid at 622, and see also *Aldridge v BT* [1989] ICR 790; [1990] IRLR 10, EAT.
25 *Dibro Ltd v Hore* [1990] ICR 370; [1990] IRLR 120, EAT.
26 *Avon CC v Foxhall and others* EAT/113/89, unreported.

on in this way must, of course, be analytical (see above), ie, it must consider the demands of the jobs under various (non-sex-related) headings such as effort, skill, and decision-making.[27]

21.22 An employer seeking to rely on a JES to show that the claim is hopeless will bear the burden of proving that the JES meets the requirements of the EqPA 1970.[28] In the absence of a JES, the burden of showing that the claim is or is not hopeless is a neutral one.[29] But when a JES is put forward, the practical effect is that the applicant has to adduce evidence to attack it as being non-analytical or sex-biased.

21.23 There is a corresponding duty under Equal Pay Directive article 1 to exclude sex-based criteria from 'job classification schemes' and to ensure there is no discrimination in the drawing-up of the criteria. The directive does not enlarge the obligations under article 141 of the treaty, but merely clarifies them, facilitates the practical application of the principle of equal pay and specifies the conditions necessary for a valid JES.[30]

21.24 A JES which indirectly discriminated against, and led to lower pay for, women would be in breach of article 141 of the treaty and of the directive.[31] The EqPA 1970 deals expressly with studies which discriminate on the grounds of sex and this can be taken to include indirect discrimination as defined by Sex Discrimination Act 1975 s1(1)(b).[31a]

Equal value claims

21.25 The right to bring a complaint based on work of equal value was introduced after the European Court of Justice found in *Commission of the European Communities v United Kingdom*[32] that the UK government had failed to fulfil its obligations under European law. Special rules of procedure applicable to such claims were subsequently introduced by the Industrial Tribunals (Rules of Procedure) (Equal Value Amendment) Regulations 1983 and are now to be found as the Equal Value Complementary Rules of Procedure in 2001 Regs[33] Sch 3.

27 See EqPA 1970 s1(5) and *Bromley v H & J Quick Ltd*, note 23 above.
28 *Bromley v H & J Quick Ltd*, note 23 above.
29 *Dennehy v Sealink UK Ltd* [1987] IRLR 120, EAT.
30 *Jenkins v Kingsgate Ltd* [1981] ICR 592 at 614; [1981] IRLR 228, ECJ.
31 *Bilka-Kaufhaus v Weber von Hartz* [1987] ICR 110 at 125; [1986] IRLR 317, ECJ.
31a As amended by the 2001 'Burden of Proof' Regs, see note 15 above.
32 [1982] ICR 578; [1982] IRLR 333.
33 Employment Tribunals (Constitution and Rules of Procedure) Regulations 2001 SI No 1171.

21.26   Practical experience of these claims indicates that, far from empowering workers to bring equal value complaints, the procedures introduced are open to abuse and often delay removal of the inequality. Cases can take many years to complete: four years for Julie Hayward,[34] seven years for Sybil Bromley,[35] over a decade for Dr Pamela Enderby and her colleagues,[36] and the applicants in the coal industry cases waited some 15 years after presenting their claims before the cases were settled.[37] All too often applicants are put off by delay, cost and legal complexity.

21.27   In *Aldridge v British Telecommunications plc*[38] Wood J said:

> The present restrictions on procedure imposed by the Rules give rise to delays which are properly described as scandalous and . . . amount to a denial of justice to women seeking remedy through the judicial process.

21.28   The situation has changed little and similar criticisms were again made by Wood J in the Employment Appeal Tribunal (EAT) in *British Coal Corporation v Smith*.[39] The Equal Opportunities Commission (EOC) made a formal complaint in 1993 to the European Commission about the UK government's failure to provide proper procedures for delivery of effective remedies. In 1996 new rules on time limits were introduced (see now Sch 3 r2, amending Sch 1 by inserting r10A of the 2001 Rules) but seem to have had little real effect, leading to the government making further proposals for procedural reform in equal pay cases.[40]

Procedural steps

21.29   It is hoped that the approach taken in relation to the procedural steps in equal value cases in this chapter may assist those involved in such

---

34   *Hayward v Cammell Laird Shipbuilders Ltd* [1988] ICR 464; [1988] IRLR 257, HL.
35   *Bromley v H & J Quick Ltd* [1988] ICR 623; [1988] IRLR 249, settled in 1993.
36   *Enderby and others v Frenchay Health Authority and Secretary of State for Health* [1991] IRLR 44, ICR 382, EAT; [1992] IRLR 15, CA; [1993] IRLR 591, ICR 112, ECJ; [1999] IRLR 155, EAT; [2000] IRLR 257, CA.
37   *Smith and others v National Coal Board* [1993] IRLR 308, EAT; [1994] IRLR 342, ICR 810, CA; [1996] 3 All ER 97, IRLR 404, ICR 515, HL.
38   [1989] ICR 790; [1990] IRLR 10, EAT.
39   [1993] ICR 529; [1993] IRLR 308 and [1996] IRLR 404.
40   These were still at the consultation stage at the time of writing, although the proposal to introduce a specific equal pay questionnaire procedure is now contained with the Employment Bill 2001 clause 42.

claims and may encourage parties to use the procedure in keeping with the aims of the treaty and directive.

Step 1: Completion of IT1/IT3

21.30   Follow normal procedure (see para 6.4). Multi-applicant cases might be best served by using 2001 Rules r1(2) to present a number of claims in one document.

Step 2: Interim stages

Requests for further particulars of IT1/IT3 and written answers to questions

21.31   These are as in other tribunal claims (see Sch 1 r4 and chapters 6, 9 and 12), except that the tribunal may also require the provision of written information relevant to the question the independent expert has been asked to determine (see Sch 3 r1, modifying Sch 1 by the insertion of r4(5A) of the 2001 Rules and see below).

Disclosure

21.32   Employers are often reluctant to make full disclosure in discrimination cases, claiming confidentiality. In *Nassé v Science Research Council*,[41] however, the House of Lords recognised that the necessary information to support a claim of discrimination is almost always in the possession of the employer, who can be ordered to disclose documents. An employer can refuse only when there is some overriding public interest in maintaining the confidentiality of documents.[42] But an employer who may be able to claim that the public interest is against disclosure of certain classes of document in its possession will not succeed on that ground in withholding *all* documents (see chapter 10).[43] Note the additional power of the tribunal under Sch 3 r1 (amending Sch 1 by inserting r4(5A)) to order discovery of documents relevant to the question the independent expert has been asked to determine (see below).

Preliminary hearing

21.33   As well as the more usual preliminary hearing to consider issues of jurisdiction, etc, tribunals are often keen to separate out legal

---

41   [1979] ICR 921; [1979] IRLR 465, HL.
42   *Halford v Sharples and others* [1992] ICR 583, CA.
43   *Commissioner of Metropolitan Police v Locker* [1993] ICR 440, EAT.

and factual issues in equal value cases to be considered at separate hearings. While this might constitute good case management in many cases, applicants and their advisers should be wary of the additional delays that this might entail (particularly where there is the possibility of appeals at each stage).

Directions hearing

21.34   These are often set up at an early stage in equal pay cases to get a clearer idea of the issues between the parties. They include considering:

– whether the claim can more conveniently be processed as a 'like work' or JES case;
– whether to consider together a number of similar claims against an employer, and whether there are by agreement any tests or sample cases – where the parties have reached such an agreement, there may be costs consequences if a party subsequently seeks to renege on this by pursuing another case which is really the same as the 'test' claim;[44]
– whether the applicant's claim that her work is of equal value may be put forward as an alternative should she fail to establish a like work claim – here the equal value claim is heard after the other claim has been dismissed;
– whether either or both parties are likely to call expert evidence and, if so, to set down a sensible time table for exchange of that evidence (particularly if this might allow the experts to reach agreement on particular issues).

Pre-hearing review (2001 Rules sch 1 r7) and application to strike out, etc (2001 Rules sch 1 r15(2)(d))

21.35   These are unlikely to be used in the light of the specific provision in step 4 below.

Conciliation

21.36   Copies of equal pay claims are sent to the Advisory, Conciliation and Arbitration Service (ACAS) and a duty is imposed under SDA 1975 s64(1), to promote the settlement of the dispute if so requested or if there is a reasonable prospect of achieving a settlement (and see chapter 3).

44   *Ashmore v British Coal Corporation* [1990] ICR 485; [1990] IRLR 283, CA.

Step 3: Invitation to adjourn

21.37 Under the 2001 Rules, the first obligation on the tribunal is to invite the parties, before hearing them on the claim itself, to apply for an adjournment for the purpose of seeking a settlement of the claim (Sch 3 r6(b), inserting r15(6A) into Sch 1). The adjournment must be by consent of all parties.

21.38 The compromise of discrimination and equal pay claims is seen as a desirable objective and the 2001 Rules relating to equal value claims reflect this perception by making specific provision for the consideration of settlement at this early stage in the procedure. There is specific provision for this in SDA 1975 s64(1). The duty to consider adjourning matters to permit settlement discussions in equal value cases is in addition to the tribunal's (or a chairman's) general discretionary power to order that proceedings be adjourned (under 2001 Regs Sch 1 r15(7)). While there are good policy reasons for encouraging parties to reach voluntary agreements in equal value cases, applicants and their advisers should always be wary of the possibility of delay that this might entail if discussions prove unsuccessful – usually there are sufficient delays inherent in equal value proceedings to permit discussions to take place without actually adjourning a hearing.

Step 4: The initial hearing

21.39 Assuming that the parties do not wish to adjourn to consider a settlement of the claim or that, having adjourned, settlement negotiations have broken down, the tribunal usually proceeds to an initial hearing at which the following matters can be raised:

– Whether an independent expert is to be appointed or whether the tribunal is to assess the question of equal value itself without referring the matter to an independent expert (EqPA 1970 s2A(1)). The parties will be given the opportunity to make representations on this issue before the tribunal determines which course to take (2001 Regs Sch 3 r2, inserting r10A(2) into Sch 1). Where a tribunal decides at this stage to proceed to determine the question of equal value itself, it may revisit the issue subsequently and refer the question to an independent expert at any later stage, providing it has again given the parties the opportunity to make representations on this course of action (2001 Regs Sch 3 r2, inserting r10A(3) into Sch 1).

– If the tribunal declines to determine the question of equal value itself under EqPA 1970 s2A(1)(a), whether there are *no reasonable grounds for determining that the work is of equal value*. This applies only to equal value claims and is designed to stop wholly unrealistic comparisons, for example, as between a refuse operative and a chief executive officer. It means that the claim is hopeless.[45] If the employer attacks in this way, the EAT had stated[46] that the tribunal has no choice but must determine this question at an initial hearing before going on to appoint an expert. However, in *Wood v William Ball Ltd*,[47] Morison J stated that this is no longer the position. Under EqPA 1970 s2A(1), the first step must be for the tribunal to consider whether it should proceed to determine the question of equal value itself or whether an independent expert's report is to be obtained (see above). It is only if the tribunal has decided on the latter course of action, that the question arises as to whether there are reasonable grounds for the claim.

– Whether there is a *genuine material factor* (GMF) defence under EqPA 1970 s1(3). If asked to consider a GMF defence at this stage, the tribunal can do so, but does not have to (2001 Regs Sch 3 r3, amending Sch 1 by inserting r11(2E)). If it finds the GMF defence is made out, the tribunal must dismiss the claim. It is generally in the employer's interest to raise the GMF defence at this stage but it is open to any party to apply to the tribunal at the initial hearing of an equal value claim to consider this question. A tribunal does not have to accede to the request at this stage, but if it does so and concludes that the defence is made out, then it must forthwith dismiss the claim.[48] On the other hand, if the tribunal does not hear the defence at this stage, the respondent can still raise it after the independent expert's report has been received: see step 7 below.

An employer not wishing the tribunal to consider the question of a GMF defence at this stage would still be well-advised to raise the point at as early a stage as possible (preferably in the notice of appearance). If an employer indicates at this stage that it does not intend to rely on any GMF defence, it may be barred from raising it subsequently.[49]

---

45 See *Bromley v H & J Quick Ltd* [1988] ICR 623 at 637; [1988] IRLR 249, CA and EqPA 1970 s2A(1)(a).

46 *Sheffield Metropolitan District Council v Siberry* [1989] ICR 208.

47 [1999] IRLR 773.

48 *Reed Packaging Ltd v Boozer and Everhurst* [1988] ICR 391; [1988] IRLR 333, EAT.

49 *Hayward v Cammell Laird Shipbuilders Ltd* [1985] ICR 71; [1984] IRLR 463, IT.

Step 5: Commissioning a report from an independent expert

21.40   Assuming the tribunal is not minded to assess the question of equal value without the assistance of a report from an independent expert (IE) and that the claim has not been dismissed at the initial hearing, the tribunal is entitled to commission an IE to prepare a report on whether the applicant's work is of equal value to that of her chosen comparator(s) (EqPA 1970 s2A(1)(b)). As already indicated, where the tribunal initially sought to proceed to determine the question of equal value itself, it can always revisit this question subsequently and can refer the matter to an IE at a later stage in the proceedings (2001 Regs Sch 3 r2, inserting r10A(3) into Sch 1).

The independent expert

21.41   The IE is a member of a panel designated as suitably qualified and independent by ACAS, although he or she cannot be a member or employee of ACAS (EqPA 1970 s2A(4)). Since 1990, members of the IE panel have adopted a self-denying ordinance for their non-statutory practices and will not accept instructions to advise, give evidence or represent anyone in a case where it is likely that an IE will be required to report.

The requirement

21.42   The tribunal will set out a written requirement for the expert's report, which will include details of the parties and of the relevant establishment at which the applicant works or worked, will set out 'the question' to be determined and will identify the comparator(s). It will also specify a date by which the IE is required to send the report to the tribunal and the length of the intervals before that date, when the IE is required to submit progress reports to the tribunal (see 2001 Regs Sch 3 r2, inserting r10A(4)(a)–(f) into Sch 1). Copies of the requirement will be supplied to the parties (2001 Regs Sch 3 r2, Sch 1 r10A(4)).

The report

21.43   The requirement stipulates that in compiling the report the expert must:

–   take no account of the difference of sex and at all times act fairly;
–   take into account all information supplied and any representations made which are relevant to the question to be determined;
–   send a written summary of information supplied and

representations made to each of the parties and invite comment on that material; and, only then,

- compile a report, which should reproduce the summary and contain an account of the representations made as well as setting out any conclusions reached and the reasons for those conclusions (2001 Regs Sch 3 r2, inserting r10A(5) into Sch 1).

21.44   The IE evaluates the relevant jobs to be compared in relation to the demands made on the holders of those jobs under headings such as effort, skill, decision-making, etc (2001 Regs Sch 3 r2, inserting r10A(1) into Sch 1). These are the same suggested headings used in EqPA 1970 s1(5) to determine whether a JES is valid. An evaluation of jobs according to headings such as these is known as 'analytical'.[50] The purpose is to make an objective comparison of the factors demanded by each job, and it is usual for there to be between four and eight, including (say) working conditions, supervision and responsibility.

21.45   It is not for the expert to take into account any GMF that may be raised by the employer, except to the limited extent that any defence may affect the demands of the job.

21.46   The parties' right to receive the summary and to make representations to the expert on this material provides the only opportunity to challenge the facts on which the expert will rely in making his or her report.[50a]

Provision of information

21.47   The tribunal has the power, on application by the IE, to order any person (other than an ACAS officer appointed to assist conciliation of the case, or where the person would otherwise have good grounds for refusing to provide that information, for example, where it is privileged, etc – see chapter 10) to furnish in writing relevant information and/or to provide documents (2001 Regs Sch 3 r1, inserting r4(5A) into Sch 1). This is a wide and unique power, since it enables the tribunal to make an order at the request of an IE, and addressed to people other than the parties. The order can require documents to be produced *and* information to be 'furnished', ie, created, put in writing and handed over.

21.48   The tribunal has no specific power under the EqPA 1970 or the 2001 Rules to order an employer to allow the IE access to the work-

---

50 See Dillon LJ in *Bromley v H & J Quick Ltd* [1988] ICR 623 at 633.
50a Except for the right to challenge the entire admissability of the report, see para 21.60 below.

place, although a respondent has been ordered to allow the applicant's expert access to the workplace,[51] under the general power to regulate proceedings in equal value cases (2001 Regs Sch 3 r3, substituting r11(1) into Sch 1). This seems to be an entirely sensible use of this general power and one which is in keeping with the spirit and intent of European law; a domestic tribunal should not be deterred in its consideration of questions of equal value by the obstructive tactics of one of the parties.

Adjournment and progress reports

21.49 While the IE is preparing the report, the proceedings will be adjourned (2001 Regs Sch 3 r2, inserting r10A(6) into Sch 1). The delays at this stage of the procedure have been the subject of much criticism by, for example, the EOC. Amendments have been made to the procedure in an attempt to prevent undue delays but with limited success in many cases. In particular, the rules require that, within the period specified in the initial requirement, the IE must send a progress report to the tribunal stating:

– whether he or she will be able to send the completed report to the tribunal by the required date; and
– if not, giving reasons for the delay and stating the date by which it is expected that the report might be ready (see 2001 Regs Sch 3 r2, inserting r10A(8) into Sch1).

21.50 The IE must thereafter provide regular progress reports in compliance with the requirement of the tribunal. In so doing, if it becomes apparent that the IE will be unable to submit the final report within the original time frame, then this must be stated, reasons given and a new date for submission provided (2001 Regs Sch 3 r2, inserting r10A(9) into Sch 1). Although, in such circumstances, the tribunal can (after receiving representations from the parties) serve notice on the IE insisting that the report is submitted by the original date or by a substituted later date (2001 Regs Sch 3 r2, inserting r10A(11)(a) and (b) into Sch 1).

21.51 If there is any reason for the delay, such as obstruction by a party to the proceedings, then the IE must say so, identifying the party, the act or omission leading to the delay and how and to what extent it has contributed to the delay (2001 Regs Sch 3 r2, inserting r10A(10) into Sch 1). In such circumstances, the tribunal can (after hearing from

---

51 *Whitmore and others v Frayling Furniture* 1985 COIT 1680/204, unreported.

that party) order costs against the party in question under 2001 Rules r14 plus costs payable to the IE (2001 Regs Sch 3 r2, inserting r10A(15) into Sch 1), or can strike out the whole or part of the originating application or notice of appearance or debar a respondent from defending the claim, as appropriate (2001 Regs Sch 3 r2, inserting r10A(14) into Sch 1).

21.52   Failure to maintain progress gives the tribunal the right, after hearing the parties, to revoke the requirement, ie, to dismiss and appoint another IE (2001 Regs Sch 3 r2, inserting r10A(11)(c) and (13) into Sch 1).

21.53   Realistically, reports by IEs will often take months, particularly where a number of applicants and/or comparators are involved. The tribunal is unlikely to delay matters further by instructing a different expert unless there are very good grounds for doing so.

Step 6: Receipt of the report

21.54   The IE will send the completed report to the tribunal, which in turn will send a copy to the parties. The tribunal will then proceed to fix a date for the hearing of the case to be resumed not less than 14 days after the date on which the report was sent to the parties (2001 Regs Sch 3 r2, inserting r10A(16) into Sch 1).

21.55   At the resumed hearing, the IE's report will be admitted as evidence in the case unless the tribunal has excluded it as inadmissible (2001 Regs Sch 3 r2, inserting r10A(17) and (18) into Sch 1 and see below).

21.56   After receiving the expert's report (assuming it is to be treated as admissible), the tribunal may at any time require that expert (or another expert from the ACAS panel) to explain any matter contained within that report. Such a requirement must be made by the tribunal in the same way as the request for the original report was made and the parties must again be given the opportunity to make any relevant representations and should be sent a copy of the expert's reply (2001 Regs Sch 3 r2, inserting r10A(20)–(23)).

Step 7: The resumed hearing

21.57   Either party may apply to the tribunal at this stage to exclude the expert's report if:

- the expert has not complied with the rules relating to the preparation, contents and presentation of the report; or
- the conclusion arrived at in the report could not reasonably have been reached; or

– for some other material reason, other than disagreement with the conclusion that the applicant's work is or is not of equal value or with the reasons for such a conclusion, the report is unsatisfactory (2001 Regs Sch 3 r2, inserting r10A(18) into Sch 1).

Equally, the tribunal may decide to exclude the IE's report of its own motion on the same grounds.

21.58 In either case, in considering whether to exclude the report, the tribunal should consider any representations made by the parties and may permit evidence from the parties or the expert to be adduced (2001 Regs Sch 3 r2, inserting r10A(19) into Sch 1).

21.59 In practice, tribunals are reluctant to exclude the expert's report at this stage and will not do so solely on the basis of a challenge to the methodology or a criticism that factors involving substantial sex bias have been deployed in the evaluation.[52]

21.60 This is, however, the last opportunity a party has to challenge the factual basis of the expert's report unless the report is inconclusive. Once a report has been admitted, no challenge can be made to the facts on which it has been based.[53]

21.61 If the tribunal determines that the expert's report should not be admitted, it must then require another report to be commissioned and the procedure will recommence. In these circumstances no further account will be taken of the first expert's report (2001 Regs Sch 3 r2, inserting r10A(24) into Sch 1).

Admission of the report and expert evidence

21.62 Otherwise, the IE's report will be admitted as evidence at the resumed hearing (2001 Regs Sch 3 r2, inserting r10A(17) into Sch 1). The report is, however, merely evidence to be taken into account by the tribunal in determining the issue of equal value; it is not conclusive, it does not change the burden of proof, and the tribunal is entitled to reach a different conclusion without necessarily being considered perverse.[54]

21.63 A tribunal may (and should, if a party so requests) require the expert to attend the resumed hearing to give evidence and be cross-examined by the parties on the contents, conclusions and reasoning of the report (2001 Regs Sch 3 r3, inserting r11(2A) into Sch 1). It is not unique in tribunal proceedings for a witness to be called by the

---

52 See, eg, the EOC's *Job Evaluation Schemes free of Sex Bias*.
53 *Hayward v Cammell Laird Shipbuilders Ltd* [1985] ICR 71; [1984] IRLR 463, IT.
54 *Tennants Textile Colours Ltd v Todd* [1989] IRLR 3, NI CA.

tribunal, it has the power to do so under 2001 Regs Sch 1 r4(5).[55] In equal value proceedings, however, it is likely that one party will seek to uphold the IE's report (assuming it to favour one side rather than another), yet there is no rule of evidence preventing leading questions being asked for that purpose. In practical terms, therefore, a party can cross-examine a favourable expert.

21.64   At this resumed hearing, either party may apply to call an expert witness and this witness will then be available for cross-examination and re-examination in the normal way (2001 Regs Sch 3 r3, inserting r11(2B) into Sch 1). A tribunal cannot order that a party be interviewed by the other party's expert.[56] Moreover, there is no express rule of evidence requiring prior disclosure to the IE or to the other party of each side's own expert's report, although this might be seen as a matter falling within the tribunal's general power to give directions and regulate its own procedure.

21.65   Other than in the provision for expert evidence, the conduct of the resumed hearing will be similar to that for tribunals generally, although no evidence of fact can be called by the parties unless the IE has been unable to reach a conclusion or the evidence goes to support or challenge a GMF defence which has been raised by the employer (2001 Regs Sch 3 r3, inserting r11(2C) and (2(D)).

55   *Clapson v British Airways Plc* [2001] IRLR 184, EAT.
56   *Lloyds Bank plc v Fox* [1989] ICR 80; [1989] IRLR 103

CHAPTER 22

Review

Scope

22.1   Underlying all proceedings of a judicial nature is the principle that there should be finality in litigation. This consideration of public policy gives rise to the general rule that tribunal decisions cannot be reopened or relitigated. You do not get two bites at the cherry.[1] Exceptions are provided in limited circumstances: when the tribunal has made an error of law the decision can be *appealed* to the Employment Appeal Tribunal (EAT) (see chapter 24), and when specific grounds exist, there is a power to *review* a tribunal's decision.

22.2   A tribunal's power of review is unusual in judicial proceedings and has been said to provide:

> . . . a useful corrective, designed to prevent any injustice being suffered as a result of the very considerable relaxation of the rules of evidence and procedure which, in the interests of informality and an absence of legalism, is encouraged at . . . tribunal hearings.[2]

22.3   This does not mean that the power is to be invoked by any party aggrieved at a tribunal decision seeking a rehearing of the case: the power is 'not intended to provide parties with the opportunity of a re-hearing at which the same evidence can be rehearsed with different emphasis, or further evidence adduced which was available before'.[3]

Clerical mistakes

22.4   Purely clerical mistakes or errors arising from an accidental slip or omission in any decision of a tribunal, or statement of reasons, or of compensation (2001 Rules r12(2) and (3)[4]), may be corrected at any time by the tribunal chairman by certificate (2001 Rules r12(8)). Where the chairman is unable to sign the certificate as required, for example, due to death or incapacity, the other members of a tribunal will sign the certificate and certify that the chairman was unable to do so (2001 Rules r12(11)).

22.5   This power may be exercised at any time and is generally referred to as 'the slip rule'. It is limited to clerical slips and arithmetical

---

1   See, eg, *Morris v Griffiths* [1977] ICR 153 at 156 EAT, per Bristow J.
2   Per Waite J in *Carryfast Ltd v Dawkins* EAT 290/83, unreported.
3   *Stevenson v Golden Wonder Ltd* [1977] IRLR 474, EAT.
4   Employment Tribunals Rules of Procedure (contained in SI 2001 No 1171, Sch 1).

mistakes, such as a reference to a limited company respondent as a 'plc', and should not be confused with the power of review.

22.6   In practice, any slips are corrected and initialed by the chairman in manuscript on the original decision, which is then sent together with the certificate of correction to the secretary so that the entry in the register can be altered (2001 Rules r12(9)). If the document was previously omitted from the register in circumstances where the tribunal sat in private, any corrected document will be sent to the parties by the secretary of tribunals (2001 Rules r12(10)).

The power to review

22.7   A tribunal can review its decision in the following circumstances (2001 Rules r13(1)):

- the decision was wrongly made as a result of an error on the part of the tribunal staff;
- a party did not receive notice of the proceedings leading to the decision;
- the decision was made in the absence of a party;
- new evidence has become available since the conclusion of the hearing, providing that its existence could not have been reasonably known of or foreseen at the time of the hearing; or
- the interests of justice require such a review.

Error by staff

22.8   'Tribunal staff' do not include the chairman or other members of the tribunal. In practice, it is rare for a review to be based on this ground, as most errors on the part of the administrative staff of tribunals would either be capable of correction under the slip rule (2001 Rules r12(8) above) or would more appropriately be considered under 2001 Rules r13(1)(b) or (c), ie, failure to give proper notice of the proceedings or reaching a decision in the absence of a party.

22.9   Furthermore, the mere fact that a member of the tribunal staff has made an error will not be sufficient for a party to succeed on an application for review on this ground: the power to review on this basis arises only when a decision was *wrongly made as a result of* the error.

No notice of proceedings

22.10   Under 2001 Rules r5(1) the secretary is obliged to send all parties a notice of hearing at least 14 days before the date fixed for that hearing. By 2001 Rules r23(4) this notice is authorised to be sent by post. The provisions of the Interpretation Act 1978 s7, relating to service of documents by post, have been held to apply to tribunal proceedings,[5] except where 'presentation' is required (see para 5.45). Section 7 provides:

> Where an Act authorises or requires any document to be sent by post . . . then, unless the contrary intention appears, the service is deemed to be effected by properly addressing, prepaying, and posting a letter containing the document, and unless the contrary is proved, to have been effected at the time at which the letter would be delivered in the ordinary course of post.

22.11   This presumption that the notice has been effectively served by committing it to the post is difficult to rebut. Nor would it be sufficient for a party to claim that the document must have been intercepted after delivery by some third party or been lost within some complicated corporate structure: parties are presumed to have made adequate arrangements for the receipt of their mail during the course of tribunal proceedings. In the case of a limited company, service at the company's registered address is deemed to have been effected, even if no reply has been received.[6]

22.12   If a notice of appearance has not been entered, for whatever reason, this is the only ground on which the respondent may apply for a review (2001 Rules r3(3)(c)).

Absence of a party

22.13   This ground does not open the way for a party to choose not to attend a hearing and subsequently apply for a review of the decision on the ground of non-attendance. A party who makes the conscious choice not to appear at a tribunal hearing must take the consequences.[7]

22.14   A party wishing to apply for a review of a tribunal decision on this ground must demonstrate a genuine reason for the original absence, such as some unforeseen illness or accident. In *Morris v Griffiths*[8] the

---

5   *Migwain Ltd (in liquidation) v TGWU* [1979] ICR 597, EAT and *T and D Transport (Portsmouth) Ltd v Linburn* [1987] ICR 696, EAT.
6   *Migwain*, note 5 above.
7   *Fforde v Black* EAT 68/80, unreported.
8   [1977] ICR 153.

EAT overturned a tribunal decision since it, the EAT, found the respondent employer's explanation as to how he fell ill on the way to the tribunal hearing, and 'had been succoured by . . . his sister who conveniently live[d] half way' was honest and gave grounds for allowing a review.

22.15   When an application is made under this head, much will depend on the view taken by the tribunal as to the creditworthiness of the party concerned; so where the question arises whether the reason given is 'genuine', an oral hearing of the application for review is required.[9]

New evidence

22.16   This must have arisen since the conclusion of the hearing to which the decision relates, provided that its existence could not have been reasonably known of or foreseen at the time of the hearing. A party wishing to apply for a review under this head must show:

- some reasonable explanation for not having produced the evidence before the tribunal, ie, the new evidence was not available before the conclusion of the original hearing and its existence could not reasonably have been known of or foreseen at that time;
- the new evidence is credible (although it may still be open to contradiction); and
- the new evidence would or might have some effect on the original tribunal decision.[10]

22.17   These conditions are those applied by the civil courts generally on appeal (see para 24.44). It has been stressed by the EAT that merely because tribunals have less formal procedures than the High Court, applications to admit fresh evidence are no more likely to be favourably entertained as a matter of course.[11] The conditions have been strictly applied by tribunals. In *Flint v Eastern Electricity Board*,[12] the tribunal did not review its decision by considering new medical evidence which could have been adduced by the employee at the original hearing, although there was clearly much sympathy for the employee and the evidence was acknowledged to be genuine and to be relevant to the tribunal's decision.

9 See *Morris*, note 8 above.
10 See *Bagga v Heavy Electricals (India) Ltd* [1972] ICR 118, NIRC.
11 *Borden (UK) Ltd v Potter* [1986] ICR 647, EAT.
12 [1975] ICR 395; [1975] IRLR 277, QBD.

22.18   A party may be unfairly confronted by evidence at the original tribunal hearing. For example if, after the respondent's case, the applicant gives evidence on matters which it has failed to put to the respondent, the respondent should apply for an adjournment at that stage to allow time to consider whether there might be evidence in rebuttal. It would be wrong to wait until after the tribunal decision and then seek to adduce evidence in rebuttal by way of review.[13] But if the party taken by surprise is unrepresented, and the tribunal fails to draw attention to the possibility of an adjournment, an application for review under 2001 Rules r13(1)(d) may succeed.[14]

22.19   Even if the evidence was not previously available and could not reasonably have been foreseen, the application will fail unless it can be shown that the new evidence is both relevant and probative and is likely to have an important influence on the result of the case. In *Wileman v Minilec Engineering Ltd*[15] it was held that the applicant's subsequent behaviour in posing for a national newspaper in a 'flimsy costume' did not meet the test of relevance, and was unlikely to have any influence in determining her complaint of sexual harassment.

22.20   In other cases, however, evidence of matters which have taken place subsequent to the tribunal decision has been held to be admissible under this rule. In *Help the Aged Housing Association (Scotland) Ltd v Vidler*[16] evidence of the applicant's subsequent employment was held to be admissible and led to a reduction in the compensation previously awarded. And in *Ladup Ltd v Barnes*[17] the EAT held that it is unjust not to allow a review where there has been a subsequent conviction in relation to the very matter (growing cannabis) for which the employee had been dismissed, when the tribunal had previously held that there had been no contributory fault. A decision which was correct at the time of the hearing may become unsound later. Yet in *Yorkshire Engineering and Welding Co Ltd v Burnham*[18] the National Industrial Relations Court (NIRC) held that a change in circumstances of a less substantial nature was not sufficient to give rise to a ground for a review of the previous award of compensation. Furthermore, generally speaking, evidence which simply goes to the

---

13 *Douglas Water Miners Welfare Society Club v Grieve* EAT 487/ 84, unreported.
14 *Grieves v Coldshield Windows Ltd* EAT 218/82, unreported.
15 [1988] ICR 318; [1988] IRLR 144, EAT.
16 [1977] IRLR 104, EAT.
17 [1982] ICR 107; [1982] IRLR 7, EAT.
18 [1974] ICR 77; [1973] IRLR 316, NIRC.

credibility of a witness will not be admitted unless it can be shown to be central to the main issue(s) of the case (see para 18.67).

22.21   When applying for a review under 2001 Rules r13(1)(d), details should be given of the new evidence which is sought to be adduced, as well as stating the reasons why it was not produced before the first hearing.[19]

Interests of justice

22.22   While this residual ground gives a wide discretion to tribunals, the discretion must be exercised judicially and with regard to the interests of *all* parties, and to the public interest in finality in litigation.[20] It has furthermore been stressed that the power to grant a review on this ground should be exercised cautiously.[21] It should, however, be exercised consistently with the right to a fair trial under article 6(1) of the European Convention on Human Rights.

22.23   It is not merely an alternative to the other grounds for review and a party will rarely succeed on this basis when the reasons for making the application have already been rejected under another head; there needs to be 'some special additional circumstance . . . or mitigating factor',[22] which leads to the conclusion that justice does in fact require a review. In *General Council of British Shipping v Deria*[23] the EAT put the test even higher, as requiring 'exceptional circumstances' which relate not to wider matters such as the unusual nature of the case or the public importance attached to it, but to factors relating to the case itself. In *Deria*, the tribunal had allowed the application for a review of the original decision (based on grounds of new evidence and the interests of justice), as the case involved 'an issue of widespread public importance and related to a technical loophole in the Race Relations Act', matters which outweighed the public interest in finality in litigation. On appeal, the EAT reversed the tribunal's decision, holding that the approach taken had been wrong in principle.

22.24   Cases which fall under 'interests of justice' alone have been divided into two categories: (1) those involving some procedural mishap, and (2) those where the tribunal's decision has been undermined by events occurring shortly thereafter.

19 *Vauxhall Motors Ltd v Henry* [1978] ITR 332, EAT.
20 *Flint*, note 12 above.
21 *Lindsay v Ironsides Ray & Vials* [1994] ICR 384, EAT.
22 *Flint*, note 12 above.
23 [1985] ICR 198, EAT.

Procedural mishaps

22.25   These include the following:

- where a party has not been given a fair opportunity to address the tribunal on a point of substance, for example, on the questions of remedy or mitigation of loss[24] (this would also be a ground of complaint under article 6(1) of the Convention);
- where a point affecting the tribunal's jurisdiction to hear the case was not raised at the original hearing;[25]
- where the originating application was withdrawn at the original hearing due in part to a mistaken view of the law on the part of the tribunal chairman and in part to a failure to disclose all relevant documents.[26]

22.26   Some procedural mishaps might involve the tribunal also correcting an error of law when reviewing the previous decision. This is not a bar to carrying out a review in such cases, even if the error of law is a major or substantial one: see *Trimble v Supertravel Ltd,*[27] where Browne-Wilkinson J stated that it was irrelevant whether the tribunal's error was minor or major, provided the erroneous decision had been reached after some procedural mishap. An application for review may even be the correct approach where a simple mistake has led to the tribunal failing to consider a question of jurisdiction, as in *British Midland Airways Ltd v Lewis,*[28] or failing to consider the award of interest on compensation in a discrimination case.

Subsequent events

22.27   Subsequent events which might give grounds for applying for a review of the original decision in the interests of justice include the following:

- where the compensatory award was made on forecasts as to earnings which subsequently are found to have been falsified by the applicant, as in *Yorkshire Engineering and Welding Co Ltd v Burnham*[29] – although in that case the application for a review failed;
- where a compensatory award has been made with no deduction

24 *Trimble v Supertravel Ltd* [1982] ICR 440; [1982] IRLR 451, EAT.
25 *British Midland Airways Ltd v Lewis* [1978] ICR 782, EAT.
26 *Harber v North London Polytechnic* [1990] IRLR 198, CA.
27 See note 24 above.
28 See note 25 above.
29 See note 18 above.

for contributory fault, and the applicant is subsequently convicted: see *Ladup v Barnes*.[30]

A decision

22.28   The power to review relates only to a *decision* of the tribunal. A decision is defined by 2001 Regs reg 2(2) as including:

> . . . a declaration, an order, including an order striking out any originating application or notice of appearance made under r4(8)(b) or 15(2), a recommendation or an award of the tribunal and a determination under r6 [entitlement to bring or contest proceedings] but does not include any other interlocutory order or any other decision on an interlocutory matter.

22.29   There is no power, therefore, to review an interim order relating to further particulars, disclosure, or joining a respondent into the case. Nor can a mandatory order striking out an originating application or notice of appearance made under 2001 Rules r7(7) be subject to a review.[31] If you want to challenge an interim order, the appropriate course of action is *either* to apply to the tribunal for further directions;[32] *or* to appeal to the EAT, if there is some error of law in the order (although most interim orders will involve a pure exercise of discretion and be un-appealable). If an interim order is made after considering representations from only one party, the order is provisional and may be reconsidered by the tribunal on an application for further direction from another party.[33]

22.30   When an originating application has been dismissed or struck out as a result of some error which gives rise to a ground for review, the applicant should apply for a review and not issue a further originating application, even if still in time to do so. The issue of a further originating application in these circumstances has been held to be vexatious,[34] and may be struck out on that ground under 2001 Rules r15(2)(d).

22.31   No distinction is made between oral and written decisions, and decisions in extended or summary form: the power to review applies to them all.

---

30   See note 17 above.
31   *Kuttapan v Croydon LBC* [1999] IRLR 349, EAT.
32   *Nikitas v Solihull MBC* [1986] ICR 291, EAT.
33   *Reddington v Straker & Sons Ltd* [1994] ICR 172, EAT.
34   *Acrow (Engineers) Ltd v Hathaway* [1981] ICR 510, EAT.

The number of applications

22.32   The tribunal can consider reviewing a particular decision more than once, although it is unclear as to whether a second consideration of the question of a review must be on new grounds. In *Raybright TV Services Ltd v Smith*[35] the NIRC held that, in exceptional circumstances, a second application for a review, made on the same grounds, was permissible. However, in *Stevensons (Dyers) Ltd v Brennan*[36] it was held that a party could not make the same application for a review more than once. At the time of both decisions the power of review was linked by rule to the county court power to order a new trial, in respect of which only one application is permissible.[37] The link no longer exists, which may undermine the judgment in *Stevensons*. On the other hand, any second application would have to be heard by a differently constituted tribunal in any event (the first would be defunct) and it may be predicted that most tribunals would be extremely reluctant to allow a party further attempts at the evidence without any new grounds.

Application of party or on tribunal's own initiative

22.33   A review can be considered either on the application of a party or of the tribunal's own initiative (2001 Rules r13(1)).

Parties

22.34   If one of the parties wishes to apply for a review, the application can either be made orally at the hearing, or in writing to the secretary within 14 days of the date on which the decision was sent to the parties. Time may be extended by the tribunal under 2001 Rules r17(1). On a written application to the secretary, the party should set out in full the grounds on which the application is made (2001 Rules r13(4)).

22.35   As a matter of practice, an application for a review *must* set out not only the grounds for seeking a review but also the grounds for contending that the decision of which a review is sought is wrong.[38] In other words, an explanation must be given together with the basis for contending that the decision was wrong on the merits.

---

35 [1973] ICR 640, NIRC.
36 [1974] ICR 194, NIRC.
37 CPR Sch 2 and County Court Rules Order 37.
38 *P J Drakard & Sons Ltd v Wilton* [1977] ICR 642, EAT.

22.36   An application for review may be refused by the president or by the chairman of the tribunal which decided the case or by a regional chairman, if he or she is of the opinion that the application has no reasonable prospect of success (2001 Rules r13(5)). Before an application is refused on this basis, however, the party applying for the review should be given the opportunity to give further reasons in writing as to the grounds on which the application is made.[39] The decision is not made by the full tribunal. In practice, when full grounds are set out and the chairman does refuse the application, the tribunal holds an oral hearing to decide whether there should be a review. If the applicant is successful at this hearing in showing that there is an arguable case, the tribunal will generally proceed with the full review hearing.

22.37   If a party seeks to review a decision under 2001 Rules r13(1)(b) and (c), ie, that it did not receive notice of the proceedings and the decision was made in its absence, the EAT has held that it would be inappropriate for the question of whether the application has reasonable prospects of success to be considered by a chairman alone, but rather it should be considered by the full tribunal so that evidence can be taken.[40] There appears to be no statutory basis for this restriction on the rule, which predates the jurisdiction for chairmen to sit alone. It is certainly consistent with the application of article 6(1) of the Convention and natural justice to allow a rehearing if a party had no notice of it, but there is no inherent injustice in the decision being made by a chairman rather than a full tribunal.

Tribunal

22.38   Only the tribunal which made the decision may review it of its own motion (2001 Rules r13(2)). It must then follow the procedure laid down under 2001 Rules r13(3). It must, within 14 days of the date on which the decision was sent to the parties, send notice to each of the parties explaining in summary form the grounds on which, and reasons why, it is proposed to review the decision and giving them an opportunity to show cause why there should not be a review. The tribunal may extend the 14 days for *itself* under 2001 Rules r17(1).

---

39   *P J Drakard*, note 37 above.
40   *Hancock v Middleton* [1982] ICR 416, EAT.

Hearing the application

22.39   If the application for a review made by a party is not refused as having no reasonable prospects of success (whether that refusal is on the papers or after an oral hearing), the review itself is then heard by the tribunal which decided the case unless (a) it is not practicable for it to be heard by that tribunal, or (b) the original decision was made by a chairman acting alone under 2001 Rules r15(8). In either case, the review will then be heard by a tribunal appointed by the president or a regional chairman (2001 Rules r13(6)).

22.40   Even if the original decision was made by a chairman sitting alone, therefore, the review will be carried out by a full tribunal (2001 Rules r13(6)(b)). Furthermore, 2001 Rules r15(8)(c) excludes the power to review a decision reached by a full tribunal from the list of instances in which a chairman can act alone (see para 1.20).

22.41   The exceptions under 2001 Rules r13(6)(a) and (b) apply only to a review on the application of a party. If the review takes place on the tribunal's own initiative, only the fully constituted original tribunal can carry out the review (2001 Rules r13(2)).

22.42   The procedure at the hearing of the review will depend on the grounds on which the application is made; some explanation of the reason for applying for a review will be required and evidence may need to be called. For instance, in an application under 2001 Rules r13(1)(c) (decision made in a party's absence), once it has been established that the ground for the application has been made out, evidence which would have been adduced at the original hearing will need to be called to demonstrate that the original decision was wrong.[41] In an application under 2001 Rules r13(1)(d) where new evidence has become available, evidence may first need to be given to establish why the existence of the evidence could not reasonably have been known or foreseen at the time of the original hearing. Then the tribunal may allow the evidence itself to be adduced and go on to consider its effect.

22.43   When evidence is called, any party resisting the application for review will have the opportunity to test that evidence, by way of cross-examination or by calling further evidence in rebuttal. The review hearing also gives both parties the opportunity to make oral submissions.

---

41   See *P J Drakard*, note 38 above.

Review and appeal

22.44   The hearing of an application for a review can continue even if the decision is also under appeal to the EAT. If the chairman of the tribunal deciding the question of review considers it undesirable to adjudicate on the application pending the hearing of the appeal, the correct procedure is for the chairman to consult with the registrar of the EAT on the most appropriate course to follow.[42] In practice, the grounds of appeal and the grounds for review may differ in nature and there may be no difficulty in allowing the two procedures to run in tandem. The delays in EAT listing make it likely that the application for review will be considered before the appeal. If the grounds do overlap, the chairman may be reluctant to proceed with any consideration of the merits of the review application, preferring the matter to be considered first by the EAT.

22.45   The distinction between grounds suitable for appeal and grounds suitable for review were considered by the EAT in *Trimble v Supertravel Ltd*,[43] where Browne-Wilkinson J stated:

> We do not think it is appropriate for a . . . tribunal to review their decision simply because it is said there was an error of law on its face. If the matter had been ventilated and properly argued, then errors of law of that kind fall to be corrected by this appeal tribunal. If, on the other hand, due to an oversight or to some procedural occurrence one or other party can with substance say that he has not had a fair opportunity to present his argument on a point of substance, then that is a procedural shortcoming in the proceedings before the tribunal which, in our view, can correctly be dealt with by a review . . . however important the point of law or fact may be. In essence, the review procedure enables errors occurring in the course of the proceedings to be corrected but would not normally be appropriate when the proceedings had given both parties a fair opportunity to present their case and the decision had been reached in the light of all relevant argument.

22.46   As the tribunal has the power to review its decision of its own initiative, a further complication may arise where a party has entered an appeal against the decision. Although the tribunal obviously considers the case to be suitable for a review, if the grounds overlap with those which form the basis of the appeal, the *Blackpole Furniture*

---

42   *Blackpole Furniture Ltd v Sullivan* [1978] ICR 558, EAT.
43   [1982] ICR 440; [1982] IRLR 451.

case[44] indicates that the tribunal should still consult the registrar of the EAT before proceeding with the question of review.

22.47   When new evidence has become available, the appropriate course is for the party seeking to adduce this evidence to apply for a review under 2001 Rules r13(1)(d) rather than seeking to do so on appeal. Indeed, when an appeal was pursued in order to adduce new evidence, costs were awarded against the unsuccessful appellant for bringing an unnecessary appeal since the proper course is to apply for a review; see *Green & Symons Ltd v Shickell and another*[45] and *William P Harrower Ltd v Hogg*.[46]

Revocation or variation of the original decision

22.48   On reviewing its decision, a tribunal may confirm its original decision or may vary or revoke it. If the original decision is revoked, the tribunal will order the case to be reheard, either before the same or a differently constituted tribunal (2001 Rules see r13(7)).

22.49   The power to vary a decision includes the power to replace the previous decision completely if appropriate:

> [T]he tribunal can . . . decide that at the original hearing the decision it came to was wrong, and the right answer is so obvious that it can go straight to that right answer . . .[47]

22.50   Furthermore, the subsequent decision may replace the original completely, even though the application for review was directed only at one aspect of the decision:

> . . . a litigant who asks a tribunal to review its decision cannot pick and choose between which parts of the decision he wishes to have reviewed. If an application is made for a review and is acceded to, then the tribunal is free to review the whole of its decision.[48]

22.51   In such cases, however, the tribunal is bound to give the parties proper warning of the potentially wider consequences than envisaged by the application for review, and to allow them adequate opportunity to be heard fully on all points potentially in issue. In *Estorffe v Smith*[49] the case was remitted to allow the parties opportunity to be heard on issues again 'at large' before the tribunal, although this was not initially envisaged in the review application.

---

44 See note 42 above.
45 EAT 528/83, unreported.
46 EAT 215/78, unreported.
47 *Stonehill Furniture Ltd v Phillippo* [1983] ICR 556, EAT.
48 *Estorffe v Smith* [1973] ITR 627, NIRC.
49 See note 48 above.

Checklist: Review of decisions

- Is there a 'decision' in respect of which an application for review might be made?
- If there is no 'decision' but only an interim order, is it possible to seek further directions from the tribunal which might lead to a reconsideration of the order or should an appeal be pursued?
- Does the party's grievance with the original decision properly fall within the limited grounds on which an application can be considered?
- If the grievance relates to a technical error in the decision, might this properly be corrected by use of the 'slip rule'?
- Is an application for review the proper course, or would an appeal be more appropriate?
- If an application for a review is made at the same time as an appeal is in progress, should the review continue or be stayed pending the outcome of the appeal?
- Is an application for review still in time or will the tribunal need also to be asked to consider extending time under 2001 Rules r17(1)? If the latter, what is the reason for the late application?
- In making the review application, detailed grounds should be presented in writing setting out both the specific ground on which the application is made and demonstrating why the original decision is wrong on the merits in the light of these grounds.
- When an application is made under 2001 Rules r13(1)(a), (b) or (c), sufficient detail should be given to demonstrate that the application is not merely technical in nature.
- When an application is made under 2001 Rules r13(1)(d), a full description of the new evidence should be provided, demonstrating how it is relevant and probative and likely to have an important effect on the original decision.
- The application should ask for the opportunity to be heard on the question of whether or not there should be a review as well as at any actual review.
- If the review is allowed and the tribunal indicates that it is likely to revoke the original decision, consider whether representations should be made as to whether the re-hearing should be before the same or a differently constituted tribunal.

CHAPTER 23

Enforcement

Introduction

23.1   Enforcement of awards by tribunals differs according to the nature of the award and the person in whose favour an award is made.

Non-monetary orders, and monetary aspects of non-monetary orders

23.2   Failure to comply with certain orders of a tribunal may lead to enforcement procedures in front of the tribunal itself. For example, non-compliance with a reinstatement or re-engagement order under Employment Rights Act 1996 (ERA 1996) s113 is enforced by the tribunal, which must award a higher sum by way of compensation (ERA 1996 s117). Failure to comply with any monetary part of an ERA 1996 s113 order, for example for back pay, is enforced through ERA 1996 s117, and not as a separate 'decision' of the tribunal in the county or sheriff court. Imaginative exploitation of the reinstatement provisions following unfair dismissal was blocked in *O'Laoire v Jackel International Ltd.*[1] The upper limit on compensation awards is raised to enable a tribunal to award more by a reinstatement order than it could had it not ordered reinstatement (ERA 1996 s124(3)). But the award remains essentially a non-monetary award, ie, an order for reinstatement under ERA 1996 s113 rather than an award of compensation under ERA 1996 s118. The former is not, therefore, amenable to enforcement in the county court (see para 23.4).

23.3   A similar provision applies to awards for failure to comply with an order following a finding of dismissal for trade union reasons under Trade Unions and Labour Relations (Consolidation) Act 1992 (TULRCA 1992) s166. A declaration by a tribunal of an individual's right not to be excluded or expelled unlawfully from a union can be enforced by an application for compensation to the tribunal or, if the individual has not been admitted or readmitted to the union, by an application direct to the EAT to assess compensation (TULRCA 1992 s176).

1   [1990] ICR 197; [1990] IRLR 70, CA.

Monetary awards

23.4 In order to obtain enforcement of an award, the decision must be registered at the county court in England and Wales, or the sheriff court in Scotland (Employment Tribunals Act 1996 (ETA 1996) s15(1) and (2)). By this method the enforcement machinery of the county court is brought into play for the purposes of a tribunal award of 'any sum payable in pursuance of a decision'. The procedure is to apply, without notice to the paying party, on Form N322 with an affidavit, verifying the sum due and producing a copy of the decision registered at the Central Office.[2]

23.5 This machinery is not available for *monetary* parts of awards for reinstatement (see para 23.2).

23.6 Once the application for enforcement has been heard (usually by a district judge) in the county court, the sum is recoverable as though it were an order of the county court. In Scotland it can be enforced 'in like manner as an extract registered decree arbitral bearing a warrant for execution' issued by the sheriff court (ETA 1996 s15(2)). This means enforcement must be effected by execution against goods, a charging order, bankruptcy proceedings, garnishee proceedings, an administration order or attachment of earnings order.

Interest

23.7 There are two provisions dealing with interest. Under the Employment Tribunals (Interest) Order 1990[3] interest becomes payable on tribunal awards after 42 days from the date of the decision. The interest rate is that specified in relation to the Judgments Act 1838.[4] So from the end of the time limit for an appeal, interest runs at the specific rate. It is therefore important to ensure that the tribunal does wherever possible make an award, rather than adjourning the matter for the parties to attempt to settle.

23.8 Separate provision is made for interest under the sex, race and disability and equal pay legislation[5] by the Employment Tribunals

---

2 Civil Procedure Rules Sch 2: County Court Rules Order 25 r12.
3 SI No 479.
4 7% in 2001.
5 But not the Part-time Workers (Prevention of Less Favourable Treatment) Regulations 2000 SI No 1551.

(Interest on Awards in Discrimination Cases) Regulations 1996.[6] Here the date from which interest begins to accrue is the date of the decision (1996 Regs reg 8(1)), but if the award of the tribunal is paid by the respondent within 14 days of the decision, no award of interest is made. Interest runs in respect of an award for injury to feelings from the date of the discriminatory act for the whole of the period up to the date of the decision. For other monetary awards in a discrimination case interest runs from the 'mid-point date' (the date half way between the start of the act or acts of discrimination and the date of calculation) to the date of calculation. The rate of interest under the 1996 Regulations is determined according to the Special Investment Account under the Court Fund Rules 1987, and in Scotland according to the Act of Sederunt (Interest in Sheriff Court Decrees or Extracts) Act 1975. Since 1 August 1999 this rate has been seven per cent.

Rights after death

23.9   Certain employment provisions may be enforced on behalf of an employee who has died before or after the commencement of proceedings (ie, ERA 1996 Parts I (so far as it relates to itemised pay statements), III, V, VI (ss50–57 and 61–63), VII, VIII, IX (ss92 and 93) and X to XII, dealing with most employment protection rights including unfair dismissal and redundancy pay: see ERA 1996 s207). Enforcement of orders made on behalf of the personal representatives of a dead employee is regulated by the Employment Tribunals Awards (Enforcement in Cases of Death) Regulations 1976.[7] This provides for awards to be made in favour of the estate of an employee who has died. It is not necessary for the personal representative to obtain letters of administration or probate or (in Scotland) confirmation (ERA 1996 s206). While there is no equivalent to ERA 1996 s206 in the discrimination legislation, claims can nevertheless be instituted or continued by virtue of section 1(1) of the Law Reform (Miscellaneous Provisions) Act 1934.[8]

---

6   SI No 2803.
7   SI No 663.
8   *Harris (personal representative of Andrews (deceased)) v Lewisham and Guy's Mental Health NHS Trust* [2000] IRLR 320, CA.

Insolvent employers

23.10 Commencement and maintenance of proceedings against insolvent respondents is dealt with at para 4.8. Some debts due are recoverable from the secretary of state, paid out of the National Insurance Fund, under ERA 1996 s167 (redundancy pay) and s182 (some other payments). Otherwise, employees rank as preferential creditors to the extent of certain elements of back pay and holidays and collect debts according to their priority in a winding-up.

CHAPTER 24

Appeals

continued

Introduction

24.1 This chapter deals in summary terms with the scope to appeal from a tribunal to the Employment Appeal Tribunal (EAT). The EAT Rules 1993,[1] as amended by the EAT (Amendment) Rules 2001,[2] and a practice direction (PD)[3] regulate the EAT's procedure. In Northern Ireland, appeal lies to the Northern Ireland Court of Appeal, in practice by way of case stated.[4]

Constitution

24.2 The EAT's powers derive from Employment Tribunals Act 1996 (ETA 1996) s20. It is almost exclusively an appellate tribunal. There are however exceptions. It can hear:

- Claims for compensation by members unjustifiably disciplined or expelled from a trade union, and individuals unlawfully excluded from membership of a union (Trade Unions and Labour Relations (Consolidation) Act 1992 (TULRCA 1992) ss67(2) and 176(2)). In each case the reference to the EAT follows a declaration in the individual's favour by a tribunal, and a failure by the union to rectify the unlawful conduct.
- Appeals on questions of law or fact from decisions of the certification officer relating to the certification and listing of a trade union (TULRCA 1992 ss3 and 4).
- A complaint under regulations 20(1), 34 and 35 of the Transnational Information and Consultation of Employees Regulations 1999 (TICE Regs 1999)[5] that an employer has failed to set up a European Works Council or information and consultation procedure. The EAT hears and determines the complaint itself, may make an order requiring steps to be taken, and in certain cases must order a penalty to be paid to the secretary of state (TICE Regs 1999 reg 21(4) and (6)).

24.3 Ironically, appeals from tribunals to the EAT are an exception to

---

1 SI No 2854
2 SI No 1128.
3 *Practice Direction (EAT: Procedure)* [1996] ICR 422; [1996] IRLR 430: see appendix C.
4 Industrial Training (NI) Order 1984 article 31 and RSC (NI) 1980 Order 61.
5 SI No 3323.

the principal statutory rule, which is that appeals lie to the High Court under Tribunals and Inquiries Act 1992 s11 and Sch 1 and Civil Procedure Rules (CPR) Part 52; 52PD/106. Only a handful of cases have been heard in this manner since the EAT was founded in 1976, mainly concerning compensation for public servants on loss or diminution of emoluments, and health and safety notices. Otherwise, appeals from tribunals under all the employment protection and discrimination legislation go to the EAT.

24.4   Appeals on questions of law from the decision of a central arbitration committee on a failure to provide information under TICE Regs 1999 regs 8 and 38(8) can be made to the EAT. Appeals on questions of law from decisions of the certification officer relating to the application of union funds for political objects (TULRCA 1992 s95); amalgamations and transfers of engagements (TULRCA 1992 s104); certain breaches of union rules (TULRCA 1992 s108C) also go to the EAT.

24.5   The President of the EAT is nominated by the Lord Chancellor (ETA 1996 s22). In practice Presidents have held office for between three and six years. Other judges, who must include one from the Court of Session, are nominated to a panel. They include judges of the High Court, circuit judges appointed under powers under Administration of Justice Act 1985 s9, and recorders and retired judges nominated to sit as temporary additional judges of the EAT (ETA 1996 s 24).

24.6   The lay members of the EAT are appointed by the Queen on the recommendation of the Lord Chancellor and the secretary of state and they must have 'special knowledge or experience of industrial relations, either as representatives of employers or representatives of workers'. There is no formal system of advertisement or nomination by representative bodies, and there is no training. In practice, most members are retired trade union national officials and serving or retired directors of corporations or service organisations. The general administration of the EAT is the responsibility of the Employment Tribunal Service.

24.7   Appeals must be heard by a judge and one member from each side of industry, and occasionally by a judge and two members from each side (ETA 1996 s28(2)). Parties may consent to a hearing with one member absent (ETA 1996 s28(3)). On appeals from decisions made by a tribunal chairman sitting alone (see para 1.20), the appeal is heard by a judge alone (ETA 1996 s28(4)).

24.8   The EAT is a superior court of record (ETA 1996 s20(3)), which means it can punish for contempt and compel attendance of witnesses. Contempt of a tribunal can be dealt with by a reference to the Divisional Court by the tribunal,[6] since the tribunal is at the same time an 'inferior court'. But it seems the reference cannot be made to the EAT even if it is chaired by a judge of the Queen's Bench Division.

24.9 The EAT sits in London and Edinburgh but can sit anywhere in England, Wales and Scotland and its decisions are binding on tribunals throughout Great Britain. In *Williams v Cowell*[7] an employee who spoke both Welsh and English claimed race discrimination as he was forced to speak English at work; his tribunal claim was heard in Welsh, in Wales, and was dismissed. He appealed against that decision and asked that either the EAT sit in Wales, or else if it sat in London, that it be conducted in Welsh. The Court of Appeal confirmed that the EAT acted contrary to neither the Welsh Language Act 1993 nor the Human Rights Act 1998, in refusing these requests. Judge LJ however added that 'it is much to be hoped that it will not be too long before the necessary administrative arrangements can be made to enable the EAT to sit in Wales on a regular basis'.

24.10 The EAT is bound by the doctrine of precedent, so it must follow judgments of the Court of Appeal. It is not bound by judgments of the divisions of the High Court. It is not bound by a decision of the Court of Session (unless it is hearing a Scottish appeal), although the latter's construction of a statute is highly persuasive. Its decisions are not binding on tribunals in Northern Ireland but they are customarily followed. The EAT will usually follow a decision of another division of the EAT, whether sitting in England, Wales or Scotland unless there are exceptional circumstances, or previous inconsistent decisions. If exceptional circumstances exist, and a previous decision is considered to be plainly wrong, the EAT will now direct that it should no longer be followed by employment tribunals.[8] When there are conflicting decisions of the EAT and the second has considered all the arguments and not followed the first, the EAT previously took the approach of following the second unless it was convinced that it was certainly wrong.[9] However this approach is no longer considered to

---

6   See CPR Procedural Guide D1–031; County Court Rules Order 29 and Rules of the Supreme Court Order 52.
7   [2000] ICR 85, CA.
8   *Tsangacos v Amalgamated Chemicals Ltd* [1997] IRLR 4 at 5; [1977] ICR 154 at 157, EAT.
9   *Colchester Estates (Cardiff) v Carlton Industries plc* [1986] Ch 80.

be correct, and the EAT will now consider the conflict, and try to resolve it in the interests of industrial harmony, giving guidance about which decision ought to be followed.[10]

24.11   There are unrestricted rights of audience before the EAT:

> Any person may appear . . . in person or be represented by Counsel or by a solicitor or by a representative of a trade union or an employer's association or by any other person . . .[11]

24.12   Legal aid is available for advice and representation at the EAT.[12]

Questions of law

24.13   With one exception (some determinations of the certification officer – see above) an appeal to the EAT lies only on a question of law (ETA 1996 s21 and TULRCA 1992 s291(2)). The EAT is jealous of its jurisdiction restricted to questions of law. When it strays outside that jurisdiction, the Court of Appeal and the Court of Session have trenchantly criticised it.[13]

Error of law

24.14   This is described as misdirection, misapplication or misunderstanding of the law.[14] If a tribunal fails to ask the right legal question or misconstrues a statute or fails to answer the correct statutory question, there is an error of law.

Perversity

24.15   In order to run a case based on perversity, it is generally necessary to have the chairman's notes so that a complete record of proceedings before the tribunal, as well as the documents, are all available to the EAT.[15] The EAT then has some material upon which it can decide that no reasonable tribunal properly considering this evidence and

10 *Digital Equipment Co Ltd v Clements (No 2)* [1997] IRLR 140 at 141, 146; [1997] ICR 237 at 239, 252, EAT.
11 ETA 1995 s28.
12 Civil Legal Aid (General) Regulations 1989 SI No 339; as amended by Community Legal Service (Funding) Order 2000 reg 149.
13 *Hereford and Worcester CC v Neale* [1986] ICR 471; [1986] IRLR 168, CA.
14 *British Telecommunications plc v Sheridan* [1990] IRLR 27, CA.
15 *Piggott Brothers & Co Ltd v Jackson* [1992] ICR 85; [1991] IRLR 309, CA.

directing itself according to the law could have reached the decision which it did. Full particulars must be given (PD para 2).

24.16 This is a more stringent test than a complaint that the tribunal made a decision contrary to the weight of evidence or did not adequately consider an aspect of the evidence. In these latter cases, the tribunal is the sole judge and arbiter of the facts, the inferences and the weight to be given to the evidence, and the EAT will not intervene.[16]

No evidence

24.17 The absence of evidence is a specific ground of appeal, although it might well fall within the category of perversity.[17] It is an error of law for a tribunal to make a decision for which there is no evidence in support. However, provided there is *some* evidence dealing with the subject matter, the tribunal decision ought not to be interfered with. If evidence on the particular subject has been given and challenged, the tribunal is entitled to accept or reject that evidence. If the evidence is unchallenged, the tribunal ought to accept it, and if it makes a decision contrary to it, the decision will fall into the 'no evidence' category.

Wrong exercise of discretion

24.18 This could form a ground within perversity but it is mentioned here because the test is much more stringent against appeals on this basis. The wrong exercise of a discretion will rarely be capable of successful challenge.[18] It includes taking into account a factor which it was improper to take into account, failing to take account of a proper factor and the exercise of a discretion 'so far beyond what any reasonable tribunal or Chairman could have decided . . .'.[19]

Bias

24.19 Bias or apparent bias is a ground for setting aside a decision of a tribunal (see paras 18.14 and 18.96). Practice Direction para 9

16 *Hollister v National Farmers Union* [1979] ICR 542; [1979] IRLR 238, CA.
17 See *Sheridan*, note 14 above.
18 *Bastick v James Lane Turf Accountants Ltd* [1979] ICR 778, EAT and *Carter v Credit Change Ltd* [1979] ICR 908; [1979] IRLR 361, CA.
19 Applying the principle found in *Associated Provincial Picture Houses Ltd v Wednesbury Corporation* [1948] IKB 223; [1947] 2 All ER 680, CA.

requires a specific complaint to be made with full and sufficient particulars in the notice of appeal, and an opportunity is given for allegations to be put in an affidavit and referred to the tribunal criticised. A successful allegation of bias or apparent bias is an error of law because it is a breach of the rules of natural justice. In *Facey v Midas Retail Security*,[20] the President, Lindsay J, set out a detailed procedure to be adopted by the EAT in cases where allegations of bias are made against the members of an employment tribunal, dealing with circumstances in which tribunal members may be required to provide sworn evidence:[21]

(i)   First, the steps outlined in the EAT Practice Direction para 9(3) will be taken and unsworn comments may then be taken from the chairman and, if necessary, other members of the employment tribunal under para 9(4);

(ii)   The EAT may next require sworn witness statements (or further ones) from persons not including members of the employment tribunal;

(iii)   The EAT may then invite, but cannot require, the chairman or other members of the employment tribunal to provide sworn written evidence-in-chief as to primary fact;

(iv)   It will in a suitable case be possible, after such an invitation, for adverse inferences to be drawn from a member's failure without good reason to provide sworn written evidence-in-chief of primary fact;

(v)   If, notwithstanding the material already collected, including whatever has been collected by way of disclosure orders, the EAT is of the view that such cross-examination will materially assist it, it may require the attendance for oral cross-examination of deponents not including the chairman or other members of the tribunal;

(vi)   The EAT is not to hear a member's cross-examination; be it as to primary or secondary fact, even where the member in question has agreed to attend;

(vii)   The EAT is not to require the attendance of a member of a tribunal for cross-examination nor to require disclosure of documents from him or her;

(viii)   The EAT is not to draw adverse inference from a member's failure to attend for cross-examination.

20   [2000] IRLR 812, EAT.
21   Ibid at 819.

Academic appeals

24.20　The EAT, like other courts and appellate jurisdictions, will not hear academic or hypothetical cases.[22] There must be a live issue between the parties which requires decision by the EAT. If the employer has been found liable for unfair dismissal, has already paid compensation in full and has said in correspondence that it would not seek to recover anything from the employee, there is no live issue.[23] A respondent wishing to appeal must make the payments subject to the appeal. Of course, there is nothing to stop an employer who succeeds in the EAT waiving the right to recover compensation already paid.

24.21　The scope of an appeal relates to the *decision* rather than the reasons for it. It follows that if there is a favourable decision, although the reasons given for it are objectionable, there is no appeal.[24] A successful party is effectively stopped from challenging the reasons or the findings unless the other side appeals, in which case the other party can cross-appeal.

Time limits

24.22　A notice of appeal must be lodged with the EAT substantially in accordance with the precedent set out in forms at the back of the EAT Rules 2001. These are fairly simple and require the nature of the claim and the grounds on which criticism is made of the tribunal to be set out. The appeal must be served with a copy of the extended written reasons for the decision 'within . . . 42 days from the date on which extended written reasons . . . were sent to the appellant' (EAT Rules 2001 r3). The 42 days begin to run on the date the document is sent to the appellant, not on the date of 'deemed service'.[25]

24.23　It follows from the rules on counting time (chapter 5 above) that if the date on the extended reasons is a Wednesday you have until the end of business on Wednesday six weeks later to serve the notice on the EAT. Since extended reasons must accompany the notice, you

22　*Sun Life Assurance v Jervis* [1944] AC 111, HL.
23　*IMI Yorkshire Imperial Ltd v Olender* [1982] ICR 69, EAT.
24　*Harrod v Ministry of Defence* [1981] ICR 8, EAT.
25　*Hammersmith and Fulham LBC v Ladejobi* [1999] ICR 673, EAT; *Mock v Inland Revenue Commissioners* [1999] IRLR 785, EAT, and see para 13.8.

effectively have only 21 days following summary reasons to apply for extended reasons in order to mount an appeal.[26]

24.24   An application for an extension of time can be made (PD para 4(b)) and the rules set out in *Marshall v Harland & Wolff Ltd*[27] will be applied to determine whether there is any justifiable excuse, what the length of the delay is, and the degree of prejudice caused to the other party. The EAT has a discretion to extend time under EAT Rules 1993 r37(as amended by EAT Rules 2001 r23). It should be borne in mind that it exercises its powers sparingly and that the test is even more strict than that applied by the Court of Appeal.[28] It is more reluctant to extend time for entering an appeal than for complying with an interim order, since the appellant has already had one chance to have a trial of the merits.[29]

24.25   No time scale is prescribed for the service of a respondent's answer and notice of cross-appeal by the rules but the Registrar, on service of a notice of appeal on a respondent, sets out the relevant time scale, which is usually 14 days. An application to extend this period is usually granted without a hearing.

Preliminary matters

Interlocutory applications

24.26   By EAT Rules 1993 r20, the registrar considers interlocutory applications must 'have regard to the just and economical disposal of the application' and may decide the matter him or herself or put it to a judge, who may decide it or put the matter to a full appeal tribunal.

24.27   An appeal lies from the registrar to a judge, who may decide it or refer it to a full appeal tribunal (EAT Rules 1993 r21). Notice of appeal must be given within five days of the decision appealed from.

Lack of jurisdiction

24.28   As a matter of practice, the registrar decides whether or not an appeal ought to be rejected for lack of jurisdiction. In this case, an appeal is

---

26   *William Hill Organisation Ltd v Gavas* [1990] IRLR 488, CA.
27   [1972] ICR 97; [1972] IRLR 90.
28   *Aziz v Bethnal Green City Challenge Co Ltd* [2000] IRLR 111, CA, approving *United Arab Emirates v Abdelghafar* [1995] IRLR 243, EAT.
29   *Costellow v Somerset CC* [1993] 1 WLR 256; [1993] 1 All ER 952, CA, applied in *Fire Brigades Union v Knowles* EAT 123/94, unreported.

not registered and a letter is sent by the registrar. If the appellant is unhappy with the result, the matter is then referred to a judge.

No arguable point of law; and directions

24.29 The 1981 Practice Direction has been superseded on this point by a procedure for preliminary hearings and directions.[30] Some cases are held by a judge to raise an obviously arguable point of law and are listed for a full hearing on the merits. But most cases are listed for preliminary hearing by a full EAT. Usually several are listed on the same day to take place before the hearing of substantive appeals. The hearing takes place with just the appellant present, although the potential respondent occasionally attends and may at the discretion of the EAT be heard. The purpose of the hearing is for the appellant to show cause why the appeal should not be rejected.

24.30 If an arguable point is raised, and in practice this means impressing at least one of the three members of the EAT, the hearing will cease and the matter will be listed for hearing before a full EAT on another date. The EAT will then make directions after considering replies from both sides to a form on which they enter estimates of length of hearing and seek other directions. If the appeal shows no arguable case, judgment will be given rejecting the appeal and this is a substantive judgment of the EAT.

24.31 The EAT can give directions at the preliminary hearing (EAT Rules 1993 r24) on its own initiative or on the application of a party. Characteristically these would deal with issues likely to be raised, duration, amendment of pleadings, consolidation and documentation (EAT Rules 1993 r24(5)). An application for the preparation by the chairman of his or her notes of evidence should be made as soon as possible, and preferably in the notice of appeal. Running a case of perversity without the chairman's notes is likely to be impossible.[31]

24.32 The EAT is increasingly reluctant to order the production of the chairman's note of evidence and will not do so merely to allow the appellant to conduct a fishing expedition. In Scotland, the chairman's note will not be supplied to parties for an appeal unless they show cause. In England a specific application must be made, citing the issues and the witnesses to which the notes are relevant (EAT PD para 7).

---

30 See [1997] IRLR 618.
31 *Hampson v Department of Education and Science* [1988] ICR 278; [1988] IRLR 87, EAT and *Piggott Brothers & Co Ltd v Jackson*, note 15 above.

24.33   An agreed note by the parties may be sufficient (EAT PD para 10). If there is disagreement, the chairman's note prevails.[32] A specific challenge to the accuracy of the chairman's notes must be made in accordance with a procedure set out in *Dexine Rubber Co Ltd v Alker*,[33] ie, submission of a competing note to the chairman with an opportunity for the chairman to agree or disagree; if the chairman's note is not accepted by the party criticising it, but is accepted by the other side, the matter can be taken no further.

Restriction orders

24.34   A party can be debarred from proceeding if the time limit for present-ing a respondent's answer has passed and also if the party fails to comply with any direction (EAT Rules 1993 r26). There is also a specific provision in ETA 1996 s33 precluding vexatious litigants from instituting or continuing proceedings. An opportunity must be given before an order is made for the party to make representations. The effect of a restriction order is that permission is required for the continuation of any further proceedings. The application is made to the EAT by the Attorney General or the Lord Advocate. The first case in which the power under ETA 1996 s33 was used, was that of *Attorney General v Wheen*.[34] Mr Wheen had instituted 15 claims in the employment tribunal, for sex, race and disability discrimination. The fact that he is a white, non-disabled man does not mean, of course that he could not be subject to discrimination, but each of his claims was without merit. Upholding the decision of the EAT, Judge LJ held:

> . . . the hallmark of a vexatious proceeding is that it (a) has little or no basis in law; (b) subjects the defendant to inconvenience, harassment and expense out of all proportion to any gain to the claimant (whatever his motive may be); and (c) involves an abuse of the court process. On the facts, that was the case here.

24.35   In *Attorney General v England*[35] the EAT showed a flexible approach when faced with applications under ETA 1996 s33, as they adjourned generally for a period of 12 months, an application to make a restric-tion order in circumstances in which Mr England, who was aged 64, said that he did not intend to institute any further proceedings.

32   *Houston v Lightwater Farms Ltd* [1990] ICR 502; [1990] IRLR 469, EAT.
33   [1977] ICR 434, EAT.
34   [2000] IRLR 461, EAT; upheld [2001] IRLR 91, CA.
35   16 May 2001, available on EAT website at wood.ccta.gov.uk/eat/ eatjudgments.nsf.

Witnesses

24.36　It is very rare for the EAT to hear live evidence, though it has power to require attendance (EAT Rules 1993 r27).

The hearing

24.37　The case will be listed before the full EAT. Parties are usually consulted about appropriate dates. Cases are given fixed dates and do not run over from one day to the next unless they are booked for more than one day. Parties are required to notify the EAT should the time estimate originally given change. Certain cases are put on the 'fast-track', ie, those which involve other applicants or new legislation or appeals from interlocutory decisions (EAT PD para 12).

24.38　　There is a requirement for skeleton arguments and a chronology to be prepared in advance (EAT PD para 8). The EAT seeks to encourage skeleton or outline arguments and professional representatives without one are usually given short shrift. They should be served on the EAT and exchanged with the other parties at least 14 days before the hearing. On a practical note, this enables the argument to be sent with the relevant papers to the lay members of the EAT so they may read them before the hearing. There is clearly an advantage to an advocate in having a written skeleton argument served in good time.

24.39　　A list of authorities should also be sent no later than the day before the hearing. The EAT encourages parties to cite from the same law report, ie, *Industrial Cases Reports* (ICR) or *Industrial Relations Law Reports* (IRLR) for the same case (EAT PD para 15). Copies are available for all three members of the EAT, but it is very useful for the members and for the advocate presenting a case for photocopies to be made of the relevant authorities so the members can mark their own versions as the argument unfolds. Each member is supplied with a copy of the relevant legislation, usually in Butterworth's *Employment Law Handbook*.

24.40　　The EAT prepares an index of the main documents and the decision of the tribunal appealed against. It selects documents it considers relevant and parties should make sure that any other relevant documents are included. Parties must make up their own bundles according to the EAT index, but often bundles used in the tribunal can be photocopied and reused without repagination. As a rule of thumb, all documents available to the tribunal below should be made available to the EAT, although there are many occasions when the scope of the appeal is much narrower and all the documents are not required. The EAT has power to admit new material but in practice it rarely does.

24.41   Hearings are in public at a dedicated building, Audit House, Victoria Embankment, London or Melville Crescent, Edinburgh, although the EAT occasionally sits in court buildings elsewhere. A restricted reporting order can be made on the same lines as can be made by a tribunal (see EAT Rules 1993 r23) in cases involving sexual misconduct. Similarly, where a sexual offence is alleged, identifying material must be omitted from the register of the EAT. There are also provisions to conceal the identity of parties or witnesses if necessary in cases concerning national security (EAT Rules 2001 r30A).

New points of law

24.42   In general, the EAT will not allow points to be taken on appeal which have not been raised at the tribunal; this is set out in the leading case of *Kumchyk v Derby CC*.[36] This is a harsh rule, particularly where parties are not represented by lawyers at a tribunal but are on appeal, where new points legitimately can be thought of and taken. The reason for the EAT's reluctance is that it would be unable to decide the appeal finally without remitting the case to the tribunal to hear more evidence.[37] On a point of pure construction, which is simply a matter of law, the EAT can and should hear additional arguments and it then can make up its own mind on the construction without the necessity for additional evidence.

24.43   The EAT may hear new points which affect the jurisdiction of the tribunal, though contrary to earlier EAT suggestions, the Court of Appeal has held in *Glennie v Independent Magazines (UK) Ltd*,[38] that the EAT does not have an unfettered discretion to decide whether justice requires a new point to be allowed to be taken. Rather the principles set out in *Kumchyk*[39] should be applied. Thus, the EAT

36 [1978] ICR 116, EAT.
37 *Kumchyk*, ibid; confirmed by CA in *Glennie v Independent Magazines (UK) Ltd* [1999] IRLR 719, and in *Mensah v East Hertfordshire NHS Trust* [1998] IRLR 531.
38 [1999] IRLR 719, CA.
39 See note 36 above.

decisions of *Russell v Elmdon Freight Terminal Ltd*[40] and *Barber v Thames Television*[41] can no longer be followed.

New evidence

24.44 An appeal can be made on the ground that new evidence has become available since the tribunal hearing. As Sir John Donaldson said:

> Such evidence will be admitted only if some reasonable explanation can be produced for its not having been put before the tribunal . . . and if the new evidence is credible and if it would or might have had a decisive effect upon the decision.[42]

These rules are essentially those for appeals to the Court of Appeal, set out in *Ladd v Marshall*.[43]

Judgment

24.45 Judgment is usually given orally immediately following the argument and a retirement of the three members to consider it. It is tape-recorded and a written revised judgment is made available. Unlike tribunals, the judgment of the EAT takes effect from the time it is given rather than the time it is published. If the EAT does not give a judgment on the day, it reserves its judgment and hands it down either in written form on a day fixed later or given orally by the judge. Sometimes a different judge hands down the judgment of the previous EAT. Majority decisions can be made: the wing members can incorporate their own words in the judgment given by the presiding judge or it can be given indirectly by the judge as part of the judgment. All judgments now appear on the EAT website.[44]

---

40 [1989] ICR 629, EAT.
41 [1991] IRLR 236, EAT.
42 *Bagga v Heavy Chemicals (India) Ltd* [1972] ICR 118, NIRC.
43 [1954] 1 WLR 1489; see *Wileman v Minilec Engineering Ltd* [1988] ICR 318; [1988] IRLR 144, EAT.
44 See appendix E.

Costs

24.46   The EAT has power to award costs (EAT Rules 1993 r4) where 'proceedings were unnecessary, improper or vexatious or ... there has
been unreasonable delay or other unreasonable conduct in bringing
or conducting the proceedings'. The 2001 amendments, which
brought significant changes to costs in tribunals, have not amended
the EAT Rules in this respect. Only a party can be ordered to pay.[44a]
The EAT can assess the costs or expenses itself, or can order costs to
be paid by agreement or to be assessed if there is no agreement. An
appeal lies from the costs officer (in the EAT or in the Supreme
Court) to a judge of the EAT.

The order

24.47   The EAT can make a reference to the European Court of Justice,
although in practice it is reluctant to do so before giving permission
to appeal to the Court of Appeal (see also para 14.11).

24.48   It can make any order the tribunal below could have made. It
can remit the case once it has allowed an appeal for rehearing by
the same or a different tribunal. It can substitute its own decision
for that of the tribunal and will do so provided that no new evidence
is required to be admitted and the EAT can tell what the tribunal
decision would have been had it, for example, applied the law correctly to the material it had. If there is any doubt, the EAT should
remit.[45]

Settlement

24.49   If the parties want to settle an appeal or reach a consent order, the
EAT follows the practice of the Court of Appeal. In principle it will not
routinely allow appeals by consent but must first be assured of the
grounds for setting aside a decision of an inferior tribunal.[46] In practice appeals are disposed of by consent where the parties agree in
writing. Sometimes, however, it is suggested that one of the parties

---

44a The Employment Bill 2001 contains proposals to alter this.
45   *O'Kelly v Trusthouse Forte plc* [1983] ICR 728; [1983] IRLR 369, CA.
46   *J Sainsbury plc v Moger* [1994] ICR 800, EAT.

should attend and explain the basis of the order sought, especially if settlement occurs shortly before the hearing date.[47]

Review and appeal

24.50 An appeal from the EAT lies to the Court of Appeal or Court of Session, but only with permission.[48] An application for permission should be made at the EAT at the conclusion of the judgment, this being an essential requirement in England and Wales, and highly desirable in Scotland. Civil Procedure Rules 52.3 states that permission to appeal will be granted more sparingly for second appeals, so that permission will be given only if the appeal would raise an important point of principle or practice, or if there is some other compelling reason for the Court of Appeal to hear it.

24.51 The time for appealing to the Court of Appeal or to the Court of Session is two weeks from the date on which the EAT order was 'sealed or otherwise perfected'.[49]

24.52 The EAT has power to review its own decision (EAT Rules 1993 r33) where:

– it was wrongly made as a result of an error on the part of the EAT;
– proper notice was not given to a party; or
– the interests of justice require it.

The EAT can review of its own initiative or on application made within 14 days of the decision.

---

47 *British Publishing Co Ltd v Fraser* [1987] ICR 517, EAT.
48 CPR Sch 1, RSC Order 59.
49 CPR 52.4(2).

Forms

Application to an Employment Tribunal

For office use

Received at ET	
Case number	
Code	
Initials	

- ♦ If you fax this form you do not need to send one in the post.
- ♦ This form has to be photocopied. Please use CAPITALS and black ink (if possible).
- ♦ Where there are tick boxes, please tick to one that applies.

1 Please give the type of complaint you want the tribunal to decide (for example, unfair dismissal, equal pay). A full list is available from the tribunal office. If you have more than one complaint list them all.

2 Please give your details

Mr ☐ Mrs ☐ Miss ☐ Ms ☐ Other _____

First names

Surname

Date of birth

Address

Postcode

Phone number

Daytime phone number

Please give an address to which we should send documents if different from above

Postcode

3 If a representative is acting for you please give details (all correspondence will be sent to your representative)

Name

Address

Postcode

Phone   Fax

Reference

4 Please give the dates of your employment

From _____ to _____

5 Please give the name and address of the employer, other organisation or person against whom this complaint is being brought

Name

Address

Postcode

Phone number

Please give the place where you worked or applied to work if different from above

Address

Postcode

6 Please say what job you did for the employer (or what job you applied for). If this does not apply, please say what your connection was with the employer

IT1(E/W)

7　Please give the number of normal basic hours worked each week

Hours per week

[   ]

9　If your complaint is not about dismissal, please give the date when the matter you are complaining about took place

[   ]

8　Please give your earning details

Basic wage or salary

£　　　:　　　per

Average take home pay

£　　　:　　　per

Other bonuses or benefits

£　　　:　　　per

10　Unfair dismissal applicants only

Please indicate what you are seeking at this stage, if you win your case

☐ Reinstatement: to carry on working in your old job as before (an order for reinstatement normally includes an award of compensation for loss of earnings).

☐ Re-engagement: to start another job or new contract with your old employer (an order for re-engagement normally includes an award of compensation for loss of earnings).

☐ Compensation only: to get an award of money.

11　Please give details of your complaint

If there is not enough space for your answer, please continue on a separate sheet and attach it to this form.

12　Please sign and date this form, then send it to the appropriate address on the back cover of this booklet (see postcode list on pages 13-16).

Signed

[   ]

Date

[   ]

IT1(E/W)

EMPLOYMENT TRIBUNALS

(London North West Region)
3rd Floor, Radius House
51 Clarendon Road
Watford WD17 1HU

Telephone 01923 281750
Fax 01923 281781

Case Number [Case number/year]

Applicant   **Respondent**
[Applicant's name]   **V**   [Respondent's name]
                                                          [Name of any other
                                                                 respondents]

ACKNOWLEDGEMENT OF APPLICATION

1. Your application has been received and registered at this office. Any future correspondence relating to your application should quote the above case number and should be sent to this office.

2. A copy of your application will be sent to each respondent whose response, if any, will be copied to you.

3. You will be given at least 14 days notice of the hearing of the case unless all parties agree to a shorter period.

4. A copy of the application will be sent to the Advisory Conciliation and Arbitration Service (ACAS) if it has power to conciliate in this case. In such cases the services of a conciliation officer are available free to the parties. ACAS is a separate organisation and not part of the Employment Tribunals. If you think it may be possible to settle the case through conciliation you can contact ACAS yourself and speak to a conciliation officer.

5. If you do not already have copies of the booklets, "How to Apply to an Employment Tribunal" you should ensure you obtain them from an Employment Service Job Centre.

To   [Applicant's name and address]   Signed
                                                          [by the Employment Tribunal]

                                                          for Regional Secretary of the Tribunals

                                                          Dated

Form IT5 E&W - 8/99

EMPLOYMENT TRIBUNALS
(London North West Region)
3rd Floor, Radius House
51 Clarendon Road
Watford, WD17 1HU

Telephone 01923 281750
Fax 01923 281781

Case Number [Case number/year]

Applicant   **Respondent**
[Applicant's name]   v   [Respondent's name]

NOTICE OF ORIGINATING APPLICATION

Employment Tribunals Rules of Procedure 2001

1. The Employment Tribunal has registered a complaint made against you by [applicant's name]. To enable you to understand how this affects you and to explain what you should do now, I am enclosing a copy of:

> (i) the originating application;
> (ii) explanatory booklet; and
> (iii) a notice of appearance form (IT3).

2. Under the Rules of Procedure you are required to enter an appearance by [compliance date]. This may be done by completing and returning the enclosed form IT3. A late Notice of Appearance may not be accepted. You can apply for an extension of time to present a late notice.

3. You will not be entitled to defend the proceedings if you fail to enter an appearance, although you will be sent a copy of the notice of hearing and the Tribunal's decision.

4. You can conduct your case yourself or appoint a representative to act for you. If you name a representative, all further communications will be sent to that representative and not to you. Help in completing your Notice of Appearance may be available from your employers' association or other professional adviser.

5. A copy of the application will be sent to the Advisory Conciliation and Arbitration Service (ACAS) if it has power to conciliate in this case. In such cases the services of a conciliation officer are available free to the parties. ACAS is a separate organisation and not part of the Employment Tribunals. If you think it may be possible to settle the case through conciliation you can contact ACAS yourself and speak to a conciliation officer.

6. If you are disabled or need any special arrangements when visiting an Employment Tribunal please inform the staff at the office dealing with this case, who will do all they can to help. Please quote the case number shown above in all future correspondence.

To [Respondent's name and address]   Signed
                                            [by the Employment Tribunal]

                                            for Regional Secretary of the Tribunals

                                            Dated

Form IT2 E&W 8/98

EMPLOYMENT TRIBUNALS

In the application of

Case Number
(please quote in all correspondence)

* This form has to be photocopied, if possible please use Black Ink and Capital letters
* If there is not enough space for your answer, please continue on a separate sheet and attach it to this form

1. Full name and address of the Respondent:

Post Code:

Telephone number:

2. If you require documents and notices to be sent to a representative or any other address in the United Kingdom please give details:

Post Code:

Reference:

Telephone number:

3. Do you intend to resist the application? (Tick appropriate box)

YES ☐   NO ☐

4. Was the applicant dismissed? (Tick appropriate box)

YES ☐   NO ☐

Please give reason below

Reason for dismissal:

5. Are the dates of employment given by the applicant correct? (Tick appropriate box)

YES ☐   NO ☐

please give correct dates below

Began on	
Ended on	

6. Are the details given by the applicant about wages/salary, take home or other bonuses correct? (Tick appropriate box)

YES ☐   NO ☐

Please give correct details below

Basic Wages/Salary	£	per
Average Take Home Pay	£	per
Other Bonuses/Benefits	£	per

PLEASE TURN OVER

For office use only
Date of receipt   Initials

Form IT3 E&W - 8/98

7. Give particulars of the grounds on which you intend to resist the application.

8. Please sign and date the form.

Signed   Dated

DATA PROTECTION ACT 1984
We may put some of the information you give on this form on to a computer. This helps us to monitor progress and produce statistics. We may also give information to:
* the other party in the case
* other parts of the DTI and organisations such as ACAS (Advisory Conciliation and Arbitration Service), the Equal Opportunities Commission or the Commission for Racial Equality.
Please post or fax this form to : The Regional Secretary

* IF YOU FAX THE FORM, DO NOT POST A COPY AS WELL
* IF YOU POST THE FORM, TAKE A COPY FOR YOUR RECORDS

Form IT3 E&W 8/98

EMPLOYMENT TRIBUNALS

(London North West Region)
3rd Floor, Radius House
51 Clarendon Road
Watford, WD17 1HU

Telephone 01923 28 1750
FAX   01923 28 1781

[Respondent's name and address]	Your Ref	[Respondent's reference]
	Our Ref	[Case number/year]
	Date	

Dear Sir or Madam

EMPLOYMENT TRIBUNALS RULES OF PROCEDURE 2001

Applicant   **V**   **Respondent**
[Applicant's name]   [Respondent's name]

Thank you for your Notice of Appearance which has been received in this case. It is being copied as indicated below.

Yours faithfully

[signed by the Employment Tribunal]
for Regional Secretary of the Tribunals

cc   [Applicant's name, address and reference]

cc   Conciliation Officer, ACAS

EMPLOYMENT TRIBUNALS
(London North West Region)
3rd Floor, Radius House
51 Clarendon Road
Watford, WD17 1HU

Telephone 01923 281750
FAX 01923 281781

[Applicant's name and address]

Your Ref   [Applicant's reference]

Our Ref   [Case number/year]

Date

[Respondent's name and address]

Your Ref   [Respondent's reference]

Dear Sir or Madam

Employment Tribunals Rules of Procedure 2001

Applicant   **Respondent**
[Applicant's name]   **V**   [Respondent's name]

Please find enclosed a copy of the Respondent's Notice of Appearance in this case (receipt of which is hereby acknowledged).

This case is shortly to be listed and a Hearing Notice will be sent to **both parties** giving details of the date and time fixed for the hearing.

In anticipation of the case being listed **both parties** should by [compliance date] disclose to the other all the documents on which it is intended to rely at the hearing. This can be done by preparing a list or sending photocopies. Each party has the right, if necessary, to inspect the original documents. If a request for voluntary disclosure and/or inspection is not complied with, an application should be made to the Tribunal when a formal order may be made. A formal order for disclosure will only be made if a request for voluntary disclosure has not been complied with. An application should be made to the Tribunal.

Both parties should bring with them to the Tribunal whatever documents either of them may wish to refer to at the hearing of the case. If there is more than one document, each page should be numbered and [six] copies should be brought to the Hearing by the parties as these will be required for use by the Tribunal.

It is essential that **both parties** comply with these requirements as a failure to do so may result in your not being permitted to rely on the documents because they have not been previously disclosed. If you bring insufficient copies of documents to the

Hearing you may be asked to go and obtain further copies (there are no public copying facilities in the building) and this could delay the start of your Hearing or may result in your case not being heard.

Yours faithfully

[signed by the Employment Tribunal]
for Regional Secretary to the Tribunals

cc   Conciliation Officer, ACAS

EMPLOYMENT TRIBUNALS
(London North West Region)
3rd Floor, Radius House
51 Clarendon Raod
Watford, WD17 1HU

Telephone 01923 281750
FAX 01923 281781

Case Number [Case number/year]

Applicant   **Respondent**
[Applicant's name]   **V**   [Respondent's name]

This case will be listed during LISTING MONTH1 or LISTING MONTH2.

(IF YOU HAVE A REPRESENTATIVE, PASS THIS FORM TO THEM)

If I do not hear from you by RETURN BY DATE, a date for hearing will be fixed and you will be informed of the time and place. Once a date has been fixed, a postponement will be allowed <u>only in exceptional circumstances</u> and requests must be made in writing, stating the full grounds.

_____

for Regional Secretary to the Tribunals

Date

(PLEASE TICK RELEVANT BOX)   Applicant [ ]   Respondent [ ]

Delete those dates on which you CANNOT attend

1	2	3	4	5	6	7	8	9	10	11	12
13	14	15	16	17	18	19	20	21	22	23	24
25	26	27	28	29	30	31					

1	2	3	4	5	6	7	8	9	10	11	12
13	14	15	16	17	18	19	20	21	22	23	24
25	26	27	28	29	30	31					

The case will be listed for one day unless there are circumstances that make you think that this case will take longer. If so, please indicate your estimate of the number of days required and give your reasons, so that appropriate arrangements can be made.

HOW MANY WITNESSES DO YOU EXPECT TO CALL?
(*Witnesses : see Booklet 2 How to apply to an Employment Tribunal or Booklet 3 What to do if taken to an Employment Tribunal*)

DATE _____ NAME IN BLOCK CAPITALS _____

IT4D2 - 8/98

EMPLOYMENT TRIBUNALS
Regional Office
(London North West Region)
3rd Floor, Radius House
51 Clarendon Road
Watford, WD17 1HU

Telephone 01923 281750
Fax 01923 281781

Case Number
[Case number/year]

Applicant	V	Respondent
[Applicant's name]		[Respondent's name]

NOTICE OF HEARING
Employment Tribunals Rules of Procedure 2001

The application will be heard by an Employment Tribunal at **[hearing venue] on [hearing date] at [hearing time]** or as soon thereafter on that day as the Tribunal can hear it.

1   It has been given [length of hearing] for its full disposal, including remedy if appropriate.

2   Any application for postponement, or to amend the hearing duration, must be in writing and state the full reasons. In the case of postponement requests, state any other unavailable dates in the eight weeks following the above hearing date(s).

3   You are responsible for ensuring that all the witnesses you may wish to call can attend on the hearing date(s).

4   All representatives must inform those they represent of the Place, date(s), time and duration of the hearing.

5   You must read carefully the contents of the enclosed booklet "Hearings at Employment Tribunals".

To   [Respondent's name and address]

and   [Applicant's name and address]

Signed

[by the Employment Tribunal]
for Regional Secretary of the Tribunals

Dated

cc ACAS/Secretary of State for Trade and Industry

Form IT4 E&W 8/98

EMPLOYMENT TRIBUNALS
(London North West Region)
3rd Floor, Radius House
51 Clarendon Road
Watford, WD17 1HU

Telephone 01923 281750
Fax 01923 281781

Case Number [Case number/year]

Applicant		**Respondent**
[Applicant's name]	v	[Respondent's name]

NOTICE OF PRE- HEARING REVIEW
Employment Tribunals Rules of Procedure 2001

1. The Tribunal has ordered a pre-hearing review to consider the Originating Application/Notice of Appearance* (Delete as appropriate) in this case. This will take place at

[hearing venue] on [hearing date] at [hearing time] or as soon thereafter on that day as the tribunal can hear it.

2. Unless there are wholly exceptional circumstances, no application for postponement will be entertained if it is received more than 14 days after the date of this notice. Any such application must be in writing and state the full grounds and any other unavailable dates in the six weeks following the above hearing date.

3. All representatives must inform those they represent of the date, time and place of the pre hearing review.

4. Please see the attached Guidance Notes about attendance at the hearing and other matters.

5. You may submit representations in writing and advance oral argument at the hearing if you wish. The Tribunal will not hear the evidence of any witnesses at this hearing.

To   [Respondent's name and address]

Signed

[by the Employment Tribunal}
for Regional Secretary of the Tribunals

Dated

and   [Applicant's name and address]

cc ACAS/Secretary of State for Trade and Industry* (Delete as appropriate)
Form IT4 PHR E&W 8/98

EMPLOYMENT TRIBUNALS
(London North West Region)
3rd Floor, Radius House
51 Clarendon Road
Watford, WD17 1HU

Telephone 01923 28 1750
FAX 01923 28 1781

[Applicant's name and address]

Your Ref   [Applicant's reference]

Our Ref   [Case number/year]

Date

Dear Sir or Madam

EMPLOYMENT TRIBUNALS RULES OF PROCEDURE 2001

Applicant	**V**	**Respondent**
[Applicant's name]		[Respondent's name]

Your case had been listed for a Pre Hearing Review. If at the hearing the Tribunal considers that the contentions put forward by a party have no reasonable prospect of success, the Tribunal may make an Order against that party requiring the payment of a deposit of an amount not exceeding £500 as a condition of being permitted to continue to take part in the proceedings.

The following information will assist the Tribunal in ascertaining the ability of a party to comply with any such Order.

Financial details:

Net wage or salary: £
(including overtime, bonus and commission)

State Benefits: £
(excluding child or single parent allowance)

Any other income: £
(including investment income)

Does anyone else contribute towards your household expenses? If yes, how much do they contribute?   £

Total Income: £

Expenditure/Outgoings

> **Rent or mortgage:** £
>
> **Community charge:** £
>
> **Travel expenses** £
> (in connection with work only)
>
> **Amenities:** £
> (gas, electricity, water rates etc.)
>
> **Food:** £
>
> **Any other regular payments:** £

If you wish to give any further information you may do so at the hearing.

You should bring documentary evidence in the form of pay slips, bank or building society statements, rent or mortgage payment books.

Please return this form before the hearing.

Yours faithfully

[signed by the Employment Tribunal]
for Regional Secretary of the Tribunals

EMPLOYMENT TRIBUNALS
(London North West Region)
3rd Floor, Radius House
51 Clarendon Road
Watford, WD17 1HU

Telephone 01923 281750
Fax 01923 281781

Case Number [Case number/year]

Applicant   **Respondent**
[Applicant's name]   v   [Respondent's name]

NOTICE OF HEARING OF A PRELIMINARY POINT
Employment Tribunals Rules of Procedure 2001

The Tribunal has ordered a preliminary hearing which will be heard by an Employment Tribunal at [hearing venue] on [hearing date] at [hearing time], or as soon thereafter on that day as the tribunal can hear it.

1. The hearing will be limited to consideration of the following preliminary issue(s); [preliminary issues]

2. You are responsible for ensuring that all the witnesses you may wish to call can attend on the hearing date.

3. Unless there are wholly exceptional circumstances, no application for postponement due to non-availability of witnesses or for other reasons will be entertained if it is received more than 14 days after the date of this notice. Any such application must be in writing and state the full grounds and any other unavailable dates in the six weeks following the above hearing date.

4. All representatives must inform those they represent of the date, time and place of the hearing.

5. Please see the attached Guidance Notes about attendance at the hearing and other matters.

6. You may submit representations in writing and advance oral argument at the hearing if you wish.

To   [Respondent's name and address]   Signed

                                            [by the Employment Tribunal]
                                            for Regional Secretary of the Tribunals

                                            Dated

And [Applicant's name and address]

cc ACAS/Secretary of State for Trade and Industry* (Delete as appropriate)
Form IT4 Prel E&W 8/98

EMPLOYMENT TRIBUNALS
3rd Floor, Radius House
51 Clarendon Road
Watford
WD17 1HU

Telephone 01923 281750
FAX 01923 281781

Case Number [Case number/year]

[Applicant's name and address]

Your Ref: [Applicant's reference]

[Respondent's name and address]

Your Ref: [Respondent's reference]

Our Ref: [Case number/year]

Dear Sirs,

Date:

Applicant   **Respondent**
[Applicant's name]   **V**   [Respondent's name]

NOTICE OF AN INTERLOCUTORY HEARING

Notice is hereby given that an Interlocutory Hearing will take place at The Employment Tribunals, [hearing venue], on [hearing date] at [hearing time] **or as soon thereafter as the Tribunal can hear it.**

ATTENDANCE

Normally a Chairman sits alone for the purpose of making Interlocutory Orders. In the great majority of cases the order is made by reference to the papers on the file without a hearing. Occasionally, where the point at issue is of importance and is strongly contested, it may be desirable to ask both parties to attend before a Chairman "in chambers" so that it can be fully argued in the presence of both of them.

In this case, the Chairman has directed that both parties should attend. It is unnecessary for any witnesses to attend.

ISSUES

The Tribunal will consider the following point(s) and make an Interlocutory Order if appropriate:

- Further particulars of the grounds on which a party relies and of any facts and contentions relating thereto.

- Discovery and/or Inspection of documents.

- The attendance of any person (including a party to the proceedings) as a witness and, if appropriate, the production by him of any document relating to the matter to be determined.

- The number of witnesses to be called.

- Date(s) for the full hearing. Prior to this Interlocutory Hearing please check your availability and any witnesses availability for a possible hearing in May and June. If expert medical evidence will be required, can dates be canvassed for the individual involved in the same period as specified above.

- The use of witness statements.

- Any other relevant matters.

To [Applicant's name and address]   Signed

                                          [by the Employment Tribunal]
                                          for Regional Secretary of the Tribunals

                                          Dated

INDUSTRIAL TRIBUNALS	Received at Tribunals		Employers claim Reference number	
			ROIT	

Employer's Claim relating to application number [......] by [......]

*This form has to be photocopied. If possible, please use BLACK INK and CAPITAL letters
*Where there are tick boxes, please tick the one that applies

1. Please give details of the person or organisation making the employer's claim

Name of Organisation or person	
Address	
	Postcode
Telephone	

Please give an address to which documents should be sent if different from above

Postcode

2. If a representative is acting for you, please give details

Name				
Address				

Postcode

Telephone	
Reference:	

3. Please give details of Employer's Claim. If there is there is not enough space for your answer please continue overleaf.

Form IT1(c) Respondent employer's claim in contract

EMPLOYMENT TRIBUNALS
(London North West Region)
3rd Floor, Radius Road
51 Clarendon Road
Watford WD17 1HU

Telephone 01923 281750
Fax 01923 281781

Case Number [Case number/year]

Applicant
[Applicant's name]

V

Respondent
[Respondent's name]

ACKNOWLEDGEMENT OF EMPLOYER'S CLAIM

1. The employer's claim has been received and registered at this office. Any future correspondence relating to the claim should quote the above case number and be sent to this office.

2. A copy has been sent to the other party to the claim, whose response, if any, will be copied to you.

3. The original claim by the applicant and the employer's claim will be heard together. You will be given at least 14 days notice of the hearing of the case unless all parties agree to a shorter period.

4. A copy of the Application will be sent to the Advisory Conciliation and Arbitration Service (ACAS) if it has power to conciliate in this case. In such cases the services of a conciliation officer are available free to the parties. ACAS is a separate organisation and not part of the Employment Tribunals. If you think it may be possible to settle the case through conciliation you can contact ACAS yourself and speak to a conciliation officer.

To   [Respondent's name and address]

Signed
[by the Employment Tribunal]

for Regional Secretary of the Tribunals

Dated

Form IT5(c) E&W - 8/98

EMPLOYMENT TRIBUNALS

(London North West Region)
3rd Floor, Radius House
51 Clarendon Road
Watford, WD17 1HU

Telephone 01923 281750
Fax 01923 281781

Case Number [Case number/year]

Applicant   **v**   **Respondent**
[Applicant's name]   [Respondent's name]

NOTICE OF EMPLOYER'S CLAIM

Employment Tribunals Rules of Procedure 2001

Employment Tribunals Extension of Jurisdiction Order (England & Wales) 1994

1. The Employment Tribunal has registered an employer's claim against you by the respondent as shown in the enclosed document.

2. Under the Rules of Procedure you are required to enter an appearance by [compliance date]. This may be done by completing and returning the enclosed form IT3 (c). A late Notice of Appearance may not be accepted. You can apply for an extension of time to present a late Notice.

3. You will not be entitled to defend the employer's claim if you fail to enter an appearance, although you will be sent a copy of the notice of hearing and the Tribunal's decision.

4. If a representative has been named on the originating application, all communications about the employer's claim will also be sent to that representative, unless you specify a different address in your notice of appearance.

5. A copy of the application will be sent to the Advisory Conciliation and Arbitration Service (ACAS) if it has power to conciliate in this case. In such cases services of a conciliation officer are available free to the parties. ACAS is a separate organisation and not part of the Employment Tribunals. If you think it may be possible to settle the case through conciliation you can contact ACAS yourself and speak to a conciliation officer.

To [Applicant's name and address]   Signed
                                            [by the Employment Tribunal]

                                            for Regional Secretary of the Tribunals
                                            Dated

Form IT2(c) E&W 8/98

EMPLOYMENT TRIBUNALS
NOTICE OF APPEARANCE BY RESPONDENT TO AN
EMPLOYER'S CLAIM

In the application of

Case Number
(please quote in all correspondence)

This form has to be photocopied. If possible please use black ink and capital letters
* If there is not enough space for your answer, please continue on a separate sheet and attach it to this form

Name and address of respondent to employer's claim:

Post Code:

Telephone number

2. If you require documents and notices to be sent to an address other than that given on your Originating **application** please give details here:

Post Code:

Telephone number:	Reference:

3. If you intend to resist the Employer's claim please give details below. If there is not enough space for your answer please continue overleaf:

EMPLOYMENT TRIBUNALS

NOTES ON TRIBUNAL DECISIONS

1.   **Please read these notes carefully. There are time limits for seeking a review of or appealing against a decision, these limits are described in paragraphs 14 and 18 below.**

2.   The decision of the Employment Tribunal is set out in the attached document. These notes are for guidance only and are not a comprehensive statement of law. They are intended to assist the persons concerned with the decision to understand how certain requirements of the decision should be carried out and what may be done if it is considered the decision is wrong.

REASONS IN EXTENDED OR SUMMARY FORM

3.   The reasons for the decision state whether they are in extended or summary form. If the reasons for your decision are given in summary form, you may request that the Tribunal give extended reasons. If you are going to appeal against the decision you will need extended reasons (see paragraph 18 below). The request for extended reasons must be made in writing within 21 days of the date on which the decision was sent to you. This date can be found stamped on the decision document. Your request should be sent in writing to the Regional Secretary of the Tribunal.

PAYMENT OF AWARDS

4.   A sum of money awarded by an Employment Tribunal is payable, without further notice, by the party against whom the award is made, direct to the party entitled to receive it, except when benefits have been paid during a period of unemployment. In such cases the whole or part of those benefits may be recovered by the Benefits Agency from the award before it is paid. In that event the appropriate notice is given in an annex attached to the Tribunal's decision.

5.   Enforcement of awards by Employment Tribunals is a matter for the County Court, under the provisions of the Employment Tribunals Act 1996, Section 15. If a sum of money awarded by the Employment Tribunals is not paid when due, a request that enforcement action should be taken may be made by the person entitled to receive it to the nearest County Court. (County Court addresses may be obtained from the public library, Citizens Advice Bureau or Legal Services Commission.) The Court will need to see:

   (a)   the decision of the Tribunal; and

   (b)   any recoupment notice that may have been served by the Benefits Agency in respect of jobseekers allowance or income support received.

   They will explain the methods of enforcement that are available. Extended written reasons for the decision are not necessary in relation to enforcement proceedings.

6.   A certified copy of the Tribunal decision for production to the County Court may, if required, be obtained without charge upon application to the Secretary of the Tribunals, 100 Southgate Street, Bury St Edmunds, IP33 2AQ.

7.   If there is any difficulty in obtaining payment of an award in redundancy payment cases, or where the employer is insolvent, the advice of the Department of Trade and Industry should first be obtained.

Their Redundancy Payment Service addresses are:

Redundancy Payment Office
7th – 9th Floor, Hagley House
83-85 Hagley Road
Birmingham
B16 8QG

Birmingham RPO is responsible for the following regions : Birmingham, Cheshire, Derbyshire, Hampshire, Herefordshire, Isle of Wight, Lancashire, Leicestershire, Lincolnshire, Manchester, Norfolk, Nottinghamshire, Rutland, Shropshire, Staffordshire, Wales, Warwickshire, West Midlands and Worcester.

Redundancy Payment Office
Ladywell House
Ladywell Road
Edinburgh
EH12 7UR

Edinburgh RPO is responsible for the following regions : Cleveland, Cumbria, Durham, Merseyside, Northumberland, Scotland, Teeside, Tyne & Wear and Yorkshire.

Redundancy Payment Office
PO Box 15
Exchange House
Watford
WD1 7SP

Watford RPO is responsible for the following regions : Bedfordshire, Berkshire, Buckinghamshire, Cambridgeshire, Cornwall, Devon, Dorset, Essex, Gloucestershire, Hertfordshire, Kent, London, Northamptonshire, Oxfordshire, Somerset, Suffolk, Sussex, Surrey and Wiltshire.

8.   If a Tribunal has made an order that a respondent should take certain actions, e.g. to reinstate or re-engage the applicant, and he fails to do so, the applicant should notify the Regional Secretary of the Tribunals.

CHANGING THE DECISION

9.   The Employment Tribunals are independent judicial bodies and their decisions may be changed only:

   (a)   if the Tribunal decides, at the request of one of the parties before it, or on its own initiative, to **review** its own decision and to change it, or

   (b)   upon the direction of a superior court or tribunal, normally following an **appeal** by one of the parties to whom the decision applies.

10.   Except as described in paragraph 9 above, no person or body has any power to change the decision of an Employment Tribunal or to set it aside and order a new hearing.

11.   Particular attention should be paid to the time limits referred to in these notes. It should not be assumed that any time limit will be extended, although in exceptional circumstances applications may be made to the Employment Tribunal, or the Employment Appeal Tribunal as the case may be, to consider an extension of time.

REVIEW OF TRIBUNAL'S DECISION

12.   In certain limited circumstances the Employment Tribunal may be asked to review and, if appropriate, change or revoke its own decision. The provisions relating to such a review are set out in Rule 13 of the Employment Tribunals (Constitution and Rules of Procedure) Regulations 2001. These Regulations are obtainable from H.M. Stationery Office bookshops or through booksellers.

13.   The grounds upon which a Tribunal has power to **review** its decision are that:

(a) the decision was wrongly made as a result of an error on the part of the Tribunal staff;

(b) a party did not receive notice of the proceedings leading to the decision; or

(c) the decision was made in the absence of a party; or

(d) new evidence has become available since the conclusion of the hearing to which the decision relates, provided that its existence could not have been reasonably known or foreseen at the time of the hearing; or

(e) the interests of justice require such a review.

14.   If you wish to apply for a review you should do so in writing to the Tribunal which dealt with your case before the end of the period of 14 days after the date on which the decision was sent to you. This date can be found stamped on the decision document. Your letter should set out the grounds for your application. In the case of an application under paragraph 13(d) a full statement of the evidence which it is sought to introduce should be supplied.

15.   A Tribunal will not agree to review its decision merely because you disagree with it. There must be valid grounds for a review. A Chairman of the Employment Tribunals has power to refuse an application for a review if, in the Chairman's opinion, it has no reasonable prospect of success.

APPEAL AGAINST TRIBUNAL'S DECISION

16.   An appeal against a Tribunal decision may (with one exception), only be made on a point of law, that is to say, if it is considered that the Tribunal has made a mistake in the application of the law relating to the issues before it. It has been held that a decision which is inconsistent with the evidence, or has been taken in the absence of evidence of matters upon which it is based, may be wrong in law. However, the Tribunal is the sole judge of the facts and no issue of law arises if the Tribunal simply misunderstood or misapplied the facts.

17.   **Notice of appeal should be in, or substantially in accordance with, the official appeal form.**

Appeal forms may be obtained from:

The Registrar, Employment Appeal Tribunal, Audit House, 58 Victoria Embankment, London EC4Y 0DS

to whom any questions relating to the time for appeal (see paragraph 18 below) should be addressed.

Appeal forms can also be obtained from the EAT Website at **www.employmentappeals.gov.uk**

18.   The notice of appeal should be accompanied by a copy of the Employment Tribunal decision and a copy of the extended written reasons for it. If you have received a decision giving only summary reasons you should request extended reasons (see paragraph 3 of this note).

The notice of appeal must be served on the Employment Appeal Tribunal within 42 days of the date on which the extended written reasons for the decision which is the subject of the appeal, were sent to you. This date can be found stamped on the decision document.

An application for review (see paragraphs 12-15 above) does not alter the time for the notice of appeal which continues to run. Action to appeal may be taken while awaiting the result of an application for review.

19. When an appeal has been made, the Employment Appeal Tribunal may wish to examine documents or other exhibits produced in evidence before the Employment Tribunal. Such exhibits will normally have been returned to the parties at the close of the Employment Tribunal hearing or subsequently. They should be retained by the parties for production, if required, at any appeal.

20. Please be advised that, except in discrimination cases and cases where an appeal has been made, it is Employment Tribunal policy to destroy all case files within 1 year of promulgation of the decision.

LEGAL ADVICE AND REPRESENTATION

Depending on your finances, you may be able to obtain legal advice about reviews and appeals. You may also be able to get representation free or at a reduced cost for an appeal before the Employment Appeal Tribunal but you will need to show:

1 that according to a test of your income and savings, you cannot afford to pay for representation yourself, and

1 that your case is strong enough to make it worthwhile paying for you to be represented.

The Legal Services Commission has contacts with the Citizens Advice Bureau, law centres, advice agencies and solicitor's firms who will be able to advise you. To find an agency or firm with a contract to do this in you area:

1 ask for the Community Legal Service Directory at your local library;

1 ring the Directory Line on 0845 608 1112 (calls charged at local rate) or minicom 0845 609 6677;

1 look for the CLS logo in the window of local agencies and solicitor's firms.

To find out more about public funding for legal services, see the Legal Services Commission's website www.legalservices.gov.uk

Issued by The Department for Education and Employment

Sex Discrimination Act 1975: The Questions Procedure

1046/1

This booklet is in four parts:

Part 1:   **Introduction** *(SD 74).*

Part 2:   **Questionnaire of the person aggrieved: The Complainant** *(SD 74(1)(a)).*

Part 3:   **Reply: The Respondent** *(SD74(1)(b)).*

Appendix: Notes on the scope of the Sex Discrimination Act 1975.

Part 1: Introduction

General

- The purpose of this introduction is to explain the questions procedure under Section 74 of the Sex Discrimination Act 1975 *(the prescribed forms, time limits for serving questions and manner of service of questions and replies under section 74 are specified in the Sex Discrimination (Questions and Replies) Order 1975 No. 2048).*

- The procedure is intended to help a person *(referred to in this booklet as the complainant)* who thinks he/she has been discriminated against by another *(the respondent)* to obtain information from that person about the treatment in question in order to:

  - decide whether or not to bring legal proceedings; and
  - if proceedings are brought, to present his/her complaint in the most effective way.

- We have devised a questionnaire which the complainant can send to the respondent. There is also a matching reply form for use by the respondent - both are included in this booklet. The questionnaire and reply form are designed to assist both the complainant and respondent to identify information which is relevant to the complaint. It is not obligatory for the questionnaire and reply form to be used: the exchange of questions and replies may be conducted, for example by letter.

- The complainant and respondent should read this booklet thoroughly before completion and retain a copy of the information supplied.

- Guidance for the complainant on the preparation of the questionnaire is set out in Part 2.

- Guidance for the respondent on the use of the reply form is set out in Part 3.

- The Appendix explains the main provisions of the Sex Discrimination Act 1975.

- If you require further information about the Act it can be found in the various leaflets published by the Equal Opportunities Commission (EOC) and also in the detailed Guide to the Sex Discrimination Act 1975. You can obtain copies of the leaflets and the Guide, as well as further copies of this booklet *(by quoting "Form SD74")* free of charge from:

The Equal Opportunities Commission	DfEE Publications
Overseas House	PO Box 5050
Quay Street	Sudbury
MANCHESTER	SUFFOLK
M3 3HN	CO10 6QZ
Telephone: 0161 833 9244	Telephone 0845 6022260
	Fax: 0845 6033360
	Text 'phone 0845 6055560
	e-mail DfEE@PrologCS.Demon.co.uk

and Employment Service Jobcentres or Citizens Advice Bureaux.

Part 1: Introduction *(continued)*

How the questions procedure can benefit both parties

- The procedure can benefit both the complainant and the respondent in the following ways:
  - if the respondent's answers satisfy the complainant and the treatment was not unlawful discrimination, there will be no need for legal proceedings.
  - If the respondent's answers do not satisfy the complainant, they should help to identify what is agreed and what is in dispute between the parties. For example, the answers, should reveal whether the parties disagree on the facts of the case, or, if they agree on the facts whether they disagree on how the Act applies. In some cases, this may lead to a settlement of the grievance, making legal proceedings unnecessary.
  - If it turns out that the complainant institutes proceedings against the respondent, the proceedings should be that much simpler because the matters in dispute will have been identified in advance.

What happens if the respondent does not reply or replies evasively

- The respondent cannot be compelled to reply to the complainant's questions. However, if the respondent deliberately, and without reasonable excuse, does not reply within a reasonable period, or replies in an evasive or ambiguous way, the respondent's position may be adversely affected should the complainant bring proceedings against him/her. The respondent's attention is drawn to these possible consequences in the note at the end of the questionnaire.

Period within which the questionnaire must be served on the respondent

- There are different time limits within which a questionnaire must be served in order to be admissible under the questions procedure in any ensuing legal proceedings. Which time limit applies depends on whether the complaint would be under the employment, training and related provisions of the Act *(in which case the proceedings would be before an industrial tribunal)* or whether it would be under the education, goods, facilities and services or premises provisions *(in which case proceedings would be before a county court or, in Scotland, sheriff court).*

Industrial tribunal proceedings

- In order to be admissible under the questions procedure in any ensuing industrial tribunal proceedings, the complainant's questionnaire must be served on the respondent either:
  - before a complaint about the treatment concerned is made to an industrial tribunal, but not more than 3 months after the treatment in question; or
  - if a complaint has already been made to a tribunal, within 21 days beginning when the complaint was received by the tribunal.

  However, where the complainant has made a complaint to the tribunal and the period of 21 days has expired, a questionnaire may still be served provided the leave of the tribunal is obtained. This may be done by sending a written application to the Secretary of the Tribunal, stating the names of the complainant and the respondent and setting out the grounds of the application. However, every effort should be made to serve the questionnaire within the period of 21 days as the leave of the tribunal to serve the questionnaire after the expiry of the period will not necessarily be obtained.

Use of the questions and replies in industrial tribunal proceedings

- If you decide to make (or have *already made)* a complaint to an industrial tribunal about the treatment concerned and if you intend to use your questions and the reply *(if any)* as evidence in the proceedings, you are advised to send copies of your questions and any reply to the Secretary of the Tribunals before the date of the hearing. This should be done as soon as the documents are available. If they are available at the time you submit your complaint to a tribunal, send the copies with your complaint to the Secretary of the Tribunal.

County or sheriff court proceedings

- In order to be admissible under the questions procedure in any ensuing county or sheriff court proceedings, the complainant's questionnaire must be served on the respondent before proceedings in respect of the treatment concerned is brought, but not more than 6 months after the treatment[1] However, where proceedings have been brought, a questionnaire may still be served provided the leave of the court has been obtained. In the case of county court proceedings, this may be done by obtaining form Ex23 from the county court office, completing it and sending it to the Registrar and the respondent, or, by applying to the Registrar at the pre-trial review. In the case of sheriff court proceedings, this may be done by making an application to a sheriff.

[1] *Where the respondent is a body in charge of a public sector educational establishment, the 6 month period begins when the complaint has been referred to the appropriate Education Minister and 2 months have elapsed or, if this is earlier, the Minister has informed the complainant that he/she requires no more time to consider the matter.*

Part 2   **The Sex Discrimination Act 1975 Section 74(1)(a)**

Questionnaire of person aggrieved: The Complainant

Note: • Before filling in this questionnaire, we advise you to prepare what you want to say on a separate piece of paper.
        • If you have insufficient room on the questionnaire for what you want to say, continue on an additional piece of paper, which should be sent with the questionnaire to the respondent.

Enter the name of the person to be   To
questioned (the respondent)

Enter the respondent's address   of

Enter your name (you are the complainant)   1. I

Enter your address   of

Please give as much relevant information as you   2.   consider that you may have discriminated against me contrary to the
can about the treatment you think may have   Sex Discrimination Act 1975.
been unlawful discrimination. Tell us about the
circumstances leading up to that treatment and
if possible give the date, place and approximate
time it happened. You should bear in mind that
in question 4 of this questionnaire you will be
asking the respondent whether he/she agrees
with what you say here.

In 3 you are telling the respondent that you think   3.   I consider that this treatment may have been unlawful because:
the treatment you have described in 2 may have
been unlawful discrimination by them against
you. It will help to identify whether there are any
legal issues between you and the respondent if
you explain why you think the treatment may
have been unlawful discrimination.

• *You do not have to complete 3. If you do not*
  wish or are unable to do so, you should
  delete the word 'because'. If you wish to
  complete 3, but feel you need more
  information about the Sex Discrimination
  Act before doing so, see the appendix
  attached.

• *If you do decide to complete 3, you may find it*
  useful to indicate what kind of discrimination
  you think the treatment may have been ie.
  whether it was:
  • *direct sex discrimination;*
  • *indirect sex discrimination;*
  • *direct discrimination against a married*
    person;
  • *indirect discrimination against a married*
    person; or
  • *victimisation;*
  and which provision of the Act you think
  may have made unlawful the kind of discrimination
  you think you may have suffered.

SD 74(1)(a) ————————————— 3 ————————————— over ▶

This is the first of your questions to the respondent. You are advised not to alter it.

4. Do you agree that the statement in 2 is an accurate description of what happened? It not, in what respect do you disagree or what is your version of what happened?

This is the second of your questions to the respondent. You are advised not to alter it.

5. Do you accept that your treatment of me was unlawful discrimination by you against me?

If not:

a) why not?

b) for what reason did I receive the treatment accorded to me?

c) how far did my sex or marital status affect your treatment of me?

The questions at 5 are especially important if you think you may have suffered direct sex discrimination, or direct discrimination against a married person, because they ask the respondent whether your sex or marital status had anything to do with your treatment. They do not ask specific questions relating to indirect sex discrimination, indirect discrimination against a married person or victimization.
Question 6 provides you with the opportunity to ask any other questions you think may be of importance. For example, if you think you have been discriminated against by having been refused a job, you may want to know what the qualifications were of the person who did get the job and why that person got the job. If you think you have suffered indirect sex discrimination (or indirect discrimination against a married person) you may find it helpful to include the following questions
Was the reason for my treatment the fact that I could not comply with a condition or requirement which is applied equally to men and women (married and unmarried persons)?'
If so,
▶ *What was the condition or requirement?*
▶ *Why was it applied?*
If you think you have been victimized you may find it helpful to include the following questions:
▶ *Was the reason for my treatment the fact that I had done or intended to do, or that you suspected I had done or intended to do, any of the following:*
 ▪ *brought proceedings under the Sex Discrimination Act 1975 or the Equal Pay Act 1970;*
 ▪ *gave evidence or information in connection with proceedings under either Act;*
 ▪ *did something else under or by reference to either Act; or*
 ▪ *made an allegation that someone acted unlawfully under either Act*

6. Other questions *(if appropriate)*:

7. My address for any reply you may wish to give to the questions I have raised is:

on page 3, at question 1 ☐   below ☐   *(Please tick the appropriate box.)*

The questionnaire must be signed and dated. If it is to be signed on behalf of (rather than by) the complainant the person signing should.:
▪ *describe himself / herself eg. 'solicitor acting for (name of complainant)'; and*
▪ *give business (or home address, if appropriate).*

Signed _____   Address *(if appropriate)*

Date _____

How to serve the papers

• We strongly advise that you retain and keep in a safe place, a copy of the completed questionnaire.
• Send the person to be questioned the **whole** of this document either to their usual last known residence or place of business or if you know they are acting through a solicitor, to that address. If your questions *(ie the introduction, the questionnaire as completed by you and the reply form)* are directed at a limited company or other corporate body or a trade union or employer's association, you should send the papers to the secretary or clerk at the registered or principal office. You should be able to find out where this is by enquiring at your public library. However, if you are unable to do so you will have to send the papers to the place where you think it is most likely they will reach the secretary or clerk. It is your responsibility to see that they receive them.
• You can deliver the papers in person or send them by post.
• If you send them by post, we advise you to use the recorded delivery service *(this will provide you with evidence of delivery).*

By virtue of section 74 of the Act, this questionnaire and any reply are (subject to the provisions of the section) admissible in proceedings under the Act and a court or tribunal may draw any such inference as is just and equitable from a failure without reasonable excuse to reply within a reasonable period, or from an evasive or equivocal reply, including an inference that the person questioned has discriminated unlawfully.

Part 3   **The Sex Discrimination Act 1975 Section 74(1)(b)**

Reply: The Respondent

Note: • Before completing this reply form, we advise you to prepare what you want to say on a separate piece of paper.
  • If you have insufficient room on the reply form for what you want to say, continue on an additional piece of paper, which should be attached to the reply form and sent to the complainant.

Enter the name of the person you are replying to (the complainant)   To

Enter the complainant's address   of

Enter your name (you are the respondent)   1. I

Enter your address   of

Complete as appropriate   hereby acknowledge receipt of the questionnaire signed by you and dated

which was served on me on *(date)*

*Please tick relevant box: you are answering question 4 of the complainants questionnaire here. If you **disagree** with the complainant's statement of events, you should explain in what respects you disagree, or your version of what happened, or both.*

2. I agree ☐ that the statement in 2 of the questionnaire is an accurate description of what happened.

I disagree ☐ with the statement in 2 of the questionnaire in that:

Please tick relevant box: you are answering question 5 of the complainant's questionnaire here. If, in answer to paragraph 4 of the questionnaire you have agreed that the statement is an accurate description of what happened but dispute that it is an unlawful description, you should state your reasons. If you have **disagreed** with the facts in the complainant's statement of events, you should answer the question on the basis of your version of the facts. We advise you to look at the attached Appendix and also the relevant parts of the 'Guide to the Sex Discrimination Act 1975'. You will need to know:

- how the Act defines discrimination - see paragraph 1 of the Appendix;
- in what situations the Act makes discrimination unlawful - see paragraph 2 of the Appendix; and
- what exceptions the Act provides - see paragraph 3 of the Appendix.

If you think that an exception (eg. the exception for employment where a person's sex is a genuine occupational qualification) applies to the treatment described in 2 of the complainant's questionnaire, you should mention this in paragraph 3a, with an explanation about why you think the exception applies.

3a. I accept ☐ that my treatment of you was unlawful discrimination by me against you.

I dispute ☐ that my treatment of you was unlawful discrimination by me against you. My reasons for so disputing are:

3b. The reason you received the treatment accorded to you is:

3c   Your sex or marital status affected my treatment of you to the following extent:

Replies to the questions in paragraph 6 of the complainant's questionnaire can be entered here.

4.

Delete the whole of this sentence if you have answered all the questions asked in the complainant's questionnaire. If you are unable or unwilling to answer the questions please tick the appropriate box and give your reasons for not answering them.

5. I have deleted *(in whole or in part)* the paragraphs numbered [ ] above

since I am unable [ ]

since I am unwilling [ ] ▶ *to reply to the relevant questions in the complainant's questionnaire for the reasons given in the box below.*

The reply form must be signed and dated. If it is to be signed on behalf of (rather than by) the respondent the person signing should:
- *describe himself / herself eg. 'solicitor acting for (name of respondent)' or 'personnel manager of (name of firm)'; and*
- *give business address (or home address if appropriate)*

Signed [ ]

Date [ ]

Address *(if appropriate)* [ ]

How to serve the reply form on the complainant
- If you wish to reply to the questionnaire we strongly advise that you do so without delay.
- You should retain, and keep in a safe place, the questionnaire sent to you and a copy of your reply.
- You can serve the reply either by delivering it in person to the complainant or by sending it by post.
- If you send it by post, we advise you to use the recorded delivery service *(this will provide you with evidence of delivery)*.
- You should send the reply form to the address indicated in paragraph 7 of the complainant's questionnaire.

Appendix

Notes on the scope of the Sex Discrimination Act 1975

Definitions of discrimination

1. The different kinds of discrimination covered by the Act are summarized below *(the reference numbers in the margin refer to the relevant paragraphs in the Guide to the Sex Discrimination Act 1975)*. Some of the explanations have been written in terms of discrimination against a woman, but the Act applies equally to discrimination against men.

   2.4 **Direct sex discrimination** arises where a woman is treated less favorably than a man is *(or would be)* treated to
   2.7 **because of her sex.**

   Indirect sex discrimination arises where a woman is treated unfavorably because she cannot comply with a condition or requirement which:
   * is *(or would be)* applied to men and women equally; and
   * is such that the proportion of women who can comply with it is considerably smaller than the proportion of men who can comply with it; and
   * is to the detriment of the woman in question because she cannot comply with it; and
   * is such that the person applying it cannot show that it is justifiable regardless of the sex of the person to whom it is applied.

   2.8 **Direct discrimination against married persons in the employment field** arises where a married person is
   to
   2.11 treated, in a situation covered by the employment provisions of the Act *(ie- those summarised under Group A in the table on page 10)*, less favourably than an unmarried person of the same sex is *(or would be)* treated **because she or he is married.**

   Indirect discrimination against married persons in the employment field arises where a married person is treated, in a situation covered by the employment provisions of the Act, unfavourably because she or he cannot comply with a condition or requirement which:
   * is *(or would be)* applied to married and unmarried persons equally; and
   * is such that the proportion of married persons who can comply with it is considerably smaller than the proportion of unmarried persons of the same sex who comply with it; and
   * is to the detriment of tile married person in question because she or he cannot comply with it; and
   * is such that the person applying it cannot show it to be justifiable irrespective of the marital status of the person to whom it is applied.

   2.12 **Victimisation** arises where a person is treated less favourably than other persons *(of either sex)* are *(or would be)* treated because the person has done *(or intends to do or is suspected of having done or intending to do)* any of the following:
   * brought proceedings under the Act or the Equal Pay Act; or
   * given evidence or information in connection with proceedings brought under either Act; or
   * done anything else by reference to either Act (eg. given information to the Equal Opportunities Commission); or
   * made an allegation that someone acted unlawfully under either Act.
   Victimisation does not, however, occur where the reason for the less favourable treatment is an allegation which was false and not made in good faith.

Unlawful discrimination

2. The provisions of the Act which make discrimination unlawful are indicated in the table over the page. Those in Group A are the employment provisions, for the purposes of which discrimination means direct sex discrimination, indirect sex discrimination, direct discrimination against married persons, indirect discrimination against married persons, and victimisation. Complaints about discrimination which is unlawful under these provisions must be made to an industrial tribunal. For detailed information about these provisions see chapter 3 of the **Guide to the Sex Discrimination Act 1975.** For the purposes of the provisions in Group B, discrimination means direct sex discrimination, indirect sex discrimination and victimisation, but not direct or indirect discrimination against married persons. Complaints about discrimination which is unlawful under these provisions must be made to a county court or, in Scotland, a sheriff court. For detailed information about these provisions see chapters 4 and 5 of the **Guide.**

Exceptions

3. Details of exceptions to the requirements of the Act not to discriminate maybe found in the **Guide.** The exceptions applying to the employment field are described in chapter 3; those applying to the educational field, in chapter 4; and those applying to the provision of goods, facilities and services and premises, in chapter 5. General exceptions are described in chapter 7.

Provisions of the Sex Discrimination Act 1975 which make discrimination unlawful	Section of Act	Paragraphs of Guide to the Act
Group A		
Discrimination by employers in recruitment and treatment of employees.	6	3.1-3.17
Discrimination against contract workers	9	3.21
Discrimination against partners	11	3.22
Discrimination by trade unions, employers' associations etc	12	3.23, 3.24
Discrimination by qualifying bodies.	13	3.25-3.28
Discrimination in vocational training.	14	3.29-3.30
Discrimination by employment agencies	15	3.31-3.34
Group B		
Discrimination by bodies in charge of educational establishments	22	4.2-4.6,4.11-4.15
Other discrimination in education	23	4.7-4.8,4.14-4.15
Discrimination in the provision of goods, facilities or services	29	5.2-5.9,5.13-5.16
Discrimination in the disposal or management of premises.	30	5.10-5.16
Discrimination by landlords against prospective assignees or sublessees	31	5.17
Discrimination by; or in relation to, barristers.	35A	5.18-5.20

Precedents

Precedents

Originating applications and notices of appearance

Marginal references are to the boxes or paragraph numbers in forms IT1 (p309), IT3 (p313) and IT5(c) (p327) (see appendix A).

Case I: Written particulars: *Originating application*

1 Determination under Employment Rights Act 1996 s11, as to the particulars of the applicant's terms and conditions of employment.

11 (1) The applicant has been employed by the respondent for more than two months (having commenced her employment on [date]). She has yet to receive a written statement of her employment particulars.

(2) The applicant therefore seeks a determination by the tribunal as to the particulars of her employment as required by Employment Rights Act 1996 s1.

Case XX: Working Time: originating application claiming breach of weekly rest period provision

1 Working Time Regulations

11 (1) The applicant is an adult worker employed by the respondent as a [job title]

(2) Pursuant to regulation 11(1) of the Working Time Regulations 1998, the applicant is entitled to an uninterrupted rest period of not less than 24 hours in each seven-day period during which she works for the respondent.

(3) In breach of regulation 11(1), during each of the following seven day periods [specify dates], the respondent has failed to permit the applicant to take an uninterrupted rest period of not less than 24 hours, but has instead required the applicant to work as follows [give particulars].

(4) The applicant claims a declaration under regulation 30 of the Working Time Regulations 1998 that her claim is well founded.

Working Time: notice of appearance defending claim of breach of weekly rest period provisions

7 (1) It is admitted that the applicant is an adult worker employed by the respondent as [job title]. The respondent's case is that it is engaged in [specify], a sector of activity excluded from regulation 11 of the Working Time Regulations ('the WTR').

(2) In the alternative, if it were held that the WTR do apply to the respondent, it

is contended that the specific characteristics of the activity on which the applicant is engaged mean that the duration of her working time is not measured or predetermined and/or can be determined by the applicant herself.

(3) In the circumstances, it is denied that the applicant can rely on regulation 11 WTR at all.

(4) In the further alternative, the respondent will rely on the [*collective or workplace agreement – identify, giving sufficient particulars to demonstrate that the agreement relied on complies with the WTR*] which [*modified or excluded*] regulation 11 of the WTR as follows [*particularise*]

(5) The respondent further contends that the applicant was permitted to take equivalent compensatory rest periods pursuant to the [*collective/workplace agreement*] as follows; [*particularise*]

(6) It is therefore denied that the applicant is entitled to the declaration claimed.

Case II: Action short of dismissal: *Originating application*

1   Action short of dismissal.

11 (1) The applicant is a member and Branch Officer of the [title]: an independent trade union, and is an employee of the respondent.

(2) On [relevant date/s], as the union Branch Officer, the applicant successfully represented a number of union members in pay negotiations with her employer. Management had agreed that the applicant should be able to represent her members during the negotiations.

(3) After the conclusion of the pay negotiations, the applicant found that she was no longer offered overtime opportunities, although these were available to other employees of the same grade as her. On [date] it was indicated to the applicant by [identify informant] that this was due to her stance during the pay negotiations.

(4) The applicant therefore believes that the respondent has taken action against her as an individual for the purpose of deterring her from, or penalising her for, participating in the activities of an independent trade union at an appropriate time. The applicant seeks a declaration to this effect and compensation.

Case XX: National minimum wage: *originating application*
Detriment

1   Whether the applicant has been subjected to a detriment contrary to s 23 National Minimum Wage Act.

11 (1) The applicant has been and remains employed by the respondent as a [specify] from [date], earning £[sum] for working [number of hours] per week, ie, £[amount] per hour.

(2) On [date], the applicant informed [identify] that she believed that she was being paid at a rate lower than the national minimum wage. The applicant stated that she [*particularise the protected act in question, ie, would refer the matter to a low pay officer and/or make a claim to an employment tribunal*] if this was not rectified.

(3) As the position was not rectified, the applicant duly [*state action taken and outcome*].

(4) On [*date/s*] the respondent took the following action against the applicant due to her raising her complaint under the National Minimum Wage Act: [*identify action taken*]. This amounted to a detriment contrary to section 23(1) of the Act.

(5) The applicant seeks an award of compensation in respect of the same.

National minimum wage: *notice of appearance* Detriment – Applicant not acting in good faith and/or denial of detriment imposed by reason of protected act

7 (1) It is admitted that the applicant is, and was at all material times, employed by the respondent as a [specify] and is paid at the rate of £[amount] per [week/month/annum].

(2) It is, however, denied that the applicant is employed to work [number of hours claimed] or does in fact work such hours as claimed. In fact the applicant is employed to work and does work [number] hours per week, giving rise to an hourly rate of pay of £[amount], ie, in excess of the national minimum wage.

(3) It is admitted that on or about [date] the applicant spoke to [identify] of the respondent and sought a pay increase which was refused. It is further admitted that the applicant then [specify such action as is admitted], alleging that the respondent was acting in breach of the National Minimum Wage Act. It is further admitted that the applicant did subsequently [*specify any further action taken, eg, contact a low pay officer . . .*].

(4) As the applicant well knew that she was paid above the National Minimum Wage, it is contended that her claim of infringement and her subsequent action in reporting the respondent was due to the refusal of her request for a pay increase and was not made in good faith.

(5) Further, and in the alternative, although it is admitted that the respondent subsequently [*identify action taken so far as admitted*], it is denied that the same amounted to a detriment imposed due to the applicant's claim of infringement and/or her action taken in respect thereof. In fact the respondent took the action complained of because [*particularise alternative reason for action in question*].

(6) It is therefore denied that the applicant is entitled to the relief claimed or any.

Case III: Unfair dismissal (capability/competence): *Originating application*

1 Unfair dismissal.

11 (1) The applicant was employed by the respondent as a [position] from [date] to [date]. The respondent is a company which carries out the business of [identify] and employs some [state number] people.

(2) On [date] the applicant was promoted against her wishes to a senior position. She was given no training in her new duties.

(3) On [date] the applicant was told by [identify by name and position] that the

respondent was not satisfied with her performance. She asked for training in her new duties and for more time. She also said that she would be happy to return to her old position. None of these suggestions was agreed. On [date] the applicant was told that she was dismissed and was not required to work out her contractual notice period, although she was paid in lieu.

(4) There were no further discussions with the applicant and she was not given the opportunity to appeal against the decision to dismiss her. In the circumstances the applicant believes that she was unfairly dismissed and claims compensation.

Unfair dismissal (capability/competence): *Notice of appearance* **alleging the claim has been presented out of time and/or that the applicant has insufficient continuity of service; alternatively contending dismissal was fair**

7 (1) It is admitted that the applicant commenced employment with the respondent on [date] as a [position]. It is further admitted that the respondent carries on business as [identify] and is a small company employing only [number] staff.

(2) It is denied that the applicant's employment terminated on [date]. The applicant was dismissed with immediate effect on [date] and was paid one week's wages in lieu of notice. In the circumstances:

   (a) the applicant's claim, having been presented on [date] has been presented more than three months after the effective date of termination and the tribunal has no jurisdiction to determine her claim out of time; alternatively

   (b) the applicant did not have one year's continuous service with the respondent as at the date of her dismissal and she has no right to bring this complaint to the employment tribunal.

(3) Without prejudice to the respondent's primary case as set out above, the respondent contends that the dismissal of the applicant was by reason of her poor performance and was in all the circumstances (including the size and administrative resources of the respondent) fair.

(4) It is denied that the applicant was promoted to a new position: she was merely asked to take up the responsibilities for which she had originally been appointed after an extended probationary period. During that probationary period, the applicant had received training whilst she worked with her predecessor in post. She was offered further training opportunities in the form of external courses on [dates] but refused to attend.

(5) It is admitted that on [date] that the respondent told the applicant that it was not satisfied with her performance. She was given a final warning as to her poor performance by [identify] but this was the last in series of warnings given to the applicant both orally and in writing on [dates].

(6) It is further denied that the applicant asked for further training. It is accepted that she asked to go back to her previous duties but this was not possible as these did not represent all the duties for the post to which she had been appointed. The respondent simply could not afford to continue to employ someone in the position of [applicant's position] who did not carry

out all the duties of that post. Ultimately the respondent felt it had no choice but to dismiss the applicant. The decision to dismiss the applicant was taken by [identify] who occupies the most senior post in the company. The applicant had no contractual right of appeal and in the circumstances there was no-one senior to whom she could have appealed.

Case IV: Unfair dismissal (capability/ill-health): *Originating application*

1 Unfair dismissal.

11 (1) The applicant was employed as a secretary by the respondent, a large company which carries on business as [identify] and employs some [state number] people. She was so employed for [number] years, from [date] to [date].

(2) On [date], the applicant began to suffer pains in her wrists and on [date] she went sick due to repetitive strain injury ('RSI') caused by her work. She was off work for three months, during which time she produced regular certificates from her GP. The applicant also underwent operative treatment for her injury and (at her own expense) undertook a re-training course to enable her to resume keyboard work without injury in the future.

(3) On [date] the applicant wrote to the respondent indicating that she would soon be ready to return to work. She received a letter in reply [date] stating that the respondent did not feel able to keep her job open any longer and that she was dismissed with immediate effect.

(4) The applicant appealed against this decision and her appeal was heard on [date]. The manager [identify] who took the decision to dismiss her also sat on the appeal panel, despite the applicant's objection. The applicant pointed out that she could return to work but [the manager] did not believe her, although he made no contact with her GP. The decision to dismiss her was upheld.

(5) In the circumstances the applicant considers her dismissal was unfair and seeks an order for re-instatement or re-engagement as well as compensation.

Unfair dismissal (capability/ill-health): *Notice of appearance* alleging application not presented in time, alternatively contending dismissal was fair

7 (1) Paragraph 1 of the originating application is admitted save that the applicant's employment was terminated on [date], not [date], which was the date of the subsequent appeal. In the circumstances it is the respondent's contention that the applicant's claim was presented more than three months after the effective date of termination and that the tribunal has no jurisdiction to hear this complaint.

(2) Without prejudice to the above, the respondent contends that in any event the dismissal of the applicant was by reason of her incapability due to ill- health and was fair in all the circumstances.

(3) For the purpose of these tribunal proceedings only, it is admitted that the applicant was off work suffering from RSI from [date]. During that time she

was examined by the respondent's doctor who confirmed that she was unfit for work. The applicant was also visited on a number of occasions [dates] by the respondent's personnel officer [identify] who suggested various alternative employment positions within the company but these were all rejected by the applicant. By [date] the respondent was experiencing extreme difficulties as a result of the applicant's absence. A further examination was undertaken by the respondent's doctor who stated his opinion that the applicant should still not return to work, notwithstanding the operative treatment and retraining she had undertaken. The respondent therefore felt it had no choice but to dismiss the applicant and notified her of its decision by letter of [date], her employment terminating on [date].

(4) The applicant appealed against this decision and her appeal was held on [date]. She was represented by her trade union officer. It is not true that the manager who took the original decision was on the appeal panel – he was present only as a witness. The appeal was a complete re-hearing of all the issues but ultimately the applicant was unsuccessful and the decision to dismiss was upheld.

Case V: Unfair dismissal (misconduct)/breach of contract/unlawful deduction of wages: *Originating application*

1 (1) Unfair dismissal and/or (2) Breach of contract: damages in lieu of notice and/or (3) Unlawful deduction of wages.

11 (1) The applicant was employed as a [position] by the respondent which operates in the [identify] business and is a large employer with some [state number] staff. She commenced her employment on [date] and was so employed until [date] on the following terms and conditions:

(a) She would receive £[amount] per week basic pay (as provided at para [ ] of her letter of appointment of [date]).

(b) She would be given a company car for private as well as business use; at the time of her dismissal the applicant enjoyed the use of a [identify] car.

(c) She would be entitled to receive notice of the termination of her employment. There being no express provision for the period of that notice; the applicant was entitled to receive reasonable notice which she contends [in all the circumstances/by reason of custom and practice/by reference to the statutory minimum] to have been [period].

(2) On [date] the applicant was informed by [identify by name and position] that she was to be suspended from her employment without pay whilst an investigation into her conduct was carried out. She was given no details of any allegations against her.

(3) On [date], the applicant was called back into work with no prior notice and attended a meeting with [identify by name and position]. She was given no further details of the allegations against her and was not afforded the opportunity to put her case. She was told that she was to be dismissed with immediate effect. The applicant sought to appeal against her dismissal and on [date], [identify person] of the respondent wrote to her stating that the decision had been reviewed but would be upheld and the appeal was therefore dismissed.

(4) In the circumstances, the applicant believes that she was unfairly dismissed.

(5) The applicant further contends that the respondent made unlawful deductions from her wages during the period of her unpaid suspension, such deduction amounting to £[amount].

(6) The applicant also complains of the respondent's breach of contract in failing to give her the [period] notice to which she was entitled, by reason of which she claims damages in lieu of notice.

Particulars of Damages Claimed

Pay in lieu of notice (£[ ] per week × [period])	£[amount]
Loss of use of car (valued according to AA Schedule at £[amount] per week × [period])	£[amount]
Total	£[amount]

Unfair dismissal (misconduct)/Breach of contract/Unlawful deduction of wages: *Notice of appearance and employer's contract claim*

7 (1) Save that the respondent contends that a reasonable period of notice in the applicant's case would amount to [period] and save that her employment was also subject to the terms set out below, paragraph (1) of the originating application is admitted.

(2) The applicant's employment was also subject to the following terms and conditions:

(a) That should she be suspended by reason of misconduct relating to dishonesty, that period of suspension would be without pay (as accepted by the applicant in writing as an addendum to the letter of appointment).

(b) That should she be found to have committed an act of gross misconduct, the respondent would be entitled to terminate her employment summarily and without any payment in lieu of notice (a term implied into the applicant's contract of employment).

(c) That on the termination of her employment with the respondent, the applicant would return any of the respondent's property forthwith, including the [make] motor car.

(3) On [date], evidence came to the respondent's attention that the applicant had [general account of allegation, eg, falsified her expenses claims in the sum of [amount]]. This allegation was put to the applicant orally by [identify] on [date]. In the absence of any satisfactory response, the applicant was suspended without pay, in accordance with the terms of her contract, whilst an investigation was carried out.

(4) At the end of the investigation, the applicant was invited to a disciplinary hearing on [date], chaired by [identify]. The applicant was asked if she would prefer the hearing to be on a later date but she stated that she wanted it held as soon as possible. She attended the hearing at which the allegations and the outcome of the investigation were put to the applicant but she was

unable to give any satisfactory response. In the circumstances, the decision to dismiss her by reason of gross misconduct was taken by [identify].

(5) The applicant appealed against this decision under the disciplinary procedure and [identify] carried out a full review of the decision. As there was no new evidence, or explanation submitted by the applicant, it was felt that a further hearing was not necessary and the decision to dismiss was upheld.

(6) In all the circumstances of the case, the respondent believes that the dismissal of the applicant by reason of her misconduct was fair.

(7) The respondent further contends that there has been no unlawful deduction of wages as the period of unpaid suspension was pursuant to a relevant provision of the applicant's contract and/or was previously consented to by the applicant.

(8) As the respondent was entitled summarily to terminate the applicant's employment for gross misconduct, it is further denied that there has been any breach of contract by reason of the failure to give the applicant notice of dismissal.

(9) In the alternative, if the respondent is found to be liable to the applicant for any breach of contract, the respondent counterclaims as follows.

Particulars of Employer's Contract Claim

(a) Since the date of her dismissal, the applicant has retained in her possession the [make] motor car belonging to the respondent and has refused to return this to the respondent.

(b) By reason of this breach of contract by the applicant, the respondent has suffered loss in the sum of £[amount].

Breach of contract and employer's contract claim: *Applicant's notice of appearance to employer's claim*

3 (1) The applicant denies, if the same is alleged by the respondent, that her employment was subject to any express or implied term that she was under an obligation to take the respondent's vehicle back to its premises.

(2) In fact, as soon as the respondent told the applicant that she had been summarily dismissed and would receive no further wages and had no further entitlement to use of the car, the applicant returned the car keys to the respondent and has made it clear that the car could be collected from her home at any time. The respondent has chosen not to collect the vehicle which remains at the applicant's premises. The applicant has not had use of the car since her dismissal.

(3) In the circumstances, it is denied that the respondent has suffered any loss by reason of the applicant's conduct as claimed or at all.

Case VI: Unfair dismissal/redundancy payment: *Originating application*

1 (1) Unfair dismissal and/or (2) Redundancy payment.

11 (1) The applicant was employed as a [position] by the respondent, a large company in the business of [identify] which employs some [number] people. The applicant was so employed from [date] to [date].

(2) On [date] the respondent announced a redundancy programme which would lead to some [number] dismissals. The applicant was given no details

as to the type or grade of employee likely to face redundancy nor as to the way in which the selection process was to take place. No further information was provided until [date] when the applicant received a letter from [identify] giving her notice that she was going to be dismissed by reason of redundancy.

(3) The applicant's employment was terminated on [date], with no further consultation and without any opportunity to appeal against the decision. Further, the respondent has refused to pay the applicant a redundancy payment.

(4) The applicant therefore claims a statutory redundancy payment. Further and/or in the alternative, the applicant believes she was unfairly dismissed.

Unfair dismissal/redundancy payment: *Notice of appearance denying applicant was an employee/alternatively accepting right to redundancy payment but contending dismissal was fair*

7 (1) The respondent carries on business as [identify], and employs a small number of staff with few administrative resources.

(2) In meeting the requirements of its business the respondent engages a number of freelance workers on contracts for services. The applicant was so engaged by the respondent to work on a number of projects from [date] to [date]. The applicant was never an employee of the respondent but remained self-employed and carried on a business on her own account: she had no staff contract and was free to take on work from other companies, including competitors of the respondent. Further, she carried out her work for the respondent in her own time, from her own premises and using her own equipment. She was self-employed for tax purposes. In the circumstances, the applicant has no entitlement to complain of unfair dismissal and/or to claim a statutory redundancy payment.

(3) Without prejudice to the above and in the alternative, if the applicant is held to have been an employee, the respondent would accept that she is entitled to a statutory redundancy payment of [£ amount] but contends that, in all the circumstances (including its size and administrative resources), her dismissal was by reason of redundancy and fair.

(4) On [date], the respondent received notification that it had lost a number of contracts, including that upon which the applicant had worked. It therefore notified all those freelance workers affected that once their current work was finished, the respondent would not be able to offer them any more work. As soon as it became apparent that the applicant was working on the last project available for her, on [date] the respondent wrote notifying her that the relationship between them would come to an end on [date].

(5) In the circumstances, there was no process of selection as only those working on the particular projects which came to an end were affected. Furthermore, those concerned were kept fully informed at all times as to the situation facing the respondent and were aware of the absence of any alternative work available. The applicant never made any complaint about the situation prior to her application to this tribunal nor did she ask to be afforded an opportunity to appeal against the decision.

Case VII: Redundancy payment: *Originating application*

1   Redundancy payment.

11 (1) The applicant was continuously employed by the respondent from [date] to [date]. At the time of her dismissal she was aged [age] years.

(2) On [date], the applicant was dismissed by the respondent by reason of redundancy and a payment was made to her of £[amount] which purported to satisfy the applicant's entitlement to a statutory redundancy payment.

(3) In fact, by reason of her [number] years service, the applicant was entitled to a statutory redundancy payment of £[amount].

(4) The applicant seeks a determination as to her right to receive a statutory redundancy payment and as to the amount of the payment to which she is entitled.

Redundancy payment: *Notice of appearance* admitting entitlement but denying amount

7 (1) The respondent accepts its obligation to pay the applicant a redundancy payment pursuant to statute on the termination of her employment on [date] by reason of redundancy.

(2) The respondent, however, contends that it has satisfied its obligation so to do by paying the applicant the sum of £[amount], calculated on the following basis:
[set out calculation]

(3) The respondent contends that the applicant's period of continuous employment commenced only on [date]. Whilst it is accepted that the applicant previously worked for the respondent from [date], that employment ended on [date] and there was therefore a break in continuity from [date] to [date].

Case VIII: Constructive unfair dismissal: *Originating application*

1 (1) Constructive unfair dismissal.

11 (1) The applicant was employed by the respondent as a [position] from [date] to [date]. During her employment she worked four days per week on a weekly shift rota.

(2) On [date], the respondent announced a change to the terms and conditions of all employees in the applicant's position. With effect from [date] it was stated that they would have to work a five-day shift rota.

(3) The applicant complained about this change and sought to invoke the grievance procedure. The respondent, however, refused to discuss the matter further or to consider making an exception in the applicant's case.

(4) The applicant considered that the proposals amounted to an anticipatory breach of the express terms of her contract of employment and/or that the respondent's behaviour amounted to a breach of the implied term to maintain trust and confidence. She considered that she could therefore no longer remain in the respondent's employment and accordingly left on [date], confirming her reasons for so doing by letter of [date].

(5) In the circumstances, the applicant considers that she has been constructively unfairly dismissed.

Constructive unfair dismissal: *Notice of appearance* denying dismissal/alleging dismissal fair, for some other substantial reason in alternative

7 (1) The respondent is a [large/medium-sized/small] company, employing some [number] people, in the business of [identify]. It is admitted that the applicant was employed as a [identify] from [date] until [date], as stated at paragraph 1 of the originating application, working a four-day rota. The applicant's written terms and conditions of employment confirmed, however, that whilst she would initially be working a four-day rota, the times and shift patterns of her employment could be changed by the respondent at any time.

(2) It is also admitted that on [date] the respondent announced that it would be changing its shift system to a five-day rota. The respondent explained at the time that this was due to changes in technology which meant that it had to adjust its working practices if it was to make full use of the equipment it had introduced and thereby remain competitive.

(3) The respondent conducted a number of meetings with the employees affected and listened to the concerns raised. It revised some of its plans in the light of those concerns, which included extending the date for implementation of the new rota to give employees more time to adjust to the arrangements. By [date] all employees concerned had agreed to work the new arrangement but for the applicant. The respondent did not feel it could treat the applicant differently to all other staff and confirmed that she too would be subject to the new rota. It is accepted that the applicant resigned from the respondent's employment on [date], stating by letter of [date] that she considered herself to have been constructively dismissed.

(4) The respondent denies that it acted in breach of contract. It was entitled to alter the applicant's shift and rota arrangements and sought to do so in a reasonable manner, giving the applicant plenty of warning of the new arrangements and spending some time consulting with all employees so affected. In the circumstances, it is also denied that the respondent's conduct amounted to a breach of its implied obligation to maintain trust and confidence.

(5) If, contrary to the respondent's case, the applicant is found to have been dismissed, the respondent contends in the alternative that the dismissal was for some other substantial reason, namely a business re-organisation necessitating a change to the rota, and was fair in all the circumstances, including its size and administrative resources.

Case IX: Unfair dismissal (transfer of undertaking): *Originating application*

1 Unfair dismissal.

11 (1) The applicant was employed as a [position] from [date] to [date] by [identify transferor] which carried on the business of [identify]. The applicant was employed in that part of the undertaking which supplied [identify service] at/to [identify premises].

(2) On [date], it was announced that the [transferor] had lost the contract to supply services at [premises] and notices of redundancy were issued to the applicant and the other staff employed in that part of the undertaking.

(3) On [date] the applicant learned that the respondent had taken over the contract to supply services at [premises] and had started to do so after a gap of only [period]. The respondent re-employed some 75% of the staff who had previously worked for [transferor] at [premises] including [managerial staff if relevant]. The respondent did not, however, seek to re-employ the applicant.

(4) In the circumstances, the applicant believes that there was a relevant transfer to the respondent of that part of the [transferor's] undertaking which involved the supply of [service] to [premises] and in which the applicant had previously been employed. Further the applicant believes that her dismissal was by reason of the transfer and was accordingly unfair.

Unfair dismissal (transfer of undertaking): *Notice of appearance* denying transfer/denying dismissal by reason of transfer/alleging economic technical or organisational reason

7 (1) The respondent makes no admissions as to the applicant's employment by [transferor].

(2) It is denied that there was a relevant transfer of an undertaking or part thereof from [transferor] to the respondent.

(3) If, contrary to the above, there is found to have been a relevant transfer, it is denied that the applicant was dismissed by reason of that transfer. The respondent understands that the applicant was dismissed on the ending of the [transferor's] contract to provide [service] at [premises]. At that stage, no tenders had been invited for a future contract nor was it necessarily envisaged that tendering would take place. The respondent therefore denies that the applicant was dismissed by reason of the transfer.

(4) In the further alternative, the respondent contends that the applicant's dismissal was due to an economic, technical or organisational reason and was, in all the circumstances, fair.

(5) On taking the provision of [service] at [premises] the respondent deployed its existing organisational structure which included a greater use of [equipment/machines] than had previously been operated by [transferor]. The respondent therefore had no need to employ staff as [applicant's position] for economic, technical and organisational reasons. Further, the respondent is a small company employing only [number] people and has few administrative resources. In the circumstances in which it took over a contract after the applicant's dismissal, the respondent believes that its actions fall within the range of responses of a reasonable employer and that the dismissal was fair.

Case X: Sex discrimination (direct: sexual harassment/victimisation): *Originating application*

1 Sex discrimination: (1) direct sex discrimination contrary to SDA 1975 s1 and (2) victimisation contrary to SDA 1975 s4.

11 (1) The applicant was employed by the respondent as a [position] from [date] and remains so employed at the date of this application.

(2) On or about [date] a new employee [identify] was appointed to the applicant's department as [position].

(3) From [date] he began to harass the applicant, subjecting her to unwanted humiliating and distressing comments and assaults of a sexual nature. In particular:

[give details of incidents complained of: particularising all allegations relied on, specifying dates and times so far as possible and indicating the sense of injury to feelings suffered by the applicant on each occasion]

(4) On [date] the applicant complained to her line manager [identify] about these matters, giving details of the incidents set out above, but was told that she would have to learn how to deal with these things herself and that nothing would be done by the respondent.

(5) On [date], the applicant was told to start working in another department, where she has less opportunity to earn commission and bonus. When she asked why this decision had been made, she was told that she clearly could not get on with the people in her old department.

(6) In the circumstances the applicant claims that she has been the subject of unlawful sex discrimination and further that she was victimised when she sought to raise a complaint of discrimination. The applicant seeks:

(a) a declaration;

(b) compensation and interest thereon;

(c) a recommendation that she be re-engaged in her former department.

Sex discrimination (direct: sexual harassment/victimisation): *Notice of appearance* denying vicarious liability/arguing took all reasonably practicable steps to avoid/disputing facts/contending applicant motivated by bad faith

7 (1) It is admitted that the applicant was employed by the respondent as a [position] from [date], and was initially so employed in [identify] department. It is further admitted that on or about [date], a new employee, [identify] commenced working in the same department as [position].

(2) The respondent accepts that there was a personality clash between the [new employee] and the applicant and that employee both made complaints to their line manager [identify] on or about [dates]. It is denied that the applicant made allegations of unlawful sex discrimination on this occasion.

(3) The respondent does not believe the allegations made in the originating application to be true but contends in any event that it took such steps as were reasonably practicable to prevent [identify new employee] acting in the manner described during the course of his employment. In particular, the respondent will rely on the fact that it operates a policy against sexual harassment in the workplace and ensures that all new employees undergo

equal opportunities training (including familiarisation with the policy on harassment) before commencing their jobs. This training was undertaken by [new employee] on [date/s].

(4) Further or alternatively, the respondent contends that the behaviour complained of could not in any event be said to have been carried out in the course of [new employee's] employment and therefore denies vicarious liability for the same.

(5) In respect of the allegations against [new employee] made by the applicant on [date], the respondent investigated them on [date/s] and came to the conclusion that they were untrue and had been made by the applicant in bad faith. On the other hand, the investigation into the allegations made by [new employee] suggested that his allegations were true. In the circumstances the respondent did not feel matters were sufficiently serious to subject the applicant to disciplinary proceedings but decided it was best for her to carry out her work in a different department. This was accordingly done on [date]. It is denied that this necessarily entails a reduced opportunity for the applicant to earn commission and bonus.

(6) If, which is denied, the respondent's decision to move the applicant is found to have been in response to a complaint about matters which could amount to unlawful discrimination, the respondent contends that the applicant made complaints which were false and which were not made in good faith and that, in the circumstances, she is not entitled to complain of victimisation.

Case XI: Race discrimination (indirect): *Originating application*

1 Indirect race discrimination.

11 (1) The applicant is of [race] origin and is a qualified [occupation]. The applicant's qualifications were obtained from [institution, country].

(2) On [date], the respondent, which carries on business as [identify], advertised for additional [positions]. The applicant answered the advertisement and applied for a position as [identify] by letter of [date].

(3) The respondent replied to the applicant's letter on [date], informing her that she had not been appointed as she did not have the additional qualification as a [qualification].

(4) The applicant could not comply with the requirement or condition that she have this additional qualification and thereby suffered a detriment.

(5) The qualification identified is only available from [institution, country]. The proportion of [identify pool, ie, by reference to occupation] of [applicant's racial origin] who can comply with this requirement or condition is considerably smaller than the number of [identify pool for comparison by reference to occupation and race] who can comply with it.

(6) The applicant therefore seeks:
  (a) a declaration;
  (b) compensation and interest thereon;
  (c) a recommendation that the respondent take action to remove the said requirement or condition.

Race discrimination (indirect): *Notice of appearance* disputing proportionality and putting forward defence of justification

7 (1) The respondent does not know of, but accepts, the applicant's racial origin but can confirm that she applied for an advertised position as a [post] with the respondent on [date]. The respondent also accepts that the applicant was notified that she was unsuccessful on [date] due to the fact that she did not hold the qualification of [identify].

(2) The requirement that the post-holder should have this qualification was applied to all candidates regardless of their race or ethnic origin. It is denied that this has a significant discriminatory effect on persons of any particular racial or ethnic group including the applicant's.

(3) Further the requirement is one which is necessary in order for that person to have the appropriate specialised skills and training to carry out the duties of the post. If, which is denied, the requirement is found to have a discriminatory effect, it is contended that its necessity for the post and thus for the respondent's business is such as to justify its imposition.

Case XII: Equal pay: *Originating application*

1 Equal pay under the Equal Pay Act 1970 and/or Article 141 of the EEC Treaty and/or the Equal Pay Directive 75/117.

11 (1) The applicant is a woman employed by the respondent as a [occupation]. The respondent is [identify business] [and as such is a state authority, in respect of which the Equal Pay Directive 75/117 has direct effect].

(2) In carrying out her duties for the respondent, the applicant is employed on like work to [name comparator], a male [identify post/department, etc] who has been so employed since [date]. Alternatively, the applicant is employed on work of equal value to [name comparator].

(3) The applicant's pay is determined by [refer to relevant contractual provision] of her contract of employment at a rate of £[identify rate]. That clause is less favourable than the comparable clause in [comparator]'s contract of employment which provides for his rate of pay to be £[identify rate in consistent manner, ie, per hour/week/etc].

(4) The applicant therefore claims:
    (a) A declaration that the term of her contract relating to pay be treated as modified so as to be not less favourable than the clause relating to pay in the contract of [comparator].
    (b) Damages: being the arrears of pay from [date] to the date of the determination herein at the rate of £[difference in pay] per week.
    (c) Interest.

Equal pay: *Notice of appearance* denying like work and raising genuine material factor defence

7 (1) The respondent admits the applicant is employed by it as a [occupation] and has been so employed since [date]. The respondent also accepts that it carries on business as [identify] [but denies that it does so as an emanation of the state and/or that the Equal Pay Directive 75/117 can be relied upon as having direct effect against it].

(2) The respondent further denies that the applicant is employed on like work to that carried out by [comparator] and/or that her work is of equal value to his.

(3) The respondent accepts the respective rates of pay cited by the applicant in her originating application but contends that any difference in rate of pay is attributable to the different nature of the work carried out and the different value given to the duties of the applicant and her comparator.

(4) If the applicant is found to be employed on like work/work of equal value to that of [comparator], the respondent alternatively contends that the whole of the difference in rate of pay is attributable to a genuine material factor other than sex, namely [specify genuine material factor relied upon, eg, the red-circling of comparator's pay when he was moved from one post to his current post].

Case XX: Disability Discrimination: *originating application* claiming unjustified less favourable treatment contrary to section 5(1) and unjustified failure to make reasonable adjustments contrary to section 5(2)

1   Unlawful discrimination on the ground of disability

11 (1) At all material times the applicant, who suffers from [describe disability] was a disabled person within the meaning of the Disability Discrimination Act 1995 ('the DDA'), who was employed by the respondent (a company employing more than 15 people) as a [describe] from [date] to [date].

(2) The respondent treated the applicant less favourably for a reason relating to her disability than it would have done a person to whom that reason did not apply, in that:
[particularise less favourable treatment complained of]

(3) The less favourable treatment was not justified in that [an applicant does not have to anticipate the respondent's defence of justification but should set out her response if she is already aware of the respondent's arguments in this regard and has a positive case by way of rebuttal]

(4) Further and/or in the alternative, the following arrangements made by the respondent/physical features of the premises occupied by the respondent subjected the applicant to a substantial disadvantage at work compared to persons who did not have her disability: [particularise the arrangements/ features relied on]

(5) The respondent failed to make the following adjustments which were reasonable and would have prevented the above arrangements/features from having that effect: [particularise].

(6) In the circumstances, the applicant claims that she has been discriminated against by the respondent on the ground of her disability and claims:
(a) damages, including damages for injury to feelings;
(b) a recommendation that [specify recommendation sought if relevant]
(c) interest
. . .
Signed:

Disability discrimination: *notice of appearance* denying disability/ less favourable treatment and pleading justification

7 (1) Although it is admitted that the applicant suffers from [*specify*], it is denied that the same amounts to a disability for the purposes of the Disability Discrimination Act 1995 ('the DDA'). In particular, the respondent does not accept that this caused the applicant any substantial impairment in her day-to-day activities [*or whatever other positive case the respondent wishes to 'plead' in this respect, although there is no obligation for the respondent to do so and it can merely put the applicant to proof on this issue*]

(2) It is accepted that the applicant was employed by the respondent as [state] from [date] until [date] but it is denied that she was [outline treatment] by reason of any disability she might suffer. The respondent [outline treatment] the applicant because of [state reason], which was unrelated to any disability. In any event, the respondent denies that the treatment complained of amounted to less favourable treatment in any respect.

(3) If, contrary to the respondent's primary case as set out above, it were to be found that it had treated the applicant less favourably on the ground of a disability, the respondent would in any event contend that was justified in doing so, in that [*particularise grounds for justification*]

(4) Moreover, it is denied that the respondent was under any duty to make reasonable adjustments in the applicant's case.

(5) In this regard, it is denied that the respondent was aware of the applicant's disability at the relevant time or that it knew or ought to have known that the applicant was likely to be affected in the way that she alleges.

(6) If, which is denied, it was under any such duty, the respondent will further contend that no reasonable adjustment could have been taken which would have been effective, practicable or within its resources in that [*give particulars*]

(7) Furthermore, the respondent will also contend that it offered the applicant the following adjustment [*particularise*] which she did not accept.

(8) In the circumstances, the respondent would in any event contend that it was justified in failing to take the steps specified by the applicant.

Interlocutory requests and responses

I: Request for further particulars of originating application (Case A III, p349)

REQUEST FOR FURTHER PARTICULARS OF THE ORIGINATING APPLICATION

Under paragraph 11(2)

OF: '. . . the applicant was promoted against her wishes to a more senior position. She was given no training in her new duties.'

REQUESTS:

1   State what was the new position to which the applicant says she was promoted, giving details as to the ways in which the applicant contends it was
'senior'.

2   Give full particulars of the 'new duties' to which the applicant refers.

Under paragraph 11(3)
OF: '. . . She asked for training in her new duties and for more time. She
also said that she would be happy to return to her old position.'

REQUESTS:

3   Please state what training the applicant sought, from whom and when. If
the applicant's alleged request was made in writing, identify the docu-
ment(s) relied upon and provide copies of the same. If made orally, give
details of each conversation, including the time, date and occasion of each
and the gist of the words used.

4   Give like details in respect of the request to return to 'her old position'.

5   State now, to what duties does the applicant mean to refer by the term 'her
old position'?

Under paragraph 11(4)
OF: '. . . In the circumstances the applicant believes that she was unfairly
dismissed and claims compensation.'

REQUESTS:

6   Give full details of the compensation claimed by the applicant, demonstrating how the same is calculated and particularising all steps taken by the
applicant to mitigate any loss claimed.

The respondent requests that the further particulars sought are supplied
within 14 days of the date of this letter. If not so supplied the respondent will
apply to the tribunal for an order, pursuant to r4(3) of the Employment
Tribunal Rules of Procedure 2001, that the applicant reply to these requests.
[signed]

Replies to request for further particulars of the originating application

FURTHER PARTICULARS OF THE ORIGINATING APPLICATION:
PURSUANT TO REQUEST/ORDER DATED [DATE]

Under paragraph 12(2)
OF: '. . . [repeat as per Request] . . . '

REQUESTS:
[repeat as per Request] . . .

ANSWERS

1   [identify title/grade of new position]. The applicant contends that this was
senior to her previous position as [identify] in that [set out reasons relied
upon].

2   The post of [identify senior post] required the applicant to undertake new
duties in that she [set out new duties relied upon].

Under paragraph 11(3)
OF: '. . . [repeat as per Request] . . . '

REQUESTS:
[repeat as per Request] . . .

ANSWERS:

3   [refer to specific course if appropriate or give general details, eg: 'sufficient training to enable the applicant to carry out her new duties'.] This was sought [orally/in writing . . . give details as appropriate].
4   [give details as appropriate].
5   [refer to previous post].

Under paragraph 11(4)
OF: '. . . [repeat as per Request] . . . '

REQUESTS:
[repeat as per Request]

ANSWERS:

6   The applicant claims a basic award and compensation for her loss of earnings from the date of her dismissal to the date of the hearing and thereafter for such period as the tribunal considers reasonable. The respondent is not entitled to seek further particulars of loss and of the applicant's attempts to mitigate that loss at this stage.

II: Request for written answers to questions

REQUEST FOR WRITTEN ANSWERS
With reference to the assertion at paragraph 7(5) of the notice of appearance:

1   Is it not the case that [identify] holds a position within the respondent senior to [identify manager who took decision to dismiss]?
2   Is it not the case that in the past the right to appeal against the decision to dismiss has been afforded to the respondent's employees?
3   If the answer to 2 is in the negative, when in the past two years has an employee been dismissed by the respondent without being afforded the right of appeal?
The applicant requests that the above questions are answered in writing within 14 days of the date of this letter. If not so answered, the applicant will apply to the tribunal for an order for the same, pursuant to r4(3) of the Employment Tribunal Rules of Procedure 2001.
[signed]

Written answers

WRITTEN ANSWERS: PURSUANT TO REQUEST/ORDER DATED [DATE]
The respondent answers as follows:

1   In response to the question [set out question] . . . the respondent states that this is not the case . . . [complete as appropriate].

[give other answers in similar form]
[Signed]

III: Request for disclosure and inspection of documents
[Address]
[Date]
Re: [employment tribunal case name and number]

REQUEST FOR DISCLOSURE AND INSPECTION OF DOCUMENTS
The applicant requests disclosure and inspection of the following documents:

1   The applicant's personnel file.
2   All notes and/or memoranda relating to the decision to dismiss the applicant including notes of meetings and/or conversations relevant to that decision.
3   [Identify such other documents as are believed to be in the respondent's possession which are relevant to the issues to be determined.]
4   All other documents relevant to the issues to be determined by the tribunal.
The applicant asks that disclosure of the above documents is provided within 14 days of the date of this letter and inspection within 7 days thereafter. As an alternative to inspection the applicant will pay reasonable photocopying and postage charges for the relevant documents. If disclosure is not so provided, the applicant will request an order for the same from the tribunal, pursuant to rule 4(5)(b) of the Employment Tribunal Rules of Procedure 2001.
[signed]

Response to request for disclosure of documents
With reference to the request dated [date], the respondent gives discovery as follows:

1   The respondent has the applicant's personnel file in its possession and will provide the applicant/her representative with a reasonable opportunity to inspect the same.
2   The respondent confirms that it has no documents under this category of the request and no such documents have ever been in its possession.
3   [answer as appropriate]
4   The respondent confirms that save for communications between it and its legal advisers, it has no other documents in its possession relevant to the issues to be determined by the tribunal in this case.
[signed]

Settlement and conciliation

The following represent suggested forms of words and general terms. Where it is sought to use a document as a means of avoiding an ET claim, however, particular care should be taken to mould the terms to the individual circumstances of the case. It is essential to check each aspect of the document you wish to utilise to ensure that it properly serves the purpose to which you intend to put it.

I: Letter before action containing offer of settlement (constructive unfair dismissal – Case A VIII, p356)

WITHOUT PREJUDICE

[Date]

[Potential respondent, address]

Letter before action: Ms A N Applicant

Dear Sirs,

We act for Ms A N Applicant, who was employed by yourselves as [position] from [date] until she was forced to resign, terminating her employment on [date].

During her employment she worked four days per week on a weekly shift rota. She informs us that on [date] you unilaterally announced a change to the terms and conditions of employment of all employees in our client's position: it was stated that with effect from [date] they would have to work a five-day shift rota.

Our client complained about this change and sought to invoke the grievance procedure. However, your personnel manager, Mr V Hardman, refused to discuss the matter further or to consider making an exception in her case. As it was quite impossible for her to work a five-day week due to personal and family commitments, she could no longer remain in your employment under the newly imposed conditions. She accordingly had no alternative but to tender her resignation on [date], confirming her reasons for so doing in a letter of [date]. She left on [date].

Your action in seeking to impose unilaterally this major change to our client's work pattern was in clear breach of an express term (clause 7) of her contract of employment. She accordingly intends to pursue a claim before an employment tribunal for constructive unfair dismissal.

However, if, within fourteen days of this letter, you undertake in writing to re-instate our client in her old position on terms and conditions no less favourable than before (and specifically including a four-day working week), to pay her the wages lost during her period of enforced unemployment and to meet our reasonable costs in this matter, she is prepared to forego her right to claim.

This offer is made without prejudice, but should such an undertaking not be forthcoming, our client will have no alternative but to proceed with her claim. Should the tribunal order re-instatement or re-engagement and award her compensation equal to or greater than her loss of wages, she reserves the right to raise this offer of settlement in relation to costs before the tribunal.

Yours faithfully,

II: Termination agreement

ACAS COT 3: SAMPLE 1

ADVISORY CONCILIATION AND ARBITRATION SERVICE

Tribunal case number . . .

AGREEMENT IN RESPECT OF AN APPLICATION MADE TO THE TRIBUNAL

Applicant	Respondent
Name [Applicant's name]	[Respondent's name]
Address [Applicant's address]	[Respondent's address]

Settlement reached as a result of a conciliation action.
We the undersigned have agreed:
That . . .

Applicant
Respondent
COT3

ACAS COT 3: SAMPLE 2

ADVISORY CONCILIATION AND ARBITRATION SERVICE

Tribunal case number . . .

AGREEMENT FOLLOWING CONCILIATION ON A CLAIM MADE BY AN APPLICANT TO ACAS (NO APPLICATION MADE TO TRIBUNAL AT TIME OF AGREEMENT) THAT ACTION HAD BEEN TAKEN BY THE RESPONDENT IN RESPECT OF WHICH A COMPLAINT OF [UNFAIR DISMISSAL] COULD BE MADE TO AN EMPLOYMENT TRIBUNAL

Applicant	Respondent
Name [Applicant's name]	[Respondent's name]
Address [Applicant's address]	[Respondent's address]

Settlement reached as a result of a conciliation action.
We the undersigned have agreed:
That

Applicant	Date
Respondent	Date
COT3	

III: Compromise agreement/contract

AN AGREEMENT to refrain from instituting or continuing with proceedings before an employment tribunal made pursuant to the provisions of section 203(2) Employment Rights Act 1996.

This [agreement/contract*] is made between:

.... ('the employee')

of ....

and

.... ('the employer')

of ....

1 The employer will pay to the employee the sum of £[*amount*] and will provide her with a reference, in the form attached to this agreement and no other, within [*specify*] days of the date of this agreement and the employee agrees to accept this sum and this reference in full and final settlement of all contractual claims outstanding at and/or arising out of the termination of her employment by the employer on [*date*].

2 The employer will further pay to the employee the sum of £[*amount*], in consideration of which the employee will refrain from [instituting a complaint against the employer before an employment tribunal][*or* continuing her complaint against the employer before the employment tribunal under Case No [*specify*] in respect of her allegation that on [*date*] the employer:

dismissed her unfairly; and/or

discriminated against her on the grounds of sex or race by (*give sufficient details to identify the particular complaint*); and/or

made an unlawful deduction from her wages by (*give sufficient details to identify the particular complaint*); and/or

took action short of dismissal against her relating to her trade union membership or activities by (*give sufficient details to identify the particular complaint*);

(*or as the case may be*).

3 The employee accepts the payment made by the employer in full and final settlement of all other claims which she has or may have against the employer arising out of her employment or the termination thereof, being claims in respect of which an employment tribunal has no jurisdiction [except any claims for damages for personal injury *or as the case may be*]

4 The employee acknowledges that, before signing this Agreement, she received independent legal advice from (*name of adviser*),[a qualified lawyer *or* certified union official *or* certified advice centre worker, *as the case may be*], as to the terms and effect of this Agreement and in particular its effect on her ability to pursue her rights before an employment tribunal.

5 The conditions regulating compromise agreements under the [list relevant statutory provisions] are satisfied in relation to this Agreement.

Signed: . . .   (employee) [date]

Signed: . . .   (employer) [date]

Statement by adviser to employee

I, [name, firm, address], confirm that I am a [eg, barrister, solicitor of the Supreme Court currently in possession of a practising certificate from the Law Society, advocate] and that I have advised the employee as to the terms of this agreement, in particular as to its effect in relation to rights to [bring] [continue] claims in the employment tribunal.

Signed: . . .

Dated: . . .

IV: Consent (Tomlin) orders

1 Decision

Settlement having been agreed between the parties in accordance with the terms set out in the Schedule hereto, by consent, this Originating Application is withdrawn upon compliance by the respondents with the terms of settlement on or before [date]. Liberty to apply on or before [date], and if no application is made by this date, this Originating Application is dismissed on withdrawal by the applicant.

Schedule

2 Decision

Settlement having been agreed between the parties in accordance with the terms endorsed on Counsels' Briefs, by consent, this Originating Application is dismissed on withdrawal by the applicant.

3 Decision

Settlement having been agreed between the parties in accordance with the terms endorsed on Counsels' Briefs, by consent, this Originating Application is withdrawn upon compliance by the respondents with the terms of settlement on or before [date] Liberty to apply on or before [date], and if no application is made by this date, this Originating Application is dismissed on withdrawal by the applicant.

Note: In the last two forms above it may be appropriate in some cases to change the words 'endorsed on Counsel's Brief' to 'endorsed in the sealed envelope annexed to this decision'.

Post-decision: reviews and appeals

I: Application to employment tribunal for review of decision

[date]

To The Assistant Secretary of the Tribunals

[address of OET]

Dear Sir/Madam,

Re: [employment tribunal case title and number]

The [applicant/respondent] applies for a review of the decision by the employment tribunal sitting at [location] on [date] that [set out summary of that decision] under rule 13(1) of the Employment Tribunal Rules of Procedure 2001 on the grounds that:

[set out grounds for application for review, eg:

The decision was wrongly made as a result of an error on the part of the staff of the tribunal in that [eg, the decision orders the respondent to pay compensation in the sum of £1,000.00 when the tribunal's calculation at paragraph [number] of the decision demonstrates that this should be £11,000.00. Alternatively this might be an accidental slip capable of correction under r10(9)].

The decision was made in the absence of the respondent [give reasons for absence, eg, who received no notification of the hearing] and who wished to contest issues relating to liability and compensation.

New evidence has become available to the applicant since the conclusion of the hearing, the existence of which she could not reasonably have known or foreseen before the hearing, namely [give details of the evidence, eg, document reference/ identity or witness and substance of evidence] which would have a material bearing on the question of [identify question considered by the tribunal to which the evidence would relate], namely [indicate how reliance is placed on that evidence].

The interests of justice require such a review as [set out grounds, eg, the tribunal's decision on compensation was made without giving the [applicant/ respondent] an opportunity to adduce evidence and address the tribunal on the question whether it was just and equitable for a full award to be made to the applicant in the light of facts discovered after her dismissal relating to [give details, indicating the evidence the respondent wished to adduce and the points upon which it would have sought to have addressed the tribunal].]

[Signed]

II: Notice of appeal to Employment Appeal Tribunal from decision by employment tribunal

IN THE EMPLOYMENT APPEAL TRIBUNAL   *EAT/*   */*

BETWEEN:

[NAME OF APPELLANT]   *Appellant*

and

[NAME OF RESPONDENT TO APPEAL]   *Respondent*

NOTICE OF APPEAL

TO:
The Registrar
Employment Appeal Tribunal
Audit House, 58 Victoria Embankment
London EC4Y 0DS
[or insert address for EAT in Scotland]

1   The appellant is [name] of [address].

2   Any communication relating to this appeal may be sent to the appellant at

[name, address and telephone number of representative or identify other address etc for service].

3   The appellant appeals from the decision of the employment tribunal sitting at [location of tribunal] on [date/s of hearing] that the [summary of tribunal's decision, ie, appellant's complaint of unfair dismissal be dismissed].

4   The only party/ies to the proceedings before the employment tribunal other than the appellant was/were [give name/s and address/es of all other parties before the tribunal or the name/s and address/es of any representative on the record].

5   A copy of the employment tribunal's decision and of the extended reasons for that decision is attached to this notice.

6   The grounds upon which this appeal are brought are that:
[set out grounds, eg:
  6.1   In concluding that [give details by reference to decision] the tribunal acted perversely in that there was no evidence of [give details] to support such a conclusion.
  6.2   The tribunal's conclusion that [give details by reference to decision] was perverse in the light of the previous findings that [give details of contradictory findings by reference to decision].
  6.3   The tribunal failed to give any reasons for its finding that [give details].
  6.4   The tribunal erred in law in construing [relevant statutory provision] as meaning [give details] when the correct approach is [set out correct construction].

Signed:
Date:

III: Respondent's answer to notice of appeal and cross-appeal to Employment Appeal Tribunal from decision of employment tribunal
[Heading as for II above]

RESPONDENT'S ANSWER
AND CROSS-APPEAL

---

1   The respondent is [name] of [address].

2   Any communication relating to this appeal may be sent to the respondent at [name, address and telephone number of representative or identify other address, etc, for service].

3   The respondent intends to resist the appeal of [name and address of appellant]. The grounds upon which the respondent will rely are [the grounds relied upon by the employment tribunal for making the decision appealed from] [and] [the following grounds:]
[set out grounds for resisting appeal, eg:
  3.1   The tribunal's finding that [give details by reference to decision] was supported by the evidence that [give details of evidence relied upon].

3.2   In relation to the tribunal's conclusion that [give details], even if the tribunal did not set out its full reasons for reaching this conclusion, these are implicit [give details by reference to decision] and/or are unnecessary given the tribunal's finding that [give details] and further the tribunal correctly construed [relevant statutory provision].

4   The respondent cross-appeals from [refer to part of tribunal decision appealed from].

5   The respondent's grounds of appeal are that:

[set out grounds of cross-appeal]

Signed

Dated

IV: Appeal to the Court of Appeal of Northern Ireland by way of case stated

IN THE BELFAST INDUSTRIAL TRIBUNAL   *Case No*

BETWEEN:

[NAME OF APELLANT]

Appellant

and

[NAME OF RESPONDENT TO APPEAL]

Respondent

APPLICATION TO STATE A CASE

To the Secretary of the Tribunals
Office of the Tribunals
Long Bridge House
20–24 Waring Street
Belfast BT1 2EB

Whereas the Appellant is dissatisfied with the decision of the Belfast industrial tribunal sitting on [date/s] as being wrong in law,

Application is hereby made pursuant to Order 61 of the Rules of the Supreme Court (Northern Ireland) 1980 that a case may be stated for the opinion of the Northern Ireland Court of Appeal.

1   By originating application of [date], the respondent claimed [set out claim]. A copy of that originating application is annexed hereto marked 'A'.

2   On [date], the appellant entered a notice of appearance in response to the claim, denying that [set out grounds of resistance]. A copy of that notice of appearance is annexed herto marked 'B'.

[set out any other relevant history of the application]

3   The respondent's application was heard by the Belfast industrial tribunal on [date/s] when the appellant contended that [summary of appellant's arguments before the tribunal].

4   By [unanimous/majority] decision registered and issued to the parties on [date], the Belfast industrial tribunal held that: [set out summary of tribunal's findings]. A copy of the tribunal's decision and the reasons for that decision is annexed hereto marked 'C'.

5   The appellant now requires the industrial tribunal to state and sign a case on the following questions of law for the opinion of the Court of Appeal of Northern Ireland:

[set out questions, eg:

5.1   Whether the industrial tribunal erred in law holding that . . . [set out question of law, referring to relevant part of tribunal decision as appropriate].

5.2   Could any reasonable tribunal on the evidence adduced and the facts found, and when properly directing itself in law, have reached the decision arrived at by this tribunal?

[signed]
[dated]

Legislation – Statutes, Regulations and Practice Directions

Legislation – Statutes, Regulations and Practice Directions

Tribunals and Inquiries Act 1992 ss1, 10, 11 and Sch 1

THE COUNCIL ON TRIBUNALS AND THEIR FUNCTIONS

The Council on Tribunals

1 (1) There shall continue to be a council entitled the Council on Tribunals (in this Act referred to as 'the Council') –

   (a) to keep under review the constitution and working of the tribunals specified in Schedule 1 (being the tribunals constituted under or for the purposes of the statutory provisions specified in that Schedule) and, from time to time, to report on their constitution and working;

   (b) to consider and report on such particular matters as may be referred to the Council under this Act with respect to tribunals other than the ordinary courts of law, whether or not specified in Schedule 1, or any such tribunal; and

   (c) to consider and report on such matters as may be referred to the Council under this Act, or as the Council may determine to be of special importance, with respect to administrative procedures involving, or which may involve, the holding by or on behalf of a Minister of a statutory inquiry, or any such procedure.

   (2) Nothing in this section authorises or requires the Council to deal with any matter with respect to which the Parliament of Northern Ireland had power to make laws.

JUDICIAL CONTROL OF TRIBUNALS ETC

Reasons to be given for decisions of tribunals and Ministers

10 (1) Subject to the provisions of this section and of section 14, where –

   (a) any tribunal specified in Schedule 1 gives any decision, or

   (b) . . .

   it shall be the duty of the tribunal or Minister to furnish a statement, either written or oral, of the reasons for the decision if requested, on or before the giving or notification of the decision, to state the reasons.

Appeals from certain tribunals

11 (1) Subject to subsection (2), if any party to proceedings before any tribunal specified in paragraph 8, 15(a) or (d), 16, 18, 24, 26, 31, 33(b), 37, 44 or 45 of Schedule 1 is dissatisfied in point of law with a decision of the tribunal he may, according as rules of court may provide, either appeal from the tribunal to the High Court or require the tribunal to state and sign a case for the opinion of the High Court.

(2) Subsection (1) shall not apply in relation to proceedings before industrial tribunals which arise under or by virtue of any of the enactments mentioned in section 136(1) of the Employment Protection (Consolidation) Act 1978.

SCHEDULE 1: TRIBUNALS UNDER GENERAL SUPERVISION OF COUNCIL

Tribunals under direct supervision of Council

1

Employment

16 The industrial tribunals for England and Wales established under section 128 of the Employment Protection (Consolidation) Act 1978.

Employment Tribunals Act 1996

PART I: EMPLOYMENT TRIBUNALS

INTRODUCTORY

Employment Tribunals

1 (1) The Secretary of State may by regulations make provision for the establishment of tribunals to be known as employment tribunals.

(2) Regulations made wholly or partly under section 128(1) of the Employment Protection (Consolidation) Act 1978 and in force immediately before this Act comes into force shall, so far as made under that provision, continue to have effect (until revoked) as if made under subsection (1) . . .

JURISDICTION

Enactments conferring jurisdictions on employment tribunals

2   Employment tribunals shall exercise the jurisdiction conferred on them by or by virtue of this Act or any other Act, whether passed before or after this Act.

Power to confer further jurisdiction on employment tribunals

3 (1) The appropriate Minister may by order provide that proceedings in respect of –

    (a) any claim to which this section applies, or

    (b) any claim to which this section applies and which is of a description specified in the order,

may, subject to such exceptions (if any) as may be so specified, be brought before an employment tribunal.

(2) Subject to subsection (3), this section applies to –

    (a) a claim for damages for breach of a contract of employment or other contract connected with employment,

    (b) a claim for a sum due under such a contract, and

    (c) a claim for the recovery of a sum in pursuance of any enactment relating to the terms or performance of such a contract,

if the claim is such that a court in England and Wales or Scotland would under the law for the time being in force have jurisdiction to hear and determine an action in respect of the claim.

(3) This section does not apply to a claim for damages, or for a sum due, in respect of personal injuries.

(4) Any jurisdiction conferred on an employment tribunal by virtue of this section in respect of any claim is exercisable concurrently with any court in England and Wales or in Scotland which has jurisdiction to hear and determine an action in respect of the claim.

(5) In this section –

    'appropriate Minister', as respects a claim in respect of which an action could be heard and determined by a court in England and Wales, means the Lord Chancellor and, as respects a claim in respect of which an action could be heard and determined by a court in Scotland, means the Lord Advocate, and

    'personal injuries' includes any disease and any impairment of a person's physical or mental condition.

(6) In this section a reference to breach of a contract includes a reference to breach of –

    (a) a term implied in a contract by or under any enactment or otherwise,

    (b) a term of a contract as modified by or under any enactment or otherwise, and

    (c) a term which, although not contained in a contract, is incorporated in the contract by another term of the contract.

MEMBERSHIP, ETC

Composition of the tribunal

4 (1) Subject to the following provisions of this section and to section 7(3A), proceedings before an employment tribunal shall be heard by –

    (a) the person who, in accordance with regulations made under section 1(1), is the chairman, and

    (b) two other members, or (with the consent of the parties) one other member, selected as the other members (or member) in accordance with regulations so made.

(2) Subject to subsection (5), the proceedings specified in subsection (3) shall be heard by the person mentioned in subsection (1)(a) alone.

(3) The proceedings referred to in subsection (2) are –
    (a) proceedings on a complaint under section 68A, 87 or 192 of the Trade Union and Labour Relations (Consolidation) Act 1992 or on an application under section 161, 165 or 166 of [that Act],
    (b) proceedings on a complaint under section 126 of the Pension Schemes Act 1993,
    (c) proceedings on a reference under section 11, 163 or 170 of the Employment Rights Act 1996, on a complaint under section 23, 34 or 188 of that Act, on a complaint under section 70(1) of the Act relating to section 64 of that Act, or on an application under section 128, 131 or 132 of that Act or for an appointment under section 206(4) of that Act,
    (ca) proceedings on a complaint under regulation 11(5) of the Transfer of Undertakings (Protection of Employment) Regulations 1981,
    (cc) proceedings on a complaint under section 11 of the National Minimum Wage Act 1998;
    (cd) proceedings on an appeal under section 19 or 22 of the National Minimum Wage Act 1998;
    (d) proceedings in respect of which an employment tribunal has jurisdiction by virtue of section 3 of this Act,
    (e) proceedings in which the parties have given their written consent to the proceedings being heard in accordance with subsection (2)(whether or not they have subsequently withdrawn it),
    (f) . . .
    (g) proceedings in which the person (or, where more than one, each of the persons) against whom the proceedings are brought does not, or has ceased to, contest the case.

(4) The Secretary of State may by order amend the provisions of subsection (3).

(5) Proceedings specified in subsection (3) shall be heard in accordance with subsection (1) if a person who, in accordance with regulations made under section 1(1), may be the chairman of an employment tribunal, having regard to –
    (a) whether there is a likelihood of a dispute arising on the facts which makes it desirable for the proceedings to be heard in accordance with subsection (1),
    (b) whether there is a likelihood of an issue of law arising which would make it desirable for the proceedings to be heard in accordance with subsection (2),
    (c) any views of any of the parties as to whether or not the proceedings ought to be heard in accordance with either of those subsections, and
    (d) whether there are other proceedings which might be heard concurrently but which are not proceedings specified in subsection (3),
decides at any stage of the proceedings that the proceedings are to be heard in accordance with subsection (1).

(6) Where (in accordance with the following provisions of this Part) the Secretary of State makes employment tribunal procedure regulations, the

regulations may provide that any act which is required or authorised by the regulations to be done by an employment tribunal and is of a description specified by the regulations for the purpose of this subsection may be done by the person mentioned in subsection (1)(a) alone.

(6A) Subsection (6) in particular enables employment tribunal procedures regulations to provide that –
  (a) the determination of proceedings in accordance with regulations under section 7(3A),(3B) or (3C)(a),
  (b) the carrying-out of pre-hearing reviews in accordance with regulations under subsection (1) of section 9 (including the exercise of powers in connection with such reviews in accordance with regulations under paragraph (b) of that subsection), or
  (c) the hearing and determination of a preliminary issue in accordance with regulations under section 9(4)(where it involves hearing witnesses other than the parties or their representatives as well as where, in accordance with regulations under section 7(3C)(b), it does not),
  may be done by the person mentioned in subsection (1)(a) alone.

(6B) Employment tribunal procedure regulations may (subject to subsection (6C)) also provide that any act which –
  (a) by virtue of subsection (6) may be done by the person mentioned in subsection (1)(a) alone, and
  (b) is of a description specified by the regulations for the purposes of this subsection,
  may be done by a person appointed as a legal officer in accordance with regulations under section 1(1); and any act so done shall be treated as done by an employment tribunal.

(6C) But regulations under subsection (6B) may not specify –
  (a) the determination of any proceedings, other than proceedings in which the parties have agreed the terms of the determination or in which the person bringing the proceedings has given notice of the withdrawal of the case, or
  (b) the carrying-out of pre-hearing reviews in accordance with regulations under section 9(1).

(7) . . .

Remuneration, fees and allowances

5 (1) The Secretary of State may pay to –
  (a) the President of the Employment Tribunals (England and Wales),
  (b) the President of the Employment Tribunals (Scotland),
  (c) any person who is a member on a full-time basis of a panel of chairmen of tribunals which is appointed in accordance with regulations made under section 1(1), and
  (d) any person who is a legal officer appointed in accordance with such regulations,
  such remuneration as he may with the consent of the Treasury determine.

  (2) The Secretary of State may pay to –
  (a) members of employment tribunals,

(b) any assessors appointed for the purposes of proceedings before employment tribunals, and

(c) any persons required for the purposes of section 2A(1)(b) of the Equal Pay Act 1970 to prepare reports,

such fees and allowances as he may with the consent of the Treasury determine.

(3) The Secretary of State may pay to any other persons such allowances as he may with the consent of the Treasury determine for the purposes of, or in connection with, their attendance at employment tribunals.

PROCEDURE

Conduct of hearings

6 (1) A person may appear before an employment tribunal in person or be represented by –

(a) counsel or a solicitor,

(b) a representative of a trade union or an employers' association, or

(c) any other person whom he desires to represent him.

(2) The Arbitration Act 1996 Part I does not apply to any proceedings before an employment tribunal.

Employment tribunal procedure regulations

7 (1) The Secretary of State may by regulations ('employment tribunal procedure regulations') make such provision as appears to him to be necessary or expedient with respect to proceedings before employment tribunals.

(2) Proceedings before employment tribunals shall be instituted in accordance with employment tribunal procedure regulations.

(3) Employment tribunal procedure regulations may, in particular, include provision –

(a) for determining by which tribunal any proceedings are to be determined,

(b) for enabling an employment tribunal to hear and determine proceedings brought by virtue of section 3 concurrently with proceedings brought before the tribunal otherwise than by virtue of that section,

(c) for treating the Secretary of State (either generally or in such circumstances as may be prescribed by the regulations) as a party to any proceedings before an employment tribunal (where he would not otherwise be a party to them) and entitling him to appear and to be heard accordingly,

(d) for requiring persons to attend to give evidence and produce documents and for authorising the administration of oaths to witnesses,

(e) for enabling an employment tribunal, on the application of any party to the proceedings before it or of its own motion, to order –

(i) in England and Wales, such discovery or inspection of documents, or the furnishing of such further particulars, as might be ordered by a county court on application by a party to proceedings before it, or

(ii) in Scotland, such recovery or inspection of documents as might be ordered by a sheriff,

(f) for prescribing the procedure to be followed in any proceedings before an employment tribunal, including provision –
   (i) . . .
   (ii) for enabling an employment tribunal to review its decisions, and revoke or vary its orders and awards, in such circumstances as may be determined in accordance with the regulations,
(g) for the appointment of one or more assessors for the purposes of any proceedings before an employment tribunal, where the proceedings are brought under an enactment which provides for one or more assessors to be appointed,
(h) for authorising an employment tribunal to require persons to furnish information and produce documents to a person required for the purposes of section 2A(1)(b) of the Equal Pay Act 1970 to prepare a report, and
(j) for the registration and proof of decisions, orders and awards of employment tribunals.

(3A) Employment tribunal procedure regulations may authorise the determination of proceedings without any hearing (and in private) where the parties have given their written consent (whether or not they have subsequently withdrawn it).

(3B) Employment tribunal procedure regulations may authorise the determination of proceedings without hearing anyone other than the person or persons by whom the proceedings are brought (or his or their representatives) where –
   (a) the person (or, where more than one, each of the persons) against whom the proceedings are brought has done nothing to contest the case, or
   (b) it appears from the application made by the person (or, where more than one, each of the persons) bringing the proceedings that he is not (or they are not) seeking any relief which an employment tribunal has power to give or that he is not (or they are not) entitled to any such relief.

(3C) Employment tribunal procedure regulations may authorise the determination of proceedings without hearing anyone other than the person or persons by whom, and the person or persons against whom, the proceedings are brought (or his or their representatives) where –
   (a) an employment tribunal is on undisputed facts bound by the decision of a court in another case to dismiss the case of the person or persons by whom, or of the person or persons against whom, the proceedings are brought, or
   (b) the proceedings relate only to a preliminary issue which may be heard and determined in accordance with regulations under section 9(4).

(4) A person who without reasonable excuse fails to comply with –
   (a) any requirement imposed by virtue of subsection (3)(d) or (h), or
   (b) any requirement with respect to the discovery, recovery or inspection of documents imposed by virtue of subsection (3)(e), or
   (c) any requirement imposed by virtue of employment tribunal procedure regulations to give written answers for the purpose of facilitating the determination of proceedings as mentioned in subsection (3A),(3B) or (3C),

is guilty of an offence and liable on summary conviction to a fine not exceeding level 3 on the standard scale.

(5) Subject to any regulations under section 11(1)(a), employment tribunal procedure regulations may include provision authorising or requiring an employment tribunal, in circumstances specified in the regulations, to send notice or a copy of –

   (a) any document specified in the regulations which relates to any proceedings before the tribunal, or

   (b) any decision, order or award of the tribunal,

   to any government department or other person or body so specified.

(6) Where in accordance with employment tribunal procedure regulations an employment tribunal determines in the same proceedings –

   (a) a complaint presented under section 111 of the Employment Rights Act 1996, and

   (b) a question referred under section 163 of that Act,

   subsection (2) of that section has no effect for the purposes of the proceedings in so far as they relate to the complaint under section 111.

Procedure in contract cases

8 (1) Where in proceedings brought by virtue of section 3 an employment tribunal finds that the whole or part of a sum claimed in the proceedings is due, the tribunal shall order the respondent to the proceedings to pay the amount which it finds due.

(2) An order under section 3 may provide that an employment tribunal shall not in proceedings in respect of a claim, or a number of claims relating to the same contract, order the payment of an amount exceeding such sum as may be specified in the order as the maximum amount which an employment tribunal may order to be paid in relation to a claim or in relation to a contract.

(3) An order under section 3 may include provisions –

   (a) as to the manner in which and time within which proceedings are to be brought by virtue of that section, and

   (b) modifying any other enactment.

(4) An order under that section may make different provision in relation to proceedings in respect of different descriptions of claims.

Pre-hearing reviews and preliminary matters

9 (1) Employment tribunal procedure regulations may include provision –

   (a) for authorising the carrying-out by an employment tribunal of a preliminary consideration of any proceedings before it (a 'pre-hearing review'), and

   (b) for enabling such powers to be exercised in connection with a pre-hearing review as may be prescribed by the regulations.

(2) Such regulations may in particular include provision –

   (a) for authorising any tribunal carrying out a pre-hearing review under the regulations to make, in circumstances specified in the regulations, an order requiring a party to the proceedings in question, if he wishes to continue to participate in those proceedings, to pay a deposit of an amount not exceeding £500, and

(b) for prescribing—

    (i) the manner in which the amount of any such deposit is to be determined in any particular case,

    (ii) the consequences of non-payment of any such deposit, and

    (iii) the circumstances in which any such deposit, or any part of it, may be refunded to the party who paid it or be paid over to another party to the proceedings.

(3) The Secretary of State may from time to time by order substitute for the sum specified in subsection (2)(a) such other sum as is specified in the order.

(4) Employment tribunal procedure regulations may also include provision for authorising an employment tribunal to hear and determine separately any preliminary issue of a description prescribed by the regulations which is raised by any case.

10 National Security

(1) If on a complaint under –

(a) section 146 of the Trade Union and Labour Relations (Consolidation) Act 1992 (detriment: trade union membership) or,

(b) section 111 of the Employment Rights Act 1996 (unfair dismissal),

it is shown that the action complained of was taken for the purpose of safeguarding national security, the employment tribunal shall dismiss the complaint.

(2) Employment tribunal procedure regulations may make provision about the composition of the tribunal (including provision disapplying or modifying section 4) for the purposes of the proceedings in relation to which –

(a) a direction is given under subsection (3), or

(b) an order is made under subsection (4).

(3) A direction may be given under this subsection by a Minister of the Crown if –

(a) it relates to particular Crown employment proceedings, and

(b) the Minister considers it expedient in the interests of national security.

(4) An order may be made under this subsection by the President or Regional Chairman in relation to particular proceedings if he considers it expedient in the interests of national security.

(5) Employment tribunal procedure regulations may make provision enabling a Minister of the Crown, if he considers it expedient in the interests of national security –

(a) to direct a tribunal to sit in private for all or part of particular Crown employment proceedings;

(b) to direct a tribunal to exclude the applicant from all or part of particular Crown employment proceedings;

(c) to direct a tribunal to exclude the applicant's representatives from all or part of particular Crown employment proceedings;

(d) to direct a tribunal to take steps to conceal the identity of a particular witness in particular Crown employment proceedings;

(e) to direct a tribunal to take steps to keep secret all or part of the reasons for its decision in particular Crown employment proceedings.

(6) Employment tribunal procedure regulations may enable a tribunal, if it considers it expedient in the interests of national security, to do anything of a kind which a tribunal can be required to do by direction under subsection (5)(a) to (e).

(7) In relation to cases where a person has been excluded by virtue of subsection (5)(b) or (c) or (6), employment tribunal procedure regulations may make provision –

    (a) for the appointment by the Attorney General, or by the Advocate General for Scotland, of a person to represent the interests of the applicant;

    (b) about the publication and registration of reasons for the tribunal's decision;

    (c) permitting an excluded person to make a statement to the tribunal before the commencement of the proceedings, or part of the proceedings, from which he is excluded.

(8) Proceedings are Crown employment proceedings for the purposes of this section if the employment to which the complaint relates –

    (a) is Crown employment, or

    (b) is connected with the performance of functions on behalf of the Crown.

(9) The reference in subsection (4) to the President or a Regional Chairman is to a person appointed in accordance with regulations under section 1(1) as –

    (a) a Regional Chairman,

    (b) President of the Employment Tribunals (England and Wales), or

    (c) President of the Employment Tribunals (Scotland).

10A   Confidential information

(1) Employment tribunal procedure regulations may enable an employment tribunal to sit in private for the purpose of hearing evidence from any person which in the opinion of the tribunal is likely to consist of –

    (a) information which he could not disclose without contravening a prohibition imposed by or by virtue of any enactment,

    (b) information which has been communicated to him in confidence or which he has otherwise obtained in consequence of the confidence reposed in him by another person, or

    (c) information the disclosure of which would, for reasons other than its effect on the negotiations with respect to any of the matters mentioned in section 178(2) of the Trade Union and Labour Relations (Consolidation) Act 1992, cause substantial injury to any undertaking of his or in which he works.

(2) The reference in subsection (1)(c) to any undertaking of a person or in which he works shall be construed –

    (a) in relation to a person in Crown employment, as a reference to the national interest,

    (b) in relation to a person who is a relevant member of the House of Lords staff, as a reference to the national interest or (if the case so requires) the interests of the House of Lords, and

(c) in relation to a person who is a relevant member of the House of Commons staff, as a reference to the national interest or (if the case so requires) in the interests of the House of Commons.

10B   Restriction of publicity in cases involving national security

(1) This section applies where a tribunal has been directed under section 10(5) or has determined under section 10(6) –
 (a) to take steps to conceal the identity of a particular witness, or
 (b) to take steps to keep secret all or part of the reasons for its decision.

(2) It is an offence to publish –
 (a) anything likely to lead to the identification of the witness, or
 (b) the reasons for the tribunal's decision of part of its reasons which it is directed or determined to keep secret.

(3) A person is guilty of an offence under this section is liable on summary conviction to a fine not exceeding level 5 on the standard scale.

(4) Where a person is charged with an offence under this section it is a defence to prove that at the time of the alleged offence he was not aware, and neither suspected nor had reason to suspect, that the publication in question was of, or included, the matter in question.

(5) Where an offence under this section committed by a body corporate is proved to have been committed with the consent or connivance of, or to be attributable to any neglect on the part of –
 (a) a director, manager, secretary or other similar officer of the body corporate, or
 (b) a person purporting to act in any such capacity,
 he as well as the body corporate is guilty of the offence and liable to be proceeded against and punished accordingly.

(6) A reference in this section to publication includes a reference to inclusion in an programme which is included in a programme service, within the meaning of the Broadcasting Act 1990.

Restriction of publicity in cases involving sexual misconduct

11 (1) Employment tribunal procedure regulations may include provision –
 (a) for cases involving allegations of the commission of sexual offences, for securing that the registration or other making available of documents or decisions shall be so effected as to prevent the identification of any person affected by or making the allegation, and provision –
 (b) for cases involving allegations of sexual misconduct, enabling an employment tribunal, on the application of any party to proceedings before it or of its own motion, to make a restricted reporting order having effect (if not revoked earlier) until the promulgation of the decision of the tribunal.

(2) If any identifying matter is published or included in a relevant programme in contravention of a restricted reporting order –
 (a) in the case of publication in a newspaper or periodical, any proprietor, any editor and any publisher of the newspaper or periodical,

(b) in the case of publication in any other form, the person publishing the matter, and

(c) in the case of matter included in a relevant programme –
   (i)   any body corporate engaged in providing the service in which the programme is included, and
   (ii) any person having functions in relation to the programme corresponding to those of an editor of a newspaper,

shall be guilty of an offence and liable on summary conviction to a fine not exceeding level 5 on the standard scale.

(3) Where a person is charged with an offence under subsection (2) it is a defence to prove that at the time of the alleged offence he was not aware, and neither suspected nor had reason to suspect, that the publication or programme in question was of, or included, the matter in question.

(4) Where an offence under subsection (2) committed by a body corporate is proved to have been committed with the consent or connivance of, or to be attributable to any neglect on the part of –

(a) a director, manager, secretary or other similar officer of the body corporate, or

(b) a person purporting to act in any such capacity,

he as well as the body corporate is guilty of the offence and liable to be proceeded against and punished accordingly.

(5) In relation to a body corporate whose affairs are managed by its members 'director', in subsection (4), means a member of the body corporate.

(6) In this section –

'identifying matter', in relation to a person, means any matter likely to lead members of the public to identify him as a person affected by, or as the person making, the allegation,

'relevant programme' has the same meaning as in the Sexual Offences (Amendment) Act 1992,

'restricted reporting order' means an order –
   (a) made in exercise of a power conferred by regulations made by virtue of this section, and
   (b) prohibiting the publication in Great Britain of identifying matter in a written publication available to the public or its inclusion in a relevant programme for reception in Great Britain,

'sexual misconduct' means the commission of a sexual offence, sexual harassment or other adverse conduct (of whatever nature) related to sex, and conduct is related to sex whether the relationship with sex lies in the character of the conduct or in its having reference to the sex or sexual orientation of the person at whom the conduct is directed,

'sexual offence' mean any offence to which section 4 of the Sexual Offences (Amendment) Act 1976, the Sexual Offences (Amendment) Act 1992 or section 274(2) of the Criminal Procedure (Scotland) Act 1995 applies (offences under the Sexual Offences Act 1956, Part I of the Criminal Law (Consolidation)(Scotland) Act 1995 and certain other enactments), and

'written publication' has the same meaning as in the Sexual Offences (Amendment) Act 1992.

Restriction of publicity in disability cases

12 (1) This section applies to proceedings on a complaint under section 8 of the Disability Discrimination Act 1995 in which evidence of a personal nature is likely to be heard by the employment tribunal hearing the complaint.

(2) Employment tribunal procedure regulations may include provision in relation to proceedings to which this section applies for –

  (a) enabling an employment tribunal, on the application of the complainant or of its own motion, to make a restricted reporting order having effect (if not revoked earlier) until the promulgation of the decision of the tribunal and

  (b) where a restricted reporting order is made in relation to a complaint which is being dealt with by the tribunal together with any other proceedings, enabling the tribunal to direct that the order is to apply also in relation to those other proceedings or such part of them as the tribunal may direct.

(3) If any identifying matter is published or included in a relevant programme in contravention of a restricted reporting order –

  (a) in the case of publication in a newspaper or periodical, any proprietor, any editor and any publisher of the newspaper or periodical,

  (b) in the case of publication in any other form, the person publishing the matter, and

  (c) in the case of matter included in a relevant programme—

    (i) any body corporate engaged in providing the service in which the programme is included, and

    (ii) any person having functions in relation to the programme corresponding to those of an editor of a newspaper,

shall be guilty of an offence and liable on summary conviction to a fine not exceeding level 5 on the standard scale.

(4) Where a person is charged with an offence under subsection (3), it is a defence to prove that at the time of the alleged offence he was not aware, and neither suspected nor had reason to suspect, that the publication or programme in question was of, or included, the matter in question.

(5) Where an offence under subsection (3) committed by a body corporate is proved to have been committed with the consent or connivance of, or to be attributable to any neglect on the part of –

  (a) a director, manager, secretary or other similar officer of the body corporate, or

  (b) a person purporting to act in any such capacity,

he as well as the body corporate is guilty of the offence and liable to be proceeded against and punished accordingly.

(6) In relation to a body corporate whose affairs are managed by its members 'director', in subsection (5), means a member of the body corporate.

(7) In this section –

'evidence of a personal nature' means any evidence of a medical, or other intimate, nature which might reasonably be assumed to be likely to cause significant embarrassment to the complainant if reported,

'identifying matter' means any matter likely to lead members of the public to identify the complainant or such other persons (if any) as may be named in the order,

'promulgation' has such meaning as may be prescribed by regulations made by virtue of this section,

'relevant programme' means a programme included in a programme service, within the meaning of the Broadcasting Act 1990,

'restricted reporting order' means an order –

(a) made in exercise of a power conferred by regulations made by virtue of this section, and

(b) prohibiting the publication in Great Britain of identifying matter in a written publication available to the public or its inclusion in a relevant programme for reception in Great Britain, and

'written publication' includes a film, a sound track and any other record in permanent form but does not include an indictment or other document prepared for use in particular legal proceedings.

Costs and expenses

13 (1) Employment tribunal procedure regulations may include provision –

(a) for the award of costs or expenses, including any allowances payable under section 5(2)(c) or (3), and

(b) for taxing or otherwise settling any such costs or expenses (and, in particular in England and Wales, for enabling such costs to be taxed in a county court).

(2) In relation to proceedings under section 111 of the Employment Rights Act 1996 –

(a) where the employee has expressed a wish to be reinstated or re-engaged which has been communicated to the employer at least seven days before the hearing of the complaint, . . .

(b) . . .

employment tribunal procedure regulations shall include provision for requiring the employer to pay the costs or expenses of any postponement or adjournment of the hearing caused by his failure, without a special reason, to adduce reasonable evidence as to the availability of the job from which the complainant was dismissed . . . or of comparable or suitable employment.

Interest

14 (1) The Secretary of State may by order made with the approval of the Treasury provide that sums payable in pursuance of decisions of employment tribunals shall carry interest at such rate and between such times as may be prescribed by the order.

(2) Any interest due by virtue of such an order shall be recoverable as a sumpayable in pursuance of the decision.

(3) The power conferred by subsection (1) includes power –

(a) to specify cases or circumstances in which interest is not payable,

(b) to provide that interest is payable only on sums exceeding a specified amount falling between specified amounts,

(c) to make provision for the manner in which and the periods by reference to which interest is to be calculated and paid,

(d) to provide that any enactment –
  (i)   does or does not apply in relation to interest payable by virtue of subsection (1), or
  (ii) applies to it with such modifications as may be specified in the order,
(e) to make provision for cases where sums are payable in pursuance of decisions or awards made on appeal from employment tribunals,
(f) to make such incidental or supplemental provision as the Secretary of State considers necessary.

(4) In particular, an order under subsection (1) may provide that the rate of interest shall be the rate specified in section 17 of the Judgments Act 1838 as that enactment has effect from time to time.

Enforcement

15 (1) Any sum payable in pursuance of a decision of an employment tribunal in England and Wales which has been registered in accordance with employment tribunal procedure regulations shall, if a county court so orders, be recoverable by execution issued from the county court or otherwise as if it were payable under an order of that court.

(2) Any order for the payment of any sum made by an employment tribunal in Scotland (or any copy of such an order certified by the Secretary of the Tribunals) may be enforced as if it were an extract registered decree arbitral bearing a warrant for execution issued by the sheriff court of any sheriffdom in Scotland.

(3) In this section a reference to a decision or order of an employment tribunal –
  (a) does not include a decision or order which, on being reviewed, has been revoked by the tribunal, and
  (b) in relation to a decision or order which on being reviewed, has been varied by the tribunal, shall be construed as a reference to the decision or order as so varied.

RECOUPMENT OF SOCIAL SECURITY BENEFITS

Power to provide for recoupment of benefits

16 (1) This section applies to payments which are the subject of proceedings before industrial tribunals and which are –
  (a) payments of wages or compensation for loss of wages,
  (b) payments by employers to employees under sections 146 to 151, sections 168 to 173 or section 192 of the Trade Union and Labour Relations (Consolidation) Act 1992,
  (c) payments by employers to employees under –
    (i)   Part III, V, VI or VII,
    (ii) section 93, or
    (iii) Part X,
    of the Employment Rights Act 1996, or
  (d) payments by employers to employees of a nature similar to, or for a purpose corresponding to the purpose of, payments within paragraph (b) or (c),

and to payments of remuneration under a protective award under section 189 of the Trade Union and Labour Relations (Consolidation) Act 1992.

(2) The Secretary of State may by regulations make with respect to payments to which this section applies provision for any or all of the purposes specified in subsection (3).

(3) The purposes referred to in subsection (2) are –
    (a) enabling the Secretary of State to recover from an employer, by way of total or partial recoupment of jobseeker's allowance or income support –
        (i) a sum not exceeding the amount of the prescribed element of the monetary award, or
        (ii) in the case of a protective award, the amount of the remuneration,
    (b) requiring or authorising an employment tribunal to order the payment of such a sum, by way of total or partial recoupment of either benefit, to the Secretary of State instead of to an employee, and
    (c) requiring an employment tribunal to order the payment to an employee of only the excess of the prescribed element of the monetary award over the amount of any jobseeker's allowance or income support shown to the tribunal to have been paid to the employee and enabling the Secretary of State to recover from the employer, by way of total or partial recoupment of the benefit, a sum not exceeding that amount.

(4) Regulations under this section may be framed –
    (a) so as to apply to all payments to which this section applies or to one or more classes of those payments, and
    (b) so as to apply to both jobseeker's allowance and income support, or to only jobseeker's allowance or income support.

(5) Regulations under this section may –
    (a) confer powers and impose duties on employment tribunals or ... other persons,
    (b) impose on an employer to whom a monetary award or protective award relates a duty –
        (i) to furnish particulars connected with the award, and
        (ii) to suspend payments in pursuance of the award during any period prescribed by the regulations,
    (c) provide for an employer who pays a sum to the Secretary of State in pursuance of this section to be relieved from any liability to pay the sum to another person,
    (cc) provide for the determination by the Secretary of State of any issue arising as to the total or partial recoupment in pursuance of the regulations of a jobseeker's allowance, unemployment benefit or income support,
    (d) confer on an employee a right of appeal to an appeal tribunal constituted under Chapter I of Part I of the Social Security Act 1998 against any decision of the Secretary of State on any such issue, and
    (e) provide for the proof in proceedings before employment tribunals (whether by certificate or in any other manner) of any amount of jobseeker's allowance or income support paid to an employee.

(6) Regulations under this section may make different provision for different cases.

Recoupment: further provisions

17 (1) Where in pursuance of any regulations under section 16 a sum has been recovered by or paid to the Secretary of State by way of total or partial recoupment of jobseeker's allowance or income support –

(a) no sum shall be recoverable under Part III or V of the Social Security Administration Act 1992, and

(b) no abatement, payment or reduction shall be made by reference to the jobseeker's allowance or income support recouped.

(2) Any amount found to have been duly recovered by or paid to the Secretary of State in pursuance of regulations under section 16 by way of total or partial recoupment of jobseeker's allowance shall be paid into the National Insurance Fund.

(3) In section 16 –

'monetary award' means the amount which is awarded, or ordered to be paid, to the employee by the tribunal or would be so awarded or ordered apart from any provision of regulations under that section, and

'the prescribed element', in relation to monetary award, means so much of that award as is attributable to such matters as may be prescribed by regulations under that section.

(4) In section 16 'income-based jobseeker's allowance' has the same meaning as in the Jobseekers Act 1995.

CONCILIATION

Conciliation

18 (1) This section applies in the case of employment tribunal proceedings and claims which could be the subject of employment tribunal proceedings –

(a) under –

(i) section 2(1) of the Equal Pay Act 1970,

(ii) section 63 of the Sex Discrimination Act 1975, or

(iii) section 54 of the Race Relations Act 1976,

(b) arising out of a contravention, or alleged contravention, of section 64, 68, 86, 137, 138, 146, 168, 169, 170, 174, 188 or 190 of the Trade Union and Labour Relations (Consolidation) Act 1992,

(c) under section 8 of the Disability Discrimination Act 1995,

(d) arising out of a contravention, or alleged contravention of section 8, 13, 15, 18(1), 21(1), 28, 92 or 135, or of Part V, VI VII or X, of the Employment Rights Act 1996,

(dd) under or by virtue of section 11, 18, 20(1)(a) or 24 of the National Minimum Wage Act 1998.

(e) which are proceedings in respect of which an employment tribunal has jurisdiction by virtue of section 3 of this Act,

(f) arising out of a contravention, or alleged contravention of a provision specified by an order under subsection (8)(b) as a provision to which this paragraph applies

(ff) under regulation 30 of the Working Time Regulations 1998.

(g) under regulation 27 or 32 of the Transnational Information and Consultation of Employees Regulations 1999, or

(h) arising out of a contravention, or alleged contravention of regulation 7(2) of the Part-time Workers (Prevention of Less Favourable Treatment) Regulations 2000.

(2) Where an application has been presented to an employment tribunal, and a copy of it has been sent to a conciliation officer, it is the duty of the conciliation officer –

(a) if he is requested to do so by the person by whom and the person against whom the proceedings are brought, or

(b) if, in the absence of any such request, the conciliation officer considers that he could act under this subsection with a reasonable prospect of success,

to endeavour to promote a settlement of the proceedings without their being determined by an employment tribunal.

(3) Where at any time –

(a) a person claims that action has been taken in respect of which proceedings could be brought by him before an employment tribunal,

(b) before any application relating to that action has been presented by him a request is made to a conciliation officer (whether by that person or by the person against whom the proceedings could be instituted) to make his services available to them,

the conciliation officer shall act in accordance with subsection (2) as if an application had been presented to an employment tribunal.

(4) Where a person who has presented a complaint to an employment tribunal under section 111 of the Employment Rights Act 1996 has ceased to be employed by the employer against whom the complaint was made, the conciliation officer shall (for the purpose of promoting a settlement of the complaint in accordance with subsection (2)) in particular –

(a) seek to promote the reinstatement or re-engagement of the complainant by the employer, or by a successor of the employer or by an associated employer, on terms appearing to the conciliation officer to be equitable, or

(b) where the complainant does not wish to be reinstated or re-engaged, or where reinstatement or re-engagement is not practicable, and the parties desire the conciliation officer to act, seek to promote agreement between them as to a sum by way of compensation to be paid by the employer to the complainant.

(5) Where at any time –

(a) a person claims that action has been taken in respect of which a complaint could be presented by him to an employment tribunal under section 111 of the Employment Rights Act 1996, but

(b) before any complaint relating to that action has been presented by him a request is made to a conciliation officer (whether by that person or by the employer) to make his services available to them,

the conciliation officer shall act in accordance with subsection (4) as if a complaint had been presented to an employment tribunal under section 111.

(6) In proceedings under this section a conciliation officer shall, where appropriate, have regard to the desirability of encouraging the use of other procedures available for the settlement of grievances.

(7) Anything communicated to a conciliation officer in connection with the performance of his functions under this section shall not be admissible in evidence in any proceedings before an employment tribunal, except with the consent of the person who communicated it to that officer.

(8) The Secretary of State may by order –

   (a) direct that further provisions of the Employment Rights Act 1996 be added to the list in subsection (1)(d), or

   (b) specify a provision of any other Act as a provision to which subsection (1)(f) applies.

Conciliation procedure

19 Employment tribunal procedure regulations shall include in relation to employment tribunal proceedings in the case of which any enactment makes provision for conciliation –

   (a) provisions requiring a copy of the application by which the proceedings are instituted, and a copy of any notice relating to it which is lodged by or on behalf of the person against whom the proceedings are brought, to be sent to a conciliation officer,

   (b) provisions securing that the applicant and the person against whom the proceedings are brought are notified that the services of a conciliation officer are available to them, and

   (c) provisions postponing the hearing of any such proceedings for such period as may be determined in accordance with the regulations for the purpose of giving an opportunity for the proceedings to be settled by way of conciliation and withdrawn.

PART II: THE EMPLOYMENT APPEAL TRIBUNAL

INTRODUCTORY

The Appeal Tribunal

20 (1) The Employment Appeal Tribunal ('the Appeal Tribunal') shall continue in existence.

   (2) The Appeal Tribunal shall have a central office in London but may sit at any time and in any place in Great Britain.

   (3) The Appeal Tribunal shall be a superior court of record and shall have an official seal which shall be judicially noticed.

   (4) Subsection 2 is subject to regulation 34 of the Transnational Information and Consultation of Employees Regulations 1999.

JURISDICTION

Jurisdiction of Appeal Tribunal

21 (1) An appeal lies to the Appeal Tribunal on any question of law arising from any decision of, or arising in any proceedings before, an employment tribunal under or by virtue of –

(a)   the Equal Pay Act 1970,
(b)   the Sex Discrimination Act 1975,
(c)   the Race Relations Act 1976,
(d)   the Trade Union and Labour Relations (Consolidation) Act 1992,
(e)   the Disability Discrimination Act 1995,
(f)   the Employment Rights Act 1996,
(ff) the National Minimum Wage Act 1998,
(fg) the Tax Credits Act 1999,
(g)   this Act
(h)   the Working Time Regulations 1998,
(i)   the Transnational Information and Consultation of Employees Regulations 1999, or
(j)   the Part-time Workers (Prevention of Less Favourable Treatment) Regulations 2000.

(2) No appeal shall lie except to the Appeal Tribunal from any decision of an employment tribunal under or by virtue of the Acts listed or the Regulations referred to in subsection (1).

(3) Subsection (1) does not affect any provision contained in, or made under, any Act which provides for an appeal to lie to the Appeal Tribunal (whether from an employment tribunal, the Certification Officer or any other person or body) otherwise than on a question to which that subsection applies.

(4) The Appeal Tribunal also has any jurisdiction in respect of matters other than appeals which is conferred on it by or under –

(a) the Trade Union and Labour Relations (Consolidation) Act 1992,
(b) this Act, or
(c) any other Act.

MEMBERSHIP, ETC

Membership of Appeal Tribunal

22 (1) The Appeal Tribunal shall consist of –

(a) such number of judges as may be nominated from time to time by the Lord Chancellor from the judges (other than the Lord Chancellor) of the High Court and the Court of Appeal,
(b) at least one judge of the Court of Session nominated from time to time by the Lord President of the Court of Session, and
(c) such number of other members as may be appointed from time to time by Her Majesty on the joint recommendation of the Lord Chancellor and the Secretary of State ('appointed Members').

(2) The appointed members shall be persons who appear to the Lord Chancellor and the Secretary of State to have special knowledge or experience of industrial relations either –

(a) as representatives of employers, or
(b) as representatives of workers (within the meaning of the Trade Union and Labour Relations (Consolidation) Act 1992).

(3) The Lord Chancellor shall, after consultation with the Lord President of the

Court of Session, appoint one of the judges nominated under subsection (1) to be the President of the Appeal Tribunal.

(4) No judge shall be nominated a member of the Appeal Tribunal except with his consent.

Temporary membership

23 (1) At any time when –

   (a) the office of President of the Appeal Tribunal is vacant, or

   (b) the person holding that office is temporarily absent or otherwise unable to act as the President of the Appeal Tribunal,

   the Lord Chancellor may nominate another judge nominated under section 22(1)(a) to act temporarily in his place.

(2) At any time when a judge of the Appeal Tribunal nominated under paragraph (a) or (b) of subsection (1) of section 22 is temporarily absent or otherwise unable to act as a member of the Appeal Tribunal –

   (a) in the case of a judge nominated under paragraph (a) of that subsection, the Lord Chancellor may nominate another judge who is qualified to be nominated under that paragraph to act temporarily in his place, and

   (b) in the case of a judge nominated under paragraph (b) of that subsection, the Lord President of the Court of Session may nominate another judge who is qualified to be nominated under that paragraph to act temporarily in his place.

(3) At any time when an appointed member of the Appeal Tribunal is temporarily absent or otherwise unable to act as a member of the Appeal Tribunal, the Lord Chancellor and the Secretary of State may jointly appoint a person appearing to them to have the qualifications for appointment as an appointed member to act temporarily in his place.

(4) A person nominated or appointed to act temporarily in place of the President or any other member of the Appeal Tribunal, when so acting, has all the functions of the person in whose place he acts.

(5) No judge shall be nominated to act temporarily as a member of the Appeal Tribunal except with his consent.

Temporary additional judicial membership

24 (1) At any time when it appears to the Lord Chancellor that it is expedient to do so in order to facilitate in England and Wales the disposal of business in the Appeal Tribunal, he may appoint a qualified person to be a temporary additional judge of the Appeal Tribunal during such period or on such occasions as the Lord Chancellor thinks fit.

(2) In subsection (1)'qualified persons' means a person who –

   (a) is qualified for appointment as a judge of the High Court under section 10 of the Supreme Court Act 1981, or

   (b) has held office as a judge of the High Court or the Court of Appeal.

(3) A person appointed to be a temporary additional judge of the Appeal Tribunal has all the functions of a judge nominated under section 22(1)(a).

Tenure of appointed members

25 (1) Subject to subsections (2) to (4), an appointed member shall hold and vacate office in accordance with the terms of his appointment.

(2) An appointed member –
  (a) may at any time resign his membership by notice in writing addressed to the Lord Chancellor and the Secretary of State, and
  (b) shall vacate his office on the day on which he attains the age of seventy.

(3) Subsection (2)(b) is subject to section 26(4) to (6) of the Judicial Pensions and Retirement Act 1993 (Lord Chancellor's power to authorise continuance of office up to the age of seventy-five).

(4) If the Lord Chancellor, after consultation with the Secretary of State, is satisfied that an appointed member –
  (a) has been absent from sittings of the Appeal Tribunal for a period longer than six consecutive months without the permission of the President of the Appeal Tribunal,
  (b) has become bankrupt or made an arrangement with his creditors, or has had his estate sequestrated or made a trust deed for behoof of his creditors or a composition contract,
  (c) is incapacitated by physical or mental illness, or
  (d) is otherwise unable or unfit to discharge the functions of a member,
  the Lord Chancellor may declare his office as a member to be vacant and shall notify the declaration in such manner as the Lord Chancellor thinks fit; and when the Lord Chancellor does so, the office becomes vacant.

Staff

26 The Secretary of State may appoint such officers and servants of the Appeal Tribunal as he may determine, subject to the approval of the Minister for the Civil Service as to numbers and terms and conditions of service.

Remuneration, pensions and allowances

27 (1) The Secretary of State shall pay –
  (a) the appointed members,
  (b) any person appointed to act temporarily in the place of an appointed member, and
  (c) the officers and servants of the Appeal Tribunal,
  such remuneration and such travelling and other allowances as he may, with the relevant approval, determine; and for this purpose the relevant approval is that of the Treasury in the case of persons within paragraph (a) or (b) and the Minister for the Civil Service in the case of persons within paragraph (c).

(2) A person appointed to be a temporary additional judge of the Appeal Tribunal shall be paid such remuneration and allowances as the Lord Chancellor may, with the approval of the Treasury, determine.

(3) If the Secretary of State determines, with the approval of the Treasury, that this subsection applies in the case of an appointed member, the Secretary of State shall –

(a) pay such pension, allowance or gratuity to or in respect of that person on his retirement or death, or

(b) make to the member such payments towards the provision of a pension, allowance or gratuity for his retirement or death,

as the Secretary of State may, with the approval of the Treasury, determine.

(4) Where –

(a) a person ceases to be an appointed member otherwise than on his retirement or death, and

(b) it appears to the Secretary of State that there are special circumstances which make it right for him to receive compensation,

the Secretary of State may make to him a payment of such amount as the Secretary of State may, with the approval of the Treasury, determine.

Composition of Appeal Tribunal

28 (1) The Appeal Tribunal may sit, in accordance with directions given by the President of the Appeal Tribunal, either as a single tribunal or in two or more divisions concurrently.

(2) Subject to subsections (3) to (5), proceedings before the Appeal Tribunal shall be heard by a judge and either two or four appointed members, so that in either case there is an equal number –

(a) of persons whose knowledge or experience of industrial relations is as representatives of employers, and

(b) of persons whose knowledge or experience of industrial relations is as representatives of workers.

(3) With the consent of the parties, proceedings before the Appeal Tribunal may be heard by a judge and one appointed member or by a judge and three appointed members.

(4) Proceedings on an appeal on a question arising from any decision of, or arising in any proceedings before, an employment tribunal consisting of the person mentioned in section 4(1)(a) alone shall be heard by a judge alone unless a judge directs that the proceedings shall be heard in accordance with subsections (2) and (3).

(5) . . .

PROCEDURE

Conduct of hearings

29 (1) A person may appear before the Appeal Tribunal in person or be represented by –

(a) counsel or a solicitor,

(b) a representative of a trade union or an employers' association, or

(c) any other person whom he desires to represent him.

(2) The Appeal Tribunal has in relation to –

(a) the attendance and examination of witnesses,

(b) the production and inspection of documents, and

(c) all other matters incidental to its jurisdiction,

the same powers, rights, privileges and authority (in England and Wales) as the High Court and (in Scotland) as the Court of Session.

Appeal Tribunal procedure rules

30 (1) The Lord Chancellor, after consultation with the Lord President of the Court of Session, shall make rules ('Appeal Tribunal procedure rules') with respect to proceedings before the Appeal Tribunal.

(2) Appeal Tribunal procedure rules may, in particular, include provision –

(a) with respect to the manner in which, and the time within which, an appeal may be brought,

(b) with respect to the manner in which any application or complaint to the Appeal Tribunal may be made,

(c) for requiring persons to attend to give evidence and produce documents and for authorising the administration of oaths to witnesses,

(d) for requiring or enabling the Appeal Tribunal to sit in private in circumstances in which an employment tribunal is required or empowered to sit in private by virtue of section 10A of this Act,

(e) for the registration and proof of any award made on an application to the Appeal Tribunal under section 67 or 176 of the Trade Union and Labour Relations (Consolidation) Act 1992, and

(f) for interlocutory matters arising on any appeal or application to the Appeal Tribunal to be dealt with otherwise than in accordance with section 28(2) to (5) of this Act.

(2A) Appeal Tribunal procedure rules may make provision of a kind which may be made by employment tribunal procedure regulations under section 10(2), (5), (6) or (7).

(2B) For the purposes of subsection (2A) –

(a) the reference in section 10(2) to section 4 shall be treated as a reference to section 28, and

(b) the reference in section 10(4) to the President or a Regional Chairman shall be treated as a reference to a judge of the Appeal Tribunal.

(2C) Section 10B shall have effect in relation to a direction to our determination of the Appeal Tribunal as it has effect in relation to a direction to or determination of an employment tribunal.

(3) Subject to Appeal Tribunal procedure rules, the Appeal Tribunal has power to regulate its own procedure.

Restriction of publicity in cases involving sexual misconduct

31 (1) Appeal Tribunal procedure rules may, as respects proceedings to which this section applies, include provision –

(a) for cases involving allegations of the commission of sexual offences, for securing that the registration or other making available of documents or decisions shall be so effected as to prevent the identification of any person affected by or making the allegation, and

(b) for cases involving allegations of sexual misconduct, enabling the Appeal Tribunal, on the application of any party to the proceedings before it or of its own motion, to make a restricted reporting order having effect (if not revoked earlier) until the promulgation of the decision of the Appeal Tribunal.

(2) This section applies to –

   (a) proceedings on an appeal against a decision of an employment tribunal to make, or not to make, a restricted reporting order, and

   (b) proceedings on an appeal against any interlocutory decision of an employment tribunal in proceedings in which the employment tribunal has made a restricted reporting order which it has not revoked.

(3) If any identifying matter is published or included in a relevant programme in contravention of a restricted reporting order –

   (a) in the case of publication in a newspaper or periodical, any proprietor, any editor and any publisher of the newspaper or periodical,

   (b) in the case of publication in any other form, the person publishing the matter, and

   (c) in the case of matter included in a relevant programme –

      (i)   any body corporate engaged in providing the service in which the programme is included, and

      (ii) any person having functions in relation to the programme corresponding to those of an editor of a newspaper,

   shall be guilty of an offence and liable on summary conviction to a fine not exceeding level 5 on the standard scale.

(4) Where a person is charged with an offence under subsection (3) it is a defence to prove that at the time of the alleged offence he was not aware, and neither suspected nor had reason to suspect, that the publication or programme in question was of, or included, the matter in question.

(5) Where an offence under subsection (3) committed by a body corporate is proved to have been committed with the consent or connivance of, or to be attributable to any neglect on the part of –

   (a) a director, manager, secretary or other similar officer of the body corporate, or

   (b) a person purporting to act in any such capacity,

   he as well as the body corporate is guilty of the offence and liable to be proceeded against and punished accordingly.

(6) In relation to a body corporate whose affairs are managed by its members 'director', in subsection (5), means a member of the body corporate.

(7) 'Restricted reporting order' means –

   (a) in subsections (1) and (3), an order –

      (i)   made in exercise of a power conferred by rules made by virtue of this section, and

      (ii) prohibiting the publication in Great Britain of identifying matter in a written publication available to the public or its inclusion in a relevant programme for reception in Great Britain, and

   (b) in subsection (2), an order which is a restricted reporting order for the purposes of section 11.

(8) In this section –

   'identifying matter', in relation to a person, means any matter likely to lead members of the public to identify him as a person affected by, or as the person making, the allegation,

'relevant programme' has the same meaning as in the Sexual Offences (Amendment) Act 1992,

'sexual misconduct' means the commission of a sexual offence, sexual harassment or other adverse conduct (of whatever nature) related to sex, and conduct is related to sex whether the relationship with sex lies in the character of the conduct or in its having reference to the sex or sexual orientation of the person at whom the conduct is directed,

'sexual offence' means any offence to which section 4 of the Sexual Offences (Amendment) Act 1976, the Sexual Offences (Amendment) Act 1992 or section 274(2) of the Criminal Procedure (Scotland) Act 1995 applies (offences under the Sexual Offences Act 1956, Part I of the Criminal Law (Consolidation)(Scotland) Act 1995 and certain other enactments), and

'written publication' has the same meaning as in the Sexual Offences (Amendment) Act 1992.

Restriction of publicity in disability cases

32 (1) This section applies to proceedings –

    (a) on an appeal against a decision of an employment tribunal to make, or not to make, a restricted reporting order, or

    (b) on an appeal against any interlocutory decision of an employment tribunal in proceedings in which the employment tribunal has made a restricted reporting order which it has not revoked.

(2) Appeal Tribunal procedure rules may, as respects proceedings to which this section applies, include provision for –

    (a) enabling the Appeal Tribunal, on the application of the complainant or of its own motion, to make a restricted reporting order having effect (if not revoked earlier) until the promulgation of the decision of the Appeal Tribunal, and

    (b) where a restricted reporting order is made in relation to an appeal which is being dealt with by the Appeal Tribunal together with any other proceedings, enabling the Appeal Tribunal to direct that the order is to apply also in relation to those other proceedings or such part of them as the Appeal Tribunal may direct.

(3) If any identifying matter is published or included in a relevant programme in contravention of a restricted reporting order –

    (a) in the case of publication in a newspaper or periodical, any proprietor, any editor and any publisher of the newspaper or periodical,

    (b) in the case of publication in any other form, the person publishing the matter, and

    (c) in the case of matter included in a relevant programme –

        (i) any body corporate engaged in providing the service in which the programme is included, and

        (ii) any person having functions in relation to the programme corresponding to those of an editor of a newspaper,

shall be guilty of an offence and liable on summary conviction to a fine not exceeding level 5 on the standard scale.

(4) Where a person is charged with an offence under subsection (3), it is a defence to prove that at the time of the alleged offence he was not aware, and neither suspected nor had reason to suspect, that the publication or programme in question was of, or included, the matter in question.

(5) Where an offence under subsection (3) committed by a body corporate is proved to have been committed with the consent or connivance of, or to be attributable to any neglect on the part of –

(a) a director, manager, secretary or other similar officer of the body corporate, or

(b) a person purporting to act in any such capacity,

he as well as the body corporate is guilty of the offence and liable to be proceeded against and punished accordingly.

(6) In relation to a body corporate whose affairs are managed by its members 'director', in subsection (5), means a member of the body corporate.

(7) 'Restricted reporting order' means –

(a) in subsection (1), an order which is a restricted reporting order for the purposes of section 12, and

(b) in subsections (2) and (3), an order –

    (i) made in exercise of a power conferred by rules made by virtue of this section, and

    (ii) prohibiting the publication in Great Britain of identifying matter in a written publication available to the public or its inclusion in a relevant programme for reception in Great Britain.

(8) In this section –

'complainant' means the person who made the complaint to which the proceedings before the Appeal Tribunal relate,

'identifying matter' means any matter likely to lead members of the public to identify the complainant or such other persons (if any) as may be named in the order,

'promulgation' has such meaning as may be prescribed by rules made by virtue of this section,

'relevant programme' means a programme included in a programme service, within the meaning of the Broadcasting Act 1990, and

'written publication' includes a film, a sound track and any other record in permanent form but does not include an indictment or other document prepared for use in particular legal proceedings.

Restrictions of vexatious proceedings

33 (1) If, on an application made by the Attorney General or the Lord Advocate under this section, the Appeal Tribunal is satisfied that a person has habitually and persistently and without any reasonable ground –

(a) instituted vexatious proceedings, whether in an employment tribunal or before the Appeal Tribunal, and whether against the same person or against different persons, or

(b) made vexatious applications in any proceedings, whether in an employment tribunal or before the Appeal Tribunal,

the Appeal Tribunal may, after hearing the person or giving him an opportunity of being heard, make a restriction of proceedings order.

(2) A 'restriction of proceedings order' is an order that –

    (a) no proceedings shall without the leave of the Appeal Tribunal be instituted in any employment tribunal or before the Appeal Tribunal by the person against whom the order is made,

    (b) any proceedings instituted by him in any employment tribunal or before the Appeal Tribunal before the making of the order shall not be continued by him without the leave of the Appeal Tribunal, and

    (c) no application (other than one for leave under this section) is to be made by him in any proceedings in any employment tribunal or before the Appeal Tribunal without the leave of the Appeal Tribunal.

(3) A restriction of proceedings order may provide that it is to cease to have effect at the end of a specified period, but otherwise it remains in force indefinitely.

(4) Leave for the institution or continuance of, or for the making of an application in, any proceedings in an employment tribunal or before the Appeal Tribunal by a person who is the subject of a restriction of proceedings order shall not be given unless the Appeal Tribunal is satisfied –

    (a) that the proceedings or application are not an abuse of the process of the tribunal in question, and

    (b) that there are reasonable grounds for the proceedings or application.

(5) A copy of a restriction of proceedings order shall be published in the London Gazette and the Edinburgh Gazette.

Costs and expenses

34 (1) Appeal Tribunal procedure rules may include provision empowering the Appeal Tribunal to order a party to any proceedings before the Appeal Tribunal to pay to any other party to the proceedings the whole or part of the costs or expenses incurred by the other party in connection with the proceedings where in the opinion of the Appeal Tribunal –

    (a) the proceedings were unnecessary, improper or vexatious, or

    (b) there has been unreasonable delay or other unreasonable conduct in bringing or conducting the proceedings.

(2) Except as provided by subsection (1), Appeal Tribunal procedure rules shall not enable the Appeal Tribunal to order the payment of costs or expenses by any party to proceedings before the Appeal Tribunal.

DECISIONS AND FURTHER APPEALS

Powers of Appeal Tribunal

35 (1) For the purpose of disposing of an appeal, the Appeal Tribunal may –

    (a) exercise any of the powers of the body or officer from whom the appeal was brought, or

    (b) remit the case to that body or officer.

(2) Any decision or award of the Appeal Tribunal on an appeal has the same effect, and may be enforced in the same manner, as a decision or award of the body or officer from whom the appeal was brought.

Enforcement of decisions etc

36 (1) Any sum payable in England and Wales in pursuance of an award of the Appeal Tribunal –

  (a) made under section 67 or 176 of the Trade Union and Labour Relations (Consolidation) Act 1992, and

  (b) registered in accordance with Appeal Tribunal procedure rules,

  is, if a county court so orders, recoverable by execution issued from the county court or otherwise as if it were payable under an order of that court.

(2) Any order by the Appeal Tribunal for the payment in Scotland of any sum in pursuance of such an award (or any copy of such an order certified by the Secretary of the Tribunals) may be enforced as if it were an extract registered decree arbitral bearing a warrant for execution issued by the sheriff court of any sheriffdom in Scotland.

(3) Any sum payable in pursuance of an award of the Appeal Tribunal under section 67 or 176 of the Trade Union and Labour Relations (Consolidation) Act 1992 shall be treated as if it were a sum payable in pursuance of a decision of an employment tribunal for the purposes of section 14 of this Act.

(4) No person shall be punished for contempt of the Appeal Tribunal except by, or with the consent of, a judge.

(5) A magistrates' court shall not remit the whole or part of a fine imposed by the Appeal Tribunal unless it has the consent of a judge who is a member of the Appeal Tribunal.

Appeals from Appeal Tribunal

37 (1) Subject to subsection (3), an appeal on any question of law lies from any decision or order of the Appeal Tribunal to the relevant appeal court with the leave of the Appeal Tribunal or of the relevant appeal court.

(2) In subsection (1) the 'relevant appeal court' means –

  (a) in the case of proceedings in England and Wales, the Court of Appeal, and

  (b) in the case of proceedings in Scotland, the Court of Session.

(3) No appeal lies from a decision of the Appeal Tribunal refusing leave for the institution or continuance of, or for the making of an application in, proceedings by a person who is the subject of a restriction of proceedings order made under section 33.

(4) This section is without prejudice to section 13 of the Administration of Justice Act 1960 (appeal in case of contempt of court).

PART III: SUPPLEMENTARY

CROWN EMPLOYMENT AND PARLIAMENTARY STAFF

Crown employment

38 (1) This Act has effect in relation to Crown employment and persons in Crown employment as it has effect in relation to other employment and other employees.

(2) In this Act 'Crown employment' means employment under or for the purposes of a government department or any officer or body exercising on behalf of the Crown functions conferred by a statutory provision.

(3) For the purposes of the application of this Act in relation to Crown employment in accordance with subsection (1) –

    (a) references to an employee shall be construed as references to a person in Crown employment, and

    (b) references to a contract of employment shall be construed as references to the terms of employment of a person in Crown employment.

(4) Subsection (1) applies to –

    (a) service as a member of the naval, military or air forces of the Crown, and

    (b) employment by an association established for the purposes of Part XI of the Reserve Forces Act 1996;

but her Majesty may by Order in Council make any provision of this Act apply to service as a member of the naval, military or air forces of the Crown subject to such exceptions and modifications as may be specified in the Order in Council.

Parliamentary staff

39 (1) This Act has effect in relation to employment as a relevant member of the House of Lords staff or a relevant member of the House of Commons staff as it has effect in relation to other employment.

(2) Nothing in any rule of law or the law of practice of Parliament prevents a relevant member of the House of Lords staff or a relevant member of the House of Commons staff from bringing before an employment tribunal proceedings of any description which could be brought before such a tribunal by a person who is not a relevant member of the House of Lords staff or a relevant member of the House of Commons staff.

(3) For the purposes of the application of this Act in relation to a relevant member of the House of Commons staff –

    (a) references to an employee shall be construed as references to a relevant member of the House of Commons staff, and

    (b) references to a contract of employment shall be construed as including references to the terms of employment of a relevant member of the House of Commons staff.

(4) In this Act 'relevant member of the House of Lords staff' means any person who is employed under a contract of employment with the Corporate Officer of the House of Lords.

(5) In this Act 'relevant member of the House of Commons staff' has the same meaning as in section 195 of the Employment Rights Act 1996; and (subject to an Order in Council under subsection (12) of that section) –

    (a) subsections (6) and (7) of that section have effect for determining who is the employer of a relevant member of the House of Commons staff for the purposes of this Act, and

    (b) subsection (8) of that section applies in relation to proceedings brought by virtue of this section.

GENERAL

Power to amend Act

40 (1) The Secretary of State may by order –

    (a) provide that any provision of this Act to which this section applies and which is specified in the order shall not apply to persons, or to employments, of such classes as may be prescribed in the order, or

    (b) provide that any provision of this Act to which this section applies shall apply to persons or employments of such classes as may be prescribed in the order subject to such exceptions and modifications as may be so prescribed.

  (2) This section applies to sections 3, 8, 16 and 17 and to section 18 so far as deriving from section 133 of the Employment Protection (Consolidation) Act 1978.

Orders, regulations and rules

41 (1) Any power conferred by this Act on a Minister of the Crown to make an order, and any power conferred by this Act to make regulations or rules, is exercisable by statutory instrument.

  (2) No recommendation shall be made to Her Majesty to make an Order in Council under section 38(4), and no order shall be made under section 3, 4(4) or 40, unless a draft of the Order in Council or order has been laid before Parliament and approved by a resolution of each House of Parliament.

  (3) A statutory instrument containing –

    (a) an order made by a Minister of the Crown under any other provision of this Act except Part II of Schedule 2, or

    (b) regulations or rules made under this Act,

is subject to annulment in pursuance of a resolution of either House of Parliament.

  (4) Any power conferred by this Act which is exercisable by statutory instrument includes power to make such incidental, supplementary or transitional provision as appears to the Minister exercising the power to be necessary or expedient.

Interpretation

42 (1) In this Act –

'the Appeal Tribunal' means the Employment Appeal Tribunal,

'Appeal Tribunal procedure rules' shall be construed in accordance with section 30(1),

'appointed member' shall be construed in accordance with section 22(1)(c),

'conciliation officer' means an officer designated by the Advisory, Conciliation and Arbitration Service under section 211 of the Trade Union and Labour Relations (Consolidation) Act 1992,

'contract of employment' means a contract of service or apprenticeship, whether express or implied, and (if it is express) whether oral or in writing, 'employee' means an individual who has entered into or works under (or, where the employment has ceased, worked under) a contract of employment,

'employer', in relation to an employee, means the person by whom the employee is (or, where the employment has ceased, was) employed,

'employers' association' has the same meaning as in the Trade Union and Labour Relations (Consolidation) Act 1992,

'employment' means employment under a contract of employment and 'employed' shall be construed accordingly,

'employment tribunal procedure regulations' shall be construed in accordance with section 7(1),

'statutory provision' means a provision, whether of a general or a special nature, contained in, or in any document made or issued under, any Act, whether of a general or special nature,

'successor', in relation to the employer of an employee, means (subject to subsection (2)) a person who in consequence of a change occurring (whether by virtue of a sale or other disposition or by operation of law) in the ownership of the undertaking, or of the part of the undertaking, for the purposes of which the employee was employed, has become the owner of the undertaking or part, and

'trade union' has the meaning given by section 1 of the Trade Union and Labour Relations (Consolidation) Act 1992.

(2) The definition of 'successor' in subsection (1) has effect (subject to the necessary modifications) in relation to a case where –

  (a) the person by whom an undertaking or part of an undertaking is owned immediately before a change is one of the persons by whom (whether as partners, trustees or otherwise) it is owned immediately after the change, or

  (b) the persons by whom an undertaking or part of an undertaking is owned immediately before a change (whether as partners, trustees or otherwise) include the persons by whom, or include one or more of the persons by whom, it is owned immediately after the change,

as it has effect where the previous owner and the new owner are wholly different persons.

(3) For the purposes of this Act any two employers shall be treated as associated if –

  (a) one is a company of which the other (directly or indirectly) has control, or

  (b) both are companies of which a third person (directly or indirectly) has control;

and 'associated employer' shall be construed accordingly.

FINAL PROVISIONS

. . .

Commencement

46 This Act shall come into force on 22 August 1996.

Extent

47   This Act does not extend to Northern Ireland.

Short title

48   This Act may be cited as the Employment Tribunals Act 1996.

SCHEDULES

. . .

SCHEDULE 2: TRANSITIONAL PROVISIONS, SAVINGS AND TRANSITORY PROVISIONS

PART I: TRANSITIONAL PROVISIONS AND SAVINGS

1   The substitution of this Act for the provisions repealed or revoked by this Act does not affect the continuity of the law.

2   Anything done, or having effect as done,(including the making of subordinate legislation) under or for the purposes of any provision repealed or revoked by this act has effect as if done under or for the purposes of any corresponding provision of this Act.

3   Any reference (express or implied) in this Act or any other enactment, or in any instrument or document, to a provision of this Act is (so far as the context permits) to be read as (according to the context) being or including in relation to times, circumstances and purposes before the commencement of this Act a reference to the corresponding provision repealed or revoked by this Act.

4   (1) Any reference (express or implied) in any enactment, or in any instrument or document, to a provision repealed or revoked by this Act is (so far as the context permits) to be read as (according to the context) being or including in relation to times, circumstances and purposes after the commencement of this Act a reference to the corresponding provision of this Act.

(2) In particular, where a power conferred by an Act is expressed to be exercisable in relation to enactments contained in Acts passed before or in the same Session as the Act conferring the power, the power is also exercisable in relation to provisions of this Act which reproduce such enactments.

5   Paragraphs 1 to 4 have effect in place of section 17(2) of the Interpretation Act 1978 (but are without prejudice to any other provision of that Act).

6   The repeal by this Act of section 130 of, and Schedule 10 to, the Employment Protection (Consolidation) Act 1978 (jurisdiction of referees under specified provisions to be exercised by employment tribunals) does not affect –

(a) the operation of those provisions in relation to any question which may arise after the commencement of this Act, or

(b) the continued operation of those provisions after the commencement of this Act in relation to any question which has arisen before that commencement.

PART II: TRANSITORY PROVISIONS

. . .

9 (1) If section 31 of the Trade Union Reform and Employment Rights Act 1993 has not come into force before the commencement of this Act, section 38 shall have effect until the relevant commencement date as if for subsection (4) there were substituted –

'(4) Subsection (1) –

(a) does not apply to service as a member of the naval, military or air forces of the Crown, but

(b) does apply to employment by an association established for the purposes of Part XI of the Reserve Forces Act 1996.'

(2) The reference in sub-paragraph (1) to the relevant commencement date is a reference –

(a) if an order has been made before the commencement of this Act appointing a day after that commencement as the day on which section 31 of the Trade Union Reform and Employment Rights Act 1993 is to come into force, to the day so appointed, and

(b) otherwise, to such day as the Secretary of State may by order appoint.

. . .

Employment Tribunals Extension of Jurisdiction (England and Wales) Order 1994 SI No 1623

Citation, commencement and interpretation

1 (1) This Order may be cited as the Employment Tribunals Extension of Jurisdiction (England and Wales) Order 1994 and comes into force on the first day after it is made.

(2) In this Order –

'contract claim' means a claim in respect of which proceedings may be brought before an Employment tribunal by virtue of article 3 or 4;

. . .

Extension of jurisdiction

3   Proceedings may be brought before an employment tribunal in respect of a claim of an employee for the recovery of damages or any other sum (other than a claim for damages, or for a sum due, in respect of personal injuries) if –

(a) the claim is one to which section [3(2)of the Employment Tribunals Act 1996] applies and which a court in England and Wales would under the law for the time being in force have jurisdiction to hear and determine;

(b) the claim is not one to which article 5 applies; and

(c) the claim arises or is outstanding on the termination of the employee's employment.

4   Proceedings may be brought before an employment tribunal in respect of a claim of an employer for the recovery of damages or any other sum (other than a claim for damages, or for a sum due, in respect of personal injuries) if –
   (a) the claim is one to which section [3(2)of the Employment Tribunals Act 1996] 131(2) applies and which a court in England and Wales would under the law for the time being in force have jurisdiction to hear and determine;
   (b) the claim is not one to which article 5 applies;
   (c) the claim arises or is outstanding on the termination of the employment of the employee against whom it is made; and
   (d) proceedings in respect of a claim of that employee have been brought before an employment tribunal by virtue of this Order.

5   This article applies to a claim for breach of a contractual term of any of the following descriptions –
   (a) a term requiring the employer to provide living accommodation for the employee;
   (b) a term imposing an obligation on the employer or the employee in connection with the provision of living accommodation;
   (c) a term relating to intellectual property;
   (d) a term imposing an obligation of confidence;
   (e) a term which is a covenant in restraint of trade.
   In this article, 'intellectual property' includes copyright, rights in performances, moral rights, design right, registered designs, patents and trade marks.

Manner in which proceedings may be brought

6   Proceedings on a contract claim may be brought before an employment tribunal by presenting a complaint to an employment tribunal.

Time within which proceedings may be brought

7   An employment tribunal shall not entertain a complaint in respect of an employee's contract claim unless it is presented –
   (a) within the period of three months beginning with the effective date of termination of the contract giving rise to the claim, or
   (b) where there is no effective date of termination, within the period of three months beginning with the last day upon which the employee worked in the employment which has terminated, or
   (c) where the tribunal is satisfied that it was not reasonably practicable for the complaint to be presented within whichever of those periods is applicable, within such further period as the tribunal considers reasonable.

8   An employment tribunal shall not entertain a complaint in respect of an employer's contract claim unless –
   (a) it is presented at a time when there is before the tribunal a complaint in respect of a contract claim of a particular employee which has not been settled or withdrawn;
   (b) it arises out of a contract with that employee; and
   (c) it is presented –

(i)   within the period of six weeks beginning with the day, or if more than one the last of the days, on which the employer (or other person who is the respondent party to the employee's contract claim) received from the tribunal a copy of an originating application in respect of a contract claim of that employee; or

(ii)   where the tribunal is satisfied that it was not reasonably practicable for the complaint to be presented within that period, within such further period as the tribunal considers reasonable.

Death and bankruptcy

9   (1) Where proceedings in respect of a contract claim have been brought before an employment tribunal and an employee or employer party to them dies before their conclusion, the proceedings shall not abate by reason of the death and the tribunal may, if it thinks it necessary in order to ensure that all matters in dispute may be effactually and completely determined and adjudicated upon, order the personal representatives of the deceased party, or other persons whom the tribunal considers appropriate, to be made parties and the proceedings to be carried on as if they had been substituted for the deceased party.

(2) Where proceedings in respect of a contract claim have been brought before an employment tribunal and the employee or employer who is the applicant party to them becomes bankrupt before their conclusion, the proceedings shall not abate by reason of the bankruptcy and the tribunal may, if it thinks it necessary in order to ensure that all matters in dispute may be effactually and completely adjudicated upon, order the person in whom the interest of the bankrupt party has vested to be made a party and the proceedings to be carried on as if he had been substituted for the bankrupt party.

Limit on payment to be ordered

10   An employment tribunal shall not in proceedings in respect of a contract claim, or in respect of a number of contract claims relating to the same contract, order the payment of an amount exceeding £25,000.

Employment Tribunals Extension of Jurisdiction (Scotland) Order 1994 SI No 1624

Citation, commencement and interpretation

1   (1) This Order may be cited as the Employment Tribunals Extension of Jurisdiction (Scotland) Order 1994 and comes into force on the first day after it is made.

(2) In this Order –
'contract claim' means a claim in respect of which proceedings may be brought before an employment tribunal by virtue of article 3 or 4; and
. . .

Extension of jurisdiction

3   Proceedings may be brought before an employment tribunal in respect of a claim of an employee for the recovery of damages or any other sum (other than a claim for damages, or for a sum due, in respect of personal injuries) if –

(a) the claim is one to which section[3(2)of the Employment Tribunals Act 1996] applies and which a court in Scotland would under the law for the time being in force have jurisdiction to hear and determine;

(b) the claim is not one to which article 5 applies; and

(c) the claim arises or is outstanding on the termination of the employee's employment.

4   Proceedings may be brought before an employment tribunal in respect of a claim of an employer for the recovery of damages or any other sum (other than a claim for damages, or for a sum due, in respect of personal injuries) if –

(a) the claim is one to which section [3(2)of the Employment Tribunals Act 1996] applies and which a court in Scotland would under the law for the time being in force have jurisdiction to hear and determine;

(b)   the claim is not one to which article 5 applies;

(c) the claim arises or is outstanding on the termination of the employment of the employee against whom it is made; and

(d) proceedings in respect of a claim of that employee have been brought before an employment tribunal by virtue of this Order.

5   This article applies to a claim for breach of a contractual term of any of the following descriptions –

(a) a term requiring the employer to provide living accommodation for the employee;

(b) a term imposing an obligation on the employer or the employee in connection with the provision of living accommodation;

(c) a term relating to intellectual property;

(d) a term imposing an obligation of confidence;

(e) a term which is a covenant in restraint of trade.

In this article,'intellectual property' includes copyright, rights in performances, moral rights, design right, registered designs, patents and trade marks.

Manner in which proceedings may be brought

6   Proceedings on a contract claim may be brought before an employment tribunal by presenting a complaint to an employment tribunal.

Time within which proceedings may be brought

7   An employment tribunal shall not entertain a complaint in respect of an employee's contract claim unless it is presented –

(a) within the period of three months beginning with the effective date of termination of the contract giving rise to the claim, or

(b) where there is no effective date of termination, within the period of three months beginning with the last day upon which the employee worked in the employment which has terminated, or

(c) where the tribunal is satisfied that it was not reasonably practicable for the complaint to be presented within whichever of those periods is applicable, within such further period as the tribunal considers reasonable.

8   An employment tribunal shall not entertain a complaint in respect of an employer's contract claim unless –

(a) it is presented at a time when there is before the tribunal a complaint in respect of a contract claim of a particular employee which has not been settled or withdrawn;

(b) it arises out of a contract with that employee; and

(c) it is presented –

   (i)   within the period of six weeks beginning with the day, or if more than one the last of the days, on which the employer (or other person who is the respondent party to the employee's contract claim) received from the tribunal a copy of an originating application in respect of a contract claim of that employee; or

   (ii) where the tribunal is satisfied that it was not reasonably practicable for the complaint to be presented within that period, within such further periods as the tribunal considers reasonable.

Death and legal incapacity

9   Where proceedings in respect of a contract claim have been brought before an employment tribunal and an employee or employer party to them dies or comes under legal incapacity before the conclusion of the proceedings, the tribunal may order any person who represents that party or his estate to be made a party to the proceedings in place of the party who has died or come under legal incapacity and the proceedings to be carried on accordingly.

Limit on payment to be ordered

10 An employment tribunal shall not in proceedings in respect of a contract claim, or in respect of a number of contract claims relating to the same contract, order the payment of an amount exceeding £25,000.

Employment Tribunals (Constitution and Rules of Procedure) Regulations 2001 SI No 1171

Citation and commencement

1   (1) These Regulations may be cited as the Employment Tribunals (Constitution and Rules of Procedure) Regulations 2001 and the Rules of Procedure contained in Schedules 1, 2, 3, 4, 5 and 6 to these Regulations may be referred to, respectively, as –

(a) the Employment Tribunals Rules of Procedure 2001;

(b) the Employment Tribunals (National Security) Complementary Rules of Procedure 2001;

(c) the Employment Tribunals (Equal Value) Complementary Rules of Procedure 2001;

(d) the Employment Tribunals (Levy Appeals) Rules of Procedure 2001;

(e) the Employment Tribunals (Improvement and Prohibition Notices Appeals) Rules of Procedure 2001; and

(f) the Employment Tribunals (Non-Discrimination Notices Appeals) Rules of Procedure 2001.

(2) These Regulations shall come into force on 16th July 2001.

Interpretation

2 (1) In these Regulations and in Schedules 1, 2, 3, 4, 5 and 6 –

'the 1975 Act' means the Sex Discrimination Act 1975;

'the 1976 Act' means the Race Relations Act 1976;

'the 1992 Act' means the Trade Union and Labour Relations (Consolidation) Act 1992;

'the 1995 Act' means the Disability Discrimination Act 1995;

'the 1996 Act' means the Employment Tribunals Act 1996;

'chairman' means the President or a member of the panel of chairmen selected in accordance with regulation 9(1), or, for the purposes of proceedings in relation to which a direction is given under section 10(3) of the 1996 Act or an order is made under section 10(4) of that Act, a member of the panel referred to in regulation 6(a) selected in accordance with regulation 9(5)(a);

'the clerk' means the person appointed as clerk to the tribunal by the Secretary or a Regional Secretary to act in that capacity at one or more hearings;

'devolution issue' means a devolution issue within the meaning of paragraph 1 of Schedule 8 to the Government of Wales Act 1998;

'hearing' means a sitting of a tribunal duly constituted for the purpose of receiving evidence, hearing addresses and witnesses or doing anything lawfully requisite to enable the tribunal to reach a decision on any question;

'the Office of the Tribunals' means the Central Office of the Employment Tribunals (England and Wales);

'panel of chairmen' means the panel appointed under regulation 5(1)(a);

'the President' means the President of the Employment Tribunals (England and Wales) or the person nominated by the Lord Chancellor to discharge for the time being the functions of the President;

'Regional Chairman' means a member of the panel of chairmen who has been appointed to the position of Regional Chairman in accordance with regulation 8(1) or who has been nominated to discharge the functions of a Regional Chairman in accordance with regulation 8(2);

'Regional Office of the Employment Tribunals' means a regional office which has been established under the Office of the Tribunals for an area specified by the President or an office established for an area within such an area;

'Regional Secretary' means the person for the time being acting as the secretary of a Regional Office of the Employment Tribunals;

'Register' means the Register of applications, appeals and decisions kept in pursuance of regulation 12;

'the relevant authority' means the Attorney General and the National Assembly for Wales;

'the Secretary' means the person for the time being appointed to act as the Secretary of the Office of the Tribunals;

'tribunal' means an employment tribunal established in pursuance of regulation 4 and in relation to any proceedings means the tribunal to which the proceedings have been referred by the President or a Regional Chairman.

(2) In these Regulations, in so far as they relate to the rules in Schedules 1, 2 and 3, and in those Schedules –

'the 1970 Act' means the Equal Pay Act 1970;

'the 1986 Act' means the Sex Discrimination Act 1986;

'Crown employment proceedings' has the meaning given by section 10(8) of the 1996 Act;

'decision' in relation to a tribunal includes –

a declaration,

an order, including an order striking out any originating application or notice of appearance made under rule 4(8)(b) or 15(2),

a recommendation or an award of the tribunal, and

a determination under rule 6,

but does not include any other interlocutory order or any other decision on an interlocutory matter;

'equal value claim' means a claim by an applicant which rests upon entitlement to the benefit of an equality clause by virtue of the operation of section 1(2)(c) of the 1970 Act;

'excluded person' means, in relation to any proceedings, a person who has been excluded from all or part of the proceedings by virtue of –

(a) a direction of a Minister of the Crown under rule 8(1)(b) or (c), or

(b) an order of the tribunal under rule 8(2)(a) read with 8(1)(b) or (c);

'expert' means a member of the panel of independent experts within the meaning of section 2A(4) of the 1970 Act;

'misconceived' includes having no reasonable prospect of success;

'report' means a report required by a tribunal to be prepared by an expert, pursuant to section 2A(1)(b) of the 1970 Act;

'respondent' means a party to the proceedings before a tribunal other than the applicant;

'special advocate' means a person appointed pursuant to rule 7A(1).

(3) In these Regulations, in so far as they relate to the rules in Schedule 4, and in that Schedule –

'the 1982 Act' means the Industrial Training Act 1982;

'the Board' means in relation to an appeal the respondent industrial training board;

'decision' includes any order which is not an interlocutory order;

'levy' means a levy imposed under section 11 of the 1982 Act.

(4) In these Regulations, in so far as they relate to the rules in Schedule 5, and in that Schedule –

'the 1974 Act' means the Health and Safety at Work etc Act 1974;

'decision' in relation to the tribunal includes a direction under rule 4(1) and any order which is not an interlocutory order;

'improvement notice' means a notice under section 21 of the 1974 Act;

'inspector' means a person appointed under section 19(1) of the 1974 Act;

'prohibition notice' means a notice under section 22 of the 1974 Act;

'respondent' means the inspector who issued the improvement notice or prohibition notice which is the subject of the appeal.

(5) In these Regulations, in so far as they relate to the rules in Schedule 6, and in that Schedule –

'the 1999 Act' means the Disability Rights Commission Act 1999;

'decision' in relation to a tribunal includes a direction under section 68(3) of the 1975 Act, under section 59(3) of the 1976 Act or, as the case may be, under paragraph 10(4) of Schedule 3 to the 1999 Act and any other order which is not an interlocutory order;

'non-discrimination notice' means a notice under section 67 of the 1975 Act, under section 58 of the 1976 Act or, as the case may be, under section 4 of the 1999 Act;

'respondent' means the Equal Opportunities Commission established under section 53 of the 1975 Act, the Commission for Racial Equality established under section 43 of the 1976 Act or, as the case may be, the Disability Rights Commission established under section 1 of the 1999 Act.

(6) Any period of time for doing any act required or permitted to be done under any of the rules in Schedules 1, 2, 3, 4, 5 and 6, or under any decision, direction, declaration, order, recommendation, award or determination of a tribunal or a chairman, shall be calculated in accordance with paragraphs (7) to (10).

(7) Where any act must or may be done within a certain number of days of or from an event, the date of that event shall not be included in the calculation. For example, a respondent receives a copy of an originating application on 1st October. He must present a written notice of appearance to the Secretary within 21 days of receiving the copy. The last day for presentation of the notice is 22nd October.

(8) Where any act must or may be done not less than a certain number of days before or after an event, the date of that event shall not be included in the calculation. For example, if a party wishes to submit representations in writing for consideration by a tribunal at the hearing of the originating application, he must submit them not less than 7 days before the hearing. If the hearing is fixed for 8th October, the representations must be submitted no later than 1st October.

(9) Where the tribunal or a chairman gives any decision, direction, declaration, order, recommendation, award or determination which imposes a time limit for doing any act, the last date for compliance shall, wherever practicable, be expressed as a calendar date.

(10) In rule 5(2) of Schedule 1, rule 8 of Schedule 4, rule 6(1) of Schedule 5 and rule 4(1) of Schedule 6, the requirement to send the notice of hearing to the parties not less than 14 days before the date fixed for the hearing shall not be construed as a requirement for service of the notice to have been effected

not less than 14 days before the hearing date, but as a requirement for the notice to have been placed in the post not less than 14 days before that date. For example, a hearing is fixed for 15th October. The last day on which the notice may be placed in the post is 1st October.

President of Employment Tribunals

3 (1) There shall be a President of the Employment Tribunals (England and Wales) who shall be appointed by the Lord Chancellor and shall be a person –
   (a) having a seven year general qualification within the meaning of section 71 of the Courts and Legal Services Act 1990;
   (b) being an advocate or solicitor admitted in Scotland of at least seven years standing; or
   (c) being a member of the Bar of Northern Ireland or solicitor of the Supreme Court of Northern Ireland of at least seven years standing.

   (2) The President may resign his office by notice in writing to the Lord Chancellor.

   (3) The President shall vacate his office at the end of the completed year of service in the course of which he attains the age of 72 years.

   (4) If the Lord Chancellor is satisfied that the President is incapacitated by infirmity of mind or body from discharging the duties of his office, or the President is adjudged to be bankrupt or makes a composition or arrangement with his creditors, the Lord Chancellor may revoke his appointment.

   (5) The functions of President under these Regulations may, if he is for any reason unable to act or during any vacancy in his office, be discharged by a person nominated for that purpose by the Lord Chancellor.

Establishment of employment tribunals

4 (1) The President shall from time to time determine the number of tribunals to be established in England and Wales for the purposes of determining proceedings.

   (2) The President or, in relation to the area specified in relation to him, a Regional Chairman shall determine at what times and in what places in England and Wales tribunals shall sit.

Panels of members of tribunals

5 (1) There shall be three panels of members of the Employment Tribunals (England and Wales), namely –
   (a) a panel of persons appointed by the Lord Chancellor consisting of persons –
       (i)   having a seven year general qualification within the meaning of section 71 of the Courts and Legal Services Act 1990;
       (ii) being an advocate or solicitor admitted in Scotland of at least seven years standing; or
       (iii) being a member of the Bar of Northern Ireland or solicitor of the Supreme Court of Northern Ireland of at least seven years standing;
   (b) a panel of persons appointed by the Secretary of State after consultation

with such organisations or associations of organisations representative of employees as he sees fit; and

(c) a panel of persons appointed by the Secretary of State after consultation with such organisations or associations of organisations representative of employers as he sees fit.

(2) Members of the panels constituted under these Regulations shall hold and vacate office under the terms of the instrument under which they are appointed but may resign their office by notice in writing, in the case of a member of the panel of chairmen, to the Lord Chancellor and, in any other case, to the Secretary of State; and any such member who ceases to hold office shall be eligible for reappointment.

Further panels in national security cases

6 For the purposes of proceedings in relation to which a direction is given under section 10(3) of the 1996 Act, or an order is made under section 10(4) of that Act, the President shall –

(a) select a panel of persons from the panel of chairmen to act as chairmen in such cases, and

(b) select –

    (i) a panel of persons from the panel referred to in regulation 5(1)(b) as persons suitable to act as members in such cases, and

    (ii) a panel of persons from the panel referred to in regulation 5(1)(c) as persons suitable to act as members in such cases.

Modification of section 4 of the Employment Tribunals Act 1996

7 (1) For the purposes of proceedings in relation to which a direction is given under section 10(3) of the 1996 Act, or an order is made under section 10(4) of that Act, section 4 of the 1996 Act shall be modified as follows.

(2) In section 4(1)(a), for the words 'in accordance with regulations made under section 1(1)' substitute the words 'in accordance with regulations 6(a) and 9(5) of the Employment Tribunals (Constitution and Rules of Procedure) Regulations 2001'.

(3) In section 4(1)(b), for the words 'in accordance with regulations so made' substitute the words 'in accordance with regulations 6(b) and 9(5) of those Regulations'.

(4) In section 4(5), for the words 'in accordance with regulations made under section 1(1)' substitute the words 'in accordance with regulation 6(a) of the Employment Tribunals (Constitution and Rules of Procedure) Regulations 2001'.

Regional Chairmen

8 (1) The Lord Chancellor may from time to time appoint Regional Chairmen from the panel of chairmen and each Regional Chairman shall be responsible for the administration of justice by tribunals in the area specified by the President in relation to him.

(2) The President or the Regional Chairman for an area may from time to time nominate a member of the panel of chairmen to discharge for the time being the functions of the Regional Chairman for that area.

Composition of tribunals

9 (1) For each hearing of any matter before a tribunal the President or the Regional Chairman shall select a chairman, who shall, subject to paragraph (5), be the President or a member of the panel of chairmen, and the President or the Regional Chairman may select himself.

(2) In any proceedings which are to be determined by a tribunal comprising a chairman (selected in accordance with paragraph (1) or (5), as the case may be) and two other members, those other members shall, subject to paragraph (5), be selected by the President or by the Regional Chairman, as to one member from the panel of persons appointed by the Secretary of State under regulation 5(1)(b) and as to the other from the panel of persons appointed under regulation 5(1)(c).

(3) In any proceedings which are to be determined by a tribunal whose composition is described in paragraph (2), or, as the case may be, paragraph (5)(b), those proceedings may, with the consent of the parties, be heard and determined in the absence of any one member other than the chairman, and in that event the tribunal shall be properly constituted.

(4) The President or the Regional Chairman may at any time select from the appropriate panel another person in substitution for the chairman or other member of the tribunal previously selected to hear any proceedings before a tribunal.

(5) For the purposes of proceedings in relation to which a direction is given under section 10(3) of the 1996 Act, or an order is made under section 10(4) of that Act –

(a) the President or the Regional Chairman shall select a chairman, who shall be the President or a member of the panel selected in accordance with regulation 6(a), and the President or the Regional Chairman may select himself, and

(b) in any such proceedings which are to be determined by a tribunal comprising a chairman (selected in accordance with sub-paragraph (a) of this paragraph) and two other members, those other members shall be selected by the President or by the Regional Chairman, as to one member from the panel selected in accordance with regulation 6(b)(i) and as to the other from the panel selected in accordance with regulation 6(b)(ii).

Overriding objective

10 (1) The overriding objective of the rules in Schedules 1, 2, 3, 4, 5 and 6 is to enable tribunals to deal with cases justly.

(2) Dealing with a case justly includes, so far as practicable –

(a) ensuring that the parties are on an equal footing;

(b) saving expense;

(c) dealing with the case in ways which are proportionate to the complexity of the issues; and

(d) ensuring that it is dealt with expeditiously and fairly.

(3) A tribunal shall seek to give effect to the overriding objective when it –

(a) exercises any power given to it by the rules in Schedules 1, 2, 3, 4, 5 and 6; or

(b) interprets any rule in Schedules 1, 2, 3, 4, 5 and 6.

(4) The parties shall assist the tribunal to further the overriding objective.

Proceedings of tribunals

11 (1) Subject to paragraphs (2) to (6), the rules in Schedule 1 shall apply in relation to all proceedings before a tribunal except where separate rules of procedure made under the provisions of any enactment are applicable.

(2) In proceedings to which the rules in Schedule 1 apply and in which any power conferred on the Minister or the tribunal by rule 8(1), (2) or (3) of Schedule 1 is exercised –

(a) rules 3, 4, 7, 10, 11, 12 and 13 of Schedule 1 shall be modified in accordance with Schedule 2; and

(b) rules 7A (special advocate) and 7B (reasons for the tribunal's decision in national security cases), as referred to in paragraph 4 of Schedule 2, shall be inserted into Schedule 1.

(3) In proceedings to which the rules in Schedule 1 apply and which involve an equal value claim –

(a) rules 4, 11, 12, 14, 15 and 23 of Schedule 1 shall be modified in accordance with Part I of Schedule 3; and

(b) rule 10A (procedure relating to expert's report), as referred to in paragraph 2 of Part I of Schedule 3, shall be inserted into Schedule 1.

(4) In proceedings to which the rules in Schedule 1 apply, and in which the rules in Schedule 1 are required to be modified in accordance with both paragraphs (2) and (3) -

(a) the insertion of rules 4(9), 7B and 12(5A) to (5D) into Schedule 1 shall be in accordance with Part II of Schedule 3; and

(b) rule 11(2) of Schedule 1 shall be modified in accordance with Part II of Schedule 3.

(5) The rules contained in Schedules 1, 2 and 3 shall apply in proceedings to which they relate where –

(a) the respondent or one of the respondents resides or carries on business in England and Wales;

(b) had the remedy been by way of action in the county court, the cause of action would have arisen wholly or partly in England and Wales; or

(c) the proceedings are to determine a question which has been referred to the tribunal by a court in England and Wales.

(6) The rules in Schedules 4, 5 and 6 shall apply in relation to proceedings before a tribunal which relate to matters arising in England and Wales and consist, respectively, in –

(a) an appeal by a person assessed to levy imposed under a levy order made under section 12 of the 1982 Act;

(b) an appeal against an improvement or prohibition notice under section 24 of the 1974 Act; and

(c) an appeal against a non-discrimination notice under section 68 of the

1975 Act, section 59 of the 1976 Act or paragraph 10 of Schedule 3 to the 1999 Act.

Register

12 (1) The Secretary shall maintain a Register at the Office of the Tribunals which shall be open to the inspection of any person without charge at all reasonable hours.

(2) The Register shall contain –

(a) details of originating applications in accordance with rule 2 of Schedule 1;

(b) details of appeals in accordance with rule 5 of Schedule 4, rule 3 of Schedule 5 and rule 2 of Schedule 6;

(c) the fact of applications in accordance with rule 4 of Schedule 5; and

(d) documents recording the decisions of tribunals and the reasons therefor.

(3) The Register, or any part of it, may be kept by means of a computer.

Proof of decisions of tribunals

13   The production in any proceedings in any court of a document purporting to be certified by the Secretary to be a true copy of an entry of a decision in the Register shall, unless the contrary is proved, be sufficient evidence of the document and of the facts stated therein.

Transitional provision

14   These Regulations shall apply in relation to all proceedings to which they relate, irrespective of when those proceedings were commenced.

Revocations

15   The instruments listed in Schedule 7 are hereby revoked.

SCHEDULE 1: THE EMPLOYMENT TRIBUNALS RULES OF PROCEDURE

Originating application

1 (1) Where proceedings are brought by an applicant, they shall be instituted by the applicant presenting to the Secretary an originating application, which shall be in writing and shall set out –

(a) the name and address of the applicant and, if different, an address within the United Kingdom to which he requires notices and documents relating to the proceedings to be sent;

(b) the names and addresses of the person or persons against whom relief is sought; and

(c) the grounds, with particulars thereof, on which relief is sought.

(2) Two or more originating applications may be presented in a single document by applicants who claim relief in respect of or arising out of the same set of facts.

(3) Where the Secretary is of the opinion that the originating application does

not seek or on the facts stated therein cannot entitle the applicant to a relief which a tribunal has power to give, he may give notice to that effect to the applicant stating the reasons for his opinion and informing him that the application will not be registered unless he states in writing that he wishes to proceed with it.

(4) An application in respect of which such a notice has been given shall not be treated as having been received for the purpose of rule 2 unless the applicant intimates in writing to the Secretary that he wishes to proceed with it; and upon receipt of such an intimation the Secretary shall proceed in accordance with that rule.

(5) In the case of an originating application in respect of a complaint under section 6(4A) of the 1986 Act relating to a term of a collective agreement, the following persons, whether or not identified in the originating application, shall be regarded as the persons against whom relief is sought and shall be treated as respondents for the purposes of these rules, that is to say –

(a) the applicant's employer (or prospective employer), and

(b) every organisation of employers and organisation of workers, and every association of or representative of such organisations, which, if the term were to be varied voluntarily, would be likely, in the opinion of the tribunal, to negotiate the variation;

provided that such an organisation or association shall not be treated as a respondent if the tribunal, having made such enquiries of the applicant and such other enquiries as it thinks fit, is of the opinion that it is not reasonably practicable to identify the organisation or association.

(6) Where proceedings are referred to a tribunal by a court, these rules shall be applied to them, except where the rules are inappropriate, as if the proceedings had been instituted by the presentation of an originating application.

(7) Paragraph (1)(b) does not apply to an originating application in respect of an application under section 3C of the Employment Agencies Act 1973 for the variation or revocation of a prohibition order, but on any application the Secretary of State shall be treated as the respondent for the purpose of these rules.

Action upon receipt of originating application

2 (1) Upon receiving an originating application the Secretary shall –

(a) send a copy of it to the respondent;

(b) give every party notice in writing of the case number of the application (which shall constitute the title of the proceedings) and of the address to which notices and other communications to the Secretary shall be sent; and

(c) send to the respondent a notice in writing which includes information, as appropriate to the case, about the means and time for entering an appearance, the consequences of failure to do so, and the right to receive a copy of the decision.

(2) The Secretary shall enter such of the details of an originating application as are referred to in paragraph (4) in the Register either within 28 days of receiving it or, if that is not practicable, as soon as reasonably practicable thereafter.

(3) The Secretary shall also, in all cases, notify the parties that, in every case where an enactment provides for conciliation, the services of a conciliation officer are available to them.

(4) The details of an originating application to be entered in the Register are –
   (a) the case number;
   (b) the date the Secretary received the application;
   (c) the name and address of the applicant;
   (d) the name and address of the respondent;
   (e) the Regional Office of the Employment Tribunals dealing with the application; and
   (f) the type of claim brought in general terms without reference to its particulars.

(5) In any case appearing to the Secretary to involve allegations of the commission of a sexual offence, where any person referred to in paragraph 4(c) or 4(d) appears to the Secretary to be a person affected by or making the allegations he shall omit from the Register the details in paragraph 4(c) or 4(d), as the case may be, relating to that person.

Appearance by respondent

3 (1) A respondent shall, within 21 days of receiving the copy of the originating application, enter an appearance to the proceedings by presenting to the Secretary a written notice of appearance –
   (a) setting out his full name and address and, if different, an address within the United Kingdom to which he requires notices and documents relating to the proceedings to be sent;
   (b) stating whether or not he intends to resist the application; and
   (c) if he does intend to resist it, setting out sufficient particulars to show on what grounds.
   Upon receipt of a notice of appearance the Secretary shall send a copy of it to each other party.

(2) Two or more notices of appearance relating to originating applications in which the relief claimed is in respect of or arises out of the same set of facts may be presented in a single document, provided that in respect of each of the originating applications to which the notices so presented relate –
   (a) the respondent intends to resist the applications and the grounds for doing so are the same in each case; or
   (b) the respondent does not intend to resist the applications.

(3) A respondent who has not entered an appearance shall not be entitled to take any part in the proceedings except –
   (a) to apply under rule 17 for an extension of the time appointed by this rule for entering an appearance;
   (b) to make an application under rule 4(1) for a direction requiring the applicant to provide further particulars of the grounds on which he relies and of any facts and contentions relevant thereto;
   (c) to make an application under rule 13(4) in respect of rule 13(1)(b);
   (d) to be called as a witness by another person;

(e) to be sent a copy of a document or corrected entry in pursuance of rule 12(5), 12(9) or 12(10);

and in the rules which follow, the word 'party' only includes such a respondent in relation to his entitlement to take such a part in the proceedings, and in relation to any such part which he takes.

Case management

4 (1) A tribunal may at any time, on the application of a party or of its own motion, give such directions on any matter arising in connection with the proceedings as appear to the tribunal to be appropriate.

(2) An application under paragraph (1) –
  (a) may be made by presenting to the Secretary a notice of application, which shall state the title of the proceedings and set out the grounds of the application, or
  (b) may be made at the hearing of the originating application.

(3) Directions under paragraph (1) may include any requirement relating to evidence (including the provision and exchange of witness statements), the provision of further particulars, and the provision of written answers to questions put to a party by the tribunal.

(4) A tribunal may appoint the time at or within which and the place at which any act required in pursuance of this rule is to be done and may direct that a copy of any document furnished pursuant to any requirement imposed under this rule be sent to the tribunal.

(5) A tribunal may, on the application of a party or of its own motion, –
  (a) require the attendance of any person in Great Britain, including a party, either to give evidence or to produce documents or both and may appoint the time and place at which the person is to attend and, if so required, to produce any document; or
  (b) require one party to grant to another such disclosure or inspection (including the taking of copies) of documents as might be granted by a court under rule 31 of the Civil Procedure Rules 1998.

(6) Every document containing a requirement imposed under paragraph (5) shall state that, under section 7(4) of the 1996 Act, any person who without reasonable excuse fails to comply with the requirement shall be liable on summary conviction to a fine, and the document shall also state the amount of the current maximum fine.

(7) Where a requirement has been imposed under paragraph (1) or (5) –
  (a) on a party in his absence; or
  (b) on a person other than a party,

that party or person may apply to the tribunal by notice to the Secretary to vary or set aside the requirement. Such notice shall be given before the time at which or, as the case may be, the expiration of the time within which the requirement is to be complied with, and the Secretary shall give notice of the application to each party, or where applicable, each party other than the party making the application.

(8) If a requirement under paragraph (1) or (5) is not complied with, the tribunal –

(a) may make an order in respect of costs under rule 14(1)(a), or
(b) before or at the hearing, may strike out the whole or part of the originat-
    ing application, or, as the case may be, the notice of appearance, and,
    where appropriate, direct that a respondent be debarred from defending
    altogether;
but a tribunal shall not exercise its powers under this paragraph unless it
has sent notice to the party who has not complied with the requirement
giving him an opportunity to show cause why the tribunal should not do so,
or the party has been given an opportunity to show cause orally why the
powers conferred by this paragraph should not be exercised.

Time and place of hearing

5   (1) The President or a Regional Chairman shall fix the date, time and place of
        the hearing of the originating application and the Secretary shall send to
        each party a notice of hearing together with information and guidance as to
        attendance at the hearing, witnesses and the bringing of documents, repre-
        sentation by another person and the making of written representations.
    (2) The Secretary shall send the notice of hearing to every party not less than 14
        days before the date fixed for the hearing except –
        (a) where the Secretary has agreed a shorter time with the parties; or
        (b) on an application for interim relief made under section 161 of the 1992
            Act or section 128 of the Employment Rights Act 1996.

Entitlement to bring or contest proceedings

6   (1) A tribunal may at any time before the hearing of an originating application,
        on the application of a party made by notice to the Secretary or of its own
        motion, hear and determine any issue relating to the entitlement of any
        party to bring or contest the proceedings to which the originating applica-
        tion relates.
    (2) A tribunal shall not determine such an issue unless the Secretary has sent
        notice to each of the parties giving them an opportunity to submit represen-
        tations in writing and to advance oral argument before the tribunal.

Pre-hearing review

7   (1) A tribunal may at any time before the hearing of an originating application,
        on the application of a party made by notice to the Secretary or of its own
        motion, conduct a pre-hearing review, consisting of a consideration of –
        (a) the contents of the originating application and notice of appearance;
        (b) any representations in writing; and
        (c) any oral argument advanced by or on behalf of a party.
    (2) If a party applies for a pre-hearing review and the tribunal determines that
        there shall be no review, the Secretary shall send notice of the determination
        to that party.
    (3) A pre-hearing review shall not take place unless the Secretary has sent
        notice to the parties giving them an opportunity to submit representations
        in writing and to advance oral argument at the review if they so wish.
    (4) If upon a pre-hearing review the tribunal considers that the contentions put

forward by any party in relation to a matter required to be determined by a tribunal have no reasonable prospect of success, the tribunal may make an order against that party requiring the party to pay a deposit of an amount not exceeding £500 as a condition of being permitted to continue to take part in the proceedings relating to that matter.

(5) No order shall be made under this rule unless the tribunal has taken reasonable steps to ascertain the ability of the party against whom it is proposed to make the order to comply with such an order, and has taken account of any information so ascertained in determining the amount of the deposit.

(6) An order made under this rule, and the tribunal's reasons for considering that the contentions in question have no reasonable prospect of success, shall be recorded in summary form in a document signed by the chairman. A copy of that document shall be sent to each of the parties and shall be accompanied by a note explaining that if the party against whom the order is made persists in participating in proceedings relating to the matter to which the order relates, he may have an award of costs made against him and could lose his deposit.

(7) If a party against whom an order has been made does not pay the amount specified in the order to the Secretary either –
   (a) within the period of 21 days of the day on which the document recording the making of the order is sent to him, or
   (b) within such further period, not exceeding 14 days, as the tribunal may allow in the light of representations made by that party within the said period of 21 days,
   the tribunal shall strike out the originating application or notice of appearance of that party or, as the case may be, the part of it to which the order relates.

(8) The deposit paid by a party under an order made under this rule shall be refunded to him in full except where rule 14(8) applies.

(9) No member of a tribunal which has conducted a pre-hearing review shall be a member of the tribunal at the hearing of the originating application.

National security

8 (1) A Minister of the Crown (whether or not he is a party to the proceedings) may, if he considers it expedient in the interests of national security, direct a tribunal by notice to the Secretary to –
   (a) sit in private for all or part of particular Crown employment proceedings;
   (b) exclude the applicant from all or part of particular Crown employment proceedings;
   (c) exclude the applicant's representatives from all or part of particular Crown employment proceedings;
   (d) take steps to conceal the identity of a particular witness in particular Crown employment proceedings.

(2) A tribunal may, if it considers it expedient in the interests of national security, by order –
   (a) do anything of a kind which a tribunal can be required to do by direction under paragraph (1);

(b) direct any person to whom any document (including any decision or record of the proceedings) has been provided for the purposes of the proceedings not to disclose any such document or the content thereof to –
  (i)   any excluded person,
  (ii) in any case in which a direction has been given under paragraph (1)(a) or an order has been made under paragraph (2)(a) read with paragraph (1)(a), to any person excluded from all or part of the proceedings by virtue of such direction or order, or
  (iii) in any case in which a Minister of the Crown has informed the Secretary in accordance with paragraph (3) that he wishes to address the tribunal with a view to the tribunal making an order under paragraph (2)(a) read with paragraph (1)(b) or (c), to any person who may be excluded from all or part of the proceedings by virtue of such an order, if an order is made, at any time before the tribunal decides whether or not to make such an order;
(c) take steps to keep secret all or part of the reasons for its decision.
The tribunal shall keep under review any order it makes under this paragraph.

(3) In any proceedings in which a Minister of the Crown considers that it would be appropriate for a tribunal to make an order as referred to in paragraph (2), he shall (whether or not he is a party to the proceedings) be entitled to appear before and to address the tribunal thereon. The Minister shall inform the Secretary by notice that he wishes to address the tribunal and the Secretary shall copy the notice to the parties.

(4) When exercising its functions, a tribunal shall ensure that information is not disclosed contrary to the interests of national security.

Dismissals in connection with industrial action

9 (1) In relation to a complaint under section 111 of the Employment Rights Act 1996 (unfair dismissal: complaint to employment tribunal) that a dismissal is unfair by virtue of section 238A of the 1992 Act (participation in official industrial action) a tribunal may adjourn the proceedings where specified civil proceedings have been brought until such time as interlocutory proceedings arising out of the specified civil proceedings have been concluded.

(2) In this rule –
  'specified civil proceedings' means legal proceedings brought by any person against another person in which it is to be determined whether an act of that other person, which induced the applicant to commit an act, or each of a series of acts, is by virtue of section 219 of the 1992 Act not actionable in tort or in delict; and
  the interlocutory proceedings shall not be regarded as having concluded until all rights of appeal have been exhausted or the time for instituting any appeal in the course of the interlocutory proceedings has expired.

The hearing

10 (1) Any hearing of an originating application shall be heard by a tribunal composed in accordance with section 4(1) and (2) of the 1996 Act.

(2) Any hearing of or in connection with an originating application shall take place in public.

(3) Notwithstanding paragraph (2), a tribunal may sit in private for the purpose of hearing evidence from any person which in the opinion of the tribunal is likely to consist of –

(a) information which he could not disclose without contravening a prohibition imposed by or by virtue of any enactment, or

(b) information which has been communicated to him in confidence, or which he has otherwise obtained in consequence of the confidence reposed in him by another person, or

(c) information the disclosure of which would, for reasons other than its effect on negotiations with respect to any of the matters mentioned in section 178(2) of the 1992 Act, cause substantial injury to any undertaking of his or any undertaking in which he works.

(4) A member of the Council on Tribunals shall be entitled to attend any hearing taking place in private in his capacity as a member.

(5) If a party wishes to submit representations in writing for consideration by a tribunal at the hearing of the originating application he shall present his representations to the Secretary not less than 7 days before the hearing and shall at the same time send a copy to each other party.

(6) The tribunal may, if it considers it appropriate, consider representations in writing which have been submitted to the Secretary less than 7 days before the hearing.

(7) The Secretary of State if he so elects shall be entitled to appear as if he were a party and be heard at any hearing of or in connection with an originating application in proceedings which may involve a payment out of the National Insurance Fund, and in that event he shall be treated for the purposes of these rules as if he were a party.

Procedure at hearing

11 (1) The tribunal shall, so far as it appears to it appropriate, seek to avoid formality in its proceedings and shall not be bound by any enactment or rule of law relating to the admissibility of evidence in proceedings before the courts of law. The tribunal shall make such enquiries of persons appearing before it and witnesses as it considers appropriate and shall otherwise conduct the hearing in such manner as it considers most appropriate for the clarification of the issues before it and generally to the just handling of the proceedings.

(2) Subject to paragraph (1), at the hearing of the originating application a party shall be entitled to give evidence, to call witnesses, to question any witnesses and to address the tribunal.

(3) If a party fails to attend or to be represented at the time and place fixed for the hearing, the tribunal may, if that party is an applicant, dismiss or, in any case, dispose of the application in the absence of that party or may adjourn the hearing to a later date; provided that before dismissing or disposing of

any application in the absence of a party the tribunal shall consider his originating application or notice of appearance, any representations in writing presented by him in pursuance of rule 10(5) and any written answer furnished to the tribunal pursuant to rule 4(3).

(4) A tribunal may require any witness to give evidence on oath or affirmation and for that purpose there may be administered an oath or affirmation in due form.

Decision of tribunal

12 (1) Where a tribunal is composed of three members its decision may be taken by a majority; and if a tribunal is composed of two members only, the chairman shall have a second or casting vote.

(2) The decision of a tribunal, which may be given orally at the end of a hearing or reserved, shall be recorded in a document signed by the chairman.

(3) The tribunal shall give reasons for its decision in a document signed by the chairman. That document shall contain a statement as to whether the reasons are given in summary or extended form and where the tribunal –
(a) makes an award of compensation, or
(b) comes to any other determination by virtue of which one party is required to pay a sum to another (excluding an award of costs or allowances),
the document shall also contain a statement of the amount of compensation awarded, or of the sum required to be paid, followed either by a table showing how the amount or sum has been calculated or by a description of the manner in which it has been calculated.

(4) The reasons for the decision of the tribunal shall be given in summary form except where –
(a) the proceedings involved the determination of an issue arising under or relating to the 1970 Act, the 1975 Act, the 1986 Act, the 1976 Act or the 1995 Act;
(b) a request that the reasons be given in extended form is made orally at the hearing by a party;
(c) such a request is made in writing by a party after the hearing either –
(i) before any document recording the reasons in summary form is sent to the parties, or
(ii) within 21 days of the date on which that document was sent to the parties; or
(d) the tribunal considers that reasons given in summary form would not sufficiently explain the grounds for its decision;
and in those circumstances the reasons shall be given in extended form.

(5) The clerk shall transmit the documents referred to in paragraphs (2) and (3) to the Secretary who shall enter them in the Register and shall send a copy of the entry to each of the parties and, where the proceedings were referred to the tribunal by a court, to that court.

(6) The document referred to in paragraph (3) shall be omitted from the Register in any case in which evidence has been heard in private and the tribunal so directs. In such a case the Secretary shall send that document to each of the parties; and where there are proceedings before a superior court relating

to the decision in question, he shall send the document to that court, together with a copy of the entry in the Register of the document referred to in paragraph (2).

(7) In any case appearing to involve allegations of a sexual offence, the document referred to in paragraph (3) shall be entered on the Register with such deletions or amendments as have been made in accordance with rule 15(6).

(8) Clerical mistakes in the documents referred to in paragraphs (2) and (3), or errors arising in those documents from an accidental slip or omission, may at any time be corrected by the chairman by certificate.

(9) If a document is corrected by certificate under paragraph (8), or if a decision is –
   (a) revoked or varied under rule 13, or
   (b) altered in any way by order of a superior court,
   the Secretary shall alter any entry in the Register which is affected to conform with the certificate or order and send a copy of any entry so altered to each of the parties and, where the proceedings were referred to the tribunal by a court, to that court.

(10) Where a document omitted from the Register pursuant to paragraph (6) is corrected by certificate under paragraph (8), the Secretary shall send a copy of the corrected document to the parties; and where there are proceedings before any superior court relating to the decision in question, he shall send a copy to that court together with a copy of the entry in the Register of the document referred to in paragraph (2), if it has been altered under paragraph (9).

(11) Where this rule requires a document to be signed by the chairman of a tribunal composed of three or two persons, but by reason of death or incapacity the chairman is unable to sign it, the document shall be signed by the other members or member of the tribunal, who shall certify that the chairman is unable to sign.

Review of tribunal's decision

13 (1) Subject to the provisions of this rule, a tribunal shall have power, on the application of a party or of its own motion, to review any decision on the grounds that –
   (a) the decision was wrongly made as a result of an error on the part of the tribunal staff;
   (b) a party did not receive notice of the proceedings leading to the decision;
   (c) the decision was made in the absence of a party;
   (d) new evidence has become available since the conclusion of the hearing to which the decision relates, provided that its existence could not have been reasonably known of or foreseen at the time of the hearing; or
   (e) the interests of justice require such a review.

(2) A tribunal may not review a decision of its own motion unless it is the tribunal which issued the decision.

(3) A tribunal may only review a decision of its own motion if –
   (a) it has sent notice to each of the parties explaining in summary form the ground upon which and reasons why it is proposed to review the

decision and giving them an opportunity to show cause why there should be no review; and

(b) such notice has been sent on or after the date of the hearing, but within 14 days of the date on which the decision was sent to the parties.

(4) An application for the purposes of paragraph (1) may be made at the hearing. If no application is made at the hearing, an application may be made to the Secretary on or after the date of the hearing, but within 14 days of the date on which the decision was sent to the parties. Such application must be in writing and must state the grounds in full.

(5) An application for the purposes of paragraph (1) may be refused by the President or by the chairman of the tribunal which decided the case or by a Regional Chairman if in his opinion it has no reasonable prospect of success.

(6) If such an application is not refused under paragraph (5) it shall be heard by the tribunal which decided the case, or –

(a) where it is not practicable for it to be heard by that tribunal, or

(b) where the decision was made by a chairman acting alone under rule 15(8),

by a tribunal appointed by either the President or a Regional Chairman.

(7) On reviewing its decision a tribunal may confirm the decision, or vary or revoke the decision; and if it revokes the decision, the tribunal shall order a re-hearing before either the same or a differently constituted tribunal.

Costs

14 (1) Where, in the opinion of the tribunal, a party has in bringing the proceedings, or a party or a party's representative has in conducting the proceedings, acted vexatiously, abusively, disruptively or otherwise unreasonably, or the bringing or conducting of the proceedings by a party has been misconceived, the tribunal shall consider making, and if it so decides, may make –

(a) an order containing an award against that party in respect of the costs incurred by another party;

(b) an order that that party shall pay to the Secretary of State the whole, or any part, of any allowances (other than allowances paid to members of tribunals) paid by the Secretary of State under section 5(2) or (3) of the 1996 Act to any person for the purposes of, or in connection with, his attendance at the tribunal.

(2) Paragraph (1) applies to a respondent who has not entered an appearance in relation to the conduct of any part in the proceedings which he has taken.

(3) An order containing an award against a party ('the first party') in respect of the costs incurred by another party ('the second party') shall be –

(a) where the tribunal thinks fit, an order that the first party pay to the second party a specified sum not exceeding £10,000;

(b) where those parties agree on a sum to be paid by the first party to the second party in respect of those costs, an order that the first party pay to the second party a specified sum, being the sum so agreed; or

(c) in any other case, an order that the first party pay to the second party the whole or a specified part of the costs incurred by the second party as assessed by way of detailed assessment (if not otherwise agreed).

(4) Where the tribunal has on the application of a party postponed the day or time fixed for or adjourned the hearing, the tribunal may make orders, of the kinds mentioned in paragraphs (1)(a) and (1)(b), against or, as the case may require, in favour of that party as respects any costs incurred or any allowances paid as a result of the postponement or adjournment.

(5) A tribunal shall make orders against a respondent of the kinds mentioned in paragraphs (1)(a) and (1)(b) as respects any costs or any allowances paid as a result of the postponement or adjournment of a hearing where, on a complaint of unfair dismissal, the applicant has expressed a wish to be reinstated or re-engaged which has been communicated to the respondent not less than 7 days before the hearing of the complaint and the postponement or adjournment has been caused by the respondent's failure, without a special reason, to adduce reasonable evidence as to the availability of the job from which the applicant was dismissed, or of comparable or suitable employment.

(6) Any costs required by an order under this rule to be assessed by way of detailed assessment may be so assessed in the County Court in accordance with the Civil Procedure Rules 1998.

(7) Where –
   (a) a party has been ordered under rule 7 to pay a deposit as a condition of being permitted to continue to participate in proceedings relating to a matter;
   (b) in respect of that matter, the tribunal has found against that party in its decision, and
   (c) there has been no award of costs made against that party arising out of the proceedings on the matter,
   the tribunal shall consider whether to award costs against that party on the ground that he conducted the proceedings relating to the matter unreasonably in persisting in having the matter determined by a tribunal; but the tribunal shall not make an award of costs on that ground unless it has considered the document recording the order under rule 7 and is of the opinion that the reasons which caused the tribunal to find against the party in its decision were substantially the same as the reasons recorded in that document for considering that the contentions of the party had no reasonable prospect of success.

(8) Where an award of costs is made against a party who has had an order under rule 7 made against him (whether the award arises out of the proceedings relating to the matter in respect of which the order was made or out of proceedings relating to any other matter considered with that matter), his deposit shall be paid in part or full settlement of the award –
   (a) where an award is made in favour of one party, to that party, and
   (b) where awards are made in favour of more than one party, to all of them or any one or more of them as the tribunal thinks fit, and if to or more than one, in such proportions as the tribunal considers appropriate,

and if the amount of the deposit exceeds the amount of the award of costs, the balance shall be refunded to the party who paid it.

Miscellaneous powers

15 (1) Subject to the provisions of these rules, a tribunal may regulate its own procedure.

(2) A tribunal may –

    (a) if the applicant at any time gives notice of the withdrawal of his originating application, dismiss the proceedings;

    (b) if both or all the parties agree in writing upon the terms of a decision to be made by the tribunal, decide accordingly;

    (c) subject to paragraph (3), at any stage of the proceedings, order to be struck out or amended any originating application or notice of appearance, or anything in such application or notice of appearance, on the grounds that it is scandalous, misconceived or vexatious;

    (d) subject to paragraph (3), at any stage of the proceedings, order to be struck out any originating application or notice of appearance on the grounds that the manner in which the proceedings have been conducted by or on behalf of the applicant or, as the case may be, respondent has been scandalous, unreasonable or vexatious; and

    (e) subject to paragraph (3), on the application of the respondent, or of its own motion, order an originating application to be struck out for want of prosecution.

(3) Before making an order under sub-paragraph (c), (d) or (e) of paragraph (2) the tribunal shall send notice to the party against whom it is proposed that the order should be made giving him an opportunity to show cause why the order should not be made; but this paragraph shall not be taken to require the tribunal to send such notice to that party if the party has been given an opportunity to show cause orally why the order should not be made.

(4) Where a notice required by paragraph (3) is sent in relation to an order to strike out an originating application for want of prosecution, service of the notice shall be treated as having been effected if it has been sent by post or delivered in accordance with rule 23(4) and the tribunal may strike out the originating application (notwithstanding that there has been no direction for substituted service in accordance with rule 23(7)) if the party does not avail himself of the opportunity given by the notice.

(5) A tribunal may, before determining an application under rule 4 or rule 19, require the party making the application to give notice of it to every other party. The notice shall give particulars of the application and indicate the address to which and the time within which any objection to the application shall be made, being an address and time specified for the purposes of the application by the tribunal.

(6) In any case appearing to involve allegations of the commission of a sexual offence, the tribunal or the Secretary shall omit from the Register, or delete from the Register or any decision, document or record of the proceedings, which is available to the public, any identifying matter which is likely to lead

members of the public to identify any person affected by or making such an allegation.

(7) A chairman may postpone the day or time fixed for, or adjourn, any hearing (particularly where an enactment provides for conciliation in relation to the case, for the purpose of giving an opportunity for the case to be settled by way of conciliation and withdrawn) and vary any such postponement or adjournment.

(8) Any act required or authorised by these rules to be done by a tribunal may be done by a chairman except –

  (a) the hearing of an originating application under rule 10;

  (b) an act required or authorised to be so done by rule 11 or 12 which the rule implies is to be done by the tribunal which is hearing or heard the originating application;

  (c) the review of a decision under rule 13(1), and the confirmation, variation or revocation of a decision, and ordering of a re-hearing, under rule 13(7).

(9) Any act required or authorised by rule 17 and paragraph (7) to be done by a chairman may be done by a tribunal or on the direction of a chairman.

(10) Any function of the Secretary may be performed by a Regional Secretary or by a person acting with the authority of the Secretary or of a Regional Secretary.

Restricted reporting orders

16 (1) In any case which involves allegations of sexual misconduct the tribunal may at any time before promulgation of its decision in respect of an originating application, either on the application of a party made by notice to the Secretary or of its own motion, make a restricted reporting order.

(2) In proceedings on a complaint under section 8 of the 1995 Act in which evidence of a personal nature is likely to be heard by the tribunal, it may at any time before promulgation of its decision in respect of an originating application, either on the application of the complainant made by notice to the Secretary or of its own motion, make a restricted reporting order.

(3) Where the tribunal makes a restricted reporting order under paragraph (2) and that complaint is being dealt with together with any other proceedings, the tribunal may direct that the order applies also in relation to those other proceedings or such part of them as the tribunal may direct.

(4) The tribunal shall not make a restricted reporting order unless it has given each party an opportunity to advance oral argument at a hearing, if they so wish.

(5) Where a tribunal makes a restricted reporting order –

  (a) it shall specify in the order the persons who may not be identified;

  (b) the order shall remain in force until the promulgation of the decision of the tribunal on the originating application to which it relates unless revoked earlier; and

  (c) the Regional Secretary shall ensure that a notice of that fact is displayed on the notice board of the tribunal with any list of the proceedings taking place before the employment tribunal, and on the door of the room in which the proceedings affected by the order are taking place.

(6) A tribunal may revoke a restricted reporting order at any time if it thinks fit.

(7) For the purposes of this rule 'promulgation' occurs on the date recorded as being the date on which the document recording the determination of the originating application was sent to the parties.

Extension of time

17 (1) A chairman may, on the application of a party or of his own motion, extend the time for doing any act appointed by or under these rules (including this rule) and may do so whether or not the time so appointed has expired.

(2) An application under paragraph (1) shall be made by presenting to the Secretary a notice of application, which shall state the title of the proceedings and shall set out the grounds of the application.

(3) The Secretary shall give notice to each of the parties of any extension of time granted under this rule.

Devolution issues

18 (1) In any proceedings in which a devolution issue arises, the Secretary shall as soon as reasonably practicable by notice inform the relevant authority thereof (unless the person to whom notice would be given is a party to the proceedings) and shall at the same time –

(a) send a copy of the notice to the parties to the proceedings; and

(b) send the relevant authority a copy of the originating application and the notice of appearance.

(2) A person to whom notice is given in pursuance of paragraph (1) may within 14 days of receipt thereof by notice to the Secretary take part as a party in the proceedings, so far as they relate to the devolution issue. The Secretary shall send a copy of the notice to the other parties to the proceedings.

Joinder and representative respondents

19 (1) A tribunal may at any time, on the application of any person made by notice to the Secretary or of its own motion, direct any person against whom any relief is sought to be joined as a party, and give such consequential directions as it considers necessary.

(2) A tribunal may likewise, on such application or of its own motion, order that any respondent named in the originating application or subsequently added, who appears to the tribunal not to have been, or to have ceased to be, directly interested in the subject of the originating application, be dismissed from the proceedings.

(3) Where there are a number of persons having the same interest in an originating application, one or more of them may be cited as the person or persons against whom relief is sought, or may be authorised by the tribunal, before or at the hearing, to defend on behalf of all the persons so interested.

Combined proceedings

20 (1) Where, in relation to two or more originating applications pending before the employment tribunals, it appears to an employment tribunal, on the application of a party made by notice to the Secretary or of its own motion, that –

(a) a common question of law or fact arises in some or all the originating applications, or

(b) the relief claimed in some or all of those originating applications is in respect of or arises out of the same set of facts, or

(c) for any other reason it is desirable to make an order under this rule,

the tribunal may order that some (as specified in the order) or all of the originating applications in respect of which it so appears to the tribunal shall be considered together, and may give such consequential directions as may be necessary.

(2) The tribunal shall only make an order under this rule if –

(a) each of the parties concerned has been given an opportunity at a hearing to show cause why such an order should not be made; or

(b) it has sent notice to all the parties concerned giving them an opportunity to show such cause.

(3) The tribunal may, on the application of a party made by notice to the Secretary or of its own motion, vary or set aside an order made under this rule but shall not do so unless it has given each party an opportunity to make either oral or written representations before the order is varied or set aside.

Transfer of proceedings

21 (1) On the application of a party made by notice to the Secretary or of his own motion, the President or a Regional Chairman may at any time, with the consent of the President of the Employment Tribunals (Scotland), direct any proceedings to be transferred to the Office of the Employment Tribunals (Scotland) if it appears to him that the proceedings could be, and would more conveniently be, determined in an employment tribunal (Scotland) established in pursuance of the Employment Tribunals (Constitution and Rules of Procedure) (Scotland) Regulations 2001; but no such direction shall be made unless notice has been sent to all parties concerned giving them an opportunity to show cause why a direction should not be made.

(2) Where proceedings have been transferred to the Office of the Employment Tribunals (England and Wales) under rule 21(1) of the Employment Tribunals Rules of Procedure (Scotland) 2001 they shall be treated as if in all respects they had been commenced by an originating application pursuant to rule 1.

References to the European Court of Justice

22 Where a tribunal makes an order referring a question to the European Court of Justice for a preliminary ruling under Article 234 of the Treaty establishing the European Community, the Secretary shall send a copy of the order to the Registrar of that Court but shall not do so until the time for appealing against the order has expired or, if an appeal is made within that time, until the appeal has been determined or otherwise disposed of.

Notices, etc

23 (1) Any notice given under these rules shall be in writing.

(2) All notices and documents required by these rules to be presented to the Secretary, other than an originating application, may be presented at the Office of the Tribunals or such other office as may be notified by the Secretary to the parties.

(3) An originating application may be presented at the Office of the Tribunals or at any Regional Office of the Employment Tribunals.

(4) All notices and documents required or authorised by these rules to be sent or given to any person hereinafter mentioned may be sent by post (subject to paragraph (6)) or delivered to or at –

   (a) in the case of a notice or document directed to the Secretary of State in proceedings to which he is not a party (or in respect of which he is treated as a party for the purpose of these rules by virtue of rule 10(7)), the offices of the Department of Trade and Industry (Employment Relations Directorate 2) at 1 Victoria Street, London, SW1H 0ET, or such other office as may be notified by the Secretary of State;

   (b) in the case of a notice or document directed to the Attorney General pursuant to rule 18, the Attorney General's Chambers, 9 Buckingham Gate, London, SW1E 7JP;

   (c) in the case of a notice or document directed to the National Assembly for Wales pursuant to rule 18, the Counsel General to the National Assembly for Wales, Crown Buildings, Cathays Park, Cardiff, CF10 3NQ;

   (d) in the case of a notice or document directed to a court, the office of the clerk of the court;

   (e) in the case of a notice or document directed to a party –

      (i) the address specified in his originating application or notice of appearance to which notices and documents are to be sent, or in a notice under paragraph (5), or

      (ii) if no such address has been specified, or if a notice sent to such an address has been returned, to any other known address or place of business in the United Kingdom or, if the party is a corporate body, the body's registered or principal office in the United Kingdom, or, in any case, such address or place outside the United Kingdom as the President or a Regional Chairman may allow;

   (f) in the case of a notice or document directed to any person (other than a person specified in the foregoing provisions of this paragraph), his address or place of business in the United Kingdom or, if the person is a corporate body, the body's registered or principal office in the United Kingdom;

   and a notice or document sent or given to the authorised representative of a party shall be deemed to have been sent or given to that party.

(5) A party may at any time by notice to the Secretary and to the other party or parties (and, where appropriate, to the appropriate conciliation officer) change the address to which notices and documents are to be sent.

(6) The recorded delivery service shall be used instead of the ordinary post –

(a) when a second set of notices or documents is sent to a respondent who has not entered an appearance under rule 3(1); and

(b) for service of an order made under rule 4(5).

(7) The President or a Regional Chairman may direct that there shall be substituted service in such manner as he may deem fit in any case he considers appropriate.

(8) In proceedings brought under the provisions of any enactment providing for conciliation the Secretary shall send copies of all documents and notices to a conciliation officer who in the opinion of the Secretary is an appropriate officer to receive them.

(9) Paragraph (8) does not apply in relation to documents or notices falling within a description of documents or notices in respect of which the Secretary and the Advisory, Conciliation and Arbitration Service have agreed that copies need not be sent.

(10) In proceedings which may involve a payment out of the National Insurance Fund, the Secretary shall, where appropriate, send copies of all documents and notices to the Secretary of State whether or not he is a party.

(11) Copies of every document and copy entry sent to the parties under rules 12(5) or 12(9) shall –

(a) in the case of proceedings under the 1970 Act, the 1975 Act or the 1986 Act, be sent to the Equal Opportunities Commission;

(b) in the case of proceedings under the 1976 Act, be sent to the Commission for Racial Equality; and

(c) in the case of proceedings under the 1995 Act, be sent to the Disability Rights Commission.

SCHEDULE 3: THE EMPLOYMENT TRIBUNALS (EQUAL VALUE) COMPLEMENTARY RULES OF PROCEDURE

For use only in proceedings involving an equal value claim

PART I: ORDINARY CASES

Modification of rule 4 of Schedule 1

1 In rule 4 of Schedule 1 (case management) –

(a) after paragraph (5), insert –

'(5A) Subject to paragraph (5B), a tribunal may, on the application of an expert who has been required by the tribunal to prepare a report –

(a) require any person whom the tribunal is satisfied may have information which may be relevant to the question or matter on which the expert is required to report to furnish, in writing, such information as the tribunal may require;

(b) require any person to produce any documents which are in the possession, custody or power of that person and which the tribunal is satisfied may contain matter relevant to the question on which the expert is required to report.

(5B) A tribunal shall not make a requirement under paragraph (5A)–

(a) of a conciliation officer who has acted in connection with the complaint under section 18 of the 1996 Act, or

(b) if it is satisfied that the person so required would have good grounds for refusing to comply with the requirement if it were a requirement made in connection with a hearing before the tribunal.

(5C) A person, whether or not a party, upon whom a requirement has been made under paragraph (5A), may apply to the tribunal by notice to the Secretary before the appointed time at or within which the requirement is to be complied with to vary or set aside the requirement. Notice of such application shall be given to the parties and to the expert upon whose application the requirement was made.'; and

(b) for paragraphs (6) and (7), substitute –

'(6) Every document containing a requirement imposed under paragraph (5) or (5A) shall state that, under section 7(4) of the 1996 Act, any person who without reasonable excuse fails to comply with the requirement shall be liable on summary conviction to a fine, and the document shall state the amount of the current maximum fine.

(7) Where a requirement has been imposed under paragraph (1),(5) or (5A) –

(a) on a party in his absence; or

(b) on a person other than a party;

that party or person may apply to the tribunal by notice to the Secretary to vary or set aside the requirement. Such notice shall be given before the time at which or, as the case may be, the expiration of the time within which the requirement is to be complied with, and the Secretary shall give notice of the application to each party, or where applicable, each party other than the party making the application.'

Insertion of rule 10A into Schedule 1

2 After rule 10 of Schedule 1, insert –

'**Procedure relating to expert's report**

10A(1) In any case involving an equal value claim where a dispute arises as to whether work is of equal value to other work in terms of the demands made on the person employed on the work (for instance under such headings as effort, skill and decision) (in this rule, hereinafter referred to as 'the question') the tribunal shall, except in cases where it is satisfied that there are no reasonable grounds for determining the question in the affirmative, determine whether to require an expert to prepare a report with respect to the question.

(2) Before determining under paragraph (1) whether to require an expert to prepare a report the tribunal shall give the parties an opportunity to make representations to the tribunal as to whether an expert should be so required.

(3) Where the tribunal has determined not to require an expert to prepare a report it may nevertheless, at any time during its consideration of the question, require an expert to prepare a report, but shall not do so unless it has

given the parties a further opportunity to make representations to the tribunal as to whether an expert should be so required.

(4) Any requirement to prepare a report shall be made in writing and shall set out –

(a) the name and address of each of the parties;

(b) the address of the establishment at which the applicant is (or, as the case may be, was) employed;

(c) the question;

(d) the identity of the person with reference to whose work the question arises;

(e) the date by which the expert is required to send his report to the tribunal; and

(f) the length of the intervals, during the currency of the requirement to prepare the report, before the expiration of which the expert must send progress reports pursuant to paragraph (8).

The Secretary shall send a copy of the requirement to each of the parties together with a notice informing them that a party who unreasonably delays the preparation of the expert's report may have an award of costs made against him, which may include an award in respect of the expert's fees, or have his originating application or notice of appearance struck out.

(5) The requirement shall stipulate that the expert shall –

(a) take account of all such information supplied and all such representations made to him as have a bearing on the question;

(b) before drawing up his report, produce and send to the parties a written summary of the said information and representations and invite the representations of the parties upon the material contained therein;

(c) make his report to the tribunal in a document which shall reproduce the summary and contain a brief account of any representations received from the parties upon it, any conclusion he may have reached upon the question and the reasons for that conclusion or, as the case may be, for his failure to reach such a conclusion;

(d) take no account of the difference of sex and at all times act fairly.

(6) Where a tribunal requires an expert to prepare a report, it shall adjourn the hearing.

(7) In paragraphs (8), (9), (11) and (12), 'the required date' means the most recent date specified as the date by which the expert must send his report to the tribunal either in the requirement made upon him under paragraph (4) or in a notice given to him under paragraph (11).

(8) Before the expiration of each interval specified in the requirement given to the expert under paragraph (4), the expert shall send a progress report to the tribunal –

(a) stating whether he considers that he will be able to send his report to the tribunal by the required date; and

(b) if he considers that he will be unable to do so, giving the reasons for the delay and the date by which he now expects to send his report to the tribunal.

Where a progress report states that the expert considers that he will be unable to send his report to the tribunal by the required date the Secretary shall send a copy to each party.

(9) If at any time when a progress report under paragraph (8) is not imminent, the expert comes to the view that he will be unable to send his report to the tribunal by the required date, he shall give notice in writing to the tribunal –

(a) stating that fact; and

(b) giving the reasons for the delay and the date by which he now expects to send his report to the tribunal.

The Secretary shall send a copy of any such notice to each party.

(10) In giving the reasons for any delay, pursuant to paragraph (8) or (9), the expert shall, in particular, state whether he considers that any action (including an omission) by a party has contributed to the delay and, if he so considers –

(i)   identify the party,

(ii)   give particulars of the action,

(iii) describe how it has contributed to the delay, and

(iv)   give an assessment of the extent to which the delay is attributable to it.

(11) On receiving a progress report under paragraph (8) or a notice under paragraph (9) stating that the expert considers that he will be unable to send his report to the tribunal by the required date, the tribunal shall do one of the following –

(a) give written notice to the expert that he is still required to send the report by the required date;

(b) give written notice to the expert substituting a later date as the required date; or

(c) if, but only if, it considers that it would be in the interests of justice to replace the expert, revoke, by notice in writing to the expert, the requirement to prepare a report, but shall not do so before it has informed the parties of the action it proposes to take and given each party the opportunity to make representations.

(12) Paragraph (11) shall also apply where the expert does not send his report to the tribunal by the required date but as if sub-paragraph (a) were excluded.

(13) Where, acting under paragraph (11), a tribunal has revoked the requirement made upon an expert to prepare a report it shall require another expert to prepare a report by proceeding under this rule as if it had just determined to require an expert to prepare a report, and the rule shall apply accordingly.

(14) Where in giving the reasons for any delay pursuant to paragraph (8) or (9), the expert has, in accordance with paragraph (10), stated that an action by a party has contributed to the delay, the tribunal shall consider whether the party has unreasonably delayed the preparation of the expert's report and, if it so considers, shall either –

(a) make an order under and in accordance with rule 14, or

(b) strike out the whole or part of the originating application, or, as the case may be of the notice of appearance and, where appropriate, direct that a respondent shall be debarred from defending altogether;

but the tribunal shall not exercise its powers under this paragraph without giving the party an opportunity to make representations.

(15) Notwithstanding rule 14(1)(b), the tribunal may, in making an order under rule 14 in pursuance of paragraph (14), order that a party shall pay to the Secretary of State the whole, or any part, of any fees and allowances paid or payable to the expert in respect of the time so far spent by him in carrying out work pursuant to the requirement to prepare a report.

(16) Where a tribunal has received the report of an expert, it shall send a copy of the report to each party and fix a date for the hearing of the case to be resumed; and the date so fixed shall be the earliest reasonably practicable date, but shall be no less than 14 days after the date on which the report is sent to the parties.

(17) Upon the resumption of the hearing of the case in accordance with paragraph (16) the report shall be admitted as evidence in the case unless the tribunal has exercised its power under paragraph (18) not to admit the report.

(18) Where the tribunal, on the application of one or more of the parties or otherwise, forms the view –

    (a) that the expert has not complied with a stipulation in paragraph (5), or

    (b) that the conclusion contained in the report is one which, taking due account of the information supplied and representations made to the expert, could not reasonably have been reached, or

    (c) that for some other material reason (other than disagreement with the conclusion that the applicant's work is or is not of equal value or with the reasoning leading to that conclusion) the report is unsatisfactory,

the tribunal may, if it thinks fit, determine not to admit the report, and in such a case the tribunal shall proceed under this rule as if it had just determined to require an expert to prepare a report, and the rule shall apply accordingly.

(19) In forming its view on the matters contained in paragraph (18)(a), (b) and (c) the tribunal shall take account of any representations of the parties thereon and may in that connection, subject to rule 11(2A) and (2B), permit any party to give evidence upon, to call witnesses and to question any witness upon any matter relevant thereto.

(20) The tribunal may, at any time after it has received the report of an expert, require that expert (or, if that is impracticable, another expert) to explain any matter contained in that report or, having regard to such matters as may be set out in the requirement, to give further consideration to the question.

(21) A requirement under paragraph (20) shall stipulate that the expert shall make his reply in writing to the tribunal, giving his explanation or, as the case may be, setting down any conclusion which may result from his further consideration and his reasons for that conclusion.

(22) Paragraphs (4), (7) to (12), (14) and (15) shall apply in relation to a requirement under paragraph (20) as if that requirement was a requirement to prepare a report except that –

(a) the duty on the Secretary under paragraph (4) to send a notice concerning unreasonable delay by the parties of the preparation of the expert's report shall not apply;

(b) for the purpose of such application the following sub-paragraphs shall be substituted for the sub-paragraphs of paragraph (11) –

'(a) give written notice to the expert that he is still required to send the reply by the required date;

(b) give written notice to the expert substituting a later date as the required date;

(c) notify the expert in writing that the requirement is cancelled without requiring another expert to fulfil it; or

(d) so notify the expert and require another expert to fulfil the requirement in accordance with paragraph (20);' and;

(c) the tribunal may decide not to require the expert to send progress reports to the tribunal if it considers the requirement to be inappropriate in the circumstances and in that event –

(i) paragraphs (4)(f) and (8) shall not apply; and

(ii) paragraph (9) shall apply if the expert at any time comes to the view that he will be unable to send his reply to the tribunal by the required date.

(23) Where the tribunal has received a reply from the expert under paragraph (21), it shall send a copy of the reply to each of the parties and shall allow the parties to make representations thereon, and the reply shall be treated as information furnished to the tribunal and be given such weight as the tribunal thinks fit.

(24) Where a tribunal has determined not to admit a report under paragraph (18), that report shall be treated for all purposes (other than the award of costs or allowances under rule 14) connected with the proceedings as if it had not been received by the tribunal and no further account shall be taken of it, and the requirement on the expert to prepare a report shall lapse.'

Modification of rule 11 of Schedule 1

3   For paragraphs (1) and (2) of rule 11 of Schedule 1, substitute –

'**Procedure at hearing**

11(1) The tribunal shall, so far as it appears to it appropriate, seek to avoid formality in its proceedings and shall not be bound by any enactment or rule of law relating to the admissibility of evidence in proceedings before the courts of law. The tribunal shall make such enquiries of persons appearing before it and witnesses as it considers appropriate and, subject to paragraphs (2A), (2B), (2C), (2D) and (2E), shall otherwise conduct the hearing in such manner as it considers most suitable to the clarification of the issues before it and generally to the just handling of the proceedings.

(2) Subject to paragraphs (1), (2A), (2B), (2C) and (2D), at the hearing of the originating application a party shall be entitled to give evidence, to call witnesses, to question any witnesses and to address the tribunal.

(2A) The tribunal may, and shall upon the application of a party, require the attendance of an expert who has prepared a report in connection with an equal value claim in any hearing relating to that claim. Where an expert attends in compliance with such requirement any party may, subject to paragraph (1), cross-examine the expert on his report and on any other matter pertaining to the question on which the expert was required to report.

(2B) At any any time after the tribunal has received the report of the expert, any party may, on giving reasonable notice of his intention to do so to the tribunal and to any other party to the claim, call one witness to give expert evidence on the question on which the tribunal has required the expert to prepare a report; and where such evidence is given, any other party may cross-examine the person giving that evidence upon it.

(2C) Except as provided in rule 10A(19) or by paragraph (2D), no party may give evidence upon, or question any witness upon, any matter of fact upon which a conclusion in the report of the expert is based.

(2D) Subject to paragraphs (2A) and (2B), a tribunal may, notwithstanding paragraph (2C), permit a party to give evidence upon, to call witnesses and to question any witness upon any such matters of fact as are referred to in paragraph (2C) if either –

(a) the matter of fact is relevant to and is raised in connection with the issue contained in subsection (3) of section 1 of the 1970 Act (defence of genuine material factor) upon which the determination of the tribunal is being sought; or

(b) the report of the expert contains no conclusion on the question of whether the applicant's work and the work of the person identified in the requirement of the tribunal under rule 10A(4) are of equal value and the tribunal is satisfied that the absence of that conclusion is wholly or mainly due to the refusal or deliberate omission of a person required by the tribunal under rule 4(5A) to furnish information or to produce documents to comply with that requirement.

(2E) A tribunal may, on the application of a party, if in the circumstances of the case, having regard to the considerations expressed in paragraph (1), it considers that it is appropriate so to proceed, hear evidence upon and permit the parties to address it upon the issue contained in subsection (3) of section 1 of the 1970 Act (defence of genuine material factor) before determining whether to require an expert to prepare a report under rule 10A.'

Modification of rule 12 of Schedule 1

4   In rule 12 of Schedule 1 (decision of tribunal) –

(a) after paragraph (4), insert –

'(4A) There shall be appended to the document referred to in paragraph (3) a copy of the report (if any) of an expert received by the tribunal in the course of the proceedings.';

(b) for paragraph (5) substitute –

'(5) The clerk shall transmit the documents referred to in paragraphs (2) and (3) and the copy of the report referred to in paragraph (4A), if any, to the Secretary who shall enter them in the Register and shall send a copy of the entry to each of the parties and where the proceedings were referred to the tribunal by a court, to that court.'; and

(c) for paragraph (6) substitute –

'(6) The document referred to in paragraph (3) and the copy of the report referred to in paragraph (4A), if any, shall be omitted from the Register in any case in which evidence had been heard in private and the tribunal so directs. In such a case the Secretary shall send that document to each of the parties; and where there are proceedings before a superior court relating to the decision in question, he shall send the document to that court, together with a copy of the entry in the Register of the document referred to in paragraph (2).'

Modification of rule 14 of Schedule 1

5　After paragraph (2) of rule 14 of Schedule 1 (costs), insert –

'(2A) For the purposes of paragraph (1)(a), the costs in respect of which a tribunal may make an order include costs incurred by the party in whose favour the order is to be made in or in connection with any investigations carried out by an expert in preparing his report.'

Modification of rule 15 of Schedule 1

6　In rule 15 of Schedule 1 (miscellaneous powers) –

(a) for paragraph (5) substitute –

'(5) A tribunal may, before determining an application under rule 4 or rule 19, require the party making the application or, in the case of an application under rule 4(5A), the expert, to give notice of it to every other party (or, in the case of an application by the expert, to the parties and any other person on whom the tribunal is asked, in the application, to impose a requirement). The notice shall give particulars of the application and indicate the address to which and the time within which any objection to the application shall be made, being an address and time specified for the purposes of the application by the tribunal.'; and

(b) after paragraph (6), insert –

'(6A) Without prejudice to paragraph (7), the tribunal shall, before proceeding to hear the parties on an equal value claim, invite them to apply for an adjournment for the purpose of seeking to reach a settlement of the claim and shall, if both or all the parties agree to such a course, grant an adjournment for that purpose.

(6B) If, after the tribunal has adjourned the hearing under rule 10A(6) but before the tribunal has received the report of the expert, the applicant gives notice under paragraph (2)(a), the tribunal shall notify the expert that the requirement to prepare a report has ceased. The notice shall be without prejudice to the operation of rule 14(2A).'

Modification of rule 23 of Schedule 1

7　For paragraph (6) of rule 23 of Schedule 1 (notices, etc), substitute –

'(6) The recorded delivery service shall be used instead of the ordinary post –

(a) when a second set of notices or documents is sent to a respondent who has not entered an appearance under rule 3(1); and

(b) for service of an order made under rule 4(5) or (5A).'

Supreme Court Practice Direction (Citation of Authorities) 2001

This practice direction is made with the concurrence of Lord Phillips of Worth Matravers MR, Dame Elizabeth Butler-Sloss P and Sir Andrew Morritt V-C.

Introduction

1 In recent years, there has been a substantial growth in the number of readily available reports of judgments in this and other jurisdictions, such reports being available either in published reports or in transcript form. Widespread knowledge of the work and decisions of the courts is to be welcomed. At the same time, however, the current weight of available material causes problems both for advocates and for courts in properly limiting the nature and amount of material that is used in the preparation and argument of subsequent cases.

2 The latter issue is a matter of rapidly increasing importance. Recent and continuing efforts to increase the efficiency, and thus reduce the cost, of litigation, whilst maintaining the interests of justice, will be threatened if courts are burdened with a weight of inappropriate and unnecessary authority, and if advocates are uncertain as to the extent to which it is necessary to deploy authorities in the argument of any given case.

3 With a view to limiting the citation of previous authority to cases that are relevant and useful to the court, this practice direction lays down a number of rules as to what material may be cited, and the manner in which that cited material should be handled by advocates. These rules are in large part such as many courts already follow in pursuit of their general discretion in the management of litigation. However, it is now desirable to promote uniformity of practice by the same rules being followed by all courts.

4 It will remain the duty of advocates to draw the attention of the court to any authority not cited by an opponent which is adverse to the case being advanced.

5 This direction applies to all courts apart from criminal courts, including within the latter category the Court of Appeal (Criminal Division).

Categories of judgments that may only be cited if they fulfil specified requirements

6.1 A judgment falling into one of the categories referred to in paragraph 6.2 below may not in future be cited before any court unless it clearly indicates that it purports to establish a new principle or to extend the present law. In respect of judgments delivered after the date of this direction, that indication must take the form of an express statement to that effect. In respect of judgments delivered before the date of this direction that indication must be present in or clearly deducible from the language used in the judgment.

6.2 Paragraph 6.1 applies to the following categories of judgment:
Applications attended by one party only

Applications for permission to appeal
Decisions on applications that only decide that the application is arguable
County court cases, unless (a) cited in order to illustrate the conventional
measure of damages in a personal injury case; or (b) cited in a county court
in order to demonstrate current authority at that level on an issue in respect
of which no decision at a higher level of authority is available.

6.3   These categories will be kept under review, such review to include
consideration of adding to the categories.

Citation of other categories of judgment

7.1   Courts will in future pay particular attention, when it is sought to cite other
categories of judgment, to any indication given by the court delivering the
judgment that it was seen by that court as only applying decided law to
the facts of the particular case; or otherwise as not extending or adding to
the existing law.

7.2   Advocates who seek to cite a judgment that contains indications of the type
referred to in paragraph 7.1 will be required to justify their decision to cite
the case.

Methods of citation

8.1   Advocates will in future be required to state, in respect of each authority that
they wish to cite, the proposition of law that the authority demonstrates, and
the parts of the judgment that support that proposition. If it is sought to cite
more than one authority in support of a given proposition, advocates must
state the reason for taking that course.

8.2   The demonstration referred to in paragraph 8.1 will be required to be contained in any skeleton argument and in any appellant's or respondent's
notice in respect of each authority referred to in that skeleton or notice.

8.3   Any bundle or list of authorities prepared for the use of any court must in
future bear a certification by the advocate responsible for arguing the case
that the requirements of this paragraph have been complied with in respect
of each authority included.

8.4   The statements referred to in paragraph 8.1 should not materially add to the
length of submissions or of skeleton arguments, but should be sufficient to
demonstrate, in the context of the advocate's argument, the relevance of the
authority or authorities to that argument and that the citation is necessary
for a proper presentation of that argument.

Authorities decided in other jurisdictions

9.1   Cases decided in other jurisdictions can, if properly used, be a valuable
source of law in this jurisdiction. At the same time, however, such authority
should not be cited without proper consideration of whether it does indeed
add to the existing body of law.

9.2   In future, therefore, any advocate who seeks to cite an authority from
another jurisdiction must (i) comply, in respect of that authority, with the
rules set out in paragraph 8 above; (ii) indicate in respect of each authority
what that authority adds that is not to be found in authority in this

jurisdiction; or, if there is said to be justification for adding to domestic authority, what that justification is; (iii) certify that there is no authority in this jurisdiction that precludes the acceptance by the court of the proposition that the foreign authority is said to establish.

9.3 For the avoidance of doubt, paragraphs 9.1 and 9.2 do not apply to cases decided in either the Court of Justice of the European Communities or the organs of the European Convention for the Protection of Human Rights and Fundamental Freedoms. Because of the status in English law of such authority, as provided by, respectively, section 3 of the European Communities Act 1972 and section 2(1) of the Human Rights Act 1998, such cases are covered by the earlier paragraphs of this direction.

Lord Woolf CJ
9 April 2001
[2001] 1 WLR 1001

Employment Appeal Tribunal Rules 1993 SI No 2854

Citation and commencement

1 (1) These Rules may be cited as the Employment Appeal Tribunal Rules 1993 and shall come into force on 16th December 1993.

   (2) As from that date the Employment Appeal Tribunal Rules 1980, the Employment Appeal Tribunal (Amendment) Rules 1985 and the Employment Appeal Tribunal (Amendment) Rules 1988 shall be revoked.

Interpretation

2 In these Rules, unless the context otherwise requires –

   'the 1978 Act' means the Employment Protection (Consolidation) Act 1978 and a section or Schedule referred to by number means the section or Schedule so numbered in the 1978 Act;

   'the 1992 Act' means the Trade Union and Labour Relations (Consolidation) Act 1992;

   'the Appeal Tribunal' means the Appeal Tribunal established under section 87 of the Employment Protection Act 1975 and continued in existence under section 135 of the 1978 Act and includes the President, a judge, a member or the Registrar acting on behalf of the Tribunal;

   'the Certification Officer' means the person appointed to be the Certification Officer under section 7(1) of the Employment Protection Act 1975 or section 254(2) of the 1992 Act, as the case may be;

   'judge' means a judge of the Appeal Tribunal nominated under section 135(2)(a) or (b) and includes a judge nominated under paragraph 5 or 6 and a judge appointed under paragraph 8 of Schedule 11 to act temporarily in the place of a judge of the Tribunal;

   'member' means a member of the Appeal Tribunal appointed under section

135(2)(c) and includes a member appointed under paragraph 7 of Schedule 11 to act temporarily in the place of a member appointed under that section;

'the President' means the judge appointed under section 135(4) to be President of the Appeal Tribunal and includes a judge nominated under paragraph 4 of Schedule 11 to act temporarily in his place;

'the Registrar' means the person appointed to be Registrar of the Appeal Tribunal and includes any officer of the Tribunal authorised by the President to act on behalf of the Registrar;

'the Secretary of Industrial Tribunals' means the person acting for the time being as the Secretary of the Central Office of the Industrial Tribunals (England and Wales) or, as may be appropriate, of the Central Office of the Industrial Tribunals (Scotland);

'taxing officer' means any officer of the Appeal Tribunal authorised by the President to assess costs or expenses.

Institution of appeal

3   (1) Every appeal to the Appeal Tribunal shall be instituted by serving on the Tribunal the following documents –

(a) a notice of appeal in, or substantially in, accordance with Form 1 or 2 in the Schedule to these Rules;

(b) a copy of the decision or order of an industrial tribunal or of the Certification Officer which is the subject of the appeal;

(c) in the case of an appeal from an industrial tribunal, a copy of the extended written reasons for the decision or order of that tribunal.

(2) The period within which an appeal to the Appeal Tribunal may be instituted is 42 days from the date on which extended written reasons for the decision or order of the industrial tribunal were sent to the appellant, or, in the case of an appeal from a decision of the Certification Officer, 42 days from the date on which the written record of that decision was so sent.

(3) Where it appears to the Registrar that the grounds of appeal stated in the notice of appeal do not give the Appeal Tribunal jurisdiction to entertain the appeal, he shall notify the appellant accordingly informing him of the reasons for the opinion and, subject to paragraphs (4) and (6) of this rule, no further action shall be taken on the appeal.

(4) Where notification has been given under paragraph (3) of this rule, the appellant may serve a fresh notice of appeal within the time remaining under paragraph (2) or within 28 days from the date on which the Registrar's notification was sent to him, whichever is the longer period.

(5) Where the appellant serves a fresh notice of appeal under paragraph (4) of this rule the Registrar shall consider such fresh notice of appeal with regard to jurisdiction as though it were an original notice of appeal lodged pursuant to paragraphs (1) and (2) of this rule.

(6) Where an appellant expresses dissatisfaction in writing with the reasons given by the Registrar, under paragraph (3) of this rule, for his opinion that the grounds of appeal stated in a notice do not give the Appeal Tribunal jurisdiction to entertain the appeal, the Registrar shall place the papers

before the President or a judge for his direction as to whether any further action should be taken on the appeal.

Service of notice of appeal

4   On Receipt of notice under rule 3, the Registrar shall seal the notice with the Appeal Tribunal's seal and shall serve a sealed copy on the appellant and on –

(a) every person who, in accordance with rule 5, is a respondent to the appeal; and

(b) The Secretary of Industrial Tribunals in the case of an appeal from an industrial tribunal; or

(c) the Certification Officer in the case of an appeal from any of his decisions; or

(d) the Secretary of State in the case of an appeal under Part VI of the 1978 Act or Chapter II of Part IV of the 1992 Act to which he is not a respondent.

Respondents to appeals

5   The respondents to an appeal shall be –

(a) in the case of an appeal from an industrial tribunal or of an appeal made pursuant to section 95 or 104 of the 1992 Act from a decision of the Certification Officer, the parties (other than the appellant) to the proceedings before the industrial tribunal or the Certification Officer;

(b) in the case of an appeal made pursuant to section 9 of the 1992 Act from a decision of the Certification Officer, that Officer.

Respondent's answer and notice of cross-appeal

6   (1) The Registrar shall, as soon as practicable, notify every respondent of the date appointed by the Appeal Tribunal by which any answer under this rule must be delivered.

(2) A respondent who wishes to resist an appeal shall, within the time appointed under paragraph (1) of this rule, deliver to the Appeal Tribunal an answer in writing in, or substantially in, accordance with Form 3 in the Schedule to these Rules, setting out the grounds on which he relies, so, however, that it shall be sufficient for a respondent to an appeal referred to in rule 5(a) who wishes to rely on any ground which is the same as a ground relied on by the industrial tribunal or the Certification Officer for making the decision or order appealed from to state that fact in his answer.

(3) A respondent who wishes to cross-appeal may do so by including in his answer a statement of the grounds of his cross-appeal, and in that event an appellant who wishes to resist the cross-appeal shall, within a time to be appointed by the Appeal Tribunal, deliver to the Tribunal a reply in writing setting out the grounds on which he relies.

(4) The Registrar shall serve a copy of every answer and reply to a cross-appeal on every party other than the party by whom it was delivered.

(5) Where the respondent does not wish to resist an appeal, the parties may deliver to the Appeal Tribunal an agreed draft of an order allowing the appeal and the Tribunal may, if it thinks it right to do so, make an order allowing the appeal in the terms agreed.

Disposal of appeal

7 (1) The Registrar shall, as soon as practicable, give notice of the arrangements made by the Appeal Tribunal for hearing the appeal to –
   (a) every party to the proceedings; and
   (b) the Secretary of Industrial Tribunals in the case of an appeal from an industrial tribunal; or
   (c) the Certification Officer in the case of an appeal from one of his decisions; or
   (d) the Secretary of State in the case of an appeal under Part VI of the 1978 Act or Chapter II of Part IV of the 1992 Act to which he is not a respondent.

   (2) Any such notice shall state the date appointed by the Appeal Tribunal by which any interlocutory application must be made.

Application in respect of exclusion or expulsion from, or unjustifiable discipline by, a trade union

8 Every application under section 67 or 176 of the 1992 Act to the Appeal Tribunal for:
   (a) an award of compensation for exclusion or expulsion from a trade union; or
   (b) one or both of the following, that is to say –
      (i) an award of compensation for unjustifiable discipline;
      (ii) an order that the union pay to the applicant an amount equal to any sum which he has paid in pursuance of any such determination as is mentioned in section 64(2)(b) of the 1992 Act;
   shall be made in writing in, or substantially in, accordance with Form 4 in the Schedule to these Rules and shall be served on the Appeal Tribunal together with a copy of the decision or order declaring that the applicant's complaint against the trade union was well-founded.

9 If on receipt of an application under rule 8(a) it becomes clear that at the time the application was made the applicant had been admitted or re-admitted to membership of the union against which the complaint was made, the Registrar shall forward the application to the Central Office of Industrial Tribunals.

Service of application under rule 8

10 On receipt of an application under rule 8, the Registrar shall seal it with the Appeal Tribunal's seal and shall serve a sealed copy on the applicant and on the respondent trade union and the Secretary of Industrial Tribunals.

Appearance by respondent trade union

11 (1) Subject to paragraph (2) of this rule, a respondent trade union wishing to resist an application under rule 8 shall within 14 days of receiving the sealed copy of the application enter an appearance in, or substantially in, accordance with Form 5 in the Schedule to these Rules and setting out the grounds on which the union relies.

   (2) Paragraph (1) above shall not require a respondent trade union to enter an appearance where the application is before the Appeal Tribunal by virtue of

having been transferred there by an industrial tribunal and, prior to that transfer, the respondent had entered an appearance to the proceedings before the industrial tribunal.

12 On receipt of the notice of appearance under rule 11 the Registrar shall serve a copy of it on the applicant.

Application for restriction of proceedings order

13 Every application to the Appeal Tribunal by the Attorney General or the Lord Advocate under section 136A for a restriction of proceedings order shall be made in writing in, or substantially in, accordance with Form 6 in the Schedule to these Rules, accompanied by an affidavit in support, and shall be served on the Tribunal.

Service of application under rule 13

14 On receipt of an application under rule 13, the Registrar shall seal it with the Appeal Tribunal's seal and shall serve a sealed copy on the Attorney General or the Lord Advocate, as the case may be, on the Secretary of Industrial Tribunals and on the person named in the application.

Appearance by person named in application under rule 13

15 A person named in an application under rule 13 who wishes to resist the application shall within 14 days of receiving the sealed copy of the application enter an appearance in, or substantially in, accordance with Form 7 in the Schedule to these Rules, accompanied by an affidavit in support.

16 On receipt of the notice of appearance under rule 15 the Registrar shall serve a copy of it on the Attorney General or the Lord Advocate, as the case may be.

Disposal of application

17 (1) The Registrar shall, as soon as practicable, give notice to the parties to an application under rule 8 or rule 13 of the arrangements made by the Appeal Tribunal for hearing the application.

(2) Any such notice shall state the date appointed by the Appeal Tribunal by which any interlocutory application must be made.

Joinder of parties

18 The Appeal Tribunal may, on the application of any person or of its own motion, direct that any person not already a party to the proceedings be added as a party, or that any party to proceedings shall cease to be a party, and in either case may give such consequential directions as it considers necessary.

Interlocutory applications

19 (1) An interlocutory application may be made to the Appeal Tribunal by giving notice in writing specifying the direction or order sought.

(2) On receipt of a notice under paragraph (1) of this rule, the Registrar shall serve a copy on every other party to the proceedings who appears to him to be concerned in the matter to which the notice relates and shall notify the

applicant and every such party of the arrangements made by the Appeal Tribunal for disposing of the application.

Disposal of interlocutory applications

20 (1) Every interlocutory application made to the Appeal Tribunal shall be considered in the first place by the Registrar who will have regard to the just and economical disposal of the application, to the expense which may be incurred by the parties in attending an oral hearing and, where applicable, to rule 23(5).

(2) Every interlocutory application other than an application for a restricted reporting order shall be disposed of by the Registrar except that any matter which he thinks should properly be decided by the President or a judge shall be referred by him to the President or a judge, who may dispose of it himself or refer it in whole or in part to the Appeal Tribunal as required to be constituted by paragraph 16(1) and (2) of Schedule 11 or refer it back to the Registrar with such directions as he thinks fit.

(3) Every interlocutory application for a restricted reporting order shall be disposed of by the President or a judge or, if he so directs, the application shall be referred to the Appeal Tribunal as required to be constituted by paragraph 16(1) and (2) of Schedule 11 who shall dispose of it.

(4) Paragraphs (2) and (3) of this rule are subject to rule 22(2).

Appeals from Registrar

21 (1) Where an application is disposed of by the Registrar in pursuance of rule 20(2) any party aggrieved by his decision may appeal to a judge and in that case (subject to rule 22(2)) the judge may determine the appeal himself or refer it in whole or in part to the Appeal Tribunal as required to be constituted by paragraph 16(1) and (2) of Schedule 11.

(2) Notice of appeal under paragraph (1) of this rule may be given to the Appeal Tribunal, either orally or in writing, within five days of the decision appealed from and the Registrar shall notify every other party who appears to him to be concerned in the appeal and shall inform every such party and the appellant of the arrangements made by the Tribunal for disposing of the appeal.

Hearing of interlocutory applications

22 (1) The Appeal Tribunal may, subject to rule 30 and, where applicable, to rule 23(6), sit either in private or in public for the hearing of any interlocutory application.

(2) Where a Minister of the Crown has given such a direction as is referred to in paragraph 16(4) of Schedule 11, any hearing of an interlocutory application shall be by the Appeal Tribunal comprised of the President alone.

Cases involving allegations of sexual misconduct or the commission of sexual offences

23 (1) This rule applies to any proceedings to which paragraph 18A of Schedule 11 applies.

(2) In any such proceedings where the appeal appears to involve allegations of

the commission of a sexual offence, the Registrar shall omit from any register kept by the Appeal Tribunal, which is available to the public, or delete from any order, judgment or other document, which is available to the public, any identifying matter which is likely to lead members of the public to identify any person affected by or making such an allegation.

(3) In any proceedings to which this rule applies where the appeal involves allegations of sexual misconduct the Appeal Tribunal may at any time before promulgation of its decision either on the application of a party or of its own motion make a restricted reporting order having effect, if not revoked earlier by the Appeal Tribunal, until the promulgation of its decision.

(4) A restricted reporting order shall specify the persons who may not be identified.

(5) The Appeal Tribunal shall not make a restricted reporting order unless it has given each party to the proceedings an opportunity to advance oral argument at a hearing, if they so wish.

(6) Any such hearing shall, subject to rule 30 or unless the Appeal Tribunal decides for any of the reasons mentioned in rule 29(2) to sit in private to hear evidence, be held in public.

(7) The Appeal Tribunal may revoke a restricted reporting order at any time where it thinks fit.

(8) Where the Appeal Tribunal makes a restricted reporting order, the Registrar shall ensure that a notice of the fact is displayed on the notice board of the Appeal Tribunal at the office in which the proceedings in question are being dealt with, on the door of the room in which those proceedings are taking place and with any list of the proceedings taking place before the Appeal Tribunal.

(9) In this rule, 'promulgation of its decision' means the date recorded as being the date on which the Appeal Tribunal's order finally disposing of the appeal is sent to the parties.

Appointment for direction

24 (1) Where it appears to the Appeal Tribunal that the future conduct of any proceedings would thereby be facilitated, the Tribunal may (either of its own motion or on application) at any stage in the proceedings appoint a date for a meeting for directions as to their future conduct and thereupon the following provisions of this rule shall apply.

(2) The Registrar shall give to every party in the proceedings notice of the date appointed under paragraph (1) of this rule and any party applying for directions shall, if practicable, before that date give to the Appeal Tribunal particulars of any direction for which he asks.

(3) The Registrar shall take such steps as may be practicable to inform every party of any directions applied for by any other party.

(4) On the date appointed under paragraph (1) of this rule, the Appeal Tribunal shall consider every application for directions made by any party and any written representations relating to the application submitted to the Tribunal and shall give such directions as it thinks fit for the purpose of securing the just, expeditious and economical disposal of the proceedings, including,

where appropriate, directions in pursuance of rule 36, for the purpose of ensuring that the parties are enabled to avail themselves of opportunities for conciliation.

(5) Without prejudice to the generality of paragraph (4) of this rule, the Appeal Tribunal may give such directions as it thinks fit as to –

(a) the amendment of any notice, answer or other document,

(b) the admission of any facts or documents;

(c) the admission in evidence of any documents;

(d) the mode in which evidence is to be given at the hearing;

(e) the consolidation of the proceedings with any other proceedings pending before the Tribunal;

(f) the place and date of the hearing.

(6) An application for further directions or for the variation of any directions already given may be made in accordance with rule 19.

Appeal Tribunal's power to give directions

25   The Appeal Tribunal may either of its own motion or on application, at any stage of the proceedings, give any party directions as to any steps to be taken by him in relation to the proceedings.

Default by parties

26   If a respondent to any proceedings fails to deliver an answer or, in the case of an application made under section 67 or 176 of the 1992 Act or section 136A, a notice of appearance within the time appointed under these Rules, or if any party fails to comply with an order or direction of the Appeal Tribunal, the Tribunal may order that he be debarred from taking any further part in the proceedings, or may make such other order as it thinks just.

Attendance of witnesses and production of documents

27 (1) The Appeal Tribunal may, on the application of any party, order any person to attend before the Tribunal as a witness or to produce any document.

(2) No person to whom an order is directed under paragraph (1) of this rule shall be treated as having failed to obey that order unless at the time at which the order was served on him there was tendered to him a sufficient sum of money to cover his costs of attending before the Appeal Tribunal.

Oaths

28   The Appeal Tribunal may, either of its own motion or on application, require any evidence to be given on oath.

Oral hearings

29 (1) Subject to paragraph (2) of this rule and to rule 30, an oral hearing at which any proceedings before the Appeal Tribunal are finally disposed of shall take place in public before, where applicable, such members of the Tribunal as (subject to paragraph 16 of Schedule 11) the President may nominate for the purpose.

(2) The Appeal Tribunal may sit in private for the purpose of –
   (a) hearing evidence which in the opinion of the Tribunal relates to matters of such a nature that it would be against the interests of national security to allow the evidence to be given in public; or
   (b) hearing evidence from any person which in the opinion of the Tribunal is likely to consist of –
      (i) information which he could not disclose without contravening a prohibition imposed by or under any enactment; or
      (ii) any information which has been communicated to him in confidence, or which he has otherwise obtained in consequence of the confidence reposed in him by another person; or;
      (iii) information the disclosure of which would cause substantial injury to any undertaking of his or any undertaking in which he works for reasons other than its effect on negotiations with respect to any of the matters mentioned in section 244(1) of the 1992 Act.

Proceedings to be conducted in private on grounds of national security

30 The Appeal Tribunal shall sit in private in circumstances in which an industrial tribunal has been required to sit in private by virtue of paragraph 1 of Schedule 9.

Drawing up, reasons for, and enforcement of orders

31 (1) Every order of the Appeal Tribunal shall be drawn up by the Registrar and a copy, sealed with the seal of the Tribunal, shall be served by the Registrar on every party to the proceedings to which it relates and –
   (a) in the case of an order disposing of an appeal from an industrial tribunal or of an order under section 136A, on the Secretary of the Industrial Tribunals; or
   (b) in the case of an order disposing of an appeal from the Certification Officer, on that Officer.

(2) The Appeal Tribunal shall, on the application of any party made within 14 days after the making of an order finally disposing of any proceedings, give its reasons in writing for the order unless it was made after the delivery of a reasoned judgment.

(3) Subject to any order made by the Court of Appeal or Court of Session and to any directions given by the Appeal Tribunal, an appeal from the Tribunal shall not suspend the enforcement of any order made by it.

Registration and proof of awards in respect of exclusion or expulsions from, or unjustifiable discipline by, a trade union

32 (1) This rule applies where an application has been made to the Appeal Tribunal under section 67 or 176 of the 1992 Act.

(2) Without prejudice to rule 31, where the Appeal Tribunal makes an order in respect of an application to which this rule applies, and that order –
   (a) makes an award of compensation, or
   (b) is or includes an order of the kind referred to in rule 8(b)(ii),
   or both, the Registrar shall as soon as may be enter a copy of the order,

sealed with the seal of the Tribunal, into a register kept by the Tribunal (in this rule referred to as 'the Register').

(3) The production in any proceedings in any court of a document, purporting to be certified by the Registrar to be a true copy of an entry in the Register of an order to which this rule applies shall, unless the contrary is proved, be sufficient evidence of the document and of the facts stated therein.

Review of decisions and correction of errors

33 (1) The Appeal Tribunal may, either of its own motion or on application, review any order made by it and may, on such review, revoke or vary that order on the grounds that –

   (a) the order was wrongly made as the result of an error on the part of the Tribunal or its staff;

   (b) a party did not receive proper notice of the proceedings leading to the order; or

   (c) the interests of justice require such review.

(2) An application under paragraph (1) above shall be made within 14 days of the date of the order.

(3) A clerical mistake in any order arising from an accidental slip or omission may at any time be corrected by, or on the authority of, a judge or member.

Costs or expenses

34 (1) Where it appears to the Appeal Tribunal that any proceedings were unnecessary, improper or vexatious or that there has been unreasonable delay or other unreasonable conduct in bringing or conducting the proceedings the Tribunal may order the party at fault to pay any other party the whole or such part as it thinks fit of the costs or expenses incurred by that other party in connection with the proceedings.

(2) Where an order is made under paragraph (1) of this rule, the Appeal Tribunal may assess the sum to be paid or may direct that it be assessed by the taxing officer, from whose decision an appeal shall lie to a judge.

(3) Rules 21 and 22 shall apply to an appeal under paragraph (2) of this rule as they apply to an appeal from the Registrar.

(4) The costs of an assisted person shall be taxed or assessed in accordance with regulation 149(7) of the Civil Legal Aid (General) Regulations 1989.

Service of documents

35 (1) Any notice or other document required or authorised by these Rules to be served on, or delivered to, any person may be sent to him by post to his address for service or, where no address for service has been given, to his registered office, principal place of business, head or main office or last known address, as the case may be, and any notice or other document required or authorised to be served on, or delivered to, the Appeal Tribunal may be sent by post or delivered to the Registrar –

   (a) in the case of a notice instituting proceedings, at the central office or any other office of the Tribunal; or

   (b) in any other case, at the office of the Tribunal in which the proceedings in question are being dealt with in accordance with rule 38(2).

(2) Any notice or other document required or authorised to be served on, or delivered to, an unincorporated body may be sent to its secretary, manager or other similar officer.

(3) Every document served by post shall be assumed, in the absence of evidence to the contrary, to have been delivered in the normal course of post.

(4) The Appeal Tribunal may inform itself in such manner as it thinks fit of the posting of any document by an officer of the Tribunal.

(5) The Appeal Tribunal may direct that service of any document be dispensed with or be effected otherwise than in the manner prescribed by these Rules.

Conciliation

36 Where at any stage of any proceedings it appears to the Appeal Tribunal that there is a reasonable prospect of agreement being reached between the parties, the Tribunal may take such steps as it thinks fit to enable the parties to avail themselves of any opportunities for conciliation, whether by adjourning any proceedings or otherwise.

Time

37 (1) The time prescribed by these Rules or by order of the Appeal Tribunal for doing any act may be extended (whether it has already expired or not) or abridged, and the date appointed for any purpose may be altered, by order of the Tribunal.

(2) Where the last day for the doing of any act falls on a day on which the appropriate office of the Tribunal is closed and by reason thereof the act cannot be done on that day, it may be done on the next day on which that office is open.

(3) An application for an extension of the time prescribed for the doing of an act, including the institution of an appeal under rule 3, shall be heard and determined as an interlocutory application under rule 20.

Tribunal offices and allocation of business

38 (1) The central office and any other office of the Appeal Tribunal shall be open at such times as the President may direct.

(2) Any proceedings before the Tribunal may be dealt with at the central office or at such other office as the President may direct.

Non-compliance with, and waiver of, rules

39 (1) Failure to comply with any requirements of these Rules shall not invalidate any proceedings unless the Appeal Tribunal otherwise directs.

(2) The Tribunal may, if it considers that to do so would lead to the more expeditious or economical disposal of any proceedings or would otherwise be desirable in the interests of justice, dispense with the taking of any step required or authorised by these Rules, or may direct that any such steps be taken in some manner other than that prescribed by these Rules.

(3) The powers of the Tribunal under paragraph (2) extend to authorising the Institution of an appeal notwithstanding that the period prescribed in rule 3(2) may not have commenced.

Transitional provisions

40 (1) Where, prior to 16th December 1993, an industrial tribunal has given full written reasons for its decision or order, those reasons shall be treated as extended written reasons for the purposes of rule 3(1)(c) and rule 3(2) and for the purposes of Form 1 in the Schedule to these Rules.

(2) Anything validly done under or pursuant to the Employment Appeal Tribunals Rules 1980 shall be treated as having been done validly for the purposes of these Rules, whether or not what was done could have been done under or pursuant to these Rules.

SCHEDULE

RULE 3

Form 1

Notice of Appeal from Decision of Industrial Tribunal

1   The appellant is (*name and address of appellant*).

2   Any communication relating to this appeal may be sent to the appellant at (*appellant's address for service, including telephone number if any*).

3   The appellant appeals from (*here give particulars of the decision of the industrial tribunal from which the appeal is brought including the date*).

4   The parties to the proceedings before the industrial tribunal, other than the appellant, were (*names and addresses of other parties to the proceedings in decision appealed from*).

5   A copy of the industrial tribunal's decision or order and of the extended written reasons for that decision or order are attached to this notice.

6   The grounds upon which this appeal is brought are that the industrial tribunal erred in law in that (*here set out in paragraphs the various grounds of appeal*).

Date   Signed

RULE 3

Form 2

Notice of Appeal from Decision of Certification Officer

1   The appellant is (*name and address of appellant*).

2   Any communication relating to this appeal may be sent to the appellant at (*appellant's address for service, including telephone number if any*).

3   The appellant appeals from (*here give particulars of the order or decision of the Certification Officer from which the appeal is brought*).

4   The appellant's grounds of appeal are (*here state the grounds of appeal*).

5   A copy of the Certification Officer's decision is attached to this notice.

Date   Signed

RULE 6

Form 3
Respondent's Answer

1 The respondent is (*name and address of respondent*).

2 Any communication relating to this appeal may be sent to the respondent at (*respondent's address for service; including telehone number if any*).

3 The respondent intends to resist the appeal of (*here give the name of appellant*). The grounds on which the respondent will rely are [the grounds relied upon by the industrial tribunal/Certification Officer for making the decision or order appealed from] [and] [the following grounds]: (*here set out any grounds which differ from those relied upon by the industrial tribunal or Certification Officer, as the case may be*).

4 The respondent cross-appeals from (*here give particulars of the decision appealed from*).

5 The respondent's grounds of appeal are: (*here state the grounds of appeal*).

Date   Signed

RULE 8

Form 4
Application to the Employment Appeal Tribunal for Compensation for Exclusion or Expulsion from a Trade Union or for Compensation
or an Order in respect of Unjustifiable Discipline

1 My name is
  My address is

2 Any communication relating to this application may be sent to me at (*state address for service, including telephone number, if any*).

3 My complaint against (*state the name and address of the trade union*) was declared to be well-founded by (*state tribunal*) on (*give date of decision or order*).

4 (*Where the application relates to exclusion or expulsion from a trade union*) I have not been admitted/re-admitted* to membership of the above-named trade union and hereby apply for compensation on the following grounds.

(*Where the application relates to unjustifiable discipline*) The determination infringing my right not to be unjustifiably disciplined has not been revoked./The trade union has failed to take all the steps necessary for securing the reversal of things done for the purpose of giving effect to the determination.*

(*Delete as appropriate)

Date   Signed

NB – A copy of the decision or order declaring the complaint against the trade union to be well-founded must be enclosed with this application.

Form 5

Notice of appearance to Application to Employment Appeal Tribunal for Compensation for Exclusion or Expulsion from a Trade Union or for Compensation or an Order in respect of Unjustifiable Discipline

1 The respondent trade union is (*name and address of union*).
2 Any communication relating to this application may be sent to the respondent at (*respondent's address for service, including telephone number, if any*).
3 The respondent intends to resist the application of (*here give name of the applicant*). The grounds on which the respondent will rely are as follows:
4 (*Where the application relates to exclusion or expulsion from the trade union, state whether or not the applicant had been admitted or re-admitted to membership on or before the date of application.*)
   (*Where the application relates to unjustifiable discipline, state whether–*
   (a) the determination infringing the applicant's right not to be unjustifiably disciplined has been revoked; and
   (b) the trade union has taken all the steps necessary for securing the reversal of anything done for the purpose of giving effect to the determination.*)

Date   Signed

Position in union

RULE 13

Form 6

Application to the Employment Appeal Tribunal Under Section 136A of the Employment Protection (Consolidation) Act 1978 for a Restriction of Proceedings Order

1 The applicant is (*the Attorney General/Lord Advocate*).
2 Any communication relating to this application may be sent to the applicant at (*state address for service, including telephone number*).
3 The application is for a restriction of proceedings order to be made against (*state the name and address of the person against whom the order is sought*).
4 An affidavit in support of the application is attached.

Date   Signed

RULE 15

Form 7

Notice of appearance to Application to the Employment Appeal Tribunal under section 136A of the Employment Protection (Consolidation) Act 1978 for a Restriction of Proceedings Order

1 The respondent is (*state name and address of respondent*).
2 Any communication relating to this application may be sent to the respondent at (*respondent's address for service, including telephone number, if any*).

3 The respondent intends to resist the application. An affidavit in support is attached to this notice.

Date   Signed

Employment Appeal Tribunal (Amendment) Rules 2001 SI No 1128

Citation, commencement and interpretation

1 (1) These Rules may be cited as the Employment Appeal Tribunal (Amendment) Rules 2001 and shall come into force on 18th April 2001.

(2) In these Rules, any reference to a rule or to the Schedule is a reference to a rule in, or to the Schedule to, the Employment Appeal Tribunal Rules 1993.

Amendment of rules

2 For rule 2 substitute –

'Interpretation

2(1) In these rules –

'the 1992 Act' means the Trade Union and Labour Relations (Consolidation) Act 1992;

'the 1996 Act' means the Employment Tribunals Act 1996;

'the 1999 Regulations' means the Transnational Information and Consultation of Employees Regulations 1999;

'the Appeal Tribunal' means the Employment Appeal Tribunal established under section 87 of the Employment Protection Act 1975 and continued in existence under section 20(1) of the 1996 Act and includes the President, a judge, a member or the Registrar acting on behalf of the Tribunal;

'the CAC' means the Central Arbitration Committee;

'the Certification Officer' means the person appointed to be the Certification Officer under section 254(2) of the 1992 Act;

'costs officer' means any officer of the Appeal Tribunal authorised by the President to assess costs or expenses;

'Crown employment proceedings' has the meaning given by section 10(8) of the 1996 Act;

'excluded person' means, in relation to any proceedings, a person who has been excluded from all or part of the proceedings by virtue of –

(a) a direction of a Minister of the Crown under rule 30A(1)(b) or (c); or

(b) an order of the Appeal Tribunal under rule 30A(2)(a) read with rule 30A(1)(b) or (c);

'judge' means a judge of the Appeal Tribunal nominated under section 22(1)(a) or (b) of the 1996 Act and includes a judge nominated under section 23(2) of, or a judge appointed under section 24(1) of, the 1996 Act to be a temporary additional judge of the Appeal Tribunal;

'member' means a member of the Appeal Tribunal appointed under section 22(1)(c) of the 1996 Act and includes a member appointed under section 23(3) of the 1996 Act to act temporarily in the place of a member appointed under that section;

'the President' means the judge appointed under section 22(3) of the 1996 Act to be President of the Appeal Tribunal and includes a judge nominated under section 23(1) of the 1996 Act to act temporarily in his place;

'the Registrar' means the person appointed to be Registrar of the Appeal Tribunal and includes any officer of the Tribunal authorised by the President to act on behalf of the Registrar;

'the Secretary of Employment Tribunals' means the person acting for the time being as the Secretary of the Central Office of the Employment Tribunals (England and Wales) or, as may be appropriate, of the Central Office of the Employment Tribunals (Scotland);

'special advocate' means a person appointed pursuant to rule 30A(4).

(2) In rules 3 and 6, 'national security appeal' means an appeal from a decision or order of an employment tribunal in respect of which the Minister directed the employment tribunal under rule 7B(3), or the employment tribunal took steps under rule 8(2)(c), of Schedule 1 to the Employment Tribunals (Constitution and Rules of Procedure) Regulations 2001 or of Schedule 1 to the Employment Tribunals (Constitution and Rules of Procedure) (Scotland) Regulations 2001(as inserted by Schedule 2, or Part II of Schedule 3, to those Regulations) to keep secret all or part of the reasons for the employment tribunal's decision or order.

(3) Any reference in these Rules to a person who was the applicant or, as the case may be, the respondent in the proceedings before an employment tribunal includes, where those proceedings are still continuing, a reference to a person who is the applicant or, as the case may be, is the respondent in those proceedings.'

3   For rule 3, substitute –

'Institution of Appeal

3(1) Every appeal to the Appeal Tribunal shall, subject to paragraphs (2) and (4), be instituted by serving on the Tribunal the following documents –

    (a) a notice of appeal in, or substantially in, accordance with Form 1, 1A or 2 in the Schedule to these rules;

    (b) a copy of the decision or order of an employment tribunal or of the Certification Officer which is the subject of the appeal; (c) in the case of an appeal from an employment tribunal, a copy of the extended written reasons for the decision or order of that tribunal; and (d) in the case of an appeal made pursuant to regulation 38(8) of the 1999 Regulations from a declaration or order of the CAC, a copy of that declaration or order.

(2) The appellant shall not be required by virtue of paragraph (1)(c) to serve on the Appeal Tribunal a copy of the extended written reasons for the decision or order of the employment tribunal in a national security appeal in relation to which –

(a) the appellant was the applicant in the proceedings before the employment tribunal; and

(b) the extended written reasons were not sent to the appellant,

but if the appellant received a document containing some of the reasons for the employment tribunal's decision or order, he shall serve on the Appeal Tribunal a copy of that document.

(3) The period within which an appeal to the Appeal Tribunal may be instituted is –

(a) 42 days from the date on which extended written reasons for the decision or order of the employment tribunal were sent to the appellant;

(b) in the case of a national security appeal in relation to which the appellant was the applicant in the proceedings before the employment tribunal, 42 days from the date on which the document containing some of the reasons for the decision or order was sent to the appellant, or if no reasons were disclosed to the appellant, 42 days from the date on which a copy of the decision or order was sent to the appellant;

(c) in the case of an appeal from a decision of the Certification Officer, 42 days from the date on which the written record of that decision was sent to the appellant;

(d) in the case of an appeal from a declaration or order of the CAC under regulation 38(8) of the 1999 Regulations, 42 days from the date on which the written notification of that declaration or order was sent to the appellant.

(4) In the case of a national security appeal, the appellant shall not set out the grounds of appeal in his notice of appeal and shall not append to his notice of appeal the extended written reasons for the decision or order of the tribunal.

(5) In a national security appeal in relation to which the appellant was the respondent in the proceedings before the employment tribunal, the appellant shall, within the period described in paragraph (3)(a), provide to the Appeal Tribunal a document setting out the grounds on which the appeal is brought.

(6) In a national security appeal in relation to which the appellant was the applicant in the proceedings before the employment tribunal –

(a) the appellant may, within the period described in paragraph (3)(b), provide to the Appeal Tribunal a document setting out the grounds on which the appeal is brought; and

(b) a special advocate appointed in respect of the appellant may, within the period described in paragraph 3(b), or within 21 days of his appointment, whichever is later, provide to the Appeal Tribunal a document setting out the grounds on which the appeal is brought or providing supplementary grounds of appeal.

(7) Where it appears to the Registrar that the grounds of appeal stated in the notice of appeal, or in the document provided under paragraph (5) or (6), do not give the Appeal Tribunal jurisdiction to entertain the appeal, he shall notify the appellant or the special advocate accordingly informing him of the

reasons for the opinion and, subject to paragraphs (8) and (10), no further action shall be taken on the appeal.

(8) Where notification has been given under paragraph (7), the appellant or the special advocate, as the case may be, may serve a fresh notice of appeal, or a fresh document under paragraph (5) or (6), within the time remaining under paragraph (3) or (6) or within 28 days from the date on which the Registrar's notification was sent to him, whichever is the longer period.

(9) Where the appellant or the special advocate serves a fresh notice of appeal or a fresh document under paragraph (8), the Registrar shall consider such fresh notice of appeal or document with regard to jurisdiction as though it were an original notice of appeal lodged pursuant to paragraphs (1) and (3), or as though it were an original document provided pursuant to paragraph (5) or (6), as the case may be.

(10) Where an appellant or a special advocate expresses dissatisfaction in writing with the reasons given by the Registrar, under paragraph (7), for his opinion that the grounds of appeal stated in a notice, or provided in a document under paragraph (5) or (6), do not give the Appeal Tribunal jurisdiction to entertain the appeal, the Registrar shall place the papers before the President or a judge for his direction as to whether any further action should be taken on the appeal.'.

4   In rule 4 –

(a) at the beginning, insert '(1)';

(b) in sub-paragraph (d), omit the words 'Part VI of the 1978 Act or';

(c) after the words 'the 1992 Act', insert the words 'or Part XI of the Employment Rights Act 1996'; and

(d) at the end insert –

'; or

    (e) the Chairman of the CAC in the case of an appeal from the CAC under regulation 38(8) of the 1999 Regulations.

(2) On receipt of a document provided under rule 3(5) –

    (a) the Registrar shall not send the document to a person in respect of whom a Minister of the Crown has informed the Registrar that he wishes to address the Appeal Tribunal in accordance with rule 30A(3) with a view to the Appeal Tribunal making an order applicable to this stage of the proceedings under rule 30A(2)(a) read with 30A(1)(b) or (c) (exclusion of a party or his representative), at any time before the Appeal Tribunal decides whether or not to make such an order; but if it decides not to make such an order, the Registrar shall, subject to sub-paragraph (b), send the document to such a person 14 days after the Appeal Tribunal's decision not to make the order; and

    (b) the Registrar shall not send a copy of the document to an excluded person, but if a special advocate is appointed in respect of such a person, the Registrar shall send a copy of the document to the special advocate.

(3) On receipt of a document provided under rule 3(6)(a) or (b), the Registrar shall not send a copy of the document to an excluded person, but shall send a copy of the document to the respondent'.

5 In rule 5 –
(a) in sub-paragraph (a), for the words 'section 95 or 104', substitute the words 'section 45D, 56A, 95, 104 or 108C';
(b) in sub-paragraph (b), for the words 'section 9', substitute the words 'section 9 or 126'; and
(c) at the end of sub-paragraph (b), insert –
'(c) in the case of an appeal made pursuant to regulation 38(8) of the 1999 Regulations from a declaration or order of the CAC, the parties (other than the appellant) to the proceedings before the CAC'.

6 In rule 6 –
(a) in paragraph (2) –
  (i) after the words 'resist an appeal shall,', insert the words 'subject to paragraph (6), and';
  (ii) after the words 'rule 5(a)', insert the words 'or 5(c)';
  (iii) for the words 'or the Certification Officer', substitute the words ', the Certification Officer or the CAC'; and
  (iv) after the word 'decision', insert the word ', declaration';
(b) in paragraph (3), after the words 'cross-appeal may,', insert the words 'subject to paragraph (6),'; and (c) after paragraph (5), insert –
'(6) In a national security appeal, the respondent shall not set out the grounds on which he relies in his answer to an appeal, nor include in his answer a statement of the grounds of any cross-appeal.
(7) In a national security appeal in relation to which the respondent was not the applicant in the proceedings before the employment tribunal, the respondent shall, within the time appointed under paragraph (1), provide to the Registrar a document, setting out the grounds on which he intends to resist the appeal, and may include in that document a statement of the grounds of any cross-appeal.
(8) In a national security appeal in relation to which the respondent was the applicant in the proceedings before the employment tribunal –
  (a) the respondent may, within the time appointed under paragraph (1) provide to the Registrar a document, setting out the grounds on which he intends to resist the appeal, and may include in that document a statement of the grounds of any cross-appeal; and
  (b) a special advocate appointed in respect of the respondent may, within the time appointed under paragraph (1), or within 21 days of his appointment, whichever is the later, provide to the Registrar a document, setting out the grounds, or the supplementary grounds, on which the respondent intends to resist the appeal, and may include in that document a statement of the grounds, or the supplementary grounds, of any cross-appeal.
(9) In a national security appeal, if the respondent, or any special advocate appointed in respect of a respondent, provides in the document containing grounds for resisting an appeal a statement of grounds of cross-appeal and the appellant wishes to resist the cross-appeal –
  (a) where the appellant was not the applicant in the proceedings before the employment tribunal, the appellant shall within a time to be appointed by the Appeal Tribunal deliver to the

Tribunal a reply in writing setting out the grounds on which he relies; and

(b) where the appellant was the applicant in the proceedings before the employment tribunal, the appellant, or any special advocate appointed in respect of him, may within a time to be appointed by the Appeal Tribunal deliver to the Tribunal a reply in writing setting out the grounds on which the appellant relies.

(10) Any document provided under paragraph (7) or (9)(a) shall be treated by the Registrar in accordance with rule 4(2), as though it were a document received under rule 3(5). (11) Any document provided under paragraph (8) or (9)(b) shall be treated by the Registrar in accordance with rule 4(3), as though it were a document received under rule 3(6)(a) or (b).'

7   In rule 7(1) –

(a) in sub-paragraph (d), for the words 'Part VI of the 1978 Act' substitute the words 'Part XI of the Employment Rights Act 1996'; and

(b) at the end of sub-paragraph (d), insert –

' ; or

(e) the Chairman of the CAC in the case of an appeal from a declaration or order of, or arising in any proceedings before, the CAC under regulation 38(8) of the 1999 Regulations'.

8   In rule 13, for the words 'section 136A', substitute the words 'section 33 of the 1996 Act'.

9   After rule 16 insert –

'Complaints under regulations 20 and 21 of the 1999 Regulations
16A Every complaint under regulation 20 or 21 of the 1999 Regulations shall be made by way of application in writing in, or substantially in, accordance with Form 4A in the Schedule to these Rules and shall be served on the Appeal Tribunal.

Service of application under rule 16A
16B On receipt of an application under rule 16A, the Registrar shall seal it with the Appeal Tribunal's seal and shall serve a sealed copy on the applicant and on the respondent.

Appearance by respondent
16C A respondent wishing to resist an application under rule 16A shall within 14 days of receiving the sealed copy of the application enter an appearance in, or substantially in, accordance with Form 5A in the Schedule to these Rules and setting out the grounds on which the respondent relies.
16D On receipt of the notice of appearance under rule 16C the Registrar shall serve a copy of it on the applicant.'

10   In rule 17, for the words 'or rule 13', substitute the words ',13 or 16A'.

11   In rule 20 –

(a) in paragraphs (2) and (3), for the words 'paragraph 16(1) and (2) of Schedule 11', substitute the words 'section 28 of the 1996 Act'; and

(b) omit paragraph (4).

12   In rule 21(1) –

(a) omit the words '(subject to rule 22(2))'; and

(b) for the words 'paragraph 16(1) and (2) of Schedule 11', substitute the words 'section 28 of the 1996 Act'.

13 In rule 22 –

(a) in paragraph (1), for the words 'rule 30', substitute the words 'any direction of a Minister of the Crown under rule 30A(1) or order of the Appeal Tribunal under rule 30A(2)(a) read with rule 30A(1),'; and

(b) omit paragraph (2).

14 In rule 23 –

(a) in paragraph (1), for the words 'paragraph 18A of Schedule 11', substitute the words 'section 31 of the 1996 Act'; and

(b) in paragraph (6), for the words 'rule 30', substitute the words 'any direction of a Minister of the Crown under rule 30A(1) or order of the Appeal Tribunal under rule 30A(2)(a) read with rule 30A(1),'.

15 In rule 23A(1), for the words 'Employment Tribunals Act 1996', substitute the words '1996 Act'.

16 In rule 26, for the words 'or section 136A', substitute the words – ', section 33 of the 1996 Act or regulation 20 or 21 of the 1999 Regulations'. .

17 In rule 27, after paragraph (1) insert –

'(1A) Where –

(a) a Minister has at any stage issued a direction under rule 30A(1)(b) or (c) (exclusion of a party or his representative), or the Appeal Tribunal has at any stage made an order under rule 30A(2)(a) read with rule 30A(1)(b) or (c); and

(b) the Appeal Tribunal is considering whether to impose, or has imposed, a requirement under paragraph (1) on any person, the Minister (whether or not he is a party to the proceedings) may make an application to the Appeal Tribunal objecting to the imposition of a requirement under paragraph (1) or, where a requirement has been imposed, an application to vary or set aside the requirement, as the case may be. The Appeal Tribunal shall hear and determine the Minister's application in private and the Minister shall be entitled to address the Appeal Tribunal thereon. The application shall be made by notice to the Registrar and the Registrar shall give notice of the application to each party.'.

18 In rule 29 –

(a) in paragraph (1) –

(i) for the words 'rule 30', substitute the words 'any direction of a Minister of the Crown under rule 30A(1)(a) or order of the Appeal Tribunal under rule 30A(2)(a) read with rule 30A(1)(a),'; and

(ii) for the words 'paragraph 16 of Schedule 11', substitute the words 'section 28 of the 1996 Act'; and

(b) for paragraph (2), substitute –

'(2) Notwithstanding paragraph (1), the Appeal Tribunal may sit in private for the purpose of hearing evidence from any person which in the opinion of the Tribunal is likely to consist of–

(a) information which he could not disclose without contravening a prohibition imposed by or by virtue of any enactment;

(b) information which has been communicated to him in confidence or which he has otherwise obtained in consequence of the confidence reposed in him by another person; or

(c) information the disclosure of which would, for reasons other than its effect on negotiations with respect to any of the matters mentioned in section 178(2) of the 1992 Act, cause substantial injury to any undertaking of his or in which he works.'.

19   For rule 30, substitute –

'**Duty of Appeal Tribunal concerning disclosure of information**

30 When exercising its functions, the Appeal Tribunal shall ensure that information is not disclosed contrary to the interests of national security.

Proceedings in cases concerning national security

30A(1) A Minister of the Crown (whether or not he is a party to the proceedings) may, if he considers it expedient in the interests of national security, direct the Appeal Tribunal by notice to the Registrar to –

(a) sit in private for all or part of particular Crown employment proceedings;

(b) exclude any party who was the applicant in the proceedings before the employment tribunal from all or part of particular Crown employment proceedings;

(c) exclude the representatives of any party who was the applicant in the proceedings before the employment tribunal from all or part of particular Crown employment proceedings;

(d) take steps to conceal the identity of a particular witness in particular Crown employment proceedings.

(2) The Appeal Tribunal may, if it considers it expedient in the interests of national security, by order –

(a) do anything of a kind which the Appeal Tribunal can be required to do by direction under paragraph (1) of this rule;

(b) direct any person to whom any document (including any decision or record of the proceedings) has been provided for the purposes of the proceedings not to disclose any such document or the content thereof –

(i)   to any excluded person;

(ii)   in any case in which a direction has been given under paragraph (1)(a) or an order has been made under paragraph (2)(a) read with paragraph (1)(a), to any person excluded from all or part of the proceedings by virtue of such direction or order; or

(iii)   in any case in which a Minister of the Crown has informed the Registrar in accordance with paragraph (3) that he wishes to address the Appeal Tribunal with a view to the Tribunal making an order under paragraph (2)(a) read with paragraph (1)(b) or (c), to any person who may be excluded from all or part of the proceedings by virtue of such an order, if an order is made, at any time before the Appeal Tribunal decides whether or not to make such an order;

(c) take steps to keep secret all or part of the reasons for any order it makes.

The Appeal Tribunal shall keep under review any order it makes under this paragraph.

(3) In any proceedings in which a Minister of the Crown considers that it

would be appropriate for the Appeal Tribunal to make an order as referred to in paragraph (2), he shall (whether or not he is a party to the proceedings) be entitled to appear before and to address the Appeal Tribunal thereon. The Minister shall inform the Registrar by notice that he wishes to address the Appeal Tribunal and the Registrar shall copy the notice to the parties.

(4) In any proceedings in which there is an excluded person, the Appeal Tribunal shall inform the Attorney General or, in the case of an appeal from an employment tribunal in Scotland, the Advocate General for Scotland, of the proceedings before it with a view to the Attorney General (or, as the case may be, the Advocate General), if he thinks it fit to do so, appointing a special advocate to represent the interests of the person who was the applicant in the proceedings before the employment tribunal in respect of those parts of the proceedings from which –

(a) any representative of his is excluded;

(b) both he and his representative are excluded; or

(c) he is excluded, where he does not have a representative.

(5) A special advocate shall have a general qualification within the meaning of section 71 of the Courts and Legal Services Act 1990, or, in the case of an appeal from an employment tribunal in Scotland, shall be –

(a) an advocate; or

(b) a solicitor who has by virtue of section 25A of the Solicitors (Scotland) Act 1980 rights of audience in the Court of Session or the High Court of Justiciary.

(6) Where the excluded person is a party to the proceedings, he shall be permitted to make a statement to the Appeal Tribunal before the commencement of the proceedings, or the part of the proceedings, from which he is excluded.

(7) Except in accordance with paragraphs (8) to (10), the special advocate may not communicate directly or indirectly with any person (including an excluded person) –

(a) (except in the case of the Appeal Tribunal or the party who was the respondent in the proceedings before the employment tribunal) on any matter contained in the documents referred to in rule 3(5), 3(6), 6(7) or 6(8)(b); or

(b) (except in the case of a person who was present) on any matter discussed or referred to during any part of the proceedings in which the Appeal Tribunal sat in private pursuant to a direction of the Minister under paragraph (1)(a) or an order of the Appeal Tribunal under paragraph (2)(a) read with paragraph (1)(a).

(8) The special advocate may apply for directions from the Appeal Tribunal authorising him to seek instructions from, or otherwise to communicate with, an excluded person –

(a) on any matter contained in the documents referred to in rule 3(5), 3(6), 6(7) or 6(8)(b); or

(b) on any matter discussed or referred to during any part of the proceedings in which the Appeal Tribunal sat in private as referred to in paragraph (7)(b).

(9) An application under paragraph (8) shall be made by presenting to the

Registrar a notice of application, which shall state the title of the proceedings and set out the grounds of the application.

(10) The Registrar shall notify the Minister of an application for directions under paragraph (8) and the Minister shall be entitled to address the Appeal Tribunal on the application.

(11) In these rules, in any case in which a special advocate has been appointed in respect of a party, any reference to a party shall (save in those references specified in paragraph (12)) include the special advocate.

(12) The references mentioned in paragraph (11) are those in rules 5 and 18, the first and second references in rule 27(1A), paragraphs (1) and (6) of this rule, the first reference in paragraph (3) of this rule, rule 34(1), the reference in item 4 of Form 1, and in item 4 of Form 1A, in the Schedule to these Rules.'.

20　In rule 31 –

(a) in paragraph (1)(a), for the words 'section 136A', substitute the words 'section 33 of the 1996 Act';

(b) at the end of paragraph (1)(a), omit the word 'or';

(c) at the end of paragraph (1)(b), insert –

'(c) in the case of an order imposing a penalty notice under regulation 20 or 21 of the 1999 Regulations, on the Secretary of State; or (d) in the case of an order disposing of an appeal from the CAC made under regulation 38(8) of the 1999 Regulations, on the Chairman of the CAC'; and

(d) at the beginning of paragraph (2), insert the words 'Subject to rule 31A,'.

21　After rule 31, insert –

'Reasons for orders in cases concerning national security

31A(1) Paragraphs (1) to (5) of this rule apply to the document setting out the reasons for the Appeal Tribunal's order prepared under rule 31(2) or any reasoned judgment of the Appeal Tribunal as referred to in rule 31(2), in any particular Crown employment proceedings in which a direction of a Minister of the Crown has been given under rule 30A(1)(a), (b) or (c) or an order of the Appeal Tribunal has been made under rule 30A(2)(a) read with rule 30A(1)(a), (b) or (c).

(2) Before the Appeal Tribunal gives its reasons in writing for any order or delivers any reasoned judgment, the Registrar shall send a copy of the reasons or judgment to the Minister.

(3) If the Minister considers it expedient in the interests of national security, he may –

(a) direct the Appeal Tribunal that the document containing its reasons for any order or its reasoned judgment shall not be disclosed to any person who was excluded from all or part of the proceedings and to prepare a further document setting out the reasons for its order, or a further reasoned judgment, but with the omission of such reasons as are specified in the direction; or

(b) direct the Appeal Tribunal that the document containing its reasons for any order or its reasoned judgment shall not be disclosed to any person who was excluded from all or part of the proceedings, but that no further document setting out the Appeal Tribunal's reasons for its order or further reasoned judgment should be prepared.

(4) Where the Minister has directed the Appeal Tribunal in accordance with paragraph (3)(a), the document prepared pursuant to that direction shall be marked in each place where an omission has been made. The document may then be given by the Registrar to the parties. (5) The Registrar shall send the document prepared pursuant to a direction of the Minister in accordance with paragraph (3)(a) and the full document without the omissions made pursuant to that direction –

(a) to whichever of the appellant and the respondent was not the applicant in the proceedings before the employment tribunal;

(b) if he was not an excluded person, to the person who was the applicant in the proceedings before the employment tribunal and, if he was not an excluded person, to his representative;

(c) if applicable, to the special advocate; and

(d) where there are proceedings before a superior court relating to the order in question, to that court.

(6) Where the Appeal Tribunal intends to take steps under rule 30A(2)(c) to keep secret all or part of the reasons for any order it makes, it shall send the full reasons for its order to the persons listed in sub-paragraphs (a) to (d) of paragraph (5), as appropriate.'.

22 In rule 34(2), for the words 'taxing officer' substitute the words 'costs officer'.

23 At the end of rule 37, insert –

'(4) An application for an extension of the time prescribed for the institution of an appeal under rule 3 shall not be heard until the notice of appeal has been served on the Appeal Tribunal.'.

24 In the Schedule, after Form 1, insert –

'FORM 1A

Rule 3

Notice of Appeal from the CAC made pursuant to regulation 38(8) of the Transnational Information and Consultation of Employees Regulations 1999

1 The appellant is (*name and address of appellant*).

2 Any communication relating to this appeal may be sent to the appellant at (*appellant's address for service, including telephone number if any*).

3 The appellant appeals from (*here give particulars of the decision, declaration or order of the CAC from which the appeal is brought including the date*).

4 The parties to the proceedings before the CAC, other than the appellant, were (*names and addresses of other parties to the proceedings resulting in decision appealed from*).

5 A copy of the CAC's decision, declaration or order appealed from is attached to this notice.

6 The grounds upon which this appeal is brought are that the CAC erred in law in that (*here set out in paragraphs the various grounds of appeal*).

Date   Signed'.

25 In the Schedule after Form 4 insert –
'FORM 4A
Rule 16A
Application under regulation 20 or 21 of the Transnational Information and Consultation of Employees Regulations 1999
1 The applicant is (*name and address of applicant*)
2 Any communication relating to this application may be sent to the applicant at (*state address for service, including telephone number, if any*).
3 The application is made against (*state identity or, where applicable, identities of respondents*) who is/are, or is/are representative of, the central or local management/the European Works Council/one or more information and consultation representatives (*delete what does not apply*).
4 The address(es) of the respondent(s) is/are
5 My complaint against the respondent(s) is that it/they failed to comply with its/their obligations under regulation 20 or 21 of the Transnational Information and Consultation of Employees Regulations 1999 as follows (*give particulars, set out in paragraphs and making reference to the specific provisions in the 1999 Regulations alleged to have been breached*).

Date   Signed'.

26 In the Schedule, after Form 5, insert –
'FORM 5A
Rule 16C
Notice of Appearance to the Employment Appeal Tribunal under regulation 20 or 21 of the Transnational Information and Consultation of Employees Regulations 1999
1 The respondent is (*name and address of respondent*)
2 Any communication relating to this application may be sent to the respondent at (*respondent's address for service, including telephone number, if any*)
3 The respondent intends to resist the application of (*here give the name or description of the applicant*)
The grounds on which the respondent will rely are as follows: (*give particulars, set out in paragraphs and making reference to the specific provisions in the Transnational Information and Consultation of Employees Regulations 1999 alleged to have been breached*)

Date   Signed

Position in respondent company or undertaking:

(*Where appropriate give position in respondent central or local management or position held in relation to respondent Works Council*)'.

27 In the Schedule in Forms 6 and 7, for the words 'section 136A of the Employment Protection (Consolidation) Act 1978', substitute the words 'section 33 of the 1996 Act'.

Transitional provision

28 The amendments to the Employment Appeal Tribunal Rules 1993 made by these Rules shall apply in relation to all proceedings to which they relate, irrespective of when those proceedings were commenced.

Employment Appeal Tribunal Practice Direction 1996

1 **Introduction**

(1) This Practice Direction supersedes *Practice Direction (EAT: Procedure)* [1981] ICR 287 issued on 17 February 1981 and *Practice Direction (EAT: Preliminary Hearing)* [1985] ICR 684 issued on 15 July 1985.

(2) The Employment Appeal Tribunal Rules 1993 (SI 1993/2854)('the Rules') came into operation on 16 December 1993*. [*NOW AMENDED BY 2001 RULES]

(3) By virtue of paragraph 17(2) of Schedule 11 to the Employment Protection (Consolidation) Act 1978 the Employment Appeal Tribunal ('the appeal tribunal') has power, subject to the Rules, to regulate its own procedure.

(4) Where the Rules do not otherwise provide, the following procedure will apply to all appeals to the appeal tribunal.

(5) The provisions of this Practice Direction are subject to any specific directions which the appeal tribunal may make in any individual case: but, subject to that, the directions set out below must be complied with in all cases.

(6) The Practice Direction comes into force on 15 April 1996.

2 **Institution of appeal**

(1) The notice of appeal must be in, or substantially in, accordance with Forms 1 or 2 of the Schedule to the Rules and, in the case of an appeal from an [employment] tribunal, a copy of the extended written reasons for the decision or order of that tribunal must also be served on the appeal tribunal.

(2) Where a request for extended written reasons has been refused by the [employment] tribunal, an appellant may appeal against that refusal and may also apply to the appeal tribunal to exercise its discretion to hear the appeal on summary reasons only.

(3) The notice of appeal must clearly identify the point of law which forms the ground of appeal from the decision of the [employment] tribunal to the appeal tribunal. It may also state the order which the appellant will ask the appeal tribunal to make at the hearing.

(4) Subject to rule 3(3) of the Rules, if it appears to the registrar that a notice of appeal or an application gives insufficient particulars of, or lacks clarity in identifying, a point of law, the registrar may postpone the decision under rule 3(3) pending amplification or clarification of the notice of appeal by the intending appellant or applicant.

(5) It is not acceptable for an appellant to state as a ground of appeal simply that 'the decision was contrary to the evidence' or that 'there was no evidence to support the decision' or that 'the decision was one that no reasonable tribunal could have reached and was perverse' or similar general grounds, unless the notice of appeal also sets out full and sufficient particulars of the matters relied on in support of those general grounds.

(6) It is not permissible for the parties (either the appellant in his notice of appeal or the respondent in the respondent's answer) to reserve a right to amend, alter or add to any pleading. No such right exists in the Rules. Amendment can only be made pursuant to an order on an interlocutory application and that should be made as soon as the need for amendment is known.

(7) The processing of the appeal will be accelerated if the appellant also serves on the appeal tribunal, with the notice of appeal, a copy of the originating application (IT1) and of the notice of appearance (IT3).

(8) A respondent who wishes to resist the appeal and/or to cross-appeal, but has not delivered a respondent's answer as directed by the registrar, may, unless leave is granted to serve an answer out of time, be precluded from taking part in the appeal.

3   **Appeals out of time**

(1) By virtue of rule 3(2) of the Rules every appeal under section 136 of the Act of 1978, or section 4 of the Employment Act 1980, to the appeal tribunal shall be instituted by serving on the appeal tribunal, within 42 days from the date on which extended written reasons for the decision or order of the [employment] tribunal were sent to the appellant, a notice of appeal. Time runs even though the question of remedy and assessment of compensation by the [employment] tribunal has been adjourned and even though an application has been made to the [employment] tribunal for a review.

(2) Every notice of appeal served after the expiration of the prescribed period of 42 days must be accompanied by a written application for an extension of time, explaining clearly and concisely the reasons for delay in serving the notice of appeal.

(3) Applications for an extension of time for appealing cannot be considered until a notice of appeal in the prescribed form has been served.

(4) Unless otherwise ordered, the application for extension of time will be considered and determined as though it were an interlocutory application to the registrar, who will normally determine the application in the first instance after inviting and considering written representations from each side. An interlocutory appeal lies from the registrar's decision to a judge. Such an appeal must be notified within five days of the decision of the registrar.

(5) In determining whether to extend the time for appealing particular attention will be paid to whether any good excuse for the delay has been shown and to the guidance contained in the decisions of the appeal tribunal, as recently summarised in *United Arab Emirates v Abdelghafar* [1995] ICR 65.

(6) It is not usually a good reason for late service of a notice of appeal that

an application for legal aid has been made, but not yet determined, or that support is being sought from, but has not yet been provided by, some other body, such as a trade union or the Equal Opportunities Commission or the Commission for Racial Equality.

(7) In any case of doubt or difficulty, a notice of appeal should be served in time and an application made to the registrar for directions.

4   **Interlocutory applications**

(1) On receipt of an interlocutory application the registrar will send a copy of the application to the other side and will indicate that, if it is not intended to oppose the application, it may be unnecessary for the parties to be heard and that the appropriate order may be made without an oral hearing.

(2) Where the application is opposed the registrar will usually determine the application on the basis of written submissions.

(3) Save where the President or a judge otherwise directs, every interlocutory application to strike out an appeal or pleading or to debar a party from taking any further part in the proceedings pursuant to the Rules will be heard on the day appointed for the hearing of the appeal immediately preceding the hearing of the appeal.

5   **Meeting for directions**

(1) In some cases the registrar may, where necessary, appoint a day when the parties should attend on an appointment for directions after the service of the respondent's answer or of a reply to a cross-appeal.

(2) The registrar will normally give written directions, including fixing a date for the hearing of the appeal.

6   **Exhibits and documents for use at the hearing**

(1) The appeal tribunal will prepare copies of all documents for use by members of the appeal tribunal at the hearing, in addition to those which the registrar is required to serve on the parties under the Rules.

(2) It is the responsibility of the parties to ensure that all documents submitted for consideration at the hearing are capable of being legibly photocopied.

(3) It is the duty of the parties or their advisers to ensure that only those documents are included which are (a) relevant to the point of law raised in the appeal *and* (b) likely to be referred to at the hearing. The relevant contract of employment should usually be included.

(4) It is the responsibility of the parties or their advisers to ensure that all exhibits and documents used before the [employment] tribunal which are considered to be necessary for use at the hearing of the appeal are sent to the appeal tribunal as soon as possible after the service of the notice of appeal and at least six weeks before the date fixed for the hearing of the appeal. This will enable the appeal tribunal staff to prepare in advance of the hearing sufficient copies, to number pages and to compile an index for the use of the members of the appeal tribunal at the hearing.

(5) At least four weeks before a full hearing a copy of the index will be sent

by the appeal tribunal to the parties or their advisers so that they may prepare their bundles of documents in the same order.

7   Chairman's notes of evidence

(This part of the Practice Direction does not apply to appeals heard in Scotland)

(1) An appellant who considers that a point of law raised in the notice of appeal cannot be argued without access to copies of the chairman's notes of evidence should submit with the notice of appeal an application for production of the chairman's notes or should make an application in writing as soon as possible after service of the notice of appeal.

(2) Any other party seeking production of chairman's notes of evidence should make a written application for them to the appeal tribunal (*not* to the [employment] tribunal) as soon as possible after the service of the notice of appeal and, in the case of a respondent, the application should accompany the respondent's answer.

(3) The application must in either case explain why it is considered necessary to refer to the chairman's notes in order to argue the point of law raised in the notice of appeal or respondent's answer. The application must identify:

(a) the issues in the notice of appeal or respondent's answer to which the notes of evidence are relevant; and

(b) the names of the witnesses whose evidence is considered relevant; and

(c) the parts of their evidence alleged to be relevant.

(4) The application will be considered in the first instance by the registrar who may determine the application on written representations.

(5) A party dissatisfied with the registrar's decision on the application may request that the matter be referred to the President or to a judge of the appeal tribunal who may direct an oral hearing of the application.

(6) The appeal tribunal will only order production of the chairman's notes and the supply of copies to the parties if satisfied that all or parts of such notes are *necessary* for the purpose of arguing the point of law on the appeal.

(7) Notes of evidence are *not* ordered to be produced and supplied to the parties to enable them to check or double check the reasoning or findings in the decision against evidence given to or submissions made at the hearing or to enable the parties to embark on a 'fishing expedition' to establish grounds of appeal or additional grounds of appeal.

8   Skeleton arguments

(This part of the Practice Direction does not apply to appeals heard in Scotland unless otherwise directed by the Employment Appeal Tribunal Office in Edinburgh)

(1) Skeleton arguments should be provided by all parties in the case of all appeals, unless the appeal tribunal otherwise directs in individual cases. It is the practice of the appeal tribunal for all the members to read the papers in advance. A well structured skeleton argument helps the members and the

parties to focus on the point of law raised by the appeal and thereby makes the oral hearing more effective.

(2) A skeleton argument should be concise and should identify and summarise the points of law, the steps or stages in the legal argument and the statutory provisions and authorities to be relied upon, identifying them by name, page and paragraph and stating the legal proposition sought to be derived from them. It is not, however, the purpose of a skeleton argument to argue the case on paper in detail.

(3) The skeleton argument should state the form of order which the party will ask the appeal tribunal to make on the appeal: for example, in the case of the appellant, whether the appeal tribunal will be asked to remit the whole or part of the case to the same [employment] tribunal or to a different [employment] tribunal or whether the appeal tribunal will be asked to substitute a different decision for that of the [employment] tribunal.

(4) The appellant's skeleton argument should be accompanied by a written chronology of events relevant to the appeal which, if possible, should be agreed by the parties. That will normally be taken as an uncontroversial document, unless corrected by the respondent or the appeal tribunal.

(5) A skeleton argument may be served by the appellant with the notice of appeal or by the respondent with the respondent's answer or cross-appeal.

(6) Skeleton arguments should be exchanged by the parties and copies should be served on the appeal tribunal not less than two weeks before the date fixed for the hearing of the full appeal. In the case of preliminary hearings, the skeleton argument should be served by the appellant on the appeal tribunal at least seven days before the hearing or, if the preliminary hearing is fixed at less than seven days' notice, as soon as possible after the hearing date has been notified.

(7) In a case where the chairman's notes of evidence have been produced the skeleton argument should identify the parts of the notes to which that party wishes to refer. The skeleton argument should cross refer to the particular passages in the notes relied on. Where practicable the skeleton argument should be prepared using the pagination in the index to the appeal bundle.

(8) The fact that settlement negotiations are in progress in relation to the appeal does not excuse delay in lodging and exchanging skeleton arguments.

(9) Where a party is represented it is the duty of the representative to obtain the instructions necessary to enable him or her to comply with this procedure within the time limits.

(10) Failure to follow this procedure may lead to an adjournment of an appeal or even to dismissal for non-compliance with the Practice Direction.

9   Complaints about the conduct of the hearing by the [employment] tribunal

(1) A party who intends to complain about the conduct of the [employment] tribunal (for example, bias or improper conduct by the chairman or lay

members or procedural irregularities at the hearing) must include in the notice of appeal full and sufficient particulars of the complaint.

(2) In any such case the registrar may inquire of the party making the complaint whether it is intended to proceed with it. If so, the registrar will give appropriate directions for the hearing.

(3) Such directions will normally include the swearing and filing of affidavits by the complainant or his or her advisers or other witnesses or by the respondent or his or her advisers or any others who can give relevant evidence as to the facts which form the basis of the complaint and the provision of further particulars of the matters relied on.

(4) When the direction has been complied with the registrar will notify the chairman of the [employment] tribunal and provide copies of the notice of appeal, the affidavits and other relevant documents to the chairman so that he has and, if appropriate, the lay members of the [employment] tribunal have, an opportunity to comment on them. Those comments will be supplied by the appeal tribunal to the parties.

(5) A copy of any affidavit or of directions for further particulars will be supplied to the other side.

(6) The appeal tribunal will not permit complaints of the kind mentioned above to be raised or developed at the hearing of the appeal unless this procedure has been followed.

10   Admissibility of documents

(1) Where an application is made by a party to an appeal to put in, at the hearing of the appeal, any agreed document which was not before the [employment] tribunal, the application should be submitted in writing as soon as practicable after the service of the respondent's answer along with copies of the documents sought to be admitted at the hearing. Such documents may include a note of evidence given to the [employment] tribunal *only* if that note is agreed by both parties.

(2) The registrar shall forthwith communicate the nature of the application and of the documents sought to be admitted to the other party and, where appropriate, to the chairman of the [employment] tribunal for comments by him and, if appropriate, by the lay members.

(3) A copy of the comments will be forwarded to the party making the application by the registrar, who will either dispose of it in accordance with the Rules or refer it for a ruling at the hearing. A copy of the comments received from the chairman and lay members of the tribunal will be sent to both parties.

11   The right to inspect the Register and certain documents and to take copies

(1) Any document lodged in the Central Office of the Employment Appeal Tribunal in London or in the office of the appeal tribunal in Edinburgh in any proceedings before the appeal tribunal shall be sealed with the seal of the appeal tribunal showing the date and time on which the document was lodged.

(2) Particulars of the time of delivery at the Central Office of the Employment Appeal Tribunal or in the office of the appeal tribunal in Edinburgh of any document for filing or lodgment, the date of the document and the title of the appeal of which the document forms part of the record shall be entered in the Register of Cases kept in the Central Office and in Edinburgh or in the file which forms part of the Register of Cases.

(3) Any person shall be entitled during office hours to inspect and request a copy of any of the following documents filed or lodged in the Central Office or the office in Edinburgh, namely:

(a) any notice of appeal or any copy thereof;

(b) any judgment or order given or made in court or any copy of such judgment or order; and

(c) with the leave of the appeal tribunal, which may be granted on any application made ex parte, any other document.

(4) A copying charge per page will be payable for those documents mentioned in (3) above.

(5) Nothing in this provision shall be taken as preventing any party to an appeal inspecting and requesting a copy of any document filed or lodged in the Central Office or the office in Edinburgh before the commencement of the appeal, but made with a view to its commencement.

12 Listing of appeals

(1) Fast-track appeals

Full appeals are normally heard in the order in which they are received. However, there are times when it is deemed expedient to hear an appeal as soon as it can be fitted into the list. Appeals are placed in this category at the discretion of the President or the registrar and will normally fall into the following categories:

(a) appeals involving new legislation or changes to [employment] tribunal procedures;

(b) appeals involving reinstatement, re-engagement or interim relief;

(c) appeals on the outcome of which other applications to the [employment] tribunal depend;

(d) appeals which are likely to go forward to the Court of Appeal or to the European Court of Justice;

(e) appeals (including appeals on time limits) against decisions of an [employment] tribunal as to a party's entitlement to bring or contest proceedings;

(f) appeals concerning trade union rights (Trade Union and Labour Relations (Consolidation) Act 1992, section 67(2));

(g) appeals against interlocutory orders and directions of an [employment] tribunal (for example, adjournments, particulars, amendments, discovery and witness orders);

(h) appeals where the parties have made a reasoned case on the merits for an expedited hearing.

(2) Estimate of length of hearing

The lay members of the appeal tribunal are part-time members. They attend when available on pre-arranged dates. They do not sit for continuous periods. Consequently any appeals which run beyond their estimated length invariably have to be adjourned part heard (often with substantial delay) until a day on which both the lay members are available so that the same tribunal may be reconvened. To avoid inconvenience to the parties and to the appeal tribunal, and to avoid additional delay and costs suffered as a result of adjournment of part heard appeals, both parties are required to ensure that the estimates of length of hearing are accurate when first given and that any change in the estimate is notified immediately to the listing office, even if it is made as late as the day of the hearing. If the tribunal concludes that the hearing is likely to exceed the estimate, it may seek to avoid such adjournment by placing each side under appropriate time limits in order to complete the presentation of the submissions within the estimated time.

(3) Listing practice in England and Wales

(a) When all the appeal documents have been received and an index com- piled, the parties will be contacted to agree a hearing date. Once the agreed date is fixed the appeal will be set down in the list. In addition to this fixed date procedure a list (called an 'undated warned list') is drawn up at the beginning of each calendar month. Parties or their representa- tives will be notified that their case has been included in this list and preferred dates will be sought. When 'fixed date' cases are settled or withdrawn, cases from the 'undated warned list' will be substituted and parties notified as soon as possible of the hearing date. If a case in that list has been 'warned' but not reached, the parties may apply for a fixed date for hearing.

(b) A party finding that the date which has been agreed causes serious difficulties may apply to the listing office before the 15th of the month in which the case first appears on the list. No change will be made to the listing, unless the listing officer agrees, but reasonable efforts will be made to accommodate parties in serious difficulties. Changes after the 15th of the month in which the list appears can only be made on applica- tion to the President or registrar of the appeal tribunal. Arrangements for the making of such an application should be through the listing office.

(c) Other cases may be put in the list by the listing officer with the consent of the parties at shorter notice: for example, where other cases have been settled or withdrawn or where it appears that they will take less time than originally estimated. Parties who wish their cases to be taken as soon as possible and at short notice should notify the listing officer.

(d) Each week an up-to-date list for the following week will be prepared, including any changes which have been made, in particular specifying cases which by then have been given fixed dates.

(4) Scotland

When the respondent's answer has been received and a copy served on the appellant, both parties will be notified in writing that the appeal must be ready for hearing in approximately six weeks. The proposed date of hearing will be notified to the parties three or four weeks ahead. Any party who wishes to apply for a different date must do so within seven days of the receipt of such notification. Thereafter a formal notice of the date fixed for the hearing will be issued not less than 14 days in advance. This will be a peremptory direction. It will not be discharged, except by the judge on cause shown.

13   Disposal of appeals by consent

(1) An appellant who wishes to abandon or withdraw an appeal should notify the respondent and the appeal tribunal immediately. If a settlement is reached the parties should inform the appeal tribunal as soon as possible.

(2) The appellant should submit to the appeal tribunal a letter signed by the appellant or on the appellant's behalf and signed also by, or on behalf of, the respondent, asking the appeal tribunal for leave to withdraw the appeal and to make a consent order in the form of an attached draft signed by both parties dismissing the appeal, together with any other agreed order.

(3) If the respondent does not agree to the proposed order (where, for example, the respondent wishes to apply for an order for costs against the appellant) the appeal tribunal should be informed. In such cases it will be necessary to fix an oral hearing to determine the outstanding matters in dispute between the parties.

(4) If the parties reach an agreement that the appeal should be *allowed* by consent and that an order made by the [employment] tribunal should be reversed or varied or the matter remitted to the [employment] tribunal on the ground that the decision contains an error of law, it is usually necessary for the matter to be heard by the appeal tribunal to determine whether there is a good reason for making the order which both parties agree should be made. In order to save costs, it may be appropriate for the appellant or a representative only to attend to argue the case for allowing the appeal and making the order that the parties wish the appeal tribunal to make.

(5) If the application for leave to withdraw an appeal is made close to the hearing date the appeal tribunal may require the attendance of the appellant and/or a representative to explain the reasons for delay in making a decision not to pursue the appeal.

14   Preliminary hearing

(This part of the Practice Direction does not apply to appeals heard in Scotland)

(1) At the discretion of the appeal tribunal appeals may be listed as ex parte preliminary hearings to determine whether the grounds in the notice of appeal raise a reasonably arguable point of law so as to give the appeal tribunal jurisdiction to entertain and determine it at a full hearing.

(2) Both parties will be notified of the decision to list the appeal as a preliminary hearing, but only the appellant and/or a representative should attend to make submissions to the appeal tribunal on the issue whether the notice of appeal raises a reasonably arguable point of law. The respondent is not required to attend the hearing and is not usually permitted to take part in it. If the appellant does not attend, the appeal may nevertheless be dealt with on written submissions and dismissed.

(3) The hearing will normally last no more than one hour.

(4) If satisfied that a reasonably arguable point of law is established, the appeal tribunal will give appropriate directions (for example, a time estimate, leave to amend the notice of appeal, or the production of chairman's notes, the exchange and lodging of skeleton arguments) to enable the appeal to proceed to a full hearing without unnecessary delay, on all or only some of the grounds of appeal.

(5) If not satisfied that a reasonably arguable point of law is raised by the appeal, the appeal tribunal will give a judgment explaining why the appeal is dismissed at that stage.

(6) Some preliminary hearings will be listed to be heard in the list of the President of the appeal tribunal and will not be assigned for hearing by a particular tribunal until the day of the hearing. The appellant and/or his representative will be notified on their arrival at the appeal tribunal of the arrangements for the hearing of the appeal.

(7) It is open to any respondent to an appeal to make a written application to the appeal tribunal on the service of the respondent's answer for the appeal to be listed as a preliminary hearing to determine whether it shall proceed further.

(8) The preliminary hearing procedure may be applied to cross-appeals as well as appeals.

15   Citation of authorities

(1) Lists of authorities, limited to those necessary for arguing the point of law on the appeal, should be sent to the librarian of the appeal tribunal using the form provided or by fax not less than 24 hours before the appeal is due to be heard.

(2) It is undesirable for parties to cite the same case from different sets of reports. The parties should, if practicable, agree upon which report will be used at the hearing.

(3) If an unreported case is to be cited by a party, it is the responsibility of the party citing such a case to provide photocopies for the use of each member of the tribunal and to the other party to the hearing. The same applies to cases not reported in the principal series of law reports, to foreign cases and to extracts from textbooks and periodicals.

(4) Parties are advised not to cite an unnecessary number of authorities either in skeleton arguments or in oral argument at the hearing. It is rarely necessary to cite more than one case for a legal proposition. It is a waste of the parties' time and of the appeal tribunal's time for parties or representatives to cite cases unnecessarily. It is of assistance to the appeal tribunal if

parties attach photocopies of the most important authorities to the skeleton arguments submitted by them and highlight the passages relied on by them.

(5) Only in exceptional circumstances will it be necessary to cite any authority at a preliminary hearing.

(6) In the case of reports of decisions of the European Court of Justice, the official report should be used where possible, though it is appreciated that there is a long time lag in the reporting of cases in the official series.

(7) It is often unnecessary for a party citing a case in oral argument to read it in full to the appeal tribunal. Whenever a case is cited in a skeleton argument or in an oral argument the legal proposition for which it is cited should be stated. References need only be made to the relevant passages in the report. If the formulation of the legal proposition based on the authority cited is not in dispute, further examination of the authority will often be unnecessary.

16 Failure to give notice of appearance

(1) If the appellant in a case has not entered a notice of appearance before the [employment] tribunal and has not applied to the [employment] tribunal for an extension of time for doing so or has applied for such an extension and been refused it, the notice of appeal will be immediately set down to be heard as a preliminary hearing.

(2) The appellant will not be permitted to pursue the appeal unless the appeal tribunal is satisfied at the preliminary hearing that:

  (i) there is a good excuse for failing to enter a notice of appearance and (if that be the case) for failing to apply for such an extension of time; and

  (ii) there is a reasonably arguable defence to the claim in the originating application.

(3) In order to satisfy the appeal tribunal on these matters, the appellant must swear and lodge with the appeal tribunal an affidavit explaining in detail the circumstances in which there has been a failure to serve a notice of appearance in time or apply for such an extension of time, the reason for that failure to do so and the facts and matters relied upon for contesting the claim on the merits. There should be exhibited to the affidavit all relevant documents and a completed draft notice of appearance (IT3).

(4) The respondent to the appeal may swear and lodge with the appeal tribunal an affidavit in reply to the appellant's affidavit.

17 Handing down judgments

(1) When the appeal tribunal reserves judgment, the parties will be notified of the date when it is ready to be handed down.

(2) Copies of the judgment may be made available to the parties or their representatives on the morning of the day on which it is handed down or, if so directed by the President or a judge of the appeal tribunal, on the previous day on request by representatives of both parties to the clerk to

the President or a judge of the appeal tribunal, subject to terms as to confidentiality. Copies will be made available to recognised law reporters.

(3) The judgment will be pronounced without being read aloud.

(4) Applications for leave to appeal to the Court of Appeal and other applications (for example, costs) may be made either when the judgment is handed down or by written application soon after.

Employment Appeal Tribunal Guidance Notes (Preliminary Hearing/Directions) 1997

The hearing

1　As from 1 October 1997, all appeals will be listed for a Preliminary Hearing/ Directions ('PHD'). At that hearing, the appellant will be required to satisfy the EAT that it is reasonably arguable that the [employment] tribunal made an error of law in their decision. If so satisfied, the appeal will be allowed to proceed to a full hearing at a later date, but the EAT will then make all necessary orders (directions), such as amendments to the notice of appeal, to ensure that the appeal may be determined efficiently and effectively. Parties are provided with a PHD form to enable them to identify the directions which they ask the EAT to make. It *must* be completed promptly (see below). If the appeal does not raise a reasonably arguable point of law, it will be dismissed at the PHD. It is not anticipated that any PHD will take longer than 30 minutes. In almost every case, it should be quickly apparent whether there is an arguable point of law.

2　The respondent to the appeal is not entitled to present arguments relating to the merits of the appeal at a PHD, but may present written or oral arguments as to the directions which the EAT should make, were the appeal to be allowed to proceed to a full hearing. It is not anticipated that, save in the more complex cases, a respondent will consider it necessary to present oral argument in relation to directions, but will be content to rely upon what has been said in the PHD form. Accordingly, the EAT does not require or expect a respondent who is not presenting a cross-appeal (see below) to attend the PHD, although he is permitted to do so for the limited purpose indicated.

Respondent's answer

3　If the appeal is allowed to proceed to a full hearing, the respondent will be required to send to the EAT an answer within 14 days of the date of the EAT's order to that effect. The EAT will only be prepared to extend time where there is good reason for the delay, which excuses a failure to comply with the time limit. A failure to act promptly may, therefore, lead to a respondent being deprived of the right to take part in the full hearing.

Respondent's cross-appeal

4   Experience shows that cross-appeals are rarely presented. In the normal course of events, a respondent to an appeal, who has been successful in the [employment] tribunal, will simply wish to persuade the EAT to uphold the decision for the same reasons which led the [employment] tribunal to reach their conclusions. There are, however, two types of cross-appeal.

(1) The first is where the respondent wishes to challenge a part of the decision of the [employment] tribunal, but only if the appeal is allowed to go to a full hearing. In such a case, the respondent may include the cross-appeal in his answer.

(2) The second is where the respondent wishes to challenge a part of the decision, whatever the outcome of the appeal. This latter type of cross-appeal will be treated in the same way as an appeal. Accordingly, the respondent *must* send to the EAT an answer and cross-appeal, when returning the PHD form. Failure to do so may deprive the respondent of the right to pursue the cross-appeal. This type of cross-appeal will be listed for hearing at the PHD, and the respondent, who will be entitled to appear, will be required to satisfy the EAT that it is reasonably arguable that the [employment] tribunal erred in law in their decision in the respects alleged in the cross-appeal. The EAT may permit the cross-appeal to be argued at a full hearing, or dismiss the whole or part of it at the PHD.

Directions

5   To enable the EAT to make appropriate directions, appellants and respondents are required to complete a PHD form within 14 days of the date when it is sent to them. Failure to complete the form within time may lead to that party being denied the opportunity of presenting or resisting an appeal or cross-appeal, and being ordered to pay costs.

6   Applications for directions after a PHD will only be entertained if the party concerned can, first, satisfy the EAT that there was a good reason for not making the application at the PHD. Such cases are likely to be exceptional. In any event, any party making a later application for directions may be ordered to pay costs, whatever its outcome. It is, therefore, important that appellants and respondents accurately complete the directions section of the PHD form.

7   These guidance notes do not cover every direction which a party might seek, but refer to those which most commonly arise.

(1) *Amendment:* If, at the PHD, the appellant is given leave to amend the notice of appeal, the EAT will specify the time within which this is to be done. Within 14 days after the EAT has sent the amended notice of appeal to the respondent, the respondent must notify the EAT of any objections to the amendment. It is unlikely that, in the absence of prejudice, there will be any ground for valid objection, but any objections will be considered and determined by the Registrar. An unreasonable objection may lead to a costs order against the party making it. If the respondent has filed an answer (and cross-appeal) by the date of the amendment of the notice of appeal, the respondent will be entitled, without leave, to

make any consequential amendment to the answer (and cross-appeal) within the same 14-day period.

(2) *Estimate of time for the appellant's/respondent's argument:* The estimate is only helpful if it is realistic. Note that the parties are being asked to estimate the time for their own arguments and *not* of the likely duration of the appeal. The estimate is to be based on the assumption that the appellant is permitted to argue all the points in the notice of appeal and that the EAT will have read the decision and the parties' skeleton arguments before the full hearing commences.

(3) *Category:* Whilst it will be the court's responsibility to give a listing category to any case, it would wish to take account of the parties' own views on the relative importance of the points at issue. A case which is important will not, for that reason, be listed before other cases. Therefore, there is no listing advantage in overstating the importance of the points at issue.

(4) *Listing:* If the appeal/cross-appeal proceeds to a full hearing, it will be listed for hearing by the EAT's listing officers.

(5) *Chairman's notes of evidence:* Parties should remember that the EAT has power to deal only with appeals on points of law. Specifically, the EAT has no power to make findings of fact nor to adjust the findings of fact made by the [employment] tribunal. The party requesting notes of evidence should identify:

(a) the issues in the notice of appeal or cross-appeal for which it is said that the notes are required; and

(b) the names of the witnesses in respect of whose evidence the notes are required; and

(a) the parts of the witnesses' evidence alleged to be necessary.

The EAT will only order production of the chairman's notes if satisfied that all or part of such notes are *necessary* for the purpose of arguing the point of law on the appeal. Notes of evidence are *not* ordered to enable the parties to check or double-check the reasoning or findings in the decision against the evidence recorded in the notes.

Other directions

8   Before completing the PHD form, each party should consider carefully whether there are any other directions that might be sought; for example, should the appeal await the outcome of another case or should it be consolidated with another appeal.

ACAS Arbitration Scheme

ACAS Arbitration Scheme (England and Wales) Order 2001

ACAS Arbitration Scheme

ACAS Arbitration Scheme (England and Wales) Order 2001 SI No 1185

Citation, commencement, interpretation and extent

1 (1) This Order may be cited as the ACAS Arbitration Scheme (England and Wales) Order 2001 and shall come into force on 21 May 2001.

(2) In this Order –
'the 1996 Act' means the Employment Rights Act 1996;
'basic amount' means such part of an award of compensation made by an arbitrator as comprises the basic amount, determined in accordance with paragraphs 118 to 134 of the Scheme;
'the Scheme' means the arbitration scheme set out in the Schedule with the exception of paragraphs 43, 94, 159, 162 to 167, 171, 177 and 178 thereof.

(3) This Order extends to England and Wales.

Commencement of the Scheme

2 The Scheme shall come into effect on 21 May 2001.

Application of Part I of the Arbitration Act 1996

3 The provisions of Part I of the Arbitration Act 1996 referred to in the Schedule at paragraphs 43, 94, 159, 162 to 167, 171, 177 and 178 and shown in italics shall, as modified in those paragraphs, apply to arbitrations conducted in accordance with the Scheme.

4 (1) Section 46(1)(b) of the Arbitration Act 1996 shall apply to arbitrations conducted in accordance with the Scheme, subject to the following modification.

(2) For 'such other considerations as are agreed by them or determined by the tribunal' in section 46(1)(b) substitute 'the Terms of Reference in paragraph 12 of the arbitration scheme set out in the Schedule to the ACAS Arbitration Scheme (England and Wales) Order 2001'.

Enforcement of re-employment orders

5 (1) Employment tribunals shall enforce re-employment orders made in arbitrations conducted in accordance with the Scheme in accordance with section 117 of the 1996 Act (enforcement by award of compensation), modified as follows.

(2) In subsection (1)(a), subsection (3) and subsection (8), for the words 'section 113' substitute in each case 'paragraph 102(i) of the Scheme'.

(3) In subsection (2) for 'section 124' substitute 'section 124(1) and (5) and subsections (9) and (10)'.

(4) In subsection (3)(a) for the words 'sections 118 to 127A' substitute the words 'sections 118 to 123, section 124(1) and (5), sections 126 and 127A and subsections (9) and (11)'.

(5) After subsection (8) insert –

'(9) Section 124(1) shall not apply to compensation awarded, or to a compensatory award made, to a person in a case where the arbitrator finds the reason (or, if more than one, the principal reason) for the dismissal (or, in a redundancy case, for which the employee was selected for dismissal) to be a reason specified in any of the enactments mentioned in section 124(1)A.

(10) In the case of compensation awarded to a person under section 117(1) and (2), the limit imposed by section 124(1) may be exceeded to the extent necessary to enable the award fully to reflect the amount specified as payable under the arbitrator's award in accordance with paragraphs 110(i) or 113(iv) of the Scheme.

(11) Where –

(a) a compensatory award is an award under subsection (3)(a) of section 117, and

(b) an additional award falls to be made under subsection (3)(b) of that section,

the limit imposed by section 124(1) on the compensatory award may be exceeded to the extent necessary to enable the aggregate of the compensatory award and additional awards fully to reflect the amount specified as payable under the arbitrator's award in accordance with paragraphs 110(i) or 113(iv) of the Scheme.

(12) In this section 'the Scheme' means the arbitration scheme set out in the Schedule to the ACAS Arbitration Scheme (England and Wales) Order 2001.'.

Awards of compensation

6 An award of a basic amount shall be treated as a basic award of compensation for unfair dismissal for the purposes of section 184(1)(d) of the 1996 Act (which specifies such an award as a debt which the Secretary of State must satisfy if the employer has become insolvent).

SCHEDULE: ACAS ARBITRATION SCHEME

I INTRODUCTION

1 The ACAS Arbitration Scheme ('the Scheme') is implemented pursuant to section 212A of the Trade Union and Labour Relations (Consolidation) Act 1992 ('the 1992 Act').

2 The Scheme provides a voluntary alternative to the employment tribunal for the resolution of unfair dismissal disputes, in the form of arbitration.

3 Resolution of disputes under the Scheme is intended to be confidential, informal, relatively fast and cost efficient. Procedures under the Scheme are non-legalistic, and far more flexible than the traditional model of the

employment tribunal and the courts. For example (as explained in more detail below), the Scheme avoids the use of formal pleadings and formal witness and documentary procedures. Strict rules of evidence will not apply, and, as far as possible, instead of applying strict law or legal precedent, general principles of fairness and good conduct will be taken into account (including, for example, principles referred to in any relevant ACAS 'Disciplinary and Grievance Procedures' Code of Practice or 'Discipline at Work' Handbook). Arbitral decisions ('awards') will be final, with very limited opportunities for parties to appeal or otherwise challenge the result.

4   The Scheme also caters for requirements imposed as a matter of law (eg, the Human Rights Act 1998, existing law in the field of arbitration and EC law).

II   THE ROLE OF ACAS

5   As more fully explained below, cases enter the Scheme by reference to ACAS, which appoints an arbitrator from a panel (see paragraphs 35–37 below) to determine the dispute. ACAS provides administrative assistance during the proceedings, and may scrutinise awards and refer any clerical or other similar errors back to the arbitrator. Disputes are determined, however, by arbitrators and not by ACAS.

Routing of communications

6   Unless in the course of a hearing, all communications between either party and the arbitrator shall be sent via the ACAS Arbitration Section.

7   Paragraph 172 below sets out the manner in which any document, notice or communication must be served on, or transmitted to, ACAS or the ACAS Arbitration Section.

III   TERMS AND ABBREVIATIONS

8   The term 'Employee' is used to denote the claimant (ie, the former employee), including any person entitled to pursue a claim arising out of a contravention, or alleged contravention, of Part X of the Employment Rights Act 1996.

9   The term 'Employer' is used to denote the respondent.

10   The term 'EC law' means:
  (i)   any enactment in the domestic legislation of England and Wales giving effect to rights, powers, liabilities, obligations and restrictions from time to time created or arising by or under the Community Treaties, and
  (ii) any such rights, powers, liabilities, obligations and restrictions which are not given effect by any such enactment.

11   With the exception of paragraph 21(i) below ('Requirements for entry into the Scheme'), references to anything being written or in writing include its being recorded by any means so as to be usable for subsequent reference.

IV   ARBITRATOR'S TERMS OF REFERENCE

12   Every agreement to refer a dispute to arbitration under this Scheme shall be taken to be an agreement that the arbitrator decide the dispute according to the following Terms of Reference:

In deciding whether the dismissal was fair or unfair, the arbitrator shall:

(i) have regard to general principles of fairness and good conduct in employment relations (including, for example, principles referred to in any relevant ACAS 'Disciplinary and Grievance Procedures' Code of Practice or 'Discipline at Work' Handbook), instead of applying legal tests or rules (eg, court decisons or legislation);

(ii) apply EC law.

The arbitrator shall not decide the case by substituting what he or she would have done for the actions taken by the Employer.

If the arbitrator finds the dismissal unfair, he or she shall determine the appropriate remedy under the terms of this Scheme.

Nothing in the Terms of Reference affects the operation of the Human Rights Act 1998 in so far as this is applicable and relevant and (with respect to procedural matters) has not been waived by virtue of the provisions of this Scheme.

V   SCOPE OF THE SCHEME

Cases that are covered by the Scheme

13   This Scheme only applies to cases of alleged unfair dismissal (ie, disputes involving proceedings, or claims which could be the subject of proceedings, before an employment tribunal arising out of a contravention, or alleged contravention, of Part X of the Employment Rights Act 1996).

14   The Scheme does not extend to other kinds of claim which are often related to, or raised at the same time as, a claim of unfair dismissal. For example, sex discrimination cases, and claims for unpaid wages are not covered by the Scheme.

15   If a claim of unfair dismissal has been referred for resolution under the Scheme, any other claim, even if part of the same dispute, must be settled separately, or referred to the employment tribunal, or withdrawn. In the event that different aspects of the same dispute are being heard in the employment tribunal as well as under the Scheme, the arbitrator may decide, if appropriate or convenient, to postpone the arbitration proceedings pending a determination by the employment tribunal.

Waiver of jurisdictional issues

16   Because of its informal nature, the Scheme is not designed for disputes raising jurisdictional issues, such as for example:

- whether or not the Employee was employed by the Employer;

- whether or not the Employee had the necessary period of continuous service to bring the claim;

- whether or not time limits have expired and/or should be extended.

17   Accordingly, when agreeing to refer a dispute to arbitration under the Scheme, both parties will be taken to have accepted as a condition of the Scheme that no jurisdictional issue is in dispute between them. The arbitrator will not therefore deal with such issues during the arbitration process, even if they are raised by the parties, and the parties will be taken to have waived any rights in that regard.

18   In particular, in agreeing to arbitration under the Scheme, the parties will be treated as having agreed that a dismissal has taken place.

Inappropriate cases

19   The Scheme is not intended for disputes involving complex legal issues. Whilst such cases will be accepted for determination (subject to the Terms of Reference), parties are advised, where appropriate, to consider applying to the employment tribunal or settling their dispute by other means.

VI   ACCESS TO THE SCHEME

20   The Scheme is an entirely voluntary system of dispute resolution: it will only apply if parties have so agreed.

Requirements for entry into the Scheme

21   Any agreement to submit a dispute to arbitration under the Scheme must satisfy the following requirements (an 'Arbitration Agreement'):
(i)   the agreement must be in writing;
(ii)   the agreement must concern an existing dispute;
(iii) the agreement must not seek to alter or vary any provision of the Scheme;
(iv)   the agreement must have been reached either:
       (a) where a conciliation officer has taken action under section 18 of the Employment Tribunals Act 1996 (a 'Conciliated Agreement') or
       (b) through a compromise agreement, where the conditions regulating such agreements under the Employment Rights Act 1996 are satisfied (a 'Compromise Agreement');
(v)   the agreement must be accompanied by a completed Waiver Form for each party, in the form of Appendix A.

22   Where an agreement fails to satisfy any one of these requirements, no valid reference to the Scheme will have been made, and the parties will have to settle their dispute by other means or have recourse to the employment tribunal.

23   Where:
(i)   a dispute concerning unfair dismissal claims as well as other claims has been referred to the employment tribunal, and
(ii)   the parties have agreed to settle the other claims and refer the unfair dismissal claim to arbitration under the Scheme,
a separate settlement must be reached referring the unfair dismissal claim to arbitration which satisfies all the requirements listed above (although it may form part of one overall settlement document).

Notification to ACAS of an Arbitration Agreement

24   All Arbitration Agreements must be notified to ACAS within six weeks of their conclusion, by either of the parties or their independent advisers or representatives, or an ACAS conciliator, sending a copy of the agreement and Waiver Forms, together with IT1 and IT3 forms if these have been completed, to the ACAS Arbitration Section.

25   For the purposes of the previous paragraph, an Arbitration Agreement is treated as 'concluded' on the date it is signed, or if signed by different people at different times, on the date of the last signature.

26   Where an Arbitration Agreement is not notified to ACAS within six weeks, ACAS will not arrange for the appointment of an arbitrator under the Scheme, unless notification within that time was not reasonably practicable. Any party seeking to notify ACAS of an Arbitration Agreement outside this period must explain in writing to the ACAS Arbitration Section the reason for the delay. ACAS shall appoint an arbitrator, in accordance with the appointment provisions below, to consider the explanation, and that arbitrator may seek the views of the other party, and may call both parties to a hearing to establish the reasons for the delay. The arbitrator shall then rule in an award on whether or not the agreement can be accepted for hearing under the Scheme.

27   Any such hearing and award will be governed by the provisions of this Scheme.

Consolidation of proceedings

28   Where all parties so agree in writing, ACAS may consolidate different arbitral proceedings under the Scheme.

VII   SETTLEMENT AND WITHDRAWAL FROM THE SCHEME

Withdrawal by the Employee

29   At any stage of the arbitration process, once an Arbitration Agreement has been concluded and the reference has been accepted by ACAS, the party bringing the unfair dismissal claim may withdraw from the Scheme, provided that any such withdrawal is in writing. Such a withdrawal shall constitute a dismissal of the claim.

Withdrawal by the Employer

30   Once an Arbitration Agreement has been concluded and the reference has been accepted by ACAS, the party against whom a claim is brought cannot unilaterally withdraw from the Scheme.

Settlement

31   Parties are free to reach an agreement settling the dispute at any stage.

32   If such an agreement is reached:
   (i)   upon the joint written request of the parties to the arbitrator or the ACAS Arbitration Section, the arbitrator (if appointed) or the ACAS

Arbitration Section (if no arbitrator has been appointed) shall terminate the arbitration proceedings;

(ii)   if so requested by the parties, the arbitrator (if appointed) may record the settlement in the form of an agreed award (on a covering proforma).

33   An agreed award shall state that it is an award of the arbitrator by consent and shall have the same status and effect as any other award on the merits of the case.

34   In rendering an agreed award, the arbitrator:

(i)   may only record the parties' agreed wording;

(ii)   may not approve, vary, transcribe, interpret or ratify a settlement in any way;

(iii)   may not record any settlement beyond the scope of the Scheme, the Arbitration Agreement or the reference to the Scheme as initially accepted by ACAS.

VIII   APPOINTMENT OF AN ARBITRATOR

The ACAS Arbitration Panel

35   Arbitrators are selected to serve on the ACAS Arbitration Panel on the basis of their practical knowledge and experience of discipline and dismissal issues in the workplace. They are recruited through an open recruitment exercise, and appointed to the Panel on the basis of standard terms of appointment. It is a condition of their appointment that they exercise their duties in accordance with the terms of this Scheme. Each appointment is initially for a period of two years, although it may be renewed by ACAS, at the latter's discretion. Payment is made by ACAS on the basis of time spent in connection with arbitral proceedings.

Appointment to a case

36   Arbitral appointments are made exclusively by ACAS from the ACAS Arbitration Panel. Parties will have no choice of arbitrator.

37   Once ACAS has been notified of a valid Arbitration Agreement, it will select and appoint an arbitrator, and notify all parties of the name of the arbitrator so appointed.

Arbitrator's duty of disclosure

38   Immediately following selection (and before an appointment is confirmed by ACAS), every arbitrator shall disclose in writing to ACAS (to be forwarded to the parties) any circumstances known to him or her likely to give rise to any justifiable doubts as to his or her impartiality, or confirm in writing that there are no such circumstances.

39   Once appointed, and until the arbitration is concluded, every arbitrator shall be under a continuing duty forthwith to disclose to ACAS (to be forwarded to the parties) any such circumstances which may have arisen since appointment.

Removal of arbitrators

40   Arbitrators may only be removed by ACAS or the court (under the provisions in paragraphs 41 to 43 below).

41   Applications under the Scheme to remove an arbitrator on any of the grounds set out in sections 24(1)(a) and (c) of the Arbitration Act 1996 shall be made in the first instance to ACAS (addressed to the ACAS Arbitration Section).

42   If ACAS refuses such an application, a party may thereafter apply to the court.

43   *(1) Sections 24(1)(a) and (c), 24(2), 24(3), 24(5) and 24(6) of the Arbitration Act 1996 shall apply to arbitrations conducted in accordance with the Scheme, subject to the following modifications.*

    (2) In subsection (1) for '(upon notice to the other parties, to the arbitrator concerned and to any other arbitrator) apply to the court' substitute '(upon notice to the other party, to the arbitrator concerned and to the Advisory, Conciliation and Arbitration Service ('ACAS')) apply to the High Court or Central London County Court'.

    (3) In subsection (2) –

      (a) omit 'If there is an arbitral or other institution or person vested by the parties with power to remove an arbitrator,';

      (b) for 'that institution or person' substitute 'ACAS'.

44   The arbitrator may continue the proceedings and make an award while an application to ACAS (as well as the court) to remove him or her is pending.

Death of an arbitrator

45   The authority of an arbitrator is personal and ceases on his or her death.

Replacement of arbitrators

46   Where an arbitrator ceases to hold office for any reason, he or she shall be replaced by ACAS in accordance with the appointment provisions above.

47   Once appointed, the replacement arbitrator shall determine whether and, if so, to what extent the previous proceedings should stand.

IX   GENERAL DUTY OF THE ARBITRATOR

48   The arbitrator shall:

    (i)   act fairly and impartially as between the parties, giving each party a reasonable opportunity of putting his or her case and dealing with that of his or her opponent, and

    (ii)   adopt procedures suitable to the circumstances of the particular case, avoiding unnecessary delay or expense, so as to provide a fair means for the resolution of the matters falling to be determined.

49   The arbitrator shall comply with the general duty (see paragraph 48 above) in conducting the arbitral proceedings, in his or her decisions on matters of procedure and evidence and in the exercise of all other powers conferred on him or her.

X   GENERAL DUTY OF THE PARTIES

50   The parties shall do all things necessary for the proper and expeditious conduct of the arbitral proceedings. This includes (without limitation) complying without delay with any determination of the arbitrator as to procedural or evidential matters, or with any order or directions of the arbitrator, and co-operating in the arrangement of any hearing.

XI   CONFIDENTIALITY AND PRIVACY

51   Arbitrations, and all associated procedures under the Scheme, are strictly private and confidential.

52   Hearings may only be attended by the arbitrator, the parties, their representatives, any interpreters, witnesses and a legal adviser if appointed. If the parties so agree, an ACAS official or arbitrator in training may also attend.

XII   ARRANGEMENTS FOR THE HEARING

Initial arrangements

53   A hearing must be held in every case, notwithstanding any agreement between the parties to a purely written procedure.

54   Once an arbitrator has been appointed by ACAS, a hearing shall be arranged as soon as reasonably practicable by him or her, with the administrative assistance of the ACAS Arbitration Section.

55   The arbitrator shall decide the date and venue for the hearing, in so far as an agreement cannot be reached with all parties within two months of the initial notification to ACAS of the Arbitration Agreement.

56   The ACAS Arbitration Section shall contact all parties with details of the date and venue for the hearing.

Expedited hearings

57   If:

(i)   before the parties have agreed to refer a dispute to arbitration under the Scheme, an employment tribunal makes an order under interim relief provisions, or

(ii)   in the arbitrator's discretion, other relevant circumstances exist, the arbitrator may expedite the hearing, on the application of any party.

Venue

58   Hearings may be held in any venue, provided that the hearing will only be held at the Employee's former workplace, or a similarly non-neutral venue, if all parties so agree.

59   Where premises have to be hired for a hearing, ACAS shall meet the reasonable costs of so doing.

Assistance

60   Where a party needs the services of an interpreter, signer or communicator at the hearing, ACAS should be so informed well in advance of the hearing.

Where an arbitrator agrees that such assistance is required, ACAS shall meet the reasonable costs of providing this.

Travelling expenses/loss of earnings

61   Every party shall meet their own travelling expenses and those of their representatives and witnesses.

62   No loss of earnings are payable by ACAS to anyone involved in the arbitration. However, where an arbitrator rules that a dismissal was unfair, he or she may include in the calculation of any compensation a sum to cover reasonable travelling expenses and loss of earnings incurred by the Employee personally in attending the hearing.

Applications for postponements of, or different venues for, initial hearings

63   Any application for a postponement of, or a different venue for, an initial hearing must be made in writing, with reasons, to the arbitrator via the ACAS Arbitration Section within 14 days of the date of the letter notifying the hearing arrangements. Such applications will be determined by the arbitrator without an oral hearing after all parties have received a copy of the application and been given a reasonable opportunity to respond.

64   If the application is rejected, the initial hearing will be held on the original date and/or in the original venue.

65   This provision does not affect the arbitrator's general discretion (set out below) with respect to postponements after an initial hearing has been fixed, or with respect to other aspects of the procedure. In particular, procedural applications may be made to the arbitrator at the hearing itself.

XIII   NON-COMPLIANCE WITH PROCEDURE

66   If a party fails to comply with any aspect of the procedure set out in this Scheme, or any order or direction by the arbitrator, or fails to comply with the general duty in section X above, the arbitrator may (in addition to any other power set out in this Scheme):

(i)   adjourn any hearing, where it would be unfair on any party to proceed; and/or

(ii)   draw such adverse inferences from the act of non-compliance as the circumstances justify.

XIV   OUTLINE OF PROCEDURE BEFORE THE HEARING

67   Once a hearing has been fixed, the following procedure shall apply, subject to any direction by the arbitrator.

Written materials

68   At least 14 days before the date of the hearing, each party shall send to the ACAS Arbitration Section (for forwarding to the arbitrator and the other party) one copy of a written statement of case, together with:

(i)   any supporting documentation or other material to be relied upon at the hearing; and where appropriate

(ii)   a list of the names and title/role of all those people who will accompany each party to the hearing or be called as a witness.

69   Written statements of case should briefly set out the main particulars of each party's case, which can then be expanded upon if necessary at the hearing itself. The statement should include an explanation of the events which led up to the dismissal, including an account of the sequence and outcome of any relevant meetings, interviews or discussions. The parties should come to the hearing prepared to address the practicability of reinstatement or re-engagement, in so far as the Employee seeks such remedies.

70   Supporting documentation or other material may include (without limitation) copies of:
(i)   contracts of employment
(ii)   letters of appointment
(iii)   written statement of particulars of employment
(iv)   time sheets and attendance records
(v)   performance appraisal reports
(vi)   warning and dismissal letters
(vii)   written reasons for dismissal, where these have been given
(viii) company handbooks, rules and procedures
(ix)   any information which will help the arbitrator to assess compensation, including (without limitation):
(a)   pay slips, P60s or wage records
(b)   details of benefits paid to the Employee such as travelling expenses and free or subsidised accommodation
(c)   guidance about, and (if available) actuarial assessments of, pension entitlements
(d)   details of any welfare benefits received
(e)   evidence of attempts to find other work, or otherwise mitigate the loss arising from the dismissal.
(x)   signed statements of any witnesses or outlines of evidence to be given by witnesses at the hearing.

71   The parties must also supply details of any relevant awards of compensation that may have been made by any other tribunal or court in connection with the subject matter of the claim.

72   Legible copies of documents must be supplied to ACAS even if they have already been supplied to an ACAS conciliator before the Arbitration Agreement was concluded.

73   No information on the conciliation process, if any, shall be disclosed by an ACAS conciliator to the arbitrator.

Submissions, evidence and witnesses not previously notified

74   Written statements of case and documentary or other material that have not been provided to the ACAS Arbitration Section prior to the hearing (in accordance with paragraph 68 above) may only be relied upon at the hearing with the arbitrator's permission.

75   All representatives and witnesses who have been listed as accompanying a

party at the hearing should be present at the start of the hearing. Witnesses who have not been included in a list submitted to the ACAS Arbitration Section prior to the hearing may only be called with the arbitrator's permission.

Requests for documents

76   Any party may request the other party to produce copies of relevant documents which are not in the requesting party's possession, custody or control. Although the arbitrator has no power to compel a party to comply, the arbitrator may draw an adverse inference from a party's failure to comply with a reasonable request.

Requests for attendance of witnesses

77   Although the arbitrator has no power to compel the attendance of anybody at the hearing, the arbitrator may draw an adverse inference if an employer who is a party to the arbitration fails or refuses to allow current employees or other workers (who have relevant evidence to give) time off from work to attend the hearing, should such an employer be so requested.

Preliminary hearings and directions

78   Where the arbitrator believes that there may be considerable differences between the parties over any issue, including the availability or exchange of documents, or the availability of witnesses, the arbitrator may call the parties to a preliminary hearing to address such issues, or he or she may give procedural directions in correspondence.

79   In the course of a preliminary hearing or in correspondence, the arbitrator may express views on the desirability of information and/or evidence being available at the hearing.

XV   OUTLINE OF PROCEDURE AT THE HEARING

Arbitrator's overall discretion

80   Subject to the arbitrator's general duty (Section IX above), and subject to the points set out below, the conduct of the hearing and all procedural and evidential matters (including applications for adjournments and changes in venue) shall be for the arbitrator to decide.

Language

81   The language of the proceedings shall be English, unless the Welsh language is applicable by virtue of the Welsh Language Act 1993 (as amended from time to time). Reference should be made to paragraph 60 above if the Welsh language is to be used.

Witnesses

82   No party or witness shall be cross-examined by a party or representative, or examined on oath or affirmation.

Examination by the arbitrator

83 The arbitrator shall have the right to address questions directly to either party or to anybody else attending the hearing, and to take the initiative in ascertaining the facts and (where applicable) the law.

Representatives

84 The parties may be accompanied by any person chosen by them to help them to present their case at the hearing, although no special status will be accorded to legally qualified representatives. Each party is liable for any fees or expenses incurred by any representatives they appoint.

Strict rules of evidence

85 The arbitrator will not apply strict rules of evidence (or any other rules) as to the admissibility, relevance or weight of any material (oral, written or other) sought to be tendered on any matters of fact or opinion.

Interim relief

86 The arbitrator shall have no power to order provisional or interim relief, but may expedite the proceedings where appropriate.

Non-attendance at the hearing

87 If, without showing sufficient cause, a party fails to attend or be represented at a hearing, the arbitrator may:
   (i)   continue the hearing in that party's absence, and in such a case shall take into account any written submissions and documents that have already been submitted by that party; or
   (ii) adjourn the hearing.

88 In the case of the non-attendance of the Employee, if the arbitrator decides to adjourn the hearing, he or she may write to the Employee to request an explanation for the non-attendance. If the arbitrator decides that the Employee has not demonstrated sufficient cause for the non-attendance, he or she may rule in an award that the claim be treated as dismissed.

Post-hearing written materials

89 No further submissions or evidence will be accepted after the end of the substantive hearing without the arbitrator's permission, which will only be granted in exceptional circumstances. Where permission is granted, any material is to be sent to the ACAS Arbitration Section, to be forwarded to the arbitrator and all other parties.

XVI   QUESTIONS OF EC LAW AND THE HUMAN RIGHTS ACT 1998

Appointment of legal adviser

90 The arbitrator shall have the power, on the application of any party or of his or her own motion, to require the appointment of a legal adviser to assist with respect to any issue of EC law or the Human Rights Act 1998 that, in the arbitrator's view and subject to paragraph 12 above (Arbitrator's Terms

of Reference), might be involved and relevant to the resolution of the dispute.

91   The legal adviser will be appointed by ACAS, to report to the arbitrator and the parties, and shall be subject to the duty of disclosure set out in paragraphs 38 and 39 above.

92   The arbitrator shall allow the legal adviser to attend the proceedings, and may order an adjournment and/or change in venue to facilitate this.

93   The parties shall be given a reasonable opportunity to comment on any information, opinion or advice offered by the legal adviser, following which the arbitrator shall take such information, opinion or advice into account in determining the dispute.

Court determination of preliminary points

94   *(1) Section 45 of the Arbitration Act 1996 shall apply to arbitrations conducted in accordance with the Scheme, subject to the following modifications.*

   (2) In subsection (1) –
   (a) for 'Unless otherwise agreed by the parties, the court' substitute 'The High Court or Central London County Court';
   (b) for 'any question of law' substitute 'any question (a) of EC law, or (b) concerning the application of the Human Rights Act 1998';
   (c) omit 'An agreement to dispense with reasons for the tribunal's award shall be considered an agreement to exclude the court's jurisdiction under this section.'.

   (3) In subsection (2)(b) omit sub-paragraph (i).

   (4) Omit subsection (4).

   (5) After subsection (6), insert –
   '(7) In this section, 'EC law' means –
   (a) any enactment in the domestic legislation of England and Wales giving effect to rights, powers, liabilities, obligations and restrictions from time to time created or arising by or under the Community Treaties, and
   (b) any such rights, powers, liabilities, obligations and restrictions which are not given effect by any such enactment.'

XVII   AUTOMATIC UNFAIRNESS

95   In deciding whether the dismissal was fair or unfair, subject to paragraph 12 above (Arbitrator's Terms of Reference), the arbitrator shall have regard to

   (i)   any provision of Part X of the Employment Rights Act 1996 (as amended from time to time) requiring a dismissal for a particular reason to be regarded as unfair, or

   (ii) any other legislative provision requiring a dismissal for a particular reason to be regarded as unfair for the purpose of Part X of the Employment Rights Act 1996.

XVIII AWARDS

Form of the award

96 The award shall be in writing, signed by the arbitrator.

97 The award (unless it is an agreed award) shall:
(i) identify the reason (or, if more than one, the principal reason) for the dismissal (or, in a redundancy case, the reason for which the employee was selected for dismissal);
(ii) contain the main considerations which were taken into account in reaching the decision that the dismissal was fair or unfair;
(iii) state the decision(s) of the arbitrator;
(iv) state the remedy awarded, together with an explanation;
(v) state the date when it was made.

Awards on different issues

98 The arbitrator may make more than one award at different times on different aspects of the matters to be determined.

99 The arbitrator may, in particular, make an award relating:
(i) to an issue affecting the whole claim, or
(ii) to a part only of the claim submitted to him or her for decision.

100 If the arbitrator does so, he or she shall specify in his or her award the issue, or the claim or part of a claim, which is the subject matter of the award.

Remedies

101 In every case, the arbitrator shall:
(i) explain to the Employee what orders for reinstatement or re-engagement may be made in an award and under what circumstances these may be granted; and
(ii) ask the Employee whether he or she wishes the arbitrator to make such an award.

102 In the event that the arbitrator finds that the dismissal was unfair:
(i) if the Employee expresses such a wish, the arbitrator may make, in an award, an order for reinstatement or re-engagement (in accordance with the provisions below); or
(ii) if no such order for reinstatement or re-engagement is made, the arbitrator shall make an award of compensation (calculated in accordance with the provisions below) to be paid by the Employer to the Employee.

103 In cases where the arbitrator finds that the dismissal was unfair by reason of the operation of EC law, the arbitrator shall apply the relevant provisions of English law with respect to remedies for unfair dismissal, in so far as these may differ from sections XIX and XX of the Scheme.

XIX AWARDS OF REINSTATEMENT OR RE-ENGAGEMENT

Definitions

104 An order for reinstatement (which must be in the form of an award) is an order that the Employer shall treat the Employee in all respects as if he or she had not been dismissed.

105   An order for re-engagement (which must be in the form of an award) is an order, on such terms as the arbitrator may decide, that the Employee be engaged by the Employer, or by a successor of the Employer or by an associated Employer, in employment comparable to that from which he or she was dismissed or in other suitable employment.

Choice of remedy

106   In exercising his or her discretion with respect to the remedy to be awarded under paragraph 102 (i) above, the arbitrator shall first consider whether to make an order for reinstatement, and in so doing shall take into account:
(i)   whether the Employee wishes to be reinstated;
(ii)   whether it is practicable for the Employer to comply with an order for reinstatement; and
(iii) where the Employee caused or contributed to some extent to the dismissal, whether it would be just to order his or her reinstatement.

107   If the arbitrator decides not to make an order for reinstatement, he or she shall then consider whether to make an order for re-engagement and, if so, on what terms. In so doing, the arbitrator shall take into account:
(i)   any wish expressed by the Employee as to the nature of the order to be made;
(ii)   whether it is practicable for the Employer (or a successor or an associated employer) to comply with an order for re-engagement, and
(iii) where the Employee caused or contributed to some extent to the dismissal, whether it would be just to order his or her re-engagement and (if so) on what terms.

108   If ordering re-engagement, the arbitrator shall do so on terms which are, so far as is reasonably practicable, as favourable as an order for reinstatement (with the exception of cases where contributory fault has been taken into account under paragraph 107(iii) above).

Permanent replacements

109   Where in any case an Employer has engaged a permanent replacement for a dismissed Employee, the arbitrator shall not take that fact into account in determining, for the purposes of paragraphs 106(ii) and 107(ii) above, whether it is practicable to comply with an order for reinstatement or re-engagement. This does not apply, however, where the Employer shows:
(i)   That it was not practicable for him or her to arrange for the dismissed Employee's work to be done without engaging a permanent replacement, or
(ii)   that:
       (a) he or she engaged the replacement after the lapse of a reasonable period, without having heard from the dismissed Employee that he or she wished to be reinstated or re-engaged, and
       (b) when the Employer engaged the replacement it was no longer reasonable for him or her to arrange for the dismissed Employee's work to be done except by a permanent replacement.

Reinstatement

110 On making an order for reinstatement, the arbitrator shall specify:

(i) any amount payable by the Employer in respect of any benefit which the Employee might reasonably be expected to have had but for the dismissal (including arrears of pay) for the period between the date of termination of employment and the date of reinstatement,

(ii) any rights and privileges (including seniority and pension rights) which must be restored to the Employee, and

(iii) the date by which the order must be complied with.

111 If the Employee would have benefited from an improvement in his or her terms and conditions of employment had he or she not been dismissed, an order for reinstatement shall require him or her to be treated as if he or she had benefited from that improvement from the date on which he or she would have done so but for being dismissed.

112 In calculating for the purposes of paragraph 110 (i) above any amount payable by the Employer, the arbitrator shall take into account, so as to reduce the Employer's liability, any sums received by the Employee in respect of the period between the date of termination of employment and the date of reinstatement by way of:

(i) wages in lieu of notice or ex gratia payments paid by the Employer, or

(ii) remuneration paid in respect of employment with another employer,

and such other benefits as the arbitrator thinks appropriate in the circumstances.

Re-engagement

113 On making an order for re-engagement the arbitrator shall specify the terms on which re-engagement is to take place, including:

(i) the identity of the employer,

(ii) the nature of the employment,

(iii) the remuneration for the employment,

(iv) any amount payable by the employer in respect of any benefit which the Employee might reasonably be expected to have had but for the dismissal (including arrears of pay) for the period between the date of termination of employment and the date of re-engagement,

(v) any rights and privileges (including seniority and pension rights) which must be restored to the Employee, and

(vi) the date by which the order must be complied with.

114 In calculating, for the purposes of paragraph 113(iv) above, any amount payable by the employer, the arbitrator shall take into account, so as to reduce the Employer's liability, any sums received by the Employee in respect of the period between the date of termination of employment and the date of re-engagement by way of:

(i) wages in lieu of notice or ex gratia payments paid by the employer, or

(ii) remuneration paid in respect of employment with another employer,

and such other benefits as the arbitrator thinks appropriate in the circumstances.

Continuity of employment

115   The Employee's continuity of employment will be preserved in the same way as it would be under an award of the employment tribunal.

XX   AWARDS OF COMPENSATION

116   When an arbitrator makes an award of compensation, instead of an award for reinstatement or re-engagement, such compensation shall consist of a *basic amount and a compensatory amount.*

117   Where paragraph 142 below applies, an award of compensation shall also include a *supplementary amount.*

The basic amount

118   (Subject to the following provisions) the *basic amount* shall be calculated by:
   (i)   determining the period, ending with the effective date of termination (see paragraph 119 below), during which the Employee has been continuously employed (see paragraph 120 below),
   (ii)   reckoning backwards from the end of that period the number of years of employment falling within that period, and
   (iii) allowing the appropriate amount (see paragraph 121 below) for each of those years of employment.

119   As to the 'effective date of termination':
   (i)   the 'effective date of termination' means:
         (a) in relation to an Employee whose contract of employment is terminated by notice, whether given by his or her Employer or by the Employee, the date on which the notice expires;
         (b) in relation to an Employee whose contract of employment is terminated without notice, the date on which the termination takes effect; and
         (c) in relation to an Employee who is employed under a contract for a fixed term which expires without being renewed under the same contract, the date on which the term expires.
   (ii)   Where:
         (a) the contract of employment is terminated by the Employer, and
         (b) the notice required by section 86 of the Employment Rights Act 1996 (as amended from time to time) to be given by an Employer would, if duly given on the material date, expire on a date later than the effective date of termination (as defined in paragraph 119(i) above),
         the later date is the effective date of termination.
   (iii) In paragraph 119(ii)(b) above, 'the material date' means:
         (a) the date when notice of termination was given by the Employer, or
         (b) where no notice was given, the date when the contract of employment was terminated by the Employer.
   (iv)   Where:
         (a) the contract of employment is terminated by the Employee, and
         (b) the material date does not fall during a period of notice given by the Employer to terminate that contract, and
         (c) had the contract been terminated not by the Employee but by

notice given on the material date by the Employer, that notice would have been required by section 86 of the Employment Rights Act 1996 (as amended from time to time) to expire on a date later than the effective date of termination (as defined in paragraph 119(i) above), the later date is the effective date of termination.

(v) In paragraph 119(iv) above, 'the material date' means:

    (a) the date when notice of termination was given by the Employee, or

    (b) where no notice was given, the date when the contract of employment was terminated by the Employee.

120 In determining 'continuous employment', the arbitrator shall have regard to Chapter I of Part XIV of the Employment Rights Act 1996 (as amended from time to time).

121 The 'appropriate amount' means:

    (i) one and a half weeks' pay for a year of employment in which the Employee was not below the age of forty-one,

    (ii) one week's pay for a year of employment (not within sub-paragraph (i) above) in which he or she was not below the age of twenty-two, and

    (iii) half a week's pay for a year of employment not within sub-paragraphs (i) or (ii) above.

122 In calculating the amount of a week's pay of an Employee, the arbitrator shall have regard to Chapter II of Part XIV of the Employment Rights Act 1996, as amended from time to time, or any other relevant statutory provision applicable to the calculation of a week's pay.

123 Where twenty years of employment have been reckoned under paragraph 118 above, no account shall be taken under that paragraph of any year of employment earlier than those twenty years.

124 Where the effective date of termination is after the sixty-fourth anniversary of the day of the Employee's birth, the amount arrived at under paragraphs 118, 121 and 123 above shall be reduced by the 'appropriate fraction' (see paragraph 125 below).

125 The 'appropriate fraction' means the fraction of which:

    (i) the numerator is the number of whole months reckoned from the sixty-fourth anniversary of the day of the Employee's birth in the period beginning with that anniversary and ending with the effective date of termination (see paragraph 119 above), and

    (ii) the denominator is twelve.

Minimum basic amounts in certain cases

126 A 'minimum basic amount' shall apply where the arbitrator has found that the dismissal was unfair, and where the reason (or, if more than one, the principal reason):

    – in a redundancy case (see paragraph 129(i) below), for selecting the Employee for dismissal, or

    – otherwise, for the dismissal

was one of the following:

Health and safety cases

(i)   having been designated by the Employer to carry out activities in connection with preventing or reducing risks to health and safety at work, the Employee carried out (or proposed to carry out) any such activities;

(ii) being a representative of workers on matters of health and safety at work or member of a safety committee:
(a) in accordance with arrangements established under or by virtue of any enactment, or
(b) by reason of being acknowledged as such by the Employer,
the Employee performed (or proposed to perform) any functions as such a representative or a member of such a committee;

Working time cases

(iii) being:
(a) a representative of members of the workforce for the purposes of Schedule 1 to the Working Time Regulations 1998 (as amended from time to time), or
(b) a candidate in an election in which any person elected will, on being elected, be such a representative,
performed (or proposed to perform) any functions or activities as such a representative or candidate;

Trustees of occupational pension schemes

(iv) being a trustee of a relevant occupational pension scheme which relates to his or her employment, the Employee performed (or proposed to perform) any functions as such a trustee;

Employee representatives

(v)   being:
(a) an employee representative for the purposes of Chapter II of Part IV of the Trade Union and Labour Relations (Consolidation) Act 1992 (redundancies) or Regulations 10 and 11 of the Transfer of Undertakings (Protection of Employment) Regulations 1981 (as amended from time to time), or
(b) a candidate in an election in which any person elected will, on being elected, be such an employee representative,
performed (or proposed to perform) any functions or activities as such an employee representative or candidate;

(vi) the Employee took part in an election of employee representatives for the purposes of Chapter II of Part IV of the Trade Union and Labour Relations (Consolidation) Act 1992 (redundancies) or Regulations 10 and 11 of the Transfer of Undertakings (Protection of Employment) Regulations 1981 (as amended from time to time);

Union membership or activities

(vii) the Employee:
(a) was, or proposed to become, a member of an independent trade union, or
(b) had taken part, or proposed to take part, in the activities of an independent trade union at an appropriate time, or

(c) was not a member of any trade union, or of a particular trade union, or of one of a number of particular trade unions, or had refused, or proposed to refuse, to become or remain a member.

(viii) For the purposes of paragraphs (vii) above to (xi) below , in defining the terms 'trade union' and 'independent trade union', the arbitrator shall have regard to sections 1 and 5 of the Trade Union and Labour Relations (Consolidation) Act 1992, as amended from time to time.

(ix) For the purposes of paragraph (vii)(b) above, an 'appropriate time' means:

(a) a time outside the employee's working hours, or

(b) a time within his or her working hours at which, in accordance with arrangements agreed with or consent given by his or her employer, it is permissible for him or her to take part in the activities of a trade union;

and for this purpose 'working hours', in relation to an Employee, means any time when, in accordance with his or her contract of employment, he or she is required to be at work.

(x) Where the reason, or one of the reasons, for the dismissal was:

(a) the employee's refusal, or proposed refusal, to comply with a requirement (whether or not imposed by his or her contract of employment or in writing) that, in the event of his or her not being a member of any trade union, or of a particular trade union, or of one of a number of particular trade unions, he or she must make one or more payments, or

(b) his or her objection, or proposed objection, (however expressed) to the operation of a provision (whether or not forming part of his or her contract of employment or in writing) under which, in the event mentioned in paragraph (x)(a) above, his or her employer is entitled to deduct one or more sums from the remuneration payable to him or her in respect of his or her employment,

the reason shall be treated as falling within paragraph (vii)(c) above.

(xi) References in paragraphs (vii) to (x) above to being, becoming or ceasing to remain a member of a trade union include references to being, becoming or ceasing to remain a member of a particular branch or section of that union or of one of a number of particular branches or sections of that trade union; and references to taking part in the activities of a trade union shall be similarly construed.

Other categories

(xii) Where the reason or principal reason for the dismissal of the Employee qualifies under any other applicable legislative provision for a minimum basic award.

127 Before any reductions are taken into account under paragraphs 130–134 below ('Reductions to the basic amount'), the 'minimum basic amount' shall not be less than:

(i) in cases within paragraph 126(i), (ii), (iii), (iv), (v) and (vi) above, the amount provided for in section 120(1) of the Employment Rights Act 1996, as amended from time to time;

(ii)   in cases within paragraph 126(vii) above, the amount provided for in section 156 of the Trade Union and Labour Relations (Consolidation) Act 1992, as amended from time to time;

(iii) in cases within paragraph 126(xii) above, the amount provided for in the relevant legislation.

Basic amount of two weeks' pay in certain cases

128   Where:

(i)   the arbitrator finds that the reason (or, where there is more than one, the principal reason) for the dismissal of the Employee is that he or she was redundant and

(ii)   the Employee:

(a) by virtue of section 138 of the Employment Rights Act 1996, as amended from time to time, is not regarded as dismissed for the purposes of Part XI of that Act, or

(b) by virtue of section 141 of that Act, as amended from time to time, is not, or (if he or she were otherwise entitled) would not be, entitled to a redundancy payment,

the basic amount shall be two weeks' pay (for the definition of 'week's pay', see paragraph 122 above).

129   For the purposes of this Scheme:

(i)   for the definition of 'redundancy', the arbitrator shall have regard to section 139 of the Employment Rights Act 1996, as amended from time to time;

(ii)   for the definition of 'redundancy payment', the arbitrator shall have regard to Part XI of the Employment Rights Act 1996, as amended from time to time.

Reductions to the basic amount

130   Where the arbitrator finds that the Employee has unreasonably refused an offer by the Employer which (if accepted) would have the effect of reinstating the Employee in his or her employment in all respects as if he or she had not been dismissed, the arbitrator shall reduce or further reduce the basic amount to such extent as he or she considers just and equitable having regard to that finding.

131   Where the arbitrator considers that any conduct of the Employee before the dismissal (or, where the dismissal was with notice, before the notice was given) was such that it would be just and equitable to reduce or further reduce the basic amount to any extent, the arbitrator shall reduce or further reduce that amount accordingly. In assessing such conduct, the arbitrator shall disregard (if relevant) those matters set out in section 155 of the Trade Union and Labour Relations (Consolidation) Act 1992, as amended from time to time.

132   The preceding paragraph does not apply in a redundancy case (see paragraph 129(i) above) unless the reason for selecting the Employee for dismissal was one of those specified in paragraph 126 above ('Minimum basic amounts in certain cases'), and in such a case, the preceding paragraph applies only to so much of the basic amount as is payable because of paragraph 126 above.

133   Where the Employee has been awarded any amount in respect of the dismissal under a dismissal procedures agreement designated under section 110 of the Employment Rights Act 1996 (as amended from time to time), the arbitrator shall reduce or further reduce the amount of the basic award to such extent as he or she considers just and equitable having regard to that award.

134   The basic amount shall be reduced or further reduced by the amount of any payment made by the Employer to the Employee on the ground that the dismissal was by reason of redundancy (whether in pursuance of Part XI of the Employment Rights Act 1996, as amended from time to time, or otherwise).

The compensatory amount

135   (Subject to the following provisions) the *compensatory amount* shall be such as the arbitrator considers just and equitable in all the circumstances having regard to the loss sustained by the Employee in consequence of the dismissal – in so far as that loss is attributable to action taken by the Employer.

136   The loss referred to in paragraph 135 above shall be taken to include:

(i)   any expenses reasonably incurred by the Employee in consequence of the dismissal, and

(ii)   (subject to (iii) below) loss of any benefit which he or she might reasonably be expected to have had but for the dismissal.

(iii)   in respect of any loss of:

– any entitlement or potential entitlement to a payment on account of dismissal by reason of redundancy (whether in pursuance of Part XI of the Employment Rights Act 1996, as amended from time to time, or otherwise) or

– any expectation of such a payment

only the loss referable to the amount (if any) by which such a payment would have exceeded the basic amount in respect of the same dismissal (as calculated under the provisions set out above – but excluding any reductions under paragraphs 130–134 above ('Reductions to the basic amount')).

137   In ascertaining the loss referred to in paragraph 135 above, the arbitrator shall apply the principle that a person has a duty to mitigate his or her loss.

138   In determining, for the purposes of paragraph 135 above, how far any loss sustained by the Employee was attributable to action taken by the Employer, no account shall be taken of any pressure which by:

(i)   calling, organising, procuring or financing a strike or other industrial action, or

(ii)   threatening to do so,

was exercised on the Employer to dismiss the Employee; and that question shall be determined as if no such pressure had been exercised.

Reductions to the compensatory amount

139   Where the arbitrator finds that the dismissal was to any extent caused or contributed to by any conduct of the Employee, he or she shall reduce the

compensatory amount by such proportion as he or she considers just and equitable having regard to that finding. In assessing such conduct, the arbitrator shall disregard (if relevant) those matters set out in section 155 of the Trade Union and Labour Relations (Consolidation) Act 1992, as amended from time to time.

140   If:

(i)   any payment was made by the Employer to the Employee on the ground that the dismissal was by reason of redundancy (whether in pursuance of Part XI of the Employment Rights Act 1996, as amended from time to time, or otherwise); and

(ii)   the amount of such a payment exceeds the basic amount that would have been payable (under the provisions set out above – excluding for this purpose reductions on account of redundancy payments (see paragraph 129 above)),

that excess goes to reduce the compensatory amount.

Internal appeal procedures

141   Where an award of compensation is to be made, and the arbitrator finds that:

(i)   the Employer provided a procedure for appealing against dismissal, and

(ii)   the Employee was, at the time of the dismissal or within a reasonable period afterwards, given written notice stating that the Employer provided the procedure and including details of it, but

(iii) the Employee did not appeal against the dismissal under the procedure (otherwise than because the Employer prevented him or her from doing so),

the arbitrator shall reduce the compensatory amount included in an award of compensation by such amount (if any) as he or she considers just and equitable.

142   Where an award of compensation is to be made, and the arbitrator finds that:

(i)   the Employer provided a procedure for appealing against dismissal, but

(ii)   the Employer prevented the Employee from appealing against the dismissal under the procedure,

the award of compensation shall include a supplementary amount, being such amount (if any) as the arbitrator considers just and equitable.

143   In determining the amount of a reduction under paragraph 141 above or a supplementary amount under paragraph 142 above, the arbitrator shall have regard to all the circumstances of the case, including in particular the chances that an appeal under the procedure provided by the Employer would have been successful.

144   The amount of such a reduction or supplementary amount shall not exceed the amount of two weeks' pay (for the definition of 'week's pay', see paragraph 122 above).

Limits on the compensatory amount

145 With the exception of:

(i) cases falling within sections 100 or 105(3), of the Employment Rights Act 1996, as amended from time to time (Health and Safety Cases), and

(ii) cases where the reason (or, if more than one, the principal reason):
(a) in a redundancy case, for selecting the Employee for dismissal, or
(b) otherwise for the dismissal,
was that the Employee made a protected disclosure (within the meaning of Part IVA of the Employment Rights Act 1996, as amended from time to time); and

(iii) cases falling within any other exception to the statutory limit,

no compensatory amount awarded by an arbitrator shall exceed the statutory limit provided for in section 124(1) of the Employment Rights Act 1996, as amended from time to time.

146 The limit referred to above applies to the amount which the arbitrator would award (apart from paragraph 145 above) in respect of the subject matter of the complaint, after taking into account:

(i) any payment made by the Employer to the Employee in respect of that matter, and

(ii) any reduction in the amount of the award required by any enactment or rule of law.

Double recovery

147 Where the same acts of the Employer are relied upon by the Employee:

(i) to ground a claim for unfair dismissal in arbitration as well as

(ii) to ground a claim in the employment tribunal for discrimination (under the Sex Discrimination Act 1975 and/or the Race Relations Act 1976 and/or the Disability Discrimination Act 1995, or any other relevant statute),

the arbitrator shall not award compensation in respect of any loss or other matter which is to be or has been taken into account by the employment tribunal in awarding compensation with respect to the discrimination claim.

In this regard, the arbitrator shall have regard to any information supplied by the parties under paragraph 71 above.

XXI ISSUE OF AWARDS AND CONFIDENTIALITY

148 The arbitrator's award shall be sent by ACAS to both parties.

149 The award shall be confidential, and shall only be issued to the parties or to their nominated advisers or representatives. Awards will not be published by ACAS, or lodged with the employment tribunal by ACAS, although awards may be retained by ACAS for monitoring and evaluation purposes, and, from time to time, ACAS may publish general summary information concerning cases heard under the Scheme, without identifying any individual cases.

XXII   CORRECTION OF AWARDS

Scrutiny of awards by ACAS

150   Before being sent to the parties, awards may be scrutinised by ACAS to check for clerical or computational mistakes, errors arising from accidental slips or omissions, ambiguities, or errors of form. Without affecting the arbitrator's liberty of decision, ACAS may refer the award back to the arbitrator (under the provisions below) in order to draw his or her attention to any such point.

Correction by the arbitrator

151   The arbitrator may, on his or her own initiative or on the application of a party or ACAS:

(i)   correct the award so as to remove any clerical or computational mistake, or error arising from an accidental slip or omission, or to clarify or remove any ambiguity in the award, or

(ii)   make an additional award in respect of any part of the claim which was presented to the arbitrator but was not dealt with in the award.

152   In so far as any such correction or additional award involves a new issue that was not previously before the parties, this power shall not be exercised without first affording the parties a reasonable opportunity to make written representations to the arbitrator.

153   Any application by a party for the exercise of this power must be made via the ACAS Arbitration Section within 28 days of the date the award was despatched to the applying party by ACAS.

154   Any correction of the award shall be made within 28 days of the date the application was received by the arbitrator or, where the correction is made by the arbitrator on his or her own initiative, within 28 days of the date of the award.

155   Any additional award shall be made within 56 days of the date of the original award.

156   Any correction of the award shall form part of the award.

XXIII   EFFECT OF AWARDS, ENFORCEMENT AND INTEREST

Effect of awards

157   Awards made by arbitrators under this Scheme are final and binding both on the parties and on any persons claiming through or under them.

158   This does not affect the right of a person to challenge an award under the provisions of the Arbitration Act 1996 as applied to this Scheme.

Enforcement

159(1)   *Section 66 of the Arbitration Act 1996 shall apply to arbitrations conducted in accordance with the Scheme, subject to the following modifications.*

(2)   *In subsection (1) for 'tribunal pursuant to an arbitration agreement' substitute 'arbitrator pursuant to the Scheme (except for an award of reinstatement or re-engagement)'.*

(3) In subsection (3) for '(see section 73)' substitute '(see section XXV of the Scheme)'.

(4) After subsection (4) insert –
'(5) In this section –
'the court' means the High Court or a county court; and
'the Scheme' means the arbitration scheme set out in the Schedule to the ACAS Arbitration Scheme (England and Wales) Order 2001.'

160 Awards of reinstatement or re-engagement will be enforced by the employment tribunal in accordance with section 117 of the Employment Rights Act 1996 (enforcement by award of compensation).

Interest

161 Awards of compensation that are not paid within 42 days of the date on which the award was despatched by ACAS to the Employer will attract interest on the same basis as for employment tribunal awards.

XXIV CHALLENGING THE AWARD

Challenges on grounds of substantive jurisdiction

162(1) *Section 67 of the Arbitration Act 1996 shall apply to arbitrations conducted in accordance with the Scheme, subject to the following modifications.*

(2) In subsection (1) –
(a) for '(upon notice to the other parties and to the tribunal) apply to the court' substitute '(upon notice to the other party, to the arbitrator and to ACAS) apply to the High Court or the Central London County Court';
(b) for '(see section 73)' substitute '(see section XXV of the Scheme)';
(c) after 'section 70(2) and (3)' insert 'as modified for the purposes of the Scheme'.

(3) After subsection (1) insert –
'(1A) In this section –
'Arbitration Agreement' means an agreement to refer a dispute to arbitration in accordance with, and satisfying the requirements of, the Scheme;
'the Scheme' means the arbitration scheme set out in the Schedule to the ACAS Arbitration Scheme (England and Wales) Order 2001; and
'substantive jurisdiction' means any issue as to –
(a) the validity of the Arbitration Agreement and the application of the Scheme to the dispute or difference in question;
(b) the constitution of the arbitral tribunal; or
(c) the matters which have been submitted to arbitration in accordance with the Arbitration Agreement.'

Challenges for serious irregularity

163(1) *Section 68 of the Arbitration Act 1996 shall apply to arbitrations conducted in accordance with the Scheme, subject to the following modifications.*

(2) In subsection (1) –
(a) for '(upon notice to the other parties and to the tribunal) apply to the court' substitute '(upon notice to the other party, to the arbitrator and to ACAS) apply to the High Court or Central London County Court';

(b) for '(see section 73)' substitute '(see Part XXV of the Scheme)';

(c) after 'section 70(2) and (3)' insert 'as modified for the purposes of the Scheme'.

(3) In subsection (2) –

(a) in paragraph (a) for 'section 33 (general duty of tribunal)' substitute 'Part IX of the Scheme (General Duty of the Arbitrator)';

(b) in paragraph (b) after 'see section 67' insert 'as modified for the purposes of the Scheme';

(c) in paragraph (c) for 'agreed by the parties' substitute 'as set out in the Scheme';

(d) in paragraph (e) for 'any arbitral or other institution or person vested by the parties with powers in relation to the proceedings or the award' substitute 'ACAS';

(e) omit paragraph (h);

(f) in paragraph (i) for 'any arbitral or other institution or person vested by the parties with powers in relation to the proceedings or the award' substitute 'ACAS'.

(4) In subsection (3) –

(a) in paragraph (b) insert 'vary the award or' before 'set the award aside';

(b) omit 'The court shall not exercise its power to set aside or to declare an award to be of no effect, in whole or in part, unless it is satisfied that it would be inappropriate to remit the matters in question to the tribunal for reconsideration.'.

(5) After subsection (4) insert –

'(5) In this section,'the Scheme' means the arbitration scheme set out in the Schedule to the ACAS Arbitration Scheme (England and Wales) Order 2001.'

Appeals on questions of EC law and the Human Rights Act 1998

164(1) *Section 69 of the Arbitration Act 1996 shall apply to arbitrations conducted in accordance with the Scheme, subject to the following modifications.*

(2) In subsection (1) –

(a) omit 'Unless otherwise agreed by the parties';

(b) for '(upon notice to the other parties and to the tribunal) appeal to the court' substitute '(upon notice to the other party, to the arbitrator and to ACAS) appeal to the High Court or Central London County Court';

(c) for 'a question of law' substitute 'a question (a) of EC law, or (b) concerning the application of the Human Rights Act 1998';

(d) omit 'An agreement to dispense with reasons for the tribunal's award shall be considered an agreement to exclude the court's jurisdiction under this section.'.

(3) In subsection (2) after 'section 70(2) and (3)' insert 'as modified for the purposes of the Scheme'.

(4) In subsection (3) –

(a) omit paragraph (b);

(b) in paragraph (c) after the words 'on the basis of the findings of fact in the award' insert ', in so far as the question for appeal raises a point of EC law, the point is capable of serious argument, and in so far as the question for appeal does not raise a point of EC law'.

(5) In subsection (7) omit 'The court shall not exercise its power to set aside an award, in whole or in part, unless it is satisfied that it would be inappropriate to remit the matters in question to the tribunal for reconsideration.'.

(6) After subsection (8) insert –

'(9) In this section –

'EC law' means –

(a) any enactment in the domestic legislation of England and Wales giving effect to rights, powers, liabilities, obligations and restrictions from time to time created or arising by or under the Community Treaties, and

(b) any such rights, powers, liabilities, obligations and restrictions which are not given effect by any such enactment; and

'the Scheme' means the arbitration scheme set out in the Schedule to the ACAS Arbitration Scheme (England and Wales) Order 2001.'

Time limits and other procedural restrictions on challenges to awards

165(1) *Section 70 of the Arbitration Act 1996 shall apply to arbitrations conducted in accordance with the Scheme, subject to the following modifications.*

(2) In subsection (1) after 'section 67, 68 or 69' insert '(as modified for the purposes of the Scheme)'.

(3) In subsection (2) –

(a) omit paragraph (a);

(b) in paragraph (b) for 'section 57 (correction of award or additional award)' substitute 'section XXII of the Scheme (Correction of Awards)'.

(4) In subsection (3) for 'of the award or, if there has been any arbitral process of appeal or review, of the date when the applicant or appellant was notified of the result of that process' substitute 'the award was despatched to the applicant or appellant by ACAS'.

(5) Omit subsection (5).

(6) After subsection (8) insert –

'(9) In this section,'the Scheme' means the arbitration scheme set out in the Schedule to the ACAS Arbitration Scheme (England and Wales) Order 2001.'

Common law challenges and saving

166 *Sections 81(1)(c) and 81(2) of the Arbitration Act 1996 shall apply to arbitrations conducted in accordance with the Scheme.*

Challenge or appeal: effect of order of the court

167(1) *Section 71 of the Arbitration Act 1996 shall apply to arbitrations conducted in accordance with the Scheme, subject to the following modifications .*

(2) In subsection (1) after 'section 67, 68 and 69' insert '(as modified for the purposes of the Scheme)'.

(3) After subsection (3) insert –

'(3A) In this section,'the Scheme' means the arbitration scheme set out in the Schedule to the ACAS Arbitration Scheme (England and Wales) Order 2001.'

(4) Omit subsection (4).

XXV   LOSS OF RIGHT TO OBJECT

168   If a party to arbitral proceedings under this Scheme takes part, or continues to take part, in the proceedings without making, either forthwith or within such time as is allowed by the arbitrator or by any provision in this Scheme, any objection:

(i)   that the arbitrator lacks substantive jurisdiction (as defined in paragraph 162 above), aside from any jurisdictional objection with respect to the circumstances of the dismissal, which will be waived in any event, as set out in paragraphs 16–18 above,

(ii)   that the proceedings have been improperly conducted,

(iii)   that there has been a failure to comply with the Arbitration Agreement or any provision of this Scheme, or

(iv)   that there has been any other irregularity affecting the arbitrator or the proceedings,

he or she may not raise that objection later, before the arbitrator or the court, unless he or she shows that, at the time he or she took part or continued to take part in the proceedings, he or she did not know and could not with reasonable diligence have discovered the grounds for the objection.

XXVI   IMMUNITY

169   An arbitrator under this Scheme is not liable for anything done or omitted in the discharge or purported discharge of his or her functions as arbitrator unless the act or omission is shown to have been in bad faith. This applies to a legal adviser appointed by ACAS as it applies to the arbitrator himself or herself.

170   ACAS, by reason of having appointed an arbitrator or nominated a legal adviser, is not liable for anything done or omitted by the arbitrator or legal adviser in the discharge or purported discharge of his or her functions.

XXVII   MISCELLANEOUS PROVISIONS

Requirements in connection with legal proceedings

171(1)   *Sections 80(1), (2), (4), (5), (6) and (7) of the Arbitration Act 1996 shall apply to arbitrations conducted in accordance with the Scheme, subject to the following modification.*

(2)   *In subsection (1) for 'to the other parties to the arbitral proceedings, or to the tribunal' substitute 'to the other party to the arbitral proceedings, or to the arbitrator, or to ACAS'.*

Service of documents and notices on ACAS or the ACAS Arbitration Section

172   Any notice or other document required or authorised to be given or served on ACAS or the ACAS Arbitration Section for the purposes of the arbitral proceedings shall be sent by pre-paid post to the following address: ACAS Arbitration Section, ACAS Head Office, Brandon House, 180 Borough High Street, London SE1 1LW, or transmitted by facsimile, addressed to the ACAS Arbitration Section, at the number stipulated in the ACAS Guide to

the Scheme, or by electronic mail, at the address stipulated in the ACAS Guide to the Scheme.

173 Paragraph 172 (above) does not apply to the service of documents on the ACAS Arbitration Section for the purposes of legal proceedings.

Service of documents or notices on any other person or entity (other than ACAS or the ACAS Arbitration Section)

174 Any notice or other document required or authorised to be given or served on any person or entity (other than ACAS or the ACAS Arbitration Section) for the purposes of the arbitral proceedings may be served by any effective means.

175 If such a notice or other document is addressed, pre-paid and delivered by post:

(i) to the addressee's last known principal residence or, if he or she is or has been carrying on a trade, profession or business, his or her last known principal business address, or

(ii) where the address is a body corporate, to the body's registered or principal office,

it shall be treated as effectively served.

176 Paragraphs 174 and 175 (above) do not apply to the service of documents for the purposes of legal proceedings, for which provision is made by rules of court.

Powers of court in relation to service of documents

177(1) *Section 77 of the Arbitration Act 1996 shall apply to arbitrations conducted in accordance with the Scheme, subject to the following modifications.*

(2) *In subsection (1) omit 'in the manner agreed by the parties, or in accordance with provisions of section 76 having effect in default of agreement,'.*

(3) *In subsection (2) for 'Unless otherwise agreed by the parties, the court' substitute 'The High Court or Central London County Court'.*

(4) *In subsection (3) for 'Any party to the arbitration agreement may apply' substitute 'ACAS or any party to the arbitration agreement may apply'.*

Reckoning periods of time

178(1) *Sections 78(2), (3), (4) and (5) of the Arbitration Act 1996 shall apply to arbitrations conducted in accordance with the Scheme, subject to the following modification.*

(2) *In subsection (2) –*

(a) *omit 'If or to the extent that there is no such agreement,';*

(b) *after 'periods of time' insert 'provided for in any provision of this Part'.*

XXVIII TERRITORIAL OPERATION OF THE SCHEME

179 The Scheme applies to disputes involving an Employer who resides or carries on business in England and Wales.

APPENDIX A – WAIVER OF RIGHTS

The ACAS Arbitration Scheme ('the Scheme') is entirely voluntary. In agreeing to refer a dispute to arbitration under the Scheme, both parties agree to waive rights that they would otherwise have if, for example, they had referred their dispute to the employment tribunal. This follows from the informal nature of the Scheme, which is designed to be a confidential, relatively fast, cost-efficient and non-legalistic process.

As required by section VI of the Scheme, as a confirmation of the parties' agreement to waive their rights, this form must be completed by each party and submitted to ACAS together with the agreement to arbitration.

A detailed description of the informal nature of arbitration under the Scheme, and the important differences between this and the employment tribunal, is contained in the ACAS Guide to the Scheme ('the ACAS Guide'), which should be read by each party before completing this form.

The Scheme is not intended for disputes involving complex legal issues, or questions of EC law. Parties to such disputes are strongly advised to consider applying to the employment tribunal, or settling their dispute by other means.

This form does not list all the differences between the Scheme and the employment tribunal, or all of the features of the Scheme to which each party agrees in referring their dispute to arbitration.

I, _____

the Applicant / Respondent / Respondent's duly authorised representative [delete as appropriate] confirm my agreement to each of the following points:

1   Unlike proceedings in the employment tribunal, all proceedings under the Scheme, including all hearings, are conducted in private. There are no public hearings, and the final award will be confidential.

2   All arbitrators under the Scheme are appointed by ACAS from the ACAS Arbitration Panel (which is a panel of impartial, mainly non-lawyer, arbitrators appointed by ACAS on fixed, but renewable, terms). The appointment process and the ACAS Arbitration Panel is described in the Scheme and the ACAS Guide. Neither party will have any choice of arbitrator.

3   Proceedings under the Scheme are conducted differently from the employment tribunal. In particular:

   – arbitrators will conduct proceedings in an informal manner in all cases;

   – the attendance of witnesses and the production of documents cannot be compelled (although failure to co-operate may be taken into account by the arbitrator);

   – there will be no oaths or affirmations, and no cross-examination of witnesses by parties or their representatives;

   – the arbitrator will take the initiative in asking questions and ascertaining the facts (with the aim of ensuring that all relevant issues are considered), as well as hearing each side's arguments;

   – the arbitrator's decision will only contain the main considerations

that have led to the result; it will not contain full or detailed reasons;
– the arbitrator has no power to order interim relief.

4   Once parties have agreed to refer their dispute to arbitration in accordance with the Scheme, the parties cannot then return to the employment tribunal.

5   In deciding whether or not the dismissal was fair or unfair, the arbitrator shall have regard to general principles of fairness and good conduct in employment relations (including, for example, principles referred to in any relevant ACAS 'Disciplinary and Grievance Procedures' Code of Practice or 'Discipline at Work' Handbook). Unlike the employment tribunal, the arbitrator will not apply strict legal tests or rules (eg, court decisions or legislation), with certain limited exceptions set out in the Scheme (see eg, paragraph 12).
Similarly, in cases that do not involve EC law, the arbitrator will calculate compensation or award any other remedy in accordance with the terms of the Scheme, instead of applying strict legal tests or rules.

6   Unlike the employment tribunal, there is no right of appeal from awards of arbitrators under the Scheme (except for a limited right to appeal questions of EC law and, aside from procedural matters set out in the Scheme, questions concerning the Human Rights Act 1998).

7   Unlike the employment tribunal, in agreeing to arbitration under the Scheme, parties agree that there is no jurisdictional argument, i.e. no reason why the claim cannot be heard and determined by the arbitrator. In particular, the arbitrator will assume that a dismissal has taken place, and will only consider whether or not this was unfair. This is explained further in the Scheme and in the ACAS Guide.

SIGNED: _____

DATED: _____

IN THE PRESENCE OF

Signature: _____

Full Name: _____

Position: _____

Address: _____

Useful addresses

Useful addresses

EMPLOYMENT TRIBUNALS: ENGLAND AND WALES

Central office
Central Office of the Employment Tribunals
19–29 Woburn Place
London WC1H 0LU
Tel: 020 7273 8575
Fax: 020 7273 8686

www.employmenttribunals.gov.uk – access to the full range of published information which is provided for users on how to apply to an employment tribunal, addresses, maps, etc.

www.ets.gov.uk – highlights the role, aims and objectives of the agency together with a vision statement.

Employment tribunal offices

Ashford
Tufton House
Tufton Street
Ashford
Kent TN23 1RJ
Tel: 01233 621346
Fax: 01233 624423

Bedford
8–10 Howard Street
Bedford MK40 3HS
Tel: 01234 351306
Fax: 01234 352315

Birmingham
1st Floor Phoenix House
1/3 Newhall Street
Birmingham B3 3NH
Tel: 0121 236 6051
Fax: 0121 236 6029

Bristol
The Crescent Centre
Temple Beck
Bristol BS1 6EZ
Tel: 0117 929 8261
Fax: 0117 925 3452

Bury St Edmunds
100 Southgate Street
Bury St Edmunds
Suffolk IP33 2AQ
Tel: 01284 762171
Fax: 01284 706064

Cardiff
2nd Floor Caradog House
1–6 St Andrew's Place
Cardiff CF10 3BE
Tel: 029 2067 8100
Fax: 029 2022 5906

Exeter
10th Floor Renslade House
Bonhay Road
Exeter EX4 3BX
Tel: 01392 279665
Fax: 01392 430063

Leeds
4th Floor Albion Tower
11 Albion Street
Leeds LS1 5ES
Tel: 0113 245 9741
Fax: 0113 242 8843

Leicester
Kings Court
5A New Walk
Leicester LE1 6TE
Tel: 0116 255 0099
Fax: 0116 255 6099

Liverpool
1st Floor Cunard Building
Pier Head
Liverpool L3 1TS
Tel: 0151 236 9397
Fax: 0151 231 1484

London North
19–29 Woburn Place
London WC1H 0LU
Tel: 020 7273 8575
Fax: 020 7273 8686

London South
Montague Court
101 London Road
West Croydon CR0 2RF
Tel: 020 8667 9131
Fax: 020 8649 9470

Manchester
Alexandra House
14–22 The Parsonage
Manchester M3 2JA
Tel: 0161 833 0581
Fax: 0161 832 0249

Newcastle
Quayside House
110 Quayside
Newcastle upon Tyne NE1 3DX
Tel: 0191 260 6900
Fax: 0191 222 1680

Nottingham
3rd Floor Byron House
2A Maid Marian Way
Nottingham NG1 6HS
Tel: 0115 947 5701
Fax: 0115 950 7612

Reading
5th Floor 30–31 Friar Street
Reading RG1 1DY
Tel: 0118 959 4917
Fax: 0118 956 8066

Sheffield
14 East Parade
Sheffield S1 2ET
Tel: 0114 276 0348
Fax: 0114 276 2551

Shrewsbury
Prospect House
Belle Vue Road
Shrewsbury SY3 7AR
Tel: 01743 358341
Fax: 01743 244186

Southampton
3rd Floor Duke's Keep
Marsh Lane
Southampton SO14 3EX
Tel: 023 8071 6400
Fax: 023 8063 5506

Stratford
44 The Broadway
Stratford
London E15 1XH
Tel: 020 8221 0921
Fax: 020 8221 0398

Watford
3rd Floor
Radius House
521 Clarendon Road
Watford
Herts WD1 1HU
Tel: 01923 281750
Fax: 01923 281781

EMPLOYMENT TRIBUNALS: SCOTLAND

Central office
Central Office of the Employment
Tribunals
Eagle Building
215 Bothwell Street
Glasgow G2 7TS
Tel: 0141 204 0730
Fax: 0141 204 0732

Employment tribunal offices

Aberdeen
Mezzanine Floor
Atholl House
84–88 Guild Street
Aberdeen AB11 6LT
Tel: 01224 593137
Fax: 01224 593138

Edinburgh
54–56 Melville Street
Edinburgh EH3 7HF
Tel: 0131 226 5584
Fax: 0131 220 6847

Dundee
13 Albert Square
Dundee DD1 1DD
Tel: 01382 221578
Fax: 01382 227136

EMPLOYMENT APPEAL TRIBUNAL

Central Office
58 Victoria Embankment
London EC4Y 0DS
Tel: 020 7273 1041
Fax: 020 7273 1045

www.employmentappeals.gov.uk

Divisional Office
52 Melville Street
Edinburgh EH3 7HF
Tel: 0131 225 3963
Fax: 0131 220 6694

CENTRAL ABRITRATION COMMITTEE

Third Floor
Discovery House
28–42 Banner Street
London EC1Y 8EQ
Tel: 020 7251 9747
Fax: 020 7251 3114

ADVISORY, CONCILIATION AND ARBITRATION SERVICE

Midlands Region

Birmingham
Warwick House
6 Highfield Road
Edgbaston
Birmingham B15 3ED
Tel: 0121 456 5856
Fax: 0121 456 5466

Nottingham
Anderson House
Clinton Avenue
Nottingham NG5 1AW
Tel: 0115 969 3355
Fax: 0115 969 3085

South and West Region

Bristol
Regent House
27a Regent Street
Clifton
Bristol BS8 4HR
Tel: 0117 946 9555
Fax: 0117 946 9501

Fleet
Westminster House
Fleet Road
Fleet
Hampshire GU13 8PD
Tel: 01252 816650
Fax: 01252 811030

Northern Region

Leeds
Commerce House
St Alban's Place
Leeds LS2 8HH
Tel: 0113 243 1371
Fax: 0113 247 0429

Newcastle
Cross House
Westgate Road
Newcastle upon Tyne NE1 4XX
Tel: 0191 261 2191
Fax: 0191 232 5452

North West Region

Manchester
Commercial Union House
2–10 Albert Square
Manchester M60 8AD
Tel: 0161 833 8585
Fax: 0161 833 8515

Liverpool
Cressington House
249 St Mary's Road
Garston
Liverpool L19 0NF
Tel: 0151 427 8881
Fax: 0151 427 2715

London, Eastern and Southern Areas

Clifton House
83–117 Euston Road
London NW1 2RB
Tel: 020 7396 5100
Fax: 020 7396 5159

Paddock Wood Office
Suites 3–5
Business Centre
1–7 Commercial Road
Paddock Wood
Kent TN12 6EN
Tel: 01892 837273
Fax: 01892 837122

Thetford Office
39 King Street
Thetford
Norfolk IP24 2AU
Tel: 01842 750 432
Fax: 01842 750 433

Scotland

Franborough House
123–157 Bothwell Street
Glasgow G2 7JR
Tel: 0141 204 2677
Fax: 0141 221 4697

Wales

3 Purbeck House
Lambourne Crescent
Llanishen
Cardiff CF14 7JR
Tel: 029 2076 1126
Fax: 029 2075 1334

Head Office

Brandon House
180 Borough High Street
London SE1 1LW
Tel: 020 7210 3000
Fax: 020 7210 3645

www.acas.org.uk

EQUAL OPPORTUNITIES COMMISSION

Overseas House
Quay Street
Manchester M3 3HN
Tel: 0161 833 9244
Fax: 0161 835 1657

www.eoc.org.uk

COMMISSION FOR RACIAL EQUALITY

Elliott House
10–12 Allington Street
London SW1E 5EH
Tel: 020 7828 7022
Fax: 020 7630 7605
www.cre.gov.uk

DISABILITY RIGHTS COMMISSION

Disability Rights Commission Helpline
Freepost MID 02164
Stratford-upon-Avon
CV37 9BR
Tel: 08457 622 633
Fax: 08457 778 878
Textphone: 08457 622 644
e-mail : ddahelp@stra.sitel.co.uk
www.drc.org.uk

FREE REPRESENTATION UNIT

4th Floor
Peer House
Verulam Street
London WC1X 5LZ
Tel: 020 7831 0692
Fax : 020 78312398

COMMUNITY LEGAL SERVICES

www.justask.org.uk

LEGAL SERVICES COMMISSION

85 Gray's Inn Road
London WC1X 8TX
Tel: 020 7759 0000
www.legalservices.gov.uk

NORTHERN IRELAND LEGAL AID BOARD

Bedford House
16–22 Bedford Sreet
Belfast BT2 7FL.
Tel: 02890 246 441
Fax: 02890 332 548

SCOTTISH LEGAL AID BOARD

44 Drumsheugh Gardens
Edinburgh EH3 7SW
Tel: 0131 226 7061
Fax: 0131 225 5195

www.slab.org.uk

TRADE UNION CONGRESS

Congress House
Great Russel Street
London WC1 3LW
Tel: 020 7636 4030
Fax: 020 636 0632

www.tuc.org.uk

NATIONAL ASSOCIATION OF CITIZEN'S ADVICE BUREAUX

Myddleton House
115–123 Pentonville Road
London N1 9LZ
Tel: 020 7833 2181
Fax: 020 7833 4371

www.nacab.org.uk

LAW CENTRES FEDERATION

Duchess House
18–19 Warren Street
London WC1P 5DP
Tel: 020 7387 8570
Fax: 020 7387 8368

THE COMMISSIONER FOR THE RIGHTS OF TRADE UNION MEMBERS

First Floor
Bank Chambers
2a Rylands Street
Warrington
Cheshire WA1 1EN
Tel: 0192 541 5771
Fax: 0192 541 5772

CERTIFICATION OFFICE FOR TRADE UNIONS AND EMPLOYER'S ASSOCIATIONS

Certification Office for Trade
Unions and Employer's
Associations
Brandon House
180 Borough High Street
London SE1 1LW
Tel: 020 7210 3734
Fax: 020 7210 3612

Index

LAG Legal Action Group

Working with lawyers and advisers to promote equal access to justice

Legal Action magazine

The only monthly magazine published specifically for legal aid practitioners and the advice sector.

2002 annual subscription: £79

Concessionary rates available for students and trainees – call the LAG office for details.

Books

LAG's catalogue includes a range of titles covering:

- community care
- crime
- debt
- education
- employment
- family
- housing
- human rights
- immigration
- personal injury
- practice & procedure
- welfare benefits
- LAG policy

Community Care Law Reports

The only law reports devoted entirely to community care issues. Compiled by an expert team and published quarterly, each issue contains:

- editorial review
- community care law update
- law reports
- guidance
- cumulative index
- full tables

Training

Accredited with the Law Society, the Bar Council and the Institute of Legal Executives, LAG provides topical training courses across a broad range of subjects, including employment law.

Conferences

LAG runs major conferences to examine issues at the cutting-edge of legal services policy and to inform practitioners of their implications.

For further information about any of Legal Action Group's activities please contact:

**Legal Action Group
242 Pentonville Road
London N1 9UN**

**DX 130400 London (Pentonville Road)
Telephone: 020 7833 2931
Fax: 020 7837 6094
e-mail: lag@lag.org.uk
www.lag.org.uk**